Automating System Administration with Perl

SECOND EDITION

Automating System Administration with Perl

*Bill—
Be sure to use this book for good and not evil!*

David N. Blank-Edelman

O'REILLY®

Beijing · Cambridge · Farnham · Köln · Sebastopol · Taipei · Tokyo

Automating System Administration with Perl, Second Edition
by David N. Blank-Edelman

Copyright © 2009 O'Reilly Media, Inc. All rights reserved.
Printed in the United States of America.

Published by O'Reilly Media, Inc., 1005 Gravenstein Highway North, Sebastopol, CA 95472.

O'Reilly books may be purchased for educational, business, or sales promotional use. Online editions are also available for most titles (*http://my.safaribooksonline.com*). For more information, contact our corporate/institutional sales department: 800-998-9938 or *corporate@oreilly.com*.

Editor: Andy Oram	**Indexer:** Lucie Haskins
Production Editor: Sarah Schneider	**Cover Designer:** Karen Montgomery
Copyeditor: Rachel Head	**Interior Designer:** David Futato
Proofreader: Kiel Van Horn	**Illustrator:** Robert Romano

Printing History:

May 2009:	Second Edition.

ISBN: 978-0-596-00639-6

[M]

1241809111

*To Cindy, ever the love of my life, and to Elijah,
a true blessing.*

Table of Contents

Preface

Do you need tools for making your system administration work easier and more efficient? You've come to the right place.

Perl is a powerful programming language that grew out of the traditional system administration toolbox. Over the years it has adapted and expanded to meet the challenges of new operating systems and new tasks. If you know a little Perl, and you need to perform system administration tasks, this is the right book for you. Readers with varying levels of both Perl programming experience and system administration experience will all find something of use within these pages.

What's New in This Edition?

A tremendous amount of work went into updating this book so it could be even better than the first edition. Here's some of what has been improved in the second edition:

New title
> My editors and I realized that the material in this book was more about how to automate your system administration work in ways that would make your working life more efficient and pleasant than it was about Perl. While Perl is still the toolshed that makes all this possible, it isn't the main focus of the book.

New material
> It's hard to know where to begin on this one. The new edition is four chapters and two appendixes bigger (with a total page count that is 50% greater) than the last one. Included in this edition are a cornucopia of new tools and techniques that you are going to love. I tried to add material on the things I wished I had sysadmin-targeted material on, including: XML and YAML best practices (using `XML::LibXML`, `XML::Twig`, and XPath); dealing with config files; more advanced LDAP topics (including updated `Net::LDAP` information); email-related topics (including POP3/ IMAP, MIME, and spam); new ways of dealing with filesystems; more advanced log file creation and parsing tools; DHCP; mapping/monitoring a network using Nmap and other tools; packet creation and sniffing; information reporting using tools like GraphViz, RRDtool, and Timeline; using SHA-2 instead of MD5;

SNMPv3; Mac OS X; converting VBScript code to Perl; geocoding; MP3 file manipulation; using Google Maps; and so on.

New advice

Part of the value of this book is the advice you can pick up from an experienced system administrator like me who has been doing this stuff for a long time and has compared notes with many other seasoned veterans. This new edition is packed with more sidebars to explain not only the *what*, but also the *why* behind the material.

Operating system and software information updates

All of the text and code has been updated and augmented to work with the latest versions of Unix- (including Linux and Mac OS X) and Windows-based operating systems.

Module and code updates/improvements

The descriptions and code in this book match the latest versions of the modules mentioned in the first edition. In cases where a module is no longer available or a better alternative has emerged, the appropriate replacement modules have been substituted. Also, all example code is now "use strict" friendly.

Errata corrected

I have attempted to address all of the errata I received from all of the printings of the first edition. I appreciate the time readers took to report errors to O'Reilly and me so I could fix them at each printing and in this edition. Special thanks go to Andreas Karrer, the German translator for the first edition. Andi pored over every single byte of the original text and submitted almost 200 (mostly layout-related) corrections, all with good cheer.

How This Book Is Structured

Each chapter in this book addresses a different system administration domain and ends with a list of the Perl modules used in that chapter and references to facilitate deeper exploration of the information presented. The chapters are as follows:

Chapter 1, Introduction

This introductory chapter describes the material covered in the book in more detail, explaining how it will serve you and what you need to get the most from it. The material in this book is powerful and is meant to be used by powerful people (e.g., Unix superusers and Windows-based operating system administrators). The introduction provides some important guidelines to help you write more secure Perl programs.

Chapter 2, Filesystems

This chapter is about keeping multiplatform filesystems tidy and ensuring that they are used properly. We'll start by looking at the salient differences between the native filesystems for each operating system. We'll then explore the process of intelligently walking or traversing filesystems from Perl and how that can be useful. Finally, we'll look at manipulating disk quotas from Perl.

Chapter 3, User Accounts

This chapter discusses how user accounts manifest themselves on two different operating systems, including what is stored for each user and how to manipulate the information from Perl. That leads into a discussion of a rudimentary account system written in Perl. In the process of building this system, we'll examine the mechanisms necessary for recording accounts in a simple database, creating these accounts, and deleting them.

Chapter 4, User Activity

Chapter 4 explores ways to automate tasks centered around user activity, introducing a number of ways to track and control process, file, and network operations initiated by users. This chapter also presents various operating system-specific frameworks and tools (e.g., Windows Management Instrumentation, GUI setup tools, *lsof*, etc.) that are helpful for user-oriented tasks on different platforms.

Chapter 5, TCP/IP Name and Configuration Services

Name and configuration services allow hosts on a TCP/IP network to communicate with each other amicably and to self-configure. This chapter takes a historical perspective by starting with host files, then moving on to the Network Information Service (NIS) and finally to the glue of the Internet, the Domain Name Service (DNS). Each step of the way, it shows how Perl can make professional management of these services easier. We'll also explore how to work with the Dynamic Host Configuration Protocol (DHCP) from Perl in this chapter.

Chapter 6, Working with Configuration Files

Almost every system or software package we touch relies heavily on configuration files to be useful in our environment. This chapter explores the tools that make writing and reading those files from Perl easy. We'll look at various formats, with special attention paid to XML and the current best practices for working with it using Perl.

Chapter 7, SQL Database Administration

Over time, more uses for relational databases are being found in the system administration realm. As a result, system administrators need to become familiar with SQL database administration. This chapter explains DBI, the preeminent SQL database framework for Perl, and provides examples of it in action for database administration.

Chapter 8, Email

This chapter demonstrates how Perl can make better use of email as a system administration tool. After discussing sending via SMTP (including MIME-based HTML messages), receiving via POP3/IMAP, and parsing via Perl, we'll explore several interesting applications, including tools for analyzing unsolicited commercial email (a.k.a. spam) and managing tech support emails.

Chapter 9, Directory Services

As the complexity of the information we deal with increases over time, so does the importance of the directory services we use to access that information. System administrators are increasingly being called upon not only to use these services, but also to build tools for their management. This chapter discusses some of the more popular directory service protocols/frameworks, such as LDAP and ADSI, and shows you how to work with them from Perl.

Chapter 10, Log Files

System administrators are often awash in a sea of log files. Every machine, operating system, and program can (and often does) log information. This chapter looks at the logging systems offered by Unix- and Windows-based operating systems and discusses approaches for analyzing logging information so it can work for you.

Chapter 11, Security

This chapter heads right into the maelstrom called "security," demonstrating how Perl can make hosts and networks more secure.

Chapter 12, SNMP

This chapter is devoted to the Simple Network Management Protocol (SNMP). It illustrates how to use this protocol to communicate with network devices (both to poll and to receive trap information).

Chapter 13, Network Mapping and Monitoring

Perl offers some excellent tools for the mapping and monitoring of networks. In this chapter, we'll look at several ways to discover the hosts on the network and the services they offer. We'll then explore helpful graphical and textual ways to present the information collected, including some of the best tools for graphing and charting the data (such as GraphViz and RRDtool).

Chapter 14, Experiential Learning

This is the chapter you don't want your boss to catch you reading.

Appendixes

Some of the chapters assume basic knowledge about topics with which you may not be familiar. For those who are new to these subjects, this book includes several mini-tutorials to bring you up to speed quickly. The appendixes provide introductions to the eXtensible Markup Language (XML), the XML Path Language (XPath), the Lightweight Directory Access Protocol (LDAP), the Structured Query Language (SQL), the Revision Control System (RCS), translating VBScript to Perl, and SNMP.

Typographical Conventions

This book uses the following typographical conventions:

Italic

> Used for file- and pathnames, usernames, directories, program names, hostnames, URLs, and new terms where they are first introduced.

`Constant width`

> Used for Perl module and function names, namespaces, libraries, commands, methods, and variables, and when showing code and computer output.

`Constant width bold`

> Used to indicate user input and for emphasis in code examples.

`Constant width italic`

> Used to indicate parts of a command line that are user-replaceable, and for code annotations.

 This icon signifies a tip, suggestion, or general note.

 This icon indicates a warning or caution.

Operating System Naming Conventions

This book is steadfastly multiplatform in its thinking. However, reading about "a Microsoft Vista/Microsoft Windows Server 2008/Microsoft Windows Server 2003/Microsoft XP script" or a "Linux/Solaris/Irix/HPUX/Mac OS X/etc. script" gets old fast. Having consulted some style guides, here's how I've chosen to handle discussing the operating system collectives:

- When writing about the Microsoft products—Microsoft Vista, Microsoft Windows Server 2008, Microsoft Windows Server 2003, and Microsoft XP (on which, by and large, all scripts were tested)—I refer to them collectively as "Windows-based operating systems," at least first time they show up in a chapter or heading. From that point on in the chapter I shorten this to simply "Windows." If something is particular to a specific Windows-based operating system, I will mention it by name.

- When writing about any of the members of the Unix family (in which I include both Linux and Mac OS X), I refer to them collectively as just "Unix," "the Unix family," or sometimes "Unix variants." If something is particular to a specific Unix vendor or release, I will mention it by name.

Coding Conventions

There are a few points I want to mention about the code in this book:

- All code examples were written and tested with `use strict;` as the first line (I highly recommend you do the same). However, given the number of examples in this book, the repetition would have taken up a significant amount of space, so to save trees and wasted bits I did not include that line in any of the examples. Please just assume that every example uses this convention.
- Almost all of the code is formatted using Steve Hancock's fabulous *perltidy* utility (*http://search.cpan.org/dist/Perl-Tidy/*) to improve readability.
- Although these examples don't reach anything like that level of perfection, much of the code has been rewritten with the advice in Damian Conway's book *Perl Best Practices (http://oreilly.com/catalog/9780596001735/)* (O'Reilly) in mind. I highly recommend reading Conway's book to improve your code and generally reinvigorate your Perl programming. The automated source code analyzer `Perl::Critic` that *Perl Best Practices* inspired was still in heavy development for much of the writing of this book, so I did not use it. You should, though, as it's another great tool.

Using Code Examples

This book is here to help you get your job done. In general, you may use the code in this book in your programs and documentation. You do not need to contact us for permission unless you're reproducing a significant portion of the code. For example, writing a program that uses several chunks of code from this book does not require permission. Selling or distributing a CD-ROM of examples from O'Reilly books *does* require permission. Answering a question by citing this book and quoting example code does not require permission. Incorporating a significant amount of example code from this book into your product's documentation *does* require permission.

We appreciate, but do not require, attribution. An attribution usually includes the title, author, publisher, and ISBN. For example: "*Automating System Administration with Perl*, Second Edition, by David N. Blank-Edelman. Copyright 2009 O'Reilly Media, Inc., 978-0-596-00639-6."

If you feel your use of code examples falls outside fair use or the permission given above, feel free to contact us at *permissions@oreilly.com*.

How to Contact Us

We have tested and verified the information in this book to the best of our ability, but you may find that features have changed (or even that we have made mistakes!). Please let us know of any errors you find, as well as your suggestions for future editions, by writing to:

O'Reilly Media, Inc.
1005 Gravenstein Highway North
Sebastopol, CA 95472
800-998-9938 (in the U.S. or Canada)
707-829-0515 (international/local)
707-829-0104 (fax)

We have a website for the book, where we'll list examples, errata, and any plans for future editions. You can access this page at:

http://www.oreilly.com/catalog/9780596006396/

The author has set up a personal website for this book. Please visit it at:

http://www.otterbook.com

To ask technical questions or comment on the book, send email to:

bookquestions@oreilly.com

For more information about our books, conferences, software, Resource Centers, and the O'Reilly Network, see the O'Reilly website:

http://www.oreilly.com

Safari® Books Online

When you see a Safari® Books Online icon on the cover of your favorite technology book, that means the book is available online through the O'Reilly Network Safari Bookshelf.

Safari offers a solution that's better than e-books. It's a virtual library that lets you easily search thousands of top tech books, cut and paste code samples, download chapters, and find quick answers when you need the most accurate, current information. Try it for free at *http://my.safaribooksonline.com/*.

Acknowledgments from the First Edition

To keep the preface from becoming too much like an Oscar acceptance speech, here's a condensed version of the acknowledgments from the first edition.

Thanks to the Perl Community, especially Larry Wall, Tom Christiansen, and the ker-jillions of programmers and hackers who poured countless hours and energy into the language and then chose to share their work with me and the rest of the Perl community.

Thanks to the SysAdmin community: members of Usenix, SAGE, and the people who have contributed to the LISA conferences over the years. Thanks to Rémy Evard for being such a great influence on my professional and personal understanding of this field as a friend, mentor, and role model. He is still one of the system administrators I want to be when I grow up.

Thanks to the reviewers of the first edition: Jerry Carter, Toby Everett, Æleen Frisch, Joe Johnston, Tom Limoncelli, John A. Montgomery, Jr., Chris Nandor, Michael Peppler, Michael Stok, and Nathan Torkington.

Thanks to the O'Reilly staff: to Rhon Porter for his illustrations, to Hanna Dyer and Lorrie LeJeune for the most amazing cover animal, and to the O'Reilly production staff. I am still thankful to Linda Mui, my editor for the first edition, whose incredible skill, finesse, and care allowed me to birth this book and raise it in a good home.

Thanks to my spiritual community: Havurat Shalom in Somerville. Thank you, M' kor HaChayim, for this book and all of the many blessings in my life.

Thanks to the Shona people of Zimbabwe for their incredible mbira music.

Thanks to my friends (Avner, Ellen, Phil Shapiro, Alex Skovronek, Jon Orwant, and Joel Segel), the faculty and staff at the Northeastern University College of Computer and Information Science (especially the folks in the CCIS Systems group), and my boss Larry Finkelstein, the Dean of the College of Computer Science.

Thanks to my nuclear family (Myra, Jason, and Steven Edelman-Blank), my cats Shimmer and Bendir (bye-bye, Bendir, I'll miss you), and my TCM pit crew (Kristen Porter and Thom Donovan).

The first edition was dedicated to Cindy, love of my life.

Acknowledgments for the Second Edition

One of the only things better than having all of these great people and things in your life is to have them remain in your life. I'm still thankful for all of the above from the first edition. Here are some of the changes and additions:

This edition had a much expanded and tremendous group of technical reviewers. I'm very grateful to Æleen Frisch, Aaron Crane, Aleksey Tsalolikhin, Andrew Langmead, Bill Cole, Cat Okita, Chaos Golubitsky, Charles Richmond, Chris Grau, Clifton Royston, Dan Wilson, Dean Wilson, Denny Allain, Derek J. Balling, Earl Gay, Eric Sorenson, Eric Toczek, Federico Lucifredi, Gordon "Fyodor" Lyon, Graham Barr, Grant McLean, Hugh Brown, James Keating, Jan Dubois, Jennifer Davis, Jerry Carter, Jesse Vincent, Joe Morri, John Levine, John Tsangaris, Josh Roberts, Justin Mason, Mark

Bergman, Michel Rodriguez, Mike DeGraw-Bertsch, Mike Stok, Neil Neely, Petr Pajas, Philip J. Hollenback, Randy Dees, Scott Murphy, Shlomi Fish, Stephen Potter, Steve Atkins, Steven Tylock, Terry Zink, Thomas Leyer, Tim Bunce, Tobias Oetiker, Toby Ovod-Everett, and Tom Regner for the time and energy they spent on making this book better. I continue to be amazed by the generosity and kindness shown by the members of the SysAdmin and Perl communities.

The editorial chain was a bit longer than usual on this book, so thanks to *all* of the editors. Starting from the first edition in chronological order: Linda Mui, Paula Ferguson, Nathan Torkington, Allison Randal, Colleen Gorman, Tatiana Apandi, Isabel Kunkle, and Andy Oram. I'm also thankful to the other O'Reilly people who have had a hand in bringing this book to fruition, including Mike Hendrickson, Rachel Head, Sarah Schneider, Rob Romano, Sanders Kleinfeld, and all the others.

I was taken with sea otters even before the first edition was published with one on the front cover, but since then my appreciation for them keeps on growing. They are an amazing species in so many ways. Unfortunately, humans historically haven't been particularly kind to the sea otters. They are still classified as an endangered species, and some of our activities actively threaten their survival. I believe they deserve our protection and our support. One organization that works toward this end is Friends of the Sea Otter (*http://www.seaotters.org*), based in Monterey, California. I'm a member, and I encourage you to join, too.

Mbira kept me sane through the arduous process of writing the first edition of this book. For this edition, I have yoga to thank for my current health and sanity. I'd like to express my profound gratitude to my teacher, Karin Stephan, and her teacher, B.K.S. Iyengar, for sharing such a wonderful union of mind and body with me.

I've tried to cut down the florid prose of the first edition's acknowledgments, but I hope you'll indulge me just one more time. The biggest change for me between these editions was the birth of our first child, Elijah. He's been a constant blessing to us, both in the noun and verb senses of the word.

## CHAPTER 1

Introduction

In my town, several of our local bus lines are powered by cables strung high above the street. One day, when going to an unfamiliar destination, I asked the driver to let me know when a particular street was approaching. He said, "I'm sorry, I can't. I just follow the wires."

These are words you will never hear from good system administrators asked to describe their jobs. System administration is a craft. It's not about following wires. System and network administration is about deciding what wires to put in place and where to put them, getting them deployed, keeping watch over them, and then eventually ripping them out and starting all over again. Good system administration is hardly ever rote, especially in multiplatform environments where the challenges come fast and furious. As in any other craft, there are better and worse ways to meet these challenges. Whether you're a full-time system administrator or a part-time tinkerer, this book will help you along that path.

Automation Is a Must

Any solution that involves fiddling with every one of your machines by hand is almost always the wrong one. This book will make that approach a thing of the past for you.

Even in the best of economic climates, system administrators always have too much to do. This is true both for the people who do this work by choice and for those who had a boss walk into their office and say, "Hey, you know about computers. We can't hire anyone else. Why don't you be in charge of the servers?" When hiring gets frozen, existing employees (including those not trained for the task) may well be asked to take on added system administration responsibilities.

Automation, when applied intelligently, is one of the few things that can actually make a difference under these circumstances. It can help people work more efficiently, often freeing up time previously spent on sysadmin scut work for more interesting things. This can improve both productivity and morale.

My editors and I changed the title of this edition of the book because we realized that the real value of the material was its ability to make your life better through automation. In this book, I'll try very hard to give you the tools you need (including the mental ones—new ways to think about your problems, for example) to improve your time at work (and, as you'll see in the last chapter, your time at play).

Related Topic: Configuration Management

Before we get started, a quick note about what this book is *not* is in order. It's not a book about configuration management, and it doesn't cover the popular tools that support configuration management, such as *cfengine*, *puppet*, and *bcfg2*.

Most environments can benefit both from having the configuration of their machines/ networks managed and from automating their everyday processes. This book focuses strictly on the second topic, but I strongly encourage you to look at the tools I mentioned in the first paragraph if you are not already using some sort of configuration management system. Once you adopt a configuration tool, you can integrate it with the scripts you'll learn to write using this book.

How Perl Can Help You

System administrators should use any and every computer language available when appropriate. So why single out Perl for a book?

The answer to this question harks back to the very nature of system administration. Rémy Evard, a colleague and friend, once described the job of a system administrator as follows:

> On one side, you have a set of resources: computers, networks, software, etc. On the other side, you have a set of users with needs and projects—people who want to get work done. Our job is to bring these two sets together in the most optimal way possible, translating between the world of vague human needs and the technical world when necessary.

System administration is often a glue job, and Perl is one of the best glue languages. Perl was being used for system administration work well before the World Wide Web came along with its voracious need for glue mechanisms. Conversations I've had with numerous system administrators at Large Installation System Administration (LISA) (*http://www.usenix.org/events/byname/lisa.html*) conferences and other venues have indicated that Perl is still the dominant language in use for the field.

Perl has several other things going for it from a system administration perspective:

- It has visible origins in the various Unix shells and the C language, which are tools many system administrators are comfortable using.

- It is available on almost all modern operating systems and does its best to present a consistent interface on each. This is important for multiplatform system administration.

- It has excellent tools for text manipulation, database access, and network programming, which are three of the mainstays of the profession.

- The core language can easily be extended through a carefully constructed module mechanism.

- A large and dedicated community of users has poured countless hours into creating modules for virtually every task. Most of these modules are collected in an organized fashion (more on these collections in a moment). This community support can be very empowering.

- It is just plain fun to program.

In the interest of full disclosure, it is important to note that Perl is not the answer to all of the world's problems. Sometimes it is not even the appropriate tool for system administration programming. There are a few things going against it:

- Perl has a somewhat dicey object-oriented programming mechanism grafted on top of it. Python or Ruby is much better in this regard.

- Perl is not always simple or internally self-consistent and is chock-full of arcane invocations. Other languages have far fewer surprises.

- Perl is powerful and esoteric enough to shoot you in the foot.

The moral here is to choose the appropriate tool. More often than not, Perl has been that tool for me, and hence it's the focus of this book.

This Book Will Show You How

In the 1966–68 *Batman* television show, the dynamic duo wore utility belts. If Batman and Robin had to scale a building, Batman would say, "Quick Robin, the Bat Grappling Hook!" or "Quick Robin, the Bat Knockout Gas!" and they'd both have the right tool at hand to subdue the bad guys. This book aims to equip you with the utility belt you need to do good system administration work.

Every chapter attempts to provide you with three things:

Clear and concise information about a system administration domain
   In each chapter, we discuss in depth one domain of the system administration world. The number of possible domains in multiplatform system administration is huge; there are far too many to be included in a single book. The best survey books on just Unix system administration—*Essential System Administration* by Æleen Frisch (O'Reilly), and *Unix System Administration Handbook*, by Evi Nemeth, Garth Snyder, Scott Seebass, and Trent H. Hein (Prentice Hall)—are two and three times, respectively, the size of this book, and we'll be looking at topics related

to three different operating systems: Unix (including variants like Linux), Windows-based operating systems, and Mac OS X.

The list of topics covered is necessarily incomplete, but I've tried to put together a good stew of system and network administration information for people with varying levels of experience in the field. Seasoned veterans and new recruits may come away from this book having learned completely different material, but everyone should find something of interest to chew on. Each chapter ends with a list of references that can help you get deeper into a topic should you so choose.

For each domain or topic—especially those that have a considerable learning curve—I've included appendixes that will give you all the information you need to get up to speed quickly. Even if you're familiar with a topic, you may find that these appendixes can round out your knowledge (e.g., showing how something is implemented on a different operating system).

Perl techniques and approaches that can be used in system administration

To get the most out of this book, you'll need some initial background in Perl. Every chapter is full of Perl code that ranges in complexity from beginner to advanced levels. Whenever we encounter an intermediate-to-advanced technique, data structure, or idiom, I'll take the time to carefully step through it, piece by piece. In the process, you should be able to pick up some interesting Perl techniques to add to your programming repertoire. My hope is that Perl programmers of all levels will be able to learn something from the examples presented in this book. And as your Perl skills improve over time, you should be able to come back to the book again and again, learning new things each time.

To further enhance the learning experience, I will often present more than one way to accomplish the same task using Perl, rather than showing a single, limited answer. Remember the Perl motto, "There's more than one way to do it." These multiple-approach examples are designed to better equip your Perl utility belt: the more tools you have at hand, the better the choices you can make when approaching a new task.

Sometimes it will be obvious that one technique is superior to the others. But this book addresses only a certain subset of situations you may find yourself in, and a solution that is woefully crude for one problem may be just the ticket for another. So bear with me. For each example, I'll try to show you both the advantages and the drawbacks of each approach (and often tell you which method I prefer).

System administration best practices and deep principles

As I mentioned at the start of this chapter, there are better and worse ways to do system administration. I've been a system and network administrator for the past 25 years in some pretty demanding multiplatform environments. In each chapter I try to bring this experience to bear as I offer you some of the best practices I've learned and the deeper principles behind them. Occasionally I'll use a personal "war story from the front lines" as the starting point for these discussions.

Hopefully the depth of the craft in system administration will become apparent as you read along.

What You Need

To get the most out of this book, you will need some technical background and some resources at hand. Let's start with the background first:

You'll need to know some Perl
> There isn't enough room in this book to teach you the basics of the Perl language, so you'll need to seek that information elsewhere before working through this material. A book like *Learning Perl (http://oreilly.com/catalog/9780596520106/)*, by Randal L. Schwartz et al. (O'Reilly), can get you in good shape to approach the code in this book.

You'll need to know the basics of your operating system(s)
> This book assumes that you have some facility with the operating system or systems you plan to administer. You'll need to know how to get around in that OS (run commands, find documentation, etc.). Background information on the more complex frameworks built into the OS (e.g., WMI on Windows or SNMP) is provided.

You may need to know the specifics of your operating system(s)
> I'll attempt to describe the differences between the major operating systems as we encounter them, but I can't cover all of the intra-OS differences. In particular, every variant of Unix is a little different. As a result, you may need to track down OS-specific information and roll with the punches should that information be different from what is described here.

For technical resources, you will need just two things:

Perl
> You will need a copy of Perl installed on or available to every system you wish to administer. The downloads section of the Perl website (*http://www.perl.com*) will help you find either the source code or the binary distribution for your particular operating system. The code in this book was developed and tested under Perl 5.8.8 and ActivePerl (5.8.8) 822. See the next section for more information about these versions.

The ability to find and install Perl modules
> A later section of this chapter is devoted to the location and installation of Perl modules, an extremely important skill for our purposes. This book assumes you have the knowledge and necessary permissions to install any modules you need.
>
> At the end of each chapter is a list of the version numbers for all of the modules used by the code in that chapter. The version information is provided because modules are updated all the time, and not all updates retain backward

compatibility. If you run into problems, this information can help you determine whether there has been a module change since this book was published.

Some Notes About the Perl Versions Used for This Book

I chose to develop and test the code in this book under Perl 5.8.8 and ActivePerl (5.8.8) 822. These choices might lead you to ask a few questions.

What About Perl 5.10?

The Perl 5 development team has done some fabulous work to produce 5.10. They've added some great features to the language that I encourage you to explore. However, 5.10 wasn't released until well after this edition was under way, and at the time of this writing no major OS distribution has shipped with it as its default version of Perl. Because I know the adoption of new versions takes a while, I didn't want to include code in the book that depended on features in the language most people couldn't use out of the box. All of the code here should work just fine on Perl 5.10, and in the interest of making this code useful to as many readers as possible, I deliberately chose to target the previous stable release.

What About Strawberry Perl?

Strawberry Perl (*http://strawberryperl.com*) is an effort to bring a more "generic" and self-sufficient version of Perl to the Win32 platform. ActiveState's Perl distribution ships with a packaging system (PPM) so users don't have to compile modules or update them via the Comprehensive Perl Archive Network (CPAN). Strawberry Perl aims to provide an environment where compilation and CPAN use are easy (or at least possible) and are the norm.

I think this is an excellent project because it is helping to push some portability back into the non-Win32 Perl community. Some great progress has been made so far, but the project is still fairly young as of this writing and it does not yet have a sufficiently large ecosystem of available modules (e.g., lots of the `Win32::` modules are missing). That ruled it out for this edition, but it is definitely something to watch.

What About Perl 6?

Ah, that's the big question, isn't it? I have the pleasure of occasionally bumping into Jesse Vincent, the current Perl 6 project manager (and author of the fabulous RT trouble ticketing system). Here's what he had to say when I asked about Perl 6:

> Perl 5 is a mature, widely deployed, production-ready language. Perl 6 is maturing rapidly, but isn't yet ready for production deployment.

There are some Perl 5 modules that let you get a taste of some planned Perl 6 features (some of which have found their way into Perl 5.10). I encourage you to try modules like `Perl6::Slurp` and `Perl6::Form`. But at this point in time, there just isn't a language implementation ready for production use, and hence there is no Perl 6 in this book. Furthermore, once Perl 6 is ready for widespread use, it will take considerable time for the necessary ecosystem of modules to be developed to replace the many, many modules we leverage in this book. I look forward to that time; perhaps you'll see a Perl 6 edition of this book some day.

Some Notes About Using Vista with the Code in This Book

The code in this book has been tested under Microsoft Vista, but there is one twist you will need to know about if you plan to use it on that platform: some of the examples in this book must be run using elevated privileges for this to work. Which things require this and which don't is somewhat idiosyncratic. For example, part of the Windows quota example in Chapter 2 works without elevated privileges and part (the important part) fails with an unhelpful error if it doesn't have them.

Under Vista's User Account Control (UAC), it is not enough to be running the code as an Administrator; you must have explicitly requested it to run at an elevated privilege level. Here are the ways I know to run Perl scripts at that privilege level (since you can't by default right-click and use "Run as administrator"). You should choose the method or methods that make the most sense in your environment:

- Use the *runas.exe* command-line utility.
- Designate that the *perl.exe* binary itself be run as an Administrator (right-click on the binary name, choose Properties, switch to the Compatibility tab, and select "Run this program as administrator."
- Use one of the Elevation Power Toys described at *http://technet.microsoft.com/en -us/magazine/2008.06.elevation.aspx* and *http://technet.microsoft.com/en-us/maga zine/2007.06.utilityspotlight.aspx* to allow Perl scripts to be Run as administrator.
- Use the command-line utility *pl2bat* to convert your Perl script into a batch file and then permit that batch file to run as Administrator. Batch files don't require any special magic (like the previous option) for this to happen.

You may be wondering if it is possible to add something to your Perl script to have it request elevated privileges as needed. Unfortunately, according to Jan Dubois (one of the top Windows Perl luminaries in the field), the answer is no. He notes that there is no way to elevate an already running process; it must be created with elevated privileges. The closest you could come would be to check whether the process was already running in this fashion (e.g., by using the `Win32` module's `IsAdminUser()` function), and if not invoke another copy of the script using something like *runas.exe*.

One last note in a similar vein: in several of the chapters I recommend using the Microsoft Scriptomatic tool to become familiar with WMI. By default this won't run under Vista because it needs elevated privileges to function, but it is an "HTML Application" (*.hta*) file. Like Perl scripts, *.hta* files can't easily be Run as administrator.

Here's a recipe for getting around this limitation so you can use this excellent tool:

1. Right-click on the Internet Explorer icon in the taskbar (the "E") and choose "Run as administrator" to run it using elevated privileges. (Warning: don't use this running copy of IE to browse to any website or load anything but the Scriptomatic file, to be on the safe side.)

2. Press the Alt key to display the IE File menu. Choose "Open..." and then press the "Browse..." button. Change the dialog filter to display "All Files" and then browse to the location of the Scriptomatic *.hta* file. Open that file and you should be all set.

Locating and Installing Modules

Much of the benefit of using Perl for system administration work comes from all of the free code available in module form. The modules mentioned in this book can be found in one of three places:

The Comprehensive Perl Archive Network
> CPAN is a huge archive of Perl source code, documentation, scripts, and modules that is replicated at over a hundred sites around the world. Information on CPAN can be found at *http://www.cpan.org*. The easiest way to find the modules in CPAN is to use the search engine at *http://search.cpan.org*. The "CPAN Search" box makes it simple to find the right modules for the job.

Individual repositories for prebuilt packages
> In a moment we'll encounter the Perl Package Manager (PPM), an especially important tool for Win32 Perl users. This tool connects to *repositories* (the most famous one is housed at ActiveState) to retrieve prebuilt module packages. A good list of these repositories can be found in the wiki at *http://win32.perl.org*. If a Win32 package we use comes from a repository other than ActiveState's, I'll be sure to point you to it.

Individual websites
> Some modules are not published to CPAN or any of the PPM repositories. I really try to avoid them if possible, but in those rare cases where they fill a critical gap, I'll tell you where to get them.

How do you install one of these modules when you find it? The answer depends on the operating system you are running. Perl now ships with documentation on this process in a file called *perlmodinstall.pod* (type `perldoc perlmodinstall` to read it). The next sections provide brief summaries of the steps required for each operating system used in this book.

Installing Modules on Unix

In most cases, the process goes like this:

1. Download the module and unpack it.
2. Run `perl Makefile.PL` to create the necessary *Makefile*.
3. Run `make` to build the package.
4. Run `make test` to run any test suites included with the module by the author.
5. Run `make install` to install it in the usual place for modules on your system.

If you want to save yourself the trouble of performing all these steps by hand, you can use the `CPAN` module by Andreas J. König (shipped with Perl), or the `CPANPLUS` module by Jos Boumans. `CPAN` allows you to perform all of those steps by typing:

```
% cpan
cpan[1]> install modulename
```

and `CPANPLUS` does the same with:

```
% cpanp
CPAN Terminal> i modulename
```

Both modules are smart enough to handle module dependencies (i.e., if one module requires another module to run, it will install both modules for you automatically). They also each have a built-in search function for finding related modules and packages. I recommend typing `perldoc CPAN` or `perldoc CPANPLUS` on your system to find out more about all of the handy features of these modules.

Installing Modules on Win32

The process for installing modules on Win32 platforms using the ActiveState distribution mirrors that for Unix, with one additional step: the Perl Package Manager (PPM). If you are comfortable installing modules by hand using the Unix instructions in the previous section, you can use a program like WinZip (*http://www.winzip.com*) to unpack a distribution and use *nmake (ftp://ftp.microsoft.com/Softlib/MSLFILES/nmake15 .exe)* instead of *make* to build and install a module.

Some modules require compilation of C files as part of their build process. A large portion of the Perl users in the Win32 world do not have the necessary software installed on their computers for this compilation, so ActiveState created PPM to handle prebuilt module distribution.

The PPM system is similar to that of the `CPAN` module. It uses a Perl program called *ppm.pl* to handle the download and installation of special archive files from PPM repositories. You can start the program either by typing `ppm` or by running `ppm-shell` from within the Perl *bin* directory:

```
C:\Perl\bin> ppm-shell
ppm 4.03
ppm> install module-name
```

PPM, like CPAN, can search the list of available and installed modules for you. Type help at the ppm> command prompt for more information on how to use these commands.

It's Not Easy Being Omnipotent

Before we continue with the book, let's take a few minutes for some cautionary words. Programs written for system administration have a twist that makes them different from most other programs: on Unix and Windows they are often run with elevated privileges (i.e., as *root* or Administrator). With this power comes responsibility. There is an extra onus on us as programmers to write secure code. We write code that can and will bypass the security restrictions placed on mere mortals. Tiny mistakes can lead to severe disruptions for our users or damage to key system files. And, if we are not careful, less "ethical" users may use flaws in our code for nefarious purposes. Here are some of the issues you should consider when you use Perl under these circumstances.

Don't Do It

By all means, use Perl. But if you can, avoid having your code run in a privileged context. Most tasks do not require *root* or Administrator privileges.

For example, your log analysis program probably does not need to run as *root*. Create another, less privileged user for this sort of automation. Have a small, dedicated, privileged program hand the data to that user if necessary, and then perform the analysis as the unprivileged user.

Drop Your Privileges As Soon As Possible

Sometimes you can't avoid running a script as *root* or Administrator. For instance, a mail delivery program you create may need to be able to write to a file as any user on the system. However, programs like these should shed their omnipotence as soon as possible during their run.

Perl programs running under Unix can set the $< and $> variables:

```
# permanently drops privs
($<,$>) = (getpwnam('nobody'),getpwnam('nobody'));
```

This sets the real and effective user IDs to *nobody*, which exists on most Unix/Linux systems as an underprivileged user (you can create the user yourself if need be). To be even more thorough, you may wish to use $(and $) to change the real and effective group IDs as well.

Windows does not have user IDs per se, but there are similar processes for dropping privileges, and you can use *runas.exe* to run processes as a different user.

Be Careful When Reading Data

When reading important data like configuration files, test for unsafe conditions first. For instance, you may wish to check that the file and all of the directories in its path are not writable (since that would make it possible for someone to tamper with them). There's a good recipe for testing this in Chapter 8 of the *Perl Cookbook (http://oreilly .com/catalog/9780596003135/)*, by Tom Christiansen and Nathan Torkington (O'Reilly).

The other concern is user input. Never trust that input from a user is palatable. Even if you explicitly print `Please answer Y or N:`, there is nothing to prevent the users from answering with 2,049 random characters (either out of malice or because they stepped away from the computer and a two-year-old came over to the keyboard instead).

User input can be the cause of even more subtle trouble. My favorite example is the "poison NULL byte" exploit reported in an article on Perl CGI problems (cited in the references section at the end of this chapter—be sure to read the whole article!). This particular exploit takes advantage of the difference between Perl's handling of a NULL (`\000`) byte in a string and the handling done by the C libraries on a system. To Perl, there is nothing special about this character, but to the libraries it indicates the end of a string.

In practical terms, this means it is possible for a user to evade simple security tests. One example given in the article is that of a password-changing program whose code looks like this:

```
if ($user ne "root"){ <call the necessary C library routine> }
```

If a malicious user manages to set `$user` to `root\000` (i.e., `root` followed by a NULL byte), the test will think that the name is not `root` and will allow the Perl script to continue. But when that string is passed to the underlying C library, the string will be treated as just `root`, and the user will have walked right past the security check. If not caught, this same exploit will allow access to random files and other resources on the system. The easiest way to avoid being caught by this exploit is to sanitize your input with something like this:

```
$input =~ tr/\000//d;
```

or better yet, only use valid data that you've explicitly extracted from the user's input (e.g., with a regular expression).

 This is just one example of how user input can get programs into trouble. Because user input can be so problematic, Perl has a security precaution called *taint mode*. See the `perlsec` manpage that ships with Perl for an excellent discussion of "taintedness" and other security precautions.

Be Careful When Writing Data

If your program can write or append to every single file on the local filesystem, you need to take special care with how, where, and when it writes data. On Unix systems, this is especially important because symbolic links make file switching and redirection easy. Unless your program is diligent, it may find itself writing to the wrong file or device. There are two classes of programs where this concern comes especially into play.

Programs that append data to a file fall into the first class. The steps your program should take before appending to a file are:

1. Check the file's attributes before opening it, using `stat()` and the normal file test operators. Make sure that it is not a hard or soft link, that it has the appropriate permissions and ownership, etc.

2. Open the file for appending.

3. `stat()` the open filehandle.

4. Compare the values from steps 1 and 3 to be sure that you have an open handle to the file you intended.

The *bigbuffy* program in Chapter 10 illustrates this procedure.

Programs that use temporary files or directories are in the second class. Chances are you've often seen code like this:

```
open(TEMPFILE,">/tmp/temp.$$") or die "unable to write /tmp/temp.$$:$!\n";
```

Unfortunately, that's not sufficiently secure on a multiuser machine. The process ID (`$$`) sequence on most machines is easily predictable, which means the next temporary filename your script will use is equally predictable. If others can predict that name they may be able to get there first, and that's usually bad news.

The easiest way to avoid this conundrum is to use Tim Jenness's `File::Temp` module, which has shipped with Perl since version 5.6. Here's how it is used:

```
use File::Temp qw(tempfile);

# returns both an open filehandle and the name of that file
my ($fh, $filename) = tempfile();
print $fh "Writing to the temp file now...\n";
```

`File::Temp` can also remove the temporary file for you automatically if desired. See the module's documentation for more details.

Avoid Race Conditions

Whenever possible, avoid writing code that is susceptible to race condition exploits. The traditional race condition starts with the assumption that the following sequence is valid:

1. Your program will amass some data.
2. Your program can then act on that data.

Here's a simple example:

1. Your program checks the timestamp on a file of bug submissions to make sure nothing has been added since you last read the file.
2. Your program modifies the contents of the file.

If users can break into this sequence at a point we'll call "step 1.5" and make some key substitutions, they may cause trouble. If they can get your program in step 2 to naively act upon different data from what it found in step 1, they have effectively exploited a race condition (i.e., their program won the race to get at the data in question). Other race conditions occur if you do not handle file locking properly.

Race conditions often show up in system administration programs that scan the file-system as a first pass and then change things in a second pass. Nefarious users may be able to make changes to the filesystem right after the scanner pass so that changes are made to the wrong file. Make sure your code does not leave such gaps open.

Enjoy

It is important to remember that system administration is fun. Not all the time, and not when you have to deal with the most frustrating of problems, but there's definitely enjoyment to be found. There is a real pleasure in supporting other people and building the infrastructures that make users' lives better. When the collection of Perl programs you've just written brings other people together for a common purpose, there is joy.

So, now that you're ready, let's get to work on those wires.

References for More Information

http://www.dwheeler.com/secure-programs/ is a HOWTO document written by David A. Wheeler for secure programming under Linux and Unix. The concepts and techniques Wheeler describes are applicable to other situations as well.

http://nob.cs.ucdavis.edu/bishop/secprog/ contains more good secure programming resources from security expert Matt Bishop.

http://www.homeport.org/~adam/review.html lists security code review guidelines by Adam Shostack.

http://www.canonical.org/~kragen/security-holes.html is an old but good paper on how to find security holes (especially in your own code) by Kragen Sitaker.

"Perl CGI Problems," by rain.forest.puppy (*Phrack Magazine*, 1999), describes CGI security vulnerabilities. It can be found online at *http://www.insecure.org/news/P55-07 .txt* or in the *Phrack* archives at *http://www.phrack.com/issues.html?issue=55*.

Perl Cookbook, Second Edition (*http://oreilly.com/catalog/9780596003135/*), by Tom Christiansen and Nathan Torkington (O'Reilly), contains many good tips on coding securely.

## CHAPTER 2

Filesystems

Perl to the Rescue

Laptops fall in slow motion. Or at least that's the way it looked when the laptop I was using to write the first edition of this book fell off a table onto a hardwood floor. The machine was still in one piece and running when I picked it up, but as I checked to see whether anything was damaged, it started to run slower and slower. Then it began to make sporadic and disturbing humming-buzzing sounds during disk access. Figuring the software slowdown was caused by a software problem, I shut down the laptop. It did not go gently into the night, refusing to shut down cleanly. This was a bad sign.

Even worse was its reluctance to boot again. Each time I tried, it began the Windows NT booting process and then failed with a "file not found" error. By now it was clear that the fall had caused some serious physical damage to the hard drive. The heads had probably skidded over the platter surface, destroying files and directory entries in their wake. Now the question was, "Did any of my files survive? Did the files for *this book* survive?"

I first tried booting into Linux, the other operating system installed on the laptop. Linux booted fine, an encouraging sign. The files for this book, however, resided on the Windows NT NTFS partition that did not boot. Using Martin von Löwis's Linux NTFS driver, available at *http://www.linux-ntfs.org* (now shipping with the Linux kernels), I mounted the partition and was greeted with what *looked* like all of my files, intact.

My ensuing attempts to copy those files off that partition would proceed fine for a while, until I reached a certain file. At that point the drive would make those ominous sounds again and the backup would fail. It was clear that if I wanted to rescue my data I was going to have to skip all the damaged files on the disk. The program I was using to copy the data (*gnutar*) had the ability to skip a list of files, but here was the problem: which files? There were over *sixteen thousand*[*] files on the filesystem at the time of impact. How was I going to figure out which files were damaged and which were fine?

---

[*] At the time, 16,000 files seemed like a lot. My current laptop has 1,096,010 files on it as I write this. I imagine if this story had happened today it would have been even more fun.

Clearly running *gnutar* again and again was not a reasonable strategy. This was a job for Perl!

I'll show you the code I used to solve this problem a little later in this chapter. For that code to make sense, we'll first need to place it into context by looking at filesystems in general and how we operate on them using Perl.

Filesystem Differences

We'll start with a quick review of the native filesystems for each of our target operating systems. Some of this may be old news to you, especially if you have significant experience with a particular operating system. Still, it's worth your while to pay careful attention to the differences between the filesystems (especially the ones you don't know) if you intend to write Perl code that will work on multiple platforms.

Unix

All modern Unix variants ship with a native filesystem whose semantics resemble those of their common ancestor, the Berkeley Fast File System (FFS). Different vendors have extended their filesystem implementations in different ways: some filesystems support POSIX access control lists (ACLs) for better security, some support journaling for better recovery, others include the ability to set special file-based attributes, and so on. We'll be writing code aimed at the lowest common denominator to allow it to work across different Unix platforms.

The top, or *root*, of a Unix filesystem is indicated by a forward slash (/). To uniquely identify a file or directory in a Unix filesystem, we construct a path starting with a slash and then add directories, separating them with forward slashes, as we descend deeper into the filesystem. The final component of this path is the desired directory or filename. Directory and filenames in modern Unix variants are case-sensitive. Almost all ASCII characters can be used in these names if you are crafty enough, but sticking to alphanumeric characters and some limited punctuation will save you hassle later.

Windows-Based Operating Systems

All current Windows-based operating systems ship with three supported filesystems: File Allocation Table (FAT), NT FileSystem (NTFS), and FAT32 (an improved version of FAT that allows for larger partitions and smaller cluster sizes).

The FAT filesystem found in these operating systems uses an extended version of the basic FAT filesystems found in DOS. Before we look at the extended version, it is important to understand the foibles of the basic FAT filesystem. In basic or real-mode FAT filesystems, filenames conform to the 8.3 specification. This means that file and directory names can consist of a maximum of eight characters, followed by a period (or *dot* as it is spoken) and a suffix of up to three characters in length. Unlike in Unix, where a period in a filename has no special meaning, in basic FAT filesystems a filename can contain only a single period as an enforced separator between the name and its extension or suffix.

Real-mode FAT was later enhanced in a version called *VFAT* or *protected-mode FAT*. This is roughly the version that current operating systems support when they say they use FAT. VFAT hides all of the name restrictions from the user. Longer filenames without separators are supported by a very creative hack: VFAT uses a chain of standard file/directory name slots to transparently shoehorn extended filename support into the basic FAT filesystem structure. For compatibility, every file and directory name can still be accessed using a special 8.3-conforming DOS alias. For instance, the directory called *Downloaded Program Files* is also available as *DOWNLO~1*.

There are four key differences between a VFAT and a Unix filesystem:

- FAT filesystems are case-insensitive. In Unix, an attempt to open a file using the wrong case (i.e., *MYFAVORITEFILE* versus *myfavoritefile*) will fail, but with FAT or VFAT, this will succeed with no problem.

- Instead of a forward slash, FAT uses the backward slash (\) as its path separator. This has a direct ramification for the Perl programmer, because the backslash is a quoting character in Perl. Paths written in single quotes with only single separators (e.g., `$path='\dir\dir\filename'`) are just fine. However, situations in which you need to place multiple backslashes next to each other (e.g., `\\server\dir\file`) are potential trouble. In those cases, you have to be vigilant in doubling any multiple backslashes. Some Perl functions and some Perl modules will accept paths with forward slashes, but you shouldn't count on this convention when programming. It is better to bite the bullet and write `\\\\winnt\\temp\\` than to learn that your code breaks because the conversion hasn't been done for you.

- FAT files and directories have special flags associated with them that are called *attributes*. Example attributes include "Read-only" and "System."

- The root of a FAT filesystem is specified starting with the drive letter on which the filesystem resides. For instance, the absolute path for a file might be specified as `c:\home\cindy\docs\resume\current.doc`.

FAT32 and NTFS filesystems have the same semantics as VFAT filesystems. They share the same support for long filenames and use the same root designator. NTFS is more sophisticated in its name support, however, because it allows these names to be specified using Unicode. Unicode is a multibyte character encoding scheme that can be used to represent all of the characters of all of the written languages on the planet.

NTFS also has some functional differences that distinguish it from the other Windows and basic Unix filesystems. Later in this chapter, we will write some code to take advantage of some of these differences, such as filesystem quotas. NTFS supports ACLs, which provide a fine-grained permission mechanism for file and directory access. It also adds some functionality that we won't touch on, including file encryption and file compression. As a related aside, Vista will only install on an NTFS-formatted filesystem.

Before we move on to another operating system, it is important to at least mention the universal naming convention (UNC). UNC is a convention for locating things (files and directories, in our case) in a networked environment. In UNC names, the drive letter and colon preceding the absolute path are replaced with *server**sharename*. This convention suffers from the same Perl backslash syntax clash we saw a moment ago, though, so it is not uncommon to see a set of leaning toothpicks like this:

```
$path = '\\\\server\\sharename\\directory\\file';
```

Mac OS X

At the time the previous edition of this book was written, OS X had just recently appeared on the horizon. Classic Mac OS used a filesystem (Mac OS Hierarchical File System, or HFS) that was a very different beast from any of the filesystems described earlier. It had very different file semantics and required special handling from Perl. Mac OS 8.1 introduced an improved variant of HFS called HFS+, which became the default filesystem format for OS X.[†] New releases of OS X saw continued development of the filesystem and its capabilities.

It has taken some time and a number of releases to get to this point, but the current HFS+ filesystem semantics don't look very different from any other Unix filesystem at this point. Files and paths are specified the same way, and HFS+ supports BSD extended attributes in the usual way (e.g., ACLs are available). If you stick to the standard Perl mechanisms for interacting with filesystems, you can generally treat HFS+ like any other Unix filesystem.

 If you do need to muck with an HFS+ filesystem in a nongeneric fashion, as I've cavalierly suggested here (i.e., if you really need to get your hands dirty and twiddle bits that are specific to HFS+), you have at least a couple of options:

- Call the Mac OS X command-line utilities directly (e.g., using chmod +a..., once *fsaclctl* has been used to turn on ACLs).
- Use Dan Kogai's MacOSX::File modules. These modules will also give you access to the "legacy" extended attributes (type, creator, etc.) that played a larger role in pre-OS X filesystem use.

[†] As an aside, you can create UFS-formatted filesystems under OS X. Full ZFS support is also on the way as of this writing.

There is one important difference between a standard UFS and a standard HFS+ filesystem. By default,‡ HFS+ is case-insensitive (albeit case-preserving): it will treat `BillyJoeBob` and `billyJoebob` exactly the same (i.e., if you try to `open()` the first but the second one is the real name of the file, you will still get a filehandle that points at the file's data). There's nothing special you have to do about this difference from a Perl perspective except be very careful about your assumptions. Be especially careful when removing files, because you can sometimes wind up targeting the wrong one.

Filesystem Differences Summary

Table 2-1 summarizes all of the differences we just discussed, along with a few more items of interest.

Table 2-1. Filesystem comparison

OS and filesystem	Path separator	Filename spec. length	Absolute path format	Relative path format	Unique features
Unix (Berkeley Fast File System and others)	/	OS-dependent number of chars	/dir/file	dir/file	OS-variant-dependent additions
Mac OS (HFS+)	/	255 Unicode chars	/dir/file	dir/file	Mac OS legacy support (e.g., creator/type attributes), BSD extended attributes
Windows-based operating systems (NTFS)	\	255 Unicode chars	Drive:\dir\file	dir\file	File encryption and compression
DOS (basic FAT)	\	8.3	Drive:\dir\file	dir\file	Attributes

Dealing with Filesystem Differences from Perl

Perl can help you write code that takes most of these filesystem quirks into account. It ships with a module called `File::Spec` that hides some of the differences between the filesystems. For instance, if we pass in the components of a path to the `catfile` method:

```
use File::Spec;

my $path = File::Spec->catfile(qw{home cindy docs resume.doc});
```

`$path` is set to `home\cindy\docs\resume.doc` on a Windows system, while on a Unix or OS X system it becomes `home/cindy/docs/resume.doc`, and so on. `File::Spec` also has methods like `curdir` and `updir` that return the punctuation necessary to describe the current and parent directories (e.g., "." and ".."). The methods in this module give you

---

‡ It is possible to create a case-sensitive HFS+ volume in current versions of OS X, but doing so can be fraught with peril. This practice has been known to break (albeit naively written) applications that did not expect anything but the default semantics. Don't do this unless you have a really good reason.

an abstract way to construct and manipulate your path specifications. If you would prefer not to have to write your code using an object-oriented syntax, the module `File::Spec::Functions` provides a more direct route to the methods found in `File::Spec`.

If you find `File::Spec`'s interface to be a little peculiar (e.g., the name `catfile()` makes sense only if you know enough Unix to understand that the `cat` command is used to con*cat*enate parts of its input together), there's a much nicer wrapper by Ken Williams called `Path::Class`. It doesn't ship with Perl like `File::Spec` does, but it is probably worth the extra installation step. Here's how it works.

First, you create either a `Path::Class::File` or a `Path::Class::Dir` object using a natural syntax that specifies the path components:

```
use Path::Class;

my $pcfile = file(qw{home cindy docs resume.doc});
my $pcdir  = dir(qw{home cindy docs});
```

`$pcfile` and `$pcdir` are now both magic. If you use them as you would any other scalar variable (in a case where you "stringify" them), they turn into a path constructed to match the current operating system. For example:

```
print $pcfile;
print $pcdir;
```

would yield `home/cindy/docs/resume.doc` and `home/cindy/docs` or `home\cindy\docs\resume.doc` and `home\cindy\docs`, as we saw earlier with `File::Spec`.

Even though `$pcfile` and `$pcdir` stringify into paths that look like strings, they are still objects. And like most other objects, there are methods that can be called on them. These methods include those found in `File::Spec` and more. Here are some examples:

```
my $absfile = $pcfile->absolute; # returns the absolute path for $pcfile
my @contents = $pcfile->slurp;   # slurps in the contents of that file
$pcfile->remove();               # actually deletes the file
```

There are two more tricks `Path::Class` can do that are worth mentioning before we move on. First, it can parse existing paths:

```
use Path::Class;

# handing it a full path (a string) instead of components
my $pcfile = file('/home/cindy/docs/resume.doc');

print $pcfile->dir();      # note: this returns a Path::Class::Dir,
                           # which we're stringify-ing
print $pcfile->parent();   # same as dir(), but can make code read better
print $pcfile->basename(); # removes the directory part of the name
```

The second trick comes in handy when you want to write code on one operating system that understands the filesystem semantics of another. For example, you may need a web application running on your Linux box to be able to instruct its users on how to find a file on their local Windows machines. To ask `Path::Class` to consider the semantics of a different operating system, you need to explicitly import two different methods: `foreign_file()` and `foreign_dir()`. These two methods each take the target operating system type as their first argument:

```
use Path::Class qw(foreign_file foreign_dir);

my $fpcfile = foreign_file('Win32', qw{home cindy docs resume.doc});
my $fpcdir  = foreign_dir('Win32', qw{home cindy});
```

Now, `$fpcfile` will yield home\cindy\docs\resume.doc even if the code is run from a Mac. This probably won't come up often, but it's very handy when you need it.

Walking or Traversing the Filesystem by Hand

By now, you're probably itching to get to some practical applications of Perl. We'll begin by examining the process of "walking the filesystem," one of the most common system administration tasks associated with filesystems. Typically this entails searching an entire set of directory trees and taking action based on the files or directories found. Each OS provides a tool for this task: under Unix it's the `find` command, under Windows it's Search, and in Mac OS it's Spotlight or the search box in the Finder (if you aren't going to run `find` from a Terminal window). All of these are useful for searching, but they lack the power to perform arbitrary and complex operations by themselves. In this section we'll explore how Perl allows us to write more sophisticated file-walking code, beginning with the very basics and ratcheting up the complexity as we go on.

To get started, let's take a common scenario that provides a clear problem for us to solve. In this scenario, we're Unix system administrators with overflowing user filesystems and empty budgets. (We're picking on Unix first, but the other operating systems will get their turns in a moment.)

We can't add more disk space without money, so we have to make better use of our existing resources. Our first step is to remove all the files on our filesystems that can be eliminated. Under Unix, good candidates for elimination are the core files left around by programs that have died nasty deaths. Most users either do not notice these files or just ignore them, leaving large amounts of disk space claimed for no reason. We need a way to search through a filesystem and delete these varmints.

To walk a filesystem by hand, we start by reading the contents of a single directory and work our way down from there. Let's ease into the process and begin with code that examines the contents of the current directory and reports if it finds either a core file or another directory to be searched.

First, we open the directory using roughly the same syntax used for opening a file. If the open fails, we exit the program and print the error message set by the `opendir()` call (`$!`):

```
opendir my $DIR, '.' or die "Can't open the current directory: $!\n";
```

This provides us with a directory handle, `$DIR` in this case, which we can pass to `readdir()` to get a list of all the files and directories in the current directory. If `readdir()` can't read that directory, our code prints an error message (which hopefully explains why it failed) and the program exits:

```
# read file/directory names in that directory into @names
my @names = readdir $DIR or die "Unable to read current dir:$!\n";
```

We then close the open directory handle:

```
closedir $DIR;
```

Now we can work with those names:

```
foreach my $name (@names) {
    next if ($name eq '.');    # skip the current directory entry
    next if ($name eq '..');   # skip the parent directory entry

    if (-d $name) {            # is this a directory?
        print "found a directory: $name\n";
        next;                  # can skip to the next name in the for loop
    }
    if ($name eq 'core') {     # is this a file named "core"?
        print "found one!\n";
    }
}
```

That's all it takes to write some very simple code that scans a single directory. This isn't even "crawling" a filesystem, though, never mind walking it. To walk the filesystem we'll have to enter all of the directories we find in the scan and look at their contents as well. If those subdirectories have subdirectories, we'll need to check them out too.

Whenever you have a hierarchy of containers and an operation that gets performed the exact same way on every container and subcontainer in that hierarchy, the situation calls out for a recursive solution (at least to computer science majors). As long as the hierarchy is not too deep and doesn't loop back on itself (i.e., all containers hold only their immediate children and do not reference other parts of the hierarchy), recursive solutions tend to make the most sense. This is the case with our example; we're going to be scanning a directory, all of its subdirectories, all of their subdirectories, and so on.

If you've never seen recursive code (i.e., code that calls itself), you may find it a bit strange at first. Writing recursive code is a bit like painting a set of *matryoshka* nesting Russian dolls, the largest of which contains a slightly smaller doll of the exact same shape, which contains another doll, and so on until you get to a very small doll in the center.

A recipe for painting these dolls might go something like this:

1. Examine the doll in front of you. Does it contain a smaller doll? If so, remove the contents and set aside the outer doll.

2. Repeat step 1 with the contents you just removed until you reach the center.

3. Paint the center doll. When it is dry, put it back in its container doll.

4. Repeat step 3 with the next-smallest doll until they're all back in their containers and you've painted the last one.

The process is the same every step of the way. If the thing in your hand has sub-things, put off dealing with it and deal with the sub-things first. If the thing you have in your hand doesn't have sub-things, do something with it, and then return to the last thing you put off and work your way back up the chain.

In coding terms, this process is typically handled by a subroutine that deals with containers. The routine first looks to see whether the current container has subcontainers. If it does, it calls *itself* again and again to deal with all of these subcontainers. If it doesn't, it performs some operation and returns back to the code that called it. If you're not familiar with code that calls itself, I recommend sitting down with a paper and a pencil and tracing the program flow until you are convinced it actually works.

Let's take a look at some recursive code now. To make our code recursive, we first encapsulate the operation of scanning a directory and acting upon its contents in a subroutine called ScanDirectory(). ScanDirectory() takes a single argument, the directory it is supposed to scan. It figures out the current directory, enters the requested directory, and scans it. When it has completed this scan, it returns to the directory from which it was called. Here's the new code:

```perl
#!/usr/bin/perl -s

# Note the use of -s for switch processing. Under Windows, you will need to
# call this script explicitly with -s (i.e., perl -s script) if you do not
# have perl file associations in place.
# -s is also considered 'retro' - many programmers prefer to load
# a separate module (from the Getopt:: family) for switch parsing.

use Cwd; # module for finding the current working directory

# This subroutine takes the name of a directory and recursively scans
# down the filesystem from that point looking for files named "core"
sub ScanDirectory {
    my $workdir = shift;

    my $startdir = cwd;     # keep track of where we began

    chdir $workdir or die "Unable to enter dir $workdir: $!\n";
    opendir my $DIR, '.' or die "Unable to open $workdir: $!\n";
    my @names = readdir $DIR or die "Unable to read $workdir: $!\n";
    closedir $DIR;

    foreach my $name (@names) {
        next if ( $name eq '.' );
        next if ( $name eq '..' );

        if ( -d $name ) {      # is this a directory?
            ScanDirectory($name);
            next;
        }
```

```
        if ( $name eq 'core' ) {    # is this a file named "core"?
                    # if -r specified on command line, actually delete the file
            if ( defined $r ) {
                unlink $name or die "Unable to delete $name: $!\n";
            }
            else {
                print "found one in $workdir!\n";
            }
        }
    }
    chdir $startdir or die "Unable to change to dir $startdir: $!\n";
}

ScanDirectory('.');
```

The most important change from the previous example is our code's behavior when it finds a subdirectory in the directory it has been requested to scan. If it finds a directory, instead of printing "found a directory!" as our previous sample did, it recursively calls itself to examine that directory first. Once that entire subdirectory has been scanned (i.e., when the call to ScanDirectory() returns), it returns to looking at the rest of the contents of the current directory.

To make our code fully functional as a core file-destroyer, we've also added file deletion functionality to it. Pay attention to how that code is written: it will only delete files if the script is started with the command-line switch -r (for remove).

We're using Perl's built-in -s switch for automatic option parsing as part of the invocation line (#!/usr/bin/perl -s). This is the simplest way to parse command-line options;* for more sophistication, we'd probably use something from the Getopt:: module family. If a command-line switch is present (e.g., -r), a global scalar variable with the same name (e.g., $r) is set when the script is run. In our code, if Perl is not invoked with -r, we revert to the past behavior of just announcing that a core file has been found.

 When you write automatic tools, you should make destructive actions harder to perform. Take heed: Perl, like most powerful languages, allows you to nuke your filesystem without breaking a sweat.

Now, lest any Windows-focused readers among you think the previous example didn't apply to you, let me point out that this code could be made useful for you as well. A single line change from:

```
    if ($name eq 'core') {
```

to:

```
    if ($name eq 'MSCREATE.DIR') {
```

---

* -s doesn't play nicely with use strict by default, so don't use it for anything but the most trivial scripts.

will create a program that deletes the annoying, hidden zero-length files certain Microsoft program installers used to leave behind. Infestation with these files isn't as much of a problem today as it used to be, but I'm sure some other file will take their place in the list of annoyances.

With this code under our belt, let's return to the quandary that started this chapter. After my laptop kissed the floor, I found myself in desperate need of a way to determine which files could be read off the disk and which were damaged.

Here's the actual code (or a reasonable facsimile) that I used:

```perl
use Cwd; # module for finding the current working directory
$|=1;    # turn off I/O buffering

sub ScanDirectory {
    my $workdir = shift;

    my $startdir = cwd;    # keep track of where we began

    chdir $workdir or die "Unable to enter dir $workdir: $!\n";

    opendir my $DIR, '.' or die "Unable to open $workdir: $!\n";
    my @names = readdir $DIR;
    closedir $DIR;

    foreach my $name (@names) {
        next if ( $name eq '.' );
        next if ( $name eq '..' );

        if ( -d $name ) {    # is this a directory?
            ScanDirectory($name);
            next;
        }
        CheckFile($name)
            or print cwd. '/' . $name . "\n";    # print the bad filename

    }
    chdir $startdir or die "Unable to change to dir $startdir:$!\n";
}

sub CheckFile {
    my $name = shift;

    print STDERR 'Scanning ' . cwd . '/' . $name . "\n";

    # attempt to read the directory entry for this file
    my @stat = stat($name);
    if ( !$stat[4] && !$stat[5] && !$stat[6] && !$stat[7] && !$stat[8] ) {
        return 0;
    }

    # attempt to open this file
    open my $T, '<', "$name" or return 0;
```

```
        # read the file one byte at a time, throw away actual data in $discard
        for ( my $i = 0; $i < $stat[7]; $i++ ) {
            my $r = sysread( $T, $discard, 1 );
            if ( $r != 1 ) {
                close $T;
                return 0;
            }
        }
        close $T;
        return 1;
    }

    ScanDirectory('.');
```

The difference between this code and our last example is the addition of a subroutine to check each file encountered. For every file, we use the `stat()` function to see if we can read that file's directory information (e.g., its size). If we can't, we know the file is damaged. If we can read the directory information, we attempt to open the file. And for a final test, we attempt to read every single byte of the file. This doesn't guarantee that the file hasn't been damaged (the contents could have been modified), but it does at least show that the file is readable.

You may wonder why this code uses an esoteric function like `sysread()` to read the files instead of using `< >` or `read()`, Perl's usual file-reading operator and function. `sysread()` gives us the ability to read the file byte-by-byte without any of the usual buffering. If a file is damaged at location X, we don't want to waste time waiting for the standard library routines to attempt to read the bytes at locations X+1, X+2, X+3, and so on as part of their usual pre-fetch; we want the code to quit trying to read the file immediately. In general you will want file reads to fetch whole chunks at a time for performance's sake, but here that's undesirable because it would mean the laptop would spend prolonged periods of time making awful noises every time it found a damaged file.

Now that you've seen the code I used, let me offer some closure to this story. After the script you just saw ran all night long (literally), it found 95 bad files out of 16,000 total. Fortunately, none of those files were files from the book you are now reading. I backed up the good files to another machine and got back to work; Perl saved the day.

Walking the Filesystem Using the File::Find Module

Now that we've explored the basics of filesystem walking, here's a faster and spiffier way to do it. Perl comes with a module called `File::Find` that allows it to emulate the Unix `find` command. The easiest way to begin using this module is to use the `find2perl` command to generate prototypical Perl code for you.

For instance, let's say you need some code to search the *home* directory for files named *beesknees*. The command line that uses the Unix `find` command is:

```
% find /home -name beesknees -print
```

Feed the same options to *find2perl*:

```
% find2perl /home -name beesknees -print
```

and it produces:

```
#! /usr/bin/perl -w
    eval 'exec /usr/bin/perl -S $0 ${1+"$@"}'
        if 0; #$running_under_some_shell

use strict;
use File::Find ();

# Set the variable $File::Find::dont_use_nlink if you're using AFS,
# since AFS cheats.

# for the convenience of &wanted calls, including -eval statements:
use vars qw/*name *dir *prune/;
*name   = *File::Find::name;
*dir    = *File::Find::dir;
*prune  = *File::Find::prune;

sub wanted;

# traverse desired filesystems
File::Find::find({wanted => \&wanted}, '/home');
exit;

sub wanted {
    /^beesknees\z/s &&
    print("$name\n");
}
```

The *find2perl*-generated code is fairly straightforward. It loads in the necessary `Find::File` module, sets up some variables for convenient use (we'll take a closer look at these a little later), and calls `File::Find::find` with the name of a "wanted" subroutine and the starting directory. We'll examine this subroutine and its purpose in just a second, since it's where all of the interesting modifications we're about to explore will live.

Before we begin modifying this code, it's important to note a few things that may not be obvious just by looking at the sample output:

- The folks who have worked on the `File::Find` module have gone to considerable trouble to make this module portable across platforms. `File::Find`'s internal routines work behind the scenes so the same Perl code for filesystem walking works for Unix, Mac OS X, Windows, VMS, and so on.

- The code generated by *find2perl* includes the obsolete use vars pragma, which was replaced by the our() function in Perl 5.6. I suspect it was left this way for backward compatibility. I just wanted to point this out just so you don't pick up this convention by mistake.

Now let's talk about the wanted() subroutine that we will modify for our own purposes. File::Find::find() calls the wanted() subroutine with the current file or directory name once for every file or directory encountered during its filesystem walk. It's up to the code in wanted() to select the "interesting" files or directories and operate on them accordingly. In the sample output shown earlier, it first checks to see if the file or directory name matches the string beesknees. If the name matches, the && operator causes Perl to execute the print statement to print the name of the file or directory that was found.

We'll have to address two practical concerns when we create our own wanted() subroutines. Since wanted() is called once per file or directory name, it is important to make the code in this subroutine short and sweet. The sooner we can exit the wanted() subroutine, the faster the File::Find::find() routine can proceed with the next file or directory, and the speedier the overall program will run. It is also important to keep in mind the behind-the-scenes portability concerns we mentioned a moment ago. It would be a shame to have a portable File::Find::find() call an OS-specific wanted() subroutine, unless this was unavoidable. Looking at the source code for the File::Find module and the perlport documentation may offer some hints on how to avoid this situation.

For our first use of File::Find, let's rewrite our previous core-destroyer example and then extend it a bit. First we type:

```
% find2perl -name core -print
```

which gives us (in excerpt):

```
use strict;
use File::Find ();

use vars qw/*name *dir *prune/;
*name    = *File::Find::name;
*dir     = *File::Find::dir;
*prune   = *File::Find::prune;

File::Find::find({wanted => \&wanted}, '.');

sub wanted {
    /^core\z/s &&
    print("$name\n");
}
```

Then we add -s to the Perl invocation line and modify the wanted() subroutine:

```
my $r;
sub wanted {
    /^core$/ && print("$name\n") && defined $r && unlink($name);
}
```

This gives us the desired deletion functionality when the user invokes the program with
-r. Here's a tweak that adds another measure of protection to our potentially destructive code:

```
my $r;
sub wanted {
    /^core$/ && -s $name && print("$name\n") &&
            defined $r && unlink($name);
}
```

This checks any file called *core* to see if it is a non-zero-length file before printing
the name or contemplating deletion. Sophisticated users sometimes create a link
to */dev/null* named *core* in their home directories to prevent inadvertent core dumps
from being stored in those directories. The -s test makes sure we don't delete links or
zero-length files by mistake. If we wanted to be even more diligent, we could make two
additional checks:

1. Open and examine the file to confirm that it is an actual core file, either from within
   Perl or by calling the Unix `file` command. Determining whether a file is an au-
   thentic core dump file can be tricky when you have filesystems remotely mounted
   over a network by machines of different architectures, all with different core file
   formats.

2. Look at the modification date of the file. If someone is actively debugging a program, she may not be happy if you delete the core file out from under her.

Before we look at any more code, it would probably be helpful to explain those
mysterious variable aliasing lines:

```
*name   = *File::Find::name;
*dir    = *File::Find::dir;
*prune  = *File::Find::prune;
```

`Find::File` makes a number of variables available to the `wanted()` subroutine as it runs.
The important ones are listed in Table 2-2.

Table 2-2. File::Find variables

Variable name	Meaning
$_	Current filename
$File::Find::dir	Current directory name
$File::Find::name	Full path of current filename (e.g., "$File::Find::dir/$_")

We'll see how these are used in our next code example.

Let's take a break from the Unix world for a bit and look at a couple of Windows-specific examples. We could make a small modification to our previous code to have it search the entire filesystem of the current drive for hidden files (i.e., those with the HIDDEN attribute set). This example works on both NTFS and FAT filesystems:

```
use File::Find ();
use Win32::File;

File::Find::find( { wanted => \&wanted }, '\\' );

my $attr;  # defined globably instead of in wanted() to avoid repeatedly
           # defining a local copy of $attr every time it is called

sub wanted {
    -f $_
        && ( Win32::File::GetAttributes( $_, $attr ) )
        && ( $attr & HIDDEN )
        && print "$File::Find::name\n";
}
```

Here's an NTFS-specific example that will look for all files that have Full Access explicitly enabled for the special group *Everyone* and print their names:

```
use File::Find;
use Win32::FileSecurity;

# determine the DACL mask for Full Access
my $fullmask = Win32::FileSecurity::MakeMask(qw(FULL));

File::Find::find( { wanted => \&wanted }, '\\' );

sub wanted {
    # this time we're happy to make sure we get a fresh %users each time
    my %users;

    ( -f $_ )
        && eval {Win32::FileSecurity::Get( $_, \%users )}
        && ( defined $users{'Everyone'} )
        && ( $users{'Everyone'} == $fullmask )
        && print "$File::Find::name\n";
}
```

In this code, we query the access control list for all files, checking whether that list includes an entry for the group *Everyone*. If it does, we compare the *Everyone* entry to the value for Full Access (computed by MakeMask()), printing the absolute path of the file when we find a match.

You may be curious about the `eval()` call that popped up in the previous code sample. Despite what the documentation says about `Win32::File Security` nicely returning errors in `$!`, when it encounters certain situations it instead throws a snit fit and exits abruptly. This is listed as a bug in the docs, but that's easy to miss.

Unfortunately, two common things give this module dyspepsia: the presence of a paging file it can't read, and the presence of a null DACL (a discretionary ACL set to null). We use `eval()` to trap and ignore this antisocial behavior.

As a related aside, some parts of the OS (e.g., Explorer) also treat a null DACL as giving the same access to Everyone our code tries to find. If we wanted to display the files with this condition, we could check `$@`.

Here is another real-life example of how useful even simple code can be. Many moons ago, I was attempting to defragment the NTFS partition on a laptop when the software reported a "Metadata Corruption Error." Perusing the website of the vendor who made the defragmentation software, I encountered a tech support note that suggested, "This situation can be caused by a long filename which contains more characters than is legal under Windows NT." It then suggested locating this file by copying each folder to a new location, comparing the number of files in the copy to the original, and then, if the copied folder has fewer files, identifying which file(s) in the original folder did not get copied to the new location.

This seemed like a ridiculous suggestion given the number of folders on my NT partition and the amount of time it would take. Instead, I whipped up the following code (edited to use current-day syntax) in about a minute using the methods we've been discussing:

```
use File::Find;

my $max;
my $maxlength;

File::Find::find( { wanted => \&wanted }, '.' );

print "max:$max\n";

sub wanted {
    return unless -f $_;
    if ( length($_) > $maxlength ) {
        $max       = $File::Find::name;
        $maxlength = length($_);
    }
    if ( length($File::Find::name) > 200 ) { print $File::Find::name, "\n"; }
}
```

This printed out the names of all the files with names longer than 200 characters, followed by the name of the largest file found. Job done, thanks to Perl.

When Not to Use the File::Find Module

When is the `File::Find` method we've been discussing *not* appropriate? Three situations come to mind:

1. If the filesystem you are traversing does not follow the normal semantics, you can't use it. For instance, in the bouncing laptop scenario described at the beginning of the chapter, the Linux NTFS filesystem driver I was using had the strange property of not listing "." or ".." in empty directories. This broke `File::Find` badly.

2. If you need to change the names of the directories in the filesystem you are traversing *while you are traversing it*, `File::Find` gets very unhappy and behaves in an unpredictable way.

3. If you need to walk a nonnative filesystem mounted on your machine (for example, an NFS mount of a Unix filesystem on a Windows machine), `File::Find` will attempt to use the native operating system's filesystem semantics.

   It is unlikely that you'll encounter these situations, but if you do, refer to the first filesystem-walking section of this chapter for information on how to traverse filesystems by hand.

Let's return to Unix to close this section with a more complex example. One idea that seems to get short shrift in many system administration contexts (but can yield tremendous benefit in the end) is the notion of empowering the user. If your users can fix their own problems with tools you provide, everybody wins.

Much of this chapter is devoted to dealing with problems that arise from filesystems being filled. Often this occurs because users do not know enough about their environment, or because it is too cumbersome to perform any basic disk-space management. Many a support request starts with "I'm out of disk space in my home directory and I don't know why." Here's a bare-bones version of a script called *needspace* that can help users with this problem. All the user has to do is type **needspace**, and the script attempts to locate items in that user's home directory that could be deleted. It looks for two kinds of files: known core/backup files and those that can be recreated automatically. Let's dive into the code:

```
use File::Find;
use File::Basename;
use strict;

# hash of fname extensions and the extensions they can be derived from
my %derivations = (
    '.dvi' => '.tex',
    '.aux' => '.tex',
    '.toc' => '.tex',
    '.o'   => '.c',
);

my %types = (
    'emacs' => 'emacs backup files',
```

```
    'tex'   => 'files that can be recreated by running La/TeX',
    'doto'  => 'files that can be recreated by recompiling source',
);

my $targets;      # we'll collect the files we find into this hash of hashes
my %baseseen;     # for caching base files
```

We start by loading the libraries we need: our friend `File::Find` and another useful library called `File::Basename`. `File::Basename` will come in handy for parsing pathnames. We then initialize a hash table with known derivations; for instance, we know that running the command TeX or LaTeX on the file *happy.tex* can generate the file *happy.dvi*, and that *happy.o* could possibly be created by running a C compiler on *happy.c*. I say "possibly" because sometimes multiple source files are needed to generate a single derived file. We can only make simple guesses based on file extensions; generalized dependency analysis is a complex problem we won't attempt to touch here.

Next, we locate the user's home directory by finding the user ID of the person running the script ($<) and feeding it to `getpwuid()`. `getpwuid()` returns password information in list form (more on this in Chapter 3), from which an array index ([7]) selects the home directory element. There are shell-specific ways to retrieve this information (e.g., querying the $HOME environment variable), but the code as written is more portable.

Once we have the home directory, we enter it and begin scanning using a `find()` call just like the ones we've seen before:

```
my $homedir = ( getpwuid($<) )[7];    # find the user's home directory

chdir($homedir)
    or die "Unable to change to your homedir $homedir:$!\n";

$| = 1;                               # print to STDOUT in an unbuffered way

print 'Scanning';
find( \&wanted, '.' );
print "done.\n";
```

Here's the `wanted()` subroutine we call. It starts by looking for *core* files and *emacs* backup and autosave files. We assume these files can be deleted without checking for their source file (perhaps not a safe assumption). If one of these files is found, its size and location is stored in a hash of hashes whose inner key is the path to the file with a value that is the size of that file.

The remaining checks for derivable files are very similar. They call the routine `BaseFileExists()` to check whether a particular file can be derived from another file in that directory. If this routine returns `true`, we store the filename and size info for later retrieval:

```
sub wanted {

    # print a dot for every dir so the user knows we're doing something
    print '.' if ( -d $_ );
```

```
    # we're only checking files
    return unless -f $_;

    # check for core files
    $_ eq 'core'
        && ( $targets->{core}{$File::Find::name} = ( stat(_) )[7] )
        && return;

    # check for emacs backup and autosave files
    ( /^#.*#$/ || /~$/ )
        && ( $targets->{emacs}{$File::Find::name} = ( stat(_) )[7] )
        && return;

    # check for derivable tex files
    ( /\.dvi$/ || /\.aux$/ || /\.toc$/ )
        && BaseFileExists($File::Find::name)
        && ( $targets->{tex}{$File::Find::name} = ( stat(_) )[7] )
        && return;

    # check for derivable .o files
    /\.o$/
        && BaseFileExists($File::Find::name)
        && ( $targets->{doto}{$File::Find::name} = ( stat(_) )[7] )
        && return;
}
```

Here's the routine that checks whether a particular file can be derived from another "base" file in the same directory (i.e., whether *happy.c* exists if we find *happy.o*):

```
sub BaseFileExists {
    my ( $name, $path, $suffix ) = File::Basename::fileparse( $_[0], '\..*' );

    # if we don't know how to derive this type of file
    return 0 unless ( defined $derivations{$suffix} );

    # easy, we've seen the base file before
    return 1
        if ( defined $baseseen{ $path . $name . $derivations{$suffix} } );

    # if file (or file to which link points) exists and has non-zero size
    # return success once we have cached the information
    return 1
        if ( -s $name . $derivations{$suffix}
        && ++$baseseen{ $path . $name . $derivations{$suffix} } );
}
```

Here's how this code works:

1. `File::Basename::fileparse()` is used to separate the path into a filename, its leading path, and its suffix (e.g., `resume.dvi`, `/home/cindy/docs/`, `.dvi`).

2. This file's suffix is checked to determine if it is one we recognize as being derivable. If not, we return `0` ("false" in a scalar context).

3. We check whether we've already seen a "base file" for this particular file, and if so return `true`. In some situations (TeX/LaTeX in particular), a single base file can yield

---

many derived files. This check speeds things up considerably because it saves us a trip to the filesystem.

4. If we haven't seen a base file for this file before, we check to see if one exists and, if so, that it's length is non-zero. If so, we cache the base file information and return 1 ("true" in a scalar context).

All that's left for us to do now is to print out the information we gathered as we walked the filesystem:

```perl
foreach my $path ( keys %{ $targets->{core} } ) {
    print 'Found a core file taking up '
        . BytesToMeg( $targets->{core}{$path} )
        . 'MB in '
        . File::Basename::dirname($path) . ".\n";
}

foreach my $kind ( sort keys %types ) {
    ReportDerivFiles( $kind, $types{$kind} );
}

sub ReportDerivFiles {
    my $kind     = shift;          # kind of file we're reporting on
    my $message  = shift;          # a message so we can describe it
    my $tempsize = 0;

    return unless exists $targets->{$kind};

    print "\nThe following are most likely $message:\n";

    foreach my $path ( keys %{ $targets->{$kind} } ) {
        $tempsize += $targets->{$kind}{$path};
        $path =~ s|^\./|~/|;          # change the path for prettier output
        print "$path ($targets->{$kind}{$path} bytes)\n";
    }
    print 'These files take up ' . BytesToMeg($tempsize) . "MB total.\n\n";
}

sub BytesToMeg {                       # convert bytes to X.XXMB
    return sprintf( "%.2f", ( $_[0] / 1024000 ) );
}
```

Before I close this section, I should note that we could extend the previous example in many ways. The sky's really the limit with this sort of program. Here are a few ideas:

- Search for web browser cache directories (a common source of missing disk space).
- Offer to delete files that are found. The operator unlink() and the subroutine rmpath from the File::Path module could be used to perform the deletion step.
- Perform more analysis on files instead of making guesses based on filenames.

Walking the Filesystem Using the File::Find::Rule Module

`File::Find` provides an easy and easy-to-understand way to walk filesystems. It has the added benefit of shipping with Perl. But after you've written a number of `File::Find`-based scripts, you may notice that you tend to write the same kind of code over and over again. At that point you might start to wonder if there are any ways to avoid repeating yourself in this fashion besides just working from a standard boilerplate you create. If you are not constrained to modules that ship with Perl, I'm happy to say there is: `File::Find::Rule`.

`File::Find::Rule` is a fabulous module by Richard Clamp (actually, potentially a family of modules, as you'll see in a second) that offers two very slick interfaces to `File::Find`. Once you have the hang of `File::Find`, I definitely recommend that you check out `File::Find::Rule`. Let's take a look at what makes it so cool.

First off, Clamp's module makes writing scripts that collect lists of certain files or directories from the filesystem much easier. With `File::Find` you have to handle both the selection and the accumulation tasks by hand, but `File::Find::Rule` does the work for you. You tell it where to begin its file walk and then provide either a series of chained methods or a list of arguments that describe the filesystem objects that interest you. It then produces either a list of what you were looking for or a way of iterating over each item it finds, one at a time. Let's start with the simplest expression and build from there:

```
use File::Find::Rule;
my @files_or_dirs = File::Find::Rule->in('.');
```

`@files_or_dirs` now contains all of the files and directories found in the current directory or its subdirectories, as specified by the `in()` method. If we only wanted the files and not the directories, we could add `file()`:

```
my @files = File::Find::Rule->file()->in('.');
```

Or if we only wanted files that ended with *.pl* (i.e., probably the Perl files):

```
my @perl_files = File::Find::Rule->file()->name('*.pl')->in('.');
```

and so on. As you can see, we are just adding more methods into the chain that essentially act as filters. `File::Find::Rule` also offers a procedural interface, so if you'd prefer something that was less object-oriented, you would rewrite the previous line of code to say:

```
my @perl_files = find( file => name => '*.pl', in => '.' );
```

I don't find that format as easy to read, but some people may prefer it.

Before I show you the second impressive thing about this module, I should mention that `File::Find::Rule` provides an iterator-based interface as well. This is handy for those cases where your selection can return a large number of items. For instance, if you asked for all of the readable files on just my laptop, the resulting array would have more than a million elements in it. It addition to that being a pretty sizable chunk of data to keep in memory, it would also take a decent amount of time to collect. You may prefer to get operating on the files as they are found, rather than twiddling your thumbs until they are all returned as a list. This is where an iterator comes in handy. To use this feature, we would call **start()** instead of **in()** at the beginning (or end, depending on your point of view) of the method chain:

```
my $ffr = File::Find::Rule->file()->name('*.pl')->start('.');
```

This code returns an object that has a **match()** method. **match()** will hand you back the very next match found (or **false** if there are none) every time you call it:

```
while ( my $perl_file = $ffr->match ){
    # do something interesting with $perl_file
}
```

This allows you to walk the filesystem one matching item at a time (kind of like the **wanted()** subroutine we saw before, but better because you're only handed the things you want).

Now on to the second benefit of using **File::Find::Rule**. You've probably already guessed that you can construct some fairly complex chains of filter methods to get back exactly what you want. If you want all of the executable Perl files over a certain size owned by a particular set of UIDs, for example, that's no problem at all. That code just looks like this:

```
use File::Find::Rule;

@interesting =
    File::Find::Rule
        ->file()
        ->executable()
        ->size('<1M')
        ->uid( 6588, 6070 )
        ->name('*.pl')
        ->in('.');
```

If you've already peeked at the **File::Find::Rule** documentation, you may have noticed that you can construct chains held together by not just a Boolean "and" relationship ("true if it is this and that and that..."). **File::Find::Rule** lets you use **or()** and **any()** to find things that have "this or that or that..." or have "at least one of any of these things true." You may also have noticed that there is a **grep()** method that can look at the contents of files found as yet another filter. But that's still not the coolest part.

Richard Clamp has designed his module so that other people can add filter methods in a seamless fashion. On first blush that may not seem all that impressive, but wait until you see some of the filter modules that are available. Here's a small taste:

- **File::Find::Rule::VCS** by Adam Kennedy adds methods that make it easy to ignore the administrative files kept around by various source control systems, such as CVS, Subversion, and Bazaar.

- **File::Find::Rule::PPI** by the same author lets you search for Perl files that contain specific Perl elements (e.g., all of the files that have POD documentation, or even those that use subroutines). This isn't just a simple `grep()`; it actually parses each of the files.

- `File::Find::Rule::ImageSize`, an add-on by creator Richard Clamp, lets you select or reject images based on their size.
- `File::Find::Rule::Permissions` by David Cantrell lets you select files and directories based on a given user's permissions (e.g., "can *nobody* change any files in this directory?")
- `File::Find::Rule::MP3Info` by Kake Pugh lets you find MP3 files based on arbitrary MP3 tags (e.g., find all songs by a certain artist, or over six minutes in length). Really. We'll see this module again in the last chapter.

There are quite a few more modules in this family. Most of them are a little more generic than the ones just listed (e.g., to allow you to search for files with various file permissions or ages), but I wanted to give you a sampling so you could see how powerful this idiom can be.

Manipulating Disk Quotas

Perl scripts like our core-killers from the last section can offer a way to deal with junk files that cause unnecessary disk-full situations. But even when run on a regular basis, they are still a reactive approach; the administrator deals with these files only after they've come into existence and cluttered the filesystem.

There's another, more proactive approach: filesystem quotas. Filesystem quotas, operating system permitting, allow you to constrain the amount of disk space a particular user can consume on a filesystem. All of the operating systems in play in this book support them in one form or another.

Though proactive, this approach is considerably more heavy-handed than cleanup scripts because it applies to all files, not just spurious ones like core dumps. Most system administrators find using a combination of automated cleanup scripts and quotas to be the best strategy: the former help prevent the latter from being necessary.

In this section, we'll mostly deal with manipulating Unix quotas from Perl (we'll take a quick peek at NTFS quotas at the end of the chapter). Before we get into Unix quota scripting, however, we should take a moment to understand how quotas are set and queried "by hand." To enable quotas on a filesystem, a Unix system administrator usually adds an entry to the filesystem mount table (e.g., */etc/fstab* or */etc/vfstab*) and then reboots the system or manually invokes the quota enable command (usually `quotaon`). Here's an example */etc/vfstab* from a Solaris box:

```
#device             device            mount  FS    fsck   mount     mount
#to mount           to fsck           point  type  pass   at boot   options
/dev/dsk/c0t0d0s7 /dev/rdsk/c0d0t0d0s7 /home  ufs   2      yes       rq
```

The `rq` option in the last column enables quotas on this filesystem. They are stored on a per-user basis. To view the quota entries for a user on all of the mounted filesystems that have quotas enabled, one can invoke the `quota` command like so:

```
$ quota -v sabrams
```

to produce output similar to this:

```
Disk quotas for sabrams (uid 670):
Filesystem    usage  quota    limit    timeleft  files  quota  limit timeleft
/home/users  228731 250000   253000                 0      0      0
```

For our next few examples, we're only interested in the first three numeric columns of this output. The first number is the current amount of disk space (in 1,024-byte blocks) being used by the user *sabrams* on the filesystem mounted at */home/users*. The second is that user's "soft quota." The soft quota is the amount after which the OS begins complaining for a set period of time, but does not restrict space allocation. The final number is the "hard quota," the absolute upper bound for this user's space usage. If a program attempts to request more storage space on behalf of the user after this limit has been reached, the OS will deny this request and return an error message like "disk quota exceeded."

If we wanted to change these quota limits by hand, we'd traditionally use the `edquota` command. `edquota` pops you into your editor of choice (specified by setting the `EDITOR` environment variable in your shell), preloaded with a small temporary text file containing the pertinent quota information. Here's an example buffer that shows a user's limits on each of the four quota-enabled filesystems. This user most likely has her home directory on */exprt/server2*, since that's the only filesystem where she has quotas in place:

```
fs /exprt/server1 blocks (soft = 0, hard = 0) inodes (soft = 0, hard = 0)
fs /exprt/server2 blocks (soft = 250000, hard = 253000) inodes (soft = 0, hard = 0)
fs /exprt/server3 blocks (soft = 0, hard = 0) inodes (soft = 0, hard = 0)
fs /exprt/server4 blocks (soft = 0, hard = 0) inodes (soft = 0, hard = 0)
```

Using `edquota` to make changes by hand may be a comfy way to edit a single user's quota limits, but it is not a viable way to deal with tens, hundreds, or thousands of user accounts. Still, as you'll see, it can be useful.

One of Unix's flaws is its lack of command-line tools for editing quota entries. Most Unix variants have C library routines for this task, but no Unix variant vendors ship common command-line tools that allow for higher-level scripting. True to the Perl motto "There's more than one way to do it" (TMTOWTDI, pronounced "tim-toady"), we are going to look at two very different ways of setting quotas from Perl: performing some tricks with `edquota` and using the `Quota` module.

Editing Quotas with edquota Trickery

The first method involves a little trickery on our part. I just described the process for manually setting a single user's quota: the `edquota` command invokes an editor to allow you to edit a small text file and then uses any changes to update the quota entries. There's nothing in this scenario mandating that an actual human has to type at a keyboard to make changes in the editor, though. In fact, there's not even a constraint on which editor has to be used. All `edquota` needs is a program it can launch that will properly change a small text file. Any valid path (as specified in the `EDITOR` environment variable) to such a program will do. Why not point `edquota` at a Perl script? In this next example, we'll look at just such a script.

Our example script will need to do double duty. First, it has to get some command-line arguments from the user, set `EDITOR` appropriately, and call `edquota`. `edquota` will then run another copy of our program to do the real work of editing this temporary file. Figure 2-1 shows a diagram of the action.

The initial program invocation must tell the second copy what to change. How it passes this information is less straightforward than one might hope. The manual page for `edquota` says: "The editor invoked is *vi(1)* unless the `EDITOR` environment variable specifies otherwise." The idea of passing command-line arguments via `EDITOR` or another environment variable is a dicey prospect at best, because we don't know how `edquota` will react. Instead, we'll have to rely on one of the other interprocess communication methods available in Perl. See the sidebar "Can We Talk?" on page 42 for some of the possibilities.

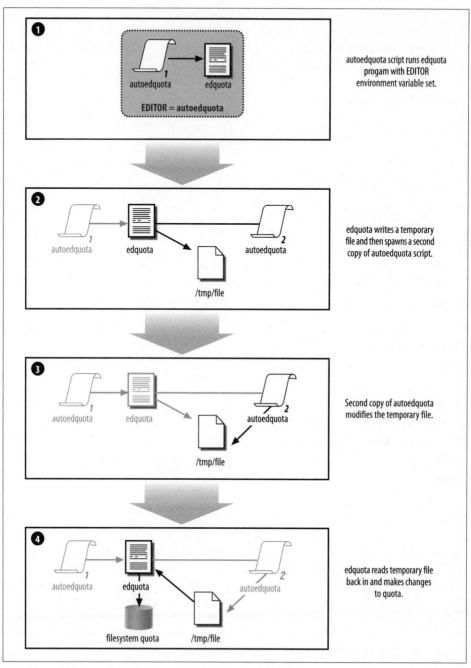

Figure 2-1. *Changing quotas using a "sleight-of-hand" approach*

In our case, we're going to choose a simple but powerful method to exchange information. Since the first process only has to provide the second one with a single set of change instructions (what quotas need to be changed and their new values), we're going to set up a standard Unix pipe between the two of them.[†] The first process will print a change request to its output, and the copy spawned by edquota will read this info as its standard input.

Can We Talk?

When you need two processes to exchange information with each other via Perl, there are a number of things you can do, including:

- Pass a temporary file between them.
- Create a named pipe and talk over that.
- Pass AppleEvents (under Mac OS X).
- Use mutexes or mutually agreed upon registry keys (under Windows).
- Have them meet at a network socket.
- Use a shared memory section.

It's up to you as the programmer to choose the appropriate communication method, though often the data will dictate this for you.

When looking at this data, you'll want to consider:

- Direction of communication (one- or two-way?)
- Frequency of communication (is this a single message or are there multiple chunks of information that need to be passed?)
- Size of data (is it a 10 MB file or 20 characters?)
- Format of data (is it a binary file or just text characters? fixed width, or character separated?)

Finally, be conscious of how complicated you want to make your script.

Let's write the program. The first thing the program has to do when it starts up is decide what role it's been asked to play. We can assume that the first invocation receives several command-line arguments (i.e., what to change) while the second, called by edquota, receives only one (the name of the temporary file). The program forces a set of command flags to be present if it is called with more than one argument, so we're pretty safe in using this assumption as the basis of our role selection. Here's the code that decides which role the script is being called for (e.g., if it's being the $EDITOR) and handles calling edquota if necessary:

[†] Actually, the pipe will be to the *edquota* program, which is kind enough to hook up its input and output streams to the Perl script being spawned.

```
#!/usr/bin/perl

use Getopt::Std;
use File::Temp qw(tempfile);

my $edquota = '/usr/sbin/edquota';    # edquota path
my $autoedq = '/bin/editquota.pl';    # full path for this script
my %opts;

# are we the first or second invocation?

# if there is more than one argument, we're the first invocation
# so parse the arguments and call the edquota binary

if ( @ARGV != 1 ) {

    # colon (:) means this flag takes an argument
    # $opts{u} = user ID, $opts{f} = filesystem name,
    # $opts{s} = soft quota amount, $opts{h} = hard quota amount
    getopt( 'u:f:s:h:', \%opts );

    die "USAGE: $0 -u <uid> -f <fsystem> -s <softq> -h <hardq>\n"
        unless ( exists $opts{u}
        and exists $opts{f}
        and exists $opts{s}
        and exists $opts{h} );

    CallEdquota();
}

# else - we're the second invocation and will have to perform the edits
else {
    EdQuota();
}
```

The code to actually call edquota over a pipe is pretty simple:

```
sub CallEdquota {
    $ENV{'EDITOR'} = $autoedq;    # set the EDITOR variable to point to us

    open my $EPROCESS, '|-', "$edquota $opts{u}"
        or die "Unable to start $edquota: $!\n";

    # send the changes line to the second script invocation
    print $EPROCESS "$opts{f}|$opts{s}|$opts{h}\n";

    close $EPROCESS;
}
```

Here's the second part of the action (the part of the script that edits the file edquota hands it):

```
sub EdQuota {
    my $tfile = $ARGV[0];         # get the name of edquota's temp file
```

```
    open my $TEMPFILE, '<', $tfile
        or die "Unable to open temp file $tfile:$!\n";

    my ( $SCRATCH_FH, $scratch_filename ) = tempfile()
        or die "Unable to open scratch file: $!\n";

    # receive line of input from first invocation and lop off the newline
    chomp( my $change = <STDIN> );
    my ( $fs, $soft, $hard ) = split( /\|/, $change );  # parse the communique

    # Read in a line from the temp file. If it contains the
    # filesystem we wish to modify, change its values. Write the input
    # line (possibly changed) to the scratch file.
    while ( my $quotaline = <$TEMPFILE> ) {
        if ( $quotaline =~ /^fs \Q$fs\E\s+/ ) {
            $quotaline
                =~ s/(soft\s*=\s*)\d+(, hard\s*=\s*)\d+/$1$soft$2$hard/;
        }
        print $SCRATCH_FH $quotaline;
    }
    close $TEMPFILE;
    close $SCRATCH_FH;

    # overwrite the temp file with our modified scratch file so
    # edquota will get the changes
    rename( $scratch_filename, $tfile )
        or die "Unable to rename $scratch_filename to $tfile: $!\n";
}
```

 This code will only work if:

1. The script starts with the "shebang" line at the beginning that indicates that it should call the Perl interpreter (rather than being treated like a shell script).

2. The file itself is marked as being executable:
   `chmod o+x /bin/editquota.pl`

The preceding code is bare bones, but it still offers a way to make automated quota changes. If you've ever had to change many quotas by hand, this should be good news. Before putting something like this into production, considerable error checking and a mechanism that prevents multiple concurrent changes should be added. In any case, you may find this sort of sleight-of-hand technique useful in other situations besides quota manipulation.

Editing Quotas Using the Quota Module

Once upon a time, the previous method (to be honest, the previous hack) was the only way to automate quota changes. Perl's XS extension mechanism provides a way to glue the C quota library into Perl, however, so it was only a matter of time before someone produced a Quota module for Perl. Thanks to Tom Zoerner and some other porting help, setting quotas from Perl is now much more straightforward—if this module supports your variant of Unix. If it doesn't, the previous method should work fine.

Here's some sample code that takes the same arguments as our last quota-editing example:

```
use Getopt::Std;
use Quota;

my %opts;
getopt( 'u:f:s:h:', \%opts );
die "USAGE: $0 -u <uid> -f <fsystem> -s <softq> -h <hardq>\n"
    unless ( exists $opts{u}
    and exists $opts{f}
    and exists $opts{s}
    and exists $opts{h} );

my $dev = Quota::getqcarg( $opts{f} )
    or die "Unable to translate path $opts{f}: $!\n";

my ( $curblock, $soft, $hard, $btimeo, $curinode, $isoft, $ihard, $itimeo )
    = Quota::query( $dev, $opts{u} )
    or die "Unable to query quota for $opts{u}: $!\n";

Quota::setqlim( $dev, $opts{u}, $opts{s}, $opts{h}, $isoft, $ihard ) == undef
    or die 'Unable to set quota: ' . Quota::strerr() . "\n";
```

After we parse the arguments, there are three simple steps. First, we use `Quota::getqcarg()` to get the correct device identifier to feed to the other quota routines. Next, we feed this identifier and the user ID to `Quota::query()` to get the current quota settings, which we need in order to avoid perturbing the quota limits we are not interested in changing (e.g., the number of files). Finally, we set the quota. That's all it takes: three lines of Perl code.

Remember, the Perl slogan states that "there's more than one way to do it," not necessarily "several equally good ways."

Editing NTFS Quotas Under Windows

There are basically two strata to be considered when you start talking about quotas in the current Windows-based operating systems. On the basic level, each NTFS filesystem can enforce quotas on a per-user, per-volume basis (i.e., a particular user can use only X amount of space on volume Y). The users can either be local to the machine or be found in Active Directory. Windows Server 2003R2 enhances this model by offering per-volume and per-folder quotas that are not tied to individual users.

The second layer to the quota story comes into play when you're administering quotas for people on a whole set of machines. It would be impractical to set up the quotas on each individual machine, so instead group policy objects (GPOs) are used to specify quota policies that can be applied to multiple machines in an organizational unit (OU).

In this section we're only going to look at the first layer, because the creation and maintenance of GPOs is a little too far off our current path to really explore here. For more info on how to mess with GPOs from Perl, I recommend you check out Robbie Allen and Laura Hunter's excellent *Active Directory Cookbook* (O'Reilly). And at the risk of increasing the hand waving to the level of a comfortable breeze, the code shown here will come with only a modicum of explanation. It uses the Windows Management Instrumentation (WMI), a technology we'll explore in depth in Chapter 4. If you're not already familiar with WMI, I'd recommend bookmarking this page and coming back to it after you've had a chance to peruse the WMI discussion in Chapter 4.

Here's some code to create a quota entry for a user named *dnb* who lives in the domain called *WINDOWS*. The entry gets created for the *C:* volume of the local machine (or, if it already exists, its values are set):

```perl
use Win32::OLE;

my $wobj = Win32::OLE->GetObject('winmgmts:\\\\.\\root\\cimv2');

# next line requires elevated privileges to work under Vista
my $quota
    = $wobj->Get(
            'Win32_DiskQuota.QuotaVolume=\'Win32_LogicalDisk.DeviceID="c:"\','
        . 'User=\'Win32_Account.Domain="WINDOWS",Name="dnb"\'' );
$quota->{Limit}        = 1024 * 1024 * 100; # 100MB
$quota->{WarningLimit} = 1024 * 1024 * 80;  #  80MB
$quota->Put_;
```

In short, this script first gets an object that references the WMI namespace. It then uses that object to retrieve an object representing the quota entry for the user (identified by the domain and username) and volume (the volume `c:`) we care about. With that object in hand, we can set the two properties of interest (`Limit` and `WarningLimit`) and push the changes back via `Put_` to make them active.[‡] If we wanted to just query the existing data, we could read those properties instead of setting them and leave off the call to `Put_`. Note that in order to perform these operations under Vista, you will need to run the script with elevated privileges (not just from an administrator account); see Chapter 1 for more information.

Querying Filesystem Usage

We've just explored a variety of methods of controlling filesystem usage, and it's only natural to want to keep track of how well they work. Let's look at a method for querying the filesystem usage on each of the operating systems discussed in this book.

[‡] In case you're curious, to set the disk quota to "no limit," the Scripting Guys at Microsoft say you need to set the value to 18446744073709551615 (seriously). See this column for details: *http://www.microsoft.com/technet/scriptcenter/resources/qanda/jan08/hey0128.mspx*.

If we wanted to query filesystem usage on a Windows machine, we could use Mike Blazer's `Win32::DriveInfo` module:

```
use Win32::DriveInfo;

my ($sectors,  $bytessect, $freeclust, $clustnum,
    $userfree, $total,     $totalfree
) = Win32::DriveInfo::DriveSpace('c');

# if quotas are in effect we can show the amount free from
# our user's perspective by printing $userfree instead
print "$totalfree bytes of $total bytes free\n";
```

`Win32::DriveInfo` can also provide other information, such as which directory letters are active and whether a drive (e.g., a CD-ROM) is in use, so it's handy to have around.

Several Unix modules are also available, including `Filesys::DiskSpace` by Fabien Tassin, `Filesys::Df` by Ian Guthrie, and `Filesys::DiskFree` by Alan R. Barclay. The first two of these make use of the Unix system call `statvfs()`, while the last one actually parses the output of the Unix command `df` on all of the systems it supports. Choosing between these modules is mostly a matter of personal preference and operating system support. I prefer `Filesys::Df` because it offers a rich feature set and does not spawn another process (a potential security risk, as discussed in Chapter 1) as part of a query. Here's one way to write code equivalent to the previous example:

```
use Filesys::Df;

my $fobj = df('/');

print $fobj->{su_bavail}* 1024 . ' bytes of ' .
      $fobj->{su_blocks}* 1024 . " bytes free\n";
```

We have to do a little bit of arithmetic (i.e., `* 1024`) because `Filesys::Df` returns values in terms of blocks, and each block is 1024 bytes on our system. (The `df()` function for this module can be passed a second optional argument for block size if necessary.) Also worth noting about this code are the two hash values we've requested. `su_bavail` and `su_blocks` are the values returned by this module for the "real" size and disk usage information. On most Unix filesystems, the `df` command will show a value that hides the standard 10% of a disk set aside for superuser overflow. If we wanted to see the total amount of space available and the current amount free from a normal user's perspective, we would have used `user_blocks` and `user_bavail` instead.

Guthrie has also written a related module called `Filesys::DfPortable`, which has very similar syntax to `Filesys::Df`. It adds Windows support for essentially the same type of disk usage queries. If you don't need the additional information about your drives that `Win32::DriveInfo` provides, it may suit your purposes on those platforms as well.

With the key pieces of Perl code we've just seen, it is possible to build more sophisticated disk monitoring and management systems. These filesystem watchdogs will help you deal with space problems before they occur.

Module Information for This Chapter

Name	CPAN ID	Version
MacOSX::File	DANKOGA	0.71
File::Find (ships with Perl)		1.12
File::Spec (ships with Perl as part of the PathTools module)	KWILLIAMS	3.2701
Path::Class	KWILLIAMS	0.16
Cwd (ships with Perl as part of the PathTools module)	KWILLIAMS	3.2701
Win32::File (ships with ActiveState Perl)	JDB	0.06
Win32::FileSecurity (ships with ActiveState Perl)	JDB	1.06
File::Basename (ships with Perl)		2.76
File::Find::Rule	RCLAMP	0.30
Getopt::Std (ships with Perl)		
File::Temp (ships with Perl)	TJENNESS	0.20
Quota	TOMZO	1.6.2
Win32::OLE (ships with ActiveState Perl)	JDB	0.1709
Win32::DriveInfo	MBLAZ	0.06
Filesys::Df	IGUTHRIE	0.92
Filesys::DfPortable	IGUTHRIE	0.85

References for More Information

For good information on platform differences for Perl programmers, the *perlport* manual page is invaluable.

Active Directory Cookbook, Second Edition, by Robbie Allen and Laura Hunter, and *Windows Server Cookbook*, by Robbie Allen (both from O'Reilly) are excellent collections of examples on how to script many of the important Windows-based operating system areas, including filesystem-related items. Allen has a website (*http://techtasks .com*) that serves as a repository for the code samples in all of the books he has authored or coauthored (and one or two others); on this site you can view all of the examples, which are in various languages (including Perl translations of all of the VBScript code), and you can buy the books and the individual code repositories. It truly is the mother lode of examples—one of the single most helpful websites you'll ever find for this sort of programming. I highly recommend supporting this worthy effort by purchasing the code (and the books!).

## CHAPTER 3

User Accounts

Here's a short pop quiz. If it weren't for users, system administration would be:

1. More pleasant
2. Nonexistent

Despite the comments you may hear from system administrators on their most beleaguered days, 2 is the best answer to this question. As I mentioned in the first chapter, ultimately system administration is about making it possible for people to use the available technology.

Why all the grumbling, then? Users introduce two things that make the systems and networks we administer significantly more complex: nondeterminism and individuality. We'll address the nondeterminism issues when we discuss user activity in the next chapter; for now, let's focus on individuality.

In most cases, users want to retain their own separate identities. Not only do they want unique names, but they want unique "stuff" too. They want to be able to say, "These are *my* files. I keep them in *my* directories. I print them with *my* print quota. I make them available from *my* web page." Modern operating systems keep an account of all of these details for each user.

But who keeps track of all of the accounts on a system or network of systems? Who is ultimately responsible for creating, protecting, and disposing with these little shells for individuals? I'd hazard a guess and say "*You*, dear reader"—or if not you personally, the tools you'll build to act as your proxy. This chapter is designed to help you with that responsibility.

Let's begin our discussion of users by addressing some of the pieces of information that form a user's identity and how that information is stored on a system. We'll start by looking at Unix and Unix-variant users, and then we'll address the same issues for Windows-based operating system users. Once we've covered identity information for both types of operating system, we'll construct a basic account system.

Unix User Identities

When exploring this topic, we'll have to putter around in a few key files that store the persistent definition of a user's identity. By "persistent definition," I mean those attributes of a user that exist during the user's entire lifespan, persisting even when he is not actively using a computer. Another word that we'll use for this persistent identity is *account*. If you have an account on a system, you can log in and become one of that system's users.

Users come into being on a system when their information is first added to the password file (or the directory service that holds the same information). They leave the scene when this entry is removed. Let's dive right in and look at how such a user identity is stored.

The Classic Unix Password File

Let's start off with the classic password file format and then get more sophisticated from there. I call this format "classic" because it is the parent of all of the other Unix password file formats currently in use. It is still in use today in many Unix variants, including Solaris, AIX, and Linux. Usually found on the system as */etc/passwd*, this file consists of lines of ASCII text, each line representing a different account on the system or a link to another directory service. A line in this file is composed of several colon-separated fields. We'll take a close look at all of these fields as soon as we see how to retrieve them.

Here's an example line from */etc/passwd*:

```
dnb:fMP.olmno4jGA6:6700:520:David N. Blank-Edelman:/home/dnb:/bin/zsh
```

There are at least two ways to go about accessing this information from Perl:

- We can access it "by hand," treating this file like any random text file and parsing it accordingly:

```
my $passwd = '/etc/passwd';
open my $PW, '<', $passwd or die "Can't open $passwd:$!\n";

my ( $name, $passwd, $uid, $gid, $gcos, $dir, $shell );
while ( chomp( $_ = <$PW> ) ) {
    ( $name, $passwd, $uid, $gid, $gcos, $dir, $shell ) = split(/:/);
    <your code here>;
}
close $PW;
```

- We can "let the system do it," in which case Perl makes available some of the Unix system library calls that parse this file for us. For instance, another way to write that last code snippet is:

```
my ( $name, $passwd, $uid, $gid, $quota, $comment, $gcos, $dir, $shell,
    $expire );
while (
    (
        $name,    $passwd, $uid, $gid,    $quota,
        $comment, $gcos,    $dir, $shell, $expire
    )
    = getpwent()
)
{
    <your code here>;
}
endpwent();
```

Using these calls offers the tremendous advantage of automatically tying in to any OS-level name service being used, such as Network Information Service (NIS), the Lightweight Directory Access Protocol (LDAP), Kerberos, or NIS+. We'll see more of these library call functions in a moment (including an easier way to use getpwent()), but for now let's look at the fields our code returns:

Name

The login name field holds the short (usually eight characters or less), unique *nom de la machine* for each account on the system. The Perl function getpwent(), which we saw earlier being used in a list context, will return the name field if we call it in a scalar context:

```
$name = getpwent(  );
```

User ID

On Unix systems, the user ID (UID) is actually more important than the login name for most things. Each file on a system is owned by a UID, not a login name. If we change the login name associated with UID 2397 in */etc/passwd* from *danielr* to *drinehart*, *danielr*'s files instantly show up as being owned by *drinehart* instead. The UID is the persistent part of a user's identity internal to the operating system. The Unix kernel and filesystems keep track of UIDs, not login names, for ownership and resource allocation, meaning that as far as the OS is concerned, multiple accounts with different login names but the same UID are actually the same account. A login name can be considered to be the part of a user's identity that is *external* to the core OS; it exists to make things easier for humans.

Here's some simple code to find the next available unique UID in a password file. This code looks for the highest UID in use and produces the next number:

```
my $passwd = '/etc/passwd';
open my $PW, '<', $passwd or die "Can't open $passwd:$!\n";
my @fields;
my $highestuid;
while ( chomp( $_ = <$PW> ) ) {
    @fields = split(/:/);
    $highestuid = ( $highestuid < $fields[2] ) ? $fields[2] : $highestuid;
}
```

```
close $PW;
print 'The next available UID is ' . ++$highestuid . "\n";
```

 This example is a little too simple for real-world use, because operating systems often come with preassigned high-numbered accounts (e.g., *nobody*, *nfsnobody*), and the UID has an upper limit. Also, many institutions also have policies about how their UIDs are assigned (certain classes of users are assigned UIDs from a predetermined range, and so on). All of these things have to be taken into account when writing code like this.

Table 3-1 lists other useful name- and UID-related Perl functions and variables.

Table 3-1. Login name- and UID-related variables and functions

Function/variable	Use
getpwnam($name)	In a scalar context, returns the UID for the specified login name; in a list context, returns all of the fields of a password entry
getpwuid($uid)	In a scalar context, returns the login name for the specified UID; in a list context, returns all of the fields of a password entry
$>	Holds the effective UID of the currently running Perl program
$<	Holds the real UID of the currently running Perl program

Primary group ID

On multiuser systems, users often want to share files and other resources with a select set of other users. Unix provides a user grouping mechanism to assist in this process. An account on a Unix system can be part of several groups, but it must be assigned to one primary group. The primary group ID (GID) field in the password file lists the primary group for that account.

Group names, GIDs, and group members are usually stored in the */etc/group* file. This file holds a listing of secondary groups. To make an account part of several secondary groups, you just list that account in several places in the file (bearing in mind that some OSs have a hard limit on the number of groups an account can join—eight used to be a common restriction). Here are a couple of lines from an */etc/group* file:

```
bin::2:root,bin,daemon
sys::3:root,bin,sys,adm
```

The first field is the group name, the second is the password (some systems allow people to join a group by entering a password), the third is the GID of the group, and the last field is a list of the users in this group.

Schemes for group ID assignment are site-specific, because each site has its own particular administrative and project boundaries. Groups can be created to model certain populations (students, salespeople, etc.), roles (backup operators, network administrators, etc.), or account purposes (backup accounts, batch processing accounts, etc.).

Dealing with group files via Perl is a very similar process to the *passwd* parsing we did earlier. We can either treat a group file as a standard text file or use special Perl functions to perform the tasks. Table 3-2 lists the group-related Perl functions and variables.

Table 3-2. Group name- and GID-related variables and functions

Function/variable	Use
getgrent()	In a scalar context, returns the group name; in a list context, returns the fields $name, $passwd, $gid, and $members
getgrnam($name)	In a scalar context, returns the group ID; in a list context, returns the same fields mentioned for getgrent()[a]
getgrgid($gid)	In a scalar context, returns the group name; in a list context, returns the same fields mentioned for getgrent()
$)	Holds the effective GID of the currently running Perl program
$(	Holds the real GID of the currently running Perl program

[a] If you list the members of a group using multiple lines in */etc/group* (e.g., if there are too many members to fit on one line), getgrgid() and getgrnam() may return only first line's information when called in a list context. In that case, you will need to manually construct the list of members using repeated getgrent() calls.

The "encrypted" password

So far we've seen three key parts of how a user's identity is stored on a Unix machine. The next field is not part of this identity, but it is used to verify that someone should be allowed to assume all of the rights, responsibilities, and privileges bestowed upon a particular user ID. This is how the computer knows that someone presenting himself as *mguerre*, for example, should be allowed to assume the UID associated with that username. Other, better forms of authentication now exist (e.g., public key cryptography), but this one has been inherited from the early days of Unix.

It is common to see a line in a password file with just an asterisk (*) for the password. Since the standard encryption algorithms won't generate an asterisk as part of the encrypted password, placing that character in the password field (by editing the password file) will effectively lock the account. This convention is usually used when an administrator wants to disable the user from logging into an account without removing the account altogether. Simply adding an asterisk to the encrypted password string will also lock the account, while making it easy to restore access without needing to know the password.

You may also see *LK* used to lock an account, and *NP* or NP used to indicate that there is no password in that file (although there might be one elsewhere, such as in */etc/shadow*; we'll deal with that in a moment).

Dealing with user passwords is a topic unto itself. Chapter 11 of this book addresses this topic.

GCOS/GECOS field

The GCOS/GECOS[*] field is the least important field (from the computer's point of view). This field usually contains the full name of the user (e.g., "Roy G. Biv"). Often, people put their titles and/or phone extensions in this field as well.

System administrators who are concerned about privacy issues on behalf of their users (as all should be) need to watch the contents of this field. It is a standard source for account-name-to-real-name mappings. On most Unix systems, this field is available as part of a world-readable */etc/passwd* file or directory service, and hence the information is available to everyone on the system. Many Unix programs, such as mail clients, also consult this field when they attach a user's login name to some piece of information. If you have any need to withhold a user's real name from other people (e.g., if that user is a political dissident, a federal witness, or a famous person), this is one of the places you must monitor.

As a side note, if you maintain a site with a less mature or professional user base, it is often a good idea to disable mechanisms that allow users to change their GCOS field values to any random string (for the same reasons that user-selected login names can be problematic). You may not want your password file to contain expletives or other unprofessional information.

Home directory

The next field contains the name of the user's *home directory*. This is the directory where the user begins his time on the system. This is also usually where the files that configure that user's environment live.

It is important for security purposes that an account's home directory be owned and writable by that account only. World-writable home directories allow trivial account hacking. There are cases, however, where even a *user*-writable home directory is problematic. For example, in restricted shell scenarios (where accounts can only log in to perform specific tasks and do not have permission to change anything on the system), a user-writable home directory is a big no-no because it could let an outsider modify the restrictions.

Here's some Perl code to make sure that every user's home directory is owned by that user and is not world-writable:

---

[*] For some amusing details on the origin of the name of this field, see the GCOS entry in the Jargon Dictionary (*http://www.jargon.org*).

```
use User::pwent;
use File::stat;

# note: this code will beat heavily upon any machine using
# automounted homedirs
while ( my $pwent = getpwent() ) {

    # make sure we stat the actual dir, even through layers of symlink
    # indirection
    my $dirinfo = stat( $pwent->dir . '/.' );
    unless ( defined $dirinfo ) {
        warn 'Unable to stat ' . $pwent->dir . ": $!\n";
        next;
    }
    warn $pwent->name
        . ''s homedir is not owned by the correct uid ('
        . $dirinfo->uid
        . ' instead '
        . $pwent->uid . ")!\n"
        if ( $dirinfo->uid != $pwent->uid );

    # world writable is fine if dir is set "sticky" (i.e., 01000);
    # see the manual page for chmod for more information
    warn $pwent->name . "'s homedir is world-writable!\n"
        if ( $dirinfo->mode & 022 and ( !$dirinfo->mode & 01000 ) );
}
endpwent();
```

This code looks a bit different from our previous parsing code because it uses two magic modules by Tom Christiansen: `User::pwent` and `File::stat`. These modules override the normal `getpwent()` and `stat()` functions, causing them to return something different from the values mentioned earlier: when `User::pwent` and `File::stat` are loaded, these functions return objects instead of lists or scalars. Each object has a method named after a field that normally would be returned in a list context. So, code like this that queries the metadata for a file to retrieve its group ID:

```
$gid = (stat('filename'))[5];
```

can be written more legibly as:

```
use File::stat;
my $stat = stat('filename');
my $gid = $stat->gid;
```

or even:

```
use File::stat;
my $gid = stat('filename')->gid;
```

User shell

The final field in the classic password file format is the user shell field. This field usually contains one of a set of standard interactive programs (e.g., *sh*, *csh*, *tcsh*, *ksh*, *zsh*), but it can actually be set to the full path of any executable program or script. This field is often set to a noninteractive program (e.g., */bin/false* or */sbin/nologin*) in order to prevent logins to daemon or locked accounts.

From time to time, people have joked (half-seriously) about setting their shells to be the Perl interpreter. Some have also contemplated embedding a Perl interpreter in the *zsh* shell (and possibly others), though this has yet to happen. However, some serious work has been done to create a Perl shell (see *http://www.focusre search.com/gregor/sw/psh/* and *http://www.pardus.nl/projects/zoidberg/*) and to embed Perl into Emacs, an editor that could easily pass for an operating system (*http://john-edwin-tobey.org/perlmacs/*). Perl has also been embedded in most of the recent *vi* editor implementations (*nvi*, *vile*, and Vim).

On occasion, you might have reason to list nonstandard interactive programs in this field. For instance, if you wanted to create a menu-driven account, you could place the menu program's name here. In these cases, you have to take care to prevent someone using the account from reaching a real shell and wreaking havoc. A common mistake is including a mail program that allows the user to launch an editor or pager for composing and reading mail, as that editor or pager could have a shell-escape function built in.

 Caution when using nonstandard interactive programs is warranted in all circumstances. For example, if you allow people to *ssh* in and you try to lock their accounts using such a program, be sure your SSH server isn't configured to pay attention to their *.ssh/ environment* files (off by default in OpenSSH). If that file is enabled, the user can play some really fun tricks by setting LD_PRELOAD.

A list of standard, acceptable shells on a system is often kept in */etc/shells*. Most FTP daemons will not allow a normal user to connect to a machine if her shell in */etc/passwd* (or the networked password file) is not on that list. On some systems, the *chsh* program also checks that file to validate any shell-changing requests from users.

Here's some Perl code to report accounts that do not have approved shells:

```
use User::pwent;

my $shells = '/etc/shells';
open my $SHELLS, '<', $shells or die "Unable to open $shells:$!\n";

my %okshell;
while (<$SHELLS>) {
    chomp;
    $okshell{$_}++;
}
close $SHELLS;

while ( my $pwent = getpwent() ) {
    warn $pwent->name . ' has a bad shell (' . $pwent->shell . ")!\n"
```

```
            unless ( exists $okshell{ $pwent->shell } );
    }
    endpwent();
```

Changes to the Password File in BSD 4.4 Systems

At the Berkeley Software Distribution (BSD) 4.3 to 4.4 upgrade point, the BSD variants added two twists to the classic password file format: additional fields were inserted between the GID and GCOS fields, and a binary database format was introduced to store account information.

Extra fields in passwd files

The first field BSD 4.4 systems added was the *class* field, which allows a system administrator to partition the accounts on a system into separate classes (e.g., different login classes might be given different resource limits, such as CPU time restrictions). BSD variants also add *change* and *expire* fields to hold an indication of when a password must be changed and when the account will expire. We'll see fields like these when we get to the next Unix password file format as well.

Perl also supports a few other fields (specific to certain operating systems) that can be found in password files. Some operating systems provide the ability to include additional information about a user, including that user's disk quota and a free-form comment. When compiled under an operating system that supports these extra fields, Perl includes the contents of the extra fields in the return values of functions like getpwent(). This is one good reason to use getpwent() in your programs instead of split()ing the password file entries by hand.

The binary database format

The second twist BSD 4.4 added to the password mechanisms was a database format, rather than plain text, for primary storage of password file information. BSD machines keep their password file information in DB format, a greatly updated version of the older Unix Database Management (DBM) libraries. This change allows the systems to quickly look up password information.

The program *pwd_mkdb* takes the name of a password text file as its argument, creates and moves into place two database files, and then moves the text file into */etc/master.passwd*. The two databases provide a shadow password scheme, differing in their read permissions and encrypted password field contents. We'll talk more about this in the next section.

Perl has the ability to work with DB files directly (we'll work with this format later, in Chapter 7), but in general I would not recommend editing the databases while the system is in use. The issue here is one of locking: it's very important not to change a crucial database like the one storing your passwords without making sure that other programs are not similarly trying to write to or read from it. Standard operating system programs like *chpasswd* and *vipw* handle this locking for you.[†] The sleight-of-hand approach we saw for quotas in Chapter 2, which used the `EDITOR` variable, can often be used with these utilities as well.

Shadow Passwords

Earlier I emphasized the importance of protecting the contents of the GCOS field, since this information is publicly available through a number of different mechanisms. Another fairly public, yet rather sensitive piece of information is the list of encrypted passwords for all of the users on the system. Even though the password information is cryptologically hidden, exposing it in a world-readable file creates a significant vulnerability, thanks to the powerful password crackers available today.[‡] Parts of the password file need to be world-readable (e.g., the UID and login name mappings), but not all of it. There's no need to provide a list of encrypted passwords to users who may be tempted to run password-cracking programs.

One very common alternative to leaving encrypted passwords exposed is to banish the encrypted password string for each user to a special file that is only readable by *root*. This second file is known as a "shadow password" file, since it contains lines that shadow the entries in the real password file. This mechanism is standard on most modern OS distributions.

With this approach, the original password file is left intact, with one small change: the encrypted password field contains a special character or characters to indicate that password shadowing is in effect. Placing an x in this field is common, though the insecure copy of the BSD database uses an asterisk (*).

 I've heard of some shadow password suites that insert a special, normal-looking string of characters in this field. If your password file goes awanderin', this provides a lovely time for the recipient, who will attempt to crack a password file of random strings that bear no relation to the real passwords.

Most operating systems take advantage of this second shadow password file to store more information about the accounts. This additional information resembles that in the surplus fields we saw in the BSD files (e.g., account expiration data and information on password changing and aging).

[†] *pwd_mkdb* may or may not perform this locking for you (depending on the BSD flavor and version), so caveat implementor.

[‡] Not to mention the highly effective technique of using rainbow tables (*http://en.wikipedia.org/wiki/Rainbow_table*).

In most cases Perl's normal password functions, such as `getpwent()`, can handle shadow password files. As long as the C libraries shipped with the OS do the right thing, so will Perl. Here's what "do the right thing" means: when your Perl script is run with the appropriate privileges (i.e., as *root*), these routines will return the encrypted password. Under all other conditions, that password will not be accessible to those routines.

Unfortunately, Perl may not retrieve the additional fields found in the shadow file. Eric Estabrooks has written `Passwd::Solaris` and `Passwd::Linux` modules that can help, but only if you are running one of those operating systems. If these fields are important to you, or you want to play it safe, the sad truth (in conflict with my earlier recommendation to use `getpwent()`) is that it is often simpler to open the shadow file by hand and parse it manually.

Windows-Based Operating System User Identities

Now that we've explored the pieces of information that Unix systems cobble together to form a user's identity, let's take a look at the same topic for Windows users. Much of this info is conceptually similar, so we'll dwell mostly on the differences between the two operating systems.

One important note before we continue: Windows systems by default store user identity information in one of two places: locally (on the machine itself, in a way not shared with other machines) or domain-wide (where it most likely lives in Active Directory on a domain controller). In the latter case, this information is shared with the user's local machine and stored on that machine for at least the duration of the user's session.

As in our discussion of Unix user identities, we'll focus here on local accounts. For more on how to work with Active Directory or other directory services, see Chapter 9.

Windows User Identity Storage and Access

Windows stores the persistent identity information for a user in a database called the *SAM* (Security Accounts Manager), or *directory*, database. The SAM database is part of the Windows registry, located at *%SYSTEMROOT%\system32\config*. The files that make up the registry are all stored in a binary format, meaning normal Perl text-manipulation idioms cannot be used to read from or write changes to this database. It is theoretically possible to use Perl's binary data operators (i.e., `pack()` and `unpack()`) with the SAM database, provided you do so when Windows is not running, but this way lie madness and misery.

Luckily, there are better ways to access and manipulate this information via Perl.

One approach is to call an external binary to interact with the OS for you. Every Windows machine has a feature-bloated command called `net` that you can use to add, delete, and view users. The `net` command is quirky and limited, though, and is generally the method of last resort.

For example, here's the net command in action on a machine with two accounts:

```
C:\> net users

User accounts for \\HOTDIGGITYDOG
----------------------------------
Administrator            Guest
The command completed successfully.
```

The output of this program could easily be parsed from Perl. There are also commercial packages that offer command-line executables to perform similar tasks.

Darn That Bitrot

Here's a sad tale of bitrot that has taken place since the first edition of this book was published. In the first edition, I recommended using several third-party modules for performing user administration tasks on Windows systems: Win32::UserAdmin (as described in the O'Reilly book *Windows NT User Administration*, with code distributed from the O'Reilly site), David Roth's Win32::AdminMisc and Win32::Perms (distributed from *http://www.roth.net/perl/packages/*), or Jens Helberg's Win32::Lanman (hidden away in his CPAN directory at *http://www.cpan.org/modules/by-authors/id/J/JH/JHEL BERG/*).

As far as I can tell, no one has touched Win32::UserAdmin in quite some time. David Roth left Perl behind when he went off to work for Microsoft back in 1999. When I spoke to David in 2005 he indicated that he was happy to continue to make the work he had done available, but that he did not have any further time to maintain and update his modules. He had hoped someone else would take on their maintenance, but that hasn't happened as of this writing. Similarly, Jens Helberg hasn't really been active in the Perl world since at least 2003.

It's a pity these modules have fallen into disrepair, because they were some of the handiest Windows modules available. I can't recommend using Win32::Lanman or Win32::AdminMisc/Win32::Perms at this point because their maintenance is so dicey, but if you still want to get a copy that can be loaded using ppm in the ActiveState distribution, there was a version of Win32::AdminMisc available for 5.10 as of this writing at *http://www.ramtek.us* (Roth's site has a 5.8 version available of both Win32::AdminMisc and Win32::Perms) and a version of Win32::Lanman for Perl 5.8 in the repository described at *http://www.bribes.org/perl/ppmdir.html*.

Instead you'll find the text in this edition almost exclusively sticks to modules like Win32API::Net that are part of the official libwin32 set of modules shepherded by Jan Dubois and plus a few other Windows modules with their own active maintainers.

Another approach is to use the Perl module Win32API::Net, which is bundled with the ActiveState Perl distribution. Here's some example code that shows the users on the local machine and some details about them. It prints out lines that look similar to the contents of */etc/passwd* under Unix:

```
use Win32API::Net qw(:User);

UserEnum( '', \my @users );
foreach my $user (@users) {
    # '3' in the following call refers to the "User info level",
    # basically a switch for how much info we want back. Here we
    # ask for one of the more verbose user info levels (3).
    UserGetInfo( '', $user, 3, \my %userinfo );
    print join( ':',
        $user, '*', $userinfo{userId},
                    $userinfo{primaryGroupId},
                    '',
                    $userinfo{comment},
                    $userinfo{fullName},
                    $userinfo{homeDir},
                    '' ),"\n";
}
```

Finally, you can use the `Win32::OLE` module to access the Active Directory Service Interfaces (ADSI) functionality built into Windows. We'll go into this topic in great detail in Chapter 9, so I won't present an example here.

We'll look at more Perl code to access and manipulate Windows users later, but for the time being let's return to our exploration of the differences between Unix and Windows users.

Windows User ID Numbers

User IDs in Windows are not created by mortals, and they cannot be reused. Unlike in Unix, where we can simply pick a UID number out of the air, the OS uniquely generates the identifier in Windows when a new user is created: a unique user identifier (which Windows calls a *relative ID*, or RID) is combined with machine and domain IDs to create a large ID number called a *security identifier*, or SID, which acts as the user's UID. An example RID is 500. The RID is part of a longer SID that looks like this:

```
S-1-5-21-2046255566-1111630368-2110791508-500
```

The RID is the number we get back as part of the `UserGetInfo()` call shown in the last code snippet. Here's the code necessary to print the RID for a particular user:

```
use Win32API::Net qw(:User);

UserGetInfo( '', $user, 3, \my %userinfo );
print $userinfo{userId},"\n";
```

You can't (by normal means) recreate a user after that user has been deleted. Even if you create a new user with the same name as the deleted user, the SID will not be the same, and the new user will not have access to the predecessor's files and resources.

This is why some Windows books recommend renaming accounts that are due to be inherited by another person. That is, if a new employee is supposed to receive all of the files and privileges of a departing employee, they suggest renaming the existing account to preserve the SID rather than creating a new account, transferring the files, and then deleting the old account. I personally find this method for account handoffs to be a little uncouth, because it means the new employee will inherit all of the corrupted and useless registry settings of his predecessor. However, it's the most expedient method, and sometimes that is important.

Part of the rationale for this recommendation comes from the pain associated with transferring ownership of files. In Unix, a privileged user can say, "Change the ownership of all of these files so that the new user owns them." In Windows, however, there's no giving of ownership; there's only taking (i.e., an admin can say, "I own these files now"). Luckily, there are two ways to get around this restriction and pretend we're using Unix's semantics. From Perl, we can:

- Call a separate binary, such as:
  - The `chown` binary from the Cygwin distribution found at *http://www.cygnus .com* (free). If you have a Unix background and work on Windows machines, you definitely should check out Cygwin. For a commercial version of Unix-like tools such as `chown`, check out the MKS Toolkit (*http://www.mkssoftware.com*).
  - The `SubInACL` binary, available for download from the Microsoft Download Center (*http://www.microsoft.com/downloads*). It has the plus of being provided by Microsoft, but it requires a small learning curve.
  - `SetACL` from *http://setacl.sourceforge.net* is similar to `SubInACL` but has its own twists. If you are considering using `SubInACL`, be sure to check out this program as well because it may be more to your liking.
- Use a Perl module such as:
  - `Win32::Security` by Toby Ovod-Everett. Here's an example of using this module to change the owner of a single file:

    ```
    use Win32::Security::NamedObject;
    my $nobj = Win32::Security::NamedObject->new('FILE',$filename);
    $nobj->ownerTrustee($NewAccountName);
    ```

    Two asides about `Win32::Security`. First, it ships with a lovely set of utility scripts, including *PermDump.pl* to show inherited and noninherited permissions and *PermFix.pl* to fix permission issues such as broken inherited permissions from files that have been moved. Second, according to the author, as of this writing `Win32::Security` can have issues with objects that have both permit and deny ACLs (if they share the same trustees), so be sure to test carefully if you use deny ACLs.
  - `Win32::OLE` by Jan Dubois to call WMI functions (see Chapter 4 for an in-depth look at WMI). This is a little tricky because it is much easier to take ownership of a file (i.e., change a file to be owned by the user running the script) than it is

to change the ownership of the file to an arbitrary user.[*] Taking ownership is performed via the `TakeOwnership()` method of the `CIM_DataFile` object in the `cimv2` namespace.

— `Win32::Perms` by Dave Roth, located at *http://www.roth.net/perl/packages* and documented at *http://www.roth.net/perl/perms*. (Be sure to read the sidebar "Darn That Bitrot" on page 60 before depending on this module.) Here's some sample code using this module that will change the owner of a directory and its contents, including subdirectories:

```
use Win32::Perms;

$my acl = new Win32::Perms( );
$acl->Owner($NewAccountName);
my $result = $acl->SetRecurse($dir);
$acl->Close( );
```

Windows Passwords Don't Play Nice with Unix Passwords

The algorithms used to obscure the passwords that protect access to a user's identity in Windows and Unix are cryptologically incompatible. Once it's been encrypted, you cannot transfer password information between these two operating system families and expect to use it for password changes or account creations, as you can when transferring encrypted passwords between different operating systems (Linux, Solaris, Irix, etc.) in the Unix family. As a result, two separate sets of passwords have to be used and/or kept in sync. This difference is the bane of every system administrator who has to administer a mixed Unix/Windows environment. Some administrators get around this by using custom authentication modules, commercial or otherwise.

As a Perl programmer, the only thing you can do if you are not using custom authentication mechanisms is to create a system whereby users provide their passwords in plain text. The plain-text passwords are then used to perform two separate password-related operations (changes, etc.), one for each OS.

Windows Groups

So far, I've been able to gloss over any distinction between storage of a user's identity on a local machine and storage in some network service, like NIS. For the information we've encountered, it hasn't really mattered if that information was used on a single system or all of the systems in a network or workgroup. But in order to talk cogently about Windows user groups and their intersection with Perl, we unfortunately have to move beyond this simplified view.

---

[*] I hunted and hunted for an example of changing ownership (versus taking it) via WMI and could not find one in any language. I don't want to claim that it is impossible, but color me dubious.

On Windows systems, a user's identity can be stored in one of two places: in the SAM database on a specific machine or in the Active Directory (AD) store on a domain controller. This is the distinction between a *local user*, who can only log into a single machine, and a *domain user*, who can log in to any of the permitted machines that participate in a domain as part of an AD instance. Often, users have information stored in both places. For example, this would allow a user to log in from any Windows machine in the domain and access his desktop environment as stored on a fileserver, or log into his own PC without referring to network resources for authentication or file sharing.

There are different kinds of groups in the Windows model. To understand the difference between them, we have to consider two things: where a group can be used (its *scope*) and what a group can contain (its *members*). The following list starts with the smallest "jurisdiction" and works outward:

Local groups
> Can be used only on the local machine to control access to resources on that machine. Can contain local accounts, domain accounts, and global groups.

Domain local groups
> Can be used to control access to resources in a domain (e.g., a shared printer). Can contain accounts, global groups, universal groups from any domain, and other domain local groups (from the same domain).

Global groups
> Often used as container groups included in other groups in any domain. Can contain accounts and other global groups from the same domain where the global group is defined.

Universal groups
> Can be used across domains and forests (i.e., sets of directory trees) in the same AD instance to hold other groups. Can contain accounts, global groups, and universal groups from the same forest where the universal group is defined

Local groups are machine-specific. People seldom add or remove local groups; they mostly just change the membership of the default groups. Given this, let's look instead at how the other kinds of groups get used.

The key to this story is the use of groups nested in other groups. Suppose you want to control access to some resource (the classic example is a shared printer) that a number of people will share. Instead of listing each person in some access list associated with the printer, it is far more convenient to say "anyone in a particular domain local group" can print to the printer. The domain local group is assigned the access to the printer.

You could just start adding users to that domain local group, and everyone you added would happily be able to print, but that approach would start to get old once you began to accumulate all the domain local groups that parts of your organization get access to as part of their job functions. If every time someone is hired into the facilities planning department you have to add them into three printer access groups, the plotter access group, plus a few others, it becomes unpleasant for you as the administrator. In addition to all of the manual labor necessary for granting access, the chance for error is pretty good.

One bad way to solve this problem would be to grant rights for each resource to the group that contains the accounts for the facilities planning department itself. That idea breaks down as soon as multiple groups need overlapping access. Let's say the facilities planning department runs out of room on its floor and needs to use some desks on another floor. The people who are moved to the new floor will need to share a printer on that floor. If the right to print to that printer is granted to each department on that floor separately, it becomes a pain to determine which departments have access (since you have to look at each department's group in turn).

The right way to fix this is to nest global groups (like the group that holds the accounts in the facilities planning department) in the domain local groups that control access to each printer. When this is done, the users in each global group are automatically given the printing rights they deserve. Dealing with situations where two departments have to share a resource is easy; you just put both global groups into the appropriate domain local group. If you need to know which groups have access to a printer, you can look at the membership of the domain local group that controls access to the printer. Figure 3-1 shows this nested group idea in a pictorial form.

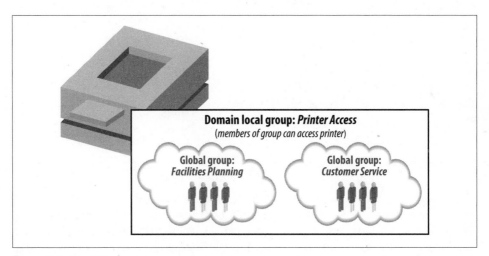

Figure 3-1. How Windows groups nest

The term "global" is a bit of a misnomer because it sounds like you should be able to insert accounts from any domain in your AD tree, but in fact global groups can only hold accounts and other groups from within the domain in which they were created. This is where universal groups fit in. Universal groups let you aggregate global groups from different domains. If you want to have a single group for all of your accounts in different domains, you can construct a universal group that nests the right global groups from each domain. You can subsequently nest this universal group in some other permission-granting group, and all of your users will inherit that permission.

This scheme would be even handier if it didn't complicate our Perl programming. We potentially have to, or at least may want to, use different modules or different functions based on group type. Here are the choices you have:

1. If you are working with universal groups, you have no choice but to use Win32::OLE to perform ADSI calls.

2. If you are working with local, domain local, or global groups, you can use ADSI (via either the WinNT or LDAP providers, depending on the group), or you may find it easier to use a module like the one we saw before: Win32API::Net. The advantage of using ADSI via Win32::OLE is consistency (you are using it for all group operations); the advantage of using Win32API::Net is that it is considerably easier (it has built-in functions for the tasks).

Let's take a quick look at each approach. If we stick to using Win32API::Net, we are immediately faced with a choice of group type: local or global? Win32API::Net has different functions for each kind of group, as listed in Table 3-3.

Table 3-3. Win32API::Net functions for local and global groups

Local functions	Global functions
LocalGroupAdd()	GroupAdd()
LocalGroupDel()	GroupDel()
LocalGroupAddMembers()	GroupAddUser()
LocalGroupDelMembers()	GroupDelUser()
LocalGroupGetMembers()	GroupGetUsers()
LocalGroupGetInfo()	GroupGetInfo()
LocalGroupSetInfo()	GroupSetInfo()
LocalGroupEnum()	GroupEnum()

The functions in the first column let you set local groups (both local to the machine and to the domain), while those in the second work strictly with global groups. The first argument to all of these functions determines where the change is made. For example, to create a group local to the machine, the first argument can be empty (''). To create a domain local group or a global group, the first argument should be the name of an appropriate domain controller. To find the appropriate domain controller, you can call GetDCName():

```
# $server is the server whose DC you need to find,
# $domainname is the domain you need the DC for,
# the answer gets placed into $dcname
GetDCName($server, $domainname, $dcname);
```

This duality means that your code may have to call two functions for the same operation. For example, if you need to obtain all of the groups a user may be in, you may have to call two functions, one for local groups and the other for global groups. The group functions in Table 3-3 are pretty self-explanatory.

Here's a quick example of adding a user to a global group:

```
use Win32API::Net qw(:Get :Group);

my $domain = 'my-domain';

# Win32::FormatMessage converts the numeric error code to something
# we can read
GetDCName('' , $domain , my $dc)
  or die Win32::FormatMessage( Win32::GetLastError() );

GroupAddUser($dc,'Domain Admins','dnbe')
  or die Win32::FormatMessage( Win32::GetLastError() );
```

 Here's a quick tip found in Roth's books (listed in the references section at the end of the chapter): your program must run with administrative privileges to access the list of local groups, but global group names are available to all users.

If we wanted to create a universal group using ADSI, we could use code like this (see Chapter 9 for a description of just what is going on here):

```
use Win32::OLE;
$Win32::OLE::Warn = 3; # throw verbose errors

# from ADS_GROUP_TYPE_ENUM in the Microsoft ADSI Doc
my %ADSCONSTANTS = (
    ADS_GROUP_TYPE_GLOBAL_GROUP        => 0x00000002,
    ADS_GROUP_TYPE_DOMAIN_LOCAL_GROUP  => 0x00000004,
    ADS_GROUP_TYPE_LOCAL_GROUP         => 0x00000004,
    ADS_GROUP_TYPE_UNIVERSAL_GROUP     => 0x00000008,
    ADS_GROUP_TYPE_SECURITY_ENABLED    => 0x80000000
);

my $groupname = 'testgroup';
my $descript  = 'Test Group';

my $group_OU = 'ou=groups,dc=windows,dc=example,dc=edu';

my $objOU = Win32::OLE->GetObject( 'LDAP://' . $group_OU );
my $objGroup = $objOU->Create( 'group', "cn=$groupname" );
$objGroup->Put( 'samAccountName', $groupname );
$objGroup->Put( 'groupType',
        $ADSCONSTANTS{ADS_GROUP_TYPE_UNIVERSAL_GROUP}
      | $ADSCONSTANTS{ADS_GROUP_TYPE_SECURITY_ENABLED} );
$objGroup->Put( 'description', $descript );
$objGroup->SetInfo;
```

Windows User Rights

The last difference between Unix and Windows user identities that we'll address is the concept of a "user right." In the traditional Unix rights schema, the actions a user can take are constrained either by file permissions or by the superuser/nonsuperuser distinction. Under Windows, the permission scheme is better explained with a superhero analogy: users (and groups) can be imbued with special powers that become part of their identities.[†] For instance, one can attach the user right `Change the System Time` to an ordinary user, allowing that user to set the system clock on the local machine.

Some people find the user rights concept confusing because they have attempted to use the Local Security Policy Editor or Group Policy/Group Policy Object Editor. The list of policies shown when you navigate to User Rights Assignment (Figure 3-2) presents the information in exactly the opposite manner that most people expect to see it: it shows a list of the possible user rights and expects you to add groups or users to a list of entities that already have this right.

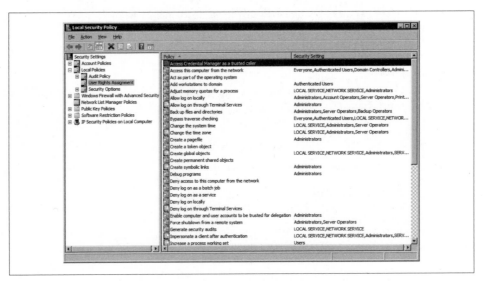

Figure 3-2. Assigning user rights via the Local Security Policy Editor

A more user-centric UI would offer a way to add user rights to or remove them from users, instead of the other way around.[‡] This is how we will operate on rights using Perl.

[†] Most modern Unix systems can use access control lists and role-based access control (RBAC) to manage user rights in similar detail, but this is not commonly done, as it is under Windows.

[‡] To their credit, the new interface for this sort of thing, the Group Policy Management Console, does improve on the situation by making the object that is receiving a policy setting paramount. It also offers the ability to script many meta-GPO operations. Unfortunately, the one thing you can't do out of the box (as of this writing) is directly twiddle the settings in a GPO from a script. Sigh.

One approach is to call the program *ntrights.exe* from the Microsoft 2000/2003 Resource Kit. The resource kit tools for 2003, including *ntrights.exe*, are (as of this writing) available for download for free from Microsoft. If you haven't heard of the resource kits, be sure to read the sidebar about them.

The Microsoft Windows Resource Kits

"You must have the Windows {Anything} Resource Kit" is the general consensus among serious Windows administrators and the media that covers this field. Microsoft Press usually publishes at least one large tome for each OS version, full of nitty-gritty operational information. It is not this information that makes these books so desirable, though; rather, it is the CD-ROMs or sometimes the direct downloads associated with the books that make them worth their weight in zlotniks. These add-ons contain a grab bag of crucial utilities for Windows administration.

Many of the utilities were contributed by the OS development groups, who wrote their own code because they couldn't find the tools they needed anywhere else. For example, there are utilities that add users, change filesystem security information, show installed printer drivers, work with roaming profiles, help with debugging domain and network browser services, and so on.

The tools in the resource kits are provided "as is," meaning there is virtually no support available for them. This no-support policy may sound harsh, but it serves the important purpose of allowing Microsoft to put a variety of useful code in the hands of administrators without having to pay prohibitive support costs. The utilities in the resource kits have a few small bugs, but on the whole they work great. Updates that fix bugs in some of these utilities have been posted to Microsoft's website.

Using *ntrights.exe* is straightforward; just call the program from Perl like you would any other (i.e., using backticks or the `system()` function). In this case, we'll call *ntrights.exe* with a command line of the form:

```
C:\> ntrights.exe +r <right name> +u <user or group name> [-m \\machinename]
```

to give a right to a user or group (on an optionally specified machine named *machinename*). To take that right away, we use a command line of the form:

```
C:\> ntrights.exe -r <right name> +u <user or group name> [-m \\machinename]
```

Unix users will be familiar with the use of the + and - characters (as in `chmod`), in this case used with the `r` switch, to give and take away privileges. The list of names of rights that can be assigned (for example, `SetSystemtimePrivilege` to set the system time) can be found in the Microsoft resource kit documentation for the `ntrights` command. If for some reason you don't want to use the resource kit tools, the Cygwin distribution that was touted earlier also provides an *editrights* utility package that can do similar things.

A second, Perl module–based approach entails using the `Win32::Lanman` module by Jens Helberg, which can be found in PPM form at *http://www.bribes.org/perl/ppmdir.html*

or in source form in Helberg's CPAN directory at *http://www.cpan.org/modules/by-au thors/id/J/JH/JHELBERG/* (this won't be found in a standard CPAN search, so you have to go to that directory directly).

 So, after all of the angst in the bitrot sidebar about modules like Win32::Lanman, why am I still describing how to use it here? I've searched high and low, and there does not appear to be (as of this writing) a reasonable substitute for this module in this context. To the best of my knowledge, you can't do these sorts of things via WMI or ADSI. I'd love to be proven wrong!

I believe it would be possible to recreate all of the Win32::Lanman calls via Win32::API, since they can both access the same underlying Win32 API, but this is beyond the depth of knowledge in Windows programming that I've ever aspired to acquire. If you do rewrite the Win32::Lanman functions listed in this section to use Win32::API (and plan to maintain/support your code), I'll be delighted to switch to your module and write about it in future editions of this book.

Let's start by looking at the process of retrieving an account's user rights. This is a multiple-step process. First, we need to load the module:

```
use Win32::Lanman;
my $server = 'servername';
```

Then, we need to retrieve the actual SID for the account we wish to query or modify. In the following sample, we'll get the *Guest* account's SID:

```
Win32::Lanman::LsaLookupNames( $server, ['Guest'], \my @info )
    or die "Unable to lookup SID: " . Win32::Lanman::GetLastError() . "\n";
```

@info now contains an array of references to anonymous hashes: one element for each account we query (in this case, it is just a single element for *Guest*). Each hash contains the following keys: domain, domainsid, relativeid, sid, and use. We only care about sid for our next step. Now we can query the rights:

```
Win32::Lanman::LsaEnumerateAccountRights( $server, ${ $info[0] }{sid},
    \my @rights )
        or die "Unable to query rights: " . Win32::Lanman::GetLastError() . "\n";
```

@rights now contains a set of names describing the rights apportioned to *Guest*.

Figuring out the API name of a user right and what it represents is tricky. The easiest way to learn which names correspond to which rights and what each right offers is to look at the software development kit (SDK) documentation at *http://msdn.microsoft .com*. This documentation is easy to find because Helberg has kept the standard SDK function names for his Perl function names. To find the names of the available rights, search the Microsoft's Developer Network site for "LsaEnumerateAccountRights"; you'll find pointers to them quickly.

This information also comes in handy for the modification of user rights. For instance, if we wanted to add a user right to allow our *Guest* account to shut down the system, we could use:

```
use Win32::Lanman;
my $server = 'servername';

Win32::Lanman::LsaLookupNames( $server, ['Guest'], \my @info )
    or die "Unable to lookup SID: " . Win32::Lanman::GetLastError() . "\n";
Win32::Lanman::LsaAddAccountRights( $server, ${ $info[0] }{sid},
    [&SE_SHUTDOWN_NAME] )
    or die "Unable to change rights: " . Win32::Lanman::GetLastError() . "\n";
```

In this case, we found the `SE_SHUTDOWN_NAME` right in the SDK doc and used `&SE_SHUTDOWN_NAME` (a subroutine defined by `Win32::Lanman`), which returns the value for this SDK constant.

`Win32::Lanman::LsaRemoveAccountRights()`, a function that takes similar arguments to those we used to add rights, is used to remove user rights.

Before we move on to other topics, it is worth mentioning that `Win32::Lanman` also provides a function that works just like the Local Security Policy Editor's broken interface, described earlier: instead of matching users to rights, we can match rights to users. If we use `Win32::Lanman::LsaEnumerateAccountsWithUserRight()`, we can retrieve a list of SIDs that have a specific user right. Enumerating this list could be useful in certain situations.

Building an Account System to Manage Users

Now that we've had a good look at user identities, we can begin to address the administration aspect of user accounts. Rather than just showing you the select Perl subroutines or function calls you need for adding and deleting users, I'll take this topic to the next level by showing these operations in a larger context. In the remainder of this chapter, we'll work toward writing a bare-bones[*] account system that starts to manage both Windows and Unix users.

Our account system will be constructed in four parts: user interface, data storage, process scripts (Microsoft would call them the "business logic"), and low-level library routines. From a process perspective, they work together (see Figure 3-3).

Requests come into the system through a user interface and get placed into an "add account queue" file for processing. We'll just call this an "add queue" from here on. A process script reads this queue, performs the required account creations, and stores information about the created accounts in a separate database. That takes care of adding the users to our system.

---

[*] Where "bare-bones" means "toy." This is really meant to be very simple code just to demonstrate the underlying concepts behind the construction of a system like this.

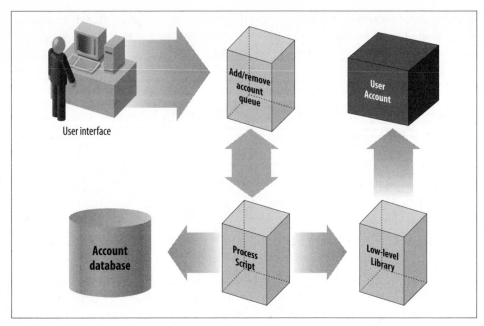

Figure 3-3. The structure of a basic account system

For removing a user, the process is similar. A user interface is used to create a "remove queue." A second process script reads this queue, deletes the indicated users from our system, and updates the central database.

We isolate these operations into separate conceptual parts because it gives us the maximum possible flexibility should we decide to change things later. For instance, if some day we decide to change our database backend, we only need to modify the database routines. Similarly, if we want our user addition process to include more steps (perhaps cross-checking against another database in human resources), we will only need to change the process script in question.

Let's start by looking at the first component: the user interface used to create the initial account queue. For the bare-bones purposes of this book, we'll use a simple text-based user interface to query for account parameters:

```
sub CollectInformation {
    use Term::Prompt;    # we'll move these use statements later
    use Crypt::PasswdMD5;

    # list of fields init'd here for demo purposes - this should
    # really be kept in a central configuration file
    my @fields = qw{login fullname id type password};
    my %record;

    foreach my $field (@fields) {
```

```
    # if it is a password field, encrypt it using a random salt before storing
        if ( $field eq 'password' ) {

            # believe it or not, we may regret the decision to store
            # the password in a hashed form like this; we'll talk about
            # this a little later on in this chapter
            $record{$field} = unix_md5_crypt(
                prompt( 'p', 'Please enter password:', '', '' ), undef );
        }
        else {
            $record{$field} = prompt( 'x', "Please enter $field:", '', '' );
        }
    }
    print "\n";
    $record{status}   = 'to_be_created';
    $record{modified} = time();
    return \%record;
}
```

This routine creates a list and populates it with the different fields of an account record. As the comment mentions, this list is inlined in the code only for brevity's sake. Good software design suggests the field name list really should be read from an additional configuration file. Ideally, that config file would also provide better prompts and validation information describing the kinds of input allowed for each field (rather than just making a distinction between password and nonpassword inputs, as we do here).

Once the list has been created, the routine iterates through it and requests the value for each field. Each value is then stored back into the record hash. At the end of the question and answer session, a reference to this hash is returned for further processing. Our next step will be to write the information to the add queue.

Before we get to that code, though, we should talk about data storage and data formats for our account system.

The Backend Database

The center of any account system is a database. Some administrators use the */etc/ passwd* file or SAM database/AD store as the only record of the users on their system, but this practice is often shortsighted. In addition to the pieces of a user's identity that we've already discussed, a separate database can be used to store metadata about each account, like its creation and expiration date, the account sponsor (if it's a guest account), the user's phone numbers, etc. And once a database is in place, it can be used for more than just basic account management; it can be useful for all sorts of niceties, such as automatic mailing list creation.

Why the Really Good System Administrators Create Account Systems

System administrators fall into roughly two categories: mechanics and architects. Mechanics spend most of their time in the trenches dealing with details. They have amazing amounts of arcane knowledge about the hardware and software they administer. If something breaks, they know just the command, file, or spanner wrench to wield. Talented mechanics can scare you with their ability to diagnose and fix problems even while standing halfway across the room from the problem machine.

Architects spend their time surveying the computing landscape from above. They think more abstractly about how individual pieces can be put together to form larger and more complex systems. Architects are concerned about issues of scalability, extensibility, and reusability.

Both types bring important skills to the system administration field. The system administrators I respect the most are those who can function as mechanics but whose preferred mindset is more closely aligned to that of an architect. They fix a problem and then spend time after the repair determining which systemic changes can be made to prevent it from occurring again. They think about how even small efforts on their part can be leveraged for future benefit.

Well-run computing environments require both architects and mechanics working in a symbiotic relationship. A mechanic is most useful while working in a solid framework constructed by an architect. In the automobile world, we need mechanics to fix cars, but mechanics rely on the car designers to engineer slow-to-break, easy-to-repair vehicles. They need infrastructure like assembly lines, service manuals, and spare-part channels to do their job well. If an architect performs her job well, the mechanic's job is made easier.

How do these roles play out in the context of our discussion? Well, a mechanic will probably use the built-in OS tools for user management. He might even go so far as to write small scripts to help make individual management tasks, like adding users, easier. On the other hand, an architect looking at the same tasks will immediately start to construct an account system. An architect will think about issues like:

- The repetitive nature of user management and how to automate as much of the process as possible.
- The sorts of information an account system collects, and how a properly built account system can be leveraged as a foundation for other functionality. For instance, LDAP directory services and automatic website generation tools could be built on top of an account system.
- Protecting the data in an account system (i.e., security).
- Creating a system that will scale if the number of users increases.
- Creating a system that other sites might be able to use.
- How other system administration architects have dealt with similar problems.

Mentioning the creation of a separate database makes some people nervous. They think, "Now I have to buy a really expensive commercial database, invest in another machine for it to run on, and hire a database administrator." If you have thousands or tens of thousands of user accounts to manage, yes, you do need to do all of those things (though you may be able to get by with a noncommercial SQL database such as PostgreSQL or MySQL). If this is the case for you, you may want to turn to Chapter 7 for more information on dealing with databases like these in Perl.

However, in this chapter when I say "database," I'm using the term in the broadest sense. A flat-file, plain-text database will work fine for smaller installations. Windows users could even use an Access database file (e.g., *database.mdb*).[†]

For portability and simplicity, we'll use the very cool module DBM::Deep by Rob Kinyon. This module provides a surprising amount of power. The documentation describes it as follows:

> A unique flat-file database module, written in pure perl. True multilevel hash/array support (unlike MLDBM, which is faked), hybrid OO / tie() interface, cross-platform FTPable files, ACID transactions, and is quite fast. Can handle millions of keys and unlimited levels without significant slow-down. Written from the ground-up in pure perl—this is NOT a wrapper around a C-based DBM. Out-of-the-box compatibility with Unix, Mac OS X, and Windows.

Choosing a Backend Database Format

The first edition of this book used plain-text files in XML format as its backend database, so I think I need to clear the air about choosing a database format. XML was used as the basis of the backend database in that edition because it offered a relatively simple data format with a number of pluses. One of those pluses was pedagogical—it was clear to me even back before the turn of the millennium that being able to sling XML was going to be an important skill for a system administrator. Over time, that prediction proved to be true well beyond my guess at the time, and XML settled into several niches in the sysadmin world. One of those niches was configuration files, so you'll find expanded and improved examples of XML use in Chapter 6. Its use for this kind of database and queue modeling isn't all that prevalent, though, so I've swapped in a different database format.

So what's the best format to use for something like this? There's a continuum of options to choose from. In rough order of increasing complexity, it goes something like this:

- Flat-file text databases of various flavors (CSV, key/value pairs, YAML, XML, etc.)
- DBM databases (*ndbm*, *gdbm*, BerkeleyDB, DBM::Deep, etc.)
- File-based SQL (e.g., SQLite via DBI using DBD::SQLite)

[†] But don't. It will lead to heartbreak and misery. I've seen it happen too many times not to say, "Friends don't let friends use Access as a multiuser database."

- Server(s)-based SQL (e.g., DBI used with MySQL, PostgreSQL, MS SQL, or Oracle)
- Some sort of object-relational mapper, or ORM (`DBIx::Class`, `Rose::DB::Object`, `Jifty::DBI`, etc.)

That last item isn't a format *per se*, it's more of a way of interacting with your data in a way that can potentially make your programming easier (read: you don't have to sling SQL). Still, it is another layer on top of any of the previous items, so I list it later even if it has the potential to simplify things.

Which format you choose will ultimately be dictated by your (present and future!) needs. I can't give an easy recipe for choosing the right one because there are so many variables (amount of data, amount of concurrent read or read/write access, portability, and so on). In this chapter we're going to use the principle of picking the simplest thing that will work (but no simpler). If I were to build a system like this for production use, I'd no doubt use some sort of SQL-based server (likely wrapped by an ORM). For the examples in this chapter we'll use `DBM::Deep` because it is highly useful in many contexts and allows us to keep on topic without digressions about SQL or DBI (for more on those topics, see Chapter 7).

Using `DBM::Deep` is a walk in the park if you've ever worked with hash references in Perl. Here's a little sample:

```
use DBM::Deep;

my $db = DBM::Deep->new('accounts.db');

# imagine we received a hash of hashes constructed from repeated
# invocations of CollectInformation()

foreach my $user ( keys %users ) {

    # could also be written as $db->put($login => $users{$login});
    $db->{$login} = $users{$login};

}

# then, later on in the program or in another program...

foreach my $login ( keys %{$db} ) {
    print $db->{$login}->{fullname}, "\n";
}
```

The two emphasized lines show that the syntax is just your standard Perl hash reference syntax. They also show that it is possible to look up the hash key and have the entire hash of a hash stored in the database come back into memory. `DBM::Deep` can also use traditional OOP calls, as demonstrated by the comment in the code.

Adding to the account queue

Let's start by returning to the cliffhanger we left off with in "Building an Account System to Manage Users" on page 71. I mentioned that we needed to write the account information we collected with CollectInformation() to our add queue file, but we didn't actually look at the code to perform this task. Let's see how the record data is written with DBM::Deep:

```perl
sub AppendAccount {
    use DBM::Deep;    # will move this to another place in the script

    # receive the full path to the file
    my $filename = shift;

    # receive a reference to an anonymous record hash
    my $record = shift;

    my $db = DBM::Deep->new($filename);

    $db->{ $record->{login} } = $record;
}
```

It really is that simple. This subroutine is just a wrapper around the addition of another key in the DBM::Deep magic hash we're keeping.

> I should fess up about two things:
>
> - This really isn't a queue in the classic sense of the word, because placing the items in the hash isn't preserving any sort of order. If that really bugs you, you could pull the items out of the hash and sort them by record modification time (one of the fields we added in CollectInformation()) before processing.
> - If you passed in two records with the same login field, the second would overwrite the first. That may actually be a desirable quality in this context. Changing this behavior would be pretty simple; all you'd need to do would be to first test for the presence of that key in the DBM::Deep data structure using exists(). The example in this chapter is intentionally meant to be toy-sized. When you write your production system, you'll be adding in all sorts of error checking and business logic appropriate to your environment.

Now we can use just one line to collect data and write it to our add queue file:

```perl
AppendAccount( $addqueue, &CollectInformation );
```

Reading this information back out of the queue files will be as easy as a hash lookup, so I'll pass on showing you the code to do that until we look at the final program.

The Low-Level Component Library

Now that we have all the data under control, including how it is acquired, written, read, and stored, let's look at how it is actually used deep in the bowels of our account system. We're going to explore the code that actually creates and deletes users. The key to this section is the notion that we are building a library of reusable components. The better you are able to compartmentalize your account system routines, the easier it will be to change only small pieces when it comes time to migrate your system to some other operating system or make changes. This may seem like unnecessary caution on our part, but the one constant in system administration work is change.

Unix account creation and deletion routines

Let's begin with the code that handles Unix account creation. Most of this code will be pretty trivial, because we're going to take the easy way out: our account creation and deletion routines will call vendor-supplied "add user," "delete user," and "change password" executables with the right arguments.

Why the apparent cop-out? We are using this method because we know the OS-specific executable will play nice with the other system components. Specifically, this method:

- Handles the locking issues for us (i.e., avoids the data corruption problems that two programs simultaneously trying to write to the password file can cause).

- Handles the variations in password file formats (including password encoding) that we discussed earlier.

- Is likely to be able to handle any OS-specific authentication schemes or password distribution mechanisms. For instance, under at least one Unix variant I have seen, the external "add user" executable can directly add a user to the NIS maps on a master server.

Drawbacks of using an external binary to create and remove accounts include:

OS variations
> Each OS has a different set of binaries, located at a different place on the system, and those binaries take slightly different arguments. In a rare show of compatibility, almost all of the major Unix variants (Linux included, BSD variants excluded) have mostly compatible add and remove account binaries called *useradd* and *userdel*. The BSD variants use *adduser* and *rmuser*, two programs with similar purposes but very different argument names. Such variations tend to increase the complexity of our code.[‡] There are some efforts (e.g., the POSIX standards) to standardize commands like these, but in practice I haven't found things to be homogenous enough to depend on any one convention.

[‡] If you want to get agitated about variations, take a look at OS X. It doesn't (at this time) even have a user-account-specific set of commands. Instead, you get to learn *dscl*, a throwback to NetInfo. Nostalgic for NeXT cubes, anyone?

Single machine scope

Most user command-line tools operate only on the local machine. If most of your users are (as is the best practice these days) in a centralized authentication store like LDAP, these commands seldom know how to create users in that central system. Windows's net command is one notable exception to this. It's pretty common for people to write their own user* commands (in Perl, even) to perform these functions.

Security concerns

The program we call and the arguments passed to it will be exposed to users wielding the ps command. If accounts are created only on a secure machine (say, a master server), this reduces the data leakage risk considerably.

Added dependency

If the executable changes for some reason or is moved, our account system is kaput.

Loss of control

We have to treat a portion of the account creation process as being *atomic*; in other words, once we run the executable we can't intervene or interleave any of our own operations. Error detection and recovery become more difficult.

These programs rarely do it all

It's likely that these programs will not perform all of the steps necessary to instantiate an account at your site. If you need to add specific user types to specific auxiliary groups, place users on a site-wide mailing list, or add users to a license file for a commercial package, you'll have to add some more code to handle these specificities. This isn't a problem with the approach itself; it's more of a heads up that any account system you build will probably require more work on your part than just calling another executable. This will not surprise most system administrators, since system administration is very rarely a walk in the park.

For the purposes of our demonstration account system, the positives of this approach outweigh the negatives, so let's take a look at some code that uses external executables. To keep things simple, we'll use show code that works under Linux on a local machine only, ignoring complexities like NIS and BSD variations. If you'd like to see a more complex example of this method in action, you may find the CfgTie family of modules by Randy Maas instructive. After the example Linux code, we'll take a quick look at some of the lessons that can be learned from other Unix variants that are less friendly to command-line administration.

Here's our basic account creation routine:

```
# these variables should really be set in a central configuration file
Readonly my $useraddex => '/usr/sbin/useradd'; # location of useradd cmd
Readonly my $homeUnixdirs => '/home';          # home directory root dir
Readonly my $skeldir      => '/home/skel';     # prototypical home directory
Readonly my $defshell     => '/bin/zsh';       # default shell
```

```perl
sub CreateUnixAccount {

    my ( $account, $record ) = @_;

    ### construct the command line, using:
    # -c = comment field
    # -d = home dir
    # -g = group (assume same as user type)
    # -m = create home dir
    # -k = copy in files from this skeleton dir
    # -p = set the password
    # (could also use -G group, group, group to add to auxiliary groups)
    my @cmd = (
        $useraddex,
        '-c',   $record->{fullname},
        '-d',   "$homeUnixdirs/$account",
        '-g',   $record->{type},
        '-m',
        '-k',   $skeldir,
        '-s',   $defshell,
        '-p',   $record->{password},
        $account
    );

    # this gets the return code of the @cmd called, not of system() itself
    my $result = 0xff & system @cmd;

    # the return code is 0 for success, non-0 for failure, so we invert
    return ( ($result) ? 0 : 1 );
}
```

This adds the appropriate entry to our password file, creates a home directory for the account, and copies over some default environment files (*.profile*, *.tcshrc*, *.zshrc*, etc.) from a skeleton directory.

For symmetry's sake, here's the simpler account deletion code:

```perl
# this variable should really be set in a central configuration file
Readonly my $userdelex => '/usr/sbin/userdel'; # location of userdel cmd

sub DeleteUnixAccount {

    my ( $account, $record ) = @_;

    ### construct the command line, using:
    # -r = remove the account's home directory for us
    my @cmd = ( $userdelex, '-r', $account );

    my $result = 0xff & system @cmd;

    # the return code is 0 for success, non-0 for failure, so we invert
    return ( ($result) ? 0 : 1 );
}
```

Unix account creation and deletion routines—a variation

Before we get to the Windows examples, I want to show you one variation on the code we just looked at because it is instructive on a number of levels. The variation I have in mind not only demonstrates a cool technical trick but also brings to sharp relief how one little difference between operating systems can cause ripples throughout your code.

Here's the innocent little detail that is about to bite us: Solaris's `useradd` command does not have a `-p` switch to set the (hashed) password on a new account. It does have a `-p` switch, but it doesn't do the same thing as its counterpart in Linux. "Ho hum," you say, "I'll just change the part of the `CreateUnixAccount()` code that sets `@cmd` to reflect the command-line argument that Solaris does use for this purpose." A quick read of the Solaris manpage for `useradd`, however, will send your naiveté packing, as you'll soon see that Solaris *doesn't have* a supported way to provide a hashed password for a new account. Instead, every account is locked until the password is changed for that account.

This impacts the code in a number of ways. First, we have to add something to `CreateUnixAccount()` so it will perform a password change after creating an account. That's easy enough. We can just add something like this:

```
$result = InitUnixPasswd( $account, $record->{'password'} ) );
return 0 if (!$result);
```

and then write an `InitUnixPasswd()` routine. But that's not the most important change to the code. The biggest change is that now we have to store the plain-text password for the account in our queue, since there's no way to use a one-way-hashed password as input into a password changing routine. Remember the ominous comment in the code presented at the very beginning of this section, for `CollectInformation()`:

```
# if it is a password field, encrypt it using a random salt before storing
    if ( $field eq 'password' ) {

            # believe it or not, we may regret the decision to store
            # the password in a hashed form like this; we'll talk about
            # this a little later on in this chapter
            $record{$field} = unix_md5_crypt(
                prompt( 'p', 'Please enter password:', '', '' ), undef );
    }
```

Here's where we regret that decision. We'll have a similar regret in a moment when we get to create accounts in Windows, because we'll need the plain-text password there too. I'm not going to show an example here, but perhaps the best middle ground would be to use a cipher module from the `Crypt::` namespace to store the password in a fashion that can be decrypted later.[*] I point all of this out because it is ripple situations along these lines that can make attempts to decouple the parts of your program hard at times.

---

[*] This means you'll have to protect the secret used to encrypt/decrypt the account password by either protecting the script or the script's config files at the OS level. This is the digression I'm not going to entertain at this point.

Once you've made all of the necessary changes to the password prompting and storing code, you then have to sit down and write the password changing code. The bucket of cold water gets dumped on your head at the point where you realize Solaris doesn't ship with a noninteractive password-changing program.[†] Setting the password requires a little sleight of hand, so we'll encapsulate that step in a separate subroutine to keep the details out of our way.

The Solaris manual pages say, "The new login remains locked until the `passwd(1)` command is executed." `passwd <accountname>` will change that account's password, which may sound simple enough. However, there's a problem lurking here. The `passwd` command expects to prompt the user for the password, and it takes great pains to make sure it is talking to a real user by interacting directly with the user's terminal device. As a result, the following will *not* work:

```
# this code DOES NOT WORK
open my $PW, "|passwd $account";
print $PW $newpasswd,"\n";
print $PW $newpasswd,"\n";
close $PW;
```

We have to be craftier than usual; somehow faking `passwd` into thinking it is dealing with a human rather than our Perl code. We can achieve this level of duplicity by using `Expect`, a Perl module by Austin Schutz (now maintained by Roland Giersig) that sets up a pseudoterminal (pty) within which another program will run. `Expect` is heavily based on the famous Tcl program *Expect* by Don Libes. This module is part of the family of bidirectional program interaction modules. We'll see its close relative, Jay Rogers's `Net::Telnet`, in Chapter 9.

These modules function using the same basic conversational model: wait for output from a program, send it some input, wait for a response, send some data, and so on. The following code starts up `passwd` in a pty and waits for it to prompt for the password. The discussion we have with `passwd` should be easy to follow:

```
Readonly my $passwdex => '/usr/bin/passwd';    # location of passwd executable

sub InitUnixPasswd {
    use Expect;                                # we'll move this later

    my ( $account, $passwd ) = @_;

    # return a process object
    my $pobj = Expect->spawn( $passwdex, $account );
    die "Unable to spawn $passwdex:$!\n" unless ( defined $pobj );

    # do not log to stdout (i.e., be silent)
    $pobj->log_stdout(0);
```

[†] If you are willing to use software that doesn't ship with Solaris for this purpose, you could look at *changepass*, part of the *cgipaf* package at *http://www.wagemakers.be/english/programs/cgipaf*.

```
    # wait for password & password re-enter prompts,
    # answering appropriately
    $pobj->expect( 10, 'New password: ' );

    # Linux sometimes prompts before it is ready for input, so we pause
    sleep 1;
    print $pobj "$passwd\r";
    $pobj->expect( 10, 'Re-enter new password: ' );
    print $pobj "$passwd\r";

    # did it work?
    $result
        = ( defined( $pobj->expect( 10, 'successfully changed' ) ) ? 1:0 );

    # close the process object, waiting up to 15 secs for
    # the process to exit
    $pobj->soft_close();

    return $result;
}
```

The Expect module meets our meager needs well in this routine, but it is worth noting that the module is capable of much more complex operations. See the documentation and tutorial included with the Expect module for more information.

Before we move on, I do want to mention one other alternative to using Expect. I don't like this alternative because it bypasses the usual password changing code path, but it may serve a purpose for you. If you don't want to script the running of passwd, Eric Estabrook's Passwd::Solaris module, mentioned earlier in this chapter, can be used to operate directly on the Solaris *etc/passwd* and *etc/shadow* files to change a user's password. It does accept a hashed password for this purpose.

 If you are going to hash your own passwords and then insert them into your *passwd* and *shadow* files, be sure that you have Solaris (9, 12/02, or later) configured for the compatible hashing algorithm in *etc/security/policy.conf*.

Windows account creation and deletion routines

The process of creating and deleting an account under Windows is slightly easier than the process under Unix, because standard API calls for these operations exist in Windows. As in Unix, we could call an external executable to handle the job (e.g., the ubiquitous net command with its USERS /ADD switch), but it is easy to use the native API calls from a handful of different modules, some of which we've mentioned earlier. Account creation functions exist in Win32::NetAdmin, Win32::UserAdmin, Win32API::Net, and Win32::Lanman, to name a few. Active Directory users will find the ADSI material in Chapter 9 to be their best route.

Picking among these Windows-centric modules is mostly a matter of personal preference. To illustrate the differences between them, we'll take a quick look behind the scenes at the native user creation API calls. These calls are described in the Network Management SDK documentation on *http://msdn.microsoft.com* (search for "NetUserAdd" if you have a hard time finding it). `NetUserAdd()` and the other calls each take a parameter that specifies the information level of the data being submitted. For instance, with information level 1, the C structure that is passed in to the user creation call looks like this:

```
typedef struct _USER_INFO_1 {
  LPWSTR    usri1_name;
  LPWSTR    usri1_password;
  DWORD     usri1_password_age;
  DWORD     usri1_priv;
  LPWSTR    usri1_home_dir;
  LPWSTR    usri1_comment;
  DWORD     usri1_flags;
  LPWSTR    usri1_script_path;
}
```

If information level 2 is used, the structure expected is expanded considerably:

```
typedef struct _USER_INFO_2 {
  LPWSTR    usri2_name;
  LPWSTR    usri2_password;
  DWORD     usri2_password_age;
  DWORD     usri2_priv;
  LPWSTR    usri2_home_dir;
  LPWSTR    usri2_comment;
  DWORD     usri2_flags;
  LPWSTR    usri2_script_path;
  DWORD     usri2_auth_flags;
  LPWSTR    usri2_full_name;
  LPWSTR    usri2_usr_comment;
  LPWSTR    usri2_parms;
  LPWSTR    usri2_workstations;
  DWORD     usri2_last_logon;
  DWORD     usri2_last_logoff;
  DWORD     usri2_acct_expires;
  DWORD     usri2_max_storage;
  DWORD     usri2_units_per_week;
  PBYTE     usri2_logon_hours;
  DWORD     usri2_bad_pw_count;
  DWORD     usri2_num_logons;
  LPWSTR    usri2_logon_server;
  DWORD     usri2_country_code;
  DWORD     usri2_code_page;
}
```

Levels 3 and 4 (4 being the one Microsoft recommends you use[‡]) look like this:

[‡] Showing you the user info level 4 structure is a bit of a tease, because as of this writing none of the Perl modules support it. It won't be too big of a loss should this still be true when you read this (level 3 and level 4 aren't that different), but I thought you should know.

```
typedef struct _USER_INFO_3 {
  LPWSTR usri3_name;
  LPWSTR usri3_password;
  DWORD usri3_password_age;
  DWORD usri3_priv;
  LPWSTR usri3_home_dir;
  LPWSTR usri3_comment;
  DWORD usri3_flags;
  LPWSTR usri3_script_path;
  DWORD usri3_auth_flags;
  LPWSTR usri3_full_name;
  LPWSTR usri3_usr_comment;
  LPWSTR usri3_parms;
  LPWSTR usri3_workstations;
  DWORD usri3_last_logon;
  DWORD usri3_last_logoff;
  DWORD usri3_acct_expires;
  DWORD usri3_max_storage;
  DWORD usri3_units_per_week;
  PBYTE usri3_logon_hours;
  DWORD usri3_bad_pw_count;
  DWORD usri3_num_logons;
  LPWSTR usri3_logon_server;
  DWORD usri3_country_code;
  DWORD usri3_code_page;
  DWORD usri3_user_id;
  DWORD usri3_primary_group_id;
  LPWSTR usri3_profile;
  LPWSTR usri3_home_dir_drive;
  DWORD usri3_password_expired;
}
```

and:

```
typedef struct _USER_INFO_4 {
  LPWSTR usri4_name;
  LPWSTR usri4_password;
  DWORD usri4_password_age;
  DWORD usri4_priv;
  LPWSTR usri4_home_dir;
  LPWSTR usri4_comment;
  DWORD usri4_flags;
  LPWSTR usri4_script_path;
  DWORD usri4_auth_flags;
  LPWSTR usri4_full_name;
  LPWSTR usri4_usr_comment;
  LPWSTR usri4_parms;
  LPWSTR usri4_workstations;
  DWORD usri4_last_logon;
  DWORD usri4_last_logoff;
  DWORD usri4_acct_expires;
  DWORD usri4_max_storage;
  DWORD usri4_units_per_week;
  PBYTE usri4_logon_hours;
  DWORD usri4_bad_pw_count;
  DWORD usri4_num_logons;
```

```
    LPWSTR usri4_logon_server;
    DWORD usri4_country_code;
    DWORD usri4_code_page;
    PSID usri4_user_sid;
    DWORD usri4_primary_group_id;
    LPWSTR usri4_profile;
    LPWSTR usri4_home_dir_drive;
    DWORD usri4_password_expired;
}
```

Without knowing anything about these parameters, or even much about C at all, you can still tell that a change in level increases the amount of information that can and must be specified as part of the user creation process. Also, it should be obvious that each subsequent information level is a superset of the previous one.

What does this have to do with Perl? Each of the modules I've mentioned makes two decisions:

- Should the notion of "information level" be exposed to the Perl programmer?
- Which information level (i.e., how many parameters) can the programmer use?

Win32API::Net and Win32::UserAdmin both allow the programmer to choose an information level. Win32::NetAdmin and Win32::Lanman do not. Of these modules, Win32::NetAdmin exposes the least number of parameters; for example, you cannot set the full_name field as part of the user creation call. If you choose to use Win32::NetAdmin, you will probably have to supplement it with calls from another module to set the additional parameters it does not expose.

Now you have some idea why the module choice really boils down to personal preference. A good strategy might be to first decide which parameters are important to you, store the values for each of these parameters in the database, and then find a comfortable module that supports them. For our demonstration subroutines we'll use Win32API::Net, to stay consistent with our previous examples. Here's the user creation and deletion code for our account system:

```
use Win32API::Net qw(:User :LocalGroup);    # for account creation
use Win32::Security::NamedObject;           # for home directory perms
use Readonly;

# each user will get a "data dir" in addition to her home directory
# (the OS will create the home dir for us with the right permissions the first
# time the user logs in)
Readonly my $homeWindirs => '\\\\homeserver\\home';  # home directory root dir
Readonly my $dataWindirs => '\\\\homeserver\\data';  # data directory root dir

sub CreateWinAccount {

    my ( $account, $record ) = @_;

    my $error;    # used to send back error messages in next call

    # ideally the default values for this sort of add would come out of a database
```

```perl
my $result = UserAdd(
    '',         # create this account on the local machine
    3,          # will specify USER_INFO_3 level of detail
    {   acctExpires => -1,     # no expiration
        authFlags   => 0,      # read only, no value necessary
        badPwCount  => 0,      # read only, no value necessary
        codePage    => 0,      # use default
        comment     => '',     # didn't ask for this from user
        countryCode => 0,      # use default
        # must use these flags for normal acct
        flags       => (
            Win32API::Net::UF_SCRIPT() & Win32API::Net::UF_NORMAL_ACCOUNT()
        ),
        fullName => $record->{fullname},
        homeDir  => "$homeWindirs\\$account",
        homeDirDrive => 'H',          # we map H: to home dir
        lastLogon    => 0,            # read only, no value necessary
        lastLogoff   => 0,            # read only, no value necessary
        logonHours   => [],           # no login restrictions
        logonServer  => '',           # read only, no value necessary
        maxStorage   => -1,           # no quota set
        name         => $account,
        numLogons    => 0,            # read only, no value necessary
        parms        => '',           # unused
        password     => $record->{password},    # plain-text passwd
        passwordAge  => 0,                       # read only
        passwordExpired =>
            0,      # don't force user to immediately change passwd
        primaryGroupId => 0x201,      # magic value as instructed by doc
        priv         => USER_PRIV_USER(),  # normal (not admin) user
        profile      => '',                # don't set one at this time
        scriptPath   => '',                # no logon script
        unitsPerWeek => 0,                 # for logonHours, not used here
        usrComment   => '',                # didn't ask for this from user
        workstations => '',                # don't specify specific wkstns
        userId       => 0,                 # read only
    },
    $error
);

return 0 unless ($result); # could return Win32::GetLastError()

# add to appropriate LOCAL group
# we assume the group name is the same as the account type
$result = LocalGroupAddMembers( '', $record->{type}, [$account] );
return 0 if (!$result);

# create data directory
mkdir "$dataWindirs\\$account", 0777
    or (warn "Unable to make datadir:$!" && return 0);

# change the owner of the directory
my $datadir = Win32::Security::NamedObject->new( 'FILE',
    "$dataWindirs\\$account" );
eval { $datadir->ownerTrustee($account) };
```

```perl
    if ($@) {
        warn "can't set owner: $@";
        return 0;
    }

    # we give the user full control of the directory and all of the
    # files that will be created within it
    my $dacl
        = Win32::Security::ACL->new( 'FILE',
        [ 'ALLOW', 'FULL_INHERIT', 'FULL', $account ],
        );

    eval { $datadir->dacl($dacl) };
    if ($@) {
        warn "can't set permissions: $@";
        return 0;
    }
}
```

The user deletion code looks like this:

```perl
use Win32API::Net qw(:User :LocalGroup);   # for account deletion
use File::Path 'remove_tree';              # for recursive directory deletion
use Readonly;

sub DeleteWinAccount {

    my ( $account, $record ) = @_;

    # Remove user from LOCAL groups only. If we wanted to also
    # remove from global groups we could remove the word "Local" from
    # the two Win32API::Net calls (e.g., UserGetGroups/GroupDelUser)
    # also: UserGetGroups can take a flag to search for indirect group
    #       membership (for example, if user is in group because that group
    #       contains another group that has that user as a member)
    UserGetLocalGroups( '', $account, \my @groups );
    foreach my $group (@groups) {
        return 0 if (! LocalGroupDelMembers( '', $group, [$account] );
    }

    # delete this account on the local machine
    # (i.e., empty first parameter)
    unless ( UserDel( '', $account ) ) {
        warn 'Can\'t delete user: ' . Win32::GetLastError();
        return 0;
    }

    # delete the home and data directory and its contents
    # remove_tree puts its errors into $err (ref to array of hash references)
    # note: remove_tree() found in File::Path 2.06+; before it was rmtree
    remove_tree( "$homeWindirs\\$account", { error => \my $err } );
    if (@$err) {
        warn "can't delete $homeWindirs\\$account\n" ;
        return 0;
    }
```

```
        remove_tree( "$dataWindirs\\$account", { error => \my $err } );
        if (@$err) {
            warn "can't delete $dataWindirs\\$account\n" ;
            return 0;
        }
        else {
            return 1;
        }
    }
```

As a quick aside, the preceding code uses the portable `File::Path` module to remove
an account's home directory. If we wanted to do something Windows-specific, like
move the home directory to the Recycle Bin instead, we could use a module called
`Win32::FileOp` by Jenda Krynicky, available at *http://jenda.krynicky.cz*. In this case,
we'd use `Win32::FileOp` and change the `rmtree()` line to:

```
# will move directories to the Recycle Bin, potentially confirming
# the action with the user if our account is set to confirm
# Recycle Bin actions
my $result = Recycle("$homeWindirs\\$account");
my $result = Recycle("$dataWindirs\\$account");
```

This same module also has a `Delete()` function that will perform the same operation
as the `remove_tree()` call, in a less portable (although quicker) fashion.

The Process Scripts

Once we have a backend database, we'll want to write scripts that encapsulate the day-
to-day and periodic processes that take place for user administration. These scripts are
based on a low-level component library (*Account.pm*) we'll create by concatenating all
of the subroutines we just wrote together into one file. To make it load properly as a
module, we'll need to add a `1;` at the end. The other change we'll make in this conversion is to move all of the module and variable initialization code to an initialization
subroutine and remove those parts (leaving behind **our** statements as necessary) from
the other subroutines. Here's the initialization subroutine we'll use:

```
sub InitAccount {

    # we use these modules in both the Linux and Win32 routines
    use DBM::Deep;
    use Readonly;
    use Term::Prompt;

    # we use these global variables for both the Linux and Win32 routines
    Readonly our $record =>
        { fields => [ 'login', 'fullname', 'id', 'type', 'password' ] };
    Readonly our $addqueue => 'add.db';    # name of add account queue file
    Readonly our $delqueue => 'del.db';    # name of del account queue file
    Readonly our $maindata => 'acct.db';   # name of main account database file

    # load the Win32-only modules and set the Win32-only global variables
    if ( $^O eq 'MSWin32' ) {
```

```
    require Win32API::Net;
    import Win32API::Net qw(:User :LocalGroup);
    require Win32::Security::NamedObject;
    require File::Path;
    import File::Path 'remove_tree';

    # location of account files
    Readonly our $accountdir => "\\\\server\\accountsystem\\";

    # mail lists, example follows
    Readonly our $maillists => $accountdir . "maillists\\";

    # home directory root
    Readonly our $homeWindirs => "\\\\homeserver\\home";

    # data directory root
    Readonly our $dataWindirs => "\\\\homeserver\\home";

    # name of account add subroutine
    Readonly our $accountadd => \&CreateWinAccount;

    # name of account del subroutine
    Readonly our $accountdel => \&DeleteWinAccount;
}

# load the Unix-only modules and set the Unix-only global variables
else {
    require Expect; # for Solaris password changes
    require Crypt::PasswdMD5;

    # location of account files
    Readonly our $accountdir => '/usr/accountsystem/';

    # mail lists, example follows
    Readonly our $maillists => '$accountdir/maillists/';

    # location of useradd executable
    Readonly our $useraddex => '/usr/sbin/useradd';

    # location of userdel executable
    Readonly our $userdelex => '/usr/sbin/userdel';

    # location of passwd executable
    Readonly our $passwdex => '/usr/bin/passwd';

    # home directory root dir
    Readonly our $homeUnixdirs => '/home';

    # prototypical home directory
    Readonly our $skeldir => '/home/skel';

    # default shell
    Readonly our $defshell => '/bin/zsh';

    # name of account add subroutine
```

```
        Readonly our $accountadd => \&CreateUnixAccount;

        # name of account del subroutine
        Readonly our $accountdel => \&DeleteUnixAccount;
    }
}
```

Let's look at some sample scripts. Here's the script that processes the add queue:

```
use Account;

# read in our low-level routines
&InitAccount;

# read the contents of the add account "queue"
my $queue = ReadAddQueue();

# attempt to create all accounts in the queue
ProcessAddQueue($queue);

# write account record to main database, or back to queue
# if there is a problem
DisposeAddQueue($queue);

# read in the add account queue to the $queue data structure
sub ReadAddQueue {

    our ( $accountdir, $addqueue );
    my $db = DBM::Deep->new( $accountdir . $addqueue );

    my $queue = $db->export();

    return $queue;
}

# iterate through the queue structure, attempting to create an account
# for each request (i.e., each key) in the structure
sub ProcessAddQueue {
    my $queue = shift;

    our $accountadd;
    foreach my $login ( keys %{$queue} ) {
        my $result = $accountadd->( $login, $queue->{$login} );
        if ( $result ) {
            $queue->{$login}{status} = 'created';
        }
        else {
            $queue->{$login}{status} = 'error';
        }
    }
}

# Now iterate through the queue structure again. For each account with
# a status of "created," append to main database. All others get written
# back to the add queue database, overwriting the record's information.
sub DisposeAddQueue {
```

```
    my $queue = shift;

    our ( $accountdir, $addqueue, $maindata );

    my $db = DBM::Deep->new( $accountdir . $addqueue );

    foreach my $login ( keys %{$queue} ) {
        if ( $queue->{$login}{status} eq 'created' ) {
            $queue->{$login}{login}         = $login;
            $queue->{$login}{creation_date} = time;
            AppendAccount( $accountdir . $maindata, $queue->{$login} );
            delete $queue->{$login};    # delete from in-memory representation
            delete $db->{$login};       # delete from disk database file
        }
    }

    # all we have left in $queue at this point are the accounts that
    # could not be created

    # merge in the queue info
    my $db = DBM::Deep->new( $accountdir . $addqueue );

    my $queue = $db->import($queue);
}
```

Our "process the delete user queue file" script is almost identical:

```
use Account;

# read in our low-level routines
&InitAccount;

# read the contents of the del account "queue"
my $queue = ReadDelQueue();

# attempt to delete all accounts in the queue
ProcessDelQueue($queue);

# write account record to main database, or back to queue
# if there is a problem
DisposeDelQueue($queue);

# read in the add account queue to the $queue data structure
sub ReadDelQueue {

    our ( $accountdir, $delqueue );
    my $db = DBM::Deep->new( $accountdir . $delqueue );

    my $queue = $db->export();

    return $queue;
}

# iterate through the queue structure, attempting to create an account
# for each request (i.e., each key) in the structure
sub ProcessDelQueue {
```

```perl
    my $queue = shift;

    our $accountdel;
    foreach my $login ( keys %{$queue} ) {
        my $result = $accountdel->( $login, $queue->{$login} );
        if ( !defined $result ) {
            $queue->{$login}{status} = 'deleted';
        }
        else {
            $queue->{$login}{status} = 'error';
        }
    }
}

# Now iterate through the queue structure again. For each account with
# a status of "deleted," change the main database information. All that
# could not get be deleted gets merged back into the del queue file,
# updating it.
sub DisposeDelQueue {
    my $queue = shift;

    our ( $accountdir, $delqueue, $maindata );

    my $maindata = DBM::Deep->new( $accountdir . $maindata );
    my $delqueue = DBM::Deep->new( $accountdir . $delqueue );

    foreach my $login ( keys %{$queue} ) {
        if ( $queue->{$login}{status} eq 'deleted' ) {
            $maintada->{$login}{deletion_date} = time;
            delete $queue->{$login};    # delete from in-memory representation
            delete $delqueue->{$login}; # delete from on disk del queue file
        }
    }

    # All we have left in $queue at this point are the accounts that
    # could not be deleted. We merge these status changes back
    # into the delete queue for future action of some sort.

    $delqueue->import($queue);
}
```

You can probably imagine writing many other process scripts. For example, we could certainly use scripts that perform data export and consistency checking tasks (e.g., does the user's home directory match up with the main database's account type? is that user in the appropriate group?). We don't have space to cover the whole array of possible programs, so let's end this section with a single example of the data export variety. Earlier I mentioned that a site might want a separate mailing list for each type of user on the system. The following code reads our main database and creates a set of files that contain usernames, with one file per user type:

```perl
use Account;    # just to get the file locations

&InitAccount;
```

```perl
# clearly this doesn't work so well on a large data set
my $database = ReadMainDatabase();

WriteFiles($database);

# read the main database into a hash of hashes
sub ReadMainDatabase {
    our ( $accountdir, $maindata );
    my $db = DBM::Deep->new( $accountdir . $maindata );

    my $database = $db->export();

    return $database;
}

# Iterate through the keys, compile the list of accounts of a certain
# type, and store them in a hash of lists. Then write out the contents of
# each key to a different file.
sub WriteFiles {

    my $database = shift;

    our ( $accountdir, $maillists );

    my %types;

    foreach my $account ( keys %{$database} ) {
        next if $database->{$account}{status} eq 'deleted';
        push( @{ $types{ $database->{$account}{type} } }, $account );
    }

    foreach my $type ( keys %types ) {
        open my $OUT, '>', $maillists . $type
            or die 'Unable to write to ' . $maillists . $type . ": $!\n";
        print $OUT join( "\n", sort @{ $types{$type} } ) . "\n";
        close $OUT;
    }
}
```

If we look at the mailing list directory, we see:

```
> dir
faculty  staff
```

Each of those files contains the appropriate list of user accounts.

Account System Wrap-Up

Now that we've explored four components of our account system, let's wrap up this section by talking about what's missing (besides oodles of functionality):

Error checking

Our demonstration code has only a modicum of error checking. Any self-respecting account system would grow another 40%–50% in code size because it would check for data and system interaction problems every step of the way.

Error reporting

The code is abysmal (for simplicity's sake) at reporting back errors in a way that could help with debugging processes gone wrong. The routines pass back a `0` to indicate failure, but what they really should be doing is handing back exceptions or exception objects that contain more detail. Often we can get that detail from the system. For example in the case of the `Win32API::Net` calls in the Windows code, we could return the information from `Win32::GetLastError()` (or `Win32::FormatMessage(Win32::GetLastError())` if we wanted to be super cool).

Object orientation

Even though I readily admit to having come to the land of object-oriented programming (OOP) late in life, I recognize that all of the global variables floating around this code are icky. The code could be much cleaner if it was rewritten to use objects instead, but I did not want to assume OOP knowledge just for the sake of this example.

Scalability

Our code could probably work in a small or mid-sized environment, but any time you see "read the entire file into memory," it should set off warning bells. To scale, we would need to change our data storage and retrieval techniques, at the very least.

Security

This is related to the first item on error checking. In addition to a few truck-sized security holes (e.g., storing plain-text passwords), we do not perform any security checks in our code. We do not confirm that the data sources we use, such as the queue files, are trustworthy. Another 20%–30% should be added to the code size to take care of this issue.

Multiuser

Perhaps the largest flaw in our code as written is that we make no provision for multiple users or even multiple scripts running at once. In theory `DBM::Deep` is handling locking for us, but the code isn't explicit enough in this regard. This is such an important issue that I'll take a few moments to discuss it before concluding this section.

Maintenance

Addressing these weaknesses, even without adding features, would dramatically increase the size and complexity of the code. The result would be a large, complex, multi-OS program with functions that are critical to the business. Does the enterprise have the staff and expertise to support ongoing software maintenance, and should that responsibility lie with the sysadmin who creates the code? These are questions that must be asked (and answered) in each environment.

One way to help with the multiuser deficiency is to carefully introduce explicit file locking. File locking allows the different scripts to cooperate. If a script plans to read or write to a file, it can attempt to lock the file first. If it can obtain a lock, it knows it is safe to manipulate the file. If it cannot lock the file (because another script is using it), it knows not to proceed with an operation that could corrupt data. Of course, there's considerably more complexity involved with locking and multiuser access in general than just this simple description reveals, as you'll see if you consult any fundamental operating or distributed systems text. It gets especially tricky when dealing with files residing on network filesystems, where there may not be a good locking mechanism. DBM::Deep's documentation makes explicit mention of not handling locking on NFS filesystems. If you don't want to trust the built-in locking, here are a few hints that may help you when you approach this topic using Perl:

- There are smart ways to cheat. My favorite method is to use the *lockfile* program distributed with the popular mail filtering program *procmail* (*http://www.procmail .org*). The *procmail* installation procedure takes great pains to determine safe locking strategies for the filesystems you are using. *lockfile* does just what its name suggests, hiding most of the complexity in the process.

- If you don't want to use an external executable, there are a plethora of locking modules available: for example, File::Flock by David Muir Sharnoff, File::LockDir from the *Perl Cookbook* by Tom Christiansen and Nathan Torkington (O'Reilly), File::Lock by Kenneth Albanowski, File::Lockf by Paul Henson, and Lockfile::Simple by Raphael Manfredi. They differ mostly in terms of their interfaces, though Lockfile::Simple attempts to perform locking without using Perl's flock() function. Shop around and pick the best one for your needs.

- Locking is easier to get right if you remember to lock before attempting to change data (or read data that could change) and unlock only *after* making sure that data has been written (e.g., after the file has been closed). For more information on this, see the previously mentioned *Perl Cookbook*, the Perl Frequently Asked Questions list (*http://faq.perl.org*), and the documentation that comes with Perl on the flock() function and the DB_File module.

This ends our look at user account administration and how it can be taken to the next level with a bit of an architectural mindset. These concepts—particularly the "self-review" of deficiencies in the account administration program—can be applied to many projects and can be very helpful in architecting system administration tools, rather than just writing scripts.

In this chapter we've concentrated on the beginning and the end of an account's life-cycle. In the next chapter, we'll examine what users do in between these two points.

Module Information for This Chapter

Name	CPAN ID	Version
User::pwent (ships with Perl)		1.00
File::stat (ships with Perl)		1.01
Passwd::Solaris	EESTABROO	1.2
Passwd::Linux	EESTABROO	1.2
Win32API::Net	JDB	0.12
Win32::Security(::NamedObject, ::ACL)	TEVERETT	0.50
Win32::OLE	JDB	0.1709
Term::Prompt	PERSICOM	1.04
Crypt::PasswdMD5	LUISMUNOZ	1.3
DBM::Deep	RKINYON	1.0014
Readonly	ROODE	1.03
Expect	RGIERSIG	1.21
File::Path (ships with Perl)	DLAND	2.07
Win32::FileOp	JENDA	0.14.1

References for More Information

Using a set of central databases from which configuration files are automatically generated is a best practice that shows up in a number of places in this book; credit for my exposure to this methodology goes to Rémy Evard. Though it is now in use at many sites, I first encountered it when I inherited the Tenwen computing environment he built (as described in the Tenwen paper at *https://www.usenix.org/publications/library/proceedings/lisa94/evard.html*). See the section "Implemented the Hosts Database" for one example of this methodology in action.

http://www.rpi.edu/~finkej/ contains a number of Jon Finke's published papers on the use of relational databases for system administration. Many of his papers were published at the LISA conference; see *http://www.usenix.org* for the archives of past proceedings.

Unix Password Files

http://www.freebsd.org/cgi/man.cgi is where the FreeBSD Project provides access to the online manual pages for *BSD and other Unix variants. This is a handy way to compare the file formats and user administration commands (useradd, etc.) for several operating systems.

Practical Unix & Internet Security, Third Edition, by Simson Garfinkel et al. (O'Reilly), is an excellent place to start for information about password files.

Windows User Administration

http://Jenda.Krynicky.cz is another site with useful Win32 modules applicable to user administration.

http://aspn.activestate.com/ASPN/Mail hosts the *Perl-Win32-Admin* and *Perl-Win32-Users* mailing lists. Both lists and their archives are invaluable resources for Windows Perl programmers.

Win32 Perl Programming: The Standard Extensions, Second Edition, and *Win32 Perl Scripting: The Administrator's Handbook*, both by Dave Roth (Sams, 2001 and 2002), are a little dated but are still some of the best references for Win32 Perl module programming available.

There are a whole slew of superb books that have Robbie Allen as author or coauthor, including *Active Directory, Third Edition* (O'Reilly), *Active Directory Cookbook, Second Edition* (O'Reilly), *Managing Enterprise AD Services* (Addison-Wesley), *Windows Server Cookbook* (O'Reilly), *Windows Server 2003 Networking Recipes* (Apress), *Windows Server 2003 Security Cookbook (orm:hideurl:ital)* (O'Reilly), and *Windows XP Cookbook (orm:hideurl:ital)* (O'Reilly). All of these are well worth reading, but it's not the books I want to gush about. Allen has a website at *http://techtasks.com* that makes all of the code samples in all of the languages (including Perl translations of all the VBScript code) from all of these books available for viewing and for purchase. It truly is the mother lode of examples—one of the single most helpful websites for this sort of programming that you'll ever find. Definitely buy the books and the code repository; this sort of effort deserves your support.

http://win32.perl.org has a wiki devoted to all things Win32-Perl related. The PPM repositories link at that site is especially helpful when you are trying to track down more modules for the ActiveState Perl distribution.

http://learning.microsoft.com is (as of this writing) the home for the Microsoft resource kits. *http://www.microsoft.com/downloads/* is (again, as of this writing, they love to shuffle URLs in Redmond) a good place to search for the freely downloadable utilities from the resource kits (search for "resource kit").

## CHAPTER 4

User Activity

In the previous chapter, we explored the parts of a user's identity and how to manage and store it. Now let's talk about how to manage users while they are active on our systems and networks.

Typical user activities fall into four domains:

Processes

Users run processes that can be spawned, killed, paused, and resumed on the machines we manage. These processes compete for a computer's finite processing power, adding resource issues to the list of problems a system administrator needs to mediate.

File operations

Most of the time, operations like writing, reading, creating, deleting, and so on take place when a specific user process interacts with files and directories in a filesystem. But under Unix, there's more to this picture. Unix uses the filesystem as a gateway to more than just file storage. Device control, input/output, and even some process control and network access operations are file operations. We dealt with filesystem administration in Chapter 2, but in this chapter we'll approach this topic from a user administration perspective.

Network usage

Users can send and receive data over network interfaces on our machines. There is material elsewhere in this book on networking, but we'll address this issue here from a different perspective.

OS-specific activities

This last domain is a catchall for the OS-specific features that users can access via different APIs. Included in this list are things like GUI element controls, shared memory usage, file-sharing APIs, sound, and so on. This category is so diverse that it would be impossible to do it justice in this book. I recommend that you track down the OS-specific web sites for information on these topics.

Process Management

We'll begin by looking at ways to deal with the first three of these domains using Perl. Because we're interested in user administration, the focus here will be on dealing with processes that other users have started.

Windows-Based Operating System Process Control

We're going to briefly look at four different ways to deal with process control on Windows, because each of these approaches opens up a door to interesting functionality outside the scope of our discussion that is likely to be helpful to you at some point. We're primarily going to concentrate on two tasks: finding all of the running processes and killing select processes.

Using external binaries

There are a number of programs available to us that display and manipulate processes. The first edition of this book used the programs *pulist.exe* and *kill.exe* from the Windows 2000 Resource Kit. Both are still available for download from Microsoft as of this writing and seem to work fine on later versions of the operating system. Another excellent set of process manipulation tools comes from the Sysinternals utility collection, which Mark Russinovich and Bryce Cogswell formerly provided on their Sysinternals web site and which is now available through Microsoft (see the references section at the end of this chapter). This collection includes a suite of utilities called *PsTools* that can do things the standard Microsoft-supplied tools can't handle.

For our first example, we're going to use two programs Microsoft ships with the operating system. The programs *tasklist.exe* and *taskkill.exe* work fine for many tasks and are a good choice for scripting in cases where you won't want to or can't download other programs to a machine.

By default `tasklist` produces output in a very wide table that can sometimes be difficult to read. Adding `/FO list` provides output like this:

```
Image Name:   System Idle Process
PID:          0
Session Name: Console
Session#:     0
Mem Usage:    16 K
Status:       Running
User Name:    NT AUTHORITY\SYSTEM
CPU Time:     1:09:06
Window Title: N/A

Image Name:   System
PID:          4
Session Name: Console
Session#:     0
Mem Usage:    212 K
```

```
Status:        Running
User Name:     NT AUTHORITY\SYSTEM
CPU Time:      0:00:44
Window Title:  N/A

Image Name:    smss.exe
PID:           432
Session Name:  Console
Session#:      0
Mem Usage:     372 K
Status:        Running
User Name:     NT AUTHORITY\SYSTEM
CPU Time:      0:00:00
Window Title:  N/A

Image Name:    csrss.exe
PID:           488
Session Name:  Console
Session#:      0
Mem Usage:     3,984 K
Status:        Running
User Name:     NT AUTHORITY\SYSTEM
CPU Time:      0:00:08
Window Title:  N/A

Image Name:    winlogon.exe
PID:           512
Session Name:  Console
Session#:      0
Mem Usage:     2,120 K
Status:        Running
User Name:     NT AUTHORITY\SYSTEM
CPU Time:      0:00:08
Window Title:  N/A
```

Another format option for `tasklist` makes using it from Perl pretty trivial: CSV (Comma/Character Separated Values). We'll talk more about dealing with CSV files in Chapter 5, but here's a small example that demonstrates how to parse that data:

```perl
use Text::CSV_XS;

my $tasklist = "$ENV{'SystemRoot'}\\SYSTEM32\\TASKLIST.EXE";
my $csv = Text::CSV_XS->new();

# /v = verbose (includes User Name), /FO CSV = CSV format, /NH - no header
open my $TASKPIPE, '-|', "$tasklist /v /FO CSV /NH"
    or die "Can't run $tasklist: $!\n";

my @columns;
while (<$TASKPIPE>) {
    next if /^$/;    # skip blank lines in the input
    $csv->parse($_) or die "Could not parse this line: $_\n";
    @columns = ( $csv->fields() )[ 0, 1, 6 ];    # grab name, PID, and User Name
    print join( ':', @columns ), "\n";
```

```
}

    close $TASKPIPE;
```

`tasklist` can also provide some other interesting information, such as the dynamic link libraries (DLLs) used by a particular process. Be sure to run it with the **/?** switch to see its usage information.

The other program I mentioned, *taskkill.exe*, is equally easy to use. It takes as an argument a task name (called the "image name"), a process ID, or a more complex filter to determine which processes to kill. I recommend the process ID format to stay on the safe side, since it is very easy to kill the wrong process if you use task names.

`taskkill` offers two different ways to shoot down processes. The first is the polite death: `taskkill.exe /PID <process id>` will ask the specified process to shut itself down. However, if we add **/F** to the command line, it forces the issue: `taskkill.exe /F /PID <process id>` works more like the native Perl `kill()` function and kills the process with extreme prejudice.

Using the Win32::Process::Info module

The second approach[*] uses the `Win32::Process::Info` module, by Thomas R. Wyant. `Win32::Process::Info` is very easy to use. First, create a process info object, like so:

```
use Win32::Process::Info;
use strict;

# the user running this script must be able to use DEBUG level privs
my $pi = Win32::Process::Info->new( { assert_debug_priv => 1 } );
```

The `new()` method can optionally take a reference to a hash containing configuration information. In this case we set the config variable `assert_debug_priv` to `true` because we want our program to use debug-level privileges when requesting information. This is necessary if getting a list of all of the process owners is important to you. If you leave this out, you'll find that the module (due to the Windows security system) will not be able to fetch the owner of some of the processes. There are some pretty scary warnings in the module's documentation regarding this setting; I haven't had any problems with it to date, but you should be sure to read the documentation before you follow my lead.

Next, we retrieve the process information for the machine:

```
    my @processinfo = $pi->GetProcInfo();
```

`@processinfo` is now an array of references to anonymous hashes. Each anonymous hash has a number of keys (such as `Name`, `ProcessId`, `CreationDate`, and `ExecutablePath`), each with its expected value. To display our process info in the same fashion as the example from the last section, we could use the following code:

---

[*] In the first edition of this book, this section was called "Using the Win32::IProc module." `Win32::IProc` shared the fate of the module I describe in the sidebar "The Ephemeral Nature of Modules" on page 127.

```
use Win32::Process::Info;

my $pi = Win32::Process::Info->new( { assert_debug_priv => 1 } );
my @processinfo = $pi->GetProcInfo();

foreach my $process (@processinfo) {
    print join( ':',
        $process->{'Name'}, $process->{'ProcessId'},
        $process->{'Owner'} ),
        "\n";
}
```

Once again, we get output like this:

```
System Idle Process:0:
System:4:
smss.exe:432:NT AUTHORITY\SYSTEM
csrss.exe:488:NT AUTHORITY\SYSTEM
winlogon.exe:512:NT AUTHORITY\SYSTEM
services.exe:556:NT AUTHORITY\SYSTEM
lsass.exe:568:NT AUTHORITY\SYSTEM
svchost.exe:736:NT AUTHORITY\SYSTEM
svchost.exe:816:NT AUTHORITY\NETWORK SERVICE
svchost.exe:884:NT AUTHORITY\SYSTEM
svchost.exe:960:NT AUTHORITY\SYSTEM
svchost.exe:1044:NT AUTHORITY\NETWORK SERVICE
svchost.exe:1104:NT AUTHORITY\LOCAL SERVICE
ccSetMgr.exe:1172:NT AUTHORITY\SYSTEM
ccEvtMgr.exe:1200:NT AUTHORITY\SYSTEM
spoolsv.exe:1324:NT AUTHORITY\SYSTEM
...
```

Win32::Process::Info provides more info about a process than just these fields (perhaps more than you will ever need). It also has one more helpful feature: it can show you the process tree for all processes or just a particular process. This allows you to display the subprocesses for each process (i.e., the list of processes that process spawned) and the subprocesses for those subprocesses, and so on.

So, for example, if we wanted to see all of the processes spawned by one of the processes just listed, we could write the following:

```
use Win32::Process::Info;
use Data::Dumper;

my $pi = Win32::Process::Info->new( { assert_debug_priv => 1 } );

# PID 884 picked for this example because it has a small number of children
my %sp = $pi->Subprocesses(884);

print Dumper (\%sp);
```

This yields:

```
$VAR1 = {
         '3320' => [],
         '884' => [
                    3320
                  ]
        };
```

which shows that this instance of *svchost.exe* (PID **884**) has one child, the process with PID **3320**. That process does not have any children.

Using the GUI control modules (Win32::Setupsup and Win32::GuiTest)

Of the approaches we'll consider, this third approach is probably the most fun. In this section we'll look at a module by Jens Helberg called `Win32::Setupsup` and a module by Ernesto Guisado, Jarek Jurasz, and Dennis K. Paulsen called `Win32::GuiTest`. They have similar functionality but achieve the same goals a little differently. We'll look primarily at `Win32::Setupsup`, with a few choice examples from `Win32::GuiTest`.

 In the interest of full disclosure, it should be mentioned that (as of this writing) `Win32::Setupsup` had not been developed since October 2000 and is kind of hard to find (see the references at the end of this chapter). It still works well, though, and it has features that aren't found in `Win32::GuiTest`; hence its inclusion here. If its orphan status bothers you, I recommend looking at `Win32::GuiTest` first to see if it meets your needs.

`Win32::Setupsup` is called "Setupsup" because it is primarily designed to supplement software installation (which often uses a program called *setup.exe*).

Some installers can be run in so-called "silent mode" for totally automated installation. In this mode they ask no questions and require no "OK" buttons to be pushed, freeing the administrator from having to babysit the install. Software installation mechanisms that do not offer this mode (and there are far too many of them) make a system administrator's life difficult. `Win32::Setupsup` helps deal with these deficiencies: it can find information on running processes and manipulate them (or manipulate them dead if you so choose).

 For instructions on getting and installing `Win32::Setupsup`, refer to the section "Module Information for This Chapter" on page 97.

With `Win32::Setupsup`, getting the list of running processes is easy. Here's an example:

```
use Win32::Setupsup;
use Perl6::Form;

my $machine = '';     # query the list on the current machine

# define the output format for Perl6::Form
my $format = '{<<<<<<<}        {<<<<<<<<<<<<<<<<<<<<<<<<<<<<<<<<}';

my ( @processlist, @threadlist );
Win32::Setupsup::GetProcessList( $machine, \@processlist, \@threadlist )
    or die 'process list error: ' . Win32::Setupsup::GetLastError() . "\n";

pop(@processlist);     # remove the bogus entry always appended to the list

print <<'EOH';
Process ID      Process Name
==========      ================================
EOH

foreach my $processlist (@processlist) {
    print form $format, $processlist->{pid}, $processlist->{name};
}
```

Killing processes is equally easy:

```
KillProcess($pid, $exitvalue, $systemprocessflag) or
    die 'Unable to kill process: ' . Win32::Setupsup::GetLastError( ) . "\n";
```

The last two arguments are optional. The second argument kills the process and sets its exit value accordingly (by default, it is set to 0). The third argument allows you to kill system-run processes (providing you have the Debug Programs user right).

That's the boring stuff. We can take process manipulation to yet another level by interacting with the windows a running process may have open. To list all of the windows available on the desktop, we use:

```
Win32::Setupsup::EnumWindows(\@windowlist) or
    die 'process list error: ' . Win32::Setupsup::GetLastError( ) . "\n";
```

@windowlist now contains a list of window handles that are converted to look like normal numbers when you print them. To learn more about each window, you can use a few different functions. For instance, to find the titles of each window, you can use GetWindowText() like so:

```
use Win32::Setupsup;

my @windowlist;
Win32::Setupsup::EnumWindows( \@windowlist )
    or die 'process list error: ' . Win32::Setupsup::GetLastError() . "\n";

my $text;
foreach my $whandle (@windowlist) {
    if ( Win32::Setupsup::GetWindowText( $whandle, \$text ) ) {
        print "$whandle: $text", "\n";
```

```
        }
    else {
        warn "Can't get text for $whandle"
            . Win32::Setupsup::GetLastError() . "\n";
    }
}
```

Here's a little bit of sample output:

```
66130: chapter04 - Microsoft Word
66184: Style
194905150:
66634: setupsup - WordPad
65716: Fuel
328754: DDE Server Window
66652:
66646:
66632: OleMainThreadWndName
```

As you can see, some windows have titles, while others do not. Observant readers might notice something else interesting about this output. Window 66130 belongs to a Microsoft Word session that is currently running (it is actually the one in which this chapter was composed). Window 66184 looks vaguely like the name of another window that might be connected to Microsoft Word. How can we tell if they are related?

Win32::Setupsup has an EnumChildWindows() function that can show us the children of any given window. Let's use it to write something that will show us a basic tree of the current window hierarchy:

```
use Win32::Setupsup;

my @windowlist;
# get the list of windows
Win32::Setupsup::EnumWindows( \@windowlist )
    or die 'process list error: ' . Win32::Setupsup::GetLastError() . "\n";

# turn window handle list into a hash
# NOTE: this conversion populates the hash with plain numbers and
# not actual window handles as keys. Some functions, like
# GetWindowProperties (which we'll see in a moment), can't use these
# converted numbers. Caveat implementor.
my %windowlist;
for (@windowlist) { $windowlist{$_}++; }

# check each window for children
my %children;
foreach my $whandle (@windowlist) {
    my @children;
    if ( Win32::Setupsup::EnumChildWindows( $whandle, \@children ) ) {

        # keep a sorted list of children for each window
        $children{$whandle} = [ sort { $a <=> $b } @children ];
```

```
            # remove all children from the hash; we won't directly
            # iterate over them
            foreach my $child (@children) {
                delete $windowlist{$child};
            }
        }
    }

# iterate through the list of windows and recursively print
# each window handle and its children (if any)
foreach my $window ( sort { $a <=> $b } keys %windowlist ) {
    PrintFamily( $window, 0, %children );
}

# print a given window handle number and its children (recursively)
sub PrintFamily {

    # starting window - how deep in a tree are we?
    my ( $startwindow, $level, %children ) = @_;

    # print the window handle number at the appropriate indentation
    print( ( ' ' x $level ) . "$startwindow\n" );

    return unless ( exists $children{$startwindow} );    # no children, done

    # otherwise, we have to recurse for each child
    $level++;
    foreach my $childwindow ( @{ $children{$startwindow} } ) {
        PrintFamily( $childwindow, $level, %children );
    }
}
```

There's one last window property function we should look at before moving on: GetWindowProperties(). GetWindowProperties() is basically a catchall for the rest of the window properties we haven't seen yet. For instance, using GetWindowProperties() we can query the process ID for the process that created a specific window. This could be combined with some of the functionality we just saw for the Win32::Process::Info module.

The Win32::Setupsup documentation contains a list of the available properties that can be queried. Let's use one of them to write a very simple program that will print the coordinates of a rectangular window on the desktop. GetWindowProperties() takes three arguments: a window handle, a reference to an array that contains the names of the properties to query, and a reference to a hash where the query results will be stored. Here's the code we need for our task:

```
use Win32::Setupsup;

# Convert window ID into a form that GetWindowProperties can cope with.
# Note: 'U' is a pack template that is only available in Perl 5.6+ releases.

my $whandle = unpack 'U', pack 'U', $ARGV[0];
```

```
my %info;
Win32::Setupsup::GetWindowProperties( $whandle, ['rect'], \%info );

print "\t" . $info{rect}{top} . "\n";
print $info{rect}{left} . ' -' . $whandle . '- ' . $info{rect}{right} . "\n";
print "\t" . $info{rect}{bottom} . "\n";
```

The output is a bit cutesy. Here's a sample showing the top, left, right, and bottom coordinates of the window with handle 66180:

```
    154
272 -66180- 903
    595
```

GetWindowProperties() returns a special data structure for only one property, rect. All of the others will simply show up in the referenced hash as normal keys and values. If you are uncertain about the properties being returned by Perl for a specific window, the *windowse* utility (*http://www.greatis.com/delphicb/windowse/*) is often helpful.

Now that we've seen how to determine various window properties, wouldn't it be spiffy if we could make changes to some of these properties? For instance, it might be useful to change the title of a particular window. With this capability, we could create scripts that used the window title as a status indicator:

```
"Prestidigitation In Progress ... 32% complete"
```

Making this change to a window is as easy as a single function call:

```
Win32::Setupsup::SetWindowText($handle,$text);
```

We can also set the rect property we just saw. This code makes the specified window jump to the position we've specified:

```
use Win32::Setupsup;

my %info;
$info{rect}{left}   = 0;
$info{rect}{right}  = 600;
$info{rect}{top}    = 10;
$info{rect}{bottom} = 500;
my $whandle = unpack 'U', pack 'U', $ARGV[0];
Win32::Setupsup::SetWindowProperties( $whandle, \%info );
```

I've saved the most impressive function for last. With SendKeys(), it is possible to send arbitrary keystrokes to any window on the desktop. For example:

```
use Win32::Setupsup;

my $texttosend = "\\DN\\Low in the gums";
my $whandle = unpack 'U', pack 'U', $ARGV[0];
Win32::Setupsup::SendKeys( $whandle, $texttosend, 0 ,0 );
```

This will send a "down cursor key" followed by some text to the specified window. The arguments to SendKeys() are pretty simple: window handle, text to send, a flag to determine whether a window should be activated for each keystroke, and an optional time between keystrokes. Special key codes like the down cursor are surrounded by backslashes. The list of available keycodes can be found in the module's documentation.

Before we move on to another tremendously useful way to work with user processes in the Windows universe, I want to briefly look at a module that shares some functionality with Win32::Setupsup but can do even more interesting stuff. Like Win32::Setupsup, Win32::GuiTest can return information about active windows and send keystrokes to applications. However, it offers even more powerful functionality.

Here's an example slightly modified from the documentation (stripped of comments and error checking, be sure to see the original) that demonstrates some of this power:

```
use Win32::GuiTest qw(:ALL);

system("start notepad.exe");
sleep 1;

MenuSelect("F&ormat|&Font");
sleep(1);

my $fontdlg = GetForegroundWindow();

my ($combo) = FindWindowLike( $fontdlg, '', 'ComboBox', 0x470 );

for ( GetComboContents($combo) ) {
    print "'$_'" . "\n";
}

SendKeys("{ESC}%{F4}");
```

This code starts up *notepad*, asks it to open its font settings by choosing the appropriate menu item, and then reads the contents of the resulting dialog box and prints what it finds. It then sends the necessary keystrokes to dismiss the dialog box and tell *notepad* to quit. The end result is a list of monospaced fonts available on the system that looks something like this:

```
'Arial'
'Arial Black'
'Comic Sans MS'
'Courier'
'Courier New'
'Estrangelo Edessa'
'Fixedsys'
'Franklin Gothic Me
'Gautami'
'Georgia'
'Impact'
'Latha'
'Lucida Console'
'Lucida Sans Unicod
'Mangal'
'Marlett'
'Microsoft Sans Ser
```

```
'Modern'
'MS Sans Serif'
```

Let's look at one more example (again, adapted from the module's documentation because it offers great example code):

```perl
use Win32::GuiTest qw(:ALL);

system 'start notepad';
sleep 1;

my $menu = GetMenu( GetForegroundWindow() );
menu_parse($menu);

SendKeys("{ESC}%{F4}");

sub menu_parse {
    my ( $menu, $depth ) = @_;
    $depth ||= 0;

    foreach my $i ( 0 .. GetMenuItemCount($menu) - 1 ) {
        my %h = GetMenuItemInfo( $menu, $i );
        print '    ' x $depth;
        print "$i  ";
        print $h{text} if $h{type} and $h{type} eq 'string';
        print "------" if $h{type} and $h{type} eq 'separator';
        print "UNKNOWN" if not $h{type};
        print "\n";

        my $submenu = GetSubMenu( $menu, $i );
        if ($submenu) {
            menu_parse( $submenu, $depth + 1 );
        }
    }
}
```

As in the previous example, we begin by spinning up *notepad*. We can then examine the menus of the application in the foreground window, determining the number of top-level menu items and then iterating over each item (printing the information and looking for submenus of each item as we go). If we find a submenu, we recursively call menu_parse() to examine it. Once we've completed the menu walk, we send the keys to close the *notepad* window and quit the application.

The output looks like this:

```
0  &File
    0  &New        Ctrl+N
    1  &Open...     Ctrl+O
    2  &Save        Ctrl+S
    3  Save &As...
    4  ------
    5  Page Set&up...
    6  &Print... Ctrl+P
    7  ------
    8  E&xit
```

```
1  &Edit
   0  &Undo      Ctrl+Z
   1  ------
   2  Cu&t       Ctrl+X
   3  &Copy      Ctrl+C
   4  &Paste     Ctrl+V
   5  De&lete    Del
   6  ------
   7  &Find...   Ctrl+F
   8  Find &Next        F3
   9  &Replace...       Ctrl+H
   10 &Go To...         Ctrl+G
   11 ------
   12 Select &All       Ctrl+A
   13 Time/&Date        F5
2  F&ormat
   0  &Word Wrap
   1  &Font...
3  &View
   0  &Status Bar
4  &Help
   0  &Help Topics
   1  ------
   2  &About Notepad
```

Triggering known menu items from a script is pretty cool, but it's even cooler to have the power to determine which menu items are available. This lets us write much more adaptable scripts.

We've only touched on a few of `Win32::GuiTest`'s advanced features here. Some of the other impressive features include the ability to read the text context of a window using `WMGetText()` and the ability to select individual tabs in a window with `SelectTabItem()`. See the documentation and the example directory (*eg*) for more details.

With the help of these two modules, we've taken process control to an entirely new level. Now it is possible to remotely control applications (and parts of the OS) without the explicit cooperation of those applications. We don't need them to offer command-line support or a special API; we have the ability to essentially script a GUI, which is useful in a myriad of system administration contexts.

Using Windows Management Instrumentation (WMI)

Let's look at one final approach to Windows process control before we switch to another operating system. By now you've probably figured out that each of these approaches is not only good for process control, but also can be applied in many different ways to make Windows system administration easier. If you had to pick the approach that would yield the most reward in the long term to learn, WMI-based scripting is probably it. The first edition of this book called Windows Management Instrumentation "Futureland" because it was still new to the scene when the book was being written. In the intervening time, Microsoft, to its credit, has embraced the WMI framework as its primary interface for administration of not just its operating systems, but also its other products, such as MS SQL Server and Microsoft Exchange.

Unfortunately, WMI is one of those not-for-the-faint-of-heart technologies that gets very complex very quickly. It is based on an object-oriented model that has the power to represent not only data, but also relationships between objects. For instance, it is possible to create an association between a web server and the storage device that holds the data for that server, so that if the storage device fails, a problem for the web server will be reported as well. We don't have the space to deal with this complexity here, so we're just going to skim the surface of WMI by providing a small and simple introduction, followed by a few code samples.

If you want to get a deeper look at this technology, I recommend searching for WMI-related content at *http://msdn.microsoft.com*. You should also have a look at the information found at the Distributed Management Task Force's website (*http://www.dmtf .org*). In the meantime, here is a brief synopsis to get you started.

WMI is the Microsoft implementation and extension of an unfortunately named initiative called the *Web-Based Enterprise Management* initiative, or WBEM for short. Though the name conjures up visions of something that requires a browser, it has virtually nothing to do with the World Wide Web. The companies that were part of the Distributed Management Task Force (DMTF) wanted to create something that could make it easier to perform management tasks using browsers. Putting the name aside, it is clearer to say that WBEM defines a data model for management and instrumentation information. It provides specifications for organizing, accessing, and moving this data around. WBEM is also meant to offer a cohesive frontend for accessing data provided by other management protocols, such as the Simple Network Management Protocol (SNMP), discussed in Chapter 12, and the Common Management Information Protocol (CMIP).

Data in the WBEM world is organized using the Common Information Model (CIM). CIM is the source of the power and complexity in WBEM/WMI. It provides an extensible data model that contains objects and object classes for any physical or logical entity one might want to manage. For instance, there are object classes for entire networks, and objects for single slots in specific machines. There are objects for hardware settings and objects for software application settings. On top of this, CIM allows us to define object classes that describe relationships between other objects.

This data model is documented in two parts: the *CIM Specification* and the *CIM Schema*. The former describes the *how* of CIM (how the data will be specified, its connection to prior management standards, etc.), while the latter provides the *what* of CIM (the actual objects). This division may remind you of the SNMP SMI and MIB relationship (see Appendix G and Chapter 12).

In practice, you'll be consulting the CIM Schema more than the CIM Specification once you get the hang of how the data is represented. The schema format (called MOF, for Managed Object Format) is fairly easy to read.

The CIM Schema has two layers:

- The *core model* for objects and classes useful in all types of WBEM interaction.
- The *common model* for generic objects that are vendor- and operating system-independent. Within the common model there are currently 15 specific areas, including Systems, Devices, Applications, Networks, and Physical.

Built on top of these two layers can be any number of *extension schemas* that define objects and classes for vendor- and OS-specific information. WMI is one WBEM implementation that makes heavy use of this extension mechanism.

A crucial part of WMI that distinguishes it from generic WBEM implementations is the Win32 Schema, an extension schema for Win32-specific information built on the core and common models. WMI also adds to the generic WBEM framework by providing Win32-specific access mechanisms to the CIM data.[†] Using this schema extension and set of data access methods, we can explore how to perform process control operations using WMI in Perl.

WMI offers two different approaches for getting at management data: object-oriented and query-based. With the former you specify the specific object or container of objects that contains the information you seek, while with the latter you construct a SQL-like[‡] query that returns a result set of objects containing your desired data. We'll give a simple example of each approach so you can see how they work.

The Perl code that follows does not appear to be particularly complex, so you may wonder about the earlier "gets very complex very quickly" description. The code looks simple because:

- We're only scratching the surface of WMI. We're not even going to touch on subjects like associations (i.e., relationships between objects and object classes).
- The management operations we are performing are simple. Process control in this context will consist of querying the running processes and being able to terminate them at will. These operations are easy in WMI using the Win32 Schema extension.
- Our samples hide the complexity of translating WMI documentation and code samples in VBScript/JScript to Perl code. See Appendix F for some help with that task.
- Our samples hide the opaqueness of the debugging process. When WMI-related Perl code fails (especially code of the object-oriented flavor), it provides very little information that would help you debug the problem. You may receive error messages, but they never say `ERROR: YOUR EXACT PROBLEM IS...`. You're more likely to

---

[†] As much as Microsoft would like to see these data access mechanisms become ubiquitous, the likelihood of finding them in a non-Win32 environment is slight. This is why I refer to them as "Win32-specific."

[‡] Microsoft provides WQL, a scaled-down query language based on SQL syntax, for this purpose. Once upon a time it also provided ODBC-based access to the data, but that approach has been deprecated in more recent OS releases.

get back a message like `wbemErrFailed 0x8004100` or just an empty data structure. To be fair to Perl, most of this opaqueness comes from Perl's role in this process: it is acting as a frontend to a set of fairly complex multilayered operations that don't concern themselves with passing back useful feedback when something fails.

I know this sounds pretty grim, so let me offer some potentially helpful advice before we actually get into the code itself:

- Look at all of the `Win32::OLE` sample code you can lay your hands on. The Active-State *Win32-Users* mailing list archive found at *http://aspn.activestate.com/ASPN/ Mail* is a good source for this code. If you compare this sample code to equivalent VBScript examples, you'll start to understand the necessary translation idioms. Appendix F and the section "Active Directory Service Interfaces" on page 354 in Chapter 9 may also help.

- Make friends with the Perl debugger, and use it to try out code snippets as part of this learning process. There are also several REPL[*]-modules available on CPAN, such as `App::REPL`, `Devel::REPL`, and `Shell::Perl`, that can make interactive prototyping easier. Other integrated development environment (IDE) tools may also offer this functionality.

- Keep a copy of the WMI SDK handy. The documentation and the VBScript code examples are very helpful.

- Use the WMI object browser in the WMI SDK frequently. It helps you get the lay of the land.

Now let's get to the Perl part of this section. Our initial task will be to determine what information we can retrieve about Windows processes and how we can interact with that information.

First we need to establish a connection to a WMI *namespace*. A namespace is defined in the WMI SDK as "a unit for grouping classes and instances to control their scope and visibility." In this case, we're interested in connecting to the root of the standard `cimv2` namespace, which contains all of the data that is interesting to us.

We will also have to set up a connection with the appropriate security privileges and impersonation level. Our program will need to be given the privilege to debug a process and to impersonate us; in other words, it has to run as the user calling the script. After we get this connection, we will retrieve a `Win32_Process` object (as defined in the Win32 Schema).

---

[*] REPL stands for Read-Eval-Print Loop, a term from the LISP (LISt Processing) world. A REPL lets you type code into a prompt, have it be executed by the language's interpreter, and then review the results.

There is a hard way and an easy way to create this connection and get the object. We'll look at both in the first example, so you get an idea of what the methods entail. Here's the hard way, with its explanation to follow:

```
use Win32::OLE('in');

my $server = ''; # connect to local machine

# get an SWbemLocator object
my $lobj = Win32::OLE->new('WbemScripting.SWbemLocator') or
    die "can't create locator object: ".Win32::OLE->LastError()."\n";

# set the impersonation level to "impersonate"
$lobj->{Security_}->{impersonationlevel} = 3;

# use it to get an SWbemServices object
my $sobj = $lobj->ConnectServer($server, 'root\cimv2') or
    die "can't create server object: ".Win32::OLE->LastError()."\n";

# get the schema object
my $procschm = $sobj->Get('Win32_Process');
```

The hard way involves:

- Getting a locator object, used to find a connection to a server object
- Setting the impersonation level so our program will run with our privileges
- Using the locator object to get a server connection to the cimv2 WMI namespace
- Using this server connection to retrieve a Win32_Process object

Doing it this way is useful in cases where you need to operate on the intermediate objects. However, we can do this all in one step using a COM moniker's display name. According to the WMI SDK, "in Common Object Model (COM), a *moniker* is the standard mechanism for encapsulating the location and binding of another COM object. The textual representation of a moniker is called a *display name*." Here's an easy way to do the same thing as the previous code snippet:

```
use Win32::OLE('in');

my $procschm = Win32::OLE->GetObject(
    'winmgmts:{impersonationLevel=impersonate}!Win32_Process')
    or die "can't create server object: ".Win32::OLE->LastError()."\n";
```

Now that we have a Win32_Process object in hand, we can use it to show us the relevant parts of the schema that represent processes under Windows. This includes all of the available Win32_Process properties and methods we can use. The code to do this is fairly simple; the only magic is the use of the Win32::OLE in operator. To explain this, we need a quick digression.

Our $procschm object has two special properties, Properties_ and Methods_. Each holds a special child object, known as a *collection object* in COM parlance. A collection object is just a parent container for other objects; in this case, they are holding the schema's property method description objects. The in operator just returns an array with references to each child object of a container object.[†] Once we have this array, we can iterate through it, returning the Name property of each child object as we go. Here's what the code looks like:

```
use Win32::OLE('in');

# connect to namespace, set the impersonation level, and retrieve the
# Win32_process object just by using a display name
my $procschm = Win32::OLE->GetObject(
    'winmgmts:{impersonationLevel=impersonate}!Win32_Process')
    or die "can't create server object: ".Win32::OLE->LastError()."\n";

print "--- Properties ---\n";
print join("\n",map {$_->{Name}}(in $procschm->{Properties_}));
print "\n--- Methods ---\n";
print join("\n",map {$_->{Name}}(in $procschm->{Methods_}));
```

The output (on a Windows XP SP2 machine) looks like this:

```
--- Properties ---
Caption
CommandLine
CreationClassName
CreationDate
CSCreationClassName
CSName
Description
ExecutablePath
ExecutionState
Handle
HandleCount
InstallDate
KernelModeTime
MaximumWorkingSetSize
MinimumWorkingSetSize
Name
OSCreationClassName
OSName
OtherOperationCount
OtherTransferCount
PageFaults
PageFileUsage
ParentProcessId
PeakPageFileUsage
PeakVirtualSize
PeakWorkingSetSize
Priority
PrivatePageCount
```

---

† See the section "Active Directory Service Interfaces" on page 354 for details on another prominent use of in.

```
ProcessId
QuotaNonPagedPoolUsage
QuotaPagedPoolUsage
QuotaPeakNonPagedPoolUsage
QuotaPeakPagedPoolUsage
ReadOperationCount
ReadTransferCount
SessionId
Status
TerminationDate
ThreadCount
UserModeTime
VirtualSize
WindowsVersion
WorkingSetSize
WriteOperationCount
WriteTransferCount
--- Methods ---
Create
Terminate
GetOwner
GetOwnerSid
SetPriority
AttachDebugger
```

Now let's get down to the business at hand. To retrieve a list of running processes, we need to ask for all instances of Win32_Process objects:

```
use Win32::OLE('in');

# perform all of the initial steps in one swell foop

my $sobj = Win32::OLE->GetObject(
    'winmgmts:{impersonationLevel=impersonate}')
    or die "can't create server object: ".Win32::OLE->LastError()."\n";

foreach my $process (in $sobj->InstancesOf("Win32_Process")){
  print $process->{Name}." is pid #".$process->{ProcessId},"\n";
}
```

Our initial display name did not include a path to a specific object (i.e., we left off !Win32_Process). As a result, we receive a server connection object. When we call the InstancesOf() method, it returns a collection object that holds all of the instances of that particular object. Our code visits each object in turn and prints its Name and ProcessId properties. This yields a list of all the running processes.

If we wanted to be a little less beneficent when iterating over each process, we could instead use one of the methods listed earlier:

```
foreach $process (in $sobj->InstancesOf("Win32_Process")){
    $process->Terminate(1);
}
```

This will terminate every process running. I do not recommend that you run this code as is; customize it for your specific needs by making it more selective.

One last note before we move on. Earlier in this section I mentioned that there are two ways to query information using WMI: the object-oriented and query-based approaches. Up to now we've been looking at the fairly straightforward object-oriented approach. Here's a small sample using the query-based approach, just to pique your interest. First, let's recreate the output from the preceding sample. The highlighted line is the key change here, because it uses WQL instead of `InstancesOf()` to retrieve all of the process objects:

```
use Win32::OLE('in');

my $sobj = Win32::OLE->GetObject('winmgmts:{impersonationLevel=impersonate}')
    or die 'can't create server object: ' . Win32::OLE->LastError() . "\n";

my $query = $sobj->ExecQuery('SELECT Name, ProcessId FROM Win32_Process');
foreach my $process ( in $query ) {
  print $process->{Name} . ' is pid #' . $process->{ProcessId}, "\n";
}
```

Now we can start throwing in SQL-like syntax in the highlighted query string. For example, if we only wanted to see the process IDs of the *svchost.exe* processes running on the system, we could write:

```
use Win32::OLE('in');

my $sobj = Win32::OLE->GetObject('winmgmts:{impersonationLevel=impersonate}')
    or die "can't create server object: " . Win32::OLE->LastError() . "\n";

my $query = $sobj->ExecQuery(
    'SELECT ProcessId FROM Win32_Process WHERE Name = "svchost.exe"');
print "SvcHost processes: "
    . join( ' ', map { $_->{ProcessId} } ( in $query) ), "\n";
```

WQL can handle queries with other SQL-like stanzas. For example, the following is valid WQL to retrieve information on all running processes that have names that begin with "svc":

```
SELECT * from Win32_Process WHERE Name LIKE "svc%"
```

If you are SQL-literate (even if the sum of your knowledge comes from Appendix D in this book), this may be a direction you want to explore.

Now you have the knowledge necessary to begin using WMI for process control. WMI has Win32 extensions for many other parts of the operating system, including the registry and the event log facility.

This is as far as we're going to delve into process control on Windows. Now let's turn our attention to another major operating system.

Unix Process Control

Strategies for Unix process control offer another multiple-choice situation. Luckily, these choices aren't nearly as complex as those that Windows offers. When we speak of process control under Unix, we're referring to three operations:

1. Enumerating the list of running processes on a machine
2. Changing their priorities or process groups
3. Terminating the processes

For the final two of these operations, there are Perl functions to do the job: `setpriority()`, `setpgrp()`, and `kill()`. The first one offers us a few options. To list running processes, you can:

- Call an external program like *ps*.
- Take a crack at deciphering */dev/kmem*.
- Look through the */proc* filesystem (for Unix versions that have one).
- Use the `Proc::ProcessTable` module.

Let's discuss each of these approaches. For the impatient reader, I'll reveal right now that `Proc::ProcessTable` is my preferred technique. You may want to just skip directly to the discussion of that module, but I recommend reading about the other techniques anyway, since they may come in handy in the future.

Calling an external program

Common to all modern Unix variants is a program called *ps*, used to list running processes. However, *ps* is found in different places in the filesystem on different Unix variants, and the command-line switches it takes are also not consistent across variants. Therein lies one problem with this option: it lacks portability.

An even more annoying problem is the difficulty in parsing the output (which also varies from variant to variant). Here's a snippet of output from *ps* on an ancient SunOS machine:

```
USER      PID %CPU %MEM    SZ  RSS TT STAT START   TIME COMMAND
dnb       385  0.0  0.0   268    0 p4 IW   Jul  2  0:00 /bin/zsh
dnb     24103  0.0  2.610504 1092 p3 S    Aug 10 35:49 emacs
dnb       389  0.0  2.5 3604 1044 p4 S    Jul  2 60:16 emacs
remy    15396  0.0  0.0   252    0 p9 IW   Jul  7  0:01 -zsh (zsh)
sys       393  0.0  0.0    28    0 ?  IW   Jul  2  0:02 in.identd
dnb     29488  0.0  0.0    68    0 p5 IW   20:15   0:00 screen
dnb     29544  0.0  0.4    24  148 p7 R    20:39   0:00 less
dnb      5707  0.0  0.0   260    0 p6 IW   Jul 24  0:00 -zsh (zsh)
root    28766  0.0  0.0   244    0 ?  IW   13:20   0:00 -:0 (xdm)
```

Notice the third line. Two of the columns have run together, making parsing this output an annoying task. It's not impossible, just vexing. Some Unix variants are kinder than others in this regard (for example, later operating systems from Sun don't have this problem), but it is something you may have to take into account.

The Perl code required for this option is straightforward: use `open()` to run *ps*, `while(<FH>){...}` to read the output, and `split()`, `unpack()`, or `substr()` to parse it. You can find a recipe for this in the *Perl Cookbook*, by Tom Christiansen and Nathan Torkington (O'Reilly).

Examining the kernel process structures

I only mention this option for completeness's sake. It is possible to write code that opens up a device like */dev/kmem* and accesses the current running kernel's memory structures. With this access, you can track down the current process table in memory and read it. However, given the pain involved (taking apart complex binary structures by hand), and its extreme nonportability (a version difference within the same operating system is likely to break your program), I'd strongly recommend against using this option.‡

If you decide not to heed this advice, you should begin by memorizing the Perl documentation for `pack()`, `unpack()`, and the header files for your kernel. Open the kernel memory file (often */dev/kmem*), then `read()` and `unpack()` to your heart's content. You may find it instructive to look at the source for programs like *top (ftp://ftp.groupsys.com/ pub/top)* that perform this task using a great deal of C code. Our next option offers a slightly better version of this method.

Using the /proc filesystem

One of the more interesting additions to Unix found in most of the current variants is the */proc* filesystem. This is a magical filesystem that has nothing to do with data storage. Instead, it provides a file-based interface for the running process table of a machine. A "directory" named after the process ID appears in this filesystem for each running process. In this directory are a set of "files" that provide information about that process. One of these files can be written to, thus allowing control of the process.

It's a really clever concept, and that's the good news. The bad news is that each Unix vendor/developer team decided to take this clever concept and run with it in a different direction. As a result, the files found in a */proc* directory are often variant-specific, both in name and format. For a description of which files are available and what they contain, you will need to consult the manual pages (usually found in sections 4, 5, or 8) for *procfs* or *mount_ procfs* on your system.

The one fairly portable use of the */proc* filesystem is the enumeration of running processes. If we want to list just the process IDs and their owners, we can use Perl's directory and `lstat()` operators:

---

‡ Later, we'll look at a module called `Proc::ProcessTable` that can do this for you without you having to write the code.

```
opendir my $PROC, '/proc' or die "Unable to open /proc:$!\n";

# only stat the items in /proc that look like PIDs
for my $process (grep /^\d+$/, readdir($PROC)){
    print "$process\t". getpwuid((lstat "/proc/$process")[4])."\n";
}

closedir $PROC;
```

If you are interested in more information about a process, you will have to open and unpack() the appropriate binary file in the */proc* directories. Common names for this file are *status* and *psinfo*. The manual pages cited a moment ago should provide details about the C structure found in this file, or at least a pointer to a C include file that documents this structure. Because these are operating system-specific (and OS version-specific) formats, you're still going to run into the problem of program fragility mentioned in the discussion of the previous option.

You may be feeling discouraged at this point because all of our options so far look like they require code with lots of special cases (one for each version of each operating system we wish to support). Luckily, we have one more option up our sleeve that may help in this regard.

Using the Proc::ProcessTable module

Daniel J. Urist (with the help of some volunteers) has been kind enough to write a module called Proc::ProcessTable that offers a consistent interface to the process table for the major Unix variants. It hides the vagaries of the different */proc* or *kmem* implementations for you, allowing you to write relatively portable code.

Simply load the module, create a Proc::ProcessTable::Process object, and run methods from that object:

```
use Proc::ProcessTable;

my $tobj = new Proc::ProcessTable;
```

This object uses Perl's tied variable functionality to present a real-time view of the system. You do not need to call a special function to refresh the object; each time you access it, it re-reads the process table.

To get at this information, you call the object method table():

```
my $proctable = $tobj->table( );
```

table() returns a reference to an array with members that are references to individual process objects. Each of these objects has its own set of methods that returns information about that process. For instance, here's how you would get a listing of the process IDs and owners:

```
use Proc::ProcessTable;

my $tobj      = new Proc::ProcessTable;
```

```
my $proctable = $tobj->table();

foreach my $process (@$proctable) {
  print $process->pid . "\t" . getpwuid( $process->uid ) . "\n";
}
```

If you want to know which process methods are available on your Unix variant, the
fields() method of your Proc::ProcessTable object ($tobj in the preceding code) will
return a list for you.

Proc::ProcessTable also adds three other methods to each process object—kill(),
priority(), and pgrp()—which are just frontends to the built-in Perl function we mentioned at the beginning of this section.

To bring us back to the big picture, let's look at some of the uses of these process control
techniques. We started to examine process control in the context of user actions, so
let's look at a few teeny scripts that focus on these actions. We will use the
Proc::ProcessTable module on Unix for these examples, but these ideas are not operating system-specific.

The first example is slightly modified from the documentation for Proc::ProcessTable:

```
use Proc::ProcessTable;

my $t = new Proc::ProcessTable;

foreach my $p (@{$t->table}){
  if ($p->pctmem > 95){
    $p->kill(9);
  }
}
```

When run on the Unix variants that provide the pctmem() method (most do), this code
will shoot down any process consuming 95% of the machine's memory. As it stands,
it's probably too ruthless to be used in real life. It would be much more reasonable to
add something like this before the kill() command:

```
print 'about to nuke '.$p->pid."\t". getpwuid($p->uid)."\n";
print 'proceed? (yes/no) ';
chomp($ans = <>);
next unless ($ans eq 'yes');
```

There's a bit of a race condition here: it is possible that the system state will change
during the delay induced by prompting the user. Given that we are only prompting for
huge processes, though, and huge processes are those least likely to change state in a
short amount of time, we're probably fine coding this way. If you wanted to be pedantic,
you would probably collect the list of processes to be killed first, prompt for input, and
then recheck the state of the process table before actually killing the desired processes.
This doesn't remove the race condition, but it does make it much less likely to occur.

There are times when death is too good for a process. Sometimes it is important to notice that a process is running while it is running so that some real-life action (like "user attitude correction") can be taken. For example, at our site we have a policy against the use of Internet Relay Chat (IRC) *bots*. Bots are daemon processes that connect to an IRC network of chat servers and perform automated actions. Though bots can be used for constructive purposes, these days they play a mostly antisocial role on IRC. We've also had security breaches come to our attention because the first (and often only) thing the intruder has done is put up an IRC bot of some sort. As a result, noting their presence on our system without killing them is important to us.

The most common bot by far is called *eggdrop*. If we wanted to look for this process name being run on our system, we could use code like this:

```
use Proc::ProcessTable;

my $logfile = 'eggdrops';
open my $LOG, '>>', $logfile or die "Can't open logfile for append:$!\n";

my $t = new Proc::ProcessTable;

foreach my $p ( @{ $t->table } ) {
    if ( $p->fname() =~ /eggdrop/i ) {
        print $LOG time . "\t"
            . getpwuid( $p->uid ) . "\t"
            . $p->fname() . "\n";
    }
}
close $LOG;
```

If you're thinking, "This code isn't good enough! All someone has to do is rename the *eggdrop* executable to evade its check," you're absolutely right. We'll take a stab at writing some less naïve bot-check code in the very last section of this chapter.

In the meantime, let's take a look at one more example where Perl assists us in managing user processes. So far all of our examples have been fairly negative, focusing on dealing with resource-hungry and naughty processes. Let's look at something with a sunnier disposition.

There are times when a system administrator needs to know which (legitimate) programs users on a system are using. Sometimes this is necessary in the context of software metering, where there are legal concerns about the number of users running a program concurrently. In those cases there is usually a licensing mechanism in place to handle the bean counting. Another situation where this knowledge comes in handy is that of machine migration. If you are migrating a user population from one architecture to another, you'll want to make sure all the programs used on the previous architecture are available on the new one.

One approach to solving this problem involves replacing every non-OS binary available to users with a wrapper that first records that a particular binary has been run and then actually runs it. This can be difficult to implement if there are a large number of binaries. It also has the unpleasant side effect of slowing down every program invocation.

If precision is not important and a rough estimate of which binaries are in use will suffice, we can use `Proc::ProcessTable` to solve this problem. Here's some code that wakes up every five minutes and surveys the current process landscape. It keeps a simple count of all the process names it finds, and it's smart enough not to count processes it saw during its last period of wakefulness. Every hour it prints its findings and starts collecting again. We wait five minutes between each run because walking the process table is usually a resource-intensive operation, and we'd prefer this program to add as little load to the system as possible:

```perl
use Proc::ProcessTable;

my $interval    = 300;   # sleep interval of 5 minutes
my $partofhour = 0;      # keep track of where in the hour we are

my $tobj = new Proc::ProcessTable;    # create new process object

my %last;         # to keep track of info from the previous run
my %current;      # to keep track of data from the current run
my %collection;   # to keep track of info over the entire hour

# forever loop, collecting stats every $interval secs
# and dumping them once an hour
while (1) {
    foreach my $process ( @{ $tobj->table } ) {

        # we should ignore ourselves
        next if ( $process->pid() == $$ );

        # save this process info for our next run
        # (note: this assumes that your PIDs won't recycle between runs,
        #  but on a very busy system that may not be the case)
        $current{ $process->pid() } = $process->fname();

        # ignore this process if we saw it during the last iteration
        next if ( $last{ $process->pid() } eq $process->fname() );

        # else, remember it
        $collection{ $process->fname() }++;
    }

    $partofhour += $interval;
    %last     = %current;
    %current = ();
    if ( $partofhour >= 3600 ) {
        print scalar localtime(time) . ( '-' x 50 ) . "\n";
        print "Name\t\tCount\n";
        print "--------------\t\t-----\n";
        foreach my $name ( sort reverse_value_sort keys %collection ) {
            print "$name\t\t$collection{$name}\n";
        }
        %collection = ();
```

```
        $partofhour = 0;
    }
    sleep($interval);
}

# (reverse) sort by values in %collection and by key name
sub reverse_value_sort {
    return $collection{$b} <=> $collection{$a} || $a cmp $b;
}
```

There are many ways this program could be enhanced. It could track processes on a per-user basis (i.e., only recording one instance of a program launch per user), collect daily stats, present its information as a nice bar graph, and so on. It's up to you where you might want to take it.

File and Network Operations

For the last section of this chapter, we're going to lump two of the user action domains together. The processes we've just spent so much time controlling do more than just suck up CPU and memory resources; they also perform operations on filesystems and communicate on a network on behalf of users. User administration requires that we deal with these second-order effects as well.

Our focus in this section will be fairly narrow. We're only interested in looking at file and network operations that *other* users are performing on a system. We're also only going to focus on those operations that we can track back to a specific user (or a specific process run by a specific user). With these blinders in mind, let's go forth.

Tracking File Operations on Windows

If we want to track other users' open files, the closest we can come involves using a former third-party command-line program called *handle*, written by Mark Russinovich (formerly of Sysinternals). See the references section at the end of this chapter for information on where to get it. *handle* can show us all of the open handles on a particular system. Here's an excerpt from some sample output:

```
System pid: 4 NT AUTHORITY\SYSTEM
   7C: File  (-W-)   C:\pagefile.sys
  5DC: File  (---)   C:\Documents and Settings\LocalService\Local Settings\
                     Application Data\Microsoft\Windows\UsrClass.dat
  5E0: File  (---)   C:\WINDOWS\system32\config\SAM.LOG
  5E4: File  (---)   C:\Documents and Settings\LocalService\NTUSER.DAT
  5E8: File  (---)   C:\WINDOWS\system32\config\system
  5EC: File  (---)   C:\WINDOWS\system32\config\software.LOG
  5F0: File  (---)   C:\WINDOWS\system32\config\software
  5F8: File  (---)   C:\WINDOWS\system32\config\SECURITY
  5FC: File  (---)   C:\WINDOWS\system32\config\default
  600: File  (---)   C:\WINDOWS\system32\config\SECURITY.LOG
  604: File  (---)   C:\WINDOWS\system32\config\default.LOG
  60C: File  (---)   C:\WINDOWS\system32\config\SAM
```

```
610: File  (---)    C:\WINDOWS\system32\config\system.LOG
614: File  (---)    C:\Documents and Settings\NetworkService\NTUSER.DAT
8E0: File  (---)    C:\Documents and Settings\dNb\Local Settings\Application
                    Data\Microsoft\Windows\UsrClass.dat.LOG
8E4: File  (---)    C:\Documents and Settings\dNb\Local Settings\Application
                    Data\Microsoft\Windows\UsrClass.dat
8E8: File  (---)    C:\Documents and Settings\dNb\NTUSER.DAT.LOG
8EC: File  (---)    C:\Documents and Settings\dNb\NTUSER.DAT
B08: File  (RW-)    C:\Program Files\Symantec AntiVirus\SAVRT
B3C: File  (R--)    C:\System Volume Information\_restore{96B84597-8A49-41EE-
                    8303-02D3AD2B3BA4}\RP80\change.log
B78: File  (R--)    C:\Program Files\Symantec AntiVirus\SAVRT\0608NAV~.TMP
------------------------------------------------------------------------
smss.exe pid: 436 NT AUTHORITY\SYSTEM
  8: File  (RW-)    C:\WINDOWS
  1C: File (RW-)    C:\WINDOWS\system32
```

You can also request information on specific files or directories:

> **handle.exe c:\WINDOWS\system32\config**

```
Handle v3.3
Copyright (C) 1997-2007 Mark Russinovich
Sysinternals - www.sysinternals.com

System          pid: 4      5E0: C:\WINDOWS\system32\config\SAM.LOG
System          pid: 4      5E8: C:\WINDOWS\system32\config\system
System          pid: 4      5EC: C:\WINDOWS\system32\config\software.LOG
System          pid: 4      5F0: C:\WINDOWS\system32\config\software
System          pid: 4      5F8: C:\WINDOWS\system32\config\SECURITY
System          pid: 4      5FC: C:\WINDOWS\system32\config\default
System          pid: 4      600: C:\WINDOWS\system32\config\SECURITY.LOG
System          pid: 4      604: C:\WINDOWS\system32\config\default.LOG
System          pid: 4      60C: C:\WINDOWS\system32\config\SAM
System          pid: 4      610: C:\WINDOWS\system32\config\system.LOG
services.exe    pid: 552    2A4: C:\WINDOWS\system32\config\AppEvent.Evt
services.exe    pid: 552    2B4: C:\WINDOWS\system32\config\Internet.evt
services.exe    pid: 552    2C4: C:\WINDOWS\system32\config\SecEvent.Evt
services.exe    pid: 552    2D4: C:\WINDOWS\system32\config\SysEvent.Evt
svchost.exe     pid: 848    17DC: C:\WINDOWS\system32\config\systemprofile\
Application Data\Microsoft\SystemCertificates\My
ccSetMgr.exe    pid: 1172   2EC: C:\WINDOWS\system32\config\systemprofile\
Application Data\Microsoft\SystemCertificates\My
ccEvtMgr.exe    pid: 1200   23C: C:\WINDOWS\system32\config\systemprofile\
Application Data\Microsoft\SystemCertificates\My
Rtvscan.exe     pid: 1560   454: C:\WINDOWS\system32\config\systemprofile\
Application Data\Microsoft\SystemCertificates\My
```

handle can provide this information for a specific process name using the **-p** switch.

Using this executable from Perl is straightforward, so we won't provide any sample code. Instead, let's look at a related and more interesting operation: auditing.

Windows allows us to efficiently watch a file, directory, or hierarchy of directories for changes. You could imagine repeatedly performing stat()s on the desired object or objects, but that would be highly CPU-intensive. Under Windows, we can ask the operating system to keep watch for us.

There is a specialized Perl module that makes this job relatively painless for us: `Win32::ChangeNotify` by Christopher J. Madsen. There is also a related helper module: `Win32::FileNotify` by Renee Baecker.

The Ephemeral Nature of Modules

In the first edition of this book, this section described how to use the module `Win32::AdvNotify` by Amine Moulay Ramdane for filesystem auditing. It was a great module; one of several superb Windows modules by the same author, it did everything `Win32::ChangeNotify` could do and considerably more.

Unfortunately, Ramdane was inexplicably strict about the distribution terms for his modules. He did not allow this module to be hosted on any website other than his own, and he did not want that site mirrored elsewhere. Source code was never released.

According to the Wayback Machine (*http://www.archive.org/web/web.php*), by April 2002 the contents of that website had disappeared, and for all practical purposes, so had the author of all those great modules. I started getting email shortly after that date from readers of the first edition looking to follow the examples in my book using Ramdane's modules. All I could do was try to suggest some alternatives. I've removed all of the demonstration code for those modules in this edition, even though most of Ramdane's modules can still be found on the Net if you're willing to hunt hard enough. The total lack of support for the modules (and the lack of potential even for someone else to support them) means it is too risky to use them at this point. Grrr.

`Win32::ChangeNotify` is pretty easy to use, but it does have one gotcha. The module uses the Win32 APIs to ask the OS to let you know if something changes in a directory. You can even specify what kind of change to look for (last write time, file or directory names/sizes, etc.). The problem is that if you ask it to watch a directory for changes, it can tell you when something changes, but not *what* has changed. It's up to the program author to determine that with some separate code. That's where `Win32::FileNotify` comes in. If you just need to watch a single file, `Win32::FileNotify` will go the extra step of double-checking whether the change the OS reported is in the file being audited.

Because they're so small, we'll look at examples of both modules. We'll start with the specific case of watching to see if a file has changed:

```
use Win32::FileNotify;

my $file = 'c:\windows\temp\importantfile';

my $fnot = Win32::FileNotify->new($file);

$fnot->wait();    # at this point, our program blocks until $file changes

... # go do something about the file change
```

And here's some code to look for changes in a directory (specifically, files coming and going):

```perl
use Win32::ChangeNotify;

my $dir = 'c:\importantdir';

# watch this directory (second argument says don't watch for changes
# to subdirectories) for changes in the filenames found there
my $cnot = Win32::ChangeNotify->new( $dir, 0, 'FILE_NAME' );

while (1) {

    # blocks for 10 secs (10,000 milliseconds) or until a change takes place
    my $waitresult = $cnot->wait(10000);

    if ( $waitresult == 1 ) {

        ... # call or include some other code here to figure out what changed

        # reset the ChangeNotification object so we can continue monitoring
        $cnot->reset;
    }
    elsif ( $waitresult == 0 ) {
        print "no changes to $dir in the last 10 seconds\n";
    }
    elsif ( $waitresult == -1 ) {
        print "something went blooey in the monitoring\n";
        last;
    }
}
```

Tracking Network Operations on Windows

That was filesystem monitoring. What about network access monitoring? There are two fairly easy ways to track network operations under Windows. Ideally, as an administrator you'd like to know which process (and therefore which user) has opened a network port. While I know of no Perl module that can perform this task, there are at least two command-line tools that provide the information in a way that could be consumed by a Perl program. The first, netstat, actually ships with the system, but very few people know it can do this (I certainly didn't for a long time). Here's some sample output:

```
> netstat -ano

Active Connections

  Proto  Local Address          Foreign Address        State          PID
  TCP    0.0.0.0:135            0.0.0.0:0              LISTENING      932
  TCP    0.0.0.0:445            0.0.0.0:0              LISTENING      4
  TCP    127.0.0.1:1028         0.0.0.0:0              LISTENING      1216
  TCP    192.168.16.129:139     0.0.0.0:0              LISTENING      4
  UDP    0.0.0.0:445            *:*                                   4
```

```
UDP    0.0.0.0:500          *:*                          680
UDP    0.0.0.0:1036         *:*                          1068
UDP    0.0.0.0:1263         *:*                          1068
UDP    0.0.0.0:4500         *:*                          680
UDP    127.0.0.1:123        *:*                          1024
UDP    127.0.0.1:1900       *:*                          1108
UDP    192.168.16.129:123   *:*                          1024
UDP    192.168.16.129:137   *:*                          4
UDP    192.168.16.129:138   *:*                          4
UDP    192.168.16.129:1900  *:*                          1108
```

The second is another tool from Mark Russinovich, formerly of Sysinternals: TcpView (or more precisely, the *tcpvcon* utility that comes in that package). It has the nice property of being able to output the information in CSV form, like so:

```
> tcpvcon -anc

TCPView v2.51 - TCP/UDP endpoint viewer
Copyright (C) 1998-2007 Mark Russinovich
Sysinternals - www.sysinternals.com

TCP,alg.exe,1216,LISTENING,127.0.0.1:1028,0.0.0.0:0
TCP,System,4,LISTENING,0.0.0.0:445,0.0.0.0:0
TCP,svchost.exe,932,LISTENING,0.0.0.0:135,0.0.0.0:0
TCP,System,4,LISTENING,192.168.16.129:139,0.0.0.0:0
UDP,svchost.exe,1024,*,192.168.16.129:123,*:*
UDP,lsass.exe,680,*,0.0.0.0:500,*:*
UDP,svchost.exe,1068,*,0.0.0.0:1036,*:*
UDP,svchost.exe,1108,*,192.168.16.129:1900,*:*
UDP,svchost.exe,1024,*,127.0.0.1:123,*:*
UDP,System,4,*,192.168.16.129:137,*:*
UDP,svchost.exe,1108,*,127.0.0.1:1900,*:*
UDP,lsass.exe,680,*,0.0.0.0:4500,*:*
UDP,System,4,*,192.168.16.129:138,*:*
UDP,svchost.exe,1068,*,0.0.0.0:1263,*:*
UDP,System,4,*,0.0.0.0:445,*:*
```

This would be trivial to parse with something like `Text::CSV::Simple` or `Text::CSV_XS`.

Let's see how we'd perform the same tasks within the Unix world.

Tracking File and Network Operations in Unix

To handle the tracking of both file and network operations in Unix, we can use a single approach.[*] This is one of few times in this book where calling a separate executable is clearly the superior method. Vic Abell has given an amazing gift to the system administration world by writing and maintaining a program called *lsof* (LiSt Open Files) that can be found at *ftp://vic.cc.purdue.edu/pub/tools/unix/lsof*. *lsof* can show in detail all of

---

[*] This is the best approach for portability. Various OSs have their own mechanisms (*inotify*, *dnotify*, etc.), and frameworks like DTrace are very cool. Mac OS X 10.5+ has a similar auditing facility to the one we saw with Windows (`Mac::FSEvents` gives you easy access to it). However, none of these options is as portable as the approach described here.

the currently open files and network connections on a Unix machine. One of the things that makes it truly amazing is its portability. The latest version as of this writing runs on at least nine flavors of Unix (the previous version supported an even wider variety of Unix flavors) and supports several OS versions for each flavor.

Here's a snippet of *lsof*'s output, showing an excerpt of the output for one of the processes I am running. *lsof* tends to output very long lines, so I've inserted a blank line between each line of output to make the distinctions clear:

```
COMMAND     PID USER   FD   TYPE       DEVICE  SIZE/OFF     NODE NAME
firefox-b 27189  dnb   cwd   VDIR      318,16168    36864 25760428 /home/dnb

firefox-b 27189  dnb   txt   VREG      318,37181   177864  6320643
 /net/csw (fileserver:/vol/systems/csw)

firefox-b 27189  dnb   txt   VREG        136,0     56874     3680
 /usr/openwin/lib/X11/fonts/Type1/outline/Helvetica-Bold.pfa

firefox-b 27189  dnb   txt   VREG      318,37181    16524   563516
 /net/csw (fileserver:/vol/systems/csw)

firefox-b 27189  dnb    0u  unix        105,43       0t0     3352
 /devices/pseudo/tl@0:ticots->(socketpair: 0x1409) (0x300034a1010)

firefox-b 27189  dnb    2u  unix        105,45       0t0     3352
 /devices/pseudo/tl@0:ticots->(socketpair: 0x140b) (0x300034a01d0)

firefox-b 27189  dnb    4u  IPv6 0x3000349cde0 0t2121076
     TCP localhost:32887->localhost:6010 (ESTABLISHED)

firefox-b 27189  dnb    6u  FIFO 0x30003726ee8      0t0  2105883
 (fifofs) ->0x30003726de0

firefox-b 27189  dnb   24r  VREG      318,37181    332618
     85700 /net/csw (fileserver:/vol/systems/csw)

firefox-b 27189  dnb   29u  unix        105,46    0t1742
     3352 /devices/pseudo/tl@0:ticots->/var/tmp/orbit-dnb/linc
-6a37-0-47776fee636a2 (0x30003cc1900->0x300045731f8)

firefox-b 27189  dnb   31u  unix        105,50       0t0
     3352 /devices/pseudo/tl@0:ticots->/var/tmp/orbit-dnb/linc
-6a35-0-47772fb086240 (0x300034a13a0)

firefox-b 27189  dnb   43u  IPv4 0x30742eb79b0    0t42210
     TCP desktop.example.edu:32897->images.slashdot.org:www (ESTABLISHED)
```

This output demonstrates some of the power of this command. It shows the current working directory (VDIR), regular files (VREG), pipes (FIFO), and network connections (IPv4/IPv6) opened by this process.

The easiest way to use *lsof* from Perl is to invoke its special "field" mode (-F). In this mode, its output is broken up into specially labeled and delimited fields, instead of the *ps*-like columns just shown. This makes parsing the output a cinch.

There is one quirk to the field mode output. It is organized into what the author calls "process sets" and "file sets." A process set is a set of field entries referring to a single process, and a file set is a similar set for a file. This all makes more sense if we turn on field mode with the 0 option. Fields are then delimited with NUL (ASCII 0) characters, and sets with NL (ASCII 12) characters. Here's a similar group of lines to those in the preceding output, this time in field mode (NUL is represented as ^@). I've added spaces between the lines again to make it easier to read:

```
p27189^@g27155^@R27183^@cfirefox-bin^@u6070^@Ldnb^@
fcwd^@a ^@l

^@tVDIR^@N0x30001b7b1d8^@D0x13e00003f28^@s36864^@i25760428^@k90^@n/home/dnb^@
ftxt^@a ^@l

^@tVREG^@N0x3000224a0f0^@D0x13e0000913d^@s177864^@i6320
643^@k1^@n/net/csw (fileserver:/vol/systems/csw)^@
ftxt^@a ^@l

^@tVREG^@N0x30001714950^@D0x8800000000^@s35064^@i2800^@k1^@n/usr/lib/nss_files.so.1

^@tVREG^@N0x300036226c0^@D0x8800000000^@s56874^@i3680^@k1^@n/usr/
openwin/lib/X11/fonts/Type1/outline/Helvetica-Bold.pfa^@
ftxt^@a ^@l

^@tunix^@F0x3000328c550^@C6^@G0x3;0x0^@N0x300034a1010^@D0x8800
000000^@o0t0^@i3352^@n/devices/pseudo/tl@0:ticots->(socketpair:
 0x1409) (0x300034a1010)^@
f1^@au^@l

^@tDOOR^@F0x3000328cf98^@C1^@G0x2001;0x1^@N0x3000178b300^@D0x13
c00000000^@o0t0^@i54^@k27^@n/var/run (swap) (door to nscd[240])^@
f4^@au^@l

^@tIPv6^@F0x300037258f0^@C1^@G0x83;0x1^@N0x300034ace50^@d0x3000349
cde0^@o0t3919884^@PTCP^@nlocalhost:32887->localhost:6010^@TST=
ESTABLISHED^@TQR=0^@TQS=8191^@TWR=49152^@TWW=13264^@
f5^@au^@l

^@tFIFO^@F0x30003724f50^@C1^@G0x3;0x0^@N0x30003726de0^@d0x30003726
de0^@o0t0^@i2105883^@n(fifofs) ->0x30003726ee8^@
f6^@au^@l

^@tFIFO^@F0x30003725420^@C1^@G0x3;0x0^@N0x30003726ee8^@d0x30003726
ee8^@o0t0^@i2105883^@n(fifofs) ->0x30003726de0^@
f7^@aw^@lW^@tVREG^@F0x30003724c40^@C1^@G0x302;0x0^@N0x30001eadbf8^
@D0x13e00003f28^@s0^@i1539532^@k1^@n/home/dnb (fileserver:/vol/homedirs/systems/dnb)^@
f8^@au^@l

^@tIPv4^@F0x30003724ce8^@C1^@G0x83;0x0^@N0x300034ac010^@d0x
300040604f0^@o0t4094^@PTCP^@ndesktop.example.edu:32931->web
-vip.srv.jobthread.com:www^@TST=CLOSE_WAIT^@TQR=0^@TQS=0^@TWR=49640^@TWW=6960^@
f44^@au^@l

^@tVREG^@F0x3000328c5c0^@C1^@G0x2103;0x0^@N0x300051cd3f8^@
```

```
D0x13e00003f28^@s276^@i16547341^@k1^@n/home/dnb (fileserver:/vol/
homedirs/systems/dnb)^@
f45^@au^@l

^@tVREG^@F0x30003725f80^@C1^@G0x3;0x0^@N0x300026ad920^@D0x
13e00003f28^@s8468^@i21298675^@k1^@n/home/dnb (fileserver:/vol/homedirs/systems/dnb)^@
f46^@au^@l

^@tIPv4^@F0x300003724a10^@C1^@G0x83;0x0^@N0x309ab62b578^@d0x30742
eb76b0^@o0t20726^@PTCP^@ndesktop.example.edu:32934->216.66.26.
161:www^@TST=ESTABLISHED^@TQR=0^@TQS=0^@TWR=49640^@TWW=6432^@
f47^@au^@l

^@tVREG^@F0x3000328c080^@C1^@G0x2103;0x0^@N0x30002186098^@D0x
13e00003f28^@s66560^@i16547342^@k1^@n/home/dnb (fileserver:/vol/
homedirs/systems/dnb)^@
f48^@au^@l
```

Let's deconstruct this output. The first line is a process set (we can tell because it begins with the letter p):

```
p27189^@g27155^@R27183^@cfirefox-bin^@u6070^@Ldnb^@
fcwd^@a ^@l
```

Each field begins with a letter identifying the field's contents (p for pid, c for command, u for uid, and L for login) and ends with a delimiter character. Together the fields on this line make up a process set. All of the lines that follow, up until the next process set, describe the open files/network connections of the process described by this process set.

Let's put this mode to use. If we wanted to show all of the open files on a system and the PIDs that are using them, we could use code like this:[†]

```
use Text::Wrap;

my $lsofexec = '/usr/local/bin/lsof';  # location of lsof executable

# (F)ield mode, NUL (0) delim, show (L)ogin, file (t)ype and file (n)ame
my $lsofflag = '-FLOtn';

open my $LSOFPIPE, '-|', "$lsofexec $lsofflag"
    or die "Unable to start $lsofexec: $!\n";

my $pid;                              # pid as returned by lsof
my $pathname;                         # pathname as returned by lsof
my $login;                            # login name as returned by lsof
my $type;                             # type of open file as returned by lsof
my %seen;                             # for a pathname cache
my %paths;                            # collect the paths as we go
```

[†] If you don't want to parse *lsof*'s field mode by hand Marc Beyer's Unix::Lsof will handle the work for you.

```
while ( my $lsof = <$LSOFPIPE> ) {

    # deal with a process set
    if ( substr( $lsof, 0, 1 ) eq 'p' ) {
        ( $pid, $login ) = split( /\0/, $lsof );
        $pid = substr( $pid, 1, length($pid) );
    }

    # deal with a file set; note: we are only interested
    # in "regular" files (as per Solaris and Linux, lsof on other
    # systems may mark files and directories differently)
    if ( substr( $lsof, 0, 5 ) eq 'tVREG' or    # Solaris
         substr( $lsof, 0, 4 ) eq 'tREG') {      # Linux
        ( $type, $pathname ) = split( /\0/, $lsof );

        # a process may have the same pathname open twice;
        # these two lines make sure we only record it once
        next if ( $seen{$pathname} eq $pid );
        $seen{$pathname} = $pid;

        $pathname = substr( $pathname, 1, length($pathname) );
        push( @{ $paths{$pathname} }, $pid );
    }
}

close $LSOFPIPE;

foreach my $path ( sort keys %paths ) {
    print "$path:\n";
    print wrap( "\t", "\t", join( " ", @{ $paths{$path} } ) ), "\n";
}
```

This code instructs *lsof* to show only a few of its possible fields. We iterate through its output, collecting filenames and PIDs in a hash of lists. When we've received all of the output, we print the filenames in a nicely formatted PID list (thanks to David Muir Sharnoff's Text::Wrap module):

```
/home/dnb (fileserver:/vol/homedirs/systems/dnb):
        12777 12933 27293 28223
/usr/lib/ld.so.1:
        10613 12777 12933 27217 27219 27293 28147 28149 28223 28352 28353
        28361
/usr/lib/libaio.so.1:
        27217 28147 28352 28353 28361
/usr/lib/libc.so.1:
        10613 12777 12933 27217 27219 27293 28147 28149 28223 28352 28353
        28361
/usr/lib/libmd5.so.1:
        10613 27217 28147 28352 28353 28361
/usr/lib/libmp.so.2:
        10613 27217 27219 28147 28149 28352 28353 28361
/usr/lib/libnsl.so.1:
        10613 27217 27219 28147 28149 28352 28353 28361
```

```
/usr/lib/libsocket.so.1:
        10613 27217 27219 28147 28149 28352 28353 28361
/usr/lib/sparcv9/libnsl.so.1:
        28362 28365
/usr/lib/sparcv9/libsocket.so.1:
        28362 28365
/usr/platform/sun4u-us3/lib/libc_psr.so.1:
        10613 12777 12933 27217 27219 27293 28147 28149 28223 28352 28353
        28361
/usr/platform/sun4u-us3/lib/sparcv9/libc_psr.so.1:
        28362 28365
...
```

For our last example of tracking Unix file and network operations, let's return to an earlier example, where we attempted to find IRC bots running on a system. There are more reliable ways to find network daemons like bots than looking at the process table. A user may be able to hide the name of a bot by renaming the executable, but he'll have to work a lot harder to hide the open network connection. More often than not, this connection is to a server running on TCP ports 6660–7000. *lsof* makes looking for these processes easy:

```
my $lsofexec = '/usr/local/bin/lsof';     # location of lsof executable
my $lsofflag = '-FLOc -iTCP:6660-7000';   # specify ports and other lsof flags

# This is a hash slice being used to preload a hash table, the
# existence of whose keys we'll check later. Usually this gets written
# like this:
#     %approvedclients = ('ircII' => undef, 'xirc' => undef, ...);
# (but this is a cool idiom popularized by Mark-Jason Dominus)
my %approvedclients;
@approvedclients{ 'ircII', 'xirc', 'pirc' } = ();

open my $LSOFPIPE, "$lsofexec $lsofflag|"
    or die "Unable to start $lsofexec:$!\n";

my $pid;
my $command;
my $login;
while ( my $lsof = <$LSOFPIPE> ) {
    ( $pid, $command, $login ) =
                    $lsof =~ /p(\d+)\000
                              c(.+)\000
                              L(\w+)\000/x;
    warn "$login using an unapproved client called $command (pid $pid)!\n"
        unless ( exists $approvedclients{$command} );
}

close $LSOFPIPE;
```

This is the simplest check we can make. It will catch users who rename *eggdrop* to something like *pine* or *-tcsh*, as well as those users who don't even attempt to hide their bots. However, it suffers from a similar flaw to our other approach. If a user is smart enough, she may rename her bot to something on our "approved clients" list. To continue our hunt, we could take at least two more steps:

- Use *lsof* to check that the file opened for that executable really is the file we expect it to be, and not some random binary in a user filesystem.
- Use our process control methods to check that the user is running this program from an existing shell. If this is the only process running for a user (i.e., if the user has logged off but left it running), it is probably a daemon and hence a bot.

This cat-and-mouse game brings us to a point that will help wrap up the chapter. In Chapter 3, we mentioned that users are fundamentally unpredictable. They do things system administrators don't anticipate. There is an old saying: "Nothing is foolproof because fools are so ingenious." It is important to come to grips with this fact as you program Perl for user administration. You'll write more robust programs as a result, and when one of your programs goes "blooey" because a user did something unexpected, you'll be able to sit back calmly and admire the ingenuity.

Module Information for This Chapter

Module	CPAN ID	Version
Text::CSV_XS	HMBRAND	0.32
Win32::Process::Info	WYANT	1.011
Win32::Setupsup	JHELBERG	1.0.1.0
Win32::GuiTest	KARASIC	1.54
Win32::OLE (ships with ActiveState Perl)	JDB	0.1703
Proc::ProcessTable	DURIST	0.41
Data::Dumper (ships with Perl)	GSAR	2.121
Win32::ChangeNotify	JDB	1.05
Win32::FileNotify	RENEEB	0.1
Text::Wrap (ships with Perl)	MUIR	2006.1117

Installing Win32::Setupsup

If you want to install `Win32::Setupsup`, you'll need to get it from a different PPM repository than the default one configured when you first installed ActiveState Perl. It can be found (as of this writing) in the very handy supplementary repository maintained by Randy Kobes at the University of Winnipeg. I'd recommend adding this repository even if you don't plan to use `Win32::Setupsup`. The easiest way to do this is from the command line, like so:

```
$ ppm repo add uwinnipeg http://theoryx5.uwinnipeg.ca/ppms/
```

or, if using Perl 5.10:

```
$ ppm repo add uwinnipeg http://cpan.uwinnipeg.ca/PPMPackages/10xx/
```

You can also add it to the GUI version of PPM4 by choosing Preferences in the Edit menu and selecting the Repositories tab. More info about this repository can be found at *http://theoryx5.uwinnipeg.ca/ppms/*.

References for More Information

http://aspn.activestate.com/ASPN/Mail/ hosts the *Perl-Win32-Admin* and *Perl-Win32-Users* mailing lists. Both lists and their archives are invaluable resources for Win32 programmers.

http://www.microsoft.com/whdc/system/pnppwr/wmi/default.mspx is the current home for WMI at Microsoft.com. This address has changed a few times since the first edition, so doing a web search for "WMI" may be a better way to locate the WMI *URL du jour* at Microsoft.

http://technet.microsoft.com/sysinternals/ is the home (as of this writing) of the *handle* program and many other valuable Windows utilities that Microsoft acquired when it bought Sysinternals and hired its principals. *http://sysinternals.com* still exists as of this writing and redirects to the correct Microsoft URL. If you can't find these utilities in any of Microsoft's websites, perhaps going to that URL will point you at the current location.

http://www.dmtf.org is the home of the Distributed Management Task Force and a good source for WBEM information.

If you haven't yet, you must download the Microsoft Scriptomatic tool (version 2 as of this writing) from *http://www.microsoft.com/technet/scriptcenter/tools/scripto2.mspx*. This Windows tool from "the Microsoft Scripting Guys" lets you poke around the WMI namespaces on your machine. When you find something you might be interested in using, it can write a script to use it for you. Really. But even better than that, it can write the script for you in VBScript, JScript, Perl, or Python. I'm raving about this tool both here and in the other chapters that mention WMI because I like it so much. If you want to use it under Vista, though, be sure to read the section on Vista in Chapter 1.

## CHAPTER 5

TCP/IP Name and Configuration Services

The majority of the conversations between computers these days take place using the *Transmission Control Protocol* running over a lower layer called the *Internet Protocol*.* These two protocols are commonly lumped together into the acronym *TCP/IP*. Every machine that participates in a TCP/IP network must be assigned at least one unique numeric identifier, called an *IP address*. IP addresses are usually written using the form *N.N.N.N* (e.g., 192.168.1.9).

While machines are content to address each other using strings of dot-separated numbers, most people are less enamored of this idea. TCP/IP would have fallen flat on its face as a protocol if users had to remember unique 12-digit sequences for every machine they wanted to contact. Mechanisms had to be invented to manage and distribute IP addresses to human-friendly name mappings. Also needed was a way to let a machine automatically determine its own TCP/IP configuration (i.e., IP address) without requiring a human to drop by and type in the information by hand.

This chapter describes the evolution of the network name services that allow us to access data at *www.oog.org* instead of at 192.168.1.9, and what takes place behind the scenes. We'll also look at the most prevalent configuration service that allows a machine to retrieve its TCP/IP configuration information from a central server. Along the way we'll combine a dash of history with a healthy serving of practical advice on how Perl can help us manage these crucial parts of any networking infrastructure.

Host Files

The first approach used to solve the problem of mapping IP addresses to names was the most obvious and simple one: creating a standard file to hold a table of IP addresses

---

* This chapter will be discussing IPv4, the current (deployed) standard. IPv6 (the next generation of IP) will potentially replace it in due course.

and their corresponding computer names. This file exists as */etc/hosts* on Unix and OS X systems and *%SystemRoot%\System32\Drivers\Etc\hosts* on machines running Windows-based operating systems. Here's an example Unix-style host file:

```
127.0.0.1     localhost
192.168.1.1   everest.oog.org     everest
192.168.1.2   rivendell.oog.org   rivendell
```

The limitations of this approach become clear very quickly. If *oog.org*'s network manager has two machines on a TCP/IP network that communicate with each other, and she wants to add a third, she has to edit the correct file on all of her machines. If *oog.org* then buys yet another machine, there will be four separate host files to be maintained (one on each machine).

As untenable as this may seem, this is what actually happened during the early days of the Internet/ARPAnet. As new sites were connected, every site on the net that wished to talk with the new site needed to update its host files. The central host repository, known as the Network Information Center (NIC)—or more precisely, the SRI-NIC, since it was housed at the Stanford Research Institute at the time—updated and published a host file for the entire network called *HOSTS.TXT*. To remain up-to-date, system administrators anonymously FTP'd this file from SRI-NIC's *NETINFO* directory on a regular basis.

Host files are still in use today, despite their limitations and the availability of the replacements we'll be talking about later in this chapter. On a small network, having an up-to-date host file that includes all of the hosts on that network is useful. It doesn't even have to reside on each machine in the network to be helpful (since the other mechanisms we'll describe later do a much better job of distributing this information). Just having one around to consult is handy for quick manual lookups and address allocation purposes.

Strangely enough, host files have made a bit of a comeback in recent years. They provide an easy way to override other network name services, which is useful in cases where you want to prevent connections to specific hosts. For example, if you find that you want to block connections to a certain web banner or web habit-tracking site, you can place its hostname in your host file with a bogus IP address. Unfortunately, virus writers have also used the same trick to break auto-update features of antivirus packages.

Host Files? Get a Horse!

Now that network name services like the Domain Name Service (DNS) and configuration services like the Dynamic Host Configuration Protocol (DHCP) are the norm and twiddling host files has become the exception, why bother talking about these files at all?

Host files are really simple. The syntax and semantics are immediately understandable to anyone who glances at such a file. That's not necessarily true for the other services we'll be exploring later in this chapter. This simplicity means that we can look at ways

---

of manipulating such files without getting distracted by the details of a specific service's implementation, configuration file syntax, etc.

The techniques we're about to explore can be applied to any of the network name and configuration services that use plain-text configuration files. We're going to initially show them in the context of manipulating host files, because that is the fastest way to demonstrate methods you'll use time and time again. Later in the chapter you'll see some of the same ideas demonstrated with other services without all of the explanation.

So, if reading about host files makes you feel like an old-timer, read for the "how" and not the "what."[†]

Perl and host files are a natural match, given Perl's predilection for text file processing. We're going to use the simple host file as a springboard for a number of different explorations.

To start, let's look at the parsing of host files. Parsing a host file can be as simple as this:

```perl
open( my $HOSTS, '<', '/etc/hosts' ) or die "Unable to open host file:$!\n";
my %addrs;
my %names;
while ( defined( $_ = <$HOSTS> ) ) {
    next if /^#/;     # skip comments lines
    next if /^\s*$/; # skip empty lines
    s/\s*#.*$//;      # delete in-line comments and preceding whitespace
    chomp;
    my ( $ip, @names ) = split;
    die "The IP address $ip already seen!\n" if ( exists $addrs{$ip} );
    $addrs{$ip} = [@names];
    for (@names) {
        die "The host name $_ already seen!\n" if ( exists $names{lc $_} );
        $names{lc $_} = $ip;
    }
}
close $HOSTS;
```

The previous code walks through an */etc/hosts* file (skipping blank lines and comments), creating two data structures for later use. The first data structure is a hash of lists of hostnames keyed by the IP address. It looks something like this:

```perl
$addrs{'127.0.0.1'}   = ['localhost'];
$addrs{'192.168.1.2'} = ['rivendell.oog.org','rivendell'];
$addrs{'192.168.1.1'} = ['everest.oog.org','everest'];
```

The second is a hash table of hostnames, keyed by name. For the same file, the %names hash would look like this:

```perl
$names{'localhost'}        = '127.0.0.1'
$names{'everest'}          = '192.168.1.1'
```

[†] Plus, a real Ol' Timer would probably point out to you that he still adds the critical machines to his *hosts* file and uses it as a backup (via *nsswitch.conf*) when he's concerned about things breaking should DNS go south.

```
$names{'everest.oog.org'}    = '192.168.1.1'
$names{'rivendell'}          = '192.168.1.2'
$names{'rivendell.oog.org'}  = '192.168.1.2'
```

Note that in the simple process of parsing this file, we've also added some functionality. Our code checks for duplicate hostnames and IP addresses (which are bad news on a TCP/IP network unless you really mean them to be there, for virtual hosts, multihomed machines, high availability, etc.). When dealing with network-related data, use every opportunity possible to check for errors and bad information. It is always better to catch problems early in the game than to have them bite you once the data has been propagated to your entire network. Because it is so important, I'll return to this topic later in the chapter.

Generating Host Files

Now we'll turn to the more interesting topic of generating host files. Let's assume we have the following host database file for the hosts on our network:

```
name: shimmer
address: 192.168.1.11
aliases: shim shimmy shimmydoodles
owner: David Davis
department: software
building: main
room: 909
manufacturer: Sun
model: M4000
-=-
name: bendir
address: 192.168.1.3
aliases: ben bendoodles
owner: Cindy Coltrane
department: IT
building: west
room: 143
manufacturer: Apple
model: Mac Pro
-=-
name: sulawesi
address: 192.168.1.12
aliases: sula su-lee
owner: Ellen Monk
department: design
building: main
room: 1116
manufacturer: Apple
model: Mac Pro
-=-
name: sander
address: 192.168.1.55
aliases: sandy micky mickydoo
owner: Alex Rollins
department: IT
```

```
building: main
room: 1101
manufacturer: Dell
model: Optiplex 740
-=-
```

The format is simple: *fieldname*: *value*, with -=- used as a separator between records. You might find that you need other fields than those listed here, or that you have too many records to make it practical to keep them in a single flat file. Though we are using a single flat file here, the concepts we'll show in this chapter are not backend-specific; for example, they could be generated from an LDAP directory (more on those in Chapter 9).

Here's some code that will parse a file like this to generate a host file:

```
my $datafile  = 'database';
my $recordsep = "-=-\n";

open my $DATAFILE, '<', "$datafile" or die "Unable to open datafile:$!\n";

{
    local $/ =
      $recordsep;     # prepare to read in database file one record at a time

    print "#\n# host file - GENERATED BY $0\n# DO NOT EDIT BY HAND!\n#\n";

    my %record;
    while (<$DATAFILE>) {
        chomp;          # remove the record separator

        # split into key1,value1,...bingo, hash of record
        %record = split /:\s*|\n/;
        print "$record{address}\t$record{name} $record{aliases}\n";
    }
    close $DATAFILE;
}
```

Here's the output:

```
#
# host file - GENERATED BY createhosts
# DO NOT EDIT BY HAND!
#
192.168.1.11    shimmer shim shimmy shimmydoodles
192.168.1.3     bendir ben bendoodles
192.168.1.12    sulawesi sula su-lee
192.168.1.55    sander sandy micky mickydoo.
```

Got "System Administration Database" Religion Yet?

In Chapter 3, I made an impassioned plea for the use of a separate administrative database to track account information. The same arguments are doubly true for network host data. In this chapter we're going to demonstrate how even a simple flat-file host database can be manipulated to produce impressive output that drives each of the services we'll be discussing. For larger sites, a "real" database would serve well. If you'd like to see an example of this output, take a quick glance ahead at the output at the end of the section "Improving the Host File Output" on page 144.

The host database approach is beautiful for a number of reasons. First, changes need to be made only to a single file or data source. Make the changes, run some scripts, and *presto!*, we've generated the configuration files needed for a number of services. These configuration files are significantly less likely to contain small syntax errors (like missing semicolons or comment characters), because they haven't been touched by human hands. If we write our code correctly, we can catch most of the other possible errors during the parsing stage.

If you haven't seen the wisdom of this "best practice" yet, you will by the end of the chapter.

Let's look at a few of the more interesting Perl techniques demonstrated in this small code sample. The first unusual thing we do is set $/ from within a small code block (delimited by the braces). In this little code block, Perl treats each chunk of text that ends in -=-\n as a single record. This means the while statement will read in an entire record at a time and assign it to $_. We place the local statement within the block so our changes to $/ don't affect any other code we might write in the future that uses this code sample.

The second interesting tidbit is the split() assignment technique. Our goal is to get each record into a hash with a key as the field name and its value as the field value. You'll see later why we go to this trouble, as we develop this example further. The first step is to break $_ into component parts using split(). The array we get back from split() is shown in Table 5-1.

Table 5-1. The array returned by split()

Element	Value
0	name
1	shimmer
2	address
3	192.168.1.11
4	Aliases
5	shim shimmy shimmydoodles
6	Owner
7	David Davis
8	Department
9	Software
10	Building
11	Main

Element	Value
12	Room
13	909
14	Manufacturer
15	Sun
16	Model
17	M4000

Take a good look at the contents of this list. Starting with the first element (element 0), we have a key/value pair list (i.e., key=Name, value=shimmer, key=Address, value=192.168.1.11...) that we can assign to populate a hash. Once this hash is created, we can print the parts we need.

Error-Checking the Host File Generation Process

Printing a bare host file is just the beginning of what we can do. One very large benefit of using a separate database that gets converted into another form is the ability to insert error-checking into the conversion process. As mentioned earlier, this can prevent simple typos from becoming a problem *before* they get a chance to propagate or be put into production use. Here's the previous code with some simple additions to check for typos:

```
my $datafile  = 'database';
my $recordsep = "-=-\n";

open my $DATAFILE, '<', "$datafile" or die "Unable to open datafile:$!\n";

{
    local $/ =
      $recordsep;    # prepare to read in database file one record at a time

    print "#\n# host file - GENERATED BY $0\n# DO NOT EDIT BY HAND!\n#\n";

    my %record;
    my %addrs;
    while (<$DATAFILE>) {
        chomp;       # remove the record separator

        # split into key1,value1,... bingo, hash of record
        %record = split /:\s*|\n/;

        # check for bad hostnames
        if ( $record{name} =~ /[^-.a-zA-Z0-9]/ ) {
            warn "!!!! $record{name} has illegal host name characters, "
              . "skipping...\n";
            next;
        }
```

```
    # check for bad aliases
    if ( $record{aliases} =~ /[^-.a-zA-Z0-9\s]/ ) {
        warn "!!!! $record{name} has illegal alias name characters, "
          . "skipping...\n";
        next;
    }

    # check for missing address
    if ( !$record{address} ) {
        warn "!!!! $record{name} does not have an IP address, "
          . "skipping...\n";
        next;
    }

    # check for duplicate address
    if ( defined $addrs{ $record{address} } ) {
        warn "!!!! Duplicate IP addr: $record{name} &
      $addrs{$record{address}}, skipping...\n";
        next;
    }
    else {
        $addrs{ $record{address} } = $record{name};
    }

    print "$record{address}\t$record{name} $record{aliases}\n";
  }
  close $DATAFILE;
}
```

Improving the Host File Output

Let's borrow from Chapter 10 on logs and add some analysis to the conversion process.
We can automatically add useful headers, comments, and separators to the data. Here's
some example output using the exact same database:

```
#
# host file - GENERATED BY createhosts3
# DO NOT EDIT BY HAND!
#
# Converted by David N. Blank-Edelman (dnb) on Sun Jun  8 00:43:24 2008
#
# number of hosts in the design department: 1.
# number of hosts in the software department: 1.
# number of hosts in the IT department: 2.
# total number of hosts: 4
#

# Owned by Cindy Coltrane (IT): west/143
192.168.1.3     bendir ben bendoodles

# Owned by Alex Rollins (IT): main/1101
192.168.1.55    sander sandy micky mickydoo

# Owned by Ellen Monk (design): main/1116
```

```
    192.168.1.12    sulawesi sula su-lee

# Owned by David Davis (software: main/909
192.168.1.11    shimmer shim shimmy shimmydoodles
```

Here's the code that produced that output, followed by some commentary:

```perl
my $datafile  = 'database';
my $recordsep = "-=-\n";

# get username on either Windows or Unix
my $user =
   ( $^O eq 'MSWin32' ) ? $ENV{USERNAME} :
                          (getpwuid($<))[6] . ' (' . (getpwuid($<))[0] . ')';

open my $DATAFILE, '<', "$datafile" or die "Unable to open datafile:$!\n";

my %addrs;
my %entries;
{
    local $/ = $recordsep;    # read in database file one record at a time

    while (<$DATAFILE>) {
        chomp;                  # remove the record separator
                                # split into key1,value1
        my @record = split /:\s*|\n/;

        my $record = {};        # create a reference to empty hash
        %{$record} = @record;   # populate that hash with @record

        # check for bad hostname
        if ( $record->{name} =~ /[^-.a-zA-Z0-9]/ ) {
            warn '!!!! '
               . $record->{name}
               . " has illegal host name characters, skipping...\n";
            next;
        }

        # check for bad aliases
        if ( $record->{aliases} =~ /[^-.a-zA-Z0-9\s]/ ) {
            warn '!!!! '
               . $record->{name}
               . " has illegal alias name characters, skipping...\n";
            next;
        }

        # check for missing address
        if ( !$record->{address} ) {
            warn '!!!! '
               . $record->{name}
               . " does not have an IP address, skipping...\n";
            next;
        }
```

```
        # check for duplicate address
        if ( defined $addrs{ $record->{address} } ) {
            warn '!!!! Duplicate IP addr:'
              . $record->{name} . ' & '
              . $addrs{ $record->{address} }
              . ", skipping...\n";
            next;
        }
        else {
            $addrs{ $record->{address} } = $record->{name};
        }

        $entries{ $record->{name} } = $record;      # add this to a hash of hashes
    }
    close $DATAFILE;
}

# print a nice header
print "#\n# host file - GENERATED BY $0\n# DO NOT EDIT BY HAND!\n#\n";
print "# Converted by $user on " . scalar(localtime) . "\n#\n";

# count the number of entries in each department and then report on it
my %depts;
foreach my $entry ( keys %entries ) {
    $depts{ $entries{$entry}->{department} }++;
}
foreach my $dept ( keys %depts ) {
    print "# number of hosts in the $dept department: $depts{$dept}.\n";
}
print '# total number of hosts: ' . scalar( keys %entries ) . "\n#\n\n";

# iterate through the hosts, printing a nice comment and the entry itself
foreach my $entry ( keys %entries ) {
    print '# Owned by ', $entries{$entry}->{owner}, ' (',
      $entries{$entry}->{department}, "): ", $entries{$entry}->{building}, '/',
      $entries{$entry}->{room}, "\n";
    print $entries{$entry}->{address}, "\t", $entries{$entry}->{name}, ' ',
      $entries{$entry}->{aliases}, "\n\n";
}
```

The most significant difference between this code example and the previous one is the data representation. Because there was no need in the previous example to retain the information from a record after it had been printed, we could use the single hash %record. But for this code, we chose to read the file into a slightly more complex data structure (a hash of hashes) so we could do some simple analysis of the data before printing it.

We could have kept a separate hash table for each field (similar to our *needspace* example in Chapter 2), but the beauty of this approach is its maintainability. If we decide later to add a serial_number field to the database, we do not need to change our program's parsing code; it will just magically appear as $record->{serial_number}.

The downside is that Perl's syntax probably makes our code look more complex than it is.

Here's an easy way to look at it: we're parsing the file in precisely the same way we did in the last example. The difference is this time we are storing each record in a newly created anonymous hash. Anonymous hashes are just like normal hash variables except they are accessed through a reference, instead of a name.

To create our larger data structure (a hash of hashes), we link this new anonymous hash back into the main hash table, %entries. When we are done, %entries has a key for each machine name. Each key has a value that is a reference to a separate new hash table containing all of the fields associated with that machine (IP address, room, etc.).

Perhaps you'd prefer to see the output sorted by IP address? No problem, just include a custom sort routine by changing this line:

```
foreach my $entry (keys %entries) {
```

to:

```
foreach my $entry (sort byaddress keys %entries) {
```

and adding:

```
sub byaddress {
    my @a = split(/\./,$entries{$a}->{address});
    my @b = split(/\./,$entries{$b}->{address});
    ($a[0]<=>$b[0]) ||
    ($a[1]<=>$b[1]) ||
    ($a[2]<=>$b[2]) ||
    ($a[3]<=>$b[3]);
}
```

 This is one of the easiest to understand ways to sort IP addresses, but it is also one of the least efficient because of all of the split() operations that have to take place. A far better way to do this is to compare packed sort keys, a technique first proposed in a paper by Uri Guttman and Larry Rosler (*http://www.sysarch.com/Perl/sort_paper.html*). Guttman's Sort::Maker module can assist you with implementing that method. The Sort::Key module by Salvador Fandiño García offers another easy way to perform highly efficient sorting in Perl. If you don't want to install a separate module just to set up a sort, search for "sort ip address perl" on the Web and you'll find other, more efficient suggestions.

Here's the relevant portion of the output, now nicely sorted:

```
# Owned by Cindy Coltrane (IT): west/143
192.168.1.3     bendir ben bendoodles

# Owned by David Davis (software): main/909
192.168.1.11    shimmer shim shimmy shimmydoodles
```

```
# Owned by Ellen Monk (design): main/1116
192.168.1.12    sulawesi sula su-lee

# Owned by Alex Rollins (IT): main/1101
192.168.1.55    sander sandy micky mickydoo
```

Make the output look good to you. Let Perl support your professional *and* aesthetic endeavors.

Incorporating a Source Code Control System

In a moment we're going to move on to the next approach to the IP address-to-name mapping problem. But before we do, we'll want to add another twist to our host file creation process, because that single file is about to take on network-wide importance. A mistake in this file will affect an entire network of machines. To give us a safety net, we'll want a way to back out of bad changes, essentially going back in time to a prior configuration state.

The most elegant way to build a time machine like this is to add a source control system to the process. Source control systems are typically used by developers to:

- Keep a record of all changes to important files.
- Prevent multiple people from changing the same file (or parts of a file) at the same time, inadvertently undoing each other's efforts.
- Allow us to revert to a previous version of a file, thus backing out of problems.

This functionality is extremely useful to a system administrator. The error-checking code we added to the conversion process in "Error-Checking the Host File Generation Process" on page 143 can help with certain kinds of typos and syntax errors, but it does not offer any protection against semantic errors (e.g., deleting an important hostname, assigning the wrong IP address to a host, or misspelling a hostname). You could add semantic error checks into the conversion process, but you probably wouldn't catch all of the possible errors. As I've quoted before, nothing is foolproof, since fools are so ingenious.

You might think it would be better to apply source control system functionality to the initial database editing process, but there are two good reasons why it is also important to apply it to the resultant output:

Time

For large data sets, the conversion process might take some time. If your network is flaking out and you need to revert to a previous revision, it's discouraging to have to stare at a Perl process chugging away to generate the file you need (presuming you can even get to Perl at that point).

Absence of database change control

If you choose to use a real database engine for your data storage (and often this is the right choice), there may not be a convenient way to apply a source control mechanism like this. You'll probably have to write your own change control mechanisms for the database editing process.

My source control system of choice[‡] is the Revision Control System (RCS). RCS has some Perl- and system administration-friendly features:

- It is multiplatform. There are ports of GNU RCS 5.7 to most Unix systems, Windows, Mac OS X, etc.
- It has a well-defined command-line interface. All functions can be performed from the command line, even on GUI-centric operating systems.
- It is easy to use. There's a small command set for basic operations that can be learned in five minutes (see Appendix E).
- It has keywords. Magic strings can be embedded in the text of files under RCS that are automatically expanded. For instance, any occurrence of `$ Date:$` in a file will be replaced with the date the file was last entered into the RCS system.
- It's free.

The source code for the GNU version of RCS is freely redistributable, and binaries for most systems are also available. A copy of the source can be found at *ftp://ftp.gnu.org/gnu/rcs*. If you've never dealt with RCS before, please take a moment to read Appendix E before going any further. The rest of this section assumes a cursory knowledge of the RCS command set.

Craig Freter has written an object-oriented module called `Rcs` that makes using RCS from Perl easy. The steps are:

1. Load the module.
2. Tell the module where your RCS command-line binaries are located.
3. Create a new `Rcs` object, and configure it with the name of the file you are using.
4. Call the necessary object methods (named after their corresponding RCS commands).

Let's add this to our host file generation code so you can see how the module works. Besides the `Rcs` module code, we've also changed things so the output is sent to a specific file and not `STDOUT`, as in our previous versions. Only the code that has changed is shown. Refer to the previous example for the omitted lines represented by "...":

```
my $outputfile = "hosts.$$"; # temporary output file
my $target     = 'hosts';    # where we want the converted data stored
...
open my $OUTPUT, '>', "$outputfile" or
  die "Unable to write to $outputfile:$!\n";

print $OUTPUT "#\n# host file - GENERATED BY $0\n# DO NOT EDIT BY HAND!\n#\n";
```

[‡] At least *in this context*. If you'd like to know why I recommend RCS over other, much spiffier source control systems (SVN, git, etc.) here, see Appendix E.

```
print $OUTPUT "# Converted by $user on " . scalar(localtime) . "\n#\n";

...
foreach my $dept ( keys %depts ) {
    print $OUTPUT "# number of hosts in the $dept department: $depts{$dept}.\n";
}
print $OUTPUT '# total number of hosts: ' . scalar( keys %entries ) . "\n#\n\n";

# iterate through the hosts, printing a nice comment and the entry itself
foreach my $entry ( keys %entries ) {
    print $OUTPUT '# Owned by ', $entries{$entry}->{owner}, ' (',
      $entries{$entry}->{department}, '): ', $entries{$entry}->{building}, '/',
      $entries{$entry}->{room}, "\n";
    print $OUTPUT $entries{$entry}->{address}, "\t", $entries{$entry}->{name},
      ' ', $entries{$entry}->{aliases}, "\n\n";
}

close $OUTPUT;

use Rcs;
Rcs->bindir('/arch/gnu/bin');

my $rcsobj = Rcs->new;
$rcsobj->file($target);
$rcsobj->co('-l');
rename( $outputfile, $target )
  or die "Unable to rename $outputfile to $target:$!\n";
$rcsobj->ci( '-u',
        '-m'
      . 'Converted by '
      . ( getpwuid($<) )[6] . ' ('
      . ( getpwuid($<) )[0] . ') on '
      . scalar localtime );
```

This code assumes the target file has been checked in at least once already.

To see the effect of this code addition, we can look at three entries excerpted from the output of `rlog hosts`:

```
revision 1.5
date: 2007/05/19 23:34:16;  author: dnb;  state: Exp;  lines: +1 -1
Converted by David N. Blank-Edelman (dnb) on Tue May 19 19:34:16 2007
----------------------------
revision 1.4
date: 2007/05/19 23:34:05;  author: eviltwin;  state: Exp;  lines: +1 -1
Converted by Divad Knalb-Namlede (eviltwin) on Tue May 19 19:34:05 2007
----------------------------
revision 1.3
date: 2007/05/19 23:33:35;  author: dnb;  state: Exp;  lines: +20 -0
Converted by David N. Blank-Edelman (dnb) on Tue May 19 19:33:16 2007
```

This example doesn't show much of a difference between file versions (see the `lines:` part of the entries), but you can see that we are tracking the changes every time the file gets created. If we needed to, we could use the `rcsdiff` command to see exactly what has changed. Under dire circumstances, if one of these changes had wreaked unexpected havoc on the network, we would be able to revert to a previous version.

Before we move on, let's do a quick review of the three techniques we have learned so far so we can be sure to bring them forward when we look at other name services:

- Generating a configuration file from an external database of some sort is a big win.
- Checking for simple errors in the data during the process, well before they can have a serious impact on the network, is a good thing.
- Incorporating a source control system into the process gives you a good way to recover from more complex errors and a way of tracking changes.

NIS, NIS+, and WINS

Developers at Sun Microsystems realized that the "edit one file per machine" approach endemic to host files didn't scale, so they invented *Yellow Pages* (YP), which was designed to distribute all the network-wide configuration file information found in files like */etc/hosts*, */etc/passwd*, */etc/services*, and so on. In this chapter, we'll concentrate on its use as a network name service to distribute machine name-to-IP address mapping information.

YP was renamed the *Network Information Service* (NIS) in 1990, shortly after British Telecom asserted (with lawyers) that it held the trademark for "Yellow Pages" in the U.K. The ghost of the name "Yellow Pages" still haunts many a Unix box today in the names used for NIS commands and library calls (e.g., *ypcat*, *ypmatch*, *yppush*).

All modern Unix variants support NIS. Mac OS X makes it easy to client off of existing NIS servers through (at least in Tiger and later releases) the Directory Access utility, found in */Applications/Utilities* (check the box next to "BSD Flat File and NIS" and click Apply). OS X also ships with the right files (*/usr/libexec/ypserv*, */var/yp/**, etc.) to serve NIS, though I've never seen it done.

The NIS and Windows story is a bit more complex. Once upon a time, back in the days of the first edition of this book, it was possible to replace one of the Windows authentication libraries with custom code that would talk to NIS servers instead of doing domain-based authentication. This was the NISGINA solution.

If you need to have a Windows machine use NIS-sourced data, your best bet at this point is to use Samba (*http://www.samba.org*) as a bridge between the two worlds. On the NIS-server front, Microsoft has also built into its Windows 2003 R2 product an NIS server that allows it to serve Active Directory-based information to NIS clients. This works well if you decide to make Active Directory the center of your authentication universe but still need to serve NIS to other, non-Windows clients. To save you some hunting, Microsoft now calls this component "Identity Management for Unix" (IdMU). You'll need to add it to your installation by hand, via Add or Remove Programs→Add/Remove Windows Components→Active Directory Services [Details].

In NIS, an administrator designates one or more machines as servers from which other machines will receive client services. One server is the *master* server, and the others are *slave* servers. The master server holds the master copies of the actual text files all machines normally use (e.g., */etc/hosts* or */etc/passwd*). Changes to these files take place on the master and are then propagated to the slave servers.

Any machine on the network that needs hostname-to-IP address mapping information can query a server instead of keeping a local copy of that information. A client can request this information from either the master or any of the slave servers. Client queries are looked up in the *NIS maps* (another name for the master's data files after they've been converted to the Unix DBM database format and propagated to the slave servers). The details of this conversion process (which involves *makedbm* and some other random munging) can be found in the *Makefile* located in */var/yp* on most machines. A collection of NIS servers and clients that share the same maps is called an *NIS domain*.

With NIS, network administration becomes considerably easier. For instance, if *oog.org* purchases more machines for its network, it is no problem to integrate them into the network. The network manager simply edits the host file on the master NIS server and pushes the new version out to the slave servers. Every client in the NIS domain now "knows" about the new machine. NIS offers one-touch administration ease coupled with some redundancy (if one server goes down, a client can ask another) and load sharing (not all of the clients in a network have to rely on a single server).

With this theory in mind, let's see how Perl can help us with NIS-related tasks. We can start with the process of getting data into NIS. You may be surprised to know that we've already done the work for this task. We can import the host files we created in the previous section into NIS by just dropping them into place in the NIS master server's source file directory and activating the usual push mechanisms (usually by typing make in */var/yp*). By default, the *Makefile* in */var/yp* uses the contents of the master server's configuration files as the source for the NIS maps.

It is usually a good idea to set up a separate directory for your NIS map source files, changing the *Makefile* accordingly. This allows you to keep separate data for your NIS master server and other members of your NIS domain. For example, you might not want to have the */etc/passwd* file for your NIS master as the password map for the entire domain, and vice versa.

A more interesting task is getting data out of NIS by querying an NIS server. The easiest way to do this is via Rik Harris's Net::NIS module (now maintained by Ed Santiago).

Here's an example of how to grab and print the entire contents of the host map with a single function call using Net::NIS, similar to the NIS command ypcat:

```
use Net::NIS;
```

```
# get our default NIS domain name
my $domain = Net::NIS::yp_get_default_domain();

# grab the map
my ( $status, $info ) = Net::NIS::yp_all( $domain, 'hosts.byname' );
foreach my $name ( sort keys %{$info} ) {
    print "$name => $info->{$name}\n";
}
```

First we query the local host for its default domain name. With this info, we can call
`Net::NIS::yp_all()` to retrieve the entire host map. The function call returns a status
variable and a reference to a hash table containing the contents of that map. We print
this information using Perl's usual dereference syntax.

If we want to look up the IP address of a single host, it is more efficient to query the
server specifically for that value:

```
use Net::NIS;

my $hostname = 'olaf.oog.org';

my $domain = Net::NIS::yp_get_default_domain();
my ( $status, $info ) =
   Net::NIS::yp_match( $domain, 'hosts.byname', $hostname );

print "$info\n";
```

`Net::NIS::yp_match()` returns a status variable and the appropriate value (as a scalar)
for the info being queried.

If the `Net::NIS` module does not compile or work for you, there's always the "call an
external program" method. For example:

```
@hosts=`<path to>/ypcat hosts`
```

or:

```
open my $YPCAT, '-|', '<path to>/ypcat hosts');
while (<YPCAT>){...}
```

Let's wind up this section with a useful example of both this technique and `Net::NIS`
in action. This small but handy piece of code will query NIS for the list of NIS servers
currently running and then query each of them in turn using the *yppoll* program. If any
of the servers fails to respond, it complains loudly:

```
use Net::NIS;

my $yppollex = '/usr/sbin/yppoll';    # full path to the yppoll executable

my $domain = Net::NIS::yp_get_default_domain();    # our NIS domain

my ( $status, $info ) = Net::NIS::yp_all( $domain, 'ypservers' );

foreach my $server ( sort keys %{$info} ) {
    my $answer = `$yppollex -h $server hosts.byname`;
```

```
        if ( $answer !~ /has order number/ ) {
            print STDERR "$server is not responding properly!\n";
        }
    }
}
```

There are a number of ways we could improve upon this code (e.g., we could check if the order number returned matched amongst the servers), but that's left as an exercise for you-know-who.

NIS+

Sun included the next version of NIS, called NIS+, with the Solaris operating system. NIS+ addresses many of the most serious problems of NIS, such as security. Unfortunately (or fortunately, since NIS+ can be a bit difficult to administer), NIS+ has not caught on in the Unix world nearly as well NIS did. Until recently, there was virtually no support for it on machines not manufactured by Sun. Thorsten Kukuk's work to bring it to Linux (*http://www.linux-nis.org/nisplus/*) has ceased, and even Sun has abandoned it for LDAP. Given its marginal status, we're not going to look at NIS+ in this book. If you do need to work with NIS+ from Perl, Harris has a `Net::NISPlus` module that's up to the task.

Windows Internet Name Server (WINS)

Let's look at one more dying protocol, for historical reasons. When Microsoft began to run its proprietary networking protocol NetBIOS over TCP/IP (NetBT), it also found a need to handle the name-to–IP address mapping question. The first shot was the *lmhosts* file, modeled after the standard host file. This was quickly supplemented with an NIS-like mechanism. Since NT version 3.5, Microsoft has offered a centralized scheme called the Windows Internet Name Server (WINS). WINS differs in several ways from NIS:

- WINS is specialized for the distribution of host-to-IP address mappings. Unlike NIS, it is not used to centralize distribution of other information (e.g., passwords, networks, port mappings, and user groups).

- WINS servers receive most of the information they distribute from preconfigured client registrations (they can be preloaded with information). Once they've received an IP address either manually or via DHCP, WINS clients are responsible for registering and re-registering their information. This is different from NIS in that client machines ask the server for information that has been preloaded and, with only one exception (passwords), do not update the information on that server.

WINS, like NIS, offers the ability to have multiple servers available for reliability and load sharing through the use of a push/pull partner model. As of Windows 2000, WINS was deprecated (read "killed off") in favor of the Dynamic Domain Name Service (DDNS), an extension to the basic DNS system we're just about to discuss.

Given that WINS, like NIS+, is about to go to the Great Protocol Graveyard to die, we're not going to explore Perl code to work with it. There is currently very little support for working directly with WINS from Perl (I know of no Perl modules designed specifically to interact with WINS). If you need to do this, your best bet may be to call some of the command-line utilities found in the Windows resource kits, such as `WINSCHK` and `WINSCL`.

Domain Name Service (DNS)

As useful as they may be, NIS and WINS suffer from flaws that make them unsuitable for "entire-Internet" uses. There are two main issues:

Scale

Even though these schemes allow for multiple servers, each server must have a complete copy of the entire network topology.[*] This topology must be duplicated to every other server, which can become a time-consuming process. WINS also suffers because of its dynamic registration model: a sufficient number of WINS clients could melt down any set of Internet-wide WINS servers with registration requests.

Administrative control

We've been talking about strictly technical issues up until now, but that's not the only side of administration. NIS, in particular, requires a single point of administration; whoever controls the master server controls the entire NIS domain led by that machine, and any changes to the network namespace must pass through that administrative gatekeeper. This doesn't work for a namespace the size of the Internet.

The Domain Name Service (DNS) was invented to deal with the flaws inherent in maintaining host files or NIS/NIS+/WINS-like systems. Under DNS, the network namespace is partitioned into a set of somewhat arbitrary "top-level domains." Each top-level domain can then be subdivided into smaller domains, each of which can in turn be partitioned, and so on. At each dividing point it is possible to designate a different party to retain authoritative control over that portion of the namespace. This handles our administrative control concern.

Network clients that reside in the individual parts of this hierarchy consult the name server closest to them in the hierarchy. If the information the client is looking for can be found on that local server, it is returned to the client. On most networks, the majority of name-to-IP address queries are for machines on that network, so the local servers handle most of the local traffic. This satisfies the scale problem. Multiple DNS servers

---

[*] NIS+ offered mechanisms for a client to search for information outside of the local domain, but they were not as flexible as those in DNS.

(also known as *secondary* or *slave servers*) can be set up for redundancy and load-balancing purposes.

If a DNS server is asked about a part of the namespace that it does not control or know about, it can either instruct the client to look elsewhere (usually higher up in the tree) or fetch the required information on behalf of the client by contacting other DNS servers.

In this scheme, no single server needs to know the entire network topology, most queries are handled locally, local administrators retain local control, and everybody is happy. DNS offers such an advantage compared to other systems that most other systems, including NIS and WINS, offer a way to integrate DNS. For instance, a Solaris NIS server can be instructed to perform a DNS query if a client asks it for a host it does not know. The results of this query are returned as a standard NIS query reply, so the client has no knowledge that any magic has been performed on its behalf. Microsoft DNS servers have similar functionality: if a client asks a Microsoft DNS server for the address of a local machine that it does not know about, the server can be configured to consult a WINS server on the client's behalf.

Generating DNS (BIND) Configuration Files

Production of DNS configuration files for the popular BIND DNS server (*https://www.isc.org/software/bind*) follows the same procedure that we used to generate host and NIS source files:

- We store data in a separate database (the same database can and probably should be the source for all of the files we've been discussing).
- We convert data to the output format of our choice, checking for errors as we go.
- We use RCS (or an equivalent source control system) to store old revisions of files.

For DNS, we have to expand the second step because the conversion process is more complicated. As we launch into these complications, you may find it handy to have *DNS and BIND* by Paul Albitz and Cricket Liu (O'Reilly) on hand for information on the DNS configuration files we'll be creating.

Creating the administrative header

DNS configuration files begin with an administrative header that provides information about the server and the data it is serving. The most important part of this header is the Start of Authority (SOA) resource record. The SOA contains:

- The name of the administrative domain served by this DNS server
- The name of the primary DNS server for that domain
- Contact info for the DNS administrator(s)
- The serial number of the configuration file (more on this in a moment)

- Refresh and retry values for secondary servers (i.e., when they synchronize with the primary server)
- Time to Live (TTL) settings for the data being served (i.e., how long the information being provided can safely be cached)

Here's an example header:

```
@ IN SOA   dns.oog.org. hostmaster.oog.org. (
                    2007052900 ; serial
                    10800      ; refresh
                    3600       ; retry
                    604800     ; expire
                    43200)     ; TTL


@                          IN  NS  dns.oog.org.
```

Most of this information is just tacked on the front of a DNS configuration file verbatim each time it is generated. The one piece we need to worry about is the serial number. Once every *X* seconds (where *X* is determined by the refresh value), secondary name servers contact their primary servers looking for updates to their DNS data. Modern secondary DNS servers (like BIND v8+ or Microsoft DNS) can also be told by their master servers to check for updates when the master data has changed. In both cases, each secondary server queries the primary server for its SOA record. If the SOA record contains a serial number higher than that server's current serial number, a zone transfer is initiated (that is, the secondary downloads a new data set). Consequently, it is important to increment this number each time a new DNS configuration file is created. Many DNS problems are caused by failures to update the serial number.

There are at least two ways to make sure the serial number is always incremented:

- Read the previous configuration file and increment the value found there.
- Compute a new value based on an external number source "guaranteed" to increment over time (like the system clock or the RCS version number of the file).

Here's some example code that uses a combination of these two methods to generate a valid header for a DNS zone file. It creates a serial number formatted as recommended in Albitz and Liu's book (YYYYMMDDXX, where YYYY=year, MM=month, DD=day, and XX=a two-digit counter to allow for more than one change per day):

```perl
# get today's date in the form of YYYYMMDD
my @localtime = localtime;
my $today     = sprintf( "%04d%02d%02d",
    $localtime[5] + 1900,
    $localtime[4] + 1,
    $localtime[3] );

# get username on either Windows or Unix
my $user =
  ( $^O eq 'MSWin32' )
  ? $ENV{USERNAME}
  : ( getpwuid($<) )[6] . ' (' . ( getpwuid($<) )[0] . ')';
```

```perl
sub GenerateHeader {
    my ($olddate,$count);

    # open old file if possible and read in serial number
    # (assumes the format of the old file)
    if ( open( my $OLDZONE, '<', $target ) ) {
        while (<$OLDZONE>) {
            last if ( $olddate, $count ) = /(\d{8})(\d{2}).*serial/;
        }
        close $OLDZONE;
    }

    # If $count is defined, we did find an old serial number.
    # If the old serial number was for today, increment last 2 digits;
    # else start a new number for today.
    my $count = ( defined $count and $olddate eq $today ) ? $count + 1 : 0;
    my $serial = sprintf( "%8d%02d", $today, $count );

    # begin the header
    my $header = "; dns zone file - GENERATED BY $0\n";
    $header .= "; DO NOT EDIT BY HAND!\n;\n";
    $header .= "; Converted by $user on " . scalar( (localtime) ) . "\n;\n";

    # count the number of entries in each department and then report
    foreach my $entry ( keys %entries ) {
        $depts{ $entries{$entry}->{department} }++;
    }
    foreach my $dept ( keys %depts ) {
        $header .=
            "; number of hosts in the $dept department: " . "$depts{$dept}.\n";
    }
    $header .=
        '; total number of hosts: ' . scalar( keys %entries ) . "\n;\n\n";

    $header .= <<"EOH";

@ IN SOA   dns.oog.org. hostmaster.oog.org. (
                        $serial ; serial
                        10800    ; refresh
                        3600     ; retry
                        604800   ; expire
                        43200)   ; TTL

@                       IN  NS  dns.oog.org.

EOH

    return $header;
}
```

Our code attempts to read in the previous DNS configuration file to determine the last serial number in use. This number then gets split into date and counter fields. If the date we've read is the same as the current date, we need to increment the counter. If not, we create a serial number based on the current date with a counter value of 00.

Once we have our serial number, the rest of the code concerns itself with writing out a pretty header in the proper form.

Generating multiple configuration files

Now that we've covered the process of writing a correct header for our DNS configuration files, there is one more complication we need to address. A well-configured DNS server has both forward (name-to-IP address) and reverse (IP address-to-name) mapping information available for every domain, or zone, it controls. Thus, two configuration files are required per zone. The best way to keep these synchronized is to create them both at the same time.

This is the last file-generation script we'll see in this chapter, so let's put together everything we've done so far. Our script will take a simple database file and generate the necessary DNS zone configuration files.

To keep this script simple, I've made a few assumptions about the data, the most important of which has to do with the topology of the network and namespace. This script assumes that the network consists of a single class-C subnet with a single DNS zone. As a result, we only create a single forward mapping file and its reverse mapping sibling file. Code to handle multiple subnets and zones (with separate files for each) would be a worthwhile addition.

Here's a quick walkthrough of what we'll do in this code:

1. Read the database file into a hash of hashes, checking the data as we go.
2. Generate a header.
3. Write out the forward mapping (name-to-IP address) file and check it into RCS.
4. Write out the reverse mapping (IP address-to-name) file and check it into RCS.

Here is the code and its output:

```
use Rcs;

my $datafile    = 'database';      # our host database
my $outputfile  = "zone.$$";       # our temporary output file
my $target      = 'zone.db';       # our target output
my $revtarget   = 'rev.db';        # our target output for the reverse mapping
my $defzone     = '.oog.org';      # the default zone being created
my $rcsbin      = '/usr/local/bin'; # location of our RCS binaries
my $recordsep   = "-=-\n";

# get today's date in the form YYYYMMDD
my @localtime = localtime;
my $today     = sprintf( "%04d%02d%02d",
    $localtime[5] + 1900,
    $localtime[4] + 1,
    $localtime[3] );

# get username on either Windows or Unix
my $user =
```

```perl
    ( $^O eq 'MSWin32' )
    ? $ENV{USERNAME}
    : ( getpwuid($<) )[6] . ' (' . ( getpwuid($<) )[0] . ')';

# read in the database file
open my $DATAFILE, '<', "$datafile" or die "Unable to open datafile:$!\n";

my %addrs;
my %entries;
{
    local $/ = $recordsep;    # read in the database file one record at a time

    while (<$DATAFILE>) {
        chomp;                    # remove the record separator
                                  # split into key1,value1
        my @record = split /:\s*|\n/;

        my $record = {};          # create a reference to empty hash
        %{$record} = @record;     # populate that hash with @record

        # check for bad hostname
        if ( $record->{name} =~ /[^-.a-zA-Z0-9]/ ) {
            warn '!!!! '
              . $record->{name}
              . " has illegal host name characters, skipping...\n";
            next;
        }

        # check for bad aliases
        if ( $record->{aliases} =~ /[^-.a-zA-Z0-9\s]/ ) {
            warn '!!!! '
              . $record->{name}
              . " has illegal alias name characters, skipping...\n";
            next;
        }

        # check for missing address
        if ( !$record->{address} ) {
            warn '!!!! '
              . $record->{name}
              . " does not have an IP address, skipping...\n";
            next;
        }

        # check for duplicate address
        if ( defined $addrs{ $record->{address} } ) {
            warn '!!!! Duplicate IP addr:'
              . $record->{name} . ' & '
              . $addrs{ $record->{address} }
              . ", skipping...\n";
            next;
        }
        else {
            $addrs{ $record->{address} } = $record->{name};
        }
```

```perl
        $entries{ $record->{name} } = $record;      # add this to a hash of hashes
    }
    close $DATAFILE;
}

my $header = GenerateHeader();

# create the forward mapping file
open my $OUTPUT, '>', "$outputfile"
  or die "Unable to write to $outputfile:$!\n";
print $OUTPUT $header;

foreach my $entry ( sort byaddress keys %entries ) {
    print $OUTPUT "; Owned by ", $entries{$entry}->{owner}, ' (',
      $entries{$entry}->{department}, "): ", $entries{$entry}->{building}, '/',
      $entries{$entry}->{room}, "\n";

    # print A record
    printf $OUTPUT "%-20s\tIN A      %s\n", $entries{$entry}->{name},
      $entries{$entry}->{address};

    # print any CNAMES (aliases)
    if ( defined $entries{$entry}->{aliases} ) {
        foreach my $alias ( split( ' ', $entries{$entry}->{aliases} ) ) {
            printf $OUTPUT "%-20s\tIN CNAME %s\n", $alias,
                $entries{$entry}->{name};
        }
    }
    print $OUTPUT "\n";
}

close $OUTPUT;

Rcs->bindir($rcsbin);
my $rcsobj = Rcs->new;
$rcsobj->file($target);
$rcsobj->co('-l');
rename( $outputfile, $target )
  or die "Unable to rename $outputfile to $target:$!\n";
$rcsobj->ci( '-u', '-m' . "Converted by $user on " . scalar(localtime) );

# now create the reverse mapping file
open my $OUTPUT, '>', "$outputfile"
  or die "Unable to write to $outputfile:$!\n";
print $OUTPUT $header;
foreach my $entry ( sort byaddress keys %entries ) {
    print $OUTPUT '; Owned by ', $entries{$entry}->{owner}, ' (',
      $entries{$entry}->{department}, '): ', $entries{$entry}->{building}, '/',
      $entries{$entry}->{room}, "\n";

    # this uses the default zone we defined at the start of the script
    printf $OUTPUT "%-3d\tIN PTR      %s$defzone.\n\n",
      ( split /\./, $entries{$entry}->{address} )[3], $entries{$entry}->{name};
```

```perl
}

close $OUTPUT;
$rcsobj->file($revtarget);
$rcsobj->co('-l');      # assumes target has been checked out at least once
rename( $outputfile, $revtarget )
    or die "Unable to rename $outputfile to $revtarget:$!\n";
$rcsobj->ci( "-u", "-m" . "Converted by $user on " . scalar(localtime) );

sub GenerateHeader {
    my ( $olddate, $count );

    # open old file if possible and read in serial number
    # (assumes the format of the old file)
    if ( open( my $OLDZONE, '<', $target ) ) {
        while (<$OLDZONE>) {
            last if ( $olddate, $count ) = /(\d{8})(\d{2}).*serial/;
        }
        close $OLDZONE;
    }

    # If $count is defined, we did find an old serial number.
    # If the old serial number was for today, increment last 2 digits;
    # else start a new number for today.
    my $count = ( defined $count and $olddate eq $today ) ? $count + 1 : 0;
    my $serial = sprintf( "%8d%02d", $today, $count );

    # begin the header
    my $header = "; dns zone file - GENERATED BY $0\n";
    $header .= "; DO NOT EDIT BY HAND!\n;\n";
    $header .= "; Converted by $user on " . scalar( (localtime) ) . "\n;\n";

    # count the number of entries in each department and then report
    my %depts;
    foreach my $entry ( keys %entries ) {
        $depts{ $entries{$entry}->{department} }++;
    }
    foreach my $dept ( keys %depts ) {
        $header .=
          "; number of hosts in the $dept department: " . "$depts{$dept}.\n";
    }
    $header .=
      '; total number of hosts: ' . scalar( keys %entries ) . "\n;\n\n";

    $header .= <<"EOH";

@ IN SOA   dns.oog.org. hostmaster.oog.org. (
                            $serial ; serial
                            10800    ; refresh
                            3600     ; retry
                            604800   ; expire
                            43200)   ; TTL

@                           IN  NS dns.oog.org.
```

```
EOH

    return $header;
}

sub byaddress {
    my @a = split( /\./, $entries{$a}->{address} );
    my @b = split( /\./, $entries{$b}->{address} );
        ( $a[0] <=> $b[0] )
     || ( $a[1] <=> $b[1] )
     || ( $a[2] <=> $b[2] )
     || ( $a[3] <=> $b[3] );
}
```

Here's the forward mapping file (*zone.db*) that gets created:

```
; dns zone file - GENERATED BY createdns
; DO NOT EDIT BY HAND!
;
; Converted by David N. Blank-Edelman (dnb); on Fri May 29 15:46:46 2007
;
; number of hosts in the design department: 1.
; number of hosts in the softwaredepartment: 1.
; number of hosts in the IT department: 2.
; total number of hosts: 4
;

@ IN SOA   dns.oog.org. hostmaster.oog.org. (
                            2007052900 ; serial
                              10800    ; refresh
                              3600     ; retry
                              604800   ; expire
                              43200)   ; TTL


@                           IN  NS  dns.oog.org.

; Owned by Cindy Coltrane (marketing): west/143
bendir              IN A     192.168.1.3
ben                 IN CNAME bendir
bendoodles          IN CNAME bendir

; Owned by David Davis (software): main/909
shimmer             IN A     192.168.1.11
shim                IN CNAME shimmer
shimmy              IN CNAME shimmer
shimmydoodles       IN CNAME shimmer

; Owned by Ellen Monk (design): main/1116
sulawesi            IN A     192.168.1.12
sula                IN CNAME sulawesi
su-lee              IN CNAME sulawesi

; Owned by Alex Rollins (IT): main/1101
sander              IN A     192.168.1.55
sandy               IN CNAME sander
```

```
micky                    IN CNAME sander
mickydoo                 IN CNAME sander
```

And here's the reverse mapping file (*rev.db*):

```
; dns zone file - GENERATED BY createdns
; DO NOT EDIT BY HAND!
;
; Converted by David N. Blank-Edelman (dnb); on Fri May 29 15:46:46 2007
;
; number of hosts in the design department: 1.
; number of hosts in the softwaredepartment: 1.
; number of hosts in the IT department: 2.
; total number of hosts: 4
;

@ IN SOA   dns.oog.org. hostmaster.oog.org. (
                       2007052900 ; serial
                          10800    ; refresh
                          3600     ; retry
                          604800   ; expire
                          43200)   ; TTL

@                              IN   NS  dns.oog.org.

; Owned by Cindy Coltrane (marketing): west/143
3   IN PTR    bendir.oog.org.

; Owned by David Davis (software): main/909
11  IN PTR    shimmer.oog.org.

; Owned by Ellen Monk (design): main/1116
12  IN PTR    sulawesi.oog.org.

; Owned by Alex Rollins (IT): main/1101
55  IN PTR    sander.oog.org.
```

This method of creating files opens up many more possibilities. Up to now, we've generated files using content from a single text-file database. We read a record from the database and wrote it out to our file, perhaps with a dash of nice formatting. Only data that appeared in the database found its way into the files we created.

Sometimes, however, it is useful to have the script itself add content during the conversion process. For instance, in the case of DNS configuration file generation, you may wish to embellish the conversion script so it inserts MX (Mail eXchange) records pointing to a central mail server for every host in your database. A trivial code change from:

```
# print A record
printf $OUTPUT "%-20s\tIN A      %s\n",
    $entries{$entry}->{name},$entries{$entry}->{address};
```

to:

```
# print A record
printf $OUTPUT "%-20s\tIN A      %s\n",
    $entries{$entry}->{name},$entries{$entry}->{address};
```

```
# print MX record
print $OUTPUT "                           IN MX 10 $mailserver\n";
```

will configure DNS so that mail destined for any host in the domain is received by the machine $mailserver instead. If that machine is configured to handle mail for its domain, you've activated a really useful infrastructure component (i.e., centralized mail handling) with just a single line of Perl code.

DNS Checking: An Iterative Approach

We've spent considerable time in this chapter on the creation of the configuration information to be served by network name services, but that's only one side of the coin for system and network administrators. Keeping a network healthy also entails checking these services once they're up and running to make sure they are behaving in a correct and consistent manner.

For instance, for a system/network administrator, a great deal rides on the question, "Are all of my DNS servers up?" In a troubleshooting situation, it's equally valuable to ask yourself "Are they all serving the same information?" or, more specifically, "Are the servers responding to the same queries with the same responses? Are they in sync as intended?" We'll put these questions to good use in this section.

In Chapter 2 we saw an example of the Perl motto "There's more than one way to do it" in action. Perl's TMTOWTDI-ness makes it an excellent prototype language in which to do "iterative development." Iterative development is one way of describing the evolutionary process that takes place when writing system administration (and other) programs to handle particular tasks. With Perl, it's all too easy to bang out a quick-and-dirty hack that gets a job done. Later, you may return to that script and rewrite it so it's more elegant. There's even likely to be yet a third iteration of the same code, this time taking a different approach to solving the problem.

In this section, we'll look at three different approaches to the same problem of DNS consistency checking. These approaches will be presented in the order you might realistically follow while trying to solve the problem and refine your solution. This ordering reflects one view on how a solution to a problem can evolve in Perl; your take on this may differ. The third approach, using the Net::DNS module, is probably the easiest and most error-proof of the bunch, but Net::DNS may not address every situation, so we're going to walk through some "roll your own" approaches first. Be sure to note the pros and cons listed after each solution has been presented.

Here's the task: write a Perl script that takes a hostname and checks a list of DNS servers to see if they all return the same information when queried about this host. To make this task simpler, we're going to assume that the host has a single, static IP address (i.e., does not have multiple interfaces or addresses associated with it).

Before we look at each approach in turn, let me show you the "driver" code we're going to use:

```perl
use Data::Dumper;

my $hostname = $ARGV[0];
my @servers = qw(nameserver1 nameserver2 nameserver3); # name servers

my %results;
foreach my $server (@servers) {
    $results{$server}
        = LookupAddress( $hostname, $server );    # populates %results
}

my %inv = reverse %results;    # invert the result hash
if (scalar keys %inv > 1) {    # see how many elements it has
    print "There is a discrepancy between DNS servers:\n";
    print Data::Dumper->Dump( [ \%results ], ['results'] ), "\n";
}
```

For each of the DNS servers listed in the @servers list, we call the LookupAddress() subroutine. LookupAddress() queries a specific DNS server for the IP address of a given hostname and returns the result so it can be stored in a hash called %results. Each DNS server has a key in %results with the IP address returned by that server as its value.

There are many ways to determine if all of the values in %results are the same (i.e., if all the DNS servers returned the same thing in response to our query). Here, we choose to invert %results into another hash table, making all of the keys into values, and vice versa. If all values in %results are the same, there should be exactly one key in the inverted hash. If not, we know we've got a situation on our hands, so we call Data::Dumper->Dump() to nicely display the contents of %results for the system administrator to puzzle over.

Here's a sample of what the output looks like when something goes wrong:

```
There is a discrepancy between DNS servers:
$results = {
            nameserver1 => '192.168.1.2',
            nameserver2 => '192.168.1.5',
            nameserver3 => '192.168.1.2',
          };
```

Let's take a look at the contestants for the LookupAddress() subroutine.

Using nslookup

If your background is in Unix, or you've done some programming in other scripting languages besides Perl, your first attempt might look a great deal like a shell script. An external program called from the Perl script does the hard work in the following code:

```perl
use Data::Dumper;

my $hostname = $ARGV[0];
```

```perl
my @servers  = qw(nameserver1 nameserver2 nameserver3 nameserver4);

my $nslookup = '/usr/bin/nslookup';

my %results;
foreach my $server (@servers) {
    $results{$server}
        = LookupAddress( $hostname, $server );    # populates %results
}

my %inv = reverse %results;      # invert the result hash
if ( scalar keys %inv > 1 ) {    # see how many elements it has
    print "There is a discrepency between DNS servers:\n";
    print Data::Dumper->Dump( [ \%results ], ['results'] ), "\n";
}

sub LookupAddress {
    my ( $hostname, $server ) = @_;
    my @results;

    open my $NSLOOK, '-|', "$nslookup $hostname $server"
        or die "Unable to start nslookup:$!\n";

    while (<$NSLOOK>) {
        next until (/^Name:/);           # ignore until we hit "Name: "
        chomp( $result = <$NSLOOK> );    # next line is Address: response
        $result =~ s/Address(es)?:\s+//; # remove the label
        push( @results, $result );
    }
    close $NSLOOK;
    return join( ', ', sort @results );
}
```

The benefits of this approach are:

- It's a short, quick program to write (perhaps even translated line by line from a real shell script).

- We didn't have to write any messy network code.

- It takes the Unix approach of using a general-purpose language to glue together other smaller, specialized programs to get a job done, rather than creating a single monolithic program.

- It may be the only approach for times when you can't code the client/server communication in Perl; for instance, when you have to talk with a server that requires a special client and there's no alternative.

The drawbacks of this approach are:

- It's dependent on another program outside the script. What if this program is not available, or its output format changes?

- It's slower, because it has to start up another process each time it wants to make a query. We could reduce this overhead by opening a two-way pipe to an *nslookup* process that stays running while we need it. This would take a little more coding skill, but it would be the right thing to do if we were going to continue down this path and further enhance this code.

- We have less control. We're at the external program's mercy for implementation details. For instance, here *nslookup* (more specifically, the resolver library *nslookup* is using) is handling server timeouts, query retries, and appending a domain search list for us.

Working with raw network sockets

If you are a "power sysadmin," you may decide calling another program is not acceptable. You might want to implement the DNS queries using nothing but Perl. This entails constructing network packets by hand, shipping them out on the wire, and then parsing the results returned from the server.

The code in this section is probably the most complicated code you'll find in this entire book; it was written by looking at the reference sources described later, along with several examples of existing networking code (including the module by Michael Fuhr/ Olaf Kolkman described in the next section). Here is a rough overview of what is going on in this approach: we query a DNS server by constructing a specific network packet header and packet contents, sending the packet to a DNS server, and then receiving and parsing the response from that server.[†]

Each and every DNS packet (of the sort we are interested in) can have up to five distinct sections:

Header
Contains flags and counters pertaining to the query or answer (always present).

Question
Contains the question being asked of the server (present for a query and echoed in a response).

Answer
Contains all the data for the answer to a DNS query (present in a DNS response packet).

Authority
Contains information on the location from which an authoritative response may be retrieved.

[†] For the nitty-gritty details, I highly recommend that you open RFC 1035 to the section entitled "Messages" and read along.

Additional

Contains any information the server wishes to return in addition to the direct answer to a query.

Our program will concern itself strictly with the first three of these sections. We'll be
using a set of pack() commands to create the necessary data structure for a DNS packet
header and packet contents. We'll pass this data structure to the IO::Socket module
that handles sending this data out as a packet. The same module will also listen for a
response on our behalf and return data for us to parse (using unpack()). Conceptually,
this process is not very difficult.

There's one twist to this process that should be noted before we look at the code. RFC
1035‡ (Section 4.1.4) defines two ways of representing domain names in DNS packets:
uncompressed and compressed. The uncompressed representation places the full domain name (for example, *host.oog.org*) in the packet, and is nothing special. However,
if the same domain name is found more than once in a packet, it is likely that a compressed representation will be used for all but the first mention. A compressed representation replaces the domain information (or part of it) with a two-byte pointer back
to the first uncompressed representation. This allows a packet to mention *host1*,
host2, and *host3* in *longsubdomain.longsubdomain.oog.org*, without having to include
the bytes for *longsubdomain.longsubdomain.oog.org* each time. We have to handle both
representations in our code, hence the decompress() routine.

Without further fanfare, here's the code:

```
use IO::Socket;
use Data::Dumper;

my $hostname = $ARGV[0];
my @servers = qw(nameserver1 nameserver2 nameserver3); # name of the name servers
my $defdomain = '.oog.org';      # default domain if not present

my %results;
foreach my $server (@servers) {
    $results{$server}
        = LookupAddress( $hostname, $server );    # populates %results
}

my %inv = reverse %results;                        # invert the result hash
if ( scalar keys %inv > 1 ) {    # see how many elements it has
    print "There is a discrepency between DNS servers:\n";
    print Data::Dumper->Dump( [ \%results ], ['results'] ), "\n";
}

sub LookupAddress {
    my ( $hostname, $server ) = @_;
    my $id = 0;
    my ( $lformat, @labels, $count, $buf );
```

‡ RFC 1035 has been updated by RFC 1101, but not in a way that impacts this discussion.

```perl
###
### Construct the packet header
###
my $header = pack(
    'n C2 n4',
    ++$id,      # query id
    1,          # qr, opcode, aa, tc, rd fields (only rd set)
    0,          # ra, z, rcode
    1,          # one question (qdcount)
    0,          # no answers (ancount)
    0,          # no ns records in authority section (nscount)
    0
);              # no additional rr's (arcount)

# if we do not have any separators in the name of the host,
# append the default domain
if ( index( $hostname, '.' ) == -1 ) {
    $hostname .= $defdomain;
}

# construct the qname section of a packet (domain name in question)
for ( split( /\./, $hostname ) ) {
    $lformat .= 'C a* ';
    $labels[ $count++ ] = length;
    $labels[ $count++ ] = $_;
}

###
### construct the packet question section
###
my $question = pack(
    $lformat . 'C n2',
    @labels,
    0,      # end of labels
    1,      # qtype of A
    1
);          # qclass of IN

###
### send the packet to the server and read the response
###
my $sock = new IO::Socket::INET(
    PeerAddr => $server,
    PeerPort => 'domain',
    Proto    => 'udp'
);

$sock->send( $header . $question );

# we know the max packet size
$sock->recv( $buf, 512 );
close($sock);

###
### unpack the header section
```

```
    ###
    my ( $id, $qr_opcode_aa_tc_rd, $ra_z_rcode, $qdcount, $ancount, $nscount,
        $arcount )
        = unpack( 'n C2 n4', $buf );

    if ( !$ancount ) {
        warn "Unable to lookup data for $hostname from $server!\n";
        return;
    }

    ###
    ### unpack the question section
    ###
    # question section starts 12 bytes in
    my ( $position, $qname ) = decompress( $buf, 12 );
    my ( $qtype, $qclass ) = unpack( '@' . $position . 'n2', $buf );

    # move us forward in the packet to end of question section
    $position += 4;

    ###
    ### unpack all of the resource record sections
    ###
    my ( $rtype, $rclass, $rttl, $rdlength, $rname, @results );
    for ( ; $ancount; $ancount-- ) {
        ( $position, $rname ) = decompress( $buf, $position );
        ( $rtype, $rclass, $rttl, $rdlength )
            = unpack( '@' . $position . 'n2 N n', $buf );
        $position += 10;

        # this next line could be changed to use a more sophisticated
        # data structure - it currently concatenates all of the answers
        push( @results,
            join( '.', unpack( '@' . $position . 'C' . $rdlength, $buf ) ) );
        $position += $rdlength;
    }

    # we sort results to deal with round-robin DNS responses
    #
    # we probably should use a custom sort routine to sort
    # them semantically, but in this case we're just looking for
    # the presence of different results from each DNS server
    return join( ', ', sort @results );
}

# handle domain information that is "compressed" as per RFC 1035
#
# we take in the starting position of our packet parse and return
# the place in the packet we left off at the end of the domain name
# (after dealing with the compressed format pointer) and the name we found
sub decompress {
    my ( $buf, $start ) = @_;
    my ( $domain, $i, $lenoct );
```

```
# get the size of the response, since we're going to have to keep track of
# where we are in that data
my $respsize = length($buf);

for ( $i = $start; $i <= $respsize; ) {
    $lenoct = unpack( '@' . $i . 'C', $buf );      # get length of label

    if ( !$lenoct ) {    # 0 signals we are done with this section
        $i++;
        last;
    }

    if ( $lenoct == 192 ) {    # we've been handed a pointer, so recurse
        $domain .= (
            decompress(
                $buf, ( unpack( '@' . $i . 'n', $buf ) & 1023 )
            )
        )[1];
        $i += 2;
        last;
    }
    else {                          # otherwise, we have a plain label
        $domain .= unpack( '@' . ++$i . 'a' . $lenoct, $buf ) . '.';
        $i += $lenoct;
    }
}
return ( $i, $domain );
}
```

Note that this code is not precisely equivalent to that from the previous example, because we're not trying to emulate all of the nuances of *nslookup*'s behavior (timeouts,
retries, searchlists, etc.). When looking at the three approaches discussed here, be sure
to keep a critical eye out for these subtle differences.

The benefits of this approach are:

- It isn't dependent on any other programs. You don't need to know the particulars
  of another programmer's work.
- It may be as fast as or faster than calling an external program.
- It is easier to tweak the parameters of the situation (timeouts, etc.).

The drawbacks of this approach are:

- It's likely to take longer to write and is more complex than the previous approach.
- It requires more knowledge external to the direct problem at hand (i.e., you may
  have to learn how to put together DNS packets by hand, something we did not
  need to know when we called nslookup).
- Our code does not deal with truncated DNS replies (if the reply is too large, most
  implementations fail over to giving a TCP response).

- You may have to handle OS-specific issues yourself (these are hidden in the previous approach by the work already done by the external program's author).

Using Net::DNS

As mentioned in Chapter 1, one of Perl's real strengths is the support of a large community of developers who churn out code for others to reuse. If there's something you need to do in Perl that seems universal, chances are good that someone else has already written a module to handle it. In our case, we can make use of Michael Fuhr's excellent **Net::DNS** module (now maintained by Olaf Kolkman) to make our job simpler. For this task, we simply have to create a new DNS resolver object, configure it with the name of the DNS server we wish to use, ask it to send a query, and then use the supplied methods to parse the response:

```
use Net::DNS;

my $hostname = $ARGV[0];

my @servers  = qw(nameserver1 nameserver2 nameserver3 nameserver4);

my %results;
foreach my $server (@servers) {
    $results{$server}
        = LookupAddress( $hostname, $server );    # populates %results
}

my %inv = reverse %results;                        # invert the result hash
if ( scalar keys %inv > 1 ) {      # see how many elements it has
    print "There is a discrepency between DNS servers:\n";
    use Data::Dumper;
    print Data::Dumper->Dump( [ \%results ], ['results'] ), "\n";
}

# only slightly modified from the example in the Net::DNS manpage
sub LookupAddress {
    my ( $hostname, $server ) = @_;

    my $res = new Net::DNS::Resolver;

    $res->nameservers($server);

    my $packet = $res->query($hostname);

    if ( !$packet ) {
        warn "Unable to lookup data for $hostname from $server!\n";
        return;
    }
    my (@results);
    foreach my $rr ( $packet->answer ) {
        push( @results, $rr->address );
    }
    return join( ', ', sort @results );
}
```

The benefits of this approach are:

- The code is legible.
- It is often faster to write.
- Depending on how the module you use is implemented (is it pure Perl or is it glue to a set of C or C++ library calls?), the code you write using this module may be just as fast as calling an external compiled program.
- It is potentially portable, depending on how much work the author of the module has done for you. Any place this module can be installed, your program can run.
- As in the first approach we looked at, writing code can be quick and easy if someone else has done the behind-the-scenes work for you. You don't have to know how the module works; you just need to know how to use it.
- Code reuse. You are not reinventing the wheel each time.

The drawbacks of this approach are:

- You're back in the dependency game. You need to make sure the module will be available for your program to run, and you need to trust that the module writer has done a decent job.
- If there is a bug in the module and the original author goes missing, you may wind up becoming the maintainer of the module.
- There may not be a module to do what you need, or it may not run on your operating system of choice.

More often than not, using a prewritten module is my preferred approach. However, any of the approaches discussed here will get the job done. TMTOWTDI, so go forth and do it!

DHCP

The Dynamic Host Configuration Protocol isn't a TCP/IP name service, but it is enough of a kissing cousin that it belongs in this chapter next to DNS. DNS lets us find the IP address associated with a hostname (or hostname associated with an IP address, in the case of a reverse lookup). DHCP lets a machine dynamically retrieve its network configuration information (including its IP address) given its Ethernet address. It is a more general and robust successor to the BOOTP and RARP protocols that used to serve a similar purpose in a more limited way.

I glossed over the complex parts of how DNS works in the previous section,* but I'm not going to be able to hand wave past the slightly more involved interaction that takes

---

* For example, we won't talk about zone transfers, non-ASCII names, or even what happens if the answer to a question can't fit in a single UDP packet. Paul Vixie wrote an excellent article on this topic for the April 2007 issue of *ACM Queue* magazine called "DNS Complexity." It's well worth a read.

place between a DHCP server and a DHCP client. Let's get that out of the way right now, before we even think about bringing Perl into the picture.

In the previous section, we could pretty much say, "DNS client asks a DNS server a question and gets an answer. Done." The worst-case scenario for the sort of queries we did might have been "DNS client asks a question, gets an answer, then has to ask another server the same question." The DHCP dance is more interesting. Here's roughly the conversation that goes on:

> **DHCP Client (to everyone):** Hey, is anyone out there? I need an address and some other configuration information.
> **DHCP Server directly to DHCP Client:** Request acknowledged by server at IP address {blah}. I can let you use the following IP address and other information: {blah, blah, blah}.
> **DHCP Client (to everyone):** OK, I'd like to use the IP address and other information that the server at IP address {blah} offered.
> **DHCP Server to DHCP Client:** OK, acknowledged. You are welcome to use that configuration for {some amount of time}.
> [half that amount of time passes]
> **DHCP Client to Server:** Hi, I'm using this IP address and configuration information: <blah, blah>. Can I continue to use it?
> **DHCP Server to Client:** OK, acknowledged. You are welcome to use that configuration for {some amount of time}.
> [client prepares to leave the network]
> **(optionally) DHCP Client to Server:** OK, done with this IP address and configuration.

There are a few variations on this conversation. For example, a client can remember its last address and lease duration (the amount of time the server said it could use the information) and ask to use it again in a broadcasted version of the third step. In that case, the server can quickly acknowledge the request, and the client is off and running with its previous address. Other variations occur when either the server or the client isn't in as sunny a mood as in the example conversation. Sometimes either side will decline a request or an offer, and then a new negotiation round occurs. For all of the gripping details, you should read the clearly written DHCP RFC (2131 as of this writing) or the *The DHCP Handbook* mentioned at the end of this chapter.

The interaction between a DHCP server and a DCHP client differs from our previous name server examples in a number of ways. Besides the number of steps, we also see the signs of:

- A negotiated handshake. The server and client have to agree that they are going to talk to each other and then agree on the configuration the client will use. Both sides need to let each other know that they agree.

- Persistent state. Once the handshake has taken place, the server keeps track of the agreement for the duration of the server-specified time (the client's lease). Halfway into the lease, the client will (under most circumstances) attempt to renew it.

 Of the protocols mentioned in this chapter, only WINS has a similar notion. Clients register with a WINS server and are required to re-register periodically so the server can maintain correct mapping information for them. DHCP is used for more than just name-to-address mapping and the rules of interaction are a little different, but DHCP and WINS are pretty similar in this regard.

These two factors make our decisions around the programming of DHCP scripts a little more interesting. Most of these decisions come down to questions of how "nice" or compliant we want our scripts to be.

Let's look at two example tasks so you can see what I mean.

Active Probing for Rogue DHCP Servers

In Chapter 13 we will work on a passive detector for rogue (i.e., unofficial/unwanted) DCHP servers using network sniffing. We'll construct something similar here, using a more active approach. The key to this approach is the first part of the sample DHCP conversation outlined previously. The first step for a client that wishes to obtain configuration information is a "hey, anybody out there?" broadcast. Any DHCP server that can hear this request is supposed to respond with a DHCP offer for the information it is configured to provide.

 Before we go much further with this example, I have to jump in with a qualification about servers being "supposed to respond" with certain information. DHCP servers—at least the good ones—are highly configurable. They can be told to respond to broadcasts only from known Ethernet addresses, network subnets, vendor classes (more on those later), and so on. All other requests are ignored, with maybe just a note left in the log file.

The code we're about to see is designed to catch servers that *aren't* configured properly. We're looking for the servers that will answer requests indiscriminately (because after all, they are the ones that can cause the most trouble). These are the rogue servers likely to still have bad default settings.

Though this code is probably too blunt to catch more subtle configuration errors, you could certainly sharpen it so it could find the more specific problems in almost-properly-configured severs as well.

For this task we're just interested in *who* answers our broadcast. We mostly don't care what they say, though that information can be helpful when tracking down the host in question. I mention this because some of the information we may send (like a fake Ethernet address) will obviously be bogus.

Given how little we care about the contents of the query we make or the response we receive, you can probably guess that we're going to be equally laissez-faire about having the script comply with the rest of the DHCP protocol. We're not going to bother to continue negotiating for a lease with the server that responds, because we don't need one. All we want to do is provoke a response from any server willing to talk to us. As a side goal, we're also going to attempt to avoid gumming any legitimate DHCP servers we run, because denial of service (DOS) attacks are seldom a good idea.

Now let's get to the code. The code we need is quick to write, thanks to the Net::DHCP::Packet module by Stephan Hadinger. This module lets us construct and deconstruct DHCP packets using an easy OOP syntax. We'll also be using the IO::Socket::INET module by Graham Barr to make the UDP sending and receiving code simpler (with one gotcha that I'll point out later). Here's our code, with explication to follow:

```
use IO::Socket::INET;
use Net::DHCP::Packet;
use Net::DHCP::Constants;

my $br_addr = sockaddr_in( '67', inet_aton('255.255.255.255') );
my $xid     = int( rand(0xFFFFFFFF) );
my $chaddr  = '0016cbb7c882';

my $socket = IO::Socket::INET->new(
    Proto     => 'udp',
    Broadcast => 1,
    LocalPort => '68',
) or die "Can't create socket: $@\n";

my $discover_packet = Net::DHCP::Packet->new(
    Xid                           => $xid,
    Chaddr                        => $chaddr,
    Flags                         => 0x8000,
    DHO_DHCP_MESSAGE_TYPE()       => DHCPDISCOVER(),
    DHO_HOST_NAME()               => 'Perl Test Client',
    DHO_VENDOR_CLASS_IDENTIFIER() => 'perl',

);

$socket->send( $discover_packet->serialize(), 0, $br_addr )
    or die "Error sending:$!\n";

my $buf = '';
$socket->recv( $buf, 4096 ) or die "recvfrom() failed:$!";
my $resp = new Net::DHCP::Packet($buf);
```

```
print "Received response from: " . $socket->peerhost() . "\n";
print "Details:\n" . $resp->toString();

close($socket);
```

Let's take a quick walk through the code. We start by defining the destination for our packets (a broadcast address†), and a couple of other constants I'll mention in a moment. We then create the socket we'll be using to send and receive packets. This socket definition specifies the protocol, the source port, and a request to set the broadcast flag on that socket. You'll note that it doesn't specify the destination for the packets ($br_addr) defined earlier in the constructor. You can't use connect() to receive a broadcast response, as detailed in the sidebar "Thank You, Lincoln Stein (Listening to Broadcasts Using IO::Socket)", so this is broken out as a separate step. You should also note that, thanks to the source and destination port numbers in the code, we're going to have to run our DHCP examples with some sort of administrative privileges (e.g., via sudo on Unix/Mac OS X). If we don't, we're in for the Permission Denied blues.

Thank You, Lincoln Stein (Listening to Broadcasts Using IO::Socket)

When writing this example, I spent a good part of a day banging my head against a particular problem. For the life of me, I couldn't get IO::Socket::INET to let me send to a broadcast address and then listen to the responses using the same socket, even though I knew this was possible. I had code that could listen for packets and code that could send broadcasts (as verified by Wireshark, a network sniffer), but I couldn't get the pieces to play nicely together.

In desperation, I did two things: I re-read the appropriate sections of Stein's excellent book *Network Programming with Perl* (Addison-Wesley) and traced the IO::Socket::INET module's operations in a debugger really carefully. In Stein's book, I found this paragraph about the connect() call being used for UDP sockets (p. 532):

> A nice side effect of connecting a datagram socket is that such a socket can receive messages only from the designated peer. Messages sent to the socket from other hosts or from other ports on the peer host are ignored.... Servers that typically must receive messages to multiple clients should generally *not* connect their sockets.

My trace of IO::Socket::INET showed that it indeed did connect() its socket if a remote address was specified (i.e., using the PeerAddr argument in the new() call), even if the remote address was the 255.255.255.255 broadcast address. That connected socket refused to listen to packets from any other host.

The code presented in this section intentionally does not specify PeerAddr when it wants to listen to responses to broadcasted packets, even though it seems like the obvious

---

† Eagle-eyed network administrators will note that we're wimping out here by sending to the "all-ones" broadcast address rather than the one specific to our subnet. Figuring out that address would add a bit of distraction in this example. There are a number of modules (such as NetAddr::IP, Net::Interface, and IO::Interface) that can help if you want to be more accurate in your target.

approach. My thanks to Lincoln Stein's book for helping me figure this out before I went batty.

Once we have the socket to be used for transiting data, it's time to bake some packets. The next line constructs a DHCP packet to our specification. Let's look at each flag in that constructor call, because they're all pretty important for understanding how things work:

Xid

> This is the transaction ID for the discussion we're about to have. The client picks a random ID for both it and the server to include in each packet being sent. This lets them both know that they are both referring to the same conversation.

Chaddr

> This is the *client hardware address* (i.e., Ethernet or MAC address). In this example I've done the simple but potentially dangerous thing of taking my laptop's Ethernet address and incrementing some of the digits. It would probably be better to either use a known idle address (like that broken Ethernet card you have sitting on your shelf) or determine the current address of your machine (assuming it isn't using DHCP at the moment).‡

Flags

> The DHCP specification allows you to set a flag to request that the response to the packet you're sending be sent as a broadcast (as opposed to a unicast reply) as well. In this case we're asking all servers that reply to do so using a broadcast response just to be safe.

DHO_DHCP_MESSAGE_TYPE

> This option sets the type of DHCP packet being sent. Here's where we say we're sending out the initial DHCP DISCOVER packet.

DHO_HOST_NAME

> Though not necessary for this particular task, this option lets our client self-identify using a name of our choice. Using this option can help make network sniffer traces easier to follow (because we can clearly identify our packets). Later, in a more complex example, we'll actually reserve a lease. In that case, it will be handy when we look at the lease database of a server (e.g., in a wireless router). It's much easier to tell which client is yours in the list if the client has supplied a recognizable name.

DHO_VENDOR_CLASS_IDENTIFIER

> Another optional flag that isn't strictly necessary, the vendor class is a concept detailed in the DHCP RFC that can help make server configuration easier. It allows

---

‡ This ostensibly simple task isn't as easy as it sounds. There is no truly portable way to get the Ethernet address of an interface on your machine. The closest you can come is using a module like Net::Address::Ethernet or Net::Ifconfig::Wrapper (which basically call *ifconfig* or *ipconfig* for you), IO::Interface::Simple (which attempts to use some of the system libraries to find the information), or even Net::SNMP::Interfaces pointed at the local host. None of these solutions works all of the time, so caveat implementor.

you to break up your network devices into different vendor classes for the purpose of assigning configurations. For example, you might want all of your Windows machines to receive a configuration that points them to your Windows Server 2003 DNS servers. If you assign them all to the same vendor class, the better DHCP servers will allow you to apply configuration directives to that set.

If specifying a DHCP packet is easy thanks to `Net::DHCP::Packet`, actually sending it is even easier. In the next line of code, we just call `send()` on a massaged (serialized) version of that packet and send it to the broadcast address and port previously defined. The middle argument of the `send()` call is for optional flags—we set it to `0`, which means we'll take the defaults.

Immediately after sending the packet, we call `recv()` to listen for a response. There are two important things to note here:

- To keep the example code as simple as possible we call `recv()` only once, which means we're only going to listen for a single packet in response to our broadcast. Ideally we would loop so we could return to listening for packets.

- A simple `recv()` call like this will block (i.e., hang) forever until it receives data. Again, we didn't do anything fancy here for simplicity's sake. There are ways to get around this limitation, such as using `alarm()` or `IO::Select`. See Lincoln Stein's book *Network Programming with Perl* (Addison-Wesley) or the examples in *Perl Cookbook* (O'Reilly) for more details.

For the purposes of illustration, we'll assume that everything goes as planned and we do receive a packet. We then take that packet apart for display using `Net::DHCP::Packet` and print it. Here's some sample output showing what we might see at this point:

```
Received response from: 192.168.0.1
Details:
op = BOOTREPLY
htype = HTYPE_ETHER
hlen = 6
hops = 0
xid = 912c020f
secs = 0
flags = 8000
ciaddr = 0.0.0.0
yiaddr = 192.168.0.2
siaddr = 0.0.0.0
giaddr = 0.0.0.0
chaddr = 0016cbb7c882
sname =
file =
Options :
 DHO_DHCP_MESSAGE_TYPE(53) = DHCPOFFER
 DHO_DHCP_SERVER_IDENTIFIER(54) = 192.168.0.1
 DHO_DHCP_LEASE_TIME(51) = 86400
 DHO_SUBNET_MASK(1) = 255.255.255.0
 DHO_ROUTERS(3) = 192.168.0.1
```

```
DHO_DOMAIN_NAME_SERVERS(6) = 68.78.7.126 68.78.7.252
padding [270] = 000000000000000000000000000000000000000000000000
000000000000000000000000000000000000000000000000000000000000
0000000000000000000000000000000000000000000000000000000000000000
000000000000000000000000000000000000000000000000000000000000
00000000000000000000000000000000000000000000000000000000000000
0000000000000000000000000000000000000000000000000000000000000000
000000000000000000000000000000000000000000000000000000000000
000000000000000000000000000000000000000000000000000000000000
```

That's a lovely offer for a lease. The next logical thing for our code to do (that it doesn't do yet) would be to check to make sure the DHCP server offering this lease is one of our authorized servers. If not, the hunt is on!

Monitoring Legitimate DHCP Servers

We can develop this last piece of code even further into yet another useful script. In the previous example we started the DHCP handshake process with a DHCPDISCOVER and received a DHCPOFFER, but we didn't consummate the transaction with the last step in the process. Leaving off at this point means we didn't hang in there long enough to see if the server would have actually given us a lease.

What if we wanted to see whether our legitimate DHCP server was properly handing out leases and other configuration information? To do that, we'd have to follow the handshake to its natural conclusion.

Here's some example code that will request a lease, print out the final packet when it receives it, and then (because we're well-mannered programmers) release that lease. I've highlighted the interesting bits that we'll talk about after you get a chance to see the new code:

```perl
use IO::Socket::INET;
use Net::DHCP::Packet;
use Net::DHCP::Constants;

my $socket = IO::Socket::INET->new(
    Proto     => 'udp',
    Broadcast => 1,
    LocalPort => '68',
) or die "Can't create socket: $@\n";

my $br_addr = sockaddr_in( '67', inet_aton('255.255.255.255') );
my $xid     = int( rand(0xFFFFFFFF) );
my $chaddr  = '0016cbb7c882';

my $discover_packet = Net::DHCP::Packet->new(
    Xid                         => $xid,
    Chaddr                      => $chaddr,
    Flags                       => 0x8000,
    DHO_DHCP_MESSAGE_TYPE()      => DHCPDISCOVER(),
    DHO_HOST_NAME()             => 'Perl Test Client',
    DHO_VENDOR_CLASS_IDENTIFIER() => 'perl',
```

```
    );

    $socket->send( $discover_packet->serialize(), 0, $br_addr )
        or die "Error sending:$!\n";

    my $buf = '';
    $socket->recv( $buf, 4096 ) or die "recvfrom() failed:$!";
    my $resp = new Net::DHCP::Packet($buf);

    my $request_packet = Net::DHCP::Packet->new(
        Xid                          => $xid,
        Chaddr                       => $chaddr,
        DHO_DHCP_MESSAGE_TYPE()       => DHCPREQUEST(),
        DHO_VENDOR_CLASS_IDENTIFIER() => 'perl',
        DHO_HOST_NAME()               => 'Perl Test Client',
        DHO_DHCP_REQUESTED_ADDRESS()  => $resp->yiaddr(),
        DHO_DHCP_SERVER_IDENTIFIER() =>
            $resp->getOptionValue( DHO_DHCP_SERVER_IDENTIFIER() ),
    );

    $socket->send( $request_packet->serialize(), 0, $br_addr )
        or die "Error sending:$!\n";

    $socket->recv( $buf, 4096 ) or die "recvfrom() failed:$!";
    $resp = new Net::DHCP::Packet($buf);

    print $resp->toString();

    my $dhcp_server = $resp->getOptionValue( DHO_DHCP_SERVER_IDENTIFIER() );

    close($socket);

    my $socket = IO::Socket::INET->new(
        Proto     => 'udp',
        LocalPort => '68',
        PeerPort  => '67',
        PeerAddr  => $dhcp_server,
    ) or die "Can't create socket: $@\n";

    my $release_packet = Net::DHCP::Packet->new(
        Xid                    => $xid,
        Chaddr                 => $chaddr,
        DHO_DHCP_MESSAGE_TYPE() => DHCPRELEASE(),
    );

    $socket->send( $release_packet->serialize() )
        or die "Error sending:$!\n";
```

You probably have the gist of what's going on here, thanks to the last example. Let's look at the ways this code expands on those ideas.

The first chunk of highlighted code shows two flags we haven't seen before:

DHO_DHCP_REQUESTED_ADDRESS

This is the address our client will request from the server. As part of the handshake, we're just parroting back the address provided to us in the reply from the DHCP server. The DHCP server sends us a packet with the `yiaddr` field set to a suggested address that it could give us (i.e., "your Internet address could be..."). In our packet, we say, "OK, we will use the address you're suggesting."

DHO_DHCP_SERVER_IDENTIFIER

When there are multiple DHCP servers on the network that can hear broadcasts and respond to them, it is important for the client to be able to indicate which server's response it is choosing to answer. It does this using the identifier (i.e., the IP address) of the server in this field.

The second piece of interesting code demonstrates the use of a new socket for the release of the lease. We need a new socket because we're done broadcasting our replies and instead need to send a unicast response to the server. We get the address of that server from the `DHO_DHCP_SERVER_IDENTIFIER` option set in the server's previous response to us.

The final addition in this example is the snippet that sends a request to relinquish the previously assigned lease. You might note that this packet has the fewest options/flags of any we've seen to date: our client just has to reference the transaction ID we've been using and the client's hardware (Ethernet) address in order to let the server know which lease to release.

With that we've seen one way to test a full `DISCOVER-OFFER-REQUEST-RELEASE` cycle. Clearly we could get even fancier and test lease renewals or closely check over the results we're receiving from our servers to make sure they make sense. If you'd like to do the former, where acting like a real DHCP client is important, I should mention in the interest of full disclosure that there is a module, `Net::DHCPClientLive` by Ming Zhang, that can make your life easier. It basically lets you test the various states a DHCP client moves through (e.g., "lease expired, attempt to renew lease") and will automatically send and receive the necessary packets to reach that state. Use it when you really need to beat up on your DHCP servers for testing purposes.

Module Information for This Chapter

Module	CPAN ID	Version
Rcs	CFRETER	1.05
Net::NIS	RIK	0.34
Data::Dumper (ships with Perl)	ILYAM	2.121
IO::Socket::INET (ships with Perl)	GBARR	1.2301
Net::DNS	OLAF	0.59
Net::DHCP::Packet	SHADINGER	0.66

References for More Information

DNS and BIND, Fifth Edition (*http://oreilly.com/catalog/9780596100575/*), by Paul Albitz and Cricket Liu (O'Reilly)

Managing NFS and NIS, Second Edition (*http://oreilly.com/catalog/9781565925106/*), by Mike Eisler et al. (O'Reilly)

The DHCP Handbook, Second Edition, by Ralph Droms and Ted Lemon (Sams)

Network Programming with Perl, by Lincoln Stein (Addison-Wesley)

Perl Cookbook, Second Edition (*http://oreilly.com/catalog/9780596003135/*), by Tom Christiansen and Nathan Torkington (O'Reilly)

RFC 849: Suggestions For Improved Host Table Distribution, by Mark Crispin (1983)

RFC 881: The Domain Names Plan and Schedule, by J. Postel (1983)

RFC 882: Domain Names: Concepts And Facilities, by P. Mockapetris (1983)

RFC 1035: Domain Names: Implementation And Specification, by P. Mockapetris (1987)

RFC 1101: NS Encoding of Network Names and Other Types, by P. Mockapetris (1989)

RFC 2131: Dynamic Host Configuration Protocol, by R. Droms (1997)

## CHAPTER 6

Working with Configuration Files

Let us consider the lowly config file. For better or worse, config files are omnipresent not just in the lives of sysadmins, but in the lives of anyone who ever has to configure software before using it. Yes, GUIs and web-based point-and-click festivals are becoming more prevalent for configuration, but even in those cases there's often some piece of configuration information that has to be twiddled before you get to the nifty GUI installer.

From the Perl programmer's point of view, the evolutionary stages of a program usually go like this. First, the programmer writes the roughest and simplest of scripts. Take for example the following script, which reads a file and adds some text to lines that begin with the string hostname: before writing the data out to a second file:

```perl
open my $DATA_FILE_H, '<', '/var/adm/data'
    or die "unable to open datafile: $!\n";
open my $OUTPUT_FILE_H, '>', '/var/adm/output'
    or die "unable to write to outputfile: $!\n";

while ( my $dataline = <$DATA_FILE_H> ) {
    chomp($dataline);
    if ( $dataline =~ /^hostname: / ) {
        $dataline .= '.example.edu';
    }
    print $OUTPUT_FILE_H $dataline . "\n";
}
close $DATA_FILE_H;
close $OUTPUT_FILE_H;
```

That's quickly replaced by the next stage, the arrival of variables to represent parts of the program's configuration:

```perl
my $datafile   = '/var/adm/data';    # input data filename
my $outputfile = '/var/adm/output';  # output data filename
my $change_tag = 'hostname: ';       # append data to these lines
my $fdqn       = '.example.edu';     # domain we'll be appending

open my $DATA_FILE_H, '<', $datafile
    or die "unable to open $datafile: $!\n";
```

```
open my $OUTPUT_FILE_H, '>', $outputfile
    or die "unable to write to $outputfile: $!\n";

while ( my $dataline = <$DATA_FILE_H> ) {
    chomp($dataline);
    if ( $dataline =~ /^$change_tag/ ) {
        $dataline .= $fdqn;
    }
    print $OUTPUT_FILE_H $dataline . "\n";
}
close $DATA_FILE_H;
close $OUTPUT_FILE_H;
```

Many Perl programs happily remain at this stage for their whole lives. However, more experienced programmers will recognize that code like this is fraught with potential peril: problems can arise as development continues and the program gets bigger and bigger, perhaps being handed off to other people to maintain.

These problems will manifest the first time someone naïvely adds code deep within the program that modifies $change_tag or $fdqn. All of a sudden, the program output changes in an unexpected and unwanted way. In a small code snippet it is easy to spot the connection between $change_tag or $fdqn and the desired results, but it can be much trickier in a program that scrolls by for screen after screen.

One approach to fixing this problem would be to rename variables like $fdqn to something more obscure, like $dont_change_this_value_yesiree_bob, but that's a bad idea. Besides consuming far too many of the finite number of keystrokes you'll be able to type in your lifetime, it wreaks havoc on code readability. There are a number of data-hiding tricks we could play instead (closures, symbol table manipulation, etc.), but they don't help with readability either and are more complex than necessary.

The best idea is to use something similar to the **use constants** pragma (see the sidebar "Constant As the Northern Star" on page 187) to make the variables read-only:

```
use Readonly;

# we've upcased the constants so they stick out
# note: this is the Perl 5.8.x syntax, see the Readonly docs for using
#       Readonly with versions of Perl older than 5.8
Readonly my $DATAFILE   => '/var/adm/data';   # input data filename
Readonly my $OUTPUTFILE => '/var/adm/output'; # output data filename
Readonly my $CHANGE_TAG => 'hostname: ';      # append data to these lines
Readonly my $FDQN       => '.example.edu';    # domain we'll be appending

open my $DATA_FILE_H, '<', $DATAFILE
    or die "unable to open $DATAFILE: $!\n";
open my $OUTPUT_FILE_H, '>', $OUTPUTFILE
    or die "unable to write to $OUTPUTFILE: $!\n";

while ( my $dataline = <$DATA_FILE_H> ) {
    chomp($dataline);
```

```
    if ( $dataline =~ /^$CHANGE_TAG/ ) {
        $dataline .= $FDQN;
    }
    print $OUTPUT_FILE $dataline . "\n";
}
close $DATA_FILE_H;
close $OUTPUT_FILE_H;
```

Constant As the Northern Star

Why not actually "use constants" instead? The `Readonly` module's documentation points out a number of reasons, the three most compelling of which are:

1. The ability to interpolate `Readonly` variables into strings (e.g., `print "Constant set to $CONSTANT\n"`)

2. The ability to lexically scope `Readonly` variables (e.g., `Readonly my $constant => "fred"`) so they can be present in only the scope you desire

3. Unlike with `use constant`, once a `Readonly` variable is defined, attempts to redefine it are rebuffed

---

Now that we've seen the *nec plus ultra* of storing configuration information within the script,[*] we've hit a wall: what happens when we decide to write a second or third script that needs similar configuration information? Copy and paste is the wrong answer. Simply duplicating the same information into a second script might seem harmless, but this would lead to Multiple Sources of Truth™.[†] That is, someday, something will change, and you'll forget to update one of these files, and then you'll spend hours trying to figure out what's gone wrong. This is the first step on to the road away from Oz and toward an unpleasant encounter with the flying monkeys and an unhappy lady with a broomstick. Don't do it.

The right answer is probably to create some sort of config file (or something more sophisticated, which we will touch on later in the chapter). The next choice once you've reached the decision to use a config file is: what format?

The answer to that question is similar to the old joke, "The wonderful thing about standards is there are so many to choose from!" Discussions of which formats are best are usually based on some mishmash of religion, politics, and personal aesthetic taste. Because I'm a flaming pluralist, we're going to take a look at how to deal with several of the most common formats, and I'll leave you to choose the best one for your application.

---

[*] There are some games we could play with __DATA__, but in general, keeping the configuration information at the beginning of the script is better form.

[†] To use Hugh Brown's special phrase for the situation.

Configuration File Formats

We'll look at four ways of storing configuration data in this chapter: in binary format, as naked delimited data, as key/value pairs, and using a markup format such as XML or YAML. I'll try to give you my humble opinion about each to help you with your decision process.

Binary

The first kind of configuration file we're going to look at is my least favorite, so let's get it out of the way quickly. Some people choose to store their configuration data on disk as basically a serialized memory dump of their Perl data structures. There are several ways to write this data structure to disk, including the old warhorse `Storable`:

```
use Storable;

# write the config file data structure out to $CONFIG_FILE
store \%config, $CONFIG_FILE; # use nstore() for platform independent file

# later (perhaps in another program), read it back in for use
my $config = retrieve($CONFIG_FILE);
```

If you need something that is pure Perl, `DBM::Deep` is another good choice. It has the benefit of producing data files that aren't platform-specific by default (though `Storable`'s `nstore()` method can help with that):

```
use DBM::Deep;

my $configdb = new DBM::Deep 'config.db';

# store some host config info to that db
$configdb->{hosts} = {
    'agatha'    => '192.168.0.4',
    'gilgamesh' => '192.168.0.5',
    'tarsus'    => '192.168.0.6',
};

# (later) retrieve the names of the hosts we've stored
print join( ' ', keys %{ $configdb->{hosts} } ) . "\n";
```

Files in a binary format are typically really fast to read, which can be quite helpful if performance is a concern. Similarly, there's something elegant about having the information stay close to the native format (i.e., a Perl data structure you're going to traverse in memory) for its entire lifespan, rather than transcoding it to and from another representation through a myriad of parsing/slicing/dicing steps.

So why is this my least favorite kind of config file? To me, the least palatable aspect is the opaque nature of the files created. I much prefer my config files to be human-readable whenever possible. I don't want to have to rely on a special program to decode the information (or encode it, when the data gets written in the first place). Besides that

---

visceral reaction, the use of binary formats also means you can't operate on the data using other standard tools at your disposal, like *grep*.[‡] Luckily, if you're looking for speed, there are other alternatives, as you'll see in a moment.

Naked Delimited Data

Also in the category of formats I tend to dislike are those that simply present a set of data in fields delimited by some character. The */etc* directory on a Unix box is lousy with them: *passwd*, *group*, and so on. Comma- or Character-Separated Value (CSV, take your pick of expansions) files are in the same category.

Reading them in Perl is pretty easy because of the built-in `split()` operator:

```
use Readonly;

Readonly my $DELIMITER => ':';
Readonly my $NUMFIELDS =>  4 ;

# open your config file and read in a line here

# now parse the data
my ( $field1, $field2, $field3, $field4, $excess ) =
    split $DELIMITER, $line_of_config, $NUMFIELDS;
```

For CSV files, a number of helpful modules can handle tricky situations like escaped characters (e.g., when commas are used in the data itself). `Text::CSV::Simple`, a wrapper around `Text::CSV_XS`, works well:

```
use Text::CSV::Simple;

my $csv_parser = Text::CSV::Simple->new;

# @data will then contain a list of lists, one entry per line of the file
my @data = $csv_parser->read_file($datafile);
```

This data format is also on my "least favored" list. Unlike the binary format, it has the benefit of being human-readable and parsable by standard tools; however, it also has the drawback of being easily human-misunderstandable and mangle-able. Without a good memory or external documentation, it is often impossible to understand the contents of the file ("what was the 7th field again?"), making it susceptible to fumble-fingering and subtle typos. It is also field-order fragile. And if that doesn't convince you not to use this format, the more you work with it, the more you'll find that individual parsers in different applications have different ideas on how to handle commas, quotes, and carriage returns within the values. CSV data seems interoperable on the surface, but it often requires a deeper understanding of the quirks of the programs producing or consuming it.

[‡] As Mark Pilgrim once said, "Never trust a format you can't edit in Emacs or *vi*" (*http://dashes.com/anil/2003/11/tools-affect-co.html#comment-2725*).

Key/Value Pairs

The most common format is the *key {something} value* style, where *{something}* is usually whitespace, a colon, or an equals sign. Some key/value pair formats (e.g., *.ini* files) throw in other twists, like section names that look like this:

```
[server section]
{setting}={value}
{setting}={value}
```

or configuration scopes (as in Apache's configuration file):

```
<Location>
    {setting} {value}
    {setting} {value}
    ...
</Location>
```

Dealing with key/value pair formats using Perl modules is initially difficult, because there are so many choices. As of this writing, there are at least 26 modules in this category on CPAN.

How do you pick which module to use? The first step is to ask yourself a number of questions that will help define your needs and winnow down the contenders.

To start, you'll want to consider just how complex you want the configuration file to be:

Will simple *.ini* files work for you? More complex *.ini* files? Apache style? Extended Apache style? Do you need sections? Do you need scoped directives? Want to write your own grammar representing the format?

Next, consider how you would like to interact with the configuration information:

Want the module to hand you back a simple data structure or an object representing the information? Prefer to treat things like magical tied hashes or Perl constants? Does the information you get back have to come back in the same order as it is listed in the config file? Would you be happy if the module figured out the config file format for you?

Finally, think about what else is important to you:

Do you care how quickly the configuration is parsed or how much memory the parsing process takes? Should it handle caching of the config for fast reload? Do you want to be able to cascade the configs (i.e., have a global config that can include other config files)? Should the configuration data be validated on parsing? Should the module both read and write config files for you?

The answers to each of these questions will point at a different module or set of modules available for your use. I don't have space to discuss all of the modules out there, so let's look at three of particular merit.

`Config::Std` is Damian Conway's config parsing module. It has the distinction of being able to read the configuration file and then update it with section order preserved and

---

comments still intact. The file format it uses looks much like that of an *.ini* file, so it should be pretty easy for most people to understand on first sight. Here's an example of the module in action (note that the examples in this section will be very simple—read: boring—because the modules are all designed to make the process of dealing with config files simple):

```
use Config::Std;

read_config 'config.cfg' => my %config;

# now work with $config{Section}{key}...
...
# and write the config file back out again
write_config %config;
```

In Conway's book *Perl Best Practices (http://oreilly.com/catalog/9780596001735/)* (O'Reilly), he suggests that if you need something more sophisticated than his simple `Config::Std` format can provide, Thomas Linden's `Config::General` can oblige. It handles files in the Apache config file family and has a much richer syntax. Actual use of the module isn't any more complex than use of `Config::Std`:

```
use Config::General;

my %config = ParseConfig( -ConfigFile => 'rcfile' );

# now work with the contents of %config...
...
# and then write the config file back out again
SaveConfig( 'configdb', \%config );
```

If `Config::General` doesn't give you enough bells and whistles, there is always `Config::Scoped`, by Karl Gaissmaier. This module parses a similarly complex format that includes scoped directives (essentially the ones used by BIND or the ISC DHCP server), can check the data being parsed, will check the permissions of the config file itself, and includes caching functionality. This caching functionality allows your program to parse the more complex format once and then quickly load in a binary representation of the format on subsequent loads if the original file hasn't changed. This gives us the speed we coveted from the first kind of file we looked at and the readability of the file formats discussed in this section. It doesn't, however, offer an easy way to programmatically update an existing configuration file, like some of the other modules we've seen. Here's a small snippet that shows how to use the caching functionality:

```
use Config::Scoped;
my $parser = Config::Scoped->new( file => 'config.cfg' );
my $config = $parser->parse;

# store the cached version on disk for later use
$parser->store_cache( cache => 'config.cfg.cache' );

# (later, in another program... we load the cached version)
my $cfg = Config::Scoped->new( file => 'config.cfg' )->retrieve_cache;
```

If you are the type of person that likes to smelt your own bits, there are also a number of other modules, such as `Config::Grammar` by David Schweikert, that allow you to define your own grammar to represent the configuration file format. I tend not to like creating custom formats if I can help it for maintainability purposes, but if this is a requirement, modules like Schweikert's can oblige.

Markup Languages

Each of the formats we've seen so far is limited in some way. Some lack readability, while others lack extensibility. Most have a certain level of unpredictability in their parsing: there's either a lack of precision in the specification or a level of rigidity to the format that can make it hard to tell whether you have parsed the data correctly. For example, with CSV files, the quoting of delimiters is handled differently depending on the parser. With binary files, one wrong element in the `unpack()` template of your program can cause it to happily start reading in garbage without any indication to the parser that something has gone wrong. Markup languages, when implemented and used intelligently, can overcome these concerns.

XML

When I started work on the first edition of this book it was clear that XML was an up-and-coming technology that deserved sysadmins' attention, and hence it found its way into the book.[*] In the intervening years XML has worked its way into many of the nooks and crannies of system administration and data handling, to the point where having some facility with it is probably essential. Given the importance of XML, we're going to spend a considerable part of this chapter discussing how to work with it.

One place where XML has started to become more prevalent is in configuration files. There are in fact a variety of XML dialects (that we won't discuss here), including DCML, NetML, and SAML, that are hoping to become the *de facto* formats for different parts of the configuration management space.

Before we dig into the mechanics of using XML it will be worthwhile to look at why it works well in this context. XML has a few properties that make it a good choice for configuration files:

- XML is a plain-text format, which means we can use our usual Perl bag o' tricks to deal with it easily.
- When kept simple (because a complex/convoluted XML document is as inscrutable as one in any other format), XML is self-describing and practically self-documenting. With a character-delimited file like */etc/passwd*, it is not always

---

[*] Most of the XML discussion in the first edition was presented using account maintenance as a backdrop, but as the use of XML matured in the world of system administration it became clear that this chapter would be a better home for this discussion.

easy to determine which part of a line represents which field. With XML, this is never a problem because an obvious tag can surround each field.

- With the right parser, XML can also be self-validating. If you use a validating parser, mistakes in an entry's format will be caught right away, since the file will not parse correctly according to its document type definition (DTD) or schema. Even without a validating parser, any XML parser that checks for well-formedness will catch many errors.[†]

- XML is flexible enough to describe virtually any set of text information you would ever desire to keep. The freedom to define almost arbitrary tags lets it be as descriptive as you'd like. This flexibility means you can use one parser library to get at all of your data, rather than having to write a new parser for each different format.

Here's an example of what I mean when I say that XML can be self-describing and self-documenting. If I write a simple XML file like this, you can probably understand the gist of it without needing a separate manual page:

```
<network>
  <host>
    <name>agatha</name>
    <addr>192.168.0.4</addr>
  </host>
  ...
</network>
```

We'll use a config file like this one, but with a slightly more complicated format, in the examples to come.

Writing XML from Perl

XML is a textual format, so there are any number of ways to write XML files from Perl. Using ordinary `print` statements to write XML-compliant text would be the simplest method, but we can do better. Perl modules like `XML::Generator` by Benjamin Holzman and `XML::Writer` by David Megginson can make the process easier and less error-prone by handling details like start/end tag matching and escaping special characters (`<`, `>`, `&`, etc.) for us.

To keep the example simple, let's say we wanted to write the teeny XML config file that we just saw.[‡] The `XML::Writer` way to do this would be:

```
use XML::Writer;
use IO::File;
```

[†] One error that is easily caught by the well-formedness check is truncated files. If the file is missing its last closing tag because some data has been lost from the end, the document will not parse correctly. This is one property YAML, which we'll look at later in this chapter, does not have.

[‡] As a quick aside, the XML specification recommends that every XML file begin with a version declaration (e.g., `<?xml version="1.0"?>`). It is not mandatory, but if we want to comply, `XML::Writer` offers the `xmlDecl()` method to create one for us.

```perl
my %hosts = (
    'name' => 'agatha',
    'addr' => '192.168.0.4',
);

my $FH = new IO::File('>netconfig.xml')
    or die "Unable to write to file netconfig.xml: $!\n";

my $xmlw = new XML::Writer( OUTPUT => $FH );

$xmlw->startTag('network');
print $FH "\n  ";

$xmlw->startTag('host');

# note that we're not guaranteed any specific ordering of the
# subelements using this code
foreach my $field ( keys %hosts ) {
    print $FH "\n      ";
    $xmlw->startTag($field);
    $xmlw->characters( $hosts{$field} );
    $xmlw->endTag;
}
print $FH "\n  ";

$xmlw->endTag;
print $FH "\n";

$xmlw->endTag;
$xmlw->end;
$FH->close();
```

Using `XML::Writer` gives us a few perks:

- The code is quite legible; anyone with a little bit of markup language experience will instantly understand the names `startTag()`, `characters()`, and `endTag()`.

- Though our data didn't need this, `characters()` is silently performing a bit of protective magic for us by properly escaping reserved entities like the greater-than symbol (>).

- Our code doesn't have to remember the last start tag we opened for later closing. `XML::Writer` handles this matching for us, allowing us to call `endTag()` without specifying *which* end tag we need.

Two drawbacks of using `XML::Writer` in this case are:

- We certainly typed more than we would have if we had just used `print` statements.

- `XML::Writer` is oriented more toward generating XML that will be parsed by a machine rather than something pretty that a human might like to read. It does have a couple of initialization-time options that allow it to provide slightly prettier output, but they still don't produce output that looks like our original example file—hence all of the icky `print $FH` statements scattered throughout the code to add whitespace.

Survey of best-practice tools to parse and manipulate XML from Perl

We're going to look at several ways to parse XML from Perl, because each way has its strengths that make it well suited for particular situations or programming styles. Knowing about all of them will allow you to pick the right tool for the job.

To make the parsing tools easier to compare and understand, we're going to use a common example XML file as input. Let's look at that now so we understand just what the data we're going to chew on looks like. Here's the full file. We'll take it apart in a second:

```
<?xml version="1.0" encoding="UTF-8"?>

<network>
    <description name="Boston">
        This is the configuration of our network in the Boston office.
    </description>
    <host name="agatha" type="server" os="linux">
        <interface name="eth0" type="Ethernet" >
            <arec>agatha.example.edu</arec>
            <cname>mail.example.edu</cname>
            <addr>192.168.0.4</addr>
        </interface>
        <service>SMTP</service>
        <service>POP3</service>
        <service>IMAP4</service>
    </host>
    <host name="gil" type="server" os="linux">
        <interface name="eth0" type="Ethernet" >
            <arec>gil.example.edu</arec>
            <cname>www.example.edu</cname>
            <addr>192.168.0.5</addr>
        </interface>
        <service>HTTP</service>
        <service>HTTPS</service>
    </host>
    <host name="baron" type="server" os="linux">
        <interface name="eth0" type="Ethernet" >
            <arec>baron.example.edu</arec>
            <cname>dns.example.edu</cname>
            <cname>ntp.example.edu</cname>
            <cname>ldap.example.edu</cname>
            <addr>192.168.0.6</addr>
        </interface>
        <service>DNS</service>
        <service>NTP</service>
        <service>LDAP</service>
        <service>LDAPS</service>
    </host>
```

```
<host name="mr-tock" type="server" os="openbsd">
    <interface name="fxp0" type="Ethernet">
        <arec>mr-tock.example.edu</arec>
        <cname>fw.example.edu</cname>
        <addr>192.168.0.1</addr>
    </interface>
    <service>firewall</service>
</host>
<host name="krosp" type="client" os="osx">
    <interface name="en0" type="Ethernet" >
        <arec>krosp.example.edu</arec>
        <addr>192.168.0.100</addr>
    </interface>
    <interface name="en1" type="AirPort">
        <arec>krosp.wireless.example.edu</arec>
        <addr>192.168.100.100</addr>
    </interface>
</host>
<host name="zeetha" type="client" os="osx">
    <interface name="en0" type="Ethernet" >
        <arec>zeetha.example.edu</arec>
        <addr>192.168.0.101</addr>
    </interface>
    <interface name="en1" type="AirPort">
        <arec>zeetha.wireless.example.edu</arec>
        <addr>192.168.100.101</addr>
    </interface>
</host>
</network>
```

This file represents a very small network consisting of three servers and two clients. Each `<host></host>` element represents a machine. The first is a server that provides mail services:

```
<host name="agatha" type="server" os="linux">
    <interface name="eth0" type="Ethernet" >
        <arec>agatha.example.edu</arec>
        <cname>mail.example.edu</cname>
        <addr>192.168.0.4</addr>
    </interface>
    <service>SMTP</service>
    <service>POP3</service>
    <service>IMAP4</service>
</host>
```

Each interface has an `<arec></arec>` associated with it to provide its DNS name (in DNS parlance, it has an A resource record). The server in the example excerpt provides three mail-related services and has a DNS CNAME element reflecting that. Other servers provide other services, and their CNAME or CNAMEs are listed accordingly. Here's a sample client:

```
<host name="krosp" type="client" os="osx">
    <interface name="en0" type="Ethernet" >
        <arec>krosp.example.edu</arec>
```

```
            <addr>192.168.0.100</addr>
        </interface>
        <interface name="en1" type="AirPort">
            <arec>krosp.wireless.example.edu</arec>
            <addr>192.168.100.100</addr>
        </interface>
    </host>
```

It is different from our example server not only because it has a different **type** attribute and has no services listed, but also because it has multiple interfaces (it is probably a laptop, since it has both wireless and Ethernet interfaces), though that could be changed if we decided to multihome any of the servers. Each interface has an address and a DNS hostname (A resource record) listed for it.

There's an interesting decision ingrained in this file. Unlike our first XML example, this file shows the use of both attributes (name, type, os) and subelements (interface, service). Choosing between the two is always a fun intellectual exercise and a great way to start a debate. In this case I was guided by one of the canonical discussions on this topic (*http://xml.coverpages.org/attrSperberg92.html*) and chose to make the pieces of information that describe a machine be attributes and the things we add to or remove from a machine (interfaces, services) be subelements. This was strictly my choice; you should do what makes sense for you.

So, let's get into the game of parsing XML files. We're going to look at the process using three different modules/approaches with roughly increasing complexity. Each module has pluses and minuses that make it better than the others for certain situations. I'll list them right at the beginning of each section so you go into each passage with the right expectations. Having at least a cursory understanding of all three will give you a complete toolkit that can tackle virtually all of your XML-related needs.[*]

Working with XML using XML::Simple

XML::Simple Pros and Cons

Benefits:

- It's the simplest module (at least on the surface) to use.
- It maps XML into a standard Perl data structure.
- It will actually use one of the other modules that we'll see in a moment (XML::LibXML) for pretty fast parsing.
- It's well documented.
- The module's maintainer is very responsive to questions, issues, etc.

---

[*] As an aside, you could also write your own code to parse XML (perhaps using some fancy regexp footwork). If you attempt this, however, you'll spend more time on the parser and less on your actual goal, with little return. If you do need a super-simple XML parser made out of regexps, modules like that also exist, though we won't be looking at them here.

Drawbacks:

- It doesn't preserve element order or format (i.e., if you read in an XML file and spit it out again, the elements won't necessarily be in the same order or have the same format).
- It can't handle "mixed content" situations (where both text and elements are embedded in another element), as in:

      <network>This is our <type>devel</type> network</network>

- All of the data gets slurped into memory by default.
- Some people are philosophically opposed to a direct transformation of XML to Perl data structures.

So when should you use this module? XML::Simple is perfect for small XML-related jobs like configuration files. It's great when your main task includes reading in an XML file or writing an XML file (although it may get a little trickier if you have to read and then write, depending on the situation). I use it for the majority of situations where XML is just a small part of the actual task at hand and not the main point.

The easiest way to read an XML config file from Perl is to use the XML::Simple module, by Grant McLean. It allows you to write simple code like this to slurp an XML file into a Perl data structure:

```
use XML::Simple;

my $config = XMLin('config.xml');

# work with $config->{stuff}
```

Turning that data structure back into XML for writing after you've made a change to it is equally as easy:

```
... (data structure already in place)

XMLout($config, OutputFile => $configfile );
```

I know what you're thinking: it can't be that easy, right? Well, let's see what happens if we feed our sample XML file to the module using its defaults. If we ran the first of our XML::Simple code samples and then dumped the resulting data structure using the debugger's x command, we'd get this output:[†]

```
0  HASH(0xa36fc8)
   'description' => HASH(0x97f5e8)
      'content' => '
         This is the configuration of our network in the Boston office.
      '
      'name' => 'Boston'
   'host' => HASH(0xa5d6ac)
```

[†] To debug XML::Simple code, it is best to use a good data-structure-dumping module like Data::Dumper, Data::Dump::Streamer, YAML, or the Perl debugger, as demonstrated here.

```
'agatha' => HASH(0xa5d424)
   'interface' => HASH(0xa38f98)
      'addr' => '192.168.0.4'
      'arec' => 'agatha.example.edu'
      'cname' => 'mail.example.edu'
      'name' => 'eth0'
      'type' => 'Ethernet'
   'os' => 'linux'
   'service' => ARRAY(0xa5da6c)
      0  'SMTP'
      1  'POP3'
      2  'IMAP4'
   'type' => 'server'
'baron' => HASH(0xa51390)
   'interface' => HASH(0xa3e228)
      'addr' => '192.168.0.6'
      'arec' => 'baron.example.edu'
      'cname' => ARRAY(0xa5d874)
         0  'dns.example.edu'
         1  'ntp.example.edu'
         2  'ldap.example.edu'
      'name' => 'eth0'
      'type' => 'Ethernet'
   'os' => 'linux'
   'service' => ARRAY(0xa5d994)
      0  'DNS'
      1  'NTP'
      2  'LDAP'
      3  'LDAPS'
   'type' => 'server'
'gil' => HASH(0xa5d61c)
   'interface' => HASH(0xa3de44)
      'addr' => '192.168.0.5'
      'arec' => 'gil.example.edu'
      'cname' => 'www.example.edu'
      'name' => 'eth0'
      'type' => 'Ethernet'
   'os' => 'linux'
   'service' => ARRAY(0xa5d964)
      0  'HTTP'
      1  'HTTPS'
   'type' => 'server'
'krosp' => HASH(0xa5d754)
   'interface' => HASH(0xa5d664)
      'en0' => HASH(0xa5d5ec)
         'addr' => '192.168.0.100'
         'arec' => 'krosp.example.edu'
         'type' => 'Ethernet'
      'en1' => HASH(0xa5d604)
         'addr' => '192.168.100.100'
         'arec' => 'krosp.wireless.example.edu'
         'type' => 'AirPort'
   'os' => 'osx'
   'type' => 'client'
'mr-tock' => HASH(0xa4ee28)
```

```
'interface' => HASH(0xa2fc50)
    'addr' => '192.168.0.1'
    'arec' => 'mr-tock.example.edu'
    'cname' => 'fw.example.edu'
    'name' => 'fxp0'
    'type' => 'Ethernet'
'os' => 'openbsd'
'service' => 'firewall'
'type' => 'server'
'zeetha' => HASH(0xa5d4b4)
    'interface' => HASH(0xa5d4cc)
        'en0' => HASH(0xa5d454)
            'addr' => '192.168.0.101'
            'arec' => 'zeetha.example.edu'
            'type' => 'Ethernet'
        'en1' => HASH(0xa5d46c)
            'addr' => '192.168.100.101'
            'arec' => 'zeetha.wireless.example.edu'
            'type' => 'AirPort'
    'os' => 'osx'
    'type' => 'client'
```

Using just the defaults, we get a pretty workable data structure. There's a hash with a key called host. This points to another hash that contains the hosts, each keyed by its name. This means we could get each host's information with a simple `$config->{host}->{hostname}`. That's all well and good, but if you peer a little harder at the data structure, a few interesting things start to stick out (in order of least to most important):

1. `XML::Simple` has preserved much of the whitespace that was included in the file just to make things prettier. When we actually want to operate on the data, we could strip the leading and trailing whitespace, but it would be much more convenient to have the parser do it for us. If we change:

   ```
   my $config = XMLin('config.xml');
   ```

   to:

   ```
   my $config = XMLin('config.xml', NormalizeSpace => 2);
   ```

   we get our wish.

2. If you look at how the `<service></service>` elements from the file have been translated into data structures for all of the server hosts, you'll notice something interesting. Take a peek at the results for, say, *agatha* and *mr-tock*. The service section for *agatha* looks like this:

   ```
   'service' => ARRAY(0xa4f2d8)
              0  'SMTP'
              1  'POP3'
              2  'IMAP4'
   ```

   while the same section for *mr-tock* looks like this:

   ```
   'service' => 'firewall'
   ```

In one case it's an array, and in the other it's a simple scalar. This difference will make coding harder, because it means we have to have two conventions for data retrieval. Why did `XML::Simple` do two different things in this case? By default `XML::Simple` converts nested elements (like those in the `<service></service>` elements) differently based on whether there is one or more than one subelement present. We can actually tune that behavior by using the `ForceArray` argument. It can take either a simple `1` to force all nested elements into arrays or, better yet, a list of element names to force only the listed elements into array form. If we instead write:

```
my $config = XMLin('config.xml', NormalizeSpace => 2, ForceArray => ['service']);
```

those two sections will look much more uniform:

```
'service' => ARRAY(0xa4f2d8)
            0  'SMTP'
            1  'POP3'
            2  'IMAP4'
...
'service' => ARRAY(0xa31fac)
            0  'firewall'
```

When to Use XML::Simple's ForceArray

You could make a good argument that one should always use `ForceArray => 1` because it provides the maximum amount of consistency. That's true, but using that setting also ensures the maximum amount of syntactic hassle. You'll quickly become annoyed at having to use an array index every time you want to get to the contents of even single subelements in the original XML file.

I'd like to suggest that you use `ForceArray` with a list of element names in the following judicious manner: if you have an element that could even conceivably contain more than one instance of a subelement (e.g., multiple `<service></service>` subelements), include it in the `ForceArray` list. If an element definitely[‡] will only have one subelement instance, you can leave it out.

Also, if you plan to use the `KeyAttr` option we'll discuss shortly, any elements listed for that option need to be listed in `ForceArray` as well.

---

3. There's another section of the `XMLin()` data structure that looks a little awry. If you look at how the `<interface></interface>` elements from the file have been translated into data structures for all of the hosts, you'll notice something interesting if you compare the results for *agatha* and *zeetha*. The interface section for *agatha* looks like this:

[‡] Experienced old-timers may snicker at the notion that you could say anything "definite" about user-supplied data ("oh, that will never happen..."), and they'd be right. To get the best assurance possible that your expectations won't be violated, you should provide a way to validate the XML file using a DTD or XML schema.

```
'interface' => HASH(0xa38f98)
            'addr' => '192.168.0.4'
            'arec' => 'agatha.example.edu'
            'cname' => 'mail.example.edu'
            'name' => 'eth0'
            'type' => 'Ethernet'
```

while the same section for *zeetha* looks like this:

```
'interface' => HASH(0xa5d4cc)
            'en0' => HASH(0xa5d454)
                'addr' => '192.168.0.101'
                'arec' => 'zeetha.example.edu'
                'type' => 'Ethernet'
            'en1' => HASH(0xa5d46c)
                'addr' => '192.168.100.101'
                'arec' => 'zeetha.wireless.example.edu'
                'type' => 'AirPort'
```

In one case it is a hash whose keys are the various components that make up the interface (address, type, etc.), while in the other it is a hash of a hash whose keys are the interface names and whose components are the sub-hash's keys. When it comes time to work with the imported data structure, we'll be forced into coding two different ways to get at basically the same kind of data.

Here, we're running into another example of single and multiple instances with the same subelement name (`<interface></interface>`) being treated differently. Let's try to apply the `ForceArray` option to this case as well:

```
my $config = XMLin('config.xml', NormalizeSpace => 2,
                              ForceArray    => ['interface']);
```

Great, now those two sections also have become much more uniform:

```
'interface' => HASH(0xa32f28)
            'eth0' => HASH(0xa32e80)
                'addr' => '192.168.0.4'
                'arec' => 'agatha.example.edu'
                'cname' => 'mail.example.edu'
                'type' => 'Ethernet'
...
'interface' => HASH(0xa2593c)
            'en0' => HASH(0xa257bc)
                'addr' => '192.168.0.101'
                'arec' => 'zeetha.example.edu'
                'type' => 'Ethernet'
            'en1' => HASH(0xa257d4)
                'addr' => '192.168.100.101'
                'arec' => 'zeetha.wireless.example.edu'
                'type' => 'AirPort'
```

But wait a second; didn't we just set something called `ForceArray`? The `<interface></interface>` elements have been converted into hash of hashes with no explicit arrays in sight. There's some magic afoot here that we really should discuss, and that leads us to our fourth comment on the default Perl data structure `XMLin()` created for us.

4. `XML::Simple` notices when nested subelements (like those we've been dealing with) have certain attributes and does something special with them. By default, if they have the attribute name, key, or id, `XML::Simple` will turn the usual array created by nested subelements into a hash keyed by that attribute. In the case we just saw, once the `<interface></interface>` elements were converted to an array, further logic kicked in because each `<interface></interface>` element has a name attribute. On the surface this may appear like a little too much "Do What I Mean" meddling, but it turns out that it yields some very usable data structures, especially if you understand how/when it works. In our example, we can now reference:

```
# can remove last two arrows
$config->{hostname}->{interface}->{interface_name}
```

The code reads well as a result.

As with the `ForceArray` option, we can tweak this behavior easily. To turn it off entirely, we can add `KeyAttr => {}`. However, the resulting data structure will have to be accessed by looping through the array of elements to find the one we need. That's a little cumbersome, so most of the time we'll instead want to write code like this:

```
# can remove last two arrows
$config->{hostname}->{interface}->{ip_addr}
```

to access a data structure with an inner part like this:

```
'interface' => HASH(0xa31c50)
        '192.168.0.101' => HASH(0xa31b18)
            'arec' => 'zeetha.example.edu'
            'name' => 'en0'
            'type' => 'Ethernet'
        '192.168.100.101' => HASH(0xa31b30)
            'arec' => 'zeetha.wireless.example.edu'
            'name' => 'en1'
            'type' => 'AirPort'
```

We'd then use a parse line like this:

```
my $config = XMLin(
    'config.xml',
    NormaliseSpace => 2,
    ForceArray  => ['interface'],           # uses square brackets
    KeyAttr     => { 'interface' => 'addr' }, # uses curly braces
);
```

The `KeyAttr` option highlighted earlier says to turn the subelements of `interface` elements (only) into a hash keyed on the interface's IP address. If for some reason you wanted to have the `addr` field also appear in the contents of that hash (instead of appearing only in the key name), you could add a + at the front of that attribute name. One last thing to point out here: we left the `ForceArray` argument in place to make sure even single `<interface></interface>` elements get turned into arrays for `KeyAttr` to transform.

The lesson to learn from that little exploration of `XML::Simple`'s default parsing behavior is that although the module is simple on the surface, you may have to do a little unexpected argument tweaking to get the results you want. `XML::Simple` has a "strict" mode you can turn on (like `use strict;`) to help guide you in the right direction, but it still takes a little work get things right sometimes. This issue becomes painfully clear when we try to round-trip the XML (i.e., read it in, modify the data, and then write it back out again).

Modifying the data we're working with is easy—we use the standard Perl data structure semantics to add/delete/modify elements of the data structure in memory. But how about writing the data?

If we use the previous parsing code example and then add this to the bottom:

```
print XMLout($config);
```

we get XML output that looks like this in part:

```
...
<host name="agatha" os="linux" type="server">
    <interface name="eth0" arec="agatha.example.edu"
 cname="mail.example.edu" type="Ethernet" />
    <service>SMTP</service>
    <service>POP3</service>
    <service>IMAP4</service>
</host>
...
```

This is hardly what we started with, and we've lost data (the interface address)! If we add a `KeyAttr` option (matching the one for `XMLin()`), as recommended by the module's strict mode, we get back the data, but not the subelement/attribute changes:

```
...
<host name="agatha" os="linux" type="server">
    <interface addr="192.168.0.4" arec="agatha.example.edu"
 cname="mail.example.edu" name="eth0" type="Ethernet" />
    <service>SMTP</service>
    <service>POP3</service>
    <service>IMAP4</service>
</host>
...
```

Unpleasant situation, no? We have a few choices at this point if we want to stick with `XML::Simple`, including:

- Changing the format of our data file. This seems a bit extreme.
- Changing the way we ask `XML::Simple` to parse our file by working hard to fine-tune our options. For example, the `XML::Simple` documentation recommends using `KeyAttr => {}` for both reading and writing in this situation. But when we tailor

the way we read in the data to make for easy writing, we lose our easy hash semantics for data lookup and manipulation.

- Performing some data manipulation after reading but before writing. We could read the data into a structure we like (just as we did before), manipulate the data to our heart's content, and then transform that data structure into one XML::Simple "likes" before writing it out. This isn't terribly hard, but you do need a good grasp of how to manipulate moderately complex data structures. It usually involves a map() call or two and a pile of punctuation.

Your situation will dictate which (if any) of these options is best. I've picked from all three choices in the past, depending what seemed to make the most sense. And sometimes, to be quite frank about it, the best way to win is not to play at all. Sometimes you need to leave the comfy harbors of XML::Simple and use another module entirely. That's just what we'll do in the next section.

Grant McLean, XML::Simple's author, says that he recommends people:

- Use XML::Simple's strict mode to avoid common mistakes.
- Switch to using XML::LibXML if they haven't gotten the results they want from XML::Simple within 5–10 minutes.

He's written an interesting article on the subject, available at *http://www .perlmonks.org/index.pl?node_id=490846.*

Working with XML using XML::LibXML

XML::LibXML Pros and Cons

Benefits:

- It provides a very fast parser.
- It has an emphasis on standards compliance (although it currently supports only XPath 1.0; XPath 2.0 support is not planned as of this writing).
- It supports both XPath and DOM, making navigating through and operating on a document pretty easy.
- It's the current default recommendation for XML parsing from Perl (as per *http:// perl-xml.sourceforge.net/faq/*).
- The module maintainer is very responsive to questions, issues, etc.
- As a bonus, it can also parse HTML and (largely) operate on it as if it were XML.

Drawbacks:

- A working and compatible version of the libxml2 library must be present on the system to be called by the module.
- The documentation is centered on describing what is supported in the module but is very light on how to go about using it. If you already know what you want to do

(perhaps because you are familiar with XML, DOM, XPath, and other related standards), this is fine, but if you're just starting out and want to understand the basics, you'll have a very hard time getting what you need from the documentation. This is by far the module's biggest drawback.

- All of the data gets slurped into memory by default.

When should you use this module? XML::LibXML is good for the vast majority of cases where you need to process reasonably sized XML documents as the main thrust of what you are trying to get done. It's fast, it behaves the way the standards suggest it should, and it's pretty easy to use, provided that you understand the basics of XPath or DOM and can figure how to use it.

XML::LibXML, maintained by Petr Pajas, has much to recommend it, including many powerful features and options. I'll just skim the surface here, to show you the most useful stuff. You'll want to consult the resources listed at the end of the chapter for the rest of the story.

Like XML::Simple, XML::LibXML slurps your entire XML document into memory by default and gives you the tools to work with that in-memory representation. Unlike XML::Simple, the interface for doing so in XML::LibXML is not your native Perl data structure semantics. Instead, the data is represented as a tree with several methods for manipulating it. If the idea of representing XML data in a tree structure doesn't make immediate sense to you, you should reach for a bookmark and insert it here. Pause reading this chapter, go read Appendix B, and then come right back. This is important because the very next paragraph is going to assume that you have at least the background provided in that appendix at your disposal.

XML::LibXML supports the two most common ways to navigate XML data represented in tree form: the W3C Document Object Model (DOM) and XPath.* Though I tend to favor XPath over DOM in my programming because I like XPath's concision and elegance, we'll look at examples using both approaches. It's good to know both methods because XML::LibXML allows you to use virtually any combination of the two that makes sense to you.

Let's start with the DOM method of getting around a tree of XML data. To make a comparison between DOM and XPath easier, we'll stick to the same sample XML document introduced in the XML::Simple section. To keep the tree mortality rate down, I won't reprint that document here.

XML::LibXML programs that use the DOM method and those that use XPath begin the same way (load the module, create a parser instance, parse the XML data):

```
use XML::LibXML;

my $prsr = XML::LibXML->new();
```

---

* DOM Level 2 Core and XPath 1.0, to be precise (as of this writing).

```
my $doc = $prsr->parse_file('config.xml');
```

To use the DOM method of walking our data, we start by retrieving the root element of the XML document:

```
my $root = $doc->documentElement();
```

From this element we can either start to explicitly walk the tree by hand or ask the module to search down the tree on our behalf. To walk the tree, we request the child nodes and iterate over them explicitly:

```
my @children = $root->childNodes;

foreach my $node (@children){
    print $node->nodeName(). "\n";
}
```

If you run the XML::LibXML code we've written so far, you'll get some very peculiar output:

```
#text
description
#text
host
#text
host
#text
host
#text
host
#text
host
#text
host
#text
```

The description and host lines make sense (those are the <description> </description> and <host></host> elements from our document), but what's with all of the #text nodes (nodes with a default name of #text)? If you were to look carefully at the contents of one of the #text nodes when the program was running, you would see:

```
x $node->data
0  '
   '
```

or, to make this even clearer:

```
x split(//,$node->data);
0  '
   '
1  ' '
2  ' '
3  ' '
4  ' '
```

The node is holding one carriage return character and four space characters. Unlike XML::Simple, which strips whitespace by default, XML::LibXML tries to preserve any whitespace it encounters when parsing a document (because it isn't always clear when the whitespace itself could be significant). It preserves the whitespace by storing it in generic text nodes in the tree. If you find the "empty" text nodes distracting and you don't need the whitespace kept around, you can ask the parser to drop all of the nodes that hold only whitespace. To do this, you set a parser option before parsing the file:

```
$prsr->keep_blanks(0);
my $doc = $prsr->parse_file('config.xml');
```

Adding this option gives us the output we'd expect (the names of all of the child nodes of <network></network>, the root element of the document):

```
description
host
host
host
host
host
host
```

Just to keep things simpler for the rest of this section, you can assume that keep_blanks(0) has been set.

The actual mechanics of walking a tree are pretty basic: you iterate over the child nodes of the node you are at, and if any of those nodes have children (you can check with hasChildNodes()), walk those as well. Most often people write recursive programs for this sort of thing; see the tree-walking code in Chapter 2 for the basic idea. To navigate by hand to a specific node someplace deeper in the tree, access the node you want at each level in the tree and descend from there:

```
my $root = $doc->documentElement();
my @children = $root->childNodes;

my $current = $children[2]; # second <host></host> element
@children = $current->childNodes();
$current = $children[1]; # first <service></service> element
print $current->textContent(); # 'HTTP'

# or, chain the steps together in a punctuation-heavy fashion (yuck):
print STDOUT (($root->childNodes())[2]->childNodes())[1]->textContent();
```

In addition to walking down the tree, we can also use nextSibling() to go sideways:

```
my $root = $doc->documentElement();
my @children = $root->childNodes;

my $current = $children[2]; # second <host></host> element
$current = $current->nextSibling; # move to third <host></host> element
```

If all this manual tree-walking code looks like a pain, there is another DOM-flavored alternative: XML::LibXML can do some of the work for us. If we know we only care about certain subelements of the element we've focused on, we can ask for just those elements using getChildrenByTagName(). This function takes the name of an element and returns only the nodes containing that element. For example, in our document we might want to only retrieve the interface definition(s) of a host:

```
my $root = $doc->documentElement();
my @children = $root->childNodes;

my $current = $children[5]; # <host></host> element for krosp
my @interface_nodes = $current->getChildrenByTagName('interface');
```

This grep()-like function saves us the effort of iterating over all of the children of a node looking for the elements of interest. If you have a sufficiently large tree, the reduction in effort can make a real difference. A more exciting method related to getChildrenByTagName() is getElementsByTagName(). getElementsByTagName() will search not only the children of the node it is called from, but everything below that node in the tree. If we wanted to retrieve all of the interface definitions for all of the hosts, we could write something like this:

```
my $root = $doc->documentElement();
my @interface_nodes = $root->getElementsByTagName('interface');
```

Once we've found the node or nodes we want in the tree, we can retrieve the child text nodes that store what you would probably consider the "contents" of an element's node (if you didn't know that that info is actually kept in a separate text sub-node):

```
foreach my $node ( @interface_nodes ) {
  $node->textContent(); # returns the contents of all child text nodes
}
```

If that node has attributes, we can list them or get their values:

```
foreach my $attribute ($node->attributes()){
   print $attribute->nodeName . ":" . $attribute->getValue() . "\n";
}
# or to retrieve a specific attribute:
print $node->getAttribute('name') if $node->hasAttribute('name');
```

Attributes of elements are stored in an associated attribute node, which is why we can call nodeName() here to get the attribute's name. Attribute nodes are associated with their elements but are not children of those element nodes in the same way the text nodes that hold the "contents"[†] of the elements are. For instance, if we call childNodes(), they are not listed as children. This is true in both the DOM and XPath specs.

[†] I'm using snarky quotes around the word "contents" here and elsewhere to indicate that an element node doesn't actually have data in it. It has one or more child text nodes that hold its data. But when you see <moo>baa-la-la</moo> it is hard not to think of "baa-la-la" as the contents of the <moo></moo> element node.

To change the "contents" of an element node, we change the data in the appropriate child text node:

```
# If we know that a node has a single child, and that child is a text
# node, we can go right to it. To test whether it is a text node, we
# could do something like the first line below.
#
# If we don't know which child (or children) of the node holds the data we
# want, we can iterate over the list returned by childNodes(), testing
# nodeType() and textContent() as we go along.

my $textnode = $node->firstChild
  if ($node->firstChild->nodeType == XML_TEXT_NODE);

$textnode->setData('new information');
```

There are various methods, such as `insertData()`, `appendData()`, and `replaceData()`, that let us operate on the text node as we would expect. Attribute modification takes place on the element node directly using the analogous call to `getAttribute()`: `setAttribute()`.

Operating on the data associated with nodes is the most common task, but sometimes we need to manipulate the node tree itself. If we want to add or delete elements (and/or their subelements) to or from an XML document, we'll need to mess with its nodes. Let's start with the second operation, deletion, because it is the easier of the two. To delete a node (perhaps deleting a whole branch of the tree at the same time), we locate that node's parent and tell it to remove the node in question:

```
my $parent = $node->parentNode;
$parent->removeChild($node);
```

Alternatively, we can chain these two steps. In case you are curious, `$node` gets a new parent (a `XML::LibXML::DocumentFragment` node) after the following is executed:

```
$node->parentNode->removeChild($node)
```

Adding an element node to a tree is a little trickier because we have to construct everything about that node before adding it to the tree. That is, we have to make the node itself, set any attributes, create text nodes and any other sub-nodes, and give those nodes values; only then can we finally connect it to the tree.

For example, let's say we wanted to add a new `<meta></meta>` element. In this element, we'll place other elements that describe the network. One such element could be `<type></type>` to help us distinguish development (or staging) networks from production networks. The XML in question would look like this (whitespace added for readability):

```
<meta>
  <type name="production">This is a production network</type>
</meta>
```

To create just that much, we'd write code like this:

```
# let's build the XML elements from the inside out
my $type = $doc->createElement('type');
$type->setAttribute( 'name', 'production' );
$type->appendTextNode('This is a production network');

my $meta = $doc->createElement('meta');

# make <type></type> a subelement, or child, of <meta></meta>
$meta->appendChild($type);
```

If you are suitably anal retentive (a good quality in a network administrator), you are probably bothered by the <description></description> element being a separate element in the document (rather than a subelement of <meta></meta>, where it rightfully belongs). To fix this, let's move it into the meta tag:

```
my $root = $doc->documentElement();

# find the <description></description> element that is a child of the
# root element and make it the last child of the <meta></meta>
# element instead
$meta->appendChild($root->getChildrenByTagName('description'));
```

Now that we have the XML fragment, let's place it into our document's node tree. If we wanted to be lazy, we could simply add it to the end of the document by making it a child of the root element ($root->appendChild($meta)), but what we really want is to have it come first in the document, since it describes the data that will follow:

```
my $root = $doc->documentElement();

# place it before the root element's current first child
$root->insertBefore($meta,$root->firstChild);
```

If you plan to insert lots of nodes, crafting them by hand can be a bit tedious. Fortunately, XML::LibXML provides a very nice shortcut called parse_balanced_chunk() that takes in XML data and returns a document fragment that can be linked into your node tree. Let's use our first <meta></meta> example to demonstrate this technique:

```
my $root = $doc->documentElement();

my $xmltoinsert = <<'EOXML';
<meta>
  <type name="production">This is a production network</type>
</meta>
EOXML

my $meta = $prsr->parse_balanced_chunk($xmltoinsert);

$root->insertBefore($meta,$root->firstChild);
```

Once you have the tree you want in memory, with whatever changes you made to the nodes or the tree itself, writing it out is a snap:

```
open my $OUTPUT_FILE, '>', $filename or
  die "Can't open $filename for writing: $!\n";
```

```
print $OUTPUT_FILE $doc->toString;
close $OUTPUT_FILE;
```

That's basically how to work with a document via the DOM model. Once you get this far into understanding XML::LibXML, the documentation may start to make more sense to you, so be sure to give the XML::LibXML::{Element, Node, Attr and Text} documentation another read for the countless methods left out of this brief introduction.

If you are one of the people who took my earlier suggestion and read the XPath appendix, you may be curious about how you can put your newfound XPath knowledge into practice. Let's look at that now.

As I mentioned before, XML::LibXML programs that use XPath start the same way as those that are DOM-based:

```
use XML::LibXML;

my $prsr = XML::LibXML->new();
$prsr->keep_blanks(0);
my $doc = $prsr->parse_file('config.xml');
```

The difference begins at the point where you want to start navigating the node tree or querying nodes from it. Instead of manually walking nodes, you can instead bring location paths into the picture using findnodes(). For comparison's sake, let's go back and redo some of the DOM examples using XPath. The first example we saw with DOM was a list of the root's child nodes. Here's the XPath equivalent:

```
my @children = $doc->findnodes('/network/*');

foreach my $node (@children){
    print "$node->nodeName()\n";
}
```

Not so exciting, I know. But now let's look at the very next example, where we had to do a lot of work to get the data associated with the first service provided by the second host in our XML config file. With XPath, all of that code gets whittled down to a line or two:

```
# we ask for the single node we're going to get back using a
# list context (the parens around $node) because findnodes()
# returns a NodeList object in a scalar context
my ($tnode) = $doc->findnodes('/network/host[2]/service[1]/text()');
print $tnode->data . "\n";

# or, if you'd like to do this in a way that allows for
# a query that could return multiple text nodes:
foreach my $tnode ($doc->findnodes('/network/host[2]/service[1]/text()')){
  print $tnode->data . "\n";
}
```

With one findnodes() call, we can locate the correct nodes and return their associated text nodes. findnodes() gives us all of the power of XPath 1.0's location paths. This power includes things like the descendant operator (//), which can easily replicate the functionality of the DOM getChildrenByTagName() and getElementByTagName() calls and add a whole new level of sophistication at the same time (thanks to XPath predicates):

```
# find all of the hosts that currently provide more than one service
my @multiservers = $doc->findnodes('//host[count(service) > 1]');

# find their names (name attribute values) instead and print them
foreach my $anode ($doc->findnodes('//host[count(service) > 1]/@name')){
  print $anode->value . "\n";
}
```

Here we've used the XPath descendant operator to find all the host element nodes in the document and then filtered that set using the XPath function count() in a predicate.

Now let's look at a simple XPath example that demonstrates the programmatic flexibility XML::LibXML offers:

```
@nodes = $doc->findnodes('/network/host[@type = "server"]//addr');
```

This XPath expression will find all servers and return their <addr></addr> element nodes. We probably don't want the nodes themselves, though; we more likely want the actual information stored in their text node children (i.e., the addresses they "hold"). There are three things you could do at this point, depending on your programming style and perhaps the larger context of the program:

1. Change the XPath expression to look more like the previous example (i.e., add a text() step):

    ```
    @nodes = $doc->findnodes('/network/host[@type = "server"]//addr/text()');
    ```

    This gets you all of the text nodes that hold the address values. We've already seen how to iterate over a list of text nodes, extracting their contents with a data() method call as we go, so I won't repeat that foreach() loop here.

2. Make additional XPath evaluation calls from each of the nodes found:

    ```
    foreach my $node (@nodes){
        print $node->find('normalize-space(./text())') . "\n";
    }
    ```

    Here we've called find() and not findnodes() because we're going to evaluate an XPath expression that will yield a string (not a node or node set). The expression we're evaluating says, "Start at the current node, find its associated text node, and normalize its value (i.e., strip the leading/trailing whitespace)." We could have left out the normalize-space() XPath function call and kept it like the other examples in this list, but this way helps show how breaking the task into two XPath calls can lead to more legible location paths in your code.

3. Switch to using DOM methods at this point:

    ```
    foreach my $node (@nodes) {
        print $node->textContent() . "\n";
    }
    ```

The last choice may seem the least sexy of the three, but it is actually one of the more important options at this point in our XPath-related discussion. XPath is superb for navigating a document or querying certain information from it, but it doesn't address how to modify that document at all. Once we've found the information we want to modify, or if we want to make some change to the tree starting at a node we've located, XPath steps out of the picture and we're back in DOM-land again. Everything we saw a little earlier in this section about how to modify the information stored in the node tree or how to mess with the tree itself now comes into play. If we want to change the data stored in a text node, we call `setData()`. If we want to remove a node, we call `removeChild()` from its parent, and so on. Even the use of `to_string()` to write out the tree is the same.

XPath and XHTML

Here's a tip that Petra Pajas, the current maintainer of `XML::LibXML`, recommended I share with you:

Beginners using XPath to parse an XHTML document (e.g., via `XML::LibXML`) often get stymied because simple XPath location paths like `/html/body` don't appear to match anything. Questions about this come up time and time again on the perl-XML mailing list because it certainly looks like it should work.

Here's the trick: XHTML has a default namespace of its own predefined (`<html xmlns="http://www.w3.org/1999/xhtml">`). See the sidebar "XML Namespaces" on page 224 for a more complete explanation, but if we were to use Perl terms, you could think of the `<html></html>` and `<body></body>` elements as living in a separate package from the default one the XPath parser would normally search. To get around this, we have to give the XPath implementation a mapping that assigns a prefix for that namespace. Once we've done this, we can successfully use location paths that include the prefix we defined. For example, `/x:html/x:body` will now do the right thing.

To create this mapping in `XML::LibXML`, we create a new `XPathContext` (a context in which we're going to do XPath work) and then register a prefix for the XHTML namespace in it. Here's a code snippet that demonstrates how this is done. The code extracts the textual contents of all paragraph nodes in a document:

```
use XML::LibXML;
use XML::LibXML::XPathContext;

my $doc = XML::LibXML->new->parse_file('index.xhtml');
my $xpath = XML::LibXML::XPathContext->new($doc);

$xpath->registerNs( x => 'http://www.w3.org/1999/xhtml' );

for my $paragraph ($xpath->findnodes('//x:p')) {
  print $paragraph->textContent,"\n";
}
```

Hope this tip saves you a bit of frustration.

To drive this point home and reinforce what you learned earlier, let's look at a more extended example of some XPath/DOM interactions used to do real work. For this example, we'll generate a DNS zone file for the wired network portion of the XML config file we've been using. To keep the focus on XML, we'll use the GenerateHeader code from Chapter 5 to generate a correct and current zone file header:

```
use XML::LibXML;
use Readonly;

Readonly my $domain => '.example.edu';

# from the programs we wrote in Chapter 5
print GenerateHeader();

my $prsr = XML::LibXML->new();
$prsr->keep_blanks(0);
my $doc = $prsr->parse_file('config.xml');

# find all of the interface nodes of machines connected over Ethernet
foreach
    my $interface ( $doc->findnodes('//host/interface[@type ="Ethernet"]') )
{

    # print a pretty comment for each machine with info retrieved via
    # DOM methods
    my $p = $interface->parentNode;
    print "\n; "
        . $p->getAttribute('name')
        . ' is a '
        . $p->getAttribute('type')
        . ' running '
        . $p->getAttribute('os') . "\n";

    # print the A record for the host
    #
    # yes, we could strip off the domain and whitespace using
    # a Perl regexp (and that might make more sense), but this is just
    # an example so you can see how XPath functions can be used
    my $arrname = $interface->find(
        " substring-before( normalize-space( arec / text() ), '$domain' ) ");

    print "$arrname \tIN A \t \t "
        . $interface->find('normalize-space(addr/text())') . " \n ";

    # find all of the CNAME RR and print them as well
    #
    # an example of using DOM and XPath methods in the same for loop
    # note: XPath calls can be computationally expensive, so you would
    # (in production) not want to place them in a loop in a loop
    foreach my $cnamenode ( $interface->getChildrenByTagName('cname') ) {
        print $cnamenode->find(
            " substring-before(normalize-space(./text()),'$domain')")
            . "\tIN CNAME\t$arrname\n";
    }
```

```
    # we could do more here, e.g., output SRV records ...
}
```

Now let's shift gears entirely and leave tree-based XML parsing behind for a bit.

Working with XML using SAX2 via XML::SAX

SAX2 via XML::SAX Pros and Cons

Benefits:

- Data can be parsed as it is received (you don't have to wait for the entire document to begin processing).

- SAX2 has become a multilingual standard. (SAX started out in the Java world but was quickly adopted by all of the major scripting languages as well. This means your Perl SAX2 code, at least at a conceptual level, will be easy for your Java, Python, Ruby, and other colleagues to understand.)

- XML::SAX makes it easy to use different parser backends with the same basic code.

- XML::SAX is object-oriented through and through.

- SAX2 has some very cool advanced features, like pipelining (multiple XML filter routines connected to each other) and easy ways to consume data from non-XML sources or export data from XML.

Drawbacks:

- You snooze, you lose. The parser will send you information a single time. If you don't save that information or you realize you should have kept the data in a different data structure for later retrieval, you're out of luck!

- XML::SAX is object-oriented through and through. If your programming experience isn't particularly oriented toward this approach, the learning curve can be steep.

- Sometimes you have to do more coding because certain operations require manual labor. Examples include collecting textual data and finding specific elements. If you want to store anything from the document being parsed (e.g., if you need a tree), you have to do that by hand.

So when is it appropriate to use XML::SAX? This module is good for large XML data sets or conditions where collecting all of the data first into an in-memory tree isn't practical. XML::SAX works well if the idea of an event-based parsing model fits the way you think about your task at hand. If you are already using XML::Parser, this would be a good next step.

So far everything we've seen for handling XML requires us to slurp all of the data into some in-memory representation before we can begin to operate on it. Even if memory prices drop, at a certain point this doesn't scale. If you have a really huge XML data set, trying to keep it all in memory probably won't work. There are also issues of timing and efficiency. If you have to bring all the data into memory before you can proceed, the actual work can't take place until the parsing is totally complete. You can't start processing if your data hasn't entirely arrived yet (e.g., if it's coming over a network pipe). Finally, this model can yield a lot of unnecessary work, especially in those cases where your program is acting as a filter to modify data (e.g., renaming all `<service>` `</service>` elements to `<protocol></protocol>` elements or some such transformation). With a tree-based model, the parser treats every element it reads the same, even though most (in this case, everything that isn't a `<service></service>` element) aren't relevant to the task at hand.

We're going to look at a standard model for XML processing that uses an approach without these disadvantages: SAX. SAX stands for Simple API for XML and is currently in its second major revision (SAX2). It provides a processing model that treats the data in an XML document as a stream of events to be handled. To understand what this means, let's take a small digression into some Perl/XML history that is still relevant to this day.

Once upon a time, James Clark, the technical lead for the XML Working Group, created a really spiffy XML parser library in C called `expat`. `expat` was a well-respected piece of code, and as the popularity of XML increased, various developers started calling it from within their code to handle the work of parsing XML documents (as of this writing, important software projects such as Apache HTTP Server and Mozilla's Firefox browser still do). Larry Wall himself actually wrote the first module for calling *expat* from Perl. This module, `XML::Parser`, was subsequently maintained by Clark Cooper, who substantially revamped it and shepherded it for quite a number of years. It is now in the capable hands of Matt Sergeant.

`XML::Parser` provides several interfaces for working with XML data. Let's take a really quick look at its `stream` style (i.e., parsing mode), because it will allow us to slide back into talking about SAX2 with considerable ease.

First, some technical background. `XML::Parser` is an event-based module, which can be described using a stockbroker analogy. Before trading begins, you leave a set of instructions with the broker for actions she should take should certain triggers occur (e.g., sell a thousand shares should the price drop below 3¼ dollars per share, buy this stock at the beginning of the trading day, and so on). With event-based programs, the triggers are called *events* and the instructions for what to do when an event happens are called *event handlers*. Handlers are usually just special subroutines designed to deal with particular events. Some people call them *callback routines*, since they are run when the main program "calls us back" after a certain condition is established. With the `XML::Parser` module, our events will be things like "started parsing the data stream," "found a start tag," and "found an XML comment," and our handlers will do things like "print the contents of the element you just found."

Before we begin to parse our data, we need to create an `XML::Parser` object. When we create this object, we'll specify which parsing mode, or *style*, to use. `XML::Parser` provides several styles, each of which behaves a little differently. The style of a parse will determine which event handlers it calls by default and the way data returned by the parser (if any) is structured.

Certain styles require that we specify an association between each event we wish to manually process and its handler. No special actions are taken for events we haven't chosen to explicitly handle. This association is stored in a simple hash table with keys that are the names of the events we want to handle, and values that are references to our handler subroutines. For the styles that require this association, we pass in the hash using a named parameter called Handlers (for example, Handlers => {Start => \&start_handler}) when we create a parser object.

We'll be using the stream style, which does not require this initialization step: it simply calls a set of predefined event handlers if certain subroutines are found in the program's namespace. The stream event handlers we'll be using are simple: StartTag, EndTag, and Text. All but Text should be self-explanatory. Text, according to the XML::Parser documentation, is "called just before start or end tags with accumulated non-markup text in the $_ variable." We'll use it when we need to know the contents of a particular element. Let's take a look at the code first, and then we'll explore a few of the interesting points it demonstrates:

```perl
use strict;
use XML::Parser;
use YAML; # needed for display, not part of the parsing

my $parser = new XML::Parser(
    ErrorContext => 3,
    Style        => 'Stream',
    Pkg          => 'Config::Parse'
);

$parser->parsefile('config.xml');
print Dump( \%Config::Parse::hosts );

package Config::Parse;

our %hosts;
our $current_host;
our $current_interface;

sub StartTag {
    my $parser  = shift;
    my $element = shift;
    my %attr    = %_; # not @_, see the XML::Parser doc

    if ( $element eq 'host' ) {
        $current_host             = $attr{name};
        $hosts{$current_host}{type} = $attr{type};
        $hosts{$current_host}{os}   = $attr{os};
    }
```

```perl
        if ( $element eq 'interface' ) {
            $current_interface = $attr{name};
            $hosts{$current_host}{interfaces}{$current_interface}{type}
                = $attr{type};
        }
    }

    sub Text {
        my $parser          = shift;
        my $text            = $_;
        my $current_element = $parser->current_element();

        $text =~ s/^\s+|\s+$//g;

        if ( $current_element eq 'arec' or $current_element eq 'addr' ) {
            $hosts{$current_host}{interfaces}{$current_interface}
                {$current_element} = $text;
        }

        if ( $current_element eq 'cname' ) {
            push(
                @{ $hosts{$current_host}{interfaces}{$current_interface}{cnames}
                    },
                $text
            );
        }

        if ( $current_element eq 'service' ) {
            push( @{ $hosts{$current_host}{services} }, $text );
        }

    }

    sub StartDocument { }
    sub EndTag        { }
    sub PI            { }
    sub EndDocument   { }
```

The StartTag() and Text() subroutines do all the work in this code. If we see a
<host> start tag, we create a new hash key for the host (found in the tag's attributes)
and store the information found in the attributes in a sub-hash keyed by its name. We
also set a global variable to keep the name of the host found in that tag in play for the
subelements nested in that <host></host> element. One such element is the
element. If we see its starting tag, we add a nested hash for
the interface to the hash being kept for the current host and similarly set a global variable
so we can use the current interface name when we subsequently parse its subelements.
This use of global variables to maintain state in a nested set of elements is a common
idiom when working with XML::Parser, although it's not particularly elegant from a
programming or program maintenance perspective (for all the "unprotected global
variables are icky" reasons). The tutorial for XML::SAX points out that it would be better

to use a closure to maintain state when using XML::Parser, but that would make our code more complex than we really need given that this is just a stepping-stone example.

The Text() subroutine deals with the elements we care about that have data in them. For <arec></arec> and <addr></addr>, which appear only once in an interface, we store the values in the appropriate interface's sub-hash. We can tell which is the appropriate interface by consulting the global variables StartTag() sets. The code that handles <cname></cname> and <service></service> tags is a hair more complex, because there can be more than one instance of these tags in an interface or host element. To handle the possibility of multiple values, their contents get pushed onto an anonymous array that will be stored in the host record.

The two other interesting parts of this code are the empty subroutines at the end and the way the data structure that gets generated by StartTag() and Text() is displayed. The empty subroutines are there because XML::Parser in stream style will print the data from any event that doesn't have a subroutine defined to handle it. We don't want any output from those events, so we define empty subroutines for them.

The data structure we create is displayed using YAML. Here's an excerpt of the program's output:

```
agatha:
  interfaces:
    eth0:
      addr: 192.168.0.4
      arec: agatha.example.edu
      cnames:
        - mail.example.edu
      type: Ethernet
  os: linux
  services:
    - SMTP
    - POP3
    - IMAP4
  type: server

...

zeetha:
  interfaces:
    en0:
      addr: 192.168.0.101
      arec: zeetha.example.edu
      type: Ethernet
    en1:
      addr: 192.168.100.101
      arec: zeetha.wireless.example.edu
      type: AirPort
  os: osx
  type: client
```

We'll be looking at YAML a little later in the chapter, so consider this a foreshadowing of some good stuff to come.

Now let's get to SAX2, because we're practically there. Similar to `XML::Parser`'s `stream` style, SAX2 is an event-based API that requires us to provide the code to handle events as the XML parser generates them. One of the main differences between `XML::Parser` and `XML::SAX` is that the latter is object-oriented through and through. This can be a bit of a stumbling block for people without an OOP background, so I will try to keep the `XML::SAX` example as simple as possible from an OOP perspective. If you really want a good grasp of how OOP in Perl functions, Damian Conway's *Object Oriented Perl: A Comprehensive Guide to Concepts and Programming Techniques* (Manning) is your best resource. The only other caveat is that we'll only be skimming the surface of the subject in this fly-by. There are further SAX2 pointers in the references section at the end of the chapter that can help you go deeper into the subject.

Enough preface; let's see some code. We need to write two kinds of code to use `XML::SAX`: the parser initialization code and the event handlers. The parser initialization for a simple parse consists of asking `XML::SAX::ParserFactory` to hand us back a parser instance:

```
use XML::SAX;
use YAML;            # needed for display, not part of the parsing

use HostHandler;     # we'll define this in a moment

my $parser = XML::SAX::ParserFactory->parser( Handler => HostHandler->new );
```

There are two things about this code snippet that aren't obvious at first glance. First, it includes `HostHandler`, which is the module we'll construct in a moment that implements the event handling class. I called it `HostHandler` because it provides the handler object the parser will use to handle the SAX2 events as they come in from parsing our host definition.[‡] The class's `new()` method returns the object used to encapsulate that code. If this seems a bit confusing, hang tight. When we return to this subject in a moment with some concrete code examples, it should all gel.

Let's get back to the parser initialization code. The second unobvious feature of this code is the module being called with the huge name of `XML::SAX::ParserFactory`. This module's purpose (I'm intentionally avoiding using the OOP parlance here) is to return a parser object from an appropriate parser-providing module. Examples of parser-providing modules include `XML::LibXML` and `XML::SAX::PurePerl`, the pure-Perl parser packaged with `XML::SAX`. `XML::SAX::ParserFactory` provides a generic way to request a parser, so you can write the same code independently of which `XML::SAX`-friendly parser module you intend to use. In this case we're letting `XML::SAX::ParserFactory` pick one for us, though there are ways of being more picky (see the documentation).

[‡] The name was arbitrary. It could have been `BobsYourUncle`, but I'd recommend sticking to something at least vaguely understandable to someone reading your code.

Once we have a parser ready to go, we aim it at our XML document just as we did with every other parser we've used to date:

```
open my $XML_DOC, '<', 'config.xml' or die "Could not open config.xml:$!";

# parse_file takes a filehandle, not a filename
$parser->parse_file($XML_DOC);

close $XML_DOC;

print Dump( \%HostHandler::hosts );
```

Now let's see where the real action in SAX lives—the event handling code. We'll take it in bite-sized pieces and use our previous XML::Parser example for comparison. As with XML::Parser, we're going to need to write a few subroutines that will fire based on what the parser finds as it moves through the document. The names are a little different, though: StartTag() becomes start_element(), EndTag() becomes end_element(), and Text() (mostly) becomes characters().

There is one big difference between the two sets of subroutines: the XML::Parser subroutines were unaffiliated subroutines that lived in a specific package, but the XML::SAX subroutines need to be class methods. If your lack of an OOP background makes you break out into a cold sweat when you hear terms like "class method," don't panic! XML::SAX makes it really easy. All you need to do is include two lines like these ahead of your subroutines, and presto, you have class methods (or more precisely, you are now overriding the default methods XML::SAX::Base provides):

```
package HostHandler;
use base 'XML::SAX::Base';
```

XML::SAX::Base handles all of the scut work associated with the parser object, including defining the new() method we called in our parser initialization code.

 If you haven't already done so, now would be a good time to shift your mental model so you are thinking solely (even on a very basic level) in terms of objects. Nothing fancy is required. Keep it as simple as this: there's a parser object, and it will encapsulate code and data for us.

The code in the object (the object's method calls) consists of subroutines that the parser will call when it finds something of interest. For example, if the parser finds a start tag for an element, the object's start_element() method is called. Other code, such as little utility routines, will also reside in this object. We can even use the object to hold data for us (e.g., the name of the host whose record we're parsing), instead of using global variables like we did in the previous section.

That's it—that's all the OOP knowledge you'll need for the rest of this section.

Let's look at the first of those method definitions. Here's the method that gets called when the parser finds the start tag for an element:

```perl
# %hosts is used to collect all of the parsed data
# (yes, we could keep this in the object itself)
my %hosts;

sub start_element {
    my ( $self, $element ) = @_;

    $self->_contents('');

    # these weird '{}something' hash keys are using James Clark notation;
    # we'll address this convention in a moment when we talk about
    # XML namespaces
    if ( $element->{LocalName} eq 'host' ) {
        $self->{current_host} = $element->{Attributes}{'{}name'}{Value};
        $hosts{ $self->{current_host} }{type}
            = $element->{Attributes}{'{}type'}{Value};
        $hosts{ $self->{current_host} }{os}
            = $element->{Attributes}{'{}os'}{Value};
    }

    if ( $element->{LocalName} eq 'interface' ) {
        $self->{current_interface} = $element->{Attributes}{'{}name'}{Value};
        $hosts{ $self->{current_host} }{interfaces}
            { $self->{current_interface} }{type}
            = $element->{Attributes}{'{}type'}{Value};
    }

    $self->{current_element} = $element->{LocalName};

    $self->SUPER::start_element($element);
}
```

This subroutine has obviously been modified from its equivalent in the XML::Parser example, so let's look at the differences. The first change is in the arguments passed to the event handler. XML::SAX passes to its handlers a reference to the parser object as the first argument and handler-specific data in the rest of the arguments. start_element() gets information in its second argument about the element the parser has just seen via a reference to a data structure that looks like this:

```
0  HASH(0xa30624)
   'LocalName' => 'host'
   'Name' => 'host'
   'NamespaceURI' => undef
   'Prefix' => ''
   'Attributes' => HASH(0xa30768)
      '{}name' => HASH(0xa3033c)
         'LocalName' => 'name'
         'Name' => 'name'
         'NamespaceURI' => ''
         'Prefix' => ''
         'Value' => 'agatha'
```

```
'{}os' => HASH(0xa307f8)
  'LocalName' => 'os'
  'Name' => 'os'
  'NamespaceURI' => ''
  'Prefix' => ''
  'Value' => 'linux'
'{}type' => HASH(0xa30678)
  'LocalName' => 'type'
  'Name' => 'type'
  'NamespaceURI' => ''
  'Prefix' => ''
  'Value' => 'server'
```

It's a hash with the fields described in Table 6-1.

Table 6-1. Contents of the hash passed to start_element()

Hash key	Contents
LocalName	The name of the element, without any namespace prefix (see the sidebar "XML Namespaces" for more info on what that means)
Name	The name of the element, including the namespace prefix
Prefix	The namespace prefix for this element (if it has one)
NamespaceURI	The URI for the element's namespace (if it has one)
Attributes	A hash of hashes containing information about the element's attributes

XML Namespaces

Up to now, I've intentionally avoided any mention of the concept of XML namespaces. They don't usually show up in smallish XML documents (like config files), and I didn't want to add an extra layer of complexity to the rest of the material. But XML::SAX provides namespace information to its event handlers, so we should give them at least a passing glance before moving on. If you'd like more detail about XML namespaces, the best place to start is the official W3C recommendation on the subject at *http://www.w3.org/TR/REC-xml-names/*.

XML namespaces are a way of making sure that elements in a document are unique and partitioned. If our document had an element called <orange></orange>, its contents or subelements could refer to either a color or a fruit. For a contrived case, imagine the situation where a design firm needs to provide information about a new juice box to a citrus grower's organization. The file could easily use <orange></orange> elements for both senses of the word. With namespaces, you can add an extra attribute (xmlns) to disambiguate an element:

```
<orange xmlns="http://colors.example.com/chart"> ... </orange>
```

Now everything in the element has a namespace associated with that URI[*] and it's clear just what kind of orange we're talking about.[†]

A slightly more complex XML namespace syntax lets you define multiple namespaces in the same element, each with its own identifying string (called a *prefix*):

```
<juicebox xmlns:color="http://colors.example.com/chart"
          xmlns:fruit="http://fruits.example.com/fruitlst">
    <color:orange>#ffa500</color:orange>
    <fruit:orange>Citrus sinensis</fruit:orange>
</juicebox>
```

In this case, we've defined two different namespaces with the prefixes `color` and `fruit`. We can then use these prefixes to label the two `<orange></orange>` subelements appropriately with *namespace*: `orange`, as in the preceding code, so there is no confusion. I did say the example was contrived....

One last related note: James Clark, source of much impressive work in the XML world (including the `expat` parser we discussed earlier in the chapter) invented an informal syntax for displaying namespaces that has become known as "James Clark notation." It uses the form `<{namespace}element_name>`. In this notation, our first example from earlier would be written as:

```
<{http://colors.example.com/chart}orange> ... </orange>
```

This syntax isn't accepted by any XML parser, but it is used in places like `XML::SAX`'s representation of attributes.

If an element has attributes (as in the sample data we just saw), the attributes are stored in their own hash of hashes data structure. The keys of that hash are the attribute names, represented in James Clark notation (see the previous sidebar). The content of each key is a hash whose keys are described in Table 6-2.

Table 6-2. Contents of the hash used to store attribute information

Hash key	Contents
LocalName	The name of the attribute without any namespace prefix
Name	The name of the attribute including the namespace prefix (if it has one)
Prefix	The namespace prefix for this element (if it has one)
NamespaceURI	The URI for the attribute's namespace (if it has one and the attribute was prefixed)
Value	The attribute's value

[*] The URI here is just used as a convenient unique string that will describe the namespace. It doesn't have to be real—the parser never opens a network connection to attempt to reach the URI. It is considered cool to have something at that URI for documentation purposes (e.g., *http://www.w3.org/1999/XSL/Transform*), but this isn't required.

[†] If it helps you understand the concept, think of XML namespaces like `package` statements in Perl. `package foo` puts all of the subsequent code (until another `package` statement comes along) into the `foo` namespace. This lets you have two scalars called `$orange` in the same program, each in its own namespace.

Our configuration file didn't use namespaces, so the attributes in our data structure all start out with empty prefixes ({}). This is what makes their hash keys look so funny.

Now that you understand how information about an element is passed into `start_element()`, hopefully the code shown earlier will start to make more sense. If you ignore the `_content()` and `SUPER::start_element()` methods (we'll get to those in a few moments), all the code is doing is either copying information out of the `$element` data structure into our `%hosts` hash or squirreling away information from `$element` (like the current element name) into the parser object‡ for later use.

That's what happens when the parse encounters a new start tag. Let's see what it does for the textual contents (as opposed to another subelement) of the element:

```perl
sub characters {
    my ( $self, $data ) = @_;

    $self->_contents( $self->_contents() . $data->{Data} );

    $self->SUPER::characters($data);
}
```

You'll notice this is much smaller than the `Text()` subroutine in our `XML::Parser` example. All it does is use a separate `_contents()` method* to collect the data it receives (ignore the second mysterious `SUPER::` line, I'll explain it soon). That method looks like this:

```perl
# stash any text passed to us in the parser object or return the
# current contents of that stash
sub _contents {
    my ( $self, $text ) = @_;

    $self->{'_contents'} = $text if defined $text;

    return $self->{'_contents'};
}
```

The `characters()` method is much smaller than the `Text()` subroutine because of a subtle but important difference in how the two work. With `Text()`, the module author guaranteed that it would receive (to quote the docs) "accumulated non-markup text." That's not the way it works for `characters()`. The `XML::SAX` tutorial says: "A SAX parser has to make no guarantees whatsoever about how many times it may call `characters` for a stretch of text in an XML document—it may call once, or it may call once for every character in the text." As a result, we can't make the same assumptions that we did before in our `XML::Parser` code about when we have the entire text contents of the element to be stored. Instead, we have to push that work into `end_element()`, because

---

‡ OOP purists will probably stomp on me with their steel-toed boots because the code isn't using "getters" and "setters" for that squirreling. I'm trying to keep the amount of code in the example down to keep the focus on `XML::SAX`, but point taken, so you can stop kicking me now.

* If just to placate the OOP thugs from the last footnote just a little bit....

by then we're certain we've collected the contents of an element. The first thing the `end_element()` handler does is retrieve the current contents of the collected data and strip the leading/following whitespace, just in case we want to store it for posterity:

```perl
sub end_element {
    my ( $self, $element ) = @_;

    my $text = $self->_contents();

    $text =~ s/^\s+|\s+$//g;    # remove leading/following whitespace

    if (    $self->{current_element} eq 'arec'
        or $self->{current_element} eq 'addr' )
    {
        $hosts{ $self->{current_host} }{interfaces}
            { $self->{current_interface} }{ $self->{current_element} }
            = $text;
    }

    if ( $self->{current_element} eq 'cname' ) {
        push(
            @{ $hosts{ $self->{current_host} }{interfaces}
                    { $self->{current_interface} }{cnames}
            },
            $text
        );
    }

    if ( $self->{current_element} eq 'service' ) {
        push( @{ $hosts{ $self->{current_host} }{services} }, $text );
    }

    $self->SUPER::end_element($element);
}

1; # to make sure the HostHandler module will load properly
```

One quick warning about this code: it makes no attempt to handle mixed content situations like this:

```xml
<element>
  This is some text in the element.
  <sub_element> This is some text in a subelement </sub_element>
  This is some more text in the element.
</element>
```

You can handle mixed content using `XML::SAX`, but it increases the complexity of the event handlers beyond what I wanted to show for a basic SAX2 example.

We're practically done with our exploration of SAX2-based XML reading. There are a number of more advanced SAX techniques that we won't have room to explore. One of those holds the secret to the lines of code in our example that began `$self->SUPER::`, so I want to at least mention it. SAX2-based coding makes it very easy to construct multistage pipelines, like Unix-style pipes. A piece of SAX2 code can take in a stream of SAX2 events, transform/filter them in some fashion, and then pass the events on to the next handler. `XML::SAX` makes it relatively easy to hook up handlers (`XML::SAX::Machine` by Barrie Slaymaker makes it *very* easy). The `$self->SUPER::` calls in each of our methods makes sure that the events get passed on correctly should our code be placed somewhere before the end of a pipeline. Even if you don't think it will happen to your code, it is good practice to include those lines.

Working with XML using a hybrid approach (XML::Twig)

XML::Twig Pros and Cons

Benefits:

- It offers a very Perl-centric approach.
- It's engineered to handle very large data sets in a memory/CPU-efficient and granular manner. It is especially good in those scenarios where you need to operate on a small portion of a much larger document. You can instruct `XML::Twig` to process only a particular element and its subelements, and it will create an in-memory representation of just that part of your data. You can then flush this document fragment from memory and replace it with the next instance of the desired element.
- It has the ability to use XPath-like selectors when choosing what data to process. These selectors make it easy to construct callbacks (i.e., give it an XPath selector and it will run a piece of code when it finds something in the document that matches the selector).
- The module offers a nice compromise between tree-based processing (similar to `XML::LibXML`'s DOM features) and stream-based processing (like the SAX2 processing model).
- It can also read HTML (it uses `HTML::TreeBuilder`'s XML export, so it needs to read the entire doc into memory).
- It has options to maintain attribute order and to pretty-print in a format that's easy to read.
- Its emphasis is on DWIM (do what I mean).
- It has superb documentation (*http://www.xmltwig.com*) and author support.

Drawbacks:

- It's not particularly standards-compliant (in the way `XML::SAX` follows SAX2 and `XML::LibXML` implements the W3C DOM model), but that may not matter to you.
- It implements only a subset of the XPath 1.0 standard (albeit a very useful subset).
- Depending on the situation, it can be slower than `XML::LibXML`.
- It uses `expat` as its underlying parser (probably not an issue because it's so solid, but `expat` doesn't see much active maintenance).

When should you use this module? `XML::Twig` is especially good for situations where you are processing a large data set but only need to operate on a smaller subset of that

---

data. Once you grok its basic way of thinking about the world (as "twigs"), it can be a pleasure for someone with Perl and a dash of XPath experience to use.

There's considerable overlap between `XML::Twig`'s functionality and the functionality of the modules we've seen so far. Like the others, Michel Rodriguez's `XML::Twig` can create and manipulate an in-memory tree representation of an XML document (DOM-like) or parse the data while providing event-based callbacks. To keep this section short and sweet, I'm going to focus on the unique features `XML::Twig` provides. The excellent documentation and the module's website (*http://www.xmltwig.com*) can provide details on the rest of its functionality.

`XML::Twig`'s main premise is that an XML document should be processed as a bunch of subtrees. In Appendix B, I introduce the notion that you can represent an XML document as a big tree structure starting from the root element of the document. `XML::Twig` takes this one step further: it allows you to select certain subtrees of that structure ("twigs") as you parse the document and operate on those twigs while ignoring the rest of the data whizzing by. This selection takes place using a subset of the XPath 1.0 specification. Before parsing, you provide a set of XPath selectors and their callbacks (the Perl code to run when the selector matches). This is similar to some of the callback-based code we've seen earlier in this chapter, except now we're thinking about firing off code based on finding subtrees of a document rather than just certain elements or parse events. Let's see how this works in practice by looking at two simple examples. We'll use the same sample XML data file for these examples as well.

First, here's a simple example of data extraction from an XML document. If we wanted to extract just the `<interface></interface>` elements and their contents, we'd write:[†]

```
use XML::Twig;

my $twig = XML::Twig->new(
    twig_roots => {
        # $_ gets set to the element here
        'host/interface' => sub { $_->print },
    },
    pretty_print => 'indented',
);

$twig->parsefile('config.xml');
```

and the output would begin like this:

```
<interface name="eth0" type="Ethernet">
    <arec>agatha.example.edu</arec>
    <cname>mail.example.edu</cname>
    <addr>192.168.0.4</addr>
</interface>
```

[†] If we didn't want to write any code at all, `XML::Twig` comes with an *xml_grep* utility that would allow us to write `xml_grep 'host/interface' config.xml`. There is an `XML::LibXML`-based version of this utility at *http://xmltwig.com/tool/*.

```
        <interface name="eth0" type="Ethernet">
          <arec>gil.example.edu</arec>
          <cname>www.example.edu</cname>
          <addr>192.168.0.5</addr>
        </interface>
        <interface name="eth0" type="Ethernet">
          <arec>baron.example.edu</arec>
          <cname>dns.example.edu</cname>
          <cname>ntp.example.edu</cname>
          <cname>ldap.example.edu</cname>
          <addr>192.168.0.6</addr>
        </interface>
    ...
```

The key here is the `twig_roots` option, which lets `XML::Twig` know that we only care about `<interface></interface>` subtrees/twigs in the data found in each `<host></host>` element. For each twig found matching that specification, we ask the module to (pretty-)print its contents.

Let's follow that extraction example with a slightly more complex transformation example. If we wanted to modify our sample document so that all of the `<service></service>` elements became `<port></port>` elements instead (complete with port numbers as attributes), we would write something like this:

```perl
use XML::Twig;
use LWP::Simple;

my %port_fix = ( 'DNS'      => 'domain',
                 'IMAP4'    => 'imap',
                 'firewall' => 'all' );
my $port_list_url = 'http://www.iana.org/assignments/port-numbers';

my %port_list = &grab_iana_list;

my $twig = XML::Twig->new(
    twig_roots => { 'host/service' => \&transform_service_tags },
    twig_print_outside_roots => 1,
);

$twig->parsefile('config.xml');

# change <service> -> <port> and add that service's port number
# as an attribute
sub transform_service_tags {
    my ( $twig, $service_tag ) = @_;

    my $port_number = (
            $port_list{ lc $service_tag->trimmed_text }
        or $port_list{ lc $port_fix{ $service_tag->trimmed_text } }
        or $port_fix{ lc $service_tag->trimmed_text }
    );

    $service_tag->set_tag('port');
    $service_tag->set_att( number => $port_number );
```

```
        $twig->flush;
    }

    # retrieve the IANA allocated port list from its URL and return
    # a hash that maps names to numbers
    sub grab_iana_list {
        my $port_page = get($port_list_url);

        # each line is of the form:
        # service       port/protocol   explanation
        # e.g.:
        # http              80/tcp      World Wide Web HTTP
        my %ports = $port_page =~ /([\w-]+)\s+(\d+)\/(?:tcp|udp)/mg;

        return %ports;
    }
```

Let's take this apart step by step. First, we (somewhat gratuitously, I admit) grab the IANA-allocated port number list and return it as a hash for further lookups. Some of the service names we've used in our example won't be found in that assignment list, so we also load up a hash with the information we'll need to fix up any lookups that fail. Then we load `XML::Twig` with the selector we need and a reference to the subroutine that it will run when it finds that selector. In the same step, we also set `twig_print_outside_roots`, which tells `XML::Twig` to pass along any data from the document that *doesn't* match the `twig_roots` selector verbatim (as opposed to simply dropping it, as in our first example). With this defined, we pull the trigger and the parse commences on our sample config file.

The parse will hum along, passing input data to output data untouched until it finds a twig that matches the selector. When this happens, the entire twig, plus the element that was parsed to yield the twig, will be sent to the handler associated with that selector. In this case, the element in question is `<service></service>` and it contains a single piece of text: the name of the service. We request the whitespace-"trimmed" version of that text and use it to look up the port number in the hash we built from the IANA data. If we don't find it in the first lookup, we try again with a fixed-up version of the name (e.g., we look up "domain" if "DNS" wasn't found). If this second attempt fails, we give up on the IANA list and pull the value we need from the fixed-up hash itself (e.g., for the service "firewall," which isn't a network service with an assigned port).

`XML::Twig` makes it very simple to perform the actual transformation. `set_tag` changes the tag name and `set_att` lets us insert a new attribute with the port number we just retrieved. The final step for the handler is to instruct `XML::Twig` to print out the contents of the twig and remove it from memory before moving on in the document. This `flush` step is optional, but it is one of the keys to `XML::Twig`'s memory efficiency. Once flushed (or purged if you don't need to print that twig), the subtree you were working on no longer resides in memory, so each new subtree found takes up essentially the same space instead of accumulating in memory, like it would in a DOM-based representation.

`XML::Twig` has a ton of other methods available that make working with XML pretty easy for a Perl programmer. This section has just presented some of the essential pieces that differentiate it from the other approaches we explored; be sure to consult the documentation for more details.

With that, we can conclude our tour of the top three best-practice approaches (as of this writing) for dealing with XML from Perl. Now that you have some best-of-breed tools in your toolkit, you should be able to handle any XML challenge that comes your way using an approach well suited to that situation.

As a final note for this section, there are a number of up-and-coming modules that will also deserve your attention as they mature. Two of the more interesting ones I'd recommend you check out if you are going to work with XML are `XML::Rules` by Jenda Krynicky and `XML::Compile` by Mark Overmeer.

But what if, after all of that, you decide XML itself is close, but not exactly the best format for your particular needs? Well....

YAML

Some people think that XML has too much markup for each piece of content and would prefer something with fewer angle brackets. For these people, there is a lighter-weight format called YAML (which stands for YAML Ain't Markup Language). It's trying to solve a different problem than XML, but it often gets pressed into service for similar reasons.

YAML tries to strike a balance between structure and concision, so it looks a little cleaner to the average eye. Here's a fairly literal translation from the sample XML config file we rubbed raw in our discussion of XML:

```
---
network:
  description:
    name: Boston
    text: This is the configuration of our network in the Boston office.
  hosts:

    - name: agatha
      os: linux
      type: server
      interface:
        - name: eth0
          type: Ethernet
          addr: 192.168.0.4
          arec: agatha.example.edu
          cname:
            - mail.example.edu
      service:
        - SMTP
        - POP3
        - IMAP4
```

```
 - name: gil
   os: linux
   type: server
   interface:
     - name: eth0
       type: Ethernet
       addr: 192.168.0.5
       arec: gil.example.edu
       cname:
         - www.example.edu
   service:
     - HTTP
     - HTTPS

 - name: baron
   os: linux
   type: server
   interface:
     - name: eth0
       type: Ethernet
       addr: 192.168.0.6
       arec: baron.example.edu
       cname:
         - dns.example.edu
         - ntp.example.edu
         - ldap.example.edu
   service:
     - DNS
     - NTP
     - LDAP
     - LDAPS

 - name: mr-tock
   os: openbsd
   type: server
   interface:
     - name: fxp0
       type: Ethernet
       addr: 192.168.0.1
       arec: mr-tock.example.edu
       cname:
         - fw.example.edu
   service:
     - firewall

 - name: krosp
   os: osx
   type: client
   interface:
     - name: en0
       type: Ethernet
       addr: 192.168.0.100
       arec: krosp.example.edu
     - name: en1
       type: AirPort
```

```
            addr: 192.168.100.100
            arec: krosp.wireless.example.edu

    - name: zeetha
      os: osx
      type: client
      interface:
        - name: en0
          type: Ethernet
          addr: 192.168.0.101
          arec: zeetha.example.edu
        - name: en1
          addr: 192.168.100.101
          type: AirPort
          arec: zeetha.wireless.example.edu
```

Already this is probably looking a little easier on the eyes. It's a fairly literal translation because it attempts to preserve all of the XML attribute names (YAML doesn't have tag attributes *per se*, so all of the attributes and the contents of each element are listed in the same way). If direct conversion weren't a priority, we'd definitely want to write our config file in an even more straightforward way. For example, here's a repeat of the YAML file we generated earlier in the chapter while mucking about with `XML::Parser`:

```
agatha:
  interfaces:
    eth0:
      addr: 192.168.0.4
      arec: agatha.example.edu
      cnames:
        - mail.example.edu
      type: Ethernet
  os: linux
  services:
    - SMTP
    - POP3
    - IMAP4
  type: server

...

zeetha:
  interfaces:
    en0:
      addr: 192.168.0.101
      arec: zeetha.example.edu
      type: Ethernet
    en1:
      addr: 192.168.100.101
      arec: zeetha.wireless.example.edu
      type: AirPort
  os: osx
  type: client
```

There's not a big difference, but hopefully you'll get a sense that it is possible to simplify your data file even further by eliminating extraneous labels.

The Perl module to parse YAML[‡] is called, strangely enough, YAML and is used like this:

```perl
use YAML qw(DumpFile); # finds and loads an appropriate YAML parser

my $config = YAML::LoadFile('config.yml');

# (later...) dump the config back out to a file
YAML::DumpFile( 'config.yml' , $config );
```

The YAML module itself is just a frontend to other YAML parsers that provides a common interface similar to what we saw with XML::SAX. By default it provides simple Load/Dump procedure calls that operate on in-memory data, though you can also use LoadFile and DumpFile to work with files. That's almost all there is to it: you either Load YAML data from some place or Dump a YAML representation of the data.

If you'd prefer a more object-oriented way of working with YAML, Config::YAML can provide it. There is also a screamingly fast parser/dumper for YAML built on the libyaml library called YAML::XS. If you don't need a pure-Perl parser, that's the recommended module to use (the YAML module will attempt to use it by default if it is available).

And with that last simple but very powerful config file format, we can start to wrap up the chapter. There are an infinite number of possible formats for config files, but at least now we've hit the highlights.

All-in-One Modules

If all this talk about picking the right module for config parsing has started to wear on you, let me ease us toward the end of this chapter with a quick look at a set of modules that can help you sidestep the choice.

Config::Context is Michael Graham's wrapper around the Config::General, XML::Simple, and Config::Scoped modules that allows you to use a single module for each of the formats those modules handle. On top of this, it also adds contexts (as in Apache), so you can use <Location></Location> tags in those file formats.

If you crave a module that supports a larger menu of config file formats, Config::Auto by Jos Boumans can handle colon/space/equals-separated key/value pairs, XML formats, Perl code, .ini formats, and BIND9-style and .irssi config file formats. Not only that, but it will (by default) guess the format it is parsing for you without further specification. If that's too magical for you, you can specify the format yourself.

[‡] One nice property of YAML is that it is language-independent. There are YAML parsers and emitters for Ruby, Python, PHP, Java, OCaml, and even JavaScript.

Advanced Configuration Storage Mechanisms

You're probably sick of talking about config files at this point (I don't blame you), so let's end this chapter with a brief mention of some of the more advanced alternatives. There are a number of other reasonable places to stash configuration information.[*] Shared memory segments can work well when performance is the key criterion. Many systems are now keeping their configuration info in databases via DBI (see Chapter 7). Others have specific network servers to distribute configuration information. These are all interesting directions to explore, but beyond the scope of this book.

Module Information for This Chapter

Modules	CPAN ID	Version
Readonly	ROODE	1.03
Storable (ships with Perl)	AMS	2.15
DBM::Deep	RKINYON	1.0013
Text::CSV::Simple	TMTM	1.00
Text::CSV_XS	JWIED	0.23
Config::Std	DCONWAY	0.0.4
Config::General	TLINDEN	2.31
Config::Scoped	GAISSMA	0.11
Config::Grammar	DSCHWEI	1.02
XML::Writer	JOSEPHW	0.606
XML::Simple	GRANTM	2.18
XML::LibXML	PAJAS	1.69
XML::SAX	GRANTM	0.96
XML::Parser	MSERGEANT	2.36
XML::Twig	MIROD	3.32
LWP::Simple (ships with Perl)	GAAS	5.810
YAML	INGY	0.68
Config::YAML	MDXI	1.42
YAML::XS	NUFFIN	0.29
Config::Context	MGRAHAM	0.10
Config::Auto	KANE	0.16

---

[*] There are also a number of other *unreasonable* places; for example, hidden in image files using Acme::Steganography::Image::Png or in a play via Acme::Playwright.

References for More Information

Some of the material in this chapter is revised and modified from a column that I originally wrote for the February 2006 issue of the USENIX Association's ;login magazine (*http://usenix.org/publications/login/*).

Perl Best Practices (*http://oreilly.com/catalog/9780596001735/*), by Damian Conway (O'Reilly), has a good section on config files.

XML and YAML

http://msdn.microsoft.com/xml and *http://www.ibm.com/developer/xml* both contain copious information. Microsoft and IBM are very serious about XML.

http://www.activestate.com/support/mailing_lists.htm hosts the *Perl-XML* mailing list. It (along with its archive) is one of the best sources on this topic.

http://www.w3.org/TR/1998/REC-xml-19980210 is the actual XML 1.0 specification. Anyone who does anything with XML eventually winds up reading the full spec, but for anything but quick reference checks, I recommend reading an annotated version like those mentioned in the next two citations.

http://www.xml.com is a good reference for articles and XML links. It also offers an excellent annotated version of the XML specification created by Tim Bray, one of its authors.

XML: The Annotated Specification, by Bob DuCharme (Prentice Hall), is another excellent annotated version of the specification, chock-full of XML code examples.

XML Pocket Reference, Third Edition (*http://oreilly.com/catalog/9780596100506/*), by Simon St.Laurent and Michael Fitzgerald (O'Reilly), is a concise but surprisingly comprehensive introduction to XML for the impatient.

Learning XML, Second Edition (*http://oreilly.com/catalog/9780596004200/*), by Erik T. Ray (O'Reilly) and *Essential XML: Beyond Markup*, by Don Box et al. (Addison-Wesley) are good places to learn the range of XML-based technologies, including XPath. The latter is much more dense and less Perl-friendly but has a level of depth I haven't found in any other reference.

Perl and XML (*http://oreilly.com/catalog/9780596002053/*), by Erik T. Ray and Jason McIntosh (O'Reilly) is worth a look as well, though it was based on the XML modules current at that time. The Perl XML world has changed some since it was published in 2002, but it is a good reference for those modules that are still in use.

http://perl-xml.sourceforge.net is a hub for Perl XML-related development. The FAQ and Perl SAX pages at that site are important material you need to read.

http://xmlsoft.org is the official website for the Gnome `libxml` library on which `XML::LibXML` is based. You'll eventually find yourself here as you try to understand some arcane part of `XML::LibXML`.

http://www.saxproject.org is the official website for SAX2.

Object Oriented Perl: A Comprehensive Guide to Concepts and Programming Techniques, by Damian Conway (Manning), is the best place to learn about OOP in Perl. Understanding OOP in Perl is crucial for using `XML::SAX` well.

http://www.xmltwig.com is the official website for `XML::Twig` and is chock-full of good documentation, tutorials, presentations, etc.

http://www.yaml.org is the home base for everything YAML-related.

## CHAPTER 7

SQL Database Administration

What's a chapter on database administration doing in a system administration book? There are several strong reasons for people with interests in Perl and system administration to become database-savvy:

- A not-so-subtle thread running through several chapters of this book is the increasing importance of databases to modern-day system administration. We've used databases (albeit simple ones) to keep track of user and machine information, but that's just the tip of the iceberg. Mailing lists, password files, and even the Windows-based operating system registry are all examples of databases you probably interact with every day. All large-scale system administration packages (e.g., offerings from CA, Tivoli, HP, and Microsoft) depend on database backends. If you are planning to do any serious system administration, you are bound to bump into a database eventually.

- Database administration is a play within a play for system administrators. Database administrators (DBAs) have to contend with, among other things:
  — Logins/users
  — Log files
  — Storage management (disk space, etc.)
  — Process management
  — Connectivity issues
  — Backups
  — Security/role-based access control (RBAC)

  Sound familiar? We can and should learn from both knowledge domains.

- Perl is a glue language, arguably one of the best. Much work has gone into Perl/ database integration, thanks mostly to the tremendous energy surrounding web development. We can put this effort to work for us. Though Perl can integrate with several different database formats (Unix DBM, Berkeley DB, etc.), we're going to pay attention in this chapter to Perl's interface with large-scale database products. We address other formats elsewhere in this book.

- Many applications we use or support require some database for storing information (e.g., Bugzilla, Request Tracker, calendars, etc.). In order to have a good understanding of the applications we support, we need to be able to mess with the storage beneath the databases and make sure they're running efficiently.

- This is going to sound a bit obvious, but another reason why sysadmins care about databases is that they store information. Sometimes it's even *our* information: logs, performance metrics (e.g., for trend analysis and capacity planning), meta-information about users and systems, and so on.

In order to be a database-literate system administrator, you have to speak a little Structured Query Language (SQL), the *lingua franca* of most commercial and several non-commercial databases. Writing scripts in Perl for database administration requires some SQL knowledge because these scripts will contain simple embedded SQL statements. See Appendix D for enough SQL to get you started. The examples in this chapter use largely the same data sets that we introduced in previous chapters to keep us from straying from the system administration realm.

Interacting with a SQL Server from Perl

Once upon a time, there were many Perl modules for interacting with different database systems. Each time you wanted to use a database by a certain vendor, you had to look for the right module for the task and then learn that module's way of doing things. If you switched databases mid-project, you likely had to rewrite all of your code to use an entirely different module. And then the DataBase Interface (DBI) by Tim Bunce came along, and things got much, much better in the Perl universe.

DBI can be thought of as "middleware." It forms a layer of abstraction that allows the programmer to write code using generic DBI calls, without having to know the specific API of any particular database. It is then up to the DBI software to hand these calls off to a database-specific layer. The DBI module calls a DataBase Dependent (DBD) driver for this. This database-specific driver takes care of the nitty-gritty details necessary for communicating with the server in question.

This is a great idea. It is so great that you see it not only in other languages (JDBC, etc.), but also in at least one OS platform: Windows has Open DataBase Connectivity (ODBC) built in. ODBC is not precisely a competitor to DBI, but there's enough overlap and it's a big enough presence in the Windows world that we're going to have to give it some attention. Windows Perl programmers largely interact with ODBC data sources, so for their sake we'll do a quick comparison. This will still be useful for non-Windows people to see because it's not uncommon for ODBC to be the only programmatic method for interacting with certain "boutique" databases.

Figure 7-1 shows the DBI and ODBC architectures. In both cases, there is a (at least) three-tiered model:

1. An underlying database (Oracle, MySQL, Sybase, Microsoft SQL Server, etc.).

2. A database-specific layer that makes the actual server-specific requests to the server on behalf of the programmer. Programmers don't directly communicate with this layer; they use the third tier. In DBI, a specific DBD module handles this layer. For example, when talking with an Oracle database, the `DBD::Oracle` module will be invoked. DBD modules are usually linked during the building process to a server-specific client library provided by the server vendor. With ODBC, a data source-specific ODBC driver provided by the vendor handles this layer.

3. A database-independent API layer. Soon, we'll be writing Perl scripts that will communicate with this layer. In DBI, this is known as the DBI layer (i.e., we'll be making DBI calls). In ODBC, one typically communicates with the ODBC Driver Manager via ODBC API calls.

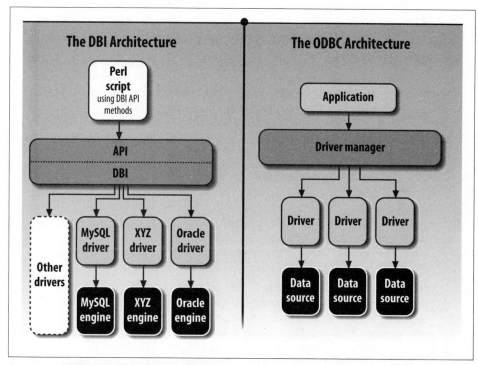

Figure 7-1. DBI and ODBC architectures

The beauty of this model is that most code written for DBI or ODBC is portable between different servers from different vendors. The API calls made are the same, independent of the underlying database—at least that's the idea, and it holds true for most database programming. Unfortunately, the sort of code we're most likely to write (i.e., database administration code) is bound to be server-specific, since virtually no two servers are administered in even a remotely similar fashion.* Experienced system administrators love portable solutions, but they don't expect them.

With the background in place, let's move as fast as possible toward writing some code. Interacting with basic DBI will be straightforward because there's only one DBI module. What about ODBC? That's an interesting question, as there are two common ways to go about interacting with ODBC in Perl: once upon a time the `Win32::ODBC` module was the primary conduit, but more recently a DBD module for the DBI framework called `DBD::ODBC` has become the preferred method interaction method (it is even now recommended by `Win32::ODBC`'s author). `DBD::ODBC` essentially subsumes the ODBC world into DBI, making it just one more data source. We'll see an example of it in action shortly.

For our DBI example code, we'll use the MySQL and Oracle servers; for ODBC, we'll use the Microsoft SQL Server.

Accessing Microsoft SQL Server from Unix

Multiplatform system administrators often ask, "How can I talk to my Microsoft SQL Server installation from my Unix machine?" If an environment's central administration or monitoring system is Unix-based, a new Microsoft SQL Server installation presents a challenge. I know of four ways to deal with this situation. Choices 2 and 3 in the following list are not Microsoft SQL Server-specific, so even if you are not using Microsoft's RDBMS in your environment you may find that these techniques come in handy some day. Your options are:

1. Build and use `DBD::Sybase`. `DBD::Sybase` will require some underlying database communication libraries, and there are two sets of libraries available that will fit the bill. The first one, the Sybase OpenClient libraries, may be available for your platform (e.g., they ship for free with some Linux distributions as part of the Sybase Adaptive Server Enterprise). Your second option is to install the FreeTDS libraries found at *http://www.freetds.org*. See the instructions on this site for building the correct protocol version for the server you will be using.

2. Use a "proxy" driver. There are two DBD proxy modules that ship with DBI: the oldest is called `DBD::Proxy`, and the more recent addition is `DBD::Gofer`. Both allow you to run a small network server on your SQL Server machine to transparently proxy requests from your Unix clients to the server.

3. Acquire and use Unix ODBC software via `DBD::ODBC`. Several vendors, including MERANT (*http://www.merant.com*) and OpenLink Software (*http://www.open linksw.com*), will sell such software to you, or you can attempt to use the work of the various open source developers. For more information, see the iODBC (*http://www.iodbc.org*) and unixODBC (*http://www.unixodbc.org*) home pages. You will

---

* Microsoft SQL Server was initially derived from Sybase source code, so it's one of the rare counter-examples.

need both an ODBC driver for your Unix platform (provided by the database vendor) and an ODBC manager (such as unixODBC or iODBC).

4. Microsoft SQL Server (starting with version 2000) can listen for database queries over HTTP or HTTPS without the need for another web server (such as IIS). The results are returned in an XML format that is easily processed with the methods we saw in Chapter 6.

Using the DBI Framework

Here are the basic steps for using DBI:[†]

1. Load the necessary Perl module.

   There's nothing special here, we just need to include this line:

   ```
   use DBI;
   ```

2. Connect to the database and receive a connection handle.

   The Perl code to establish a DBI connection to a MySQL database and return a database handle looks like this:

   ```
   # connect to the database named $database using the given
   # username and password, and return a database handle
   my $database = 'sysadm';
   my $dbh = DBI->connect("DBI:mysql:$database",$username,$pw);
   die "Unable to connect: $DBI::errstr\n" unless (defined $dbh);
   ```

   DBI will load the low-level DBD driver (DBD::mysql) for us prior to actually connecting to the server. We then test if the connect() succeeded before continuing. DBI provides RaiseError and PrintError options for connect(), should we want DBI to test the return code of all DBI operations in that session and automatically complain about errors when they happen. For example, if we used this code:

   ```
   $dbh = DBI->connect("DBI:mysql:$database",
                       $username,$pw,{RaiseError => 1});
   ```

   DBI would call die for us if the connect() failed.

3. Send SQL commands to the server.

   With our Perl module loaded and a connection to the database server in place, it's showtime! Let's send some SQL commands to the server. We'll use some of the SQL tutorial queries from Appendix D for examples. These queries will use the Perl q convention for quoting (i.e., *something* is written as q{*something*}), just so we don't have to worry about single or double quotes in the actual queries themselves. Here's the first of the two DBI methods for sending commands:

[†] For more information on DBI, see *Programming the Perl DBI* (*http://oreilly.com/catalog/9781565926998/*) by Alligator Descartes and Tim Bunce (O'Reilly).

```
my $results=$dbh->do(q{UPDATE hosts
                       SET bldg = 'Main'
                       WHERE name = 'bendir'});
die "Unable to perform update:$DBI::errstr\n" unless (defined $results);
```

$results will receive either the number of rows updated, or undef if an error occurs. Though it is useful to know how many rows were affected, that's not going to cut it for statements like SELECT, where we need to see the actual data. This is where the second method comes in.

To use the second method, you first prepare a SQL statement for use and then ask the server to execute it. Here's an example:

```
my $sth = $dbh->prepare(q{SELECT * from hosts}) or
    die 'Unable to prep our query:'.$dbh->errstr."\n";
my $rc = $sth->execute or
    die 'Unable to execute our query:'.$dbh->errstr."\n";
```

prepare() returns a new creature we haven't seen before: the *statement handle*. Just as a database handle refers to an open database connection, a statement handle refers to a particular SQL statement we've prepare()d. Once we have this statement handle, we use execute to actually send the query to our server. Later, we'll be using the same statement handle to retrieve the results of our query.

You might wonder why we bother to prepare() a statement instead of just executing it directly. prepare()ing a statement gives the DBD driver (or more likely, the database client library it calls) a chance to parse and mull over the SQL query. Once a statement has been prepare()d, we can execute it repeatedly via our statement handle without parsing it (or deciding how the query will be played out in the server) over and over again. Often this is a major efficiency win. In fact, the default do() DBI method does a prepare() and then an execute() behind the scenes for each statement it is asked to execute.

Like the do call we saw earlier, execute() returns the number of rows affected. If the query affects zero rows, the string 0E0 is returned to allow a Boolean test to succeed. -1 is returned if the number of rows affected is unknown by the driver.

Before we move on to how the results of a query are retrieved, it is worth mentioning one more twist on the prepare() theme that is supported by most DBD modules: *placeholders*, also called *positional markers*, allow you to prepare() a SQL statement that has holes in it to be filled at execute() time. This allows you to construct queries on the fly without paying most of the parse-time penalty. The question mark character (?) is used as the placeholder for a single scalar value. Here's some Perl code to demonstrate the use of placeholders:[‡]

[‡] This demonstrates the most common case, where the placeholders represent simple strings to be filled into the query. If you'll be substituting in more complex data types, like SQL datetimes, you'll need to use the DBI bind_param() method before calling execute().

```
my @machines = qw(bendir shimmer sander);
my $sth = $dbh->prepare(q{SELECT name, ipaddr FROM hosts WHERE name = ?});
foreach my $name (@machines){
    $sth->execute($name);
    do-something-with-the-results
}
```

Each time we go through the `foreach` loop, the `SELECT` query is executed with a different `WHERE` clause. Multiple placeholders are straightforward:

```
$sth->prepare(
    q{SELECT name, ipaddr FROM hosts
    WHERE (name = ? AND bldg = ? AND dept = ?)});
$sth->execute($name,$bldg,$dept);
```

The other bonus you get by using placeholders is automatic quoting of the arguments.

Now that we know how to retrieve the number of rows affected by non-`SELECT` SQL queries, let's look into retrieving the results of our `SELECT` requests.

4. Retrieve `SELECT` results.

   DBI offers three different approaches for retrieving the results of a query. We're going to look at each of them in turn because they all come in handy at one time or another, depending on the situation and programming context.

   Two of these mechanisms are similar to the cursors idea we discussed briefly in Appendix D. With these mechanisms we expect to iterate over the results one row at a time, calling some method each time we want the next row of results returned to our program.

   The first of these mechanisms—using `bind_col()` or `bind_columns()` with `fetchrow_arrayref()`—is often the best tack, because it is both the most efficient and the most "magical" of the choices. Let's take a look at how it works. After the `execute()`, we tell DBI to place the answers we get back into the scalar or the collection of scalars (list or hash) of our choosing. That binding between the results and the variables is done like this:

   ```
   # imagine we just finished a query like SELECT first,second,third FROM table
   my $first;
   my $second;
   my $third;
   $sth->bind_col(1, \$first);  # bind first column of search result to $first
   $sth->bind_col(2, \$second); # bind second column
   $sth->bind_col(3, \$third);  # bind third column, and so on

   # or perform all of the binds in one shot:
   $sth->bind_columns(\$first, \$second, \$third);
   ```

   Binding to whole arrays or to elements in a hash is equally as easy using the magical `\(...)` syntax:

   ```
   $sth->bind_columns( \(@array) ); # $array[0] gets the first column
                                    # $array[1] get the second column...
   ```

```
# we can only bind to the hash elements, not to the hash itself
$sth->bind_col(1, \$hash{first} );
$sth->bind_col(2, \$hash{second} );
```

Now, each time we call `fetch()`, those variables magically get populated with another row from the results of our query:

```
while ($sth->fetch){
    # do something with $first, $second and $third
    #    or $array[0], $array[1],...
    #        or $hash{first}, $hash{second}
}
```

It turns out that `fetch()` is actually an alias for the method call `fetchrow_arrayref()`, giving us a nice segue to the second method of retrieving SELECT results from DBI. If you find the magical nature of binding columns to be a bit too magical or you'd prefer to receive the results back as a Perl data structure so you can manipulate the data, there are a number of methods you can call.

In DBI, we call one of the methods in Table 7-1 to return data from the result set.

Table 7-1. DBI methods for returning data

Name	Returns	Returns if no more rows
`fetchrow_arrayref()`	An array reference to an anonymous array with values that are the columns of the next row in a result set	`undef`
`fetchrow_array()`	An array with values that are the columns of the next row in a result set	An empty list
`fetchrow_hashref()`	A hash reference to an anonymous hash with keys that are the column names and values that are the values of the columns of the next row in a result set	`undef`
`fetchall_arrayref()`	A reference to an array of arrays data structure	A reference to an empty array
`fetchall_hashref($key_field)`	A reference to a hash of hashes. The top-level hash is keyed by the unique values returned from the $key_field column, and the inner hashes are structured just like the ones we get back from `fetchrow_hashref()`	A reference to an empty hash

Two kinds of methods are listed: single row (`fetchrow_`) methods and entire data set (`fetchall_`) methods. The `fetchrow_` methods return a single row from the returned results, just like what we've seen so far. `fetchall_` methods take this one step further and return the entire result set in one fell swoop (essentially by running the appropriate `fetchrow_` as many times as necessary to retrieve the data). Be careful to limit the size of your queries when using this method because it does pull the entire result set into memory. If you have a terabyte-sized result set, this may prove to be a bit problematic.

Let's take a look at these methods in context. For each of these examples, assume the following was executed just previously:

```
$sth = $dbh->prepare(q{SELECT name,ipaddr,dept from hosts}) or
    die 'Unable to prepare our query: '.$dbh->errstr."\n";
$sth->execute or die "Unable to execute our query: ".$dbh->errstr."\n";
```

Here's `fetchrow_arrayref()` in action:

```
while (my $aref = $sth->fetchrow_arrayref){
    print 'name: '   . $aref->[0] . "\n";
    print 'ipaddr: ' . $aref->[1] . "\n";
    print 'dept: '   . $aref->[2] . "\n";
}
```

 Just a quick warning about using `fetchrow_arrayref()` like this: any time you rely on the order of the elements in an array when you store/retrieve data (i.e., which field is which array element), you've created a booby trap in your code that is just waiting to spring on you. All you (or someone else working on your code) have to do is naïvely change the previous SELECT statement, and all bets about what is versus what should be in `$aref->[2]` are off.

The DBI documentation mentions that `fetchrow_hashref()` is less efficient than `fetchrow_arrayref()` because of the extra processing it entails, but it can yield more readable and potentially more maintainable code. Here's an example:

```
while (my $href = $sth->fetchrow_hashref){
    print 'name: '   . $href->{name}  . "\n";
    print 'ipaddr: ' . $href->{ipaddr}. "\n";
    print 'dept: '   . $href->{dept}  . "\n";
}
```

Finally, let's look at `fetchall_arrayref()`. Each reference returned looks exactly like something we'd receive from `fetchrow_arrayref()`, as shown in Figure 7-2.

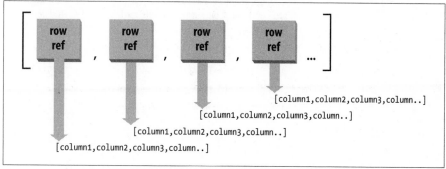

Figure 7-2. The data structure returned by fetchrow_arrayref()

Here's some code that will print out the entire query result set:

```
$aref_aref = $sth->fetchall_arrayref;
foreach my $rowref (@$aref_aref){
    print 'name: '   . $rowref->[0] . "\n";
    print 'ipaddr: ' . $rowref->[1] . "\n";
    print 'dept: '   . $rowref->[2] . "\n";
    print '-'x30,"\n";
}
```

This code sample is specific to our particular data set because it assumes a certain number of columns in a certain order. For instance, we assume the machine name is returned as the first column in the query ($rowref->[0]).

We can use some of the magic attributes (often called metadata) of statement handles to rewrite our result-retrieval code to make it more generic. Specifically, if we look at $sth->{NUM_OF_FIELDS} after a query, it will tell us the number of fields (columns) in our result set. $sth->{NAME} contains a reference to an array containing the names of each column. Here's a more generic way to write the last example:

```
my $aref_aref = $sth->fetchall_arrayref;
my $numfields = $sth->{NUM_OF_FIELDS};
foreach my $rowref (@$aref_aref){
    for (my $i=0; $i < $numfields; $i++){
        print $sth->{NAME}->[$i].": ".$rowref->[$i]."\n";
    }
    print '-'x30,"\n";
}
```

Be sure to see the DBI documentation for more metadata attributes.

The last method for returning data is through a series of "shortcut" methods, listed in Table 7-2, that prepare a SQL statement, execute it, and then return the data using one of the methods we saw earlier.

Table 7-2. DBI shortcut methods

Name	Combines these methods into a single method
selectcol_arrayref($stmnt)	prepare($stmnt),execute(), (@{fetchrow_arrayref()})[0] (i.e., returns the first column for each row, though the column number(s) can be changed via an optional Columns argument)
selectrow_array($stmnt)	prepare($stmnt),execute(),fetchrow_array()
selectrow_arrayref($stmnt)	prepare($stmnt),execute(),fetchrow_arrayref()
selectrow_hashref($stmnt)	prepare($stmnt),execute(),fetchrow_hashref()
selectall_arrayref($stmnt)	prepare($stmnt),execute(),fetchall_arrayref()
selectall_hashref($stmnt)	prepare($stmnt),execute(),fetchall_hashref()

5. Close the connection to the server.

   In DBI, this is simply:

```
# disconnects handle from database
$dbh->disconnect;
```

Using ODBC from Within DBI

The basic steps for using ODBC from DBI are pretty much identical to the steps we just discussed, with one twist. The hardest part is dealing with the arguments in the initial connect() call. ODBC requires one preliminary step before making a connection: we need to create a *data source name* (DSN). A DSN is a named reference that stores the configuration information (e.g., server and database name) needed to reach an information source like a SQL server. DSNs come in two flavors, *user* and *system*, distinguishing between connections available to a single user on a machine and connections available to any user or service.[*]

DSNs can be created either through the ODBC control panel under Windows (see Figure 7-3), or programmatically via Perl.

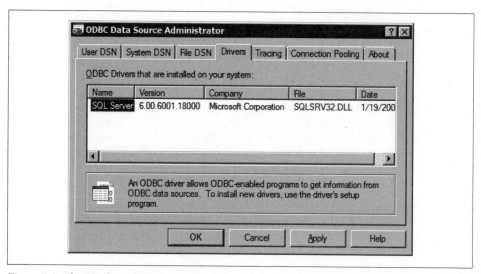

Figure 7-3. The Windows ODBC control panel

We'll take the latter route, if just to keep the snickering down among the Unix folks (see the upcoming note for a better reason). Here's some code to create a user DSN to our SQL Server database:

---

[*] There's a third flavor, *file*, that writes the DSN configuration information out to a file so it can be shared among several computers, but it isn't created by the Win32::ODBC method call we're about to use.

```
use Win32::ODBC;  # we only use this to create DSNs; everything else is
                  # done via DBI through DBD::ODBC

# Creates a user DSN to a Microsoft SQL Server
# Note: to create a system DSN, substitute ODBC_ADD_SYS_DSN
# for ODBC_ADD_DSN - be sure to use a system DSN for
# situations where your code will be run as another user
# (e.g., in a web application)
#
if (Win32::ODBC::ConfigDSN(
    ODBC_ADD_DSN,
    'SQL Server',
    ('DSN=PerlSysAdm',
    'DESCRIPTION=DSN for PerlSysAdm',
    'SERVER=mssql.example.edu', # server name
    'ADDRESS=192.168.1.4',      # server IP addr
    'DATABASE=sysadm',          # our database
    'NETWORK=DBMSSOCN',         # TCP/IP Socket Lib
    ))){
    print "DSN created\n";
}
else {
    die "Unable to create DSN:" . Win32::ODBC::Error(  ) . "\n";
}
```

Should you create your DSNs manually or automatically? This is a superb question with no definitive answer. On the one hand, DSNs are compact descriptions of how to access potentially critical or sensitive data. This would lead one to be very cautious about who sets them up and tests them, and how (suggesting that a manual approach would be better). If a DSN is intentionally deleted from a machine, having it automatically created again may be undesirable. On the other hand, manual configuration is easy to get wrong and, in general, doesn't scale for more than a few servers or applications.

The best answer is probably to write and test a set of special setup scripts that can be run either manually or as part of your automated initial configuration process. This should help avoid the pitfalls.

Once you have a DSN in place, you can reference it in the **connect()** call. For example, if we wanted to connect to the database via the DSN created by the previous code, the connect process would look like this:

```
use DBI;

$dbh = DBI->connect('DBI:ODBC:PerlSysAdm',$username,$pw);
die "Unable to connect: $DBI::errstr\n" unless (defined $dbh);
```

From that point on, you can put the rest of your DBI expertise to work. See the **DBD::ODBC** documentation for details on the additional features the driver provides and on the few ODBC-specific concerns worth mentioning. You now know how to work with a database from Perl using both DBI and ODBC, so let's put your knowledge to the test with some more extended examples from the database administration realm.

Server Documentation

A great deal of time and energy goes into the configuration of a SQL server and the objects that reside on it. Having a way to document this sort of information can come in handy in a number of situations. If a database gets corrupted and there's no backup, you may be called upon to recreate all of its tables. You may have to migrate data from one server to another; knowing the source and destination configurations can be important. Even for your own database programming, being able to see a table map can be very helpful.

To give you a taste of the nonportable nature of database administration, let me show you an example of the same simple task as written for three different SQL servers using both DBI and ODBC (via `Win32::ODBC`). Each of these programs does the exact same thing: prints out a listing of all of the databases on a server, their tables, and the basic structure of each table. These scripts could easily be expanded to show more information about each object. For instance, it might be useful to show which columns in a table had NULL or NOT NULL set. The output of all three programs looks roughly like this:

```
---sysadm---
        hosts
                name [char(30)]
                ipaddr [char(15)]
                aliases [char(50)]
                owner [char(40)]
                dept [char(15)]
                bldg [char(10)]
                room [char(4)]
                manuf [char(10)]
                model [char(10)]
---hpotter---
        customers
                cid [char(4)]
                cname [varchar(13)]
                city [varchar(20)]
                discnt [real(7)]
        agents
                aid [char(3)]
                aname [varchar(13)]
                city [varchar(20)]
                percent [int(10)]
        products
                pid [char(3)]
                pname [varchar(13)]
                city [varchar(20)]
                quantity [int(10)]
                price [real(7)]
```

```
    orders
            ordno [int(10)]
            month [char(3)]
            cid [char(4)]
            aid [char(3)]
            pid [char(3)]
            qty [int(10)]
            dollars [real(7)]
...
```

It will be to your advantage to look at all three examples, even if you don't use or plan to ever use the particular database server in question. We'll be looking at several different methods for querying the information in these sections, all of which you will want to know about.

MySQL Server via DBI

Here's a DBI way of pulling the information just presented from a MySQL server. MySQL's SHOW command makes this task pretty easy:

```
use DBI;

print 'Enter user for connect: ';
chomp(my $user = <STDIN>);
print 'Enter passwd for $user: ';
chomp(my $pw = <STDIN>);

my $start= 'mysql'; # connect initially to this database

# connect to the start MySQL database
my $dbh = DBI->connect("DBI:mysql:$start",$user,$pw,
                       { RaiseError => 1, ShowErrorStatement => 1 });

# find the databases on the server
my $sth=$dbh->prepare(q{SHOW DATABASES});
$sth->execute;

my @dbs = ( );
while (my $aref = $sth->fetchrow_arrayref) {
    push(@dbs,$aref->[0]);
}

# find the tables in each database
foreach my $db (@dbs) {
    print "---$db---\n";

    $sth=$dbh->prepare(qq{SHOW TABLES FROM $db});
    $sth->execute;

    my @tables=(  );
    while (my $aref = $sth->fetchrow_arrayref) {
        push(@tables,$aref->[0]);
    }
```

```perl
    # find the column info for each table
    foreach my $table (@tables) {
        print "\t$table\n";

        $sth=$dbh->prepare(qq{SHOW COLUMNS FROM $table FROM $db});
        $sth->execute;

        while (my $aref = $sth->fetchrow_arrayref) {
            print "\t\t",$aref->[0],' [',$aref->[1],"]\n";
        }
    }
}
$dbh->disconnect;
```

A few quick comments about this code:

- MySQL 5.x (a fairly new release as of this writing) has a special metadata database called `INFORMATION_SCHEMA` that contains tables that can be queried using ordinary `SELECT` statements to retrieve the same information as we're getting from the `SHOW` commands. If you are using a 5.x version of MySQL, you'll want to use that mechanism instead to get the table and column information. Querying this information is slower than querying normal data in your database, however, so be wary of doing so if performance is important to you.

- We connect to a starting database only to satisfy the DBI connect semantics; this context is not necessary thanks to the `SHOW` commands.

- If you thought the `SHOW TABLES` and `SHOW COLUMNS` prepare and execute statements looked like excellent candidates for placeholders, you're absolutely right. Unfortunately, this particular DBD driver/server combination doesn't support placeholders in this context (at least, not when this book was being written). If you can use placeholders in situations like this, definitely do. They offer some protection against SQL injection attacks, thanks to their automatic quoting property (mentioned earlier).

- We prompt for a database user and password interactively because the alternatives (hard-coding them into the script or passing them on the command line, where they can be found by anyone running a process table dump) are even worse evils. This prompt will echo the password characters as typed. To be really careful, we should use something like `Term::Readkey` to turn off character echo.

- And finally, a tip from Tim Bunce himself. Notice that we're using `RaiseError` and `ShowErrorStatement` in the initial connect to the database. This asks DBI to handle the checking for and reporting of errors, which we would normally have to include with an `or die "something"` after each DBI call. It helps declutter your code considerably.

Oracle Server via DBI

Here's an Oracle equivalent. This example sparks a whole bunch of commentary, so peruse the code and then we'll talk about it:

```
use DBI;
use DBD::Oracle qw(:ora_session_modes);

print 'Enter passwd for sys: ';
chomp(my $pw = <STDIN>);

my $dbh =
    DBI->connect( 'DBI:Oracle:perlsysadm', 'sys', $pw,
    { RaiseError => 1, AutoCommit => 0, ora_session_mode => ORA_SYSDBA } );

my ( $catalog, $schema, $name, $type, $remarks ); # table_info returns this
my $sth = $dbh->table_info( undef, undef, undef, 'TABLE' );

my (@tables);

while ( ( $catalog, $schema, $name, $type, $remarks ) = $sth->fetchrow_array() )
{
    push( @tables, [ $schema, $name ] );
}

for my $table ( sort @tables ) {
    $sth = $dbh->column_info( undef, $table->[0], $table->[1], undef );

    # if you encounter an ORA-24345 error from the following fetchrow_arrayref(),
    # you can set $sth->{LongTruncOk} = 1 here as described in the DBD::Oracle doc

    print join( '.', @$table ), "\n";
    while ( my $aref = $sth->fetchrow_arrayref ) {

        # [3] = COLUMN_NAME, [5] = TYPE_NAME, [6] = COLUMN_SIZE
        print "\t\t", $aref->[3], ' [', lc $aref->[5], "(", $aref->[6], ")]\n";
    }
}

$sth->finish;
$dbh->disconnect;
```

Here is the promised commentary:

- First, a general comment to set the scene: Oracle has a different notion of what the word "database" means than most other servers. The other servers discussed in this chapter each have a model where a user owns a database in which he is permitted to create a set of tables. This is why the previous example first found the list of the databases on the server, then stepped into each database, and finally listed the tables inside it. Oracle doesn't have this additional level of hierarchy. Yes, there are databases in Oracle, but they are more like chunks of storage, often containing many tables owned by many users. The nearest equivalent to our previous usage of the word "database" in Oracle is the *schema*. A schema is the collection of objects (tables, indices, etc.) owned by a user. Tables are usually referenced as *SCHEMA.TABLENAME*. The preceding code connects to a single database instance called "perlsysadm" and shows its contents.

- Ideally this code would connect to the database using an account that was specially privileged for this kind of work. To make the code more generic for example purposes, it attempts to connect to the database as the standard Oracle systems user *sys*. This user has permission to look at all tables in the database. To connect to this database as this user, one has to request special SYSDBA privileges, hence the funky parameter `ora_session_mode => ORA_SYSDBA` in the initial connect. If you have another user with that privilege granted, you will want to change the code to use that user instead of the all-powerful, all-knowing *sys*.

- Besides that connection parameter, the code is surprisingly database server-independent. In contrast to the previous MySQL example, where the SHOW commands did the heavy lifting, here we use the standard DBI `table_info()` and `column_info()` calls to retrieve the information we need. Oracle has at least one similar command (DESCR *tablename*) that returns more information about a table, but sticking with the most generic method possible will improve code portability between separate database servers.

- The example code is actually doing more work than it needs to do. To keep the code close in structure to the previous example, it first queries for the list of tables, then iterates over each table in a sorted order, and then queries the column info for that table. It turns out that `column_info()` is perfectly happy to retrieve information on all of the columns of all of the tables in the database in a single invocation if you just leave out the schema and table name (`column_info(undef,undef,undef,undef)`); furthermore, the DBI specification says the command should return the information to you in sorted order, so the `sort()` call also becomes unnecessary.

Microsoft SQL Server via ODBC

The DBI/DBD::ODBC-based code to show the same database/table/column information from Microsoft SQL Server is basically a combination of the two previous examples. First we use a database-specific query[†] to get the list of databases, and then we can use the DBI standard calls of `table_info()` and `column_info()` to retrieve the information we need.

One small but significant set of changes is in the initial connect string: the `connect()` uses `'dbi:ODBC:{DSN_name_here}'` (with some predefined DSN), a different privileged user is entered (see the following note), and the `ora_session_mode` option is removed.

[†] If your user has the ability to access all databases on the server and you'd prefer not to grovel around in a system table, `select catalog_name from information_schema.schemata` is another query that can be used to retrieve this information on a relatively recent version of SQL Server.

One of the things that changed between SQL Server 2000 and SQL Server 2005 is the visibility of the metadata (i.e., the list of all objects, etc.). With the 2000 version of the server, virtually any user on the system could enumerate these objects, but with 2005 this is considerably more locked down: a user must have the VIEW ANY DEFINITION permission to retrieve the same info as before.

These changes yield a program that looks like the following:

```
use DBI;

# this assumes a privileged user called mssqldba; your
# username will probably be different
print 'Enter passwd for mssqldba: ';
chomp(my $pw = <STDIN>);

# assumes there is a predefined DSN with the name "PerlSys"
my $dbh =
    DBI->connect( 'dbi:ODBC:PerlSys', 'mssqldba', $pw, { RaiseError => 1 });

# fetch the names of all of the databases
my (@dbs) =
    map { $_->[0] }
    @{ $dbh->selectall_arrayref("select name from master.dbo.sysdatabases") };

my ( $catalog, $schema, $name, $type, $remarks );  # table_info returns this
foreach my $db (@dbs) {

    my $sth = $dbh->table_info( $db, undef, undef, 'TABLE' );

    my (@tables);

    while ( ( $catalog, $schema, $name, $type, $remarks ) =
        $sth->fetchrow_array() ) {
        push( @tables, [ $schema, $name ] );
    }

    for my $table ( sort @tables ) {
        $sth = $dbh->column_info( $db, $table->[0], $table->[1], undef );
        print join( '.', @$table ), "\n";
        while ( my $aref = $sth->fetchrow_arrayref ) {

            # [3] = COLUMN_NAME, [5] = TYPE_NAME, [6] = COLUMN_SIZE
            print "\t\t", $aref->[3], ' [', lc $aref->[5], "(", $aref->[6],
                ")]\n";
        }
    }
}
$dbh->disconnect;
```

Just to give you one more way to approach the problem, here's some code that uses the legacy Win32::ODBC module. This code looks different from our previous two examples in a number of ways. First off, it uses the native-ODBC style of retrieving information (see the `Win32::ODBC` docs). It may also look strange because we are relying on a few of the special stored procedures that ship with the server to retrieve the info we need (e.g., `sp_columns()`), using a really icky calling convention. This particular example is included on the off chance that you'll find yourself in a situation that requires the use of `Win32::ODBC` and you'd like an example to help you begin the process.

Here's the code:

```perl
use Win32::ODBC;

print 'Enter user for connect: ';
chomp(my $user = <STDIN>);
print 'Enter passwd for $user: ';
chomp(my $pw = <STDIN>);

my $dsn='sysadm'; # name of the DSN we will be using

# find the available DSNs, creating $dsn if it doesn't exist already
die 'Unable to query available DSN's'.Win32::ODBC::Error()."\n"
    unless (my %dsnavail = Win32::ODBC::DataSources());
if (!defined $dsnavail{$dsn}) {
    die 'unable to create DSN:'.Win32::ODBC::Error()."\n"
        unless (Win32::ODBC::ConfigDSN(ODBC_ADD_DSN,
        "SQL Server",
        ("DSN=$dsn",
        "DESCRIPTION=DSN for PerlSysAdm",
        "SERVER=mssql.happy.edu",
        "DATABASE=master",
        "NETWORK=DBMSSOCN", # TCP/IP Socket Lib
    )));
}

# connect to the master database via the DSN we just defined
#
# the DSN specifies DATABASE=master so we don't have to
# pick it as a starting database explicitly
my $dbh = new Win32::ODBC("DSN=$dsn;UID=$user;PWD=$pw;");
die "Unable to connect to DSN $dsn:".Win32::ODBC::Error()."\n"
    unless (defined $dbh);

# find the databases on the server, Sql returns an error number if it fails
if (defined $dbh->Sql(q{SELECT name from sysdatabases})){
    die 'Unable to query databases:'.Win32::ODBC::Error()."\n";
}

my @dbs = ( );
my @tables = ( );
my @cols = ( );
# ODBC requires a two-step process of fetching the data and then
# accessing it with a special call (Data)
while ($dbh->FetchRow()){
    push(@dbs, $dbh->Data("name"));
}
$dbh->DropCursor(); # this is like DBI's $sth->finish()
```

```perl
# find the user tables in each database
foreach my $db (@dbs) {
    if (defined $dbh->Sql("use $db")){
        die "Unable to change to database $db:" .
            Win32::ODBC::Error() . "\n";
    }
    print "---$db---\n";
    @tables=();

    if (defined $dbh->Sql(q{SELECT name from sysobjects
                              WHERE type="U"})){
        die "Unable to query tables in $db:" .
            Win32::ODBC::Error() . "\n";
    }
    while ($dbh->FetchRow()) {
        push(@tables,$dbh->Data("name"));
    }
    $dbh->DropCursor();

    # find the column info for each table
    foreach $table (@tables) {
        print "\t$table\n";
        if (defined $dbh->Sql(" {call sp_columns (\'$table\')} ")){
            die "Unable to query columns in $table:" .
                Win32::ODBC::Error() . "\n";
        }
        while ($dbh->FetchRow()) {
            @cols=$dbh->Data("COLUMN_NAME","TYPE_NAME","PRECISION");
            print "\t\t",$cols[0]," [",$cols[1],"(",$cols[2],")]\n";
        }
        $dbh->DropCursor();
    }
}
$dbh->Close();

die "Unable to delete DSN:".Win32::ODBC::Error()."\n"
    unless (Win32::ODBC::ConfigDSN(ODBC_REMOVE_DSN,
        "SQL Server","DSN=$dsn"));
```

Database Logins

As mentioned earlier, database administrators have to deal with some of the same issues system administrators contend with, like maintaining logins and accounts. For instance, at my day job we teach database programming classes. Each student who takes a class gets a login on our Oracle server and her very own (albeit small) database quota on that server to play with. Here's a simplified version of the code we use to create these databases and logins:

```perl
use DBI;

my $userquota   = 10000; # K of user space given to each user
my $usertmpquota =  2000; # K of temp tablespace given to each user
```

```perl
my $admin = 'system';
print "Enter passwd for $admin: ";
chomp(my $pw = <STDIN>);
my $user=$ARGV[0];

# generate a *bogus* password based on username reversed
# and padded to at least 6 chars with dashes
# note: this is a very bad algorithm; better to use something
# like Crypt::GeneratePassword
my $genpass = reverse($user) . '-' x (6-length($user));

my $dbh = DBI->connect("dbi:Oracle:instance",$admin,$pw,{PrintError => 0});
die "Unable to connect: $DBI::errstr\n"
    unless (defined $dbh);

# prepare the test to see if user name exists
my $sth = $dbh->prepare(q{SELECT USERNAME FROM dba_users WHERE USERNAME = ?})
    or die 'Unable to prepare user test SQL: '.$dbh->errstr."\n";

my $res = $sth->execute(uc $user);
$sth->fetchrow_array;
die "user $user exists, quitting" if ($sth->rows > 0);
if (!defined $dbh->do (
    qq {
        CREATE USER ${LOGIN} PROFILE DEFAULT
        IDENTIFIED BY ${PASSWORD}
        DEFAULT TABLESPACE USERS TEMPORARY TABLESPACE TEMP
        QUOTA $usertmpquota K ON TEMP QUOTA $userquota K ON USERS
        ACCOUNT UNLOCK
    })){
    die 'Unable to create database:'.$dbh->errstr."\n";
}

# grant the necessary permissions
$dbh->do("GRANT CONNECT TO ${LOGIN}") or
    die "Unable to grant connect privs to ${LOGIN}:".$dbh->errstr."\n";

# perhaps a better approach would be to explicity grant the parts of
# RESOURCE the users need rather than grant them everything and
# removing things like UNLIMITED TABLESPACE later
$dbh->do("GRANT RESOURCE TO ${LOGIN}") or
    die "Unable to grant resource privs to ${LOGIN}:".$dbh->errstr."\n";

# set the correct roles
$dbh->do("ALTER USER ${LOGIN} DEFAULT ROLE ALL") or
    die "Unable to use set correct roles for ${LOGIN}:".$dbh->errstr."\n";

# make sure the quotas are enforced
$dbh->do("REVOKE UNLIMITED TABLESPACE FROM ${LOGIN}") or
    die "Unable to revoke unlimited tablespace from ${LOGIN}:".$dbh->errstr."\n";

$dbh->disconnect;
```

We could use a similar script to delete these accounts and their databases when the class has concluded:

```
use DBI;

$admin = 'system';
print "Enter passwd for $admin: ";
chomp(my $pw = <STDIN>);
my $user=$ARGV[0];

my $dbh = DBI->connect("dbi:Oracle:instance",$admin,$pw,{PrintError => 0});
die "Unable to connect: $DBI::errstr\n"
    if (!defined $dbh);

die "Unable to drop user ${user}:".$dbh->errstr."\n"
    if (!defined $dbh->do("DROP USER ${user} CASCADE"));

$dbh->disconnect;
```

You might find it useful to code up a variety of login-related functions. Here are a few ideas:

Password checker
> Connect to the server and get a listing of databases and logins. Attempt to connect using weak passwords (login names, blank passwords, default passwords).

User mapping
> Generate a listing of which logins can access which databases.

Password control
> Write a pseudo-password expiration system.

Monitoring Space Usage on a Database Server

For our final example, we'll take a look at a way to monitor the storage space of a SQL server. This sort of routine monitoring is similar in nature to the network service monitoring we'll see in Chapter 13.

To get technical for a moment, database servers are places to hold stuff. Running out of space to hold stuff is known as either "a bad thing" or "a very bad thing." As a result, programs that help us monitor the amount of space allocated and used on a server are very useful indeed. Let's look at a DBI program designed to evaluate the space situation on an Oracle server.

Here's a snippet of output from a program that illustrates graphically each user's space usage in relationship to her predefined quota. Each section shows a bar chart of the percentage of used versus allocated space in the USERS and TEMP tablespaces. In the following chart, u stands for user space and t stands for temp space. For each bar, the percentage of space used and the total available space are indicated:

```
                    |uuuuuuu                          |15.23%/5MB
    hpotter--------|                                 |
                    |                                 |0.90%/5MB
```

```
                     |uuuuuuu                                    |15.23%/5MB
       dumbledore-----|                                          |
                     |                                           |1.52%/5MB


                     |uuuuuuuu                                   |16.48%/5MB
       hgranger-------|                                          |
                     |                                           |1.52%/5MB


                     |uuuuuuu                                    |15.23%/5MB
       rweasley-------|                                          |
                     |t                                          |3.40%/5MB


                     |uuuuuuuuuuuuuuuuuuuuuuuuuuu                 |54.39%/2MB
       hagrid--------|                                           |
                     |- no temp quota                            |
```

Here's how we generated this output:

```perl
use DBI;
use DBD::Oracle qw(:ora_session_modes);
use POSIX;     # for ceil rounding function

use strict;

print 'Enter passwd for sys: ';
chomp( my $pw = <STDIN> );

# connect to the server
my $dbh = DBI->connect( 'DBI:Oracle:', 'sys', $pw,
    { RaiseError => 1, ShowErrorStatement => 1, AutoCommit => 0,
      ora_session_mode => ORA_SYSDBA } );

# get the quota information
my $sth = $dbh->prepare(
    q{SELECT USERNAME,TABLESPACE_NAME,BYTES,MAX_BYTES
        FROM SYS.DBA_TS_QUOTAS
        WHERE TABLESPACE_NAME = 'USERS' or TABLESPACE_NAME = 'TEMP'}
    );

$sth->execute;

# bind the results of the query to these variables, later to be stored in %qdata
my ( $user, $tablespace, $bytes_used, $bytes_quota, %qdata );
$sth->bind_columns( \$user, \$tablespace, \$bytes_used, \$bytes_quota );

while ( defined $sth->fetch ) {
    $qdata{$user}->{$tablespace} = [ $bytes_used, $bytes_quota ];
}

$dbh->disconnect;

# show this information graphically
foreach my $user ( sort keys %qdata ) {
    graph(
        $user,
```

```
            $qdata{$user}->{'USERS'}[0],     # bytes used
            $qdata{$user}->{'TEMP'}[0],
            $qdata{$user}->{'USERS'}[1],     # quota size
            $qdata{$user}->{'TEMP'}[1]
    );
}

# print out nice chart given username, user and temp sizes,
# and usage info
sub graph {
    my ( $user, $user_used, $temp_used, $user_quota, $temp_quota ) = @_;

    # line for user space usage
    if ( $user_quota > 0 ) {
        print ' ' x 15 . '|'
            . 'd' x POSIX::ceil( 49 * ( $user_used / $user_quota ) )
            . ' ' x ( 49 - POSIX::ceil( 49 * ( $user_used / $user_quota ) ) )
            . '|';

        # percentage used and total M for data space
        printf( "%.2f", ( $user_used / $user_quota * 100 ) );
        print "%/" . ( $user_quota / 1024 / 1000 ) . "MB\n";
    }

    # some users do not have user quotas
    else {
        print ' ' x 15 . '|- no user quota' . ( ' ' x 34 ) . "|\n";
    }

    print $user . '-' x ( 14 - length($user) ) . '-|' . ( ' ' x 49 ) . "|\n";

    # line for temp space usage
    if ( $temp_quota > 0 ) {
        print ' ' x 15 . '|'
            . 't' x POSIX::ceil( 49 * ( $temp_used / $temp_quota ) )
            . ' ' x ( 49 - POSIX::ceil( 49 * ( $temp_used / $temp_quota ) ) )
            . '|';

        # percentage used and total M for temp space
        printf( "%.2f", ( $temp_used / $temp_quota * 100 ) );
        print "%/" . ( $temp_quota / 1024 / 1000 ) . "MB\n";
    }

    # some users do not have temp quotas
    else {
        print ' ' x 15 . '|- no temp quota' . ( ' ' x 34 ) . "|\n";
    }
    print "\n";
}
```

Writing this code wasn't particularly hard because Oracle provides a lovely view called SYS.DBA_TS_QUOTAS that contains the tablespace quota information we need in an easy-to-query fashion. This ease is highly database server-specific; other servers can make you work harder for this information (e.g., with Sybase you need to add up segments when computing database sizes).

This small program just scratches the surface of the sort of server monitoring we can do. It would be easy to take the results we get from SYS.DBA_TS_QUOTAS and graph them over time to get a better notion of how our server is being used. There are lots of other things we can (and probably should) monitor, including CPU usage and various database performance metrics (cache hit rates, etc.). There are entire books on "Tuning Database *X*" from which you can get a notion of the key parameters to watch from a Perl script. Let creeping featurism be your muse.

Module Information for This Chapter

Module	CPAN ID	Version
DBI	TIMB	1.50
DBD::mysql	RUDY	2.9008
DBD::Oracle	PYTHIAN	1.17
DBD::ODBC	JURL	1.13
Win32::ODBC (from *http://www.roth.net*)	JDB	970208

References for More Information

There are a number of good SQL tutorials on the Web, including *http://www.sqlzoo.net* and *http://www.sqlcourse.com*. Search for "SQL tutorial" and you'll find a bunch more. Reading them can give you a good jumpstart into using the language.

http://home.fnal.gov/~dbox/SQL_API_Portability.html is a swell guide to the vagaries of the more popular database engines. Though its focus is on writing portable code, as you saw in this chapter, often one needs to know database-specific commands to help administer a server.

DBI

http://dbi.perl.org is the official DBI home page. It's quite dated in places (according to Tim Bunce), but this should be your first stop.

Programming the Perl DBI (http://oreilly.com/catalog/9781565926998/), by Alligator Descartes and Tim Bunce (O'Reilly), is a great DBI resource.

http://gmax.oltrelinux.com/dbirecipes.html has some useful DBI recipes for common tasks.

Microsoft SQL Server

In addition to the Microsoft SQL Server information available at the Microsoft website (*http://www.microsoft.com/sql*), there's a tremendous amount of information at *http://www.sqlserverfaq.com*. Microsoft's training materials for Microsoft SQL Server administration from MS Press are also quite good.

ODBC

http://www.microsoft.com/odbc contains Microsoft's ODBC information. You'll need to dig a little because it has been subsumed (as of this writing) into their larger Data Access and Storage Center rubric. You may also want to search for ODBC on the *http://msdn.microsoft.com* site, looking carefully at the library material on ODBC in the MDAC SDK.

http://www.roth.net/perl/odbc/ is the official `Win32::ODBC` home page. (For legacy purposes. You should use `DBD::ODBC` whenever possible.)

Win32 Perl Programming: The Standard Extensions, by Dave Roth (Macmillan), the author of `Win32::ODBC`, is still a good reference for Windows Perl module-based programming.

Oracle

The Oracle universe is very large. There are many, many Oracle-related books and websites. One site I find really useful is *http://www.orafaq.com*; this is a fabulous resource for getting answers to both basic and more sophisticated Oracle questions.

The Documentation and Tutorials paths on *http://otn.oracle.com* are a great source for in-depth information about the different releases of Oracle databases.

## CHAPTER 8

Email

Unlike the other chapters in this book, this chapter does not discuss how to administer a particular service, technology, or knowledge domain. Instead, we're going to look at how to use email from Perl as a tool for system administration.

Email is a great notification mechanism: often we want a program to tell us when something goes wrong, provide the results of an automatic process (like a late-night *cron* or scheduler service job), or let us know when something we care about changes. In this chapter we'll explore how to send mail from Perl for these purposes and then look at some of the pitfalls associated with the practice of sending ourselves mail.

We'll also look at how Perl can be used to fetch and post-process mail we receive to make it more useful to us. Perl can be useful for dealing with spam and managing user questions.

This chapter will assume that you already have a solid and reliable mail infrastructure. We're also going to assume that your mail system, or one that you have access to, uses protocols that follow the IETF specifications for sending and receiving mail. The examples in this chapter will use protocols like SMTP (Simple Mail Transfer Protocol, RFC 2821) and expect messages to be RFC 2822-compliant. We'll go over these terms in due course.

Sending Mail

Let's talk about the mechanics of sending email before we tackle the more sophisticated issues. The traditional (Unix) Perl mail-sending code often looks something like this example from the Perl Frequently Asked Questions list (*http://faq.perl.org*):

```
# assumes we have sendmail installed in /usr/sbin
# sendmail install directory varies based on OS/distribution
open my $SENDMAIL, '|-', '|/usr/sbin/sendmail -oi -t -odq' or
  die "Can't fork for sendmail: $!\n";
print $SENDMAIL <<'EOF';
From: User Originating Mail <me@host>
To: Final Destination <you@otherhost>
```

```
Subject: A relevant subject line

Body of the message goes here after the blank line
in as many lines as you like.
EOF
close(SENDMAIL) or warn "sendmail didn't close nicely";
```

 A common error (which has its roots in Perl4 when made by Perl old-timers) is to write something like this, including the @ sign directly in a double-quoted string:

```
$address = "fred@example.com"; # array interpolates
```

This line needs to be changed to one of the following to work properly:

```
$address = "fred\@example.com";
$address = 'fred@example.com';
$address = q{ fred@example.com };
$address = join('@', 'fred', 'example.com');
```

Code that calls *sendmail* (like the preceding example) works fine in many circumstances, but it doesn't work on any operating system that lacks a mail transport agent called "sendmail" (e.g., Windows-based operating systems). If you're using such an OS you have a few choices, which are described in the next few sections.

Getting sendmail (or a Similar Mail Transport Agent)

Various *sendmail* and *sendmail*-like ports (most of which are commercial) are available for Windows. If you want a free version of something that can potentially pretend to be *sendmail*, try the Cygwin *exim* port (*http://cygwin.com/packages/exim*). If you'd like something more lightweight and are willing to make small modifications to your Perl code to support different command-line arguments, programs like *blat (http://www.blat .net)* will do the trick.

The advantage of this approach is that it offloads much of the mail-sending complexity from your script. A good mail transport agent (MTA) handles the process of retrying a destination mail server if it's unreachable, selecting the right destination server (finding and choosing between Mail eXchanger DNS records), rewriting the headers if necessary, dealing with bounces, and so on. If you can avoid having to take care of all of that in Perl, that's often a good thing.

Using the OS-Specific IPC Framework to Drive a Mail Client

On Mac OS X or Windows, you can drive a mail client using the native interprocess communication (IPC) framework.

Mac OS X ships with the Postfix MTA installed, but only minimally configured. If you don't want to bother setting it up, you can ask Perl to use AppleScript to drive the built-in mail client (often called *Mail.app*):

```
use MacPerl;

my $to      = 'user@example.com';
my $subject = 'Hi there';
my $body    = 'message body';

MacPerl::DoAppleScript(<<EOAS);
tell application "Mail"
  set theNewMessage to make new outgoing message with properties
    {subject:"$subject", content:"$body", visible:true}
  tell theNewMessage
    make new to recipient at end of to recipients with properties
      {address:"$to"}
    send
  end tell
end tell
EOAS
```

This code executes a very simple AppleScript that creates and sends a message. There are a number of ways to drive AppleScript on Mac OS X from Perl; search CPAN for "AppleScript" to see some of them. This particular module, part of `Mac::Carbon` by Chris Nandor, happens to ship with Mac OS X 10.5 and is one of the more efficient methods.

Under Windows, we can use the `Win32::OLE` module to control the relatively ubiquitous Outlook:[*]

```
use Win32::OLE;
use Win32::OLE::Const 'Microsoft Outlook';

my $outl = Win32::OLE->new('Outlook.Application');
my $ol   = Win32::OLE::Const->Load($outl);

my $message = $outl->CreateItem(olMailItem);

$message->Recipients->Add('user@example.edu');
$message->{Subject} = 'Perl to Outlook Test';
$message->{Body}    = "Hi there!\n\nLove,\nPerl\n";

$message->Send;
```

To drive Outlook, we request an Outlook `Application` object and use it to create a mail message for sending. To make our lives easier during that process, we use `Win32::OLE::Const` to suck in the OLE constants associated with Outlook. This gives us `olMailItem`, and from there things are straightforward.

The preceding code is pretty simple, but we still had to know more than should have been necessary about how to talk to Outlook. Figuring out how to expand upon this idea (e.g., how to attach a file or move messages around in Outlook folders) would

---

[*] The code shown here controls Outlook using the `Application` object, found in reasonably modern versions of Outlook (2000 and beyond). The first edition of this book predated those Outlook versions, so it described how to do this task using the lower-level MAPI calls. This is a much easier tack to take.

require more probing of the MSDN website for clues. To make this easier, the developer known as "Barbie" created `Mail::Outlook`, which allows us to write code like this instead:

```
use Mail::Outlook;

my $outl    = new Mail::Outlook();

my $message = $outl->create();

$message->To('user@example.edu');
$message->Subject('Perl to Outlook Test');
$message->Body("Hi there!\n\nLove,\nPerl\n");
$message->Attach(@files);

$message->send() or die "failed to send message";
```

Ultimately, programs that rely on AppleScript or `Application` objects are equally as non-portable as those that call a program called "sendmail." They offload some of the work, but they're relatively inefficient. Such approaches should probably be your methods of last resort.

Speaking the Mail Protocols Directly

Our final choice is to write code that speaks to the mail server in its native language. Most of this language is documented in RFC 2821. Here's a basic SMTP conversation. The data we send is in bold:

```
% telnet example.com 25          - connect to the SMTP port on example.com
Trying 192.168.1.10 ...
Connected to example.com.
Escape character is '^]'.
220 mailhub.example.com ESMTP Sendmail 8.9.1a/8.9.1; Sun, 13
  Apr 2008 15:32:16 -0400 (EDT)
HELO client.example.com          - identify the machine we are connecting from
                                   (can also use EHLO)
250 mailhub.example.com Hello dnb@client.example.com [192.168.1.11],
  pleased to meet you
MAIL FROM: <dnb@example.com>    - specify the sender
250 <dnb@example.com>... Sender ok
RCPT TO: <dnb@example.com>       - specify the recipient
250 <dnb@example.com>... Recipient ok
DATA                             - begin to send message, note we send
                                   several key header lines
354 Enter mail, end with "." on a line by itself
From: David N. Blank-Edelman <dnb@example.com>
To: dnb@example.com
Subject: SMTP is a fine protocol

Just wanted to drop myself a note to remind myself how much I love SMTP.
    Peace,
       dNb
.                                - finish sending the message
```

```
250 PAA26624 Message accepted for delivery
QUIT                         - end the session
221 mailhub.example.com closing connection
Connection closed by foreign host.
```

It's not difficult to script a network conversation like this; we could use the IO::Socket module, or even something like Net::Telnet, which we'll see in the next chapter. However, there are good mail modules out there that make our job easier, such as Jenda Krynicky's Mail::Sender, Milivoj Ivkovic's Mail::Sendmail, the Mail::Mailer module in Graham Barr's *MailTools* package, and Email::Send (maintained by Ricardo Signes for the Perl Email Project). All four of these packages are operating system-independent and will work almost anywhere a modern Perl distribution is available. We'll look at Email::Send for two reasons: because it offers a single interface to two of the mail-sending methods we've discussed so far, and because it offers us a good entry into the phalanx of modules connected to the Perl Email Project.

 A late-breaking tip: after this book went to production, Ricardo Signes, the developer who maintains Email::Send (and most of the Perl Email Project modules), announced he was going to deprecate Email::Send in favor of a new module called Email::Sender. Email::Sender isn't fully written yet (e.g., there is an Email::Sender::Simple module on the way that will make using that module even easier) and hasn't had the same level of field testing Email::Send has seen. Signes says he'll still maintain Email::Send for a year or so, so I would recommend sticking with it until it is clear Email::Sender is ripe.

Sending vanilla mail messages with Email::Send

Email::Send will happily send a mail message stored in plain text in a scalar variable along the lines of:

```
my $message = <<'EOM';
From: motherofallthings@example.org
To: dnb@example.edu
Subject: advice

I am the mother-of-all-things and all things should wear a sweater.

    Love,
      Mom
EOM
```

You can also get some free error checking by using an object from another of the Perl Email Project's modules: Email::Simple. Email::Simple and its plug-in module Email::Simple::Creator make it easy to programmatically construct email messages using an object-oriented approach. This is less prone to errors than writing email messages like the one in our last code snippet directly into your program. Let's see these modules in action; then we can bring Email::Send back into the picture to actually send the message we create.

`Email::Simple::Creator` takes the hassle out of creating a message by providing a straightforward `create()` method. It takes two arguments, `header` (containing a list of headers and their contents) and `body` (a scalar with the body of the message), like so:

```
use Email::Simple;
use Email::Simple::Creator;
use Email::Send;

my $message = Email::Simple->create(
   header => [
       From    => 'motherofallthings@example.org',
       To      => 'dnb@example.edu',
       Subject => 'Test Message from Email::Simple::Creator',
   ],
     body => "Hi there!\n\tLove,\n\tdNb",
);
```

Easy, no? Now let's look at how this message gets sent. If we wanted to directly send the message via SMTP, we'd write:

```
my $sender = Email::Send->new({mailer => 'SMTP'});
$sender->mailer_args([Host => 'smtp.example.edu']);
$sender->send($message) or die "Unable to send message!\n";
```

To send it using *sendmail*, or whatever is pretending to be *sendmail* on the system (e.g., Exim or Postfix), we'd change this to:

```
my $sender = Email::Send->new({mailer => 'Sendmail'});
$Email::Send::Sendmail::SENDMAIL = '/usr/sbin/sendmail';
$sender->send($message) or die "Unable to send message: $!\n";
```

You might note that the code is setting the package variable `$Email::Send::Sendmail::SENDMAIL`. This is required because `Email::Send::Sendmail`, at least as of this writing, makes no attempt to find the *sendmail* binary any place other than in the current path (a strange choice because the binary is very rarely in users' paths). We have to help it out by pointing it to the correct location.

There are a number of other possible values for `mailer`, corresponding to various `Email::Send::` helper modules. One of my favorites is `'test'`, which uses `Email::Send::Test`. The `Email::Send::Test` module lets your application think it is sending mail, but actually "traps" all outgoing mail and stores it in an array for your inspection. This is a great way to debug mail-sending code before accidentally irritating thousands of recipients with a mistake you didn't catch until after the mail was sent.

Sending mail messages with attachments using Email::Send

Once people find sending mail via Perl is so easy, they often want to do more complicated things in this vein. Despite email being a poor medium for file transfer, it is pretty common to find yourself needing to send mail with arbitrary attachments. That process can get complex quickly, though, because you're now on the path down the rabbit hole known as the Multipurpose Internet Mail Extensions (MIME) standards. Described in RFCs 2045, 2046, 2047, 2077, 4288, and 4289 (yes, it takes at least six standards documents to document this beast), MIME is a standard for including various kinds of content within an email message.

We don't have the space in this chapter to do anything but skim the surface of MIME, so I'll just note that a MIME message is composed of parts, each of which is labeled with a content type and other metadata, such as how it is represented or encoded. There is an `Email::MIME` module in the Perl Email Project (maintained by Ricardo Signes) for working with MIME in this context. Luckily for us, `Email::MIME` has a helper plug-in module called `Email::MIME::Creator` (also maintained by Signes) that makes creating attachments much less painful than usual. Let's look at some example code first, and then we'll talk about how it works:

```
use Email::Simple;
use Email::MIME::Creator;
use File::Slurp qw(slurp);
use Email::Send;

my @mimeparts = (
    Email::MIME->create(
        attributes => {
            content_type => 'text/plain',
            charset      => 'US-ASCII',
        },
        body => "Hi there!\n\tLove,\n\tdNb\n",
    ),
    Email::MIME->create(
        attributes => {
            filename     => 'picture.jpg',
            content_type => 'image/jpeg',
            encoding     => 'base64',
            name         => 'picture.jpg',
        },
        body => scalar slurp('picture.jpg'),
    ),
);
my $message = Email::MIME->create(
    header => [
        From    => 'motherofallthings@example.org',
        To      => 'dnb@example.edu',
        Subject => 'Test Message from Email::MIME::Creator',
    ],
    parts => [@mimeparts],
);

my $sender = Email::Send->new({mailer => 'Sendmail'});
$Email::Send::Sendmail::SENDMAIL = '/usr/sbin/sendmail';
$sender->send($message) or die "Unable to send message!\n";
```

The first step is to create the two parts that will make up the message: the plain-text part (the body of the message a user will see) and the attachment part. This is again pretty straightforward, with the only tricky part being the actual inclusion of the file being attached. `Email::MIME->create()` needs a scalar value containing the entire contents of the file being attached. One of the easiest and most efficient ways to suck an entire file into a variable is to use Dave Rolsky's `File::Slurp` module. Being explicit about what type of value we expect to get back from the `slurp()` call ensures that we get the scalar value we need.

After defining the two MIME parts for the message and loading them with data, we now need to construct the message consisting of those two parts. The second call to `Email::MIME->create()` creates the message consisting of our required headers and the parts objects we just created. With this message in hand, sending the actual message is just like the vanilla send shown earlier.

Sending HTML mail messages using Email::Send

I'm loath to show you how to do this because I personally dislike HTML mail, but if it gets around that you know how to send mail programmatically, someday someone is going to come to you and demand you send HTML mail messages for him. If that person is your boss, you can say "HTML mail is icky" as many times as you want, but it probably won't get you out of the assignment. To help you keep your job, I'll show you one example of how this is done—just don't tell anyone you learned this from me.

HTML mail messages are just another example of using MIME to transport non-plain-text data in a mail message. Given that, you could construct a mail message using the same `Email::MIME::Creator` technique demonstrated in the last section. This would be relatively straightforward for a very basic, text-only page if you already knew the MIME metadata for each part of the HTML message. However, it starts to get a little tricky if you want to have things like images rendered in the HTML page, particularly if you'd prefer to send those things within the message itself. There are a couple of reasons to embed images: URL-sourced images make for a slow message display, and, more importantly, many email clients block URL-based images for security reasons (so spammers cannot use them as web bugs to confirm that the messages were received).

Luckily, there's a similar message-creation module called `Email::MIME::CreateHTML`, created and maintained by programmers at the BBC, that can handle all the heavy lifting for us. Here's a very simple example of sending HTML mail with a plain-text alternative:

```
use Email::MIME::CreateHTML;
use Email::Send;

my $annoyinghtml=<<HTML;
<html>
  <body>
    Hi there!<br />
      Love,<br />
      <em>dNb</em>
  <body>
<html>
HTML

my $message = Email::MIME->create_html(
    header => [
        From    => 'motherofallthings@example.org',
```

```
        To      => 'dnb@example.edu',
        Subject => 'Test Message from Email::MIME::CreateHTML',
    ],
    body => $annoyinghtml,
    text_body => "Hi there!\n\tLove,\n\tdNb",
);

my $sender = Email::Send->new( { mailer => 'Sendmail' } );
$Email::Send::Sendmail::SENDMAIL = '/usr/sbin/sendmail';
$sender->send($message) or die "Unable to send message!\n";
```

Our part in the process is super-simple—we're just passing in scalar values that contain the HTML and plain-text versions of the message. The HTML we're passing in doesn't have any external references to images and such, but if it did, the method `Email::MIME->create_html` would have parsed them out of the message and attached the files for us accordingly. You'll also notice that the actual sending of the message is handled in exactly the same way as in our previous examples. This is one of the benefits of using `Email::Send`.

One last comment about this code before we move on: `Email::MIME::CreateHTML` removes the need for a lot of complex fiddling around, but there's a price to pay for all the power under the hood. In order to work its magic, `Email::MIME::CreateHTML` depends on a relatively large list of other modules (each with its own dependencies). Installing these dependencies isn't a problem, thanks to the `CPAN.pm` and `CPANPLUS` modules, but if you're looking for something lightweight you'll want to look for another way to create your mail messages.

Common Mistakes in Sending Email

Now that you know how to send email, you can begin using email as a notification method. Once you start to write code that performs this function, you'll quickly find that the issue of *how* to send mail is not nearly as interesting as the questions of *when* and *what* to send.

This section explores those questions by taking a contrary approach. If we look at when and how *not* to send mail, we'll get a deeper insight into these issues.[†] Let's begin by exploring some of the most common mistakes made by system administration programs that send mail.

Overzealous Message Sending

By far, the most common mistake is sending too much mail. It's a great idea to have scripts send mail. If there's a service disruption, normal email and email sent to a pager

---

[†] This assumes that you've decided email is still the best communication method for your purposes. When making that decision, you should take into account that it can be subject to large delays, isn't generally secure, etc.

are good ways to bring this problem to the attention of a human. But under most circumstances, it is a very *bad* idea to have your program send mail about the problem every five minutes or so. Overzealous mail generators tend to be quickly added to the mail filters of the very humans who should be reading the messages, with the end result being that important mail is routinely and automatically ignored.

Controlling the frequency of mail

The easiest way to avoid what I call "mail beaconing" is to build into the programs safeguards to gate the delay between messages. If your script runs constantly, it's easy to stash the time when the last mail message was sent in a variable like this:

```
my $last_sent = time;
```

If your program is started up every *N* minutes or hours via Unix's *cron* or the Windows Task Scheduler service mechanisms, this information can be written to a one-line file and read again the next time the program is run. Be sure in this case to pay attention to some of the security precautions outlined in Chapter 1.

Depending on the situation, you may be able to get fancy about your delay times. One suggestion is to perform an exponential backoff where you have a routine that gives the OK to send mail once every minute (2^0), then every two minutes (2^1), every four minutes (2^2), every eight minutes (2^3), and so on until you reach some upper limit like "once a day."

Alternatively, sometimes it is more appropriate to have your program act like a two-year-old, complaining more often as time goes by. In that case you can do an exponential ramp-up where the routine initially gives the OK to send messages starting with the maximum delay value (say, "once a day") and becomes exponentially more permissive until it reaches a minimum value, like "every five minutes."

Controlling the amount of mail

Another subclass of the "overzealous message sending" syndrome is the "everybody on the network for themselves" problem. If all the machines on your network decide to send you a piece of mail at the same time, you may miss something important in the subsequent message blizzard. A better approach is to have them all report to a central repository of some sort.‡ The information can then be collated and mailed out later in a single message.

---

‡ One good tool (under Unix) for the central reporting of status is *syslog* (or one of its descendants, such as *syslog-ng*). To be able to use this tool effectively in this context, however, you need to be able to control its configuration on the receiving end. That's not always an option, for any number of technical and administrative reasons, so this chapter presents another method. For more info on dealing with *syslog* logs, see Chapter 10.

Let's consider a moderately contrived example. For this scenario, assume each machine in your network drops a one-line file into a shared directory.* Named for the machine, that file will contain that machine's summary of the results of last night's scientific computation. The single line in the file might be of this form:

```
hostname success-or-failure number-of-computations-completed
```

A program that collates the information and mails the results might look like this:

```perl
use Email::Simple;
use Email::Simple::Creator;
use Email::Send;
use Text::Wrap;
use File::Spec;

# the list of machines reporting in
my $repolist = '/project/machinelist';

# the directory where they write files
my $repodir = '/project/reportddir';

# send mail "from" this address
my $reportfromaddr = 'project@example.com';

# send mail to this address
my $reporttoaddr = 'project@example.com';

my $statfile;     # the name of the file where status reports are recorded
my $report;       # the report line found in each statfile
my %success;      # the succesful hosts
my %fail;         # the hosts that failed
my %missing;      # the list of hosts missing in action (no reports)

# Now we read the list of machines reporting in into a hash.
# Later, we'll depopulate this hash as each machine reports in,
# leaving behind only the machines that are missing in action.

open my $LIST, '<', $repolist or die "Unable to open list $repolist:$!\n";
while (<$LIST>) {
    chomp;
    $missing{$_} = 1;
}
close $LIST;

# total number of machines that should be reporting
my $machines = scalar keys %missing;

# Read all of the files in the central report directory.
# Note: this directory should be cleaned out automatically
#       by another script.
opendir my $REPO, $repodir or die "Unable to open dir $repodir:$!\n";
```

---

* Another good rendezvous spot for status information like this would be in a database. A third possibility would be to have all of the mail sent to another mailbox. You could then have a separate Perl program retrieve the messages via POP3 and post-process them.

```perl
while ( defined( $statfile = readdir($REPO) ) ) {
    next unless -f File::Spec->catfile( $repodir, $statfile );

    # open each status file and read in the one-line status report
    open my $STAT, File::Spec->catfile( $repodir, $statfile )
        or die "Unable to open $statfile:$!\n";

    chomp( $report = <$STAT> );

    my ( $hostname, $result, $details ) = split( ' ', $report, 3 );

    warn "$statfile said it was generated by $hostname!\n"
        if ( $hostname ne $statfile );

    # hostname is no longer considered missing
    delete $missing{$hostname};

    # populate these hashes based on success or failure reported
    if ( $result eq 'success' ) {
        $success{$hostname} = $details;
    }
    else {
        $fail{$hostname} = $details;
    }
    close $STAT;
    # we could remove the $statfile here to clean up for the
    # next night's run, but only if that works in your setup
}
closedir $REPO;

# construct a useful subject for our mail message
my $subject;
if ( scalar keys %success == $machines ) {
    $subject = "[report] Success: $machines";
}
elsif ( scalar keys %fail == $machines or
        scalar keys %missing >= $machines ) {
    $subject = "[report] Fail: $machines";
}
else {
    $subject
        = '[report] Partial: '
        . keys(%success)
        . ' ACK, ' .
        keys(%fail) . ' NACK'
        . ( (%missing) ? ', ' . keys(%missing) . ' MIA' : '' );
}

# create the body of the message
my $body = "Run report from $0 on " . scalar localtime(time) . "\n";

if ( keys %success ) {
    $body .= "\n==Succeeded==\n";
    foreach my $hostname ( sort keys %success ) {
```

```
            $body .= "$hostname: $success{$hostname}\n";
        }
    }

    if ( keys %fail ) {
        $body .= "\n==Failed==\n";
        foreach my $hostname ( sort keys %fail ) {
            $body .= "$hostname: $fail{$hostname}\n";
        }
    }

    if ( keys %missing ) {
        $body .= "\n==Missing==\n";
        $body .= wrap( '', '', join( ' ', sort keys %missing ) ), "\n";
    }

    my $message = Email::Simple->create(
        header => [
            From    => $reportfromaddr,
            To      => $reporttoaddr,
            Subject => $subject,
        ],
        body => $body,
    );

    my $sender = Email::Send->new( { mailer => 'Sendmail' } );
    $Email::Send::Sendmail::SENDMAIL = '/usr/sbin/sendmail';
    $sender->send($message) or die "Unable to send message!\n";
```

The code first reads in a list of the machine names that will be participating in this scheme. Later, it will use a hash based on this list to check whether there are any machines that have not placed a file in the central reporting directory. We'll open each file in this directory and extract the status information. Once we've collated the results, we construct a mail message and send it out.

Here's an example of the resulting message:

```
Date: Mon, 14 Apr 2008 13:06:09 -0400 (EDT)
Message-Id: <200804141706.NAA08780@example.com>
Subject: [report] Partial: 3 ACK, 4 NACK, 1 MIA
To: project@example.com
From: project@example.com

Run report from reportscript on Mon Apr 14 13:06:08 2008

==Succeeded==
barney: computed 23123 oogatrons
betty: computed 6745634 oogatrons
fred: computed 56344 oogatrons

==Failed==
bambam: computed 0 oogatrons
dino: computed 0 oogatrons
pebbles: computed 0 oogatrons
wilma: computed 0 oogatrons
```

```
==Missing==
mrslate
```

Another way to collate results like this is to create a custom logging daemon and have each machine report in over a network socket. Let's look at the code for the server first. This example reuses code from the previous example. We'll talk about the important new bits right after you see the listing:

```perl
use IO::Socket;
use Text::Wrap;     # used to make the output prettier

# the list of machines reporting in
my $repolist = '/project/machinelist';

# the port number clients should connect to
my $serverport = '9967';

my %success;       # the succesful hosts
my %fail;          # the hosts that failed
my %missing;       # the list of hosts missing in action (no reports)

# load the machine list using a hash slice (end result is a hash
# of the form %missing = { key1 => undef, key2 => undef, ...})
@missing{ loadmachines() } = ();
my $machines = keys %missing;

# set up our side of the socket
my $reserver = IO::Socket::INET->new(
    LocalPort => $serverport,
    Proto     => "tcp",
    Type      => SOCK_STREAM,
    Listen    => 5,
    Reuse     => 1
) or die "Unable to build our socket half: $!\n";

# start listening on it for connects
while ( my ( $connectsock, $connectaddr ) = $reserver->accept() ) {

    # the name of the client that has connected to us
    my $connectname
        = gethostbyaddr( ( sockaddr_in($connectaddr) )[1], AF_INET );

    chomp( my $report = $connectsock->getline );

    my ( $hostname, $result, $details ) = split( ' ', $report, 3 );

    # if we've been told to dump our info, print out a ready-to-go mail
    # message and reinitialize all of our hashes/counters
    if ( $hostname eq 'DUMPNOW' ) {
        printmail($connectsock);
        close $connectsock;
        undef %success;
        undef %fail;
        undef %missing;
```

```perl
        @missing{ loadmachines() } = ();     # reload the machine list
        my $machines = keys %missing;
        next;
    }

    warn "$connectname said it was generated by $hostname!\n"
        if ( $hostname ne $connectname );

    delete $missing{$hostname};

    if ( $result eq 'success' ) {
        $success{$hostname} = $details;
    }
    else {
        $fail{$hostname} = $details;
    }
    close $connectsock;
}
close $reserver;

# Prints a ready-to-go mail message. The first line is the subject,
# and subsequent lines are all the body of the message.
sub printmail {
    my $socket = shift;

    my $subject;
    if ( keys %success == $machines ) {
        $subject = "[report] Success: $machines";
    }
    elsif ( keys %fail == $machines or keys %missing >= $machines ) {
        $subject = "[report] Fail: $machines";
    }
    else {
        $subject
            = '[report] Partial: '
            . keys(%success)
            . ' ACK, ' .
            keys(%fail) . " NACK"
            . ( (%missing) ? ', ' . keys(%missing) . ' MIA' : '' );
    }

    print $socket "$subject\n";

    print $socket "Run report from $0 on " . scalar localtime(time) . "\n";

    if ( keys %success ) {
        print $socket "\n==Succeeded==\n";
        foreach my $hostname ( sort keys %success ) {
            print $socket "$hostname: $success{$hostname}\n";
        }
    }

    if ( keys %fail ) {
        print $socket "\n==Failed==\n";
        foreach my $hostname ( sort keys %fail ) {
```

```
                print $socket "$hostname: $fail{$hostname}\n";
            }
        }

        if ( keys %missing ) {
            print $socket "\n==Missing==\n";
            print $socket wrap( '', '', join( ' ', sort keys %missing ) ), "\n";
        }
    }

    # loads the list of machines from the given file
    sub loadmachines {
        my @missing;
        open my $LIST, '<', $repolist or die "Unable to open list $repolist:$!\n";
        while (<$LIST>) {
            chomp;
            push( @missing, $_ );
        }
        close $LIST;
        return @missing;
    }
```

Besides moving some of the code sections to their own subroutines, the key change is the addition of the networking code. The `IO::Socket` module makes the process of opening and using sockets pretty painless. Sockets are usually described using a telephone metaphor. We start by setting up our side of the socket (`IO::Socket->new()`), essentially turning on our phone, and then wait for a call from a network client (`IO::Socket->accept()`). Our program will pause (or "block") until a connection request comes in. As soon as it arrives, we note the name of the connecting client. We then read a line of input from the socket.

This line of input is expected to look just like those we read from the individual files in our previous example. The one difference is the magic hostname DUMPNOW. If we see this hostname, we print the subject and body of a ready-to-mail message to the connecting client and reset all of our counters and hash tables. The client is then responsible for actually sending the mail it receives from the server. Let's look at our sample client and what it can do with this message:

```
use IO::Socket;

# the port number clients should connect to
my $serverport = '9967';

# the name of the server
my $servername = 'reportserver';

# name-to-IP address mapping
my $serveraddr     = inet_ntoa( scalar gethostbyname($servername) );
my $reportfromaddr = 'project@example.com';
my $reporttoaddr   = 'project@example.com';

my $reserver = IO::Socket::INET->new(
    PeerAddr => $serveraddr,
```

```
        PeerPort => $serverport,
        Proto    => 'tcp',
        Type     => SOCK_STREAM
) or die "Unable to build our socket half: $!\n";

if ( $ARGV[0] ne '-m' ) {
    print $reserver $ARGV[0];
}
else {

    # These 'use' statements will load their respective modules when the
    # script starts even if we don't get to this code block. We could use
    # require/import instead (like we did in Chapter 3), but the goal here
    # is to just make it clear that these modules come into play when we
    # use the -m switch.

    use Email::Simple;
    use Email::Simple::Creator;
    use Email::Send;

    print $reserver "DUMPNOW\n";
    chomp( my $subject = <$reserver> );
    my $body = join( '', <$reserver> );

    my $message = Email::Simple->create(
        header => [
            From    => $reportfromaddr,
            To      => $reporttoaddr,
            Subject => $subject,
        ],
        body => $body,
    );

    my $sender = Email::Send->new( { mailer => 'Sendmail' } );
    $Email::Send::Sendmail::SENDMAIL = '/usr/sbin/sendmail';
    $sender->send($message) or die "Unable to send message!\n";
}

close $reserver;
```

First, we open up a socket to the server. In most cases, we pass it our status information (received on the command line as $ARGV[0], i.e., `script.pl "dino fail computed 0 oogatrons"`) and drop the connection. If we were really going to set up a logging client/server like this, we would probably encapsulate this client code in a subroutine and call it from within a much larger program after its processing had been completed.

If this script is passed an -m flag, it instead sends "DUMPNOW" to the server and reads the subject line and body returned by the server. Then this output is fed to Email::Send and sent out via mail using the same code we saw earlier.

To limit the example code size and keep the discussion on track, the server and client code presented here is as bare bones as possible. There's no error or input checking, access control or authentication (anyone on the Net who can get to our server can feed and receive data from it), persistent storage (what if the machine goes down?), or any of a number of other routine precautions in place. On top of this, we can only handle a single request at a time. If a client should stall in the middle of a transaction, we're sunk. For more sophisticated server examples, I recommend you check out the client/server treatments in Lincoln Stein's *Network Programming With Perl* (Addison-Wesley) and Tom Christiansen and Nathan Torkington's *Perl Cookbook (http://oreilly.com/cat alog/9780596003135/)* (O'Reilly). Jochen Wiedmann's `Net::Daemon` module will also help you write more sophisticated daemon programs.

Now that we've dealt with regulating the volume of mail sent, let's move on to other common mistakes made when writing system administration programs that send mail.

Subject Line Waste

A `Subject` line is a terrible thing to waste. When sending mail automatically, it is possible to generate a useful `Subject` line on the fly for each message. This means there is very little excuse to leave someone with a mailbox that looks like this:

```
Super-User      File history database merge report
Super-User      File history database merge report
Super-User      File history database merge report
Super-User      File history database merge report
Super-User      File history database merge report
Super-User      File history database merge report
Super-User      File history database merge report
```

when it could look like this:

```
Super-User      Backup OK, 1 tape, 1.400 GB written.
Super-User      Backup OK, 1 tape, 1.768 GB written.
Super-User      Backup OK, 1 tape, 2.294 GB written.
Super-User      Backup OK, 1 tape, 2.817 GB written.
Super-User      Backup OK, 1 tape, 3.438 GB written.
Super-User      Backup OK, 3 tapes, 75.40 GB written.
```

or even like this:

```
Super-User      Backup of Hostname OK, 1 tape, 1.400 GB written.
Super-User      Backup of Hostname:/usr OK, 1 tape, 1.768 GB written.
```

Your `Subject` line should provide a concise and explicit summary of the situation. It should be very clear from that line whether the program generating the message is reporting success, failure, or something in between. A little more programming effort will pay off handsomely in reduced time reading mail.

Insufficient Information in the Message Body

As with the `Subject` line, in the message body a little specificity goes a long way. If your script is going to complain about problems or error conditions via email, it should strive to provide certain pieces of information. They boil down to the canonical questions of journalism:

Who?

Which script is complaining? Include the contents of `$0` (if you haven't set it explicitly) to show the full path to the current script. Mention the version of your script if it has one.

Where?

Give some indication of the place in your script where trouble occurred. The Perl function `caller()` returns all sorts of useful information for this purpose:

```
# Note: what caller() returns can be specific to a
# particular Perl version, so be sure to see the perlfunc docs
($package, $filename, $line, $subroutine, $hasargs, $wantarray,
 $evaltext, $is_require) = caller($frames);
```

`$frames` is the number of stack frames (if you've called subroutines from within subroutines) desired. Most often you'll want `$frames` set to 1. Here's a sample list returned by the `caller()` function when it's called in the middle of the server code from our last full code example:

```
('main','repserver',32,'main::printmail',1,undef)
```

This shows that the script was in the `main` package while running from the filename `repserver` at line 32 in the script. At that point it was executing code in the `main::printmail` subroutine (which has arguments and has not been called in a list context).

If you want to be even kinder to the people who will read your mail, you can pair `caller()` up with the `Carp` module shipped with Perl to output diagnostic information that is (at best guess) most relevant to the issue at hand. For our purposes, we'll want to use the `longmess()` routine, explicitly imported because the module does not export it by default:

```
use Carp qw(longmess);
```

`longmess()` provides the contents of the warning message that would be produced if one called a `warn()`-like substitute called `cluck()`. In addition to printing out this warning, it also produces a whole stack backtrace that can be helpful for determining exactly where in a long program things failed.

When?

Describe the program state at the time of the error. For instance, what was the last line of input read?

Why?

If you can, answer the reader's unspoken question: "Why are you bothering me with a mail message?" The answer may be as simple as "the accounting data has not been fully collated," "DNS service is not available now," or "the machine room is on fire." This provides context to the reader (and perhaps some motivation to investigate).

What?

Finally, don't forget to mention what went wrong in the first place.

Here's some simple Perl code that covers all of these bases:

```perl
use Text::Wrap;
use Carp qw(longmess);

sub problemreport {

    # $shortcontext should be a one-line description of the problem
    # $usercontext should be a detailed description of the problem
    # $nextstep should be the best suggestion for how to remedy the problem
    my ( $shortcontext, $usercontext, $nextstep ) = @_;
    my ( $filename, $line, $subroutine ) = ( caller(1) )[ 1, 2, 3 ];
    my $report = '';

    $report .= "Problem with $filename: $shortcontext\n";
    $report .= "*** Problem report for $filename ***\n\n";
    $report .= fill( '', ' ', "- Problem: $usercontext" ) . "\n\n";
    $report
        .= "- Location: line $line of file $filename in " . "$subroutine\n\n";
    $report .= longmess('Stack trace ') . "\n";
    $report .= '- Occurred: ' . scalar localtime(time) . "\n\n";
    $report .= "- Next step: $nextstep\n";

    return $report;
}

sub fireperson {
    my $report = problemreport( 'the computer is on fire', <<EOR, <<EON);
While running the accounting report, smoke started pouring out of the
back of the machine. This occurred right after we processed the
pension plan.
EOR
Please put fire out before continuing.
EON

    print $report;

}

fireperson();
```

`problemreport()` will output a problem report, subject line first, suitable for feeding to `Email::Send` as per our previous examples. `fireperson()` is an example test of this subroutine.

 One last tip: if you are going to write code that sends mail in response to mail you receive (e.g., an auto-responder of some sort), you should definitely read RFC 3834, *Recommendations for Automatic Responses to Electronic Mail*.

Now that we've explored sending mail, let's take a look at the other edge of the sword.

Fetching Mail

The attraction of being able to send mail programmatically is probably pretty easy to see, but it may not be as clear why you might want to be able to fetch or receive mail with similar mechanical ease. One reason is mail server testing. If you run a mail server, this capability lets you test that server's functionality beyond the usual sending tests. Ideally you would test mail fetching as if you were one of your server's clients. I also recommend doing round-trip tests where you attempt both to send a piece of mail through your server and to retrieve it again. This type of check isn't perfect by any means because mail paths aren't always symmetric, but it's much better than just checking whether your MTA is still listening on a socket.

Even if you don't run any mail servers, there are still good reasons for knowing how to fetch mail. For example, if you think you can do a better job of filtering spam than your ISP does, you may want to pull down all incoming mail, check it, and then act on the spam messages before your usual mail-reading client sees them. Similarly, if you want to do more sophisticated filtering or processing of your mail than is possible at your ISP, you could use the information in this section to fetch the mail and work on it locally.

Talking POP3 to Fetch Mail

The POP3 protocol (documented in RFC 1939) is relatively simple, so we'll start there. Here's the usual set of steps a POP3 client will perform each time it connects to a POP3 server:

1. Connect and authenticate as a known user.
2. See if there is new mail (more on this step in a bit).
3. Request the contents of the oldest unseen message and squirrel it away on the local machine.
4. Request that the server delete the message just fetched (the server marks the message for deletion).
5. Repeat steps 3 and 4 for every remaining new message.
6. Signal that it is finished with the connection and close it. The server actually removes the messages marked for deletion in step 4.

One of the pleasant things about this protocol is its simplicity: those six steps show almost all of the operations available.[†] There are a couple of details about those operations that need to be mentioned, though.

[†] One operation we're not going to discuss that you may want to use at some point is the RFC-optional TOP command. It asks the server for the headers of a message plus the top *N* lines of the body of a message.

First, how does the client determine if there are new messages? If the client always requests that the server delete the messages it downloads (as in step 4), the answer is easy: any messages on the server at connection time are new. But a client doesn't always want the mail messages to be deleted right after downloading them; sometimes it makes more sense to leave them in place. This is most often the case when the user wants to have two mail readers look at the same mail (e.g., home and office machines). In this case, one of the clients downloads the mail; the other both downloads it and asks the server to delete those messages.

The client that doesn't ask the server to delete the mail needs a way to remember which messages it has seen before. This is usually handled with an RFC-optional command called UIDL. The UIDL command asks the server to return a "unique-id listing" for a single message or each message on the server. The client caches these unique identifiers and later downloads only the messages whose UIDLs are not in the cache.

There are a number of POP3 Perl modules out there that can make using POP3 really simple. The one I tend to use most is Mail::POP3Client, because it makes SSL connections easy (by default POP3 sends passwords in the clear) and provides methods that mostly map directly to the names of the operations found in RFC 1939. That "mostly" part is my one quibble with this module, because sometimes it makes up its own names for things that have perfectly good (but different) names in the RFC. For example, it provides Retrieve() (which is an alias for HeadAndBody()), while RFC 1939 calls that method RETR. I'd prefer that the module's methods could be directly inferred from the RFC, even as an option.

Here's some sample code that shows how to connect securely, display a count of messages in a mailbox, and print out the contents of its first message:

```
use Mail::POP3Client;

my $pop3 = new Mail::POP3Client(
    USER     => 'user',
    PASSWORD => 'secretsquirrel',
    HOST     => 'pop3.example.edu',
    USESSL   => 'true',
    );

die 'Connection failed: ' . $pop3->Message() . "\n"
    if $pop3->Count() == -1;

print 'Number of messages in this mailbox: ' . $pop3->Count() . "\n\n";
print "The first message looks like this: \n" . $pop3->Retrieve(1) . "\n";

$pop3->Close();
```

There's not much to this code as written because there doesn't have to be much. If we wanted to extend it, we could call Delete(*message #*) to mark a message for deletion or Uidl() if we wanted to get back UIDLs for all messages or a particular one. Both the Head() and HeadAndBody() methods will return either a scalar or an array based on their calling context, so it's easy to get a mail header or message in the form desired by packages like `Mail::SpamAssassin`, discussed later in this chapter.

Talking IMAP4rev1 to Fetch Mail

IMAP4rev1, called IMAP4 from this point on, is a significantly more powerful (read: complex) protocol documented in RFC 3501. Its basic model is different from that of POP3. With POP3 it is assumed that the POP3 client polls the POP3 server and downloads mail periodically, while with IMAP4 a client connects to a server for the duration of the mail reading session.‡ With POP3 the client is expected to handle all of the sophisticated work, like deciding what messages to download, while with IMAP4 the discussion between the server and the client is much richer, so the protocol has to be considerably smarter. Smarter how? Here are some of the characteristics of IMAP4:

- It can deal with a whole hierarchical structure of mail folders and the contents of each folder. According to RFC 3051, "IMAP4rev1 includes operations for creating, deleting, and renaming mailboxes, checking for new messages, permanently removing messages, setting and clearing flags, RFC 2822 and RFC 2045 parsing, searching, and selective fetching of message attributes, texts, and portions thereof."

- It has a much more sophisticated understanding of the structure of an individual mail message. POP3 lets us grab a mail message's headers or the headers plus the first *N* lines of the message body. IMAP4 lets us ask for just "the text part of the message" in messages that have lots of attachments and doodads. It does this by building MIME into the official specification.

- It lets a client send a whole bunch of commands to the server at once and receive the results back in whatever fashion the server chooses to send them. This is different from the standard process of having a client send a command and then wait for the server to respond before it can send a second command. Each IMAP4 command and response is prefaced with a unique "tag" that allows both the client and the server to keep track of what has been asked and answered.

- It has a "disconnected mode" that allows clients to connect to a server, cache as much information as they need, and then disconnect. The user can then potentially operate on that cache as if the connection was still in place. When the connection returns, the client can play the changes made to the local mail store back to the server and the server will catch the client up on what happened while the client was out of touch. This mode allows you to sit on a plane without network access, deleting and filing mail, later to have those changes be reflected on the server once you get back on the network.

With all of this power comes the price of complexity. You won't want to do much IMAP4 programming without RFC 3501 close at hand. Even that only gets you so far,

---

‡ Warning: there's a little bit of hand waving going on in this statement, because IMAP4 has something known as "disconnected mode" that doesn't fit this description. We'll talk about that in just a moment.

because different server authors have decided to implement certain edge cases differently. You may have to play around a bit to get the results you want when it comes to more advanced IMAP4 programming.

For the example code we're about to see, I'll be using my current preferred IMAP module, `Mail::IMAPClient` (originally by David J. Kernen, rewritten and now maintained by Mark Overmeer). This is the same module that forms the basis of the superb *imapsync* program (*http://www.linux-france.org/prj/imapsync/dist/*), a great tool for migrating data from one IMAP4 server to another. In addition to *imapsync*'s vote of confidence, I like this module because it is mostly complete when it comes to features while still offering the ability to send raw IMAP4 commands should it become necessary. The other module that I would consider looking at is `Mail::IMAPTalk` by Rob Mueller, the primary developer behind Fastmail.fm. Even though it hasn't been updated in a few years, the module's author assures me that the current release still works well and is in active use.

For our first IMAP4 example, here's some code that connects (securely) to a user's mailbox, finds everything that was previously labeled as spam by SpamAssassin (it adds the header `X-Spam-Flag: YES`), and moves those messages to a *SPAM* folder. We'll start with connecting to the IMAP server:

```
use IO::Socket::SSL;
use Mail::IMAPClient;

my $s = IO::Socket::SSL->new(PeerAddr =>'imap.example.com',
                             PeerPort => '993',
                             Proto    => 'tcp');
die $@ unless defined $s;

my $m = Mail::IMAPClient->new(User     => 'user', Socket=>$s,
                              Password => 'topsecret');
```

`Mail::IMAPClient` does not have SSL built-in in the same way that `Mail::POP3Client` does, so we're forced to construct an SSL-protected socket by hand and pass it to `Mail::IMAPClient`. Without specifying this connection, all communication, including the password, would be sent in clear text.

Chained to an Old Version

If you rely on *imapsync*, you may find yourself in the unfortunate position of having to keep an old version of `Mail::IMAPClient` around because, as of this writing, *imapsync* doesn't yet completely work with the 3.x rewrite of `Mail::IMAPClient`. If this is still the case when you read this text, you are going to find that the code in this section won't work as written. There are two non-obvious changes of the hair-pulling kind that you'll need to make if you are going to use your own secure socket.

First, `Mail::IMAPClient` doesn't properly handle the greeting that comes back from the server. You'll need to "eat" the greeting yourself right after the socket is created using code like this:

```
my $greeting = <$s>;
my ( $id, $answer ) = split /\s+/, $greeting;
die "connect problem: $greeting" if $answer ne 'OK';
```

Second, `Mail::IMAPClient` doesn't know that it is connected and doesn't automatically initiate a login sequence, so the following is necessary right after the call to `new()`:

```
$m->State( Mail::IMAPClient::Connected() );
$m->login() or die 'login(): ' . $m->LastError();
```

Both of these issues get fixed in the 3.x versions of `Mail::IMAPClient`, so hopefully the module will play nicely with *imapsync* in the future.

STOP THE PRESSES: Literally as this book was being produced, a set of patches that purport to fix a number of the major incompatibilities with the latest `Mail::IMAPClient` version came across the *imapsync* mailing list. Looks like hope is in sight—perhaps by the time you have the chance to read this sidebar it will be a non-issue. The moral of the story: sometimes an application you use can lock you into a specific version of a Perl module.[*]

Once connected, the first thing one typically does is tell the server which folder to operate on. In this case, we'll select the user's *INBOX*:

```
$m->select('INBOX');
```

Now let's get to work and look for all of the messages in the *INBOX* with the `X-Spam-Flag` header set to `YES`:

```
my @spammsgs = $m->search(qw(HEADER X-Spam-Flag YES));
die $@ if $@;
```

`@spammsgs` now contains the list of messages we want to move, so we move each one in turn, close the folder, and log out of the server:

```
foreach my $msg (@spammsgs){
    $m->move('SPAM', $msg) or die 'move failed: '.$m->LastError;
}
$m->close(); # expunges currently selected folder
$m->logout;
```

There's a hidden detail in the last two lines of code that I feel compelled to mention. You might remember from the POP3 discussion that we talked about messages being "marked as deleted." The same tombstoning process takes place here as well. Deletes are always a two-step process in IMAP4: we first flag messages as `\Deleted`, then expunge messages marked with that flag. When we requested that a message be moved, the server copied the message to the new folder and marked the message in the source folder as being deleted. Ordinarily you would need to `expunge()` the source folder to actually remove the message, but RFC 3501 says that performing a `CLOSE` operation on a folder implicitly expunges that folder.

---

[*] The `local::lib` module by Matt S. Trout, now maintained by Christopher Nehren, can help a considerable amount with module version lock-in like this.

Let's look at one more IMAP4 example that will offer a good segue into our next section on processing mail. Earlier in this section we mentioned IMAP4's ability to work with a message's component MIME parts. Here's some code that demonstrates this at work. To save a tree or two of book paper, I'll leave out the initial module load, object creation, secure connection to the server, and mailbox selection code, because it's exactly the same as what we've already seen:

```
my @digests = $m->search(qw(SUBJECT digest));

foreach my $msg (@digests) {

  my $struct = $m->get_bodystructure($msg);
  next unless defined $struct;

  # Messages in a mailbox get assigned both a sequence number and
  # a unique identifier. By default Mail::IMAPClient works with UIDs.
  print "Message with UID $msg (Content-type: ",$struct->bodytype,'/',
        $struct->bodysubtype,
            ") has this structure:\n\t",
            join("\n\t",$struct->parts) ,"\n\n";
}

$m->logout;
```

This code searches for all of the messages in the currently selected folder that have "digest" in the Subject line. Then the loop examines the structure of each message and prints the MIME parts of each. Here's some sample output for two messages in my *INBOX*:

```
Message with UID 2457 (Content-type: TEXT/PLAIN) has this structure:
        HEAD
        1

Message with UID 29691 (Content-type: MULTIPART/MIXED) has this structure:
        1
        2
        3
        3.1
        3.1.HEAD
        3.1.1
        3.1.2
        3.2
        3.2.HEAD
        3.2.1
        3.2.2
        3.3
        3.3.HEAD
        3.3.1
        3.3.2
        4
```

Once you know the MIME part you're looking for, you can call bodypart_string() with the message UID and the MIME part number to retrieve it. For example, the following:

```
print $m->bodypart_string(29691,'4');
```

prints out the footer of the message with UID 29691:

```
Perl-Win32-Database mailing list
   Perl-Win32-Database@listserv.ActiveState.com
   To unsubscribe: http://listserv.ActiveState.com/mailman/mysubs
```

Mail::IMAPClient uses the Parse::RecDescent module to take apart MIME messages. Its parser works most of the time, but I have found that some messages cause it to malfunction. If you find yourself doing a good deal of MIME-related mail processing, you may want to call on one of the dedicated MIME-processing modules, such as Email::MIME, or even use the Mail::IMAPTalk module mentioned earlier. We'll see an example of using Email::MIME in the next section.

This discussion of extracting parts of messages leads us right into our next subject.

Processing Mail

It is useful to be able to fetch mail, but that's just the beginning. In this section we'll explore what can be done with that mail once it has been transferred.

Let's start with the basics and look at the tools available for the dissection of both a single mail message and an entire mailbox. For the first topic, we will again turn to modules provided by the Perl Email Project.

In the first edition of this book the examples in this section used the Mail::Internet, Mail::Header, and Mail::Folder modules. I've switched to the modules from the Perl Email Project for consistency's sake, but the first edition's modules are all still viable (especially now that the first two are being updated regularly under the stewardship of Mark Overmeer). Mark is also the author of Mail::Box, a copiously featured package for mail handling. If the modules from the Perl Email Project don't provide what you need, you should definitely take a look at Mail::Box.

Dissecting a Single Message

The Email::Simple module offers a convenient way to slice and dice the headers of an RFC 2822-compliant mail message. RFC 2822 dictates the format of a mail message, including the names of the acceptable header lines and their formats.

To use Email::Simple, feed it a scalar variable that contains a mail message:

```
use Email::Simple;

my $message = <<'EOM';
```

```
From user@example.edu Mon Aug  6 05:43:22 2007
Received: from localhost (localhost [127.0.0.1])
        by zimbra.example.edu (Postfix) with ESMTP id 6A39577490A
        for <dnb@example.edu>; Mon,  6 Aug 2007 05:43:22 -0400 (EDT)
Received: from zimbra.example.edu ([127.0.0.1])
        by localhost (zimbra.example.edu [127.0.0.1]) (amavisd-new, port 10024)
        with ESMTP id OIIgygSczEdt for <dnb@zimbra.example.edu>;
        Mon,  6 Aug 2007 05:43:22 -0400 (EDT)
Received: from amber.example.edu (amber.example.edu [192.168.16.51])
        by zimbra.example.edu (Postfix) with ESMTP id 2828A774909
        for <dnb@zimbra.example.edu>; Mon,  6 Aug 2007 05:43:22 -0400 (EDT)
Received: from chinese.example.edu ([192.168.16.212])
        by amber.example.edu with esmtps (TLSv1:DHE-RSA-AES256-SHA:256)
        (Exim 4.50)
        id 1IHzA6-0002GV-7g
        for dnb@example.edu; Mon, 06 Aug 2007 05:46:06 -0400
Date: Mon, 6 Aug 2007 05:46:06 -0400 (EDT)
From: My User <user@example.edu>
To: "David N. Blank-Edelman" <dnb@example.edu>
Subject: About mail server
Message-ID: <Pine.GSO.4.58.0708060544550.2793@chinese.example.edu>

Hi David,

Boy, that's a spiffy mail server you have there!

Best,

Your User
EOM

my $esimple = Email::Simple->new($message);
```

There are two methods on the `$esimple` object that you would typically call at this point: `header('`*field*`')` and `body()`. The `body()` method returns the body of the message, as you'd expect, but the `header()` method is a little more interesting. It returns either all of the headers with that field (if called in a list context), or the first one (if called in a scalar context):

```
my @received       = $esimple->header('Received');
my $first_received = $esimple->header('Received');
```

One difference between `Email::Simple` and some other mail-parsing modules is that `Email::Simple` returns only the data for the header, and not the entire line from the mail including that header. For example:

```
print scalar $esimple->header('Date')
```

prints:

```
Mon, 6 Aug 2007 05:46:06 -0400 (EDT)
```

not:

```
Date: Mon, 6 Aug 2007 05:46:06 -0400 (EDT)
```

If for some reason you need to know which header fields are present in a message, the `header_names()` method will return that information.

The other kind of mail message dissection one often does beyond just header/body processing is the extraction of certain contents from the body of the message. In the case of a MIME-encoded message, for example, we may want to extract an attachment from the contents of the mail and save it as a different file. Here's an example of using `Email::MIME` to that end:

```
use Email::MIME;
use File::Slurp qw(slurp write_file);

my $message = slurp('mime.txt');

my $parsed = Email::MIME->new($message);

foreach my $part ($parsed->parts) {
    if ($part->content_type =~ /^application\/pdf;/i){
        write_file ($part->filename, $part->body);
    }
}
```

This code uses `slurp()` to bring in the contents of a message stored in *mime.txt* and then parses it (this is done automatically by the `new()` method). We then iterate over each MIME part and decide whether it is a PDF file based on the MIME content type. If it is, we write that part of the message out to a file using the filename provided in the MIME header (or one autogenerated by `Email::MIME` if the sender didn't specify a name). It is important to note that this code is less than ideal in at least two ways. First, it looks only at the top-level MIME parts in the message when looking for the attachment. That approach won't work if the attachment is embedded in another part (e.g., when someone forwards the entire contents of a message, attachments included, as an attachment itself).[†] The second and much more serious problem with this code is that it trusts the filename as specified in the header. Real code would be much more paranoid (see the cautionary note in the following sidebar).

Don't Cut Corners When Parsing Mail

Here's a quick warning that should accompany all of the mail-parsing material that we've just covered. Parsing mail is tricky business for at least two reasons: the complexity of the data and "the bad guys." Your code needs to be robust and complete.

Here's a good example that demonstrates the first peril: many people write code that uses simple regular expressions to validate email addresses. Don't be one of them. The RFC 2822 syntax is sufficiently complex that I can almost guarantee that some day your code will break if you cut corners like this. It is far better to use a tool such as

---

[†] You might think that looking for embedded attachments using recursive `parts()` calls or the `subparts()` method would be a good exercise to leave to the reader, but I'll make it easier than that: there is a separate module called `Email::MIME::Attachment::Stripper`, also maintained by Ricardo Signes, that does this work for you.

the `Email::Valid` module, currently maintained by Ricardo Signes, or the `Mail::Message::Field::*` modules in the `Mail::Box` package. Look first to modules like `Regexp::Common` (e.g., the `net` module) for parsing IP addresses and so on. Packages like these can help you manage the complexity of the data. You can also use Perl's `-T` switch (taint mode) to look carefully at how data is being passed around in your script.

As for "the bad guys," they mostly appear when you're parsing mail received by spammers and other nogoodniks. As Bill Cole, someone who has worked in the anti-spam community for over a decade, said to me in an email he gave me permission to publish:

> Spammers toss all sorts of pathological garbage at filters, both as stupid accident and as conscious attack. Spam filtering is no place to assume that someone else has validated your input as meeting any sort of norm. You really need to protect yourself in any code that looks at email, because even if you are being shielded in principle by some other tool (e.g., `MIMEDefang`, *sendmail*, whatever) you have to assume that someday spam will start coming in that gets malicious content through that armor to your code.

Before we end this section, I'd like to give two examples of "deep" parsing of a message. For this kind of parsing, we're going to take apart the message body itself. To keep things simple for the example, I'm going to assume that the message body is plain text and is not encoded in any way, as in the previous MIME examples. You should be able to use the modules mentioned earlier to whittle down a message to this point if you need to deal with more complex message formats.

For the first example, we'll explore how to do keyword scanning efficiently. Let's say it's important to quarantine all messages that contain any words on a special "dirty words" list. The key to efficient scanning of a message text (especially when given a whole list of items) is to pass over the same text as few times as possible—ideally, only once. Sure, we could do this:

```perl
my @dirty_words = qw ( sod ground soil earth filth mud shmutz );

foreach my $word (@dirty_words){
    return 'dirty' if ($body =~ /$word/is);
}
```

But that would drag the regular expression engine over the whole message again and again, and it would force the regexp engine to reparse/recompile the regexp each time. There are a number of ways to get around this problem, but one of the most efficient is to combine the strings using regular expression alternation. We could jam all of the words together, with pipe characters (|) separating them:

```perl
my $wordalt = join('|',@dirty_words);
my $regex = qr/$wordalt/is;

return 'dirty' if ($message =~ $regex);
```

That's a bit better, but we can still go one step further. If you stare at your list of dirty words for a while, you'll probably notice that they have some things in common (lexicographically). Several of them will start with the same letters, which means we could start optimizing the regexp using shorthand like so(d|il). Perl 5.10+'s regular expression engine will do some of this optimization for us. If you really have a need for speed and/or if you're working with an earlier version of the Perl interpreter, you can use modules like Aaron Crane's Text::Match::FastAlternatives or David Landgren's Regexp::Assemble. The former is made exactly for the case we're describing here and is even faster than the 5.10+ optimized regular expression engine. Regexp::Assemble isn't as fast, but it has a number of additional features that may make it a good choice for more complicated tasks. Here's a quick example of Text::Match::FastAlternatives in action:

```
use Text::Match::FastAlternatives;
use Email::Simple;
use File::Slurp qw(slurp);

my $message = slurp('message.txt');
my $esimple = Email::Simple->new($message);

my @dirty_words = qw ( sod ground soil earth filth mud shmutz );

# this gets much more impressive when the size of the list is huge
my $matcher = Text::Match::FastAlternatives->new( @dirty_words );

print 'dirty' if $matcher->match( $esimple->body() );
```

There are two important restrictions that should be mentioned when talking about Text::Match::FastAlternatives. First, it only works with data consisting of printable ASCII characters (a problem if you are scanning email messages that use a different character set); second, and more importantly, it only performs case-sensitive matches. If we wanted to catch both "filth" and "Filth," we'd probably have to rewrite the last two lines of the code to look like this instead:

```
my $matcher = Text::Match::FastAlternatives->new( map { lc } @dirty_words );

print 'dirty' if $matcher->match( lc $esimple->body() );
```

Text::Match::FastAlternatives usually gives enough of a speed boost to your program that you probably won't mind having to downcase everything first.

So that's looking for keywords. What if you wanted to find more sophisticated content? Sometimes it is useful to extract URIs from a message. As mentioned in the sidebar "Don't Cut Corners When Parsing Mail" on page 293, Regexp::Common is one module that can make this task easier/safer:

```
use File::Slurp qw(slurp);
use Email::Simple;
use Regexp::Common qw /URI/;
```

```
my $esimple = Email::Simple->new( scalar slurp $ARGV[0] );
my $body = $esimple->body;

while ( $body =~ /$RE{URI}{HTTP}{-keep}/g ) {
  print "$1\n";
}
```

This code uses a regular expression from Regexp::Common to find all URIs in a message. The use of the -keep flag means we capture those URIs into $1. We'll discuss something more interesting to do with the URIs a little later in this chapter.

Dissecting a Whole Mailbox

Taking this subject to the next level, where we slice and dice entire mailboxes, is straightforward. If our mail is stored in the classical Unix mbox, maildir, or mh format, we can use Email::Folder from the Perl Email Project (also currently maintained by Ricardo Signes). Even many common non-Unix mail agents, like Eudora, store their mail in classical Unix mbox format, so this module can be useful on multiple platforms.

The drill is very similar to the examples we've seen before:

```
use Email::Folder;

my $folder = Email::Folder->('FilenameOrDirectory');
```

The new() constructor takes the filename (for mbox format storage) or the directory where mail is stored (for the maildir and mh formats) to parse. It returns a folder object instance, which represents a mail folder containing a number of messages.[‡] We can retrieve messages from that folder as Email::Simple objects. We can either retrieve all of the messages:

```
my @messages = $folder->messages;
```

or retrieve one message at a time:

```
foreach my $message ($folder->next_message){
    ... # do something with that message object
}
```

$message will contain an Email::Simple object instance. With this object instance, you can use all of the methods we just discussed. For example, if you need just the Subject header of the same message:

```
$subject = $message->header('Subject');
```

These methods can be chained, so the following code will get the Subject line for the next message in the mailbox:

```
$subject = $folder->next_message->header('Subject');
```

[‡] This folder representation does not depend on how the messages are actually stored, be they messages kept in a single file (for mbox format) or one file per message (for maildir/mh format).

`Email::Folder` by itself is very basic.[*] If you need to do anything beyond simply dicing a folder, you should consider using the `Mail::Box` package mentioned earlier.

Into the Fray Again

Of all the material that was updated in this second edition of the book, the sections on spam turned out to be some of the most challenging. The war between spammers and the anti-spam community escalated to such an extent in the interim that the approach and tools presented in the first edition seem ridiculously naïve to me now, even though the advice I gave was good at the time.

Once upon a time, you could help fight the good fight by first identifying the origin of a message and then complaining to the ISP that sent the mail. However, in the current age, which is populated with legions of zombie machines herded into massive botnets doing spammers' bidding, reporting one sending host just isn't going to make an appreciable dent. The advice to locate and report the host is so outdated, it would be like someone telling you to be sure to keep the pointy part of your pike upright as you entered a modern battlefield.

Truth be told, when I first started to rewrite this section I wasn't sure what Perl tools would be helpful, not just at the time I was writing it, but for the shelf life of this edition. It's very hard to predict how the battle between good and evil will rage in the coming years, especially given how far things have progressed since the publication of the last edition. To figure out what to present to you, dear reader, I wound up turning to a group of people who I knew had some of the greatest expertise and experience in the anti-spam realm. They were kind enough to offer a slew of suggestions, many of which I've incorporated into the section "Dealing with Spam" and the rest of the chapter. Hopefully this will provide you with some best-practices advice that will serve you well for some time to come.

Dealing with Spam

So far in this chapter we've looked at general tools for slicing and dicing mail messages and briefly touched on some of the applications that could benefit from a pile of finely chopped message parts. One (unfortunately increasingly large) application domain for these techniques is that surrounding the handling of unsolicited commercial email, or "spam" for short.

SpamAssassin

As the sidebar "Into the Fray Again" mentions, dealing with spam from any angle has become a tricky business. Thus, it behooves us to bring to bear on the problem as much firepower as possible. Ideally, we'd like to use software assembled from the collective

---

[*] There are additional `Email::Folder::` helper modules available that allow you to specify a folder on a POP3, IMAP(s), or Exchange server and parse it as if it were local. Still basic, sure, but cool nonetheless.

intelligence of lots of people working on the issue. The easiest way for us to do that is to do something unusual for this book and focus on how to program using just one Perl-based anti-spam tool: Apache SpamAssassin (*http://spamassassin.apache.org*). The SpamAssassin Perl API is provided by the `Mail::SpamAssassin` set of modules. The API has stayed stable for the last five years and is likely to continue to be useful for quite a few more years to come. Another reason to look at this module is that it provides quite a few handy utility functions for mail processing. The package provides easy ways to decode HTML and MIME structures, extract readable URLs, perform blacklist look-ups, and much more. This in itself makes it worth exploring.

Like most Perl modules that are indistinguishable from magic, `Mail::SpamAssassin` makes the hardest thing the easiest to do. Want to figure out whether a message is spam (according to SpamAssassin)? It's this easy, though there is more going on here than meets the eye:

```perl
use Mail::SpamAssassin;
use File::Slurp qw(slurp);

my $spama   = Mail::SpamAssassin->new();
my $message = $spama->parse(scalar slurp 'message.txt');
my $status  = $spama->check($message);

print (($status->is_spam()) ? 'spammy!' : "hammy!" . "\n");

$status->finish();
$message->finish();
```

This code requires three steps to answer the spam/not spam question: create the `Mail::SpamAssassin` object, use it to parse a mail message into an object it can use, and then call the check() method from that object. We could actually do this in two steps if we eliminated the parse step and called check_message_text() instead of check(). The check_message_text() method will work on a plain mail message, but if we eliminate the parsing step we don't get a cool message object that can be used later if we need to query or manipulate parts of the original message. Let's look at some of the things we can do with that message object.

The first thing we can do is extract RFC 2822-related parts of the message, such as the headers. For example, to get a list of all of the Received headers, we can write:

```perl
use Mail::SpamAssassin;
use File::Slurp qw(slurp);

my $spama   = Mail::SpamAssassin->new();
my $message = $spama->parse(scalar slurp 'message.txt');

my @received = $message->header('Received');
# or, to retrieve only the last one (as opposed to the first one,
# which most packages give you when called in a scalar context):
# my $received = $message->header('Received');

$message->finish();
```

`Mail::SpamAssassin` can also help us extract MIME parts found in the message. For example, to print all the HTML parts of a message, we could write code like this:

```
use Mail::SpamAssassin;
use File::Slurp qw(slurp);

my $sa       = Mail::SpamAssassin->new();
my $message  = $sa->parse( scalar slurp 'mime.txt' );
my @html_parts = $message->find_parts( qr(text/html), 1 );

foreach my $part (@html_parts) {
    print @{ $part->raw() };
}

$message->finish();
```

Let's talk for a second about the two highlighted lines, because we've already seen the others. The first line calls `find_parts()`. This method does a complete MIME parse of the message, walks the potentially complex structure of the message, and returns pointers (`Mail::SpamAssassin::Message::Node` objects, to be precise) to the parts that match the regular expression provided. The second parameter (`1`) tells the method to return only the individual parts found. Without that parameter, `find_parts()` will also return the containing parts should the desired type be found nested in some other part.

To see all of the parts of the message after a full parse has been completed (see the sidebar "Parse As Little As Possible"), we can call `content_summary()` on the object. This will return output that looks like this:

```
DB<1> x $message->content_summary();
0  'multipart/mixed'
1  'multipart/alternative,text/plain,text/html'
2  'application/pdf'
```

Parse As Little As Possible

One gotcha that you may encounter is that `Mail::SpamAssassin` doesn't do a complete MIME parse of a message until it has no choice but to take that extra step. This can be confusing if you expect the **parse()** method to return an object that reflects a complete parse. Not so! It only initially parses the headers of a message.

This will throw you the first time you try to use `content_summary()` and don't see all the parts you'd expect in a message. The easiest way to deal with this is to first do a `find_parts()`, perhaps something like this:

```
$message->find_parts(qr/./,1);
```

This unexpected behavior shows that this is a highly optimized spam-fighting tool, not just yet another general-purpose mail-parsing module. Ideally, you want messages to pass through `Mail::SpamAssassin` as quickly as possible so it can process high volumes of mail. To this end, the less work/parsing the module has to do initially per message, the better.

Once we've found the parts of a message that we need, we can print them in their raw form as we do in our sample code, decode them (e.g., from base64 encoding), render them as text (e.g., for HTML parts), and so on.

 Right about now you may be experiencing some feelings of déjà vu, because it seems like we've already seen how to handle most of these parsing tasks using other modules from the Perl Email Project. You're not imagining things; there is definitely some overlap between these two sets of mail-handling modules.

So how do you choose which mail-handling package to use? My inclination is to avoid mixing and matching modules from different packages. If you're doing only generic mail parsing and don't need anything that `Mail::SpamAssassin` provides, stick with the `Email::` modules. If you do need something anti-spam-related, you want to be paranoid about the input messages, and/or you want to use some of the convenience functions (like those we're about to see), go with `Mail::SpamAssassin`.

We've just looked at the functionality provided to us if we `parse()` a message to receive a `Mail::SpamAssassin::Message` object, but it turns out that there are a number of benefits to `check()`ing a message as well. These benefits go beyond just the ability to decide whether or not a message is spam.

Running `check()` on a message object or `check_message_text()` on a plain-text message returns a `Mail::SpamAssassin::PerMsgStatus` object. We called `$status->is_spam()` earlier in this chapter to check whether the object was classified as spam, but there are other methods that we could call as well. Here are some of the ones I find most handy:

`get_content_preview()`
Returns a small, text-only excerpt from the first few lines of a message.

`get_decoded_body_text_array()`, `get_decoded_stripped_body_text_array()`
Returns a message body with all encoded data (base64, etc.) decoded and all of the non-text parts (e.g., attachments) removed. The `..._stripped_...` method will also try to render HTML message parts into their text equivalents.

`get_uri_list()`, `get_uri_detail_list()`
Retrieves a list of the URIs mentioned in the message. The `..._detail_...` method provides a data structure with more details about the URIs.

`get()`
Very similar to the `header()` functionality we've seen, but with a couple of helpful twists.

Let's look at the URI-related methods in more detail.

There may be multiple reasons to extract all of the URIs found in a message. In the context of SpamAssassin, doing so offers another tool for spam detection. When sending spam related to products or services for sale over the Internet, spammers usually include URLs in the messages so people can go to the sites that sell their wares. If you extracted the URLs, you could then conceivably filter based on the URLs themselves. You could even look for the domains mentioned in those URLs and then, once you've identified a set of spammer's domains, look for messages that contain them and deal with them accordingly. The SURBL blacklists (*http://www.surbl.org*) are predicated on this idea (they list the domains extracted from known spam messages) and tend to be very effective. This is the use for URIs foreshadowed at the end of "Dissecting a Single Message" on page 291.

The `get_uri_detail_list()` method returns a data structure like this (from the documentation):

```
raw_uri => {
    types => { a => 1, img => 1, parsed => 1 },
    cleaned => [ canonified_uri ],
    anchor_text => [ "click here", "no click here" ],
    domains => { domain1 => 1, domain2 => 1 },
  }
```

The hash of a hash data structure requires us to do a little work to get the list of unique domains mentioned in the URIs, but it's not that hard:

```perl
use Mail::SpamAssassin;
use File::Slurp qw(slurp);
use List::MoreUtils qw(uniq);

my $sa      = Mail::SpamAssassin->new();
my $status  = $sa->check_message_text( scalar slurp 'spam.txt' );
my $uris    = $status->get_uri_detail_list();

my @domains;

foreach my $uri ( keys %{$uris} ) {
    next if $uri =~ /^mailto:/;
    push( @domains, keys %{ $uris->{$uri}->{domains} } );
}

print join( "\n", uniq @domains );
```

Once you have a set of unique domains, you can look them up in a blacklist like those available at surbl.org (*http://www.surbl.org*). Each blacklisted domain is recorded as a DNS "A" resource record (hostname) entry under the *surbl.org* domain. This provides an easy way to check whether a domain has been blacklisted: simply prepend the domain name in question to *multi.surbl.org* (e.g., *makemoneyfast.com.multi.surbl.org*) and performing a DNS lookup for the resulting hostname. This can be done using `Net::DNS`, as demonstrated in Chapter 5. If the hostname resolves, you can take action accordingly, because that domain is in the blacklist.

To finish this section, let's briefly look at the `get()` method. To use `get()`, we first run `check()` on the message object or `check_message_text()` on the message. These methods each return a status object from which a `get()` method call can be made. The `get()` method extracts headers just as `Email::Simple`'s `header()` method does, but the additional parsing done by a `check()` gives it a few extra superpowers. For example, `header('From')` will return the `From` header from a message, but `get('From:addr')` takes an extra step and returns just the address part of that header. Likewise, `get('From:name')` will return just the "name" part of the header. For instance, if the header contains:

```
David Blank-Edelman <dnb@example.edu>
```

we can use the `:addr` form to return "dnb@example.edu" and the `:name` form to return "David Blank-Edelman". The `get()` method also provides a set of pseudo-headers that can be queried. These are typically aggregates of other headers. For example, if you want to retrieve all of the stated recipients of a message (`Bccs` aside), using `ToCc` as the header name will get that list for you.

SpamAssassin allows you to configure "trusted" and "untrusted" hosts at install time. This helps it distinguish between hosts that are locally controlled and those in the big, bad, scary Internet for the purpose of determining how likely they are to contribute to the "spaminess" of a message. There are several `get()` pseudo-headers that return information based on this distinction, but I think the most interesting ones are `X-Spam-Relays-Untrusted` and `X-Spam-Relays-Trusted`. Here's an example set of received headers from a real piece of spam:

```
Received: from smtp.abac.com (smtp.abac.com [208.137.248.30])
        by amber.example.edu (8.8.6/8.8.6) with ESMTP id FAA29389
        for <user@ccs.example.edu>; Tue, 2 Dec 1997 05:51:56 -0500 (EST)
Received: from smtp.abac.com (la-ppp-109.abac.com [209.60.248.109])
        by smtp.abac.com (8.8.7/8.8.7) with SMTP id CAA01384;
        Tue, 2 Dec 1997 02:53:33 -0800 (PST)
Received: from mailhost.nowhere.com (alt1.nowhere.com (208.137.887.15))
  by nowhere.com (8.8.5/8.6.5) with SMTP id GAA00064 for <>;
  Tue, 02 Dec 1997 01:49:32 -0600 (EST)
```

Asking for `X-Spam-Relays-Untrusted` gives us (slightly reformatted):

```
[ ip=208.137.248.30 rdns=smtp.abac.com helo=smtp.
abac.com by=amber.example.edu ident= envfrom= intl=0 id=FAA29389 auth= msa=0 ]

[ ip=209.60.248.109 rdns=la-ppp-109.abac.com helo=smtp.abac.com
by=smtp.abac.com ident= envfrom= intl=0 id=CAA01384 auth= msa=0 ]
```

SpamAssassin has parsed the headers into a form that makes it easy to see the inconsistencies (to put it charitably) between the information the sender presented to us and the actual origins of the message. This is most clear in the last line of the output, corresponding to the second `Received` header in the input, where the sender claimed to be from *smtp.abac.com* but instead was actually coming from (presumably) a dial-up line at *la-ppp-109.abac.com*.

Feedback loops

There's another side to the spam discussion that often gets forgotten. We've just looked at how you deal with messages you've received to determine if they are spam. But what if you're on the other side of the fence and want to avoid being labeled a spammer due to the mail you send?

Legitimate bulk email senders and people who run email systems, especially the large ones, actually have some goals in common. Both want people to receive the mail they have opted to receive, and neither wants to be part of a process that leaves the users feeling like they've received spam. The bulk emailer doesn't want to send something the user does not want to receive, and the email system administrator doesn't want to anger the users by continuing to deliver mail they don't desire.

This common ground gives the two parties a reason to collaborate. One thing they can do is share information about which messages are considered to be spam, either because the service provider uses software that has tagged it as such, or because the recipient has actually pressed a mark this as spam button in her mail client. In either case, the sender will generally want to know that this has taken place so that the recipient's address can be removed from its database, and so on. That's where feedback loops come into play.

Some of the large email providers let bulk-email-sending companies subscribe to a feedback loop. This loop sends information back to the sender about the messages the email provider has received (from the bulk-email company) that were labeled as spam. The best collection of available feedback loops I know about at the time of this writing can be found in the Spamhaus FAQ mentioned in the references section at the end of this chapter.

You may be wondering what role Perl can play in all of this. A number of the big players in the arena got together and hashed out a standardized format for the reports that are sent as part of a feedback loop. This format is called the Abuse Reporting Format (ARF) and is documented in the draft specification also pointed to in the references section. It's a MIME-based format that automated systems can use to send and receive this sort of spam report. The availability of this common format makes it easier to write Perl scripts that can parse incoming reports and act on them.

You may be saying "MIME? Great!† We went over MIME parsing before, I know how to do that!" And if you said this, you wouldn't be wrong. However, there are two specialized Perl packages that make handling ARF reports a little easier than rolling your own code based on the standard Perl MIME parsers. I'll show you an example of parsing an ARF message using `Email::ARF::Report`, from the Perl Email Project. If you plan to send ARF messages, you may also want to look at `MIME::ARF`, by Steve Atkins (found at *http://wordtothewise.com/resources/mimearf.html*).

---

† Or, if you're as ambivalent about MIME as I am, you may choose a word that begins with a letter a little earlier in the alphabet.

Just so we know what we're dealing with, Table 8-1 shows the three mandatory parts of an ARF message. The example text comes from the ARF spec.

Table 8-1. ARF message structure

Part	Contents	Example
1	Human-readable information	This is an email abuse report for an email message received from IP 10.67.41.167 on Thu, 8 Mar 2005 14:00:00 EDT. For more information about this format please see http://www.mipassoc.org/arf/.
2	Machine-readable metadata	Feedback-Type: abuse User-Agent: SomeGenerator/1.0 Version: 0.1
3	Full copy of message or message headers	From: <somespammer@example.net> Received: from mailserver.example.net (mailserver.example.net [10.67.41.167]) by example.com with ESMTP id M63d4137594e46; Thu, 08 Mar 2005 14:00:00 -0400 To: <Undisclosed Recipients> Subject: Earn money MIME-Version: 1.0 Content-type: text/plain Message-ID: 8787KJKJ3K4J3K4J3K4J3.mail@example.net Date: Thu, 02 Sep 2004 12:31:03 -0500 Spam Spam Spam Spam Spam Spam Spam Spam Spam

Please refer to the ARF spec to see these parts in the context of a full email message. Taking apart a message like this is pretty easy with `Email::ARF::Report`. Here's example code that prints some information from the original message copied into an ARF report:

```
use Email::ARF::Report;
use File::Slurp qw(slurp);

my $message = slurp('arfsample1.txt');

my $report = Email::ARF::Report->new($message);

foreach my $header (qw(to date subject message-id)) {
    print ucfirst $header . ': '
        . $report->original_email->header($header) . "\n";
}
```

If this looks remarkably like the `Email::Simple` code we looked at earlier, that's no coincidence. `Email::ARF::Report` parses an ARF message and provides methods to retrieve parts of that report. In this case we're using the method `original_email()` to access the original message. `original_email()` is kind enough to return an `Email::Simple` object, so we can put to use all of our previous knowledge and call the `header()` method on that object as desired. Once we've extracted the information we need from the report, we can do whatever we like with that info (unsubscribe the user, etc.).

But spam is such an unpleasant subject. Let's move on to a cheerier topic, such as interacting with users via email.

Support Mail Augmentation

Even if you don't have a "help desk" at your site, you probably have some sort of support email address for user questions and problems. Email as a medium for support communications has certain advantages:

- It can be stored and tracked, unlike hallway conversations.
- It is asynchronous; the system administrator can read and answer mail during the more rational nighttime hours.
- It can be a unicast, multicast, or broadcast medium. If 14 people write in, it's possible to respond to all of them simultaneously when the problem is resolved.
- It can easily be forwarded to someone else who might know the answer or have authority over that service domain.

These are all strong reasons to make email an integral part of any support relationship. However, email does have certain disadvantages:

- If there is a problem with your email system itself, or if the user is having email-related problems, another medium must be used.
- Users can and will type anything they want into an email message. There's no guarantee that this message will contain the information you need to fix the problem or assist the user. You may not gain even a superficial understanding of the purpose of the email. This leads us to the conundrum we'll attempt to address in this section.

My favorite support email of all time is reproduced in its entirety here, with only the name of the sender changed to protect the guilty:

```
Date: Sat, 28 Sep 1996 12:27:35 -0400 (EDT)
From: Special User <user@example.com>
To: systems@example.com
Subject: [Req. #9531] printer help

something is wrong and I have know idea what
```

If the user hadn't mentioned "printer" in the subject of the mail, we would have had no clue where to begin and would probably have chalked the situation up to existential angst. Granted, this was perhaps an extreme example. More often, you'll receive mail like this:

```
From: Another user <user2@example.com>
Subject: [Req #14563] broken macine
To: systems@example.com
Date: Wed, 11 Mar 1998 10:59:42 -0500 (EST)

There is something wrong with the following machine:

      krakatoa.example.com
```

A user does not send mail devoid of contextual content like this out of malice. I believe the root cause of these problems is an impedance mismatch between the user's and the system administrator's mental model of the computing environment.

For most users, the visible structure of the computing environment is limited to the client machine they are logged into, the nearby printer, and their storage (i.e., home directory). For a system administrator, the structure of the computing environment is considerably different. It consists of a set of servers providing services to clients, all of which may have a multitude of different peripheral devices. Each machine may have a different set of software installed and a different state (system load, configuration, etc.).

To users, the question "Which machine is having a problem?" may seem strange. They're talking about *the* computer, the one they're using *now*. Isn't that obvious? To a system administrator, a request for "help with *the* printer" is equally odd; after all, there are likely many printers in his charge.

So too it goes with the specifics of a problem. System administrators around the world grit their teeth every day when they receive mail that says, "My machine isn't working, can you help me?" They know "not working" could indicate a whole panoply of symptoms, each with its own array of causes. To a user that has experienced three screen freezes in the last week, however, "not working" is unambiguous.

One way to address this disconnect is to constrain the material sent in email. Some sites force the users to send in trouble reports using a custom support application or web form. The problem with this approach is that very few users enjoy engaging in a click-and-scroll fest just to report a problem or ask a question. The more pain is involved in the process, the less likely it is that someone will go to the trouble of using these mechanisms. It doesn't matter how carefully constructed or beautifully designed your web form is if no one is willing to use it. Hallway requests will become the norm again. Back to square one?

Well, with the help of Perl, maybe not. Perl can help us augment normal mail receiving to assist us in the support process. One of the first steps in this process for a system administrator is the identification of locus: "Where is the problem? Which printer? Which machine?" And so on.

Let's take a look at a program I call *suss*, which demonstrates the augmentation I have in mind in a simple fashion. It looks at an email message and attempts to guess the name of the machine associated with that message. The upshot of this is that we can often determine the hostname for the "My machine has a problem" category of email without having to engage in a second round of email with the vague user. That hostname is typically a good starting point in the troubleshooting process.

suss uses an extremely simple algorithm to guess the name of the machine in question (basically just a hash lookup for every word in the message). First it examines the message subject, then the body of the message, and finally it looks at the initial `Received` header on the message. Here's a simplified version of the code that expects to be able to read an */etc/hosts* file to determine the names of our hosts:[‡]

```perl
use Email::Simple;
use List::MoreUtils qw(uniq);
use File::Slurp qw(slurp);
my $localdomain = ".example.edu";

# read in our host file
open my $HOSTS, '<', '/ccs/etc/hosts' or die "Can't open hosts file\n";
my $machine;
my %machines;
while ( defined( $_ = <$HOSTS> ) ) {
    next if /^#/;           # skip comments
    next if /^$/;           # skip blank lines
    next if /monitor/i;     # an example of a misleading host

    $machine = lc( (split)[1] );    # extract the first host name & downcase
    $machine =~ s/\Q$localdomain\E//oi;   # remove our domain name
    $machines{$machine}++ unless $machines{$machine};
}
close $HOSTS;

# parse the message
my $message = new Email::Simple( scalar slurp( $ARGV[0] ) );

my @found;

# check in the subject line
if ( @found = check_part( $message->header('Subject'), \%machines ) ) {
    print 'subject: ' . join( ' ', @found ) . "\n";
    exit;
}

# check in the body of the message
if ( @found = check_part( $message->body, \%machines ) ) {
    print 'body: ' . join( ' ', @found ) . "\n";
    exit;
}

# last resort: check the last Received line
my $received = ( reverse $message->header('Received') )[0];
$received =~ s/\Q$localdomain\E//g;
if ( @found = check_part( $received, \%machines ) ) {
    print 'received: ' . join( ' ', @found ) . "\n";
```

[‡] In real life you would probably want to use something considerably more sophisticated to get a host list, like a cached copy of a DNS zone transfer or perhaps a walk of an LDAP tree.

```
    }

    # find all unique matches from host lookup table in given part of message
    sub check_part {
        my $part     = shift;     # the text from that message part
        my $machines = shift;     # a reference to the machine lookup table

        $part =~ s/[^\w\s]//g;
        $part =~ s/\n/ /g;

        return uniq grep { exists $machines->{$_} } split( ' ', lc $part );
    }
```

One comment on this code: the simplicity of our word check becomes painfully apparent when we encounter perfectly reasonable hostnames like *monitor* in sentences like "My monitor is broken." If you have hostnames that are likely to appear in support messages, you'll either have to special-case them, as we do with `next if /monitor/i;`, or preferably create a more complicated parsing scheme.

Let's take this code out for a spin. Here are two real support messages:

```
Received: from strontium.example.com (strontium.example.com [192.168.1.114])
        by mailhub.example.com (8.8.4/8.7.3) with ESMTP id RAA27043
        for <systems>; Thu, 29 Mar 2007 17:07:44 -0500 (EST)
From: User Person <user@example.com>
Received: (user@localhost)
        by strontium.example.com (8.8.4/8.6.4) id RAA10500
        for systems; Thu, 29 Mar 2007 17:07:41 -0500 (EST)
Message-Id: <199703272207.RAA10500@strontium.example.com>
Subject: [Req #11509] Monitor
To: systems@example.com
Date: Thu, 29 Mar 2007 17:07:40 -0500 (EST)

Hi,
My monitor is flickering a little bit and it is tiresome
whe working with it to much.
Is it possible to fix it or changing the monitor?

Thanks.

User.
-------------------------------------
Received: from example.com (user2@example.com [192.168.1.7])
        by mailhost.example.com (8.8.4/8.7.3) with SMTP id SAA00732
        for <systems@example.com>; Thu, 29 Mar 2007 18:34:54 -0500 (EST)
Date: Thu, 29 Mar 2007 18:34:54 -0500 (EST)
From: Another User <user2@example.com>
To: systems@example.com
Subject: [Req #11510] problems with two computers
Message-Id: <Pine.SUN.3.95.970327183117.23440A-100000@example.com>

In Jenolen (in room 292), there is a piece of a disk stuck in it. In intrepid,
there is a disk with no cover (or whatever you call that silver thing) stuck in
it. We tried to turn off intrepid, but it wouldn't work. We (the proctor on duty
and I) tried to get the disk piece out, but it didn't work. The proctor in charge
```

```
decided to put signs on them saying 'out of order'

AnotherUser
```

Aiming our code at these two messages yields:

```
received: strontium
```

and:

```
body: jenolen intrepid
```

Both hostname guesses were right on the money, and that's with just a little bit of simple code. To take things one step further, let's assume we got this email from a user who doesn't realize we're responsible for a herd of 30 printers:

```
Received: from [192.168.1.118] (buggypeak.example.com [192.168.1.118])
        by mailhost.example.com (8.8.6/8.8.6) with SMTP id JAA16638
        for <systems>; Tue, 7 Aug 2007 09:07:15 -0400 (EDT)
Message-Id: <v02130502b1ecb78576a9@[192.168.1.118]>
Date: Tue, 7 Aug 2007 09:07:16 -0400
To: systems@example.com
From: user@example.com (Nice User)
Subject: [Req #15746] printer

Could someone please persuade my printer to behave and print like a nice printer
should?  Thanks much :)

-Nice User.
```

Fortunately, we can use Perl and a basic observation to help us make an educated guess about which printer is causing the problem. Users tend to print to printers that are geographically close to the machines they are using at the time. If we can determine which machine the user sent the mail from, we can probably figure out which printer she's using. There are many ways to retrieve a machine-to-printer mapping (e.g., from a separate file, from a field in the host database we mentioned in Chapter 5, or even a directory service from LDAP). Here's some code that uses a simple hostname-to-associated printer database:

```
use Email::Simple;
use File::Slurp qw(slurp);
use DB_File;

my $localdomain = '.example.com';
my $printdb     = 'printdb';

# parse the message
my $message = new Email::Simple( scalar slurp $ARGV[0] );

# check in the subject line
my $subject = $message->header('Subject');

if ( $subject =~ /print(er)?/i ) {
```

```
# find sending machine
my $received = ( reverse $message->header('Received') )[0];
my ($host) = $received =~ /\((\S+)\Q$localdomain\E \[/;

tie my %printdb, 'DB_File', $printdb
    or die "Can't tie $printdb database:$!\n";

print "Problem on $host may be with printer " . $printdb{$host} . ".\n";

untie %printdb;

}
```

If the message mentions "print," "printer," or "printing" in its subject line, we pull out the hostname from the `Received` header. We know the format our mail hub uses for `Received` headers, so we can construct a regular expression to extract this information. (If this does not match your MTA's format, you may have to fiddle with the regexp a little bit.) With the hostname in hand, we can look up the associated printer in a Berkeley DB database. The end result:

```
Problem on buggypeak may be with the printer called prints-charming.
```

If you take a moment to examine the fabric of your environment, you will see other ways to augment the receiving of your support email. The examples in this section were small and designed to get you thinking about the possibilities.

The *suss* program, with rules specific to your environment, could become a frontend to almost any kind of ticketing system. Combining it with the earlier concepts of using Perl to retrieve and parse mail would allow you to build a system that lets users send mail to a "catachall" address, such as "helpdesk@example.com," where it's automatically parsed. If there's good confidence about the determination of the subject of the question (the `Mail::SpamAssassin` rules provide an example of that kind of scoring), the mail could automatically be forwarded to the person designated for handling that type of problem.

Perl gives you many ways to analyze your email, place it in a larger context, and then act upon that information. I'll leave it to you to consider other kinds of help programs that read mail (perhaps mail sent by other programs) could provide you.

Module Information for This Chapter

Module	CPAN ID	Version
Mac::Carbon	CNANDOR	0.77
Win32::OLE (ships with ActiveState Perl)	JDB	0.1709
Mail::Outlook (found in *MailTools*)	BARBIE	0.13
Email::Send	RJBS	2.192

Module	CPAN ID	Version
Email::Simple	RJBS	2.003
Email::Simple::Creator	RJBS	1.424
Email::MIME	RJBS	1.861
Email::MIME::Creator	RJBS	1.454
File::Slurp	DROLSKY	9999.13
Email::MIME::CreateHTML	BBC	1.026
Text::Wrap (found in *Text-Tabs+Wrap* and also ships with Perl)	MUIR	2006.1117
File::Spec (found in *PathTools* and also ships with Perl)	KWILLIAMS	3.2701
IO::Socket (found in IO and also ships with Perl)	GBARR	1.30
Carp (ships with Perl)		1.08
Mail::POP3Client	SDOWD	2.18
Mail::IMAPClient	MARKOV	3.08
Mail::IMAPTalk	ROBM	1.03
IO::Socket::SSL	SULLR	1.13
Mail::Box	MARKOV	2.082
Text::Match::FastAlternatives	ARC	1.00
Regexp::Common	ABIGAIL	2.122
Email::Folder	RJBS	0.854
Mail::SpamAssassin	JMASON	3.24
List::MoreUtils	VPARSEVAL	0.22
Email::ARF::Report	RJBS	3.01
DB_File (ships with Perl)	PMQS	1.817

References for More Information

The POP3 and IMAPv4 sections of this chapter are revised and modified from a column I originally wrote for the February 2008 issue of the USENIX Association's ;login magazine (*http://usenix.org/publications/login/*).

Network Programming with Perl, by Lincoln Stein (Addison-Wesley), is one of the best books on programming network servers in Perl.

Perl Cookbook (http://oreilly.com/catalog/9780596003135/), by Tom Christiansen and Nathan Torkington (O'Reilly), also addresses the programming of network servers.

http://www.cauce.org is the website of the Coalition Against Unsolicited Commercial Email. There are many sites devoted to fighting spam; this site is a good place to start. It has pointers to many other sites, including those that go into greater detail about the analysis of mail headers for this process.

http://emailproject.perl.org is the home page for the Perl Email Project.

http://www.spamhaus.org/faq/ has a number of good anti-spam-related FAQ lists, including one on ISP spam issues that addresses feedback loops and other ways ISPs can address spam issues for and with their customers.

http://wordtothewise.com/resources/arf.html and *http://mipassoc.org/arf/index.html* are two good resources for information on the ARF standard. The latest draft of the standard itself (as of this writing) can be found at *http://www.ietf.org/internet-drafts/draft -shafranovich-feedback-report-07.txt*. (See *http://www.ietf.org/internet-drafts/* for the latest draft.)

If you'd like to experiment with high-volume mail handling from a server perspective (especially in the anti-spam context), there are two very interesting pieces of software you may want to investigate: *qpsmtpd (http://smtpd.develooper.com)* and Traffic Control (*http://www.mailchannels.com*). The first is an open source package, and the second is a commercial package free for use under some conditions. Both are SMTP handlers/ daemons written in Perl that are meant to sit in front of a standard MTA and proxy only good mail to it. What makes these two interesting for this chapter in particular is their plug-in functionality. A user can write plug-ins in Perl to change or direct how messages that pass through these packages are processed. Often these plug-ins attempt to do some sort of spam/ham determination, but really, the sky is the limit.

You may also want to take a look at these RFCs:

- *RFC 1939: Post Office Protocol - Version 3*, by J. Myers and M. Rose (1996)
- *RFC 2045: Multipurpose Internet Mail Extensions (MIME) Part One: Format of Internet Message Bodies*, by N. Freed and N. Borenstein (1996)
- *RFC 2046: Multipurpose Internet Mail Extensions (MIME) Part Two: Media Types*, by N. Freed and N. Borenstein (1996)
- *RFC 2047: MIME (Multipurpose Internet Mail Extensions) Part Three: Message Header Extensions for Non-ASCII Text*, by K. Moore (1996)
- *RFC 2077: The Model Primary Content Type for Multipurpose Internet Mail Extensions*, S. Nelson and C. Parks (1997)
- *RFC 2821: Simple Mail Transfer Protocol*, by J. Klensin (2001)
- *RFC 2822: Internet Message Format*, by P. Resnick (2001)
- *RFC 3501: INTERNET MESSAGE ACCESS PROTOCOL - VERSION 4rev1*, by M. Crispin (2003)
- *RFC 3834: Recommendations for Automatic Responses to Electronic Mail*, by K. Harrenstien and K. Moore (2004)
- *RFC 4288: Media Type Specifications and Registration Procedures*, by N. Freed and J. Klensin (2005)
- *RFC 4289: Multipurpose Internet Mail Extensions (MIME) Part Four: Registration Procedures*, N. Freed and J. Klensin (2005)

## CHAPTER 9

Directory Services

The larger an information system gets, the harder it becomes to find anything in that system, or even to know what's available. As networks grow and become more complex, they are well served by some sort of directory. Network users might make use of a directory service to find other users for email and messaging services. A directory service might advertise resources on a network, such as printers and network-available disk areas. Public-key and certificate infrastructures could use a directory service to distribute information. In this chapter we'll look at how to use Perl to interact with some of the more popular directory services, including Finger, WHOIS, LDAP, and Active Directory (via Active Directory Service Interfaces).

What's a Directory?

In Chapter 7, I suggested that all the system administration world is a database. Directories are a good example of this characterization. For the purpose of our discussion, we'll distinguish between "databases" and "directories" by observing a few salient characteristics of directories:

Networked
> Directories are almost always networked. Unlike a database, which may live on the same machine as its clients (e.g., the venerable */etc/passwd* file), directory services are usually provided over a network.

Simple communication/data manipulation
> Databases often have complex query languages for data queries and manipulation. We looked at the most common of these, SQL, in Chapter 7 (and in Appendix D). Communicating with a directory is a much simpler affair. A directory client typically performs only rudimentary operations and does not use a full-fledged language as part of its communication with the server. As a result, any queries made are often much simpler.

Hierarchical
> Modern directory services encourage the building of tree-like information structures, whereas databases on the whole do not.

Read-many, write-few
> Modern directory servers are optimized for a very specific data traffic pattern. Under normal use, the number of reads/queries to a directory service far outweighs the number of writes/updates.

If you encounter something that looks like a database (and is probably backended by a database) but has the preceding characteristics, you're probably dealing with a directory. In the four directory services we're about to discuss, these characteristics will be easy to spot.

Finger: A Simple Directory Service

Finger and WHOIS are good examples of simple directory services. Finger exists primarily to provide read-only information about a machine's users (although we'll see some more creative uses shortly). Later versions of Finger, like the GNU Finger server and its derivatives, expanded upon this basic functionality by allowing you to query one machine and receive back information from all the machines on your network.

Churn Your Own Butter, Too?

I think you'd be hard-pressed to find a site running Finger these days (the World Wide Web and privacy concerns drove it to near extinction)—so why is it still in the book?

I'm including a very short discussion of Finger here for one reason: it is an excellent training-wheels protocol. The protocol itself is simple, which makes it ideal for learning to deal with text-based network services that don't have their own custom client modules. You'll be happy you paid attention to this little slice of history the first time you need to interact with a service like that.

Finger was one of the first widely deployed directory services. Once upon a time, if you wanted to locate a user's email address at another site, or even within your own, the `finger` command was the best option. `finger harry@hogwarts.edu` would tell you whether Harry's email address was `harry`, `hpotter`, or something more obscure (along with listing all of the other Harrys at that school). Finger's popularity has waned over time as web home pages have become prevalent and the practice of freely giving out user information has become problematic.

Using the Finger protocol from Perl provides another good example of TMTOWTDI. In 2000, when I first looked on CPAN for a module to perform Finger operations, there were none available. If you look now, you'll find Dennis Taylor's `Net::Finger` module, which he published six months or so after my initial search. We'll see how to use it in a moment, but in the meantime, let's pretend it doesn't exist and take advantage of this opportunity to learn how to use a more generic module to talk to a specific protocol when the "perfect" module doesn't exist.

The Finger protocol itself is a very simple TCP/IP-based text protocol. Defined in RFC 1288, it calls for a standard TCP connection to port 79. The client passes a simple CRLF-terminated[*] string over the connection. This string either requests specific user information or, if empty, asks for information about all the machine's users. The server responds with the requested data and closes the connection at the end of the data stream. You can see this in action by *telnet*ing to the Finger port directly on a remote machine:[†]

```
$ telnet quake.geo.berkeley.edu 79
Trying 136.177.20.1...
Connected to gldfs.cr.usgs.gov.
Escape character is '^]'.
/W quake<CR><LF>
                RAPID EARTHQUAKE LOCATION SERVICE
          U.S. Geological Survey, Menlo Park, California.
     U.C. Berkeley Seismological Laboratory, Berkeley, California.
        (members of the Council of the National Seismic System)
...
DATE-(UTC)-TIME  LAT    LON     DEP   MAG  Q  COMMENTS
yy/mm/dd hh:mm:ss deg.   deg.   km
-------------------------------------------------------------------
09/01/12 16:29:37 36.03N 120.59W   4.5  2.3Md A*  20 km NW  of  Parkfield, CA
09/01/13 08:17:38 38.81N 122.82W   2.4  2.1Md A*   2 km NNW of  The Geysers, CA
09/01/13 11:51:09 40.66N 124.04W  23.6  2.5Md B*  12 km NE  of  Fortuna, CA
09/01/13 18:27:01 36.80N 121.51W   5.5  2.4Md A*   5 km SSE of  San Juan Bautista, CA
09/01/14 00:29:11 39.37N 123.27W   3.1  2.2Md B*   8 km ESE of  Willits, CA
09/01/14 01:48:23 38.24N 118.69W  12.0  2.3Md C*  17 km WSW of  Qualeys Camp, NV
09/01/14 02:06:57 38.24N 118.69W   6.0  2.2Md C*  17 km WSW of  Qualeys Camp, NV
09/01/14 03:44:02 38.82N 122.83W   2.1  2.1Md A*   3 km NW  of  The Geysers, CA
09/01/14 05:08:21 36.74N 121.34W   9.1  3.4Ml A*   6 km SSW of  Tres Pinos, CA
09/01/14 07:46:02 39.04N 123.34W   0.1  2.2Md C*  17 km SW  of  Ukiah, CA
09/01/14 10:24:53 40.42N 125.07W   1.2  3.1Ml C*  67 km W   of  Petrolia, CA
09/01/14 17:32:54 38.84N 122.83W   1.9  2.2Md A*   5 km NNW of  The Geysers, CA
09/01/14 17:57:34 36.56N 121.16W   6.7  2.4Md A*   4 km NNW of  Pinnacles, CA

...
$
```

In this example we've connected directly to *quake.geo.berkeley.edu*'s Finger port. We typed the username "quake" (with a /W to ask for verbose information), and the server returned information about that user.

I chose this particular host and user just to show you some of the variety of information that used to be available via Finger servers back in the early days of the Internet. Finger servers got pressed into service for all sorts of tasks. You used to be able to send Finger requests to soda machines, hot tubs, and sensor machines of all sorts. The Finger

---

[*] Carriage return + linefeed; i.e., ASCII 13 + ASCII 10.

[†] There used to be a whole battalion of earthquake information Finger servers. This is the only one of the 16 I tried that was still working as of this writing. If you don't get a response from this server, you'll have to trust me that it did return this data once upon a time.

example just shown, for instance, allows anyone anywhere on the planet to see information on earthquakes recorded by seismic sensors.

Unfortunately, making interesting information like this available via Finger seems to be a dying art. At the time of this writing, none of the Finger hosts listed in Bennet Yee's "Internet Accessible Coke Machines" and "Internet Accessible Machines" pages (*http://www.bennetyee.org/ucsd-pages/fun.html*) were operational. HTTP has almost entirely supplanted the Finger protocol for these sorts of tasks. There may still be Finger servers available on the Internet, but they are mostly set up for internal use.

Even though Finger servers are less prevalent today than they used to be, the simplicity of the protocol itself makes it a good place to start if you are looking to learn how to roll your own simple network service clients. Let's take the network communication we just performed using a *telnet* binary back to the world of Perl. With Perl, we can also open up a network socket and communicate over it. Instead of using lower-level socket commands, we'll use Jay Rogers's Net::Telnet module.‡

Net::Telnet will handle all of the connection setup work for us and provide a clean interface for sending and receiving data over this connection. Though we won't use them in this example, Net::Telnet also provides some handy pattern-scanning mechanisms that allow programs to watch for specific responses from the other server.

Here's a Net::Telnet version of a simple Finger client. This code takes an argument of the form *user@finger_server*. If the username is omitted, the server will return a list of all users it considers active. If the hostname is omitted, we query the local host:

```
use Net::Telnet;

my($username,$host) = split(/\@/,$ARGV[0]);
$host = $host ? $host : 'localhost';

# create a new connection
my $cn = new Net::Telnet(Host => $host,
                         Port => 'finger');

# send the username down this connection
# /W for verbose information as per RFC 1288
unless ($cn->print("/W $username")){
    $cn->close;
    die 'Unable to send finger string: '.$cn->errmg."\n";
}

# grab all of the data we receive, stopping when the
# connection is dropped
my ($ret,$data);
while (defined ($ret = $cn->get)) {
    $data .= $ret;
}
```

---

‡ If Net::Telnet didn't fit the bill so nicely, another alternative would be Expect.pm (written by Austin Schutz and now maintained by Roland Giersig), driving *telnet* or another network client.

```
# close the connection
$cn->close;

# display the data we collected
print $data;
```

You may have noticed the /W in the string we passed to `print()`: RFC 1288 specifies that a /W switch can be prepended to the username sent to the server to request it to provide "a higher level of verbosity in the user information output."

If you needed to connect to another TCP-based text protocol besides Finger, you'd use very similar code. For example, the following code connects to a daytime server (which shows the local time on a machine):

```
use Net::Telnet;

my $host = $ARGV[0] ? $ARGV[0] : 'localhost';

my $cn = new Net::Telnet(Host => $host,
                         Port => 'daytime'); port 13

my ($ret,$data);
while (defined ($ret = $cn->get)) {
    $data .= $ret;
}
$cn->close;

print $data;
```

Now you have a sense of how easy it is to create generic TCP-based network clients. If someone has taken the time to write a module specifically designed to handle a protocol, it can be even easier. In the case of Finger, you can use Taylor's `Net::Finger` to turn the whole task into a single function call:

```
use Net::Finger;

# finger() takes a user@host string and returns the data received
print finger($ARGV[0]);
```

Just to present all of the options, there's also the fallback position of calling another executable (if it exists on the machine), like so:

```
my($username,$host) = split('@',$ARGV[0]);
$host = $host ? $host : 'localhost';

# location of finger executable
my $fingerex = ($^O eq 'MSWin32') ?
               $ENV{'SYSTEMROOT'}.'\\System32\\finger' :
                '/usr/bin/finger';  # (could also be /usr/ucb/finger)

print `$fingerex ${username}\@${host}`
```

Now you've seen three different methods for performing Finger requests. The third method is probably the least ideal because it requires spawning another process.

`Net::Finger` will handle simple Finger requests; for everything else, `Net::Telnet` or any of its kin should work well for you.

The WHOIS Directory Service

WHOIS is another useful read-only directory service. WHOIS provides a service like a telephone directory for machines, networks, and the people who run them. Some larger organizations (such as IBM, UC Berkeley, and MIT) provide WHOIS services, but the most important WHOIS servers by far are those run by the InterNIC and other Internet registries such as RIPE (European IP address allocations) and APNIC (Asia/Pacific address allocations).

If you have to contact a system administrator at another site to report suspicious network activity, you can use WHOIS to get the contact info.[*] GUI and command-line tools are available, making WHOIS queries possible on most operating systems. All of the registrars also have web-based WHOIS query pages. Under Unix, a typical query using a command-line interface looks like this:

```
% whois -h whois.educause.net brandeis.edu
<instructional paragraph omitted>
Registrant:
    Brandeis University
    Library and Technology Services MS017
    415 South Street
    Waltham, MA 02453-2728
    UNITED STATES

Administrative Contact:
    Director for Networks & Systems
    Brandeis University
    Library and Technology Services
    MS017 PO Box 9110
    Waltham, MA 02454-9110
    UNITED STATES
    (781) 736-4569
    noc@brandeis.edu

Technical Contact:
    NetSys
    Brandeis University
    Library and Technology Services
    MS017 PO Box 9110
    Waltham, MA 02454-9110
    UNITED STATES
    (781) 736-4571
    hostmaster@brandeis.edu
```

---

[*] If you feel a breeze after reading this sentence, that's because there's a lot of hand waving behind this overly simplistic statement. In a page or two the reality of the situation will make its entrance.

```
Name Servers:
    LILITH.UNET.BRANDEIS.EDU       129.64.99.12
    FRASIER.UNET.BRANDEIS.EDU      129.64.99.11
    NS1.UMASS.EDU
    NS2.UMASS.EDU
    NS3.UMASS.EDU


Domain record activated:     27-May-1987
Domain record last updated: 11-Jun-2008
Domain expires:              31-Jul-2009
```

If you need to track down the owner of a particular IP address range, WHOIS is also the right tool:

```
% whois -h whois.arin.net 129.64.2
OrgName:   Brandeis University
OrgID:     BRANDE
Address:   415 South Street
City:      Waltham
StateProv: MA
PostalCode: 02454
Country:   US

NetRange:  129.64.0.0 - 129.64.255.255
CIDR:      129.64.0.0/16
NetName:   BRANDEIS
NetHandle: NET-129-64-0-0-1
Parent:    NET-129-0-0-0-0
NetType:   Direct Assignment
NameServer: LILITH.UNET.BRANDEIS.EDU
NameServer: FRASIER.UNET.BRANDEIS.EDU
Comment:
RegDate:   1987-09-04
Updated:   2002-10-24

TechHandle: ZB114-ARIN
TechName:   Brandeis University Information Technology
TechPhone:  +1-781-736-4800
TechEmail:  hostmaster@brandeis.edu

# ARIN WHOIS database, last updated 2009-01-13 19:10
# Enter ? for additional hints on searching ARIN's WHOIS database.
```

The previous sessions used a command-line WHOIS client like that found in Unix and Mac OS X distributions. Windows-based operating systems do not ship with such a client, but that shouldn't stop users of Windows systems from accessing this information. There are many fine free and shareware clients available; the *cygwin* distribution contains one, and the `Net::Whois::Raw` module introduced in a few paragraphs also provides a client.

A recent wise footnote warned you that there was some hand waving going on. Let's dispense with that now and get to the reality of the situation: as of this writing, the WHOIS situation on the Internet continues to be in considerable flux. Several of the previous Perl solutions for doing WHOIS queries are now, quite frankly, in shambles as a result of this situation.

Let me try to explain without going too deep into the morass. Once upon a time there was one registry for all Internet-related WHOIS information. This made it easy to write Perl code that created a query and properly parsed the response. For political and perhaps technical reasons, the Pangaea of registries was split into different subregistries. This meant that WHOIS query code had to become smarter about where to send a query and how to parse the response (thanks to variations in the different output formats of new severs as they were introduced).

Even with this added complexity, the Perl module authors were able to keep up. The changes in the WHOIS landscape happened infrequently enough that authors were able to release new versions to handle them. Some created frameworks for plugging in new server formats and locations. Vipul Ved Prakash wrote one good example of this, called Net::XWhois.

As the registrar churn continued and even accelerated, the amount of bitrot in this area became more and more apparent. Net::Whois, now maintained by Dana Hudes but last updated in 1999, doesn't work much of the time: a change to the registry provider for the top-level domain (TLD) *.org* broke Net::XWhois's lookups for those sites, and so on. For a while, none of the existing modules really could be trusted to work.

Before we break out the guitar and start to compose a blues number about this sad state of affairs, it turns out there is a ray of hope that can help us get out of this situation. The fine folks at CenterGate Research Group LLC set up the domain *whois-servers.net*. In this domain, they've registered CNAMEs for all the TLDs on the Internet. These CNAMEs point to the name of the registrar for each TLD. For example, to find the registrar for the *.com* TLD, we could type:

```
$ host com.whois-servers.net
com.whois-servers.net is an alias for whois.verisign-grs.com.
whois.verisign-grs.com has address 199.7.52.74
```

It would be easy enough to use a module like Net::DNS to retrieve this information, but luckily, at least one module author has beaten us to it. The Net::Whois::Raw module, maintained by Walery Studennikov, uses *whois-servers.net* and is still being actively developed. Using it is as trivial as using Net::Finger was in the last section:

```
use Net::Whois::Raw;

my $whois = whois('example.org');
```

Puny as this code sample is, there are a couple of small details behind it that you'll want to know. First, using the default options, as we've done here, only queries the *whois-servers.net* name servers for top-level domains not already in the module's hardcoded registrar table. To always rely on *whois-servers.net* for registrar info, you need to import and set an option like this:

```
use Net::Whois::Raw;

$Net::Whois::Raw::USE_CNAMES = 1;
my $whois = whois('example.org');
```

The second detail worth knowing about is the $OMIT_MSG option, set in the same way $USE_CNAMES was in this the last example. $OMIT_MSG will do its best to remove the lengthy copyright disclaimers most WHOIS servers return these days. It uses a set of hardcoded regular expressions, though, so rely on it with caution.

$OMIT_MSG aside, Net::Whois::Raw just returns the results of a WHOIS query in raw form: it makes no attempt to parse the information returned, like Net::Whois and Net::Xwhois used to do. That's probably a wise decision on the author's part, because the format of the response seems to change from registrar to registrar. All of the successful queries will have fields of some sort. You'll likely find at least Name, Address, and Domain fields in the response, but who knows how they'll be formatted, what order they'll appear in, etc. This can make WHOIS data really annoying to parse and render the resulting programs brittle. To get away from this problem, we have to look at more complex directory protocols, like LDAP.

 One final idea before we leave this section. There's one other approach we haven't discussed because it also can be a bit dicey. There are a few public services that provide WHOIS proxy servers that attempt to do the work for you. You can query them like any other server, and you'll get results based on someone's code that works hard to query the right places on your behalf and format the output in a reasonable way. Two such services are found at whois.geektools.com (sponsored by Center-Gate Research Group; see *http://www.geektools.com*) for general WHOIS queries and whois.pwhois.org (see *http://pwhois.org*) for data based on the global routing tables. In both cases you can just point a standard whois client at them (e.g., whois -h whois.geektools.com and whois -h pwhois.org 18.0.0.0) and they will do the right thing. The key issues with using public servers like these for your mission-critical application are: a) they typically have usage limits (to prevent abuse), and b) someone else is running them, so if they go down, sorry! But for the occasional query, they can be very handy.

LDAP: A Sophisticated Directory Service

The Lightweight Directory Access Protocol, or LDAP (including its Active Directory implementation), is a much richer and more sophisticated directory service than the ones we've considered thus far. There are two widely deployed versions of the LDAP protocol out there: version 2 and version 3. Anything that is version-specific will be clearly noted as such.

This protocol is the industry standard for directory access. System administrators have embraced LDAP because it offers them a way to centralize and make available all sorts of infrastructure information. Besides the standard "company directory" examples, applications include:

- NIS-to-LDAP gateways
- Authentication databases of all sorts (e.g., for use on the Web)
- Resource advertisement (i.e., which machines and peripherals are available)

LDAP is also the basis of other sophisticated directory services, such as Microsoft's Active Directory (explored later, in the section "Active Directory Service Interfaces" on page 354).

Even if your environment doesn't use LDAP to provide anything but a fancy phone book, there are still good reasons to learn how to use the protocol. LDAP servers themselves can be administered using the same protocol they serve, similar to SQL database servers being administered via SQL. To this end, Perl offers an excellent glue environment for automating LDAP administrative tasks. Before we get there, though, it's important that you understand LDAP itself.

Appendix C contains a quick introduction to LDAP for the uninitiated. The biggest barrier new system administrators encounter when they begin to learn about LDAP is the unwieldy nomenclature it inherited from its parent protocol, the X.500 Directory Service. LDAP is a simplified version of part of X.500, but unfortunately the distillation process did not make the terminology any easier to swallow. Taking a few moments with Appendix C to get the language under your belt will make understanding how to use LDAP from Perl easier.

LDAP Programming with Perl

Like so many other system administration tasks in Perl, a good first step toward LDAP programming is the selection of the required Perl module. LDAP is not the most complex protocol out there, but it is not a plain-text protocol. As a result, cobbling together something that speaks LDAP is not a trivial exercise. Luckily, there are two modules available for this purpose: `Net::LDAPapi` (a.k.a. `PerLDAP` and `Mozilla::LDAP`) by Leif Hedstrom and Clayton Donley, and Graham Barr's `Net::LDAP`. In the first edition of this book, the code examples used both modules. Since then, `Net::LDAP` has continued to evolve[†] while `PerLDAP` has suffered bitrot for about 10 years. Though you'll occasionally see a piece of `PerlLDAP` code go by, at this point I can only recommend using `Net::LDAP` and will use it exclusively in the code we're about to explore.[‡]

For demonstration servers, we'll be using the commercial (formerly Sun One, formerly iPlanet, formerly Netscape) JES Directory Server and the free OpenLDAP server (found

---

[†] Quanah Gibson-Mount recently (around January 2008) took over `Net::LDAPapi` and published the first update of the module to CPAN since 1998.

[‡] As an aside, Donley, one of the original authors, himself uses `Net::LDAP` in his book *LDAP Programming, Management and Integration* (Manning).

at *http://www.sun.com* and *http://www.openldap.org*) almost interchangeably. Both come with nearly identical command-line utilities that you can use to prototype and crosscheck your Perl code.

The Initial LDAP Connection

Connecting with authentication is the usual first step in any LDAP client/server transaction. In LDAP-speak this is known as "binding to the server." Binding to a server before sending commands to it was required in LDAPv2, but this requirement was relaxed for LDAPv3.

When you bind to an LDAP server, you are said to be doing so in the context of a specific *distinguished name* (DN), described as the *bind DN* for that session. This is similar to logging in as a particular user on a multiuser system. On such a system, your current login (for the most part) determines your level of access to data on the system; with LDAP, it is the bind DN context that determines how much data on the LDAP server you can see and modify. There is also a special DN known as the *root distinguished name* (which is not given an acronym to avoid confusing it with the term "relative distinguished name"). The root distinguished name is the DN context that has total control over the whole tree; it's similar to being logged in as *root* under Unix/ Mac OS X or *Administrator* on Windows. Some servers also refer to this as the *manager DN*.

If a client provides no authentication information (e.g., DN and password) as part of a bind, or does not bother to bind before sending commands, this is known as *anonymous binding*. Anonymously bound clients typically receive very restricted access to a server's data.

There are two flavors of binding in the LDAPv3 specification: simple and SASL. Simple binding uses plain-text passwords for authentication. SASL (Simple Authentication and Security Layer) is an extensible authentication framework defined in RFC 2222 that allows client/server authors to plug in a number of different authentication schemes, such as Kerberos and one-time passwords. When a client connects to a server, it requests a particular authentication mechanism. If the server supports this mechanism, it will begin the challenge/response dialogue specific to that mechanism to authenticate the client. During this dialogue, the client and server may also negotiate a security layer (e.g., "all traffic between us will be encrypted using TLS") for use after the initial authentication has been completed.

Some LDAP servers and clients add one more authentication method to the standard simple and SASL choices. This method comes as a by-product of running LDAP over an encrypted channel via the Secure Sockets Layer (SSL) or its successor, Transport Layer Security (TLS). To set up this channel, LDAP servers and clients exchange public-key cryptography certificates just like a web server and browser do for HTTPS. Once the channel is in place, some LDAP servers can be told to use a trusted client's certificate for authentication without having to bother with other authentication info.

There are two ways to handle SSL/TLS connections. In LDAPv2 days, some servers started to provide SSL-encrypted connections on a separate port designated for this purpose (port 636). A client could connect to this special port and immediately negotiate an SSL connection before performing any LDAP operations. This is often referred to as LDAPS, just like the HTTP/HTTPS analogue. However, HTTPS differs from LDAPS in one very important respect: LDAPS isn't part of the LDAP specifications and hence isn't a "real" protocol, even though quite a few servers still implement it.

RFC 2830 defines the real extension to the LDAPv3 protocol for this purpose. In LDAPv3, clients can connect to the standard LDAP port (port 389) and request an encrypted connection by making a Start TLS request. Servers that implement this extension to the protocol (most do at this point) will then begin the process of negotiating a TLS-encrypted connection through which the normal authentication and other LDAP requests will take place.

To keep our examples from getting too complicated, we'll stick to simple authentication and unencrypted transport sessions in everything but the upcoming sidebar on this topic.

Here's how you do a simple bind and unbind in Perl:

```
use Net::LDAP;

# create a Net::LDAP object and connect to server
my $c = Net::LDAP->new($server, port => $port) or
    die "Unable to connect to $server: $@\n";

# use no parameters to bind() for anonymous bind
# $binddn is presumably set to something like:
#    "uid=bucky,ou=people,dc=example,dc=edu"
my $mesg = $c->bind($binddn, password => $passwd);
if ($mesg->code){
    die 'Unable to bind: ' . $mesg->error . "\n";
}
...
$c->unbind(); # not strictly necessary, but polite
```

All Net::LDAP methods—e.g., bind()—return a message response object. When we call that object's code() method it will return the result code of the last operation. The result code for a successful operation (LDAP_SUCCESS) is 0, hence the test in the preceding code.

Using Encryption for LDAP Communications

Given the wild and woolly nature of today's network life, it would be irresponsible of me not to show you how to encrypt your LDAP communications (either the initial authentication or subsequent operations).

Luckily, the simple methods are pretty easy.

First, you have to determine what encryption methods the server you are using implements. The choices are (in order of decreasing preference):

1. Start TLS
2. LDAPS
3. SASL

You may be surprised that I listed SASL last, so let's get that question out of the way first. Yes, SASL is the most flexible of the methods available, but it also requires the most work on your part. The most common reason to use SASL is for times when Kerberos (via the GSSAPI mechanism in SASL[*]) is used as the authentication source. Another scenario would be for server configurations that don't require encryption for simple queries (e.g., a company directory), but require them for operations where the information will be updated (e.g., updating your own record). In that case they might use SASL since simple binds are performed in clear text. Other uses exist but are relatively rare.

It is much more common to use the first two choices in my list: Start TLS and LDAPS. These are both easy from `Net::LDAP`:

- For Start TLS, call the `start_tls()` method after you use `new()` but before making a `bind()` call.

- For LDAPS, either use the `Net::LDAPS` module and add additional certificate-related parameters to `new()`, or use the normal `Net::LDAP` module but feed an `ldaps://` URI to `new()` along with additional certificate-related parameters.

Performing LDAP Searches

The D in LDAP stands for Directory, and the one operation you'll perform most often on a directory is a search. Let's start our exploration of LDAP functionality by looking at how to find information. An LDAP search is specified in terms of:

Where to begin the search
> This is called the *base DN* or *search base*. A base DN is simply the DN of the entry in the directory tree where the search should begin.

Where to look
> This is known as the search *scope*. The scope can be either *base* (search just the base DN), *one* (search everything one level below the base DN, not including the base DN itself), or *sub* (search the base DN and all of the parts of the tree below it).

---

[*] For generic Kerberos authentication, the `Authen::SASL` package (plus its dependent modules) by Graham Barr works fine. If you need to do anything funky like connect to an Active Directory server explicitly authenticated by Kerberos, you'll probably need to use Mark Adamson's hooks into the Cyrus-SASL libraries (`Authen::SASL::Cyrus`). This module has some issues, so be sure to look at the `Net::LDAP` mailing list archives before you head down that twisted path.

What to look for

This is called the *search filter*. We'll discuss filters and how they are specified in just a moment.

What to return

To speed up the search operation, you can select which attributes the search filter returns for each entry it finds. It is also possible to request that the search filter only return attribute names and not their values. This is useful for those times when you want to know which entries have a certain attribute, but you don't care what value that attribute contains.

Be Prepared to Carefully Quote Attribute Values

A quick tip before we do any more Perl programming: if you have an attribute in your relative distinguished name with a value that contains one of the characters "+", "(space)," ",", """, ">", "<", or ";", you must specify the value surrounded by quotation marks or with the offending character escaped by a backslash (\). If the value contains quotation marks, those marks must be escaped using backslashes. Backslashes in values are also escaped with more backslashes. Later versions of `Net::LDAP::Util` (0.32+) have an `escape_dn_value()` function to help you with this.

Insufficient quoting will bite you if you are not careful (of course, avoiding these characters all together in your directory's RDNs wouldn't hurt either).

In Perl, a search looks like this:[†]

```
...
my $searchobj = $c->search(base   => $basedn,
                          scope  => $scope,
                          filter => $filter);
die 'Bad search: ' . $searchobj->error() if $searchobj->code();
```

Let's talk about the mysterious `$filter` parameter before we get into a fully fleshed-out code example. Simple search filters are of the form:[‡]

```
<attribute name> <comparison operator> <attribute value>
```

where `<comparison operator>` is specified in RFC 2254 as one of the operators listed in Table 9-1.

[†] Because we do it exactly the same way each time, and to save space, the module load, creation of the connection object, and bind steps have been replaced with an ellipsis in this and later code examples.

[‡] Filters also have restrictions on the characters that can be used without special handling. `escape_filter_value()` in version 0.32+ of `Net::LDAP::Util` can help with this.

Table 9-1. LDAP comparison operators

Operator	Means
=	Exact value match. Can also be a partial value match if * is used in the `<attribute value>` specification (e.g., `cn=Tim O*`).
=*	Match all entries that have values for `<attribute name>`, independent of what the values are. By specifying * instead of `<attribute value>`, we test for the presence of that particular attribute in an entry (e.g., `cn=*` would select entries that have cn attributes).
~=	Approximate value match.
>=	Greater than or equal to value.
<=	Less than or equal to value.

Before you get excited because these look like Perl operators, I have bad news: they have nothing to do with the Perl operators. Two misleading constructs to a Perl person are ~= and =*. The first has nothing to do with regular expression matches; instead, it finds matches that approximate the stated value. The definition of "approximate" in this case is server-dependent. Most servers use an algorithm called soundex, originally invented for census taking, to determine the matching values. It attempts to find words that "sound like" the given value (in English) but are spelled differently.[*]

The other construct that may clash with your Perl knowledge is the = operator. In addition to testing for exact value matches (both string and numeric), = can also be used with prefix and suffix asterisks as wildcard characters, similar to shell globbing. For example, `cn=fi*` will yield all of the entries that have a common name that begins with the letters "fi". `cn=*ink*` likewise performs just as you would suspect, finding each entry whose common name attribute has the letters "ink" in it.

We can take two or more of these simple `<attribute name>` `<comparison operator>` `<attribute value>` search forms and string them together with Boolean operators to make a more complex filter. This takes the form:

```
(<boolean operator> (<simple1>) (<simple2>) (<simple3>) ... )
```

People with LISP experience will have no problem with this sort of syntax; everyone else will just have to remember that the operator that combines the simple search forms is written first. To filter entries that match both criteria A *and* B, you would use `(&(A)(B))`. For entries that match criteria A *or* B *or* C, you would use `(|(A)(B)(C))`. The exclamation mark negates a specific criterion: A *and not* B is written `(&(A)(!(B)))`. Compound filters can be compounded themselves to make arbitrarily complex search filters. Here is an example of a compound search filter that finds all of the Finkelsteins who work in Boston:

```
(&(sn=Finkelstein)(l=Boston))
```

---

[*] If you want to play with the soundex algorithm, Mark Mielke's `Text::Soundex` module provides a Perl implementation.

To find anyone with the last name Finkelstein or Hodgkin:

```
(|(sn=Finkelstein)(sn=Hodgkin))
```

To find all of the Finkelsteins who do not work in Boston:

```
(&(sn=Finkelstein)(!(l=Boston)))
```

To find all the Finkelsteins or Hodgkins who do not work in Boston:

```
(&(|(sn=Finkelstein)(sn=Hodgkin))(!(l=Boston)))
```

Here are two code examples that take an LDAP server name and an LDAP filter and return the results of the query:

```
use Net::LDAP;
use Net::LDAP::LDIF;

my $server = $ARGV[0];
my $port   = getservbyname('ldap','tcp') || '389';
my $basedn = 'c=US';
my $scope  = 'sub';

# anonymous bind
my $c = Net::LDAP->new($server, port=>$port) or
    die "Unable to connect to $server: $@\n";
my $mesg = $c->bind();
if ($mesg->code){
    die 'Unable to bind: ' . $mesg->error . "\n";
}

my $searchobj = $c->search(base   => $basedn,
                           scope  => $scope,
                           filter => $ARGV[1]);
die "Bad search: " . $searchobj->error() if $searchobj->code();

# print the return values from search() found in our $searchobj
if ($searchobj){
    my $ldif = Net::LDAP::LDIF->new('-', 'w');
    $ldif->write_entry($searchobj->entries());
    $ldif->done();
}
```

Here's an excerpt from some sample output:

```
$ ldapsrch ldap.example.org '(sn=Pooh)'
...
dn: cn="bear pooh",mail=poohbear219@hotmail.com,c=US,o=hotmail.com
mail: poohbear219@hotmail.com
cn: bear pooh
o: hotmail.com
givenname: bear
surname: pooh
...
```

Before we develop this example any further, let's explore the code that processes the results returned by search(). You may be wondering what all of that Net::LDAP::LDIF stuff was. This is a sneak peek at a format called LDAP Data Interchange Format, or LDIF. Hang on for just a couple more sections and we'll talk about LDIF in detail.

More interesting at the moment is that innocuous call to `$searchobj->entries()`. Net::LDAP's programming model resembles the protocol definition of RFC 2251. LDAP search results are returned in LDAP `Message` objects. The code we just saw calls the `entries()` method to return a list of all of the entries returned in these packets. We then use a method from the adjunct module `Net::LDAP::LDIF` to dump out these entries en masse.

Let's tweak our previous example a little bit. Earlier in this chapter I mentioned that we could construct speedier searches by limiting the attributes that are returned by a search. With the `Net::LDAP` module, this is as simple as adding an extra parameter to our `search()` method call:

```
...
# could also add "typesonly => 1" to return just attribute types
#(i.e., no values at all)
my @attr = qw( sn cn );
my $searchobj = $c->search(base   => $basedn,
                           scope  => $scope,
                           filter => $ARGV[1],
                           attrs  => \@attr);
```

Note that `Net::LDAP` takes a reference to an array for that additional argument, not values in the array.

Entry Representation in Perl

These code samples may provoke some questions about entry representation and manipulation—for example, how are entries themselves stored and manipulated in a Perl program? I'll answer a few of those questions as a follow-up to our LDAP searching discussion here and then provide a more in-depth exploration in the upcoming sections on addition and modification of entries.

After you conduct a search with `Net::LDAP`, all of the results are available encapsulated by a single `Net::LDAP::Search` object. To get at the individual attributes for the entries in this object, you can take one of two approaches.

First, you can ask the module to convert all of the returned entries (represented as `Net::LDAP::Entry` objects) into one large user-accessible data structure. `$searchobj->as_struct()` returns a hash-of-hash-of-lists data structure. That is, it returns a reference to a hash whose keys are the DNs of the returned entries. The values for these keys are references to anonymous hashes keyed on the attribute names. These keys yield references to anonymous arrays that hold the actual values for those attributes. Figure 9-1 makes this clearer.

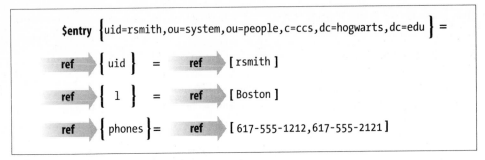

Figure 9-1. Data structure returned by as_struct()

To print the first value of the cn attribute for each entry in this data structure, you could use code like this:

```
my $searchstruct = $searchobj->as_struct;
foreach my $dn (keys %$searchstruct){
    print $searchstruct->{$dn}{cn}[0],"\n";
}
```

Alternatively, you can first use any one of these methods to unload an individual entry object from the object a search returns:

```
# return a specific entry number
my $entry   = $searchobj->entry($entrynum);

# acts like Perl shift() on entry list
my $entry   = $searchobj->shift_entry;

# acts like Perl pop() on entry list
my $entry   = $searchobj->pop_entry;

# return all of the entries as a list
my @entries = $searchobj->entries;
```

Once you have an entry object, you can use one of the method calls in Table 9-2.

Table 9-2. Key Net::LDAP entry methods (see Net::LDAP::Entry for more)

Method call	Returns
$entry->get_value($attrname)	The value(s) of that attribute in the given entry. In a list context, returns all of the values. In a scalar context, returns just the first one.
$entry->attributes()	The list of attribute names for that entry.

It is possible to chain these method calls together in a fairly legible fashion. For instance, this line of code will retrieve the first value of the cn attribute in the first returned entry:

```
my $value = $searchobj->entry(1)->get_value('cn')
```

Now that you know how to access individual attributes and values returned by a search, let's look at how to get this sort of data into a directory server in the first place.

Adding Entries with LDIF

Before we get into the generic methods for adding entries to an LDAP directory, let's look at a technique useful mostly to system and directory administrators. This technique uses a data format that helps you to bulk-load data into a directory server. We're going to explore ways of writing and reading LDIF.

LDIF, defined by Gordon Good in RFC 2849, offers a simple text representation of a directory entry. Here's a simple LDIF example taken from that RFC:

```
version: 1
    dn: cn=Barbara Jensen, ou=Product Development, dc=airius, dc=com
    objectclass: top
    objectclass: person
    objectclass: organizationalPerson
    cn: Barbara Jensen
    cn: Barbara J Jensen
    cn: Babs Jensen
    sn: Jensen
    uid: bjensen
    telephonenumber: +1 408 555 1212
    description: A big sailing fan.

    dn: cn=Bjorn Jensen, ou=Accounting, dc=airius, dc=com
    objectclass: top
    objectclass: person
    objectclass: organizationalPerson
    cn: Bjorn Jensen
    sn: Jensen
    telephonenumber: +1 408 555 1212
```

The format should be almost self-explanatory to you by now. After the LDIF version number, each entry's DN, `objectClass` definitions, and attributes are listed. A line separator alone on a line (i.e., a blank line) separates individual entries.

Our first task is to learn how to write LDIF files from extant directory entries. In addition to giving us practice data for the next section (where we'll read LDIF files), this functionality is useful because once we have an LDIF file, we can massage it any way we like using Perl's usual text-manipulation idioms. LDIF has a few twists (e.g., how it handles special characters and long lines), so it is a good idea to use `Net::LDAP::LDIF` to handle the production and parsing of your LDIF data whenever possible.

You already saw how to print out entries in LDIF format, during our discussion of LDAP searches. Let's change the code we used in that example so it writes to a file. Instead of using this line:

```
my $ldif = Net::LDAP::LDIF->new('-', 'w');
```

we use:

```
my $ldif = Net::LDAP::LDIF->new($filename, 'w');
```

to print the output to the specified filename instead of the standard output channel.

Let's work in the opposite direction now, reading LDIF files instead of writing them. The module object methods we're about to explore will allow us to easily add entries to a directory.[†]

When you read in LDIF data via Perl, the process is exactly the reverse of what we used in the previous LDIF-writing examples. Each entry listing in the data gets read in and converted to an entry object instance that is later fed to the appropriate directory modification method. Net::LDAP handles the data reading and parsing for you, so this is a relatively painless process.

In the following examples, we're using the *root* or *manager* DN user context for demonstration purposes. In general, if you can avoid using this context for everyday work, you should. Good practice for setting up an LDAP server includes creating a powerful account or account group (which is not the *root* DN) for directory management. Keep this security tip in mind as you code your own applications.

With Net::LDAP, the LDIF entry addition code is easier to write:

```perl
use Net::LDAP;
use Net::LDAP::LDIF;

my $server   = $ARGV[0];
my $LDIFfile = $ARGV[1];
my $port     = getservbyname('ldap','tcp') || '389';
my $rootdn   = 'cn=Manager, ou=Systems, dc=ccis, dc=hogwarts, dc=edu';
my $pw       = 'secret';

# read in the LDIF file specified as the second argument on the command line;
# last parameter is "r" for open for read, "w" would be used for write
my $ldif = Net::LDAP::LDIF->new($LDIFfile,'r');

# copied from the deprecated read() command in Net::LDAP::LDIF
my ($entry,@entries);
push(@entries,$entry) while $entry = $ldif->read_entry;

my $c = Net::LDAP-> new($server, port => $port) or
          die "Unable to connect to $server: $@\n";

my $mesg = $c->bind(dn => $rootdn, password => $pw);
if ($mesg->code){
    die 'Unable to bind: ' . $mesg->error . "\n"; }

for (@entries){
    my $res = $c->add($_);
    warn 'Error in add for '. $_->dn().': ' . $res->error()."\n"
      if $res->code();
```

[†] LDIF files can also contain a special changetype: directive that instructs the LDIF reader to delete or modify entry information rather than just adding it. Net::LDAP has direct support for changetype: via its Net::LDAP::LDIF::read_entry() method.

```
}

$c->unbind();
```

Adding Entries with Standard LDAP Operations

It's time to look under the hood of the entry addition process, so we can see how to create and populate entries manually, instead of just reading them from a file like we did in the last subsection. `Net::LDAP` supports two ways to go about creating entries in a directory. Feel free to choose the one that feels the most comfortable to you.

If you are used to working with Perl data structures and like your programming to be terse and to the point, you can feed the `add()` method a naked data structure for single-step entry addition:

```
my $res = $c->add(
  dn => 'uid=jay, ou=systems, ou=people, dc=ccis, dc=hogwarts, dc=edu',
  attr => ['cn'          => 'Jay Sekora',
           'sn'          => 'Sekora',
           'mail'        => 'jayguy@ccis.hogwarts.edu',
           'title'       => ['Sysadmin','Part-time Lecturer'],
           'uid'         => 'jayguy',
    'objectClass' => [qw(top person organizationalPerson inetOrgPerson)]]
                 );
die 'Error in add: ' . $res->error()."\n" if $res->code();
```

Here, we're passing two arguments to `add()`: the first is a DN for the entry, and the second is a reference to an anonymous array of attribute/value pairs. You'll notice that multivalued attributes like `title` are specified using a nested anonymous array.

If you'd prefer to take things one step at a time, you can construct a new `Net::LDAP::Entry` object and feed that object to `add()` instead:

```
use Net::LDAP;
use Net::LDAP::Entry;
...
my $entry = Net::LDAP::Entry->new;

$entry->dn(
  'uid=jayguy, ou=systems, ou=people, dc=ccs, dc=hogwarts, dc=edu');

# these add statements could be collapsed into a single add()
$entry->add('cn'    => 'Jay Sekora');
$entry->add('sn'    => 'Sekora');
$entry->add('mail'  => 'jayguy@ccis.hogwarts.edu');
$entry->add('title' => ['Sysadmin','Part-time Lecturer']);
$entry->add('uid'   => 'jayguy');
$entry->add('objectClass' =>
               [qw(top person organizationalPerson inetOrgPerson)]);

# we could also call $entry->update($c) instead
# of add() if we felt like it
my $res = $c->add($entry);
die 'Error in add: ' . $res->error()."\n" if $res->code();
```

One thing that may be a bit confusing in this last example is the double use of the method name add(). There are two very different method calls being made here that unfortunately have the same name. The first is from a Net::LDAP::Entry object ($entry->add())—this adds new attributes and their values to an existing entry. The second, $c->add($entry), is a method call to our Net::LDAP connection object asking it to add our newly constructed Net::LDAP::Entry object to the directory. If you pay attention to the piece of the call before the arrow, you'll be fine. If this double use of the same name bothers you too much, you could replace the second add() call with a Net::LDAP::Entry update() call, as mentioned in the final code comment.

Deleting Entries

Deleting entries from a directory is easy (and irrevocable, so be careful). Here is a code snippet, again with the bind code left out for brevity's sake:

```
...
my $res = $c->delete($dn);
die 'Error in delete: ' . $res->error() . "\n" if $res->code();
```

It is important to note that delete() operates on a single entry at a time. With most servers, if you want to delete an entire subtree, you will need to first search for all of the child entries of that subtree using a scope of sub or one and then iterate through the return values, deleting as you go; once you've deleted all the children, you can remove the top of that subtree. However, the following sidebar details a few shortcuts that may work for you.

Deleting an Entire Directory Subtree

As of this writing, the somewhat laborious process described in the text for deleting a whole subtree from a directory is the correct canonical method for performing that task. There are a couple of easier approaches you can take in some cases, though:

- Use someone else's code—OpenLDAP ships with a command-line tool called ldapdelete that has a -r option for recursive deletions. No, you won't get closer to your Net::LDAP merit badge by calling another executable from your program, but it does make the code considerably easier to write.

- Use an unofficial LDAP control—we haven't talked about LDAP controls yet in this chapter (we'll get to them in another few sections), so for the moment feel free to treat the following code snippet as a magic incantation for deleting whole subtrees:

```
my $res =
    $ldap->delete($dn, control =>
        {type => LDAP_CONTROL_TREE_DELETE});
```

There are two complications with using this code. First, it uses a control that was proposed as a standard but never made it to the RFC stage (the last version was *draft-armijo-ldap-treedelete-02.txt*), and hence is "unofficial." Second, most LDAP

---

servers don't implement it. I wouldn't mention it except that the one notable exception that does implement it is Active Directory. Caveat implementor.

Modifying Entry Names

For our final look at LDAP operations, we will focus on two kinds of modifications to LDAP entries. The first kind of modification we'll consider is a change of DN or RDN.

Here's an example of the `Net::LDAP` code used to change the relative distinguished name for an entry:

```
# $oldDN could be something like
#    "uid=johnny,ou=people,dc=example,dc=edu"
# $newRDN could be something like
#    "uid=pedro"
my $res = $c->moddn($oldDN,
                    newrdn      => $newRDN,
                    deleteoldrdn => 1);
die 'Error in rename: ' . $res->error()."\n" if $res->code();
```

Here's a quick review, in case you're fuzzy on this RDN concept. LDAP servers store their entries in a tree-like form. But unlike some tree-based protocols (e.g., SNMP, which we'll see later), LDAP doesn't let you pick a specific entry out of the tree by its numeric position. For instance, you can't just say "give me the third entry found in the fourth branch to the left." Instead, you need to identify a unique path to that entry. LDAP makes it easy to find a unique path by dictating that at each level of the tree an individual entry must have something that sets it apart from every other entry at that level in the tree. Since every step of your path is guaranteed to be unique at that level, the whole path is guaranteed to be a unique way to locate a specific entry.‡

It is the RDN that keeps each entry unique at a particular level of the tree. This is why we're fussing so much about this single line of code. When you change the RDN, you are changing the entry's name at that level. The actual operation is pretty simple; it's just important to understand what's happening.

Before we move on to the second kind of rename, there's one small detail worth mentioning. You probably noticed the `deleteoldrdn` parameter being set in the code and may have wondered about it. When we think about renaming objects in almost all contexts (e.g., filename changes), we don't worry about what happens to the old name after the operation has been completed. If you rename a file, the file gets a new name, and the information about what the file *was* called is lost to the mists of time. With LDAP, you have a choice:

---

‡ There's some moderate hand waving going on here because LDAP directory "trees" (snarky quotes provided for the benefit of readers with a computer science background) can have symlink-like aliases and other complications that make it possible to find an entry using two very different paths. This isn't a problem for the discussion at hand, but it's worth noting to keep ourselves honest.

- You can change the RDN and toss the old RDN information (`deleteoldrdn => 1`). This is almost always the right choice.
- You can change the RDN and keep the old RDN information as an additional value in the entry (`deleteoldrdn => 0`). Don't do this unless you have a good reason.

Since this is so weird, here's a quick example that will make it clear. Let's assume we start off with an entry that looks in part like this:

```
dn: uid=gmarx, ou=People, dc=freedonia, dc=com
cn: Julius Henry Marx
sn: Marx
uid: gmarx
```

If we execute code that includes these lines:

```
my $oldDN  = "uid=gmarx, ou=People, dc=freedonia, dc=com";
my $newRDN = "uid=cspaulding";
my $res    = $c->moddn($oldDN, newrdn => $newRDN, deleteoldrdn => 1);
```

the entry will look like this:

```
dn: uid=cspaulding, ou=People, dc=freedonia, dc=com
cn: Julius Henry Marx
sn: Marx
uid: cspaulding
```

Nothing special here; it looks just like we'd expect. If we had run the same code with the last line changed to this:

```
my $res    = $c->moddn($oldDN, newrdn => $newRDN, deleteoldrdn => 0);
```

the entry would look like this:

```
dn: uid=cspaulding, ou=People, dc=freedonia, dc=com
cn: Julius Henry Marx
sn: Marx
uid: gmarx
uid: cspaulding
```

That's clearly not what we want. As mentioned earlier, you'll almost always[*] want to set `deleteoldrdn` to 1. Time to move on.

The second kind of entry name modification is the more drastic one. To move an entry to a different spot in the directory tree, you need to change its distinguished name. Version 3 of LDAP introduces a more powerful renaming operation that allows arbitrary entry relocations within the directory tree hierarchy. `Net::LDAP`'s `moddn()` function gives us access to that when called with the additional parameter `newsuperior`. If we add it like so:

---

[*] To keep you from spending all day racking your brain looking for a case where you would want to keep the old RDN, here's one idea: imagine you were changing all of your usernames due to a company merger and you wanted the ability to look up users by their old names after the renaming. There are better ways to implement this, but you asked....

```
# $oldDN could be something like
#    "uid=johnny,ou=people,dc=example,dc=edu"
# $newRDN could be something like
#    "uid=pedro"
# $parenDN could be something like
#    ou=boxdweller, dc=example,dc=edu
$result = $c->moddn($oldDN,
                       newrdn       => $newRDN,
                       deleteoldrdn => 1,
                       newsuperior  => $parentDN);
    die 'Error in rename: ' . $res->error()."\n" if $res->code();
```

the entry located at $oldDN will be moved to become the child of the DN specified in $parentDN. Using this method to move entries in a directory tree is more efficient than the add() or delete() sequence previously required by the protocol, but it is not supported by all LDAP servers. Other server-dependent caveats may be applicable here as well: for example, the server you are using may not allow you to modify the DN of an entry that has children. In any case, if you've carefully designed your directory tree structure, you'll hopefully have to relocate entries less often.

Modifying Entry Attributes

Let's move on to the more common operation of modifying the attributes and attribute values in an entry. We'll start with an example of this process as part of a global search-and-replace. Here's the scenario: one of the facilities at your company is moving from Pittsburgh to Los Angeles. This code will change all of the entries with a Pittsburgh location:

```
use Net::LDAP;

my $server = $ARGV[0];
my $port   = getservbyname('ldap','tcp') || '389';
my $basedn = 'dc=ccis,dc=hogwarts,dc=edu';
my $scope  = 'sub';
my $rootdn = 'cn=Manager, ou=Systems, dc=ccis, dc=hogwarts, dc=edu';
my $pw     = 'secret';

my $c = Net::LDAP->new($server, port => $port) or
  die "Unable to init for $server: $@\n";
my $mesg = $c->bind(dn => $rootdn, password => $pw);
if ($mesg->code){
    die 'Unable to bind: ' . $mesg->error . "\n";
}

my $searchobj = $c->search(base  => $basedn, filter => '(l=Pittsburgh)',
                           scope => $scope,  attrs => [''],
                           typesonly => 1);
die 'Error in search: '.$searchobj->error()."\n" if ($searchobj->code());

if ($searchobj){
    @entries = $searchobj->entries;
    for (@entries){
```

```
            # we could also use replace {'l' => 'Los Angeles'} here
            $res=$c->modify($_->dn(), # dn() yields the DN of that entry
                    delete => {'l' => 'Pittsburgh'},
                    add    => {'l' => 'Los Angeles'});

            die 'unable to modify, errorcode #'.$res->error() if $res->code();
    }
}
$c->unbind( );
```

The crucial part of this code is the use of the mega-method called modify(), toward the end of the example. modify() takes the DN of the entry to be changed and a set of parameters that tells it just how to modify that entry. Table 9-3 lists the possible choices.

Table 9-3. Net::LDAP entry modification methods

Parameter	Effect
add => {$attrname => $attrvalue}	Adds a named attribute with the given value.
add => {$attrname => [$attrvalue1, $attrvalue2...]}	Adds a named attribute with the specified set of values.
delete => {$attrname => $attrvalue}	Deletes a named attribute with the specified value.
delete => {$attrname => []}	Deletes an attribute or set of attributes independent of their value or values.
delete => [$attrname1, $attrname2...]	
replace => {$attrname => $attrvalue}	Like add, but replaces the current named attribute value. If $attrvalue is a reference to an empty anonymous list ([ ]), this becomes a synonym for the delete operation.

Be sure to pay attention to the punctuation in Table 9-3. Some parameters call for a reference to an anonymous hash, while others call for a reference to an anonymous array. Mixing the two will cause problems.

If you find yourself needing to make several changes to an entry, as we did in our code example, you can combine several of these parameters in the same call to modify(). However, there's a potential problem lurking here. When you call modify() with a set of parameters, like so:

```
$c->modify($dn,replace => {'l' => 'Medford'},
                add     => {'l' => 'Boston'},
                add     => {'l' => 'Cambridge'});
```

there's no guarantee that the additions you specify will take place after the replacement. This code could have an unpredictable, if not downright unpleasant, result.

If you need your operations to take place in a specific order, you'll need to use a slight twist on the normal syntax. Instead of using a set of discrete parameters, pass in a single array containing a queue of commands. In this version, modify() takes a changes parameter whose value is a list. This list is treated as a set of pairs: the first half of the pair is the operation to be performed, and the second half is a reference to an anonymous array of data for that operation. For instance, if we wanted to ensure that the operations in the previous code snippet happened in order, we could write:

```
$c->modify($dn, changes =>
             [ replace => ['l' => 'Medford'],
               add     => ['l' => 'Boston'],
               add     => ['l' => 'Cambridge']
             ]);
```

Take careful note of the punctuation: it is different from that in the earlier examples.

Deeper LDAP Topics

If you've read up to this point and things are starting to make sense to you, you've got all the basic skills for using LDAP from Perl ready to roll. If you're chomping at the bit to see how this is all put together in some more complete examples, you can skip to the next section, "Putting It All Together" on page 348, and come back here when you're done. If you can hold on for a little while longer, in this section we'll touch on a few advanced topics to give you a really thorough grounding in this stuff.

Referrals and references

The hardest part of understanding LDAP referrals and references is simply keeping the two of them distinct in your memory. In LDAPv2, referrals were pretty simple (so simple, in fact, that they really didn't exist in the spec). If you asked an LDAPv2 server for data it didn't have, the server could return a default referral that said, "I don't know anything about that. Why don't you go look over here at this LDAP URL instead?" An LDAP client could then use that URL (whose format is defined in RFC 2255) to determine the name of the server to query and the base DN. For example, if your LDAP client asked the server responsible for ou=sharks,dc=jeromerobbins,dc=org about ou=jets,dc=jeromerobbins,dc=org, it could return a response that said "Sorry, ask ldap://robertwise.org/ou=jets,dc=robertwise,dc=org instead." Your client could then attempt to connect to the LDAP server running on robertwise.org and retry its query.

LDAPv3 made this concept a little more complex, by adding the LDAPv2 behavior to the spec and expanding upon it. Now, when a server is queried for data it knows it doesn't have, it can return a response like "Sorry, never heard of that. Why don't you check over yonder at this URL or set of URLs?" The client is then free to choose for itself which URL to follow to get its information.

The second enhancement to the referral concept in LDAPv3 came in the form of *continuation references*. Continuation references are a type of referral (see, I told you it was hard to keep the two things straight![†]) that only comes into play during an LDAP search. If the server realizes during a search that more information for that search could be found at another server, it is free to return a continuation reference along with the other entries being returned. This continuation reference says, "Hey, I couldn't answer the entire question, but I think I know who can. Try asking over at this URL (or set of URLs) for the rest of your data." It is then up to the client to query all of those additional servers to complete its query. Continuation references usually come into play when dealing with a very large directory tree where parts of the tree have been split onto multiple servers for load management.

Let's see how all this manifests itself in Perl code. Though they are related, we'll examine referrals and continuation references separately. To deal with referrals, here are the steps:

1. When the operation has completed, check to see if we've received any referrals. If not, just proceed.

2. If we did receive a referral, extract an LDAP URL[‡] from the response and dissect it into its component parts.

3. Bind to the appropriate server based on this information and query it. Go back to step 1 (since we might have received another referral).

The code for these steps is pretty easy:

1. Check for a referral:

```
use Net::LDAP qw(LDAP_REFERRAL); # be sure to import this constant
use URI::LDAP; # going to use this to dissect our LDAP URL

# bind as usual
...
# perform a search as usual
my $searchobj = $c->search(...);

# check if we've received a referral
if ($searchobj->code() == LDAP_REFERRAL) {
```

2. Extract an LDAP URL:

```
# the return code indicates we have referrals, so retrieve all of them
my @referrals = $searchobj->referrals();
```

---

† To make it easier for you to remember the difference between referrals and references, I'll always refer to references as "continuation references."

‡ RFC 2251, the LDAPv3 spec, says that while multiple URLs can be returned as part of the referral process, "All the URLs MUST be equally capable of being used to progress the operation." This means you get to choose which one to follow. The level of difficulty of your strategy for making that choice can be low (pick the first one, pick a random one), medium (pick the one with the shortest ping time), or high (pick the closest one in your network topology). It's your call.

```
# RFC 2251 says we can choose any of them - let's pick the first one
my $uri = URI->new($referrals[0]);
```

3. Bind and query again using the new info (dissecting the URL we received as necessary with `URI::LDAP` method calls):

```
$c->unbind();
my $c = Net::LDAP-> new ($uri->host(), port => $uri->port()) or
die 'Unable to init for ' . $uri->$host . ": $@\n";
my $mesg = $c->bind(dn => $rootdn, password => $pw);
if ($mesg->code){
    die 'Unable to bind: ' . $mesg->error . "\n";
}

# RFC 2251 says we must use the filter in the referral URL if one
# is returned; otherwise, we should use the original filter
#
# Note: we're using $uri->_filter() instead of just $uri->filter()
# because the latter returns a default string when no filter is
# present in the URL. We want to use our original filter in that case
# instead of the default of (objectClass=*).
$searchobj = $c->search(base    => $uri->dn(),
                        scope => $scope,
                        filter => $uri->_filter() ? $uri->_filter() :
                                                    $filter,
                        ...);
}
```

You may find it easier to think about referral processing as just sophisticated error handling (because that is essentially what it is). You query a server and it replies, "Sorry, can't handle your request. Please try again, but this time, try again at this server on this port with this baseDN and filter."

It is important to note that the preceding code isn't as sophisticated or as rigorous as it could be. The first flaw is that, while RFC 2251 states that almost all LDAP operations can return a referral, the code only checks for this condition after the search operation (not after the initial bind). I would recommend that you sit down and have a good long think before you decide to follow referrals from bind operations, even if the spec says you should. If you are going to present your authentication credentials to some other server besides the one you originally intended, be sure you completely trust both servers (perhaps by checking the server certificates) first. Similar dire warnings apply to following referrals during the other LDAP operations.

The second flaw is that there's nothing (besides good directory architecture practices) stopping the second server you query from handing you back another reference for you to chase. It is highly inefficient to keep a client hopping from server to server, so you shouldn't see this in the real world, but it is possible.

And finally, in the same category of "you shouldn't see this," the code doesn't check for referral loops where server A says to go talk to server B, which sends you back to server A. It is easy to keep a list of the servers you've contacted to avoid this issue if you think it may happen for some reason. Caveat implementor.

Now that you have referrals under your belt, let's move on to continuation references. Continuation references are marginally easier to deal with; they occur only during a search operation and they come into play only if a search can successfully begin (i.e., if the place you've asked to start searching from really exists in the tree). Unlike the referrals we just talked about, receiving a continuation reference is not an error condition that requires restarting the whole operation. Continuation references are more like outstanding IOUs to a dull-witted debt collector. If your program were the debt collector, it would ask a server for information it felt entitled to have, and the server might say, "I'm sorry, I can't make the entire payment (of LDAP entries you are looking for), but you can get the rest by asking at these three places...." Instead of trying to collect the whole amount from a single other server (as with a referral), your program will dutifully trudge off and try to get the rest of the information from all the additional sources. Those sources are, unfortunately, allowed to send you on a further chase to other places as well.

From a coding perspective, the difference between continuation references and referrals is twofold:

1. The methods for determining whether a referral or a continuation reference is in play are very different. For a referral, we check the result code of an operation and then call the `referrals()` method. For a continuation reference, we examine the data we receive back from the server and then call the `references()` method if we find a continuation reference:

   ```
   ... # bind and search have taken place
   if ($searchobj){
       my @returndata = $searchobj->entries;
       foreach my $entry (@returndata){
           if ($entry->isa('Net::LDAP::Reference')){
           # @references is a list of LDAP URLs
            push(@references,$entry->references());
           }
       }
   }
   ```

2. Unlike with referrals, where we have a choice for which URLs to follow, we're supposed to follow all continuation references. Most people code this using a recursive subroutine[*] along the lines of:

   ```
   ... # assume a search has taken place that has yielded continuation
       # references
   foreach my $reference (@references){
       ChaseReference($reference)
   }

   sub ChaseReference ($reference){
       my $reference = shift;
   ```

[*] For a refresher on recursion, see Chapter 2.

```
# this code should look very familiar because we stole it almost
# verbatim from the previous example on referrals

# dissect the LDAP URL, bind to the indicated server, and search it
my $uri = URI->new($reference);
my $c = Net::LDAP-> new ($uri->host(), port => $uri->port()) or
die 'Unable to init for ' . $uri->$host . ": $@\n";
my $mesg = $c->bind(dn => $rootdn, password => $pw);
if ($mesg->code){
    die 'Unable to bind: ' . $mesg->error . "\n";
}

my $searchobj = $c->search(base => $uri->dn(),
                           scope => $scope,
                           filter => $uri->_filter() ? $uri->_filter() :
                                                        $filter,
                    ...);
# assuming we got a result, collect the entries and the references into
# different lists
if ($searchobj){
    my @returndata = $searchobj->entries;
    my @references = ();
    foreach my $entry (@returndata){
        if ($entry->isa('Net::LDAP::Reference')){
        # @references will contain a list of LDAP URLs
        push(@references,$entry->references());
      }
        else { push @entries, $entry );
      }
}

# now, chase any more references we received from that last search
# (here's the recursion part)
foreach my $reference (@references){
    ChaseReference($reference)
}
}
```

Now, if you wanted to be a troublemaker, you might ask whether any of the operations in this code could return referrals, and whether the code should be handling these cases. "Yes" and "Yes." Next question?

Seriously though, the code presented so far on this topic has been intentionally kept as simple as possible to help explain the concepts and keep referrals and continuation references distinct in your mind. If you wanted to write the most robust code possible to handle these cases, you'd probably need to write wrapper subroutines around each LDAP operation that are prepared to handle referrals and deal with continuation references during searches.

Controls and extensions

The best explanation I've ever heard for LDAP controls comes from Gerald Carter's book *LDAP System Administration* (O'Reilly). Carter described them as "adverbs" for

LDAP operations: they modify, change, or enhance an ordinary LDAP operation. For example, if you wanted a server to pre-sort the results of a search, you would use the Server Side Sorting control, as documented by RFC 2891. Let's look at some code that presumes the server supports this control (not all do—for example, the Sun JES Directory Server does, but the OpenLDAP server does not).

In most cases, the first step is to locate the Net::LDAP::Control subclass module for that particular control. All of the common controls have one.[†] In this case we'll be using Net::LDAP::Control::Sort. Using this module, we create a control object:

```
use Net::LDAP;
use Net::LDAP::Control::Sort;

...

# create a control object that will ask to sort by surname
$control = Net::LDAP::Control::Sort->new(order => 'sn');
```

Once we have the control object, it is trivial to use it to modify a search:

```
# this should return back the entries in a sorted order
$searchobj= $c->search (base    => $base,
                        scope   => $scope,
                        filter  => $filter,
                        control => [$control]);
```

Some controls require more effort than others to use, but now you have the basic idea.

Extensions (also called "extended operations" in some contexts) are like controls, only more powerful. Instead of modifying a basic LDAP operation, they actually allow for extending the basic LDAP protocol to include entirely new operations. Examples of new operations added to the LDAP world through this mechanism include Start TLS (RFC 2830) for secure transmission of LDAP data and LDAP Password Modify (RFC 3062) for changing passwords stored on an LDAP server.

Using extensions from Perl is usually a very simple affair, because all of the common extensions exist in their own module as part of Net::LDAP. For example, using Password Modify is this easy:

```
use Net::LDAP;
use Net::LDAP::Extension::SetPassword;

... # usual connection and bind here
$res = $c->set_password( user        => $username,
                         oldpassword => $oldpw,
                         newpassword => $newpw, );
die 'Error in password change : ' . $res->error()."\n" if $res->code();
```

[†] If you get unlucky and can't find one for the control you want to use, it's not hard to roll your own. The controls included with Net::LDAP should provide enough examples to get you all or most of the way there.

If you need to use an extension that isn't already implemented in the package, then your best bet is to cheat by copying a module file such as `Net::LDAP::Extension::Set Password` and modifying it accordingly.

One question you may have had while reading this section is, "How do I know which controls and extensions are supported by the server I'm using?" Besides looking at the server's documentation or source code (if available), you could also query the root DSE. That's the subject of the next section.

The root DSE

The hardest thing about dealing with this topic is hacking through the overgrown terminology inherited from X.500 just to get to the actual meaning. Machete in hand, here's how it goes:

> A DSE is a DSA-specific entry. *What's a DSA, you ask?*
> A DSA is a directory system agent. *What's a directory system agent?*
> A directory system agent is a server (an LDAP server, in this case).

Besides the ability to impress all your friends at party with your command of X.500 terminology, why do you care about any of this? The root DSE is a special entry in a directory server that contains information about that server. If you interrogate the root DSE, RFC 2251 says you should be able to find the following attributes:

namingContexts
> Which suffixes/directory trees (e.g., dc=ccis, dc=hogwarts, dc=edu) the server is ready to serve.

subschemaSubentry
> The location in the directory where you can query the server's schema (see Appendix C for an explanation of LDAP schemas).

altServer
> According to RFC 2251, a list of "alternative servers in case this one is later unavailable" (this is stated without noting the irony). This information might come in handy if you were storing the data for future queries after your first contact with the server, but it still seems like the time you'll be most interested in this information (i.e., during an outage) is the time when it is least accessible.

supportedExtension
> The list of extensions this server can handle.

supportedControl
> The list of controls that can be used with this server.

supportedSASLMechanisms
> The list of available SASL mechanisms (e.g., Kerberos).

supportedLDAPVersion
> Which LDAP versions the server is willing to speak (as of this writing, probably 2 and 3).

Getting this info from Perl is really easy. `Net::LDAP` has a `Net::LDAP::RootDSE` module that gets called like this:

```
use Net::LDAP;
use Net::LDAP::RootDSE;

my $server = 'ldap.hogwarts.edu';

my $c = Net::LDAP->new($server) or
  die "Unable to init for $server: $@\n";

my $dse = $c->root_dse();

# let's find out which suffixes can be found on this server
print join("\n",$dse->get_value('namingContexts')),"\n";
```

This code returns something like this (i.e., a list of suffixes served from that server):

```
dc=hogwarts,dc=edu
o=NetscapeRoot
```

You may have noticed we're missing the usual "bind happens here" ellipsis we've seen in most of the code examples up until this point. That's because `Net::LDAP::RootDSE` is actually arranging for an anonymous `bind()` followed by a `search()` to happen on our behalf behind the scenes. If you looked at the LDAP server log after this operation, you'd see what was really going on:

```
[16/May/2004:21:25:46 -0400] conn=144 op=0
  msgId=1 - SRCH base="" scope=0 filter="(objectClass=*)" attrs="subsch
emaSubentry namingContexts altServer supportedExtension supportedControl
  supportedSASLMechanisms supportedLDAPVersion"
```

This says we're performing a search with a baseDN of an empty string (meaning the root DSE), a scope of 0 (which is "base"), a filter for anything in that entry, and a list of specific attributes to return. If you ever want to query this information for attributes in the root DSE not normally returned by `Net::LDAP::RootDSE`, now you know how to do it.

DSML

Our last advanced topic before we look at a small sample application is the Directory Services Markup Language (DSML). DSML comes in two flavors: version 1 and version 2. For our purposes, you can think of DSMLv1 as a slightly improved version of LDIF in XML. Acronym parking lot aside, this means that DSML represents entry data in XML instead of the LDIF format we learned about in "Adding Entries with LDIF" on page 331. It slightly improves on LDIF in this regard because it has an explicit standard for representing not just entries but also directory schemas (mentioned in Appendix C). That's the good news. The bad news is that DMSLv1 can't actually represent directory operations like LDIF can (via `changetype: delete`). This deficiency was remedied in the more complex DSMLv2. As of this writing, the Perl world hasn't caught up yet, so the only modules available specific to DSML are for version 1 only.

However, if DSMLv1 is your bag, `Net::LDAP::DSML` offers a handy way to write DSMLv1-formatted files (though as of this writing, it can't read them[‡]). The process is very similar to the one we used for writing LDIF:

```perl
use Net::LDAP;
use Net::LDAP::DSML;

open my $OUTPUTFILE, '>', 'output.xml'
  or die "Can't open file to write:$!\n";

my $dsml = Net::LDAP::DSML->new(output      => $OUTPUTFILE,
                                pretty_print => 1 )
                          or die "OUTPUTFILE problem: $!\n";

... # bind and search here to @entries

$dsml->start_dsml();

foreach my $entry (@entries){
    $dsml->write_entry($entry);
}

$dsml->end_dsml();
close $OUTPUTFILE;
```

When we run this code (with the ellipsis replaced with real code), we get output like this (hand-indented for clarity):

```xml
<?xml version="1.0" encoding="UTF-8"?>
<dsml:dsml xmlns:dsml="http://www.dsml.org/DSML">
  <dsml:directory-entries>
    <dsml:entry dn="ou=People, dc=hogwarts,dc=edu">
      <dsml:objectclass>
        <dsml:oc-value>top</dsml:oc-value>
        <dsml:oc-value>organizationalunit</dsml:oc-value>
      </dsml:objectclass>
    </dsml:entry>
  </dsml:directory-entries>
  <dsml:directory-entries>
    <dsml:entry dn="uid=colinguy,ou=People, dc=hogwarts,dc=edu">
      <dsml:attr name="cn">
        <dsml:value>Colin Johnson</dsml:value>
      </dsml:attr>
      <dsml:attr name="uid">
        <dsml:value>colinguy</dsml:value>
      </dsml:attr>
      <dsml:objectclass>
        <dsml:oc-value>top</dsml:oc-value>
        <dsml:oc-value>person</dsml:oc-value>
        <dsml:oc-value>organizationalPerson</dsml:oc-value>
        <dsml:oc-value>inetorgperson</dsml:oc-value>
```

[‡] If you want to read DSML, you can use any of the XML reading modules (e.g., `XML::Simple`), to read the data and then hand it to the `Net::LDAP` calls we saw in the section "Adding Entries with Standard LDAP Operations" on page 333.

```
      </dsml:objectclass>
    </dsml:entry>
  </dsml:directory-entries>
</dsml:dsml>
```

This all begs the question, "Why use DSML instead of LDIF for entry representation?" It's a reasonable question. DSML is meant to be an abstract representation of directory data (and directory operations, in version 2) in XML form. If you are doing lots of inter-organizational directory sharing, or you find a use for this abstraction, DSML might be right for you. But if you plan to stick to the LDAP arena and you don't need the inter-operability XML provides, stick to LDIF. LDIF is (on the whole) simpler, well tested, and well supported by directory vendors.

Putting It All Together

Now that we've toured all of the major LDAP areas (and even some of the minor ones), let's write some small system administration-related scripts. We'll import our machine database from Chapter 5 into an LDAP server and then generate some useful output based on LDAP queries. Here are a couple of listings from that flat file, just to remind you of the format:

```
name: shimmer
address: 192.168.1.11
aliases: shim shimmy shimmydoodles
owner: David Davis
department: software
building: main
room: 909
manufacturer: Sun
model: M4000
-=-
name: bendir
address: 192.168.1.3
aliases: ben bendoodles
owner: Cindy Coltrane
department: IT
building: west
room: 143
manufacturer: Apple
model: Mac Pro
-=-
```

The first thing we need to do is prepare the directory server to receive this data. We're going to use nonstandard attributes, so we'll need to update the server's schema. Different servers handle this process in different ways. For instance, the Sun JES Directory Server has a pleasant Directory Server Console GUI for changing details like this. Other servers require modifications to a text configuration file. With OpenLDAP, we could use something like this in a file that the master configuration file includes to define our own object class for a machine:

```
objectclass machine
        requires
                objectClass,
                cn
        allows
                address,
                aliases,
                owner,
                department,
                building,
                room,
                manufacturer,
                model
```

Once we've configured the server properly, we can think about importing the data. One approach would be to bulk load it using LDIF. If the sample from our flat-file database reminded you of the LDIF format, you were right on target. This similarity makes the translation easy. Still, we'll have to watch out for a few snares:

Continuation lines

> Our flat-file database does not have any entries with values spanning several lines, but if it did we'd need to make sure that the output conformed to the LDIF standard. The LDIF standard dictates that all continuation lines must begin with exactly one space.

Entry separators

> Our database uses the adorable character sequence -=- between each entry. Two line separators (i.e., a blank line) must separate LDIF entries, so we'll need to axe this character sequence when we see it in the input.

Attribute separators

> Right now our data has only one multivalued attribute: `aliases`. LDIF deals with multivalued attributes by listing each value on a separate line. If we encounter multiple aliases, we'll need special code to print out a separate line for each. If it weren't for this misfeature in our data format, the code to go from our format to LDIF would be a single line of Perl.

Even with these snares, the conversion program is still pretty simple:

```perl
my $datafile    = 'database';
my $recordsep   = "-=-\n";
my $suffix      = 'ou=data, ou=systems, dc=ccis, dc=hogwarts, dc=edu';
my $objectclass = <<"EOC";
objectclass: top
objectclass: machine
EOC

open my $DATAFILE, '<', $datafile or die "unable to open $datafile:$!\n";

print "version: 1\n"; #
```

```
while (<$DATAFILE>) {
    # print the header for each entry
    if (/name:\s*(.*)/){
        print "dn: cn=$1, $suffix\n";
        print $objectclass;
        print "cn: $1\n";
        next;
    }
    # handle the multivalued aliases attribute
    if (s/^aliases:\s*//){
        my @aliases = split;
        foreach my $name (@aliases){
            print "aliases: $name\n";
        }
        next;
    }
    # handle the end of record separator
    if ($_ eq $recordsep){
        print "\n";
        next;
    }
    # otherwise, just print the attribute as we found it
    print;
}

close $DATAFILE;
```

If we run this code, it prints an LDIF file that looks (in part) like this:

```
version: 1
dn: cn=shimmer, ou=data, ou=systems, dc=ccis, dc=hogwarts, dc=edu
objectclass: top
objectclass: machine
cn: shimmer
address: 192.168.1.11
aliases: shim
aliases: shimmy
aliases: shimmydoodles
owner: David Davis
department: software
building: main
room: 909
manufacturer: Sun
model: M4000

dn: cn=bendir, ou=data, ou=systems, dc=ccis, dc=hogwarts, dc=edu
objectclass: top
objectclass: machine
cn: bendir
address: 192.168.1.3
aliases: ben
aliases: bendoodles
owner: Cindy Coltrane
department: IT
building: west
```

```
room: 143
manufacturer: Apple
model: Mac Pro
...
```

With this LDIF file, we can use one of the bulk-load programs that come with our
servers to load our data into the server. For instance, *ldif2ldbm*, packaged with both
the OpenLDAP and Sun JES Directory Servers, reads an LDIF file and imports it directly
into the directory server's native backend format without having to go through LDAP.
Though you can only use this program while the server is not running, it can provide
the quickest way to get lots of data into a server. If you can't take the server offline, you
can use the LDIF-reading Perl code we developed earlier to feed a file like this to an
LDAP server.

To throw one more option into the mix, here's some code that skips the intermediate
step of creating an LDIF file and imports our data directly into an LDAP server:

```perl
use Net::LDAP;
use Net::LDAP::Entry;

my $datafile  = 'database';
my $recordsep = '-=-';
my $server    = $ARGV[0];
my $port      = getservbyname('ldap','tcp') || '389';
my $suffix    = 'ou=data, ou=systems, dc=ccis, dc=hogwarts, dc=edu';
my $rootdn    = 'cn=Manager, ou=Systems, dc=ccis, dc=hogwarts, dc=edu';
my $pw        = 'secret';

my $c = Net::LDAP-> new ($server,port => $port) or
  die "Unable to init for $server: $@\n";
my $mesg = $c->bind(dn => $rootdn,password => $pw);
if ($mesg->code){
    die 'Unable to bind: ' . $mesg->error . "\n";
}

open my $DATAFILE, '<', $datafile or die "unable to open $datafile:$!\n";

while (<$DATAFILE>) {
    chomp;
    my $entry;
    my $dn;
    # at the start of a new record, create a new entry object instance
    if (/^name:\s*(.*)/){
        $dn="cn=$1, $suffix";
        $entry = Net::LDAP::Entry->new;
        $entry->add('cn',$1);
        next;
    }
    # special case for multivalued attribute
    if (s/^aliases:\s*//){
        $entry->add('aliases',[split()]);
        next;
    }
```

```
    # if we've hit the end of the record, add it to the server
    if ($_ eq $recordsep){
        $entry->add('objectclass',['top','machine']);
        $entry->dn($dn);
        my $res = $c->add($entry);
        warn 'Error in add for ' . $entry->dn() . ':' .
             $res->error()."\n"   if $res->code();
        undef $entry;
        next;
    }

    # add all of the other attributes
    $entry->add(split(':\s*')); # assume single valued attributes
}

close $DATAFILE;
$c->unbind();
```

Now that we've imported the data into a server, we can start to do some interesting things. To save space, in the following examples the header at the top that sets our configuration variables and the code that binds us to a server will not be repeated.

So what can we do with this data when it resides in an LDAP server? We can generate a host file on the fly:

```
use Net::LDAP;

...

my $searchobj = $c->search (base   => $basedn,
                            scope  => 'one',
                            filter => '(objectclass=machine)',
                            attrs  => ['cn','address','aliases']);
die 'Bad search: ' . $searchobj->error() if $searchobj->code();

if ($searchobj){
    print "#\n\# host file - GENERATED BY $0\n
           # DO NOT EDIT BY HAND!\n#\n";
    foreach my $entry ($searchobj->entries()){
        print $entry->get_value(address),"\t",
              $entry->get_value(cn)," ",
              join(' ', $entry->get_value(aliases)),"\n";
    }
}
$c->close();
```

Here's the output:

```
#
# host file - GENERATED BY ldap2hosts
# DO NOT EDIT BY HAND!
#
192.168.1.11    shimmer shim shimmy shimmydoodles
192.168.1.3     bendir ben bendoodles
192.168.1.12    sulawesi sula su-lee
192.168.1.55    sander sandy mickey mickeydoo
```

We can also find the names of all of our machines made by Apple:

```
use Net::LDAP;
...
my $searchobj = $c->search(base   => $basedn,
                           filter => '(manufacturer=Apple)',
                           scope  => 'one',
                           attrs  => ['cn']);
die 'Bad search: ' . $searchobj->error() if $searchobj->code();

if ($searchobj){
    foreach my $entry ($searchobj->entries){
        print $entry->get_value('cn'),"\n";
    }
}

$c->unbind();
```

Here's the output:

```
bendir
sulawesi
```

We can generate a list of machine owners:

```
use Net::LDAP;
...
my $searchobj = $c->search(base   => $basedn,
                           filter => '(manufacturer=Apple)',
                           scope  => 'one',
                           attrs  => ['cn','owner']);
die 'Bad search: ' . $searchobj->error() if $searchobj->code();

my $entries = $searchobj->as_struct;

foreach my $dn (sort byOwner keys %{entries}){
    print $entries->{$dn}->{owner}->[0]. ":\t" .
          $entries->{$dn}->{cn}->[0]."\n";
}

# to sort our data structure by owner instead of its DN key
sub byOwner
    { $entries->{$a}->{owner}->[0] <=>  $entries->{$b}->{owner}->[0]    }
```

Here's the output:

```
Alex Rollins:   sander
Cindy Coltrane: bendir
David Davis:    shimmer
Ellen Monk:     sulawesi
```

And we can check to see if the current user ID is the owner of the current Unix machine (maybe some kind of pseudo-authentication):

```
use Net::LDAP;
use Sys::Hostname;

$user = (getpwuid($<))[6];
```

```
my $hostname = hostname;
my $hostname =~ s/\..*//;               # strip domain name off of host

...

my $searchobj = $c->search (base     => "cn=$hostname,$suffix",
                            scope    => 'base',
                            filter   => "(owner=$user)"
                            typesonly => 1);

if ($searchobj){
    print "Owner ($user) can log on to machine $hostname.\n";
}
else {
    print "$user is not the owner of this machine ($hostname).\n";
}
```

These snippets should give you an idea of some of the system administration uses for LDAP access through Perl, and provide inspiration to write your own code. In the next section we'll take these ideas to the next level and look at a whole administration framework based on the conceptual groundwork laid by LDAP.

Not (Really) a Database

Before we move on to ADSI, I just want to offer a quick note about one way *not* to use LDAP. It might be tempting to use an LDAP server as your central repository for all information (as discussed in Chapter 7). Heck, to a certain extent Microsoft uses Active Directory in this fashion.

This is up for debate, but I believe this isn't the best of ideas for a homegrown system. LDAP makes things look very database-like, but it doesn't have the power of a good relational database. It is very forgiving about what is stored (vis-à-vis data validation), doesn't really use a relational model, has a limited query language, etc.

My preference is to keep most information in a relational database and feed an LDAP server from it. This gives you the power of both models without having to work as hard to make LDAP into something it is not. Microsoft has a considerable amount of code in its management tools and APIs to allow it to use LDAP as a central data store. You probably don't want to have to write code like that. If you do decide to go this route, be sure to think carefully about it first.

Active Directory Service Interfaces

For the final section of this chapter, we'll discuss a platform-dependent directory service framework that is heavily based on the material we've just covered.

Microsoft created a sophisticated LDAP-based directory service called Active Directory for use at the heart of its Windows administration framework. Active Directory serves as the repository for all of the important configuration information (users, groups, system policies, software installation support, etc.) used in a network of Windows machines.

During the development of Active Directory, the folks at Microsoft realized that a higher-level applications interface to this service was needed. They invented Active Directory Service Interfaces (ADSI) to provide this interface. To their credit, the developers at Microsoft also realized that their new ADSI framework could be extended to cover other system administration realms, such as printers and Windows services. This coverage makes ADSI immensely useful to people who script and automate system administration tasks. Before we show this power in action, we need to cover a few basic concepts and terms.

ADSI Basics

You can think of ADSI as a wrapper around any directory service that wishes to participate in the ADSI framework. There are *providers*, as these ADSI glue implementations are called, for LDAP, Security Accounts Manager (i.e., local/WinNT-domain style) databases, and Novell Directory Services, among others. In ADSI-speak, each of these directory services and data domains are called *namespaces*. ADSI gives you a uniform way to query and change the data found in these namespaces.

To understand ADSI, you have to know a little about the Microsoft Component Object Model (COM) upon which ADSI is built. There are many books about COM, but we can distill the basics down to these key points:

- Everything we want to work with via COM is an *object*.[*]

- Objects have *interfaces* that provide a set of *methods* for us to use to interact with these objects. From Perl, we can use the methods provided by or inherited from the interface called IDispatch. Luckily, most of the ADSI methods provided by the ADSI interfaces and their children (e.g., IADsUser, IADsComputer, IADsPrintQueue) are inherited from IDispatch.

- The values encapsulated by an object, which is queried and changed through these methods, are called *properties*. We'll refer to two kinds of properties in this chapter: *interface-defined properties* (those that are defined as part of an interface) and *schema-defined properties* (those that are defined in a schema object—more on this in just a moment). Unless I refer explicitly to "schema properties" in the following discussion, you can assume we're using interface properties.

This is standard object-oriented programming fare, but it starts to get tricky when the nomenclature for ADSI/COM and other object-oriented worlds, like LDAP, collide.

---

[*] COM is in fact the protocol used to communicate with these objects as part of the larger framework called Object Linking and Embedding (OLE). In this section, I've tried to keep us out of the Microsoft morass of acronyms, but if you want to dig deeper, some good resources are available at *http://www.microsoft.com/com*.

For instance, in ADSI we speak of two different kinds of objects: *leaf* and *container*. Leaf objects encapsulate real data; container objects hold, or *parent*, other objects. In LDAP-speak, a close translation for these terms might be "entry" and "branching point." On the one hand we talk about objects with properties, and on the other we talk about entries with attributes. So how do you deal with this discrepancy, since both names refer to the exact same data?

Here's one way to think about it: an LDAP server does indeed provide access to a tree full of entries and their associated attributes. When you use ADSI instead of native LDAP to get at an entry in that tree, ADSI sucks the entry out of the LDAP server, wraps it up in a few layers of shiny wrapping paper, and hands it to you as a COM object. You use the necessary methods to get the contents of that parcel, which are now called "properties." If you make any changes to the properties of this object, you can hand the object back to ADSI, which will take care of unwrapping the information and putting it back in the LDAP tree for you.

A reasonable question at this point is, "Why not go directly to the LDAP server?" There are three good answers:

- Once we know how to use ADSI to communicate with one kind of directory service, we know how to communicate with them all (or at least the ones that have ADSI providers).
- ADSI's encapsulation can make directory service programming a little easier.
- Microsoft tells us to use ADSI. Using Microsoft's supported API is almost always the right decision.

To head in the direction of ADSI programming from Perl, we need to introduce *ADsPaths*. ADsPaths give us a unique way to refer to objects in any of our namespaces. They look like this:

```
<progID>:<path to object>
```

where `<progID>` is the programmatic identifier for a provider and `<path to object>` is a provider-specific way of finding the object in its namespace. The two most common progIDs are `LDAP` and `WinNT` (`WinNT` uses the SAM databases mentioned in Chapter 3).

Here are some ADsPath examples taken from the ADSI SDK documentation:

```
WinNT://MyDomain/MyServer/User
WinNT://MyDomain/JohnSmith,user
LDAP://ldapsvr/CN=TopHat,DC=DEV,DC=MSFT,DC=COM,O=Internet
LDAP://MyDomain.microsoft.com/CN=TopH,DC=DEV,DC=MSFT,DC=COM,O=Internet
```

It's no coincidence that these look like URLs, since both URLs and ADsPaths serve roughly the same purpose: they both try to provide an unambiguous way to reference a piece of data made available by different data services. In the case of `LDAP` ADsPaths, we are using the LDAP URL syntax from the RFC mentioned in Appendix C (RFC 2255).

The `<progID>` portion is *case-sensitive*. Using `winnt`, `ldap`, or `WINNT` instead of `WinNT` and `LDAP` will cause your programs to fail. Also be sure to note that there are some characters that can't be used in an ADsPath without being escaped with a backslash or represented in hexadecimal format.[†] At the time of this writing, they were the line feed and carriage return, `,`, `;`, `"`, `#`, `+`, `<`, `=`, `>`, and `\`.

We'll look more closely at ADsPaths when we discuss the two namespaces, `WinNT` and `LDAP`, referenced earlier. Before we get there, let's see how ADSI in general is used from Perl.

The Tools of the ADSI Trade

Any machine running Windows 2000 or later has ADSI built into the OS. I recommend downloading the ADSI SDK found at *http://www.microsoft.com/adsi*, because it provides this documentation and a handy ADSI object browser called *ADsVW*. The SDK comes with ADSI programming examples in a number of languages, including Perl. Unfortunately, the examples in the current ADSI distribution rely on the deprecated `OLE.pm` module, so while you might be able to pick up a few tips, you should not use these examples as your starting point. At this URL you will also find crucial ADSI documentation including *adsi25.chm*, a compressed HTML help file that contains some of the best ADSI documentation available.

Before you begin to code, you will also want to pick up Toby Everett's ADSI object browser (written in Perl) from *http://public.activestate.com/authors/tobyeverett/*. It will help you navigate around the ADSI namespaces. Be sure to visit this site early in your ADSI programming career. It hasn't been updated in a while, but it remains a good starting place for using ADSI from Perl.

One last tip: even if it makes you queasy, it is in your best interest to gain just enough familiarity with VBScript to be able to read scripts written in that language. The deeper you get into ADSI, the more VBScript code you'll find yourself reading and adapting. Appendix F and some of the references listed at the end of this chapter should help a bit with this learning process.

Using ADSI from Perl

The `Win32::OLE` family of modules, maintained by Jan Dubois, gives us a Perl bridge to ADSI (which is built on COM as part of OLE). After loading the main module, we use it to request an ADSI object:

[†] There's an old vaudeville skit where a man goes to the doctor and complains, "Doc, my arm hurts when I move it like this," only to receive the advice, "So, don't move it like that!" I have to offer the same advice. Don't set up a situation where you might need to use these characters in an ADsPath. You'll only be asking for trouble.

```
use Win32::OLE;

$adsobj = Win32::OLE->GetObject($ADsPath) or
    die "Unable to retrieve the object for $ADsPath\n";
```

 Here are two tips that may save you some consternation. First, if you run these two lines of code in the Perl debugger and examine the contents of the object reference that is returned, you might see something like this:

```
DB<3> x $adsobj
0  Win32::OLE=HASH(0x10fe0d4)
      empty hash
```

Don't panic. Win32::OLE uses the power of tied variables. The seemingly empty data structure you see here will magically yield information from our object when we access it properly.

Second, if your GetObject call returns something like this (especially from within the debugger):

```
Win32::OLE(0.1403) error 0x8007202b:
      "A referral was returned from the server"
```

it often means you've requested an LDAP provider ADsPath for an LDAP tree that doesn't exist on your server. This is usually the result of a simple typo: e.g., you typed LDAP://dc=exampel,dc=com when you really meant LDAP://dc=example,dc=com.

Win32::OLE->GetObject() takes an OLE *moniker* (a unique identifier to an object, which in this case is an ADsPath) and returns an ADSI object for us. This call also handles the process of *binding* to the object, which is a process you should be familiar with from our LDAP discussion. By default we bind to the object using the credentials of the user running the script.

Perl's hash reference syntax is used to access the interface property values of an ADSI object:

```
$value = $adsobj->{key}
```

For instance, if that object had a Name property defined as part of its interface (and they all do), you could retrieve it like this:

```
print $adsobj->{Name}."\n";
```

Interface property values can be assigned using the same notation:

```
$adsobj->{FullName}= "Oog";  # set the property in the cache
```

An ADSI object's properties are stored in an in-memory cache called the *property cache*. The first request for an object's properties populates this cache. Subsequent queries for the same property will retrieve the information from this cache, *not from the directory service*. If you want to populate the cache by hand, you can call that object instance's `GetInfo()` or `GetInfoEx()` method (an extended version of `GetInfo()`) using the syntax we'll see in a moment.

Because the initial fetch is automatic, `GetInfo()` and `GetInfoEx()` are often overlooked. Though we won't see any in this book, there are cases where you will need them. Here are two example cases:

1. Some object properties are only fetched by an explicit `GetInfoEx()` call. For example, many of the properties of Microsoft Exchange 5.5's LDAP provider were not available without calling `GetInfoEx()` first. See *http://public.activestate.com/au thors/tobyeverett/* for more details on this inconsistency.

2. If you have a directory that multiple people can change, an object you may have just retrieved could be changed while you are still working with it. If this happens, the data in your property cache for that object will be stale. `GetInfo()` and `GetInfoEx()` will refresh this cache for you.

To actually update the backend directory service and data source provided through ADSI, you *must* call the special method `SetInfo()` after changing an object. `SetInfo()` flushes the changes from the property cache to the actual directory service or data source.

Calling methods from an ADSI object instance is easy:

```
$adsobj->Method($arguments...)
```

So, if we changed an object's properties, we might use this line right after the code that made the change:

```
$adsobj->SetInfo();
```

This would flush the data from the property cache back into the underlying directory service or data source.

One `Win32::OLE` call you'll want to use often is `Win32::OLE->LastError()`. This will return the error, if any, that the last OLE operation generated. Using the `-w` switch with Perl (e.g., `perl -w script`) also causes any OLE failures to complain in a verbose manner. Often these error messages are all the debugging help you have, so be sure to make good use of them.

The ADSI code we've seen so far should look like fairly standard Perl to you, because on the surface, it is. Now let's introduce a few of the plot complications.

Dealing with Container/Collection Objects

Earlier, I mentioned that there are two kinds of ADSI objects: leaf and container objects. Leaf objects represent pure data, whereas container objects (also called "collection objects" in OLE/COM terms) contain other objects. Another way to distinguish between the two in the ADSI context is by noting that leaf objects have no children, but container objects do.

Container objects require special handling, since most of the time we're interested in the data encapsulated by their child objects. There are two ways to access these objects from Perl. `Win32::OLE` offers a special function called `in()` for this purpose, though it is not available by default when the module is loaded in the standard fashion. We have to use the following line at the beginning of our code to make use of it:

```
use Win32::OLE qw(in);
```

`in()` will return a list of references to the child objects held by the specified container. This allows us to write easy-to-read Perl code like:

```
foreach $child (in $adsobj){
    print $child->{Name}
}
```

Alternatively, we can load one of `Win32::OLE`'s helpful progeny, called `Win32::OLE::Enum`. So `Win32::OLE::Enum->new()` will create an enumerator object from one of our container objects:

```
use Win32::OLE::Enum;

$enobj = Win32::OLE::Enum->new($adsobj);
```

We can then call a few methods on this enumerator object to get at `$adsobj`'s children. `$enobj->Next()` will return a reference to the next child object instance (or the next *N* objects if given an optional parameter). `$enobj->All()` returns a list of object instance references. `Win32::OLE::Enum` offers a few more methods (see the documentation for details), but these are the ones you'll use most often.

Identifying a Container Object

You can't know if an object is a container object *a priori*. There is no way to ask an object itself about its "containerness" from Perl. The closest you can come is to try to create an enumerator object and fail gracefully if this does not succeed. Here's some code that does just that:

```
use Win32::OLE;
use Win32::OLE::Enum;

eval {$enobj = Win32::OLE::Enum->new($adsobj)};
print 'object is ' . ($@ ? 'not ' : '') . "a container\n";
```

Alternatively, you can look to other sources that describe the object. This segues nicely into our third plot complication.

So How Do You Know Anything About an Object?

We've avoided the biggest and perhaps the most important question until now. In a moment we'll be dealing with objects in two of our namespaces. You already know how to retrieve and set object properties and how to call object methods for these objects, but only if you already know the names of these properties and methods. Where do these names come from? How do you find them in the first place?

There's no single place to find an answer to these questions, but there are a few sources we can draw upon to get most of the picture. The first place is the ADSI documentation—especially the help file mentioned in the earlier sidebar, "The Tools of the ADSI Trade" on page 357. This file contains a huge amount of helpful material. For the answer to our question about property and method names, the place to start in the file is Active Directory Service Interfaces 2.5→ADSI Reference→ADSI System Providers.

The documentation is sometimes the only place to find method names, but there's a second, more interesting approach we can take when looking for property names: we can use metadata that ADSI itself provides. This is where the schema properties concept I mentioned earlier comes into the picture (see the first part of the section "ADSI Basics" on page 355 if you don't recall the schema/interface property distinction).

Every ADSI object has a property called Schema that yields an ADsPath to its schema object. For instance, the following code:

```
use Win32::OLE;

$ADsPath = 'WinNT://BEESKNEES,computer';
$adsobj  = Win32::OLE->GetObject($ADsPath) or
    die "Unable to retrieve the object for $ADsPath\n";
print 'This is a '.$adsobj->{Class}."object, schema is at:\n".
    $adsobj->{Schema},"\n";
```

will print:

```
This is a Computer object, schema is at:
WinNT://DomainName/Schema/Computer
```

The value of $adsobj->{*Schema*} is an ADsPath to an object that describes the schema for the objects of class Computer in that domain. Here we're using the term "schema" in the same way we used it when talking about LDAP schemas. In LDAP, schemas define which attributes can and must be present in entries of specific object classes. In ADSI, a schema object holds the same information about objects of a certain class and their schema properties.

If we want to see the possible attribute names for an object, we can look at the values of two properties in its schema object: MandatoryProperties and OptionalProperties. Let's change the print statement from our last example to the following:

```
$schmobj = Win32::OLE->GetObject($adsobj->{Schema}) or
    die "Unable to retrieve the object for $ADsPath\n";
print join("\n",@{$schmobj->{MandatoryProperties}},
                @{$schmobj->{OptionalProperties}}),"\n";
```

This prints:

```
Owner
Division
OperatingSystem
OperatingSystemVersion
Processor
ProcessorCount
```

Now we know the possible schema interface property names in the WinNT namespace for our Computer objects. Pretty nifty, eh?

Schema properties are retrieved and set in a slightly different manner than interface properties. Recall that interface properties are retrieved and set like this:

```
# retrieving and setting INTERFACE properties
$value = $obj->{property};
$obj->{property} = $value;
```

Schema properties are retrieved and set using special methods:

```
# retrieving and setting SCHEMA properties
$value = $obj->Get('property');
$obj->Put('property','value');
```

Everything we've talked about so far regarding interface properties holds true for schema properties as well (i.e., the property cache, SetInfo(), etc.). Besides the need to use special methods to retrieve and set values, the only other place where you'll need to distinguish between the two is in their names. Sometimes the same object may have two different names for essentially the same property: one for the interface property and one for the schema property. For example, these two lines retrieve the same basic setting for a user:

```
$len = $userobj->{PasswordMinimumLength};  # the interface property
$len = $userobj->Get('MinPasswordLength'); # the same schema property
```

There are two kinds of properties because interface properties exist as part of the underlying COM model. When developers define an interface as part of developing a program, they also define the interface properties. Later, if they want to extend the property set, they have to modify both the COM interface and any code that uses that interface. In ADSI, developers can change the schema properties in a provider without having to modify the underlying COM interface for that provider. It is important to become comfortable with dealing with both kinds of properties, because sometimes a certain piece of data in an object is made available only from within one kind.

On a practical note, if you are just looking for interface or schema property names and don't want to bother writing a program to find them, I recommend using Toby Everett's ADSI browser, mentioned earlier. Figure 9-2 is a sample screen shot of this browser in action.

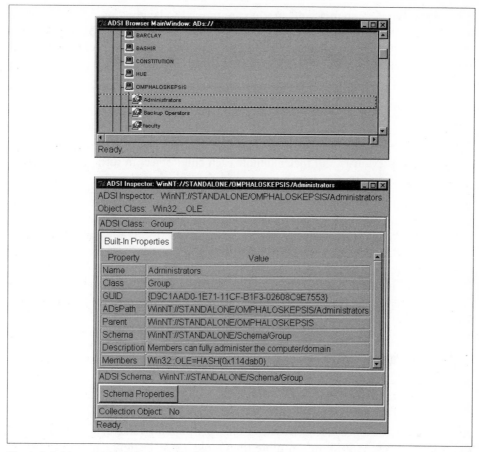

Figure 9-2. Everett's ADSI browser displaying an Administrators group object

Alternatively, the *General* folder of the SDK samples contains a program called *ADSIDump* that can dump the contents of an entire ADSI tree for you.

Searching

This is the last complication we'll discuss before moving on. In the section "LDAP: A Sophisticated Directory Service" on page 321, we spent considerable time talking about LDAP searches. But here in ADSI-land, we've breathed hardly a word about the subject. This is because from Perl (and any other language that uses the same OLE automation interface), searching with ADSI is a pain—that is, subtree searches, or searches that entail anything but the simplest of search filters, are excruciatingly painful (other types of search are not so bad). Complex searches are troublesome because they require you to step out of the ADSI framework and use a whole different methodology to get at your data (not to mention learn more Microsoft acronyms).

But people who do system administration are trained to laugh at pain, so let's take a look. We'll start with simple searches before tackling the hard stuff. Simple searches that encompass one object (scope of **base**) or an object's immediate children (scope of **one**) can be handled manually with Perl. Here's how:

- For a single object, retrieve the properties of interest and use the normal Perl comparison operators to determine if this object is a match:

    ```
    if ($adsobj->{cn} eq 'Mark Sausville' and $adsobj->{State} eq 'CA'){...}
    ```

- To search the children of an object, use the container object access techniques we discussed previously and then examine each child object in turn. We'll see some examples of this type of search in a moment.

If you want to do more complex searches, like those that entail searching a whole directory tree or subtree, you need to switch to using a different "middleware" technology called ActiveX Data Objects (ADO). ADO offers scripting languages an interface to Microsoft's OLE DB layer. OLE DB provides a common database-oriented interface to data sources such as relational databases and directory services. In our case we'll be using ADO to talk to ADSI (which then talks to the actual directory service). Because ADO is a database-oriented methodology, the code you are about to see relates to the ODBC material we covered in Chapter 7.

ADO only works when talking to the LDAP ADSI provider. It will not work for the `WinNT` namespace.

ADO is a whole subject in itself that is only peripherally related to the subject of directory services, so we'll do no more than look at one example and a little bit of explanation before moving on to some more relevant ADSI examples. For more information on ADO itself, search the Microsoft website for the term "ADO" and check out this Wikipedia page: *http://en.wikipedia.org/wiki/ActiveX_Data_Objects*.

Here's some code that displays the names of all of the groups to be found in a given domain:

```
use Win32::OLE qw(in);

# get the ADO object, set the provider, open the connection
$c = Win32::OLE->new('ADODB.Connection');
$c->{Provider} = 'ADsDSOObject';
$c->Open('ADSI Provider');
die Win32::OLE->LastError() if Win32::OLE->LastError();

# prepare and then execute the query
$ADsPath = 'LDAP://ldapserver/dc=example,dc=com';
$rs = $c->Execute("<$ADsPath>;(objectClass=Group);Name;SubTree");
die Win32::OLE->LastError() if Win32::OLE->LastError();
```

```
until ($rs->EOF){
    print $rs->Fields(0)->{Value},"\n";
    $rs->MoveNext;
}

$rs->Close;
$c->Close;
```

After loading the modules, this block of code gets an ADO `Connection` object instance, sets that object instance's provider name, and then instructs it to open the connection. This connection is opened on behalf of the user running the script, though we could have set some other object properties to change this.

We then perform the actual search using `Execute()`. This search can be specified using one of two "dialects," SQL or ADSI.[‡] The ADSI dialect, as shown, uses a command string consisting of four arguments, separated by semicolons.

 Be careful of this ADSI ADO provider quirk: there cannot be any white-space around the semicolons, or the query will fail.

The arguments are:

- An ADsPath (in angle brackets) that sets the server and base DN for the search
- A search filter (using the same LDAP filter syntax we saw before)
- The name or names (separated by commas) of the properties to return
- A search scope of either `Base`, `OneLevel`, or `SubTree` (as per the LDAP standard)

`Execute()` returns a reference to the first of the ADO `RecordSet` objects returned by our query. We ask for each `RecordSet` object in turn, unpacking the objects it holds and printing the `Value` property returned by the `Fields()` method for each of these objects. The `Value` property contains the value we requested in our command string (the name of the `Group` object). Here's an excerpt from sample output from a Windows Server 2003 machine:

```
Domain Computers
Domain Users
RAS and IAS Servers
Users
Domain Guests
Group Policy Creator Owners
Enterprise Admins
Server Operators
Account Operators
```

[‡] The mention of SQL in this context leads into an interesting aside: Microsoft SQL Server can be configured to know about ADSI providers in addition to normal databases. This means that you can execute SQL queries against SQL Server and have it actually query `ActiveDirectory` objects via ADSI instead of normal databases. Pretty cool.

```
Print Operators
Replicator
Domain Controllers
Schema Admins
Remote Desktop Users
Network Configuration Operators
Incoming Forest Trust Builders
Performance Monitor Users
Terminal Server License Servers
Pre-Windows 2000 Compatible Access
Performance Log Users
Windows Authorization Access Group
Backup Operators
Domain Admins
Administrators
Cert Publishers
Guests
DnsAdmins
DnsUpdateProxy
Debugger Users
```

Performing Common Tasks Using the WinNT and LDAP Namespaces

Now that we've safely emerged from our list of complications, we can turn to performing some common administrative tasks using ADSI from Perl. The goal is to give you a taste of the things you can do with the ADSI information we've presented. Then you can use the code we're going to see as starter recipes for your own programming.

For these tasks, we'll use one of two namespaces. The first namespace is WinNT, which gives us access to the local Windows SAM database that includes objects like local users, groups, printers, services, etc.

The second is our friend LDAP. LDAP becomes the provider of choice when we move on to the LDAP-based Active Directory of Windows 2000 and beyond. Most of the WinNT objects can be accessed via LDAP as well. But even with Windows Server 2003, there are still tasks that can only be performed using the WinNT namespace (like the creation of local machine accounts).

The code that works with these different namespaces looks similar (after all, that's part of the point of using ADSI), but you should note two important differences. First, the ADsPath format is slightly different. The WinNT ADsPath takes one of these forms, according to the ADSI SDK:

```
WinNT:[//DomainName[/ComputerName[/ObjectName[,className]]]]
WinNT:[//DomainName[/ObjectName[,className]]]
WinNT:[//ComputerName,computer]
WinNT:
```

The `LDAP` ADsPath looks like this:

```
LDAP://HostName[:PortNumber][/DistinguishedName]
```

Note that the properties of the objects in the `LDAP` and `WinNT` namespaces are similar, but they are not the same. For instance, you can access the same user objects from both namespaces, but you can only get to some Active Directory properties for a particular user object through the `LDAP` namespace.

It's especially important to pay attention to the differences between the schemas found in the two namespaces. For example, the `User` class for `WinNT` has no mandatory properties, while the `LDAP` `User` class has several. With the `LDAP` namespace, you need to populate at least the `cn` and `samAccountName` properties to successfully create a `User` object.

With these differences in mind, let's look at some actual code. To save space, we're going to omit most of the error checking, but you'll want to run your scripts with the `-w` switch and liberally sprinkle lines like this throughout your code:

```
die 'OLE error :'.Win32::OLE->LastError() if Win32::OLE->LastError();
```

 In the examples that follow, you'll find that I flip-flop between using the `WinNT` and `LDAP` namespaces. This is to give you a sense of how to use both of them. Deciding which one to use depends largely on the task at hand and the size of the Active Directory implementation in play.

Sometimes the decision is made for you. For example, you need to use `WinNT` when dealing with local machine users/services and for printer queue control; conversely, you need to use `LDAP` to access some user properties in AD, AD control objects, and so on.

For other tasks, you have a choice. In those cases `LDAP` is usually preferred (despite being a bit more complex) because it is more efficient. With the `LDAP` namespace, you can operate directly on an object deep in the AD tree without having to enumerate through a list of objects as you would when using `WinNT`. If your AD implementation is relatively small, this efficiency gain may not matter to you and the ease of using `WinNT` may be more compelling. It is largely your choice.

Working with Users via ADSI

To dump the list of users using the `WinNT` namespace:

```
use Win32::OLE qw(in);

# 'WinNT://CurrentComputername,computer' - accounts local to this computer
# 'WinNT://DCname, computer'    - accounts for the client's current domain
# 'WinNT://DomainName/DCName,computer'          - to specify the domain

my $ADsPath= 'WinNT://DomainName/DCName,computer';
my $c = Win32::OLE->GetObject($ADsPath) or die "Unable to get $ADsPath\n";
```

```
foreach my $adsobj (in $c){
    print $adsobj->{Name},"\n" if ($adsobj->{Class} eq 'User');
}
```

If you wanted to use the LDAP namespace instead of the WinNT namespace to do an exhaustive (i.e., entire-tree) search for users, you would need to use the ADO-based method demonstrated in the section on searching.

To create a user (local to the machine) and set that user's full name:

```
use Win32::OLE;

my $ADsPath='WinNT://LocalMachineName,computer';
my $c = Win32::OLE->GetObject($ADsPath) or die "Unable to get $ADsPath\n";

# create and return a User object
my $u = $c->Create('user',$username);
$u->SetInfo();  # we have to create the user before we modify it

# no space between "Full" and "Name" allowed with WinNT namespace
$u->{FullName} = $fullname;
$u->SetInfo();
```

The equivalent code to create a global user (you can't create local users using the LDAP namespace) in Active Directory looks like this:

```
use Win32::OLE;

# This creates the user under the cn=Users branch of your directory tree.
# If you keep your users in a sub-OU of Users, just change the next line.
my $ADsPath= 'LDAP://ldapserver,CN=Users,dc=example,dc=com';

my $c = Win32::OLE->GetObject($ADsPath) or die "Unable to get $ADsPath\n";

# create and return a User object
my $u=$c->Create('user','cn='.$commonname);
$u->{samAccountName} = $username;
# IMPORTANT: we have to create the user in the dir before we modify it
$u->SetInfo();

# space between "Full" and "Name" required with LDAP namespace (sigh)
$u->{'Full Name'} = $fullname;
$u->SetInfo();
```

Deleting a local user requires just a small change:

```
use Win32::OLE;

my $ADsPath= 'WinNT://DomainName/ComputerName,computer';
my $c = Win32::OLE->GetObject($ADsPath) or die "Unable to get $ADsPath\n";

# delete the User object; note that we are bound to the container object
$c->Delete('user',$username);
$c->SetInfo();
```

Changing a user's password is a single method's work:

```
use Win32::OLE;

# or 'LDAP://cn=$username,ou=staff,ou=users,dc=example,dc=com' (for example)
my $ADsPath= 'WinNT://DomainName/ComputerName/'.$username;
my $u = Win32::OLE->GetObject($ADsPath) or die "Unable to get $ADsPath\n";

$u->ChangePasssword($oldpassword,$newpassword);
$u->SetInfo();
```

Working with Groups via ADSI

You can enumerate the available groups using the `WinNT` namespace with just a minor tweak of our user enumeration code. The one changed line is:

```
print $adsobj->{Name},"\n" if ($adsobj->{Class} eq 'Group');
```

If you want to enumerate groups using the `LDAP` namespace, it is best to use ADO (see the section "Searching" on page 363).

Creation and deletion of groups involves the same `Create()` and `Delete()` methods we just saw for user account creation and deletion; the only difference is the first argument needs to be `'group'`. For example:

```
my $g = $c->Create('group',$groupname);
```

To add a user to a group (specified as a `GroupName`) once you've created it:

```
use Win32::OLE;

my $ADsPath= 'WinNT://DomainName/GroupName,group';

my $g = Win32::OLE->GetObject($ADsPath) or die "Unable to get $ADsPath\n";

# this uses the ADsPath to a specific user object
$g->Add($userADsPath);
```

With the `WinNT` namespace, the same rules we saw earlier about local versus domain (global) users apply here as well. If we want to add a domain user to our group, our `$userADsPath` should reference the user at a DC for that domain. If we want to use the `LDAP` namespace for this task, we explicitly point at the group in the directory tree:

```
my $ADsPath= 'LDAP://cn=GroupName,ou=Groups,dc=example,dc=com';
```

To remove a user from a group, use:

```
$c->Remove($userADsPath);
```

Working with File Shares via ADSI

Now we start to get into some of the more interesting ADSI work. It is possible to use ADSI to instruct a machine to start sharing a part of its local storage with other computers:

```
use Win32::OLE;

my $ADsPath= 'WinNT://ComputerName/lanmanserver';

my $c = Win32::OLE->GetObject($ADsPath) or die "Unable to get $ADsPath\n";

my $s = $c->Create('fileshare',$sharename);
$s->{path}        = 'C:\directory';
$s->{description} = 'This is a Perl created share';
$s->SetInfo();
```

File shares are deleted using the `Delete()` method.

 Before we move on to other tasks, let me take this opportunity to remind you to closely consult the SDK documentation before using any of these ADSI objects. Sometimes, you'll find useful surprises. If you look in the ADSI 2.5 help file at Active Directory Service Interfaces 2.5→ADSI Reference→ADSI Interfaces→Persistent Object Interfaces→IADsFileShare, you'll see that a `fileshare` object has a `CurrentUserCount` property that shows how many users are currently connected to this file share. This could be a very handy detail.

Working with Print Queues and Print Jobs via ADSI

Here's how to determine the names of the queues on a particular server and the models of the printers being used to serve those queues:

```
use Win32::OLE qw(in);

my $ADsPath='WinNT://DomainName/PrintServerName,computer';

my $c = Win32::OLE->GetObject($ADsPath) or die "Unable to get $ADsPath\n";

foreach my $adsobj (in $c){
    print $adsobj->{Name}.':'.$adsobj->{Model}."\n"
      if ($adsobj->{Class} eq 'PrintQueue');
}
```

Once you have the name of a print queue, you can bind to it directly to query and control it:

```
use Win32::OLE qw(in);

# this table comes from this section in the ADSI 2.5 SDK:
# 'Active Directory Service Interfaces 2.5->ADSI Reference->
# ADSI Interfaces->Dynamic Object Interfaces->IADsPrintQueueOperations->
# IADsPrintQueueOperations Property Methods' (phew)

my %status =
  (0x00000001 => 'PAUSED',         0x00000002 => 'PENDING_DELETION',
   0x00000003 => 'ERROR' ,         0x00000004 => 'PAPER_JAM',
   0x00000005 => 'PAPER_OUT',      0x00000006 => 'MANUAL_FEED',
   0x00000007 => 'PAPER_PROBLEM',  0x00000008 => 'OFFLINE',
```

```
    0x00000100 => 'IO_ACTIVE',        0x00000200 => 'BUSY',
    0x00000400 => 'PRINTING',         0x00000800 => 'OUTPUT_BIN_FULL',
    0x00001000 => 'NOT_AVAILABLE',    0x00002000 => 'WAITING',
    0x00004000 => 'PROCESSING',       0x00008000 => 'INITIALIZING',
    0x00010000 => 'WARMING_UP',       0x00020000 => 'TONER_LOW',
    0x00040000 => 'NO_TONER',         0x00080000 => 'PAGE_PUNT',
    0x00100000 => 'USER_INTERVENTION', 0x00200000 => 'OUT_OF_MEMORY',
    0x00400000 => 'DOOR_OPEN',        0x00800000 => 'SERVER_UNKNOWN',
    0x01000000 => 'POWER_SAVE');

my $ADsPath = 'WinNT://PrintServerName/PrintQueueName';

my $p = Win32::OLE->GetObject($ADsPath) or die "Unable to get $ADsPath\n";

print 'The printer status for ' . $c->{Name} . ' is ' .
    ((exists $p->{status}) ? $status{$c->{status}} : 'NOT ACTIVE') . "\n";
```

The `PrintQueue` object offers the set of print queue control methods you'd hope for: `Pause()`, `Resume()`, and `Purge()`. These allow us to control the actions of the queue itself. But what if we want to examine or manipulate the actual jobs in this queue?

To get at the actual jobs, you call a `PrintQueue` object method called `PrintJobs()`. `PrintJobs()` returns a collection of `PrintJob` objects, each of which has a set of properties and methods. For instance, here's how to show the jobs in a particular queue:

```
use Win32::OLE qw(in);

# this table comes from this section in the ADSI 2.5 SDK:
# 'Active Directory Service Interfaces 2.5->ADSI Reference->
# ADSI Interfaces->Dynamic Object Interfaces->IADsPrintJobOperations->
# IADsPrintJobOperations Property Methods' (double phew)

my %status = (0x00000001 => 'PAUSED',   0x00000002 => 'ERROR',
              0x00000004 => 'DELETING', 0x00000010 => 'PRINTING',
              0x00000020 => 'OFFLINE',  0x00000040 => 'PAPEROUT',
              0x00000080 => 'PRINTED',  0x00000100 => 'DELETED');

my $ADsPath = 'WinNT://PrintServerName/PrintQueueName';

my $p = Win32::OLE->GetObject($ADsPath) or die "Unable to get $ADsPath\n";

$jobs = $p->PrintJobs();
foreach my $job (in $jobs){
  print $job->{User} . "\t" . $job->{Description} . "\t" .
        $status{$job->{status}} . "\n";
}
```

Each job can be `Pause()`d and `Resume()`d as well.

Working with Windows-Based Operating System Services via ADSI

For our last set of examples, we're going to look at how to locate, start, and stop the services on a Windows machine. Like the other examples in this chapter, these code snippets must be run from an account with sufficient privileges on the target computer to effect changes.

To list the services on a computer and their statuses, we could use this code:

```
use Win32::OLE qw(in);

# this table comes from this section in the ADSI 2.5 SDK:
# 'Active Directory Service Interfaces 2.5->ADSI Reference->
# ADSI Interfaces->Dynamic Object Interfaces->IADsServiceOperations->
# IADsServiceOperations Property Methods'

my %status =
   (0x00000001 => 'STOPPED',            0x00000002 => 'START_PENDING',
    0x00000003 => 'STOP_PENDING',       0x00000004 => 'RUNNING',
    0x00000005 => 'CONTINUE_PENDING',   0x00000006 => 'PAUSE_PENDING',
    0x00000007 => 'PAUSED',             0x00000008 => 'ERROR');

my $ADsPath = 'WinNT://DomainName/ComputerName,computer';

my $c = Win32::OLE->GetObject($ADsPath) or die "Unable to get $ADsPath\n";

foreach my $adsobj (in $c){
  print $adsobj->{DisplayName} . ':' . $status{$adsobj->{status}} . "\n"
     if ($adsobj->{Class} eq 'Service');
}
```

To start, stop, pause, or continue a service, we call the obvious methods (Start(), Stop(), etc.). Here's how we might start the Network Time service on a Windows machine if it were stopped:

```
use Win32::OLE;

my $ADsPath = 'WinNT://DomainName/ComputerName/W32Time,service';

my $s = Win32::OLE->GetObject($ADsPath) or die "Unable to get $ADsPath\n";

$s->Start();
# may wish to check status at this point, looping until it is started
```

To avoid potential user and computer name conflicts, the previous code can also be written as:

```
use Win32::OLE;

my $d = Win32::OLE->GetObject('WinNT://Domain');
my $c = $d->GetObject('Computer', $computername);
my $s = $c->GetObject('Service', 'W32Time');

$s->Start();
```

Stopping it is just a matter of changing the last line to:

```
$s->Stop();
# may wish to check status at this point, sleep for a second or two
# and then loop until it is stopped
```

These examples should give you some idea of the amount of control using ADSI from Perl can give you over your system administration work. Directory services and their interfaces can be a very powerful part of your computing infrastructure.

Module Information for This Chapter

Name	CPAN ID	Version
Net::Telnet	JROGERS	3.03
Net::Finger	FIMM	1.06
Net::Whois::Raw	DESPAIR	0.34
Net::LDAP	GBARR	0.32
Sys::Hostname (ships with Perl)		1.11
Win32::OLE (ships with ActiveState Perl)	JDB	0.17

References for More Information

The following sections list some resources you might want to consult for further information on the topics discussed in this chapter.

RFC 1288: The Finger User Information Protocol, by D. Zimmerman (1991), defines Finger.

ftp://sipb.mit.edu/pub/whois/whois-servers.list is a list of most major WHOIS servers.

RFC 954: NICNAME/WHOIS, by K. Harrenstien, M. Stahl, and E. Feinler (1985), defines WHOIS.

LDAP

http://ldap.perl.org is the home page for Net::LDAP.

http://www.openldap.org is the home page for OpenLDAP, a free LDAP server under active development.

JXplorer (*http://www.jxplorer.org*) and Apache Directory Studio (*http://directory .apache.org/studio/*) are both good, free GUI LDAP browsers that work with all of the LDAP servers I've ever used.

led (http://sourceforge.net/projects/led/) and *ldapdiff (https://launchpad.net/ldapdiff/)* are two handy command-line utilities to help with the editing of LDAP entries/trees. The first pops you into an editor of your choice to edit an LDIF representation of an entry, and the second helps with showing the difference between a live LDAP tree and an LDIF file (and patching it accordingly if you'd like).

You might also want to consult the following sources on LDAP:

- *Implementing LDAP*, by Mark Wilcox (Wrox Press)
- *LDAP-HOWTO*, by Mark Grennan (1999), available at *http://www.grennan.com/ldap-HOWTO.html*
- *Understanding and Deploying LDAP Directory Services*, Second Edition, by Tim Howes et al. (Addison-Wesley)
- *RFC 1823: The LDAP Application Program Interface*, by T. Howes and M. Smith (1995)
- *RFC 2222: Simple Authentication and Security Layer* (SASL), by J. Myers (1997)
- *RFC 2251: Lightweight Directory Access Protocol* (v3), by M. Wahl, T. Howes, and S. Kille (1997)
- *RFC 2252: Lightweight Directory Access Protocol (v3): Attribute Syntax Definitions*, by M. Wahl et al. (1997)
- *RFC 2254: The String Representation of LDAP Search Filters*, by T. Howes (1997)
- *RFC 2255: The LDAP URL Format*, by T. Howes and M. Smith (1997)
- *RFC 2256: A Summary of the X.500(96) User Schema for Use with LDAPv3*, by M. Wahl (1997)
- *RFC 2849: The LDAP Data Interchange Format (LDIF)—Technical Specification*, by Gordon Good (2000)
- *Understanding LDAP*, by Heinz Jonner et al. (1998), available at *http://www.redbooks.ibm.com/abstracts/sg244986.html* (a superb "Redbook" introduction to LDAP)
- *LDAP System Administration (http://oreilly.com/catalog/9781565924918/)*, by Gerald Carter (O'Reilly)
- *LDAP Programming, Management, and Integration*, by Clayton Donley (Manning)

ADSI

http://cwashington.netreach.net is a good (non-Perl-specific) site on scripting ADSI and other Microsoft technologies.

http://msdn.microsoft.com/en-us/library/aa772170.aspx is the canonical source for ADSI information.

http://public.activestate.com/authors/tobyeverett/ contains Toby Everett's collection of documentation on using ADSI from Perl.

http://www.15seconds.com is another good (non-Perl-specific) site on scripting ADSI and other Microsoft technologies.

http://isg.ee.ethz.ch/tools/realmen/ presents a whole system-management infrastructure for Windows written almost entirely in Perl.

Robbie Allen, author/coauthor of a slew of superb books on Windows and AD, has a website at *http://techtasks.com* where you can find the code samples from all of his books. It truly is the mother lode of examples—one of the single most helpful websites for ADSI programming that you'll ever find. For more on Allen's contributions, see the references at the end of Chapter 3.

You might also want to check out these sources:

- *Active Directory (http://oreilly.com/catalog/9780596004668/)*, Second Edition, by Alistair G. Lowe-Norris (O'Reilly)
- *Managing Enterprise Active Directory Services*, by Robbie Allen and Richard Puckett (Addison-Wesley)
- *Microsoft Windows 2000 Scripting Guide: Automating System Administration* (Microsoft Press)

## CHAPTER 10

Log Files

If this weren't a book on system administration, an entire chapter on log files would seem peculiar. But system administrators have a very special relationship with log files. System administrators are expected to be like Doctor Doolittle, who could talk to the animals: able to communicate with a large menagerie of software and hardware. Much of this communication takes place through log files, so we become log file linguists. Perl can be a big help in this process.

It would be impossible to touch on all the different kinds of processing and analysis you can do with logs in a single chapter. Entire books have been devoted to just statistical analysis of this sort of data, and companies have been founded to sell products to help analyze it. However, this chapter does present some general approaches to the topic and some relevant Perl tools, to whet your appetite for more.

Reading Text Logs

Logs come in different flavors, so we need several approaches for dealing with them. The most common type of log file is one composed entirely of lines of text: popular server packages like Apache (Web), BIND (DNS), and *sendmail* (email) spew log text in voluminous quantities (especially in debug mode). Most logs on Unix machines look similar because they are created by a centralized logging facility known as *syslog*. For our purposes, we can treat files created by *syslog* like any other text files.

Here's a simple Perl program to scan for the word "error" in a text-based log file:

```
open my $LOG, '<', "$logfile" or die "Unable to open $logfile:$!\n";
while(my $line = <$LOG>){
    print if $line =~ /\berror\b/i;
}
close $LOG;
```

Perl-savvy readers are probably itching to turn it into a one-liner. For those folks:

```
perl -ne 'print if /\berror\b/i' logfile
```

Reading Binary Log Files

Sometimes it's not that easy writing programs to deal with log files. Instead of nice, easily parsable text lines, some logging mechanisms produce nasty, gnarly binary files with proprietary formats that can't be parsed with a single line of Perl. Luckily, Perl isn't afraid of these miscreants. Let's look at a few approaches we can take when dealing with these files. We're going to look at two different examples of binary logs: Unix's *wtmp* file and Windows-based operating system event logs.

Back in Chapter 4, we touched briefly on the notion of logging in and logging out of a Unix host. Login and logout activity is tracked in a file called *wtmpx* (or *wtmp*) on most Unix variants. It is common to check this file whenever there is a question about a user's connection habits (e.g., what hosts does this person usually log in from?). It tends to live in different places depending on the operating system (e.g., Solaris has it in */var/adm*, Linux in */var/log*[*]).

On Windows, the event logs play a more generalized role. They are used as a central clearinghouse for logging practically all activity that takes place on these machines, including login and logout activity, OS messages, security events, etc. Their role is analogous to the Unix *syslog* service we mentioned earlier.

Using unpack()

Perl has a function called `unpack()` especially designed to parse binary and structured data. Let's take a look at how we might use it to deal with the *wtmpx* files. The format of *wtmp* and *wtmpx* differs from Unix variant to Unix variant. For this specific example, we'll look at the *wtmpx* file found on Solaris 10 and the Linux 2.6 *wtmp*. Here's a plain-text translation of the first two records in a Solaris 10 *wtmpx* file:

```
0000000   d   n   b  \0  \0  \0  \0  \0  \0  \0  \0  \0  \0  \0  \0  \0
0000020  \0  \0  \0  \0  \0  \0  \0  \0  \0  \0  \0  \0  \0  \0  \0  \0
0000040   t   s   /   1   p   t   s   /   1  \0  \0  \0  \0  \0  \0  \0
0000060  \0  \0  \0  \0  \0  \0  \0  \0  \0  \0  \0  \0  \0  \0  \0  \0
0000100  \0  \0  \0  \0  \0  \0   #  346  \0 007  \0  \0  \0  \0  \0  \0
0000120   D   9   .  253  \0  \t 313 234  \0  \0  \0  \0  \0  \0  \0  \0
0000140  \0  \0  \0  \0  \0  \0  \0  \0  \0  \0  \0  \0  \0  \0  \0  \0
0000160  \0   '   p   o   o   l   -   1   4   1   -   1   5   4   -   1
0000200   2   1   -   5   .   b   o   s   .   e   a   s   t   .   v   e
0000220   r   i   z   o   n   .   n   e   t  \0  \0  \0  \0  \0  \0  \0
0000240  \0  \0  \0  \0  \0  \0  \0  \0  \0  \0  \0  \0  \0  \0  \0  \0
*
0000560  \0  \0  \0   T   d   n   b  \0  \0  \0  \0  \0  \0  \0  \0  \0
0000600  \0  \0  \0  \0  \0  \0  \0  \0  \0  \0  \0  \0  \0  \0  \0  \0
0000620  \0  \0  \0  \0   t   s   /   2   p   t   s   /   2  \0  \0  \0
0000640  \0  \0  \0  \0  \0  \0  \0  \0  \0  \0  \0  \0  \0  \0  \0  \0
0000660  \0  \0  \0  \0  \0  \0  \0  \0  \0  \0   $   R  \0 007  \0  \0
```

---

[*] And Mac OS X has, sigh, its own logging framework called the Apple System Log facility. It does keep */var/run/utmpx* up-to-date at the same time, though.

```
0000700   \0  \0  \0  \0   D   9   /  212  \0 016   L  315  \0  \0  \0  \0
0000720   \0  \0  \0  \0  \0  \0  \0  \0   \0  \0  \0  \0  \0  \0  \0  \0
0000740   \0  \0  \0  \0  \0   '   p   o   o   l   -   1   4   1   -   1
0000760   5   4   -   1   2   1   -   5   .   b   o   s   .   e   a   s
0001000   t   .   v   e   r   i   z   o   n   .   n   e   t  \0  \0  \0
0001020   \0  \0  \0  \0  \0  \0  \0  \0  \0  \0  \0  \0  \0  \0  \0  \0
*
0001340   \0  \0  \0  \0  \0  \0  \0   T
```

Unless you are already familiar with the structure of this file, that "ASCII dump" (as it is called) of the data probably looks like line noise or some other kind of semirandom garbage. So how do we become acquainted with this file's structure?

The easiest way to understand the format of this file is to look at the source code for programs that read and write to it. If you are not literate in the C language, this may seem like a daunting task. Luckily, we don't actually have to understand or even look at most of the source code; we can just examine the portion that defines the file format.

All of the operating system programs that read and write to the *wtmp* file get their file definitions from a single, short C include file, which is very likely to be found at */usr/include/utmp.h* or *utmpx.h*. The part of the file we need to look at begins with a definition of the C data structure that will be used to hold the information. If you search for `struct utmp {`, you'll find the portion we need. The next lines after `struct utmp {` define each of the fields in this structure. These lines should each be commented using the /* *text* */ C comment convention.

Just to give you an idea of how different two versions of *wtmpx* can be, let's compare the relevant excerpts on these two operating systems.

Here's an excerpt from Solaris 10's *utmpx.h*:

```
/*
 * This data structure describes the utmp *file* contents using
 * fixed-width data types. It should only be used by the implementation.
 *
 * Applications should use the getutxent(3c) family of routines to interact
 * with this database.
 */

struct futmpx {
        char    ut_user[32];            /* user login name */
        char    ut_id[4];               /* inittab id */
        char    ut_line[32];            /* device name (console, lnxx) */
        pid32_t ut_pid;                 /* process id */
        int16_t ut_type;                /* type of entry */
        struct {
                int16_t e_termination;  /* process termination status */
                int16_t e_exit;         /* process exit status */
        } ut_exit;                      /* exit status of a process */
        struct timeval32 ut_tv;         /* time entry was made */
        int32_t ut_session;             /* session ID, user for windowing */
        int32_t pad[5];                 /* reserved for future use */
        int16_t ut_syslen;              /* significant length of ut_host */
```

```
            char    ut_host[257];              /* remote host name */
    };
```

And here's an excerpt from Linux 2.6's *bits/utmp.h*:

```
    struct utmp
    {
      short int ut_type;            /* Type of login.  */
      pid_t ut_pid;                 /* Process ID of login process.  */
      char ut_line[UT_LINESIZE];    /* Device name.  */
      char ut_id[4];                /* Inittab ID.  */
      char ut_user[UT_NAMESIZE];    /* Username.  */
      char ut_host[UT_HOSTSIZE];    /* Hostname for remote login.  */
      struct exit_status ut_exit;   /* Exit status of a process marked
                                       as DEAD_PROCESS.  */
      /* The ut_session and ut_tv fields must be the same size when compiled
         32- and 64-bit. This allows data files and shared memory to be
         shared between 32- and 64-bit applications.  */
    #if __WORDSIZE == 64 && defined __WORDSIZE_COMPAT32
      int32_t ut_session;           /* Session ID, used for windowing.  */
      struct
      {
        int32_t tv_sec;             /* Seconds.  */
        int32_t tv_usec;            /* Microseconds.  */
      } ut_tv;                      /* Time entry was made.  */
    #else
      long int ut_session;          /* Session ID, used for windowing.  */
        struct timeval ut_tv;       /* Time entry was made.  */
    #endif

      int32_t ut_addr_v6[4];        /* Internet address of remote host.  */
      char __unused[20];            /* Reserved for future use.  */
    };
```

These files provide all the clues we need to compose the necessary unpack() statement. unpack() takes a data format template as its first argument. It uses this template to determine how to disassemble the (usually) binary data it receives in its second argument. unpack() will take apart the data as instructed, returning a list in which each element corresponds to an element of your template.

Let's construct our template piece by piece, based on the C structure from the Solaris *utmpx.h* include file. There are many possible template letters we can use. I've translated the ones we'll use in Table 10-1, but you should check the pack() section of the *perlfunc* manual page for more information. Constructing these templates is not always straightforward; C compilers occasionally pad out values to satisfy alignment constraints. The command pstruct that ships with Perl can often help with quirks like these.

Table 10-1. Translating the utmpx.h C code to an unpack() template

C code	unpack() template	Template letter/repeat # translation
`char ut_user[32];`	A32	ASCII string (space-padded), 32 bytes long
`char ut_id[4];`	A4	ASCII string (space-padded), 4 bytes long
`char ut_line[32];`	A32	ASCII string (space-padded), 32 bytes long
`pid32_t ut_pid;`	l	A signed "long" value (4 bytes, which may not be the same as the size of a true long value on some machines)
`int16_t ut_type;`	s	A signed "short" value
`struct {`	s	A signed "short" value
`int16_t e_termination;`		
`int16_t e_exit;`	s	A signed "short" value
`} ut_exit;`		
	x2	Compiler-inserted padding
`struct {`	l	A signed "long" value
`time32_t tv_sec;`		
`int32_t tv_usec`	l	A signed "long" value
`} ut_tv;`		
`int32_t ut_session;`	l	A signed "long" value
`int32_t pad[5];`	x20	Skip 20 bytes for padding
`int16_t ut_syslen;`	s	A signed "short" value
`char ut_host[257];`	Z257	ASCII string, null-terminated up to 257 bytes including \0
	x	Compiler-inserted padding

Having constructed our template, let's use it in a real piece of code:

```
# template for Solaris 9/10 wtmpx
my $template = 'A32 A4 A32 l s s s x2 l l l x20 s Z257 x';

my $recordsize = length( pack( $template, () ) );

open my $WTMP, '<', '/var/adm/wtmpx'  or die "Unable to open wtmpx:$!\n";

my ($ut_user, $ut_id,                 $ut_line,   $ut_pid,
    $ut_type, $ut_e_termination, $ut_e_exit, $tv_sec,
    $tv_usec, $ut_session,          $ut_syslen, $ut_host,
) = ();

# read wtmpx one record at a time
my $record;
```

```
while ( read( $WTMP, $record, $recordsize ) ) {

    # unpack it using our template
    (   $ut_user, $ut_id,                $ut_line,   $ut_pid,
        $ut_type, $ut_e_termination, $ut_e_exit, $tv_sec,
        $tv_usec, $ut_session,          $ut_syslen, $ut_host
    ) = unpack( $template, $record );

    # this makes the output more readable - the value 8 comes
    # from /usr/include/utmp.h:
    # #define DEAD_PROCESS     8
    if ( $ut_type == 8 ) {
        $ut_host = '(exit)';
    }
    print "$ut_line:$ut_user:$ut_host:" . scalar localtime($tv_sec) . "\n";
}

close $WTMP;
```

Here's the output of this little program:

```
pts/176:vezt:c-61-212-209-21.hsd1.ma.comcast.net:Wed Apr 16 06:37:44 2008
pts/176:vezt:(exit):Wed Apr 16 06:38:03 2008
pts/147:birnou:pool-50-29-232-81.bos.eas.veriz.net:Wed Apr 16 08:09:27 2008
pts/17:croche:ce-23-213-189-154.nycap.res.rr.com:Wed Apr 16 08:34:18 2008
pts/17:croche:(exit):Wed Apr 16 08:34:45 2008
pts/139:hermd:d-66-249-250-270.hsd1.ut.comc.net:Wed Apr 16 09:45:57 2008
pts/139:hermd:(exit):Wed Apr 16 09:58:55 2008
```

One small comment on the code before we move on: read() takes a number of bytes to read as its third argument. Rather than hardcoding in a record size like "32", we use a handy property of the pack() function. When handed an empty list, pack() returns a null or space-padded string the size of a record. This allows us to feed pack() an arbitrary record template and have it tell us how big a record it is:

```
my $recordsize = length( pack( $template, () ) );
```

You Know You're a Power User When...

Of all the methods we'll look at for accessing logging information, the unpack() method is the one with the greatest potential to leave you feeling like a power user. This is the one you'll need to use if you find the other methods are failing due to data corruption. For example, I've heard of cases where the *wtmpx* file became damaged in a way that left the *last* executable just sputtering error messages. When that happens it's sometimes possible to write code that will skip the damaged part (via sysread() in concert with unpack()) and allow you to recover the rest of the file. You'll definitely have earned your superhero cape the first time you succeed in one of these situations.

The unpack() method is not the only intra-Perl method for accessing the *wtmp/x* data. At least one module uses the vendor-approved system calls (getutxent(), etc.) for reading these files. We'll use that module in an example a little later.

Calling an OS (or Someone Else's) Binary

Sifting through *wtmp* files is such a common task that Unix systems ship with a command called `last` for printing a human-readable dump of the binary file. Here's some sample output showing approximately the same data as the output of our previous example:

```
vezt      pts/176     c-61-212-209-21. Wed Apr 16 06:37 - 06:38  (00:00)
birnou    pts/147     pool-50-29-232-8 Wed Apr 16 08:09    still logged
croche    pts/17      ce-23-213-189-15 Wed Apr 16 08:34 - 08:34  (00:00)
hermd     pts/139     d-66-249-250-270 Wed Apr 16 09:45 - 09:58  (00:12)
```

We can easily call binaries like *last* from Perl. This code will show all the unique usernames found in our current *wtmpx* file:

```
# location of the last command binary
my $lastexec = '/bin/last';

open my $LAST, '-|', "$lastexec" or die "Unable to run $lastexec:$!\n";
my %seen;
while(my $line = <$LAST>){
    last if $line =~ /^$/;
    my $user = (split(' ', $line))[0];
    print "$user\n" unless exists $seen{$user};
    $seen{$user}='';
}
close $LAST or die "Unable to properly close pipe:$!\n";
```

So why use this method when `unpack()` looked like it could serve all your needs? Portability. As you've seen, the format of the *wtmp/x* file differs from Unix variant to Unix variant. On top of this, a single vendor may change the format of *wtmp/x* between OS releases, rendering your perfectly good `unpack()` template invalid.

However, one thing you *can* reasonably depend on is the continued presence of a `last` command that will read this format, independent of any underlying format changes. If you use the `unpack()` method, you have to create and maintain separate template strings for each different *wtmp* format you plan to parse.[†]

The biggest disadvantage of using this method rather than `unpack()` is the increased sophistication of the field parsing you need to do in the program. With `unpack()`, all the fields are automatically extracted from the data for you. Using our *last* example, you may find yourself with `split()` or regular expression-resistant output like this, all in the same output:

```
user    console                    Wed Oct 14 20:35 - 20:37  (00:01)
user    pts/12      208.243.191.21 Wed Oct 14 09:19 - 18:12  (08:53)
user    pts/17      208.243.191.21 Tue Oct 13 13:36 - 17:09  (03:33)
reboot  system boot                Tue Oct  6 14:13
```

---

† There's a bit of hand waving going on here, since you still have to track where the *last* executable is found in each Unix environment and compensate for any differences in the format of each program's output.

Your eye has little trouble picking out the columns, but any program that parses this output will have to deal with the missing information in lines 1 and 4. `unpack()` can still be used to tease apart this output because it has fixed field widths, but that's not always possible. There are other techniques for writing more sophisticated parsers, but that's probably more work than you desire.

Using the OS's Logging API

For this approach, let's switch our focus to the Windows Event Log Service. As mentioned earlier, Windows machines unfortunately do not log to plain-text files. The only supported way to get to the log file data is through a set of special API calls. Most users rely on the Event Viewer program, shown in Figure 10-1, to retrieve this data for them.

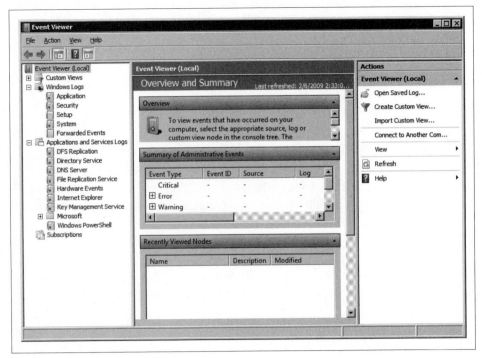

Figure 10-1. The Windows Event Viewer

Luckily, there is a Perl module (written by Jesse Dougherty and later updated by Martin Pauley and Bret Giddings) that allows easy access to the Event Log API calls.[‡] We'll walk through a more complex version of this program later in this chapter, but for now

---

[‡] Log information in Windows can also be retrieved using the Window Management Instrumentation (WMI) framework we touched on in Chapter 4, but `Win32::EventLog` is easier to use and understand. If you need to parse Event Log data stored on a non-Windows machine, `Parse::EventLog` by John Eaglesham makes a valiant attempt.

here's a simple program that dumps a listing of events in the *System* event log in a *syslog-like* format:

```
use Win32::EventLog;
# each event has a type - this is a translation of the common types
my %type = (1  => 'ERROR',
            2  => 'WARNING',
            4  => 'INFORMATION',
            8  => 'AUDIT_SUCCESS',
            16 => 'AUDIT_FAILURE');

# if this is set, we also retrieve the full text of every
# message on each Read()
$Win32::EventLog::GetMessageText = 1;

# open the System event log
my $log = new Win32::EventLog('System')
  or die "Unable to open system log:$^E\n";

my $event = '';
# read through it one record at a time, starting with the first entry
while ($log->Read((EVENTLOG_SEQUENTIAL_READ|EVENTLOG_FORWARDS_READ),
             1,$entry)){
    print scalar localtime($entry->{TimeGenerated}).' ';
    print $entry->{Computer}.'['.($entry->{EventID} &
          0xffff).'] ';
    print $entry->{Source}.':'.$type{$entry->{EventType}}.': ';
    print $entry->{Message};
}
```

Command-line utilities like *last* that dump event logs into plain ASCII format also exist for Windows. We'll see one of these utilities in action later in this chapter, and shortly we'll see an example of using the Unix equivalent of an OS logging API for *wtmp* data.

Structure of Log File Data

In addition to the format in which log files present their data, it is important to think about the contents of these files, because *what* the data represents and *how* it is represented both contribute to our plan of attack when programming. With log file contents, often a distinction can be made between data that is *stateful* and data that is *stateless*. Let's take a look at a couple of examples that will make this distinction clear.

Here's a three-line snippet from an Apache web server log. Each line represents a request answered by the web server:

```
esnet-118.dynamic.rpi.edu - - [13/Dec/2008:00:04:20 -0500] "GET home/u1/tux/
tuxedo05.gif

HTTP/1.0" 200 18666 ppp-206-170-3-49.okld03.pacbell.net - - [13/Dec/2008:00:04:21
 -0500] "GET home/u2/news.htm

HTTP/1.0" 200 6748 ts007d39.ftl-fl.concentric.net - - [13/Dec/2008:00:04:22 -0500]
 "GET home/u1/bgc.jpg HTTP/1.1" 304 -
```

Here are a few lines from a printer daemon log file:

```
Aug 14 12:58:46 warhol  printer: cover/door open
Aug 14 12:58:58 warhol  printer: error cleared
Aug 14 17:16:26 warhol  printer: offline or intervention needed
Aug 14 17:16:43 warhol  printer: error cleared
Aug 15 20:40:45 warhol  printer: paper out
Aug 15 20:40:48 warhol  printer: error cleared
```

In both cases, each line of the log file is independent of every other line in the file. We can find patterns or aggregate lines together to gather statistics, but there's nothing inherent in the data that connects the log file entries to each other.

Now consider some slightly doctored entries from a *sendmail* mail log:

```
Dec 13 05:28:27 mailhub sendmail[26690]: FAA26690:
from=<user@has.a.godcomplex.com>, size=643, class=0, pri=30643, nrcpts=1,
msgid=<200812131032.CAA22824@has.a.godcomplex.com>, proto=ESMTP,
 relay=user@has.a.godcomplex.com [216.32.32.176]

Dec 13 05:29:13 mailhub sendmail[26695]: FAA26695: from=<root@host.example.edu>,
size=9600, class=0, pri=39600, nrcpts=1,
msgid=<200812131029.FAA15005@host.example.edu>, proto=ESMTP,
 relay=root@host.example.edu [192.168.16.69]

Dec 13 05:29:15 mailhub sendmail[26691]: FAA26690: to=<user@host.example.edu>,
 delay=00:00:02, xdelay=00:00:01, mailer=local, stat=Sent

Dec 13 05:29:19 mailhub sendmail[26696]: FAA26695: to="|IFS=' '&&exec /usr/bin/
procmail -f-||exit 75 #user", ctladdr=user (6603/104), delay=00:00:06,
xdelay=00:00:06, mailer=prog, stat=Sent
```

Unlike in the previous examples, there is a definite connection between the lines in this file. Figure 10-2 makes that connection explicit.

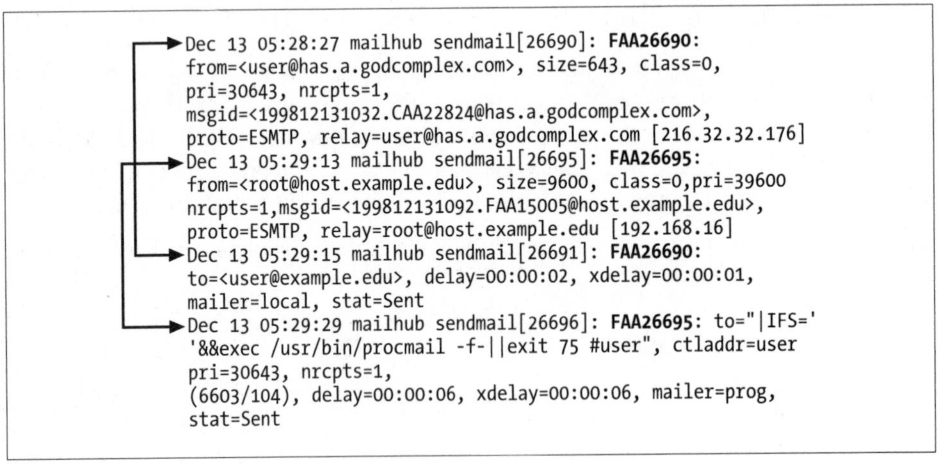

Figure 10-2. Related entries in the sendmail log

Each line has at least one partner entry that shows the source and destination(s) of each message. When a message enters the system it is assigned a unique "Message-ID," highlighted in the figure, which identifies that message while it is in play. This message ID allows us to associate related lines in an interleaved log file, essentially giving a message an existence or "state" in between entries in the log file.

Sometimes we care about the "distance" between state transitions. Take, for instance, the *wtmpx* file we looked at earlier in this chapter: in that file we're interested not only in when a user logs in and out (the two state transitions in the log), but also in the time between these two events (i.e., how long the user was logged in).

The most sophisticated log files can add another twist. Here are some excerpts from a POP (Post Office Protocol) server's log file while the server is in debug mode. The names and IP addresses have been changed to protect the innocent:

```
Jan 14 15:53:45 mailhub popper[20243]: Debugging turned on
Jan 14 15:53:45 mailhub popper[20243]: (v2.53) Servicing request from
"client" at 129.X.X.X
Jan 14 15:53:45 mailhub popper[20243]: +OK QPOP (version 2.53) at mailhub starting.
Jan 14 15:53:45 mailhub popper[20243]: Received: "USER username"
Jan 14 15:53:45 mailhub popper[20243]: +OK Password required for username.
Jan 14 15:53:45 mailhub popper[20243]: Received: "pass xxxxxxxxx"
Jan 14 15:53:45 mailhub popper[20243]: +OK username has 1 message (26627 octets).
Jan 14 15:53:46 mailhub popper[20243]: Received: "LIST"
Jan 14 15:53:46 mailhub popper[20243]: +OK 1 messages (26627 octets)
Jan 14 15:53:46 mailhub popper[20243]: Received: "RETR 1"
Jan 14 15:53:46 mailhub popper[20243]: +OK 26627 octets
<message text appears here>
Jan 14 15:53:56 mailhub popper[20243]: Received: "DELE 1"
Jan 14 15:53:56 mailhub popper[20243]: Deleting message 1 at offset 0 of length 26627
Jan 14 15:53:56 mailhub popper[20243]: +OK Message 1 has been deleted.
Jan 14 15:53:56 mailhub popper[20243]: Received: "QUIT"
Jan 14 15:53:56 mailhub popper[20243]: +OK Pop server at mailhub signing off.
Jan 14 15:53:56 mailhub popper[20243]: (v2.53) Ending request
  from "user" at (client) 129.X.X.X
```

Not only do we encounter connections ("Servicing request from...") and disconnections ("Ending request from..."), but we have information detailing what took place in between these state transitions.

Each of the middle events also provides potentially useful "distance" information. If there was a problem with our POP server, we might look to see how long each step in the output took.

In the case of an FTP server, you may be able to draw some conclusions from this data about how people interact with your site. On average, how long do people stay connected before they transfer files? Do they pause between commands for a long time? Do they always travel from one part of your site to another before downloading the same file? The interstitial data can be a rich source of information.

Dealing with Log File Information

Once you've learned how to access your logging data programmatically, two important applications start begging to be addressed: logging information space management and log analysis. Let's look at each in turn.

Space Management of Logging Information

The downside to having programs that can provide useful or verbose logging output is the amount of disk space this output can consume. This is a concern for all three operating systems covered in this book: Unix, Mac OS X, and Windows. Windows is probably the least troublesome of the lot, because its central logging facility has built-in autotrimming support.

Usually, the task of keeping the log files down to a reasonable size is handed off to the system administrator. Most Unix vendors provide some sort of automated log size management mechanism with the OS, but it often handles only the select set of log files shipped with the machine. As soon as you add another service to a machine that creates a separate log file, it becomes necessary to tweak (or even toss) the vendor-supplied solution.

Log rotation

The usual solution to the space problem is to *rotate* the log files. (We'll explore an unusual solution in the next subsection.) After a specific interval has passed or a certain file size has been reached, we rename the current log file (e.g., *logfile* becomes *logfile.0*). The logging process is then continued into an empty file. The next time the specified interval or limit is reached, we repeat the process, first renaming the original backup file (e.g., renaming *logfile.0* to *logfile.1*) and then renaming the current log file to *logfile.0*. This process is repeated until a set number backup files have been created, at which point the oldest backup file is deleted. Figure 10-3 illustrates this process.

This method allows us to keep on hand a reasonable, finite amount of log data. Table 10-2 provides one recipe for log rotation and the Perl functions needed to perform each step.

Table 10-2. A recipe for log rotation in Perl

Process	Perl
Move the older backup logs out of the way (i.e., move each one to a new name in the sequence).	rename(), or File::Copy::move() if moving files across filesystems.
If necessary, signal the process creating this particular log file to close the current file and cease logging to disk until told otherwise.	kill() for programs that take signals; system() or `` (back-ticks) if another administrative program has to be called for this purpose.
Copy or move the log file that was just in use to another file.	File::Copy to copy, rename() to rename (or File::Copy::move() if moving files across filesystems).

Process	Perl
If necessary, truncate the current log file.	`truncate()` or `open my $FILE,'>','`*`filename`*`'.`
If necessary, signal the logging process to resume logging.	See row 2 of this table.
If desired, compress or post-process the copied file.	`system()` or ` `` ` (backticks) to run a compression program; `Compress::Zlib` or other code for post-processing.
Delete other, older log file copies.	`stat()` to examine file sizes and dates; `unlink()` to delete files.

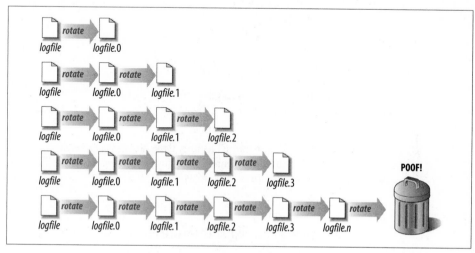

Figure 10-3. A pictorial representation of log rotation

There are many variations on this theme. Everyone and their aunt's vendors have written their own scripts for log rotation. Thus, it should come as no surprise that there's a Perl module to handle log rotation. Let's look at `Logfile::Rotate`, by Paul Gampe.

`Logfile::Rotate` uses the object-oriented programming convention of first creating a new log file object instance and then running a method of that instance. First, we create a new instance with the parameters found in Table 10-3.

Table 10-3. Logfile::Rotate parameters

Parameter	Purpose
`File`	Name of log file to rotate
Count (optional, default: 7)	Number of backup files to keep around
Gzip (optional, default: Perl's default *gzip* executable name as found during the Perl build—must be in your path)	Full path to *gzip* compression program executable
Post	Code to be executed after the rotation has been completed, as in row 5 of Table 10-2

Here's some example code that uses these parameters:

```perl
use Logfile::Rotate;
my $logfile = new Logfile::Rotate(
                File  => '/var/adm/log/syslog',
                Count => 5,
                Gzip  => '/usr/local/bin/gzip',
                Post  =>
                    sub {
                        open my $PID, '<', '/etc/syslog.pid' or
                            die "Unable to open pid file:$!\n";
                        chomp(my $pid = <$PID>);
                        close $PID;
                        kill 'HUP', $pid;
                        }
            );
# Log file locked (really) and loaded. Now let's rotate it.
$logfile->rotate();
# make sure the log file is unlocked (destroying object unlocks file)
undef $logfile;
```

 The preceding code has *three* potential security flaws. See if you can pick them out before looking at the sidebar "Identifying and Fixing Insecure Code" for the answers and tips on how to avoid all three.

Identifying and Fixing Insecure Code

Now that you've pored over the `Logfile::Rotate` code looking for security holes, let's talk about them. Since this module is often run by a privileged user (such as *root*), there are a few concerns:

1. The /usr/local/bin/gzip command will be run as that privileged user. We've done the right thing by calling the command with a full path (*important!*), but it behooves you to check just who has filesystem permissions to modify/replace that executable. One perhaps slightly safer way to sidestep this problem (presuming you retain total control over who can install Perl modules) is to change the line to `Gzip => 'lib'`. This causes `Logfile::Rotate` to call `Compress::Zlib` instead of calling out to a separate binary to do the compression.

2. In the `Post` section, the code happily reads /etc/syslog.pid without seeing if that file could be tampered with by a malicious party. Is the file world-writable? Is it a link to something else? Does the right user own the file? Our code doesn't care, but it should. It would be easy to check its permissions via `stat()` before proceeding.

3. In the same section, the code blithely sends a HUP signal to the PID number it read from the file just mentioned. It makes no attempt to determine if that process ID actually refers to a running *syslog* process. More defensive coding would check the process table first (perhaps with one of the process table listing strategies we discussed in Chapter 4) before sending the signal.

> These are the most blatant problems with the code. Be sure to read the section on safe scripting in Chapter 1 for more thoughts on the matter.

Circular buffering

We've just discussed the traditional log rotation method for dealing with storage of ever-growing logs. Now let me show you a more unusual approach that you can add to your toolkit.

Here's a common scenario: you're trying to debug a server daemon that provides a torrent of log output. You're only interested in a small part of the total output, perhaps just the lines the server produces after you run some sort of test with a special client. Saving all of the log output to disk as usual would fill your disk quickly. Rotating the logs as often as would be needed with this volume of output would slow down the server. What do you do?

I wrote a program called *bigbuffy* to deal with this conundrum. The approach is pretty straightforward. *bigbuffy* reads from its usual "standard" or "console" input one line at a time. These lines are stored in a circular buffer of a set size (see Figure 10-4). When the buffer is full, it starts filling from the top again. This read/store process continues until *bigbuffy* receives a signal from the user. Upon receiving this signal, it dumps the current contents of the buffer to a file and returns to its normal cycle. What's left behind on disk is essentially a window into the log stream, showing just the data you need.

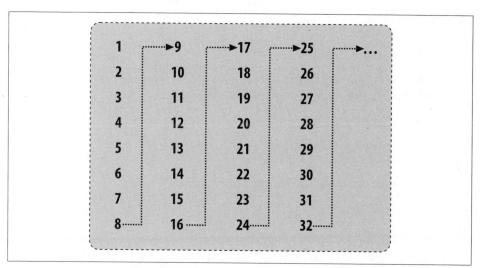

Figure 10-4. Logging to a circular buffer

bigbuffy can be paired with a service-monitoring program like those found in Chapter 13. As soon as the monitor detects a problem, it can signal *bigbuffy* to dump its log buffer, leaving you with a snapshot of the log localized to the failure instance (assuming your buffer is large enough and your monitor noticed the problem in time).

Here's a simplified version of *bigbuffy*. The code is longer than the examples we've seen so far in this chapter, but it's not very complex. We'll use it in a moment as a springboard for addressing some important issues, such as input blocking and security:

```perl
use Getopt::Long;

my @buffer;                  # buffer for storing input
my $dbuffsize = 200;         # default circular buffer size (in lines)
my $whatline  = 0;           # start line in circular buffer
my $dumpnow   = 0;           # flag to indicate dump requested

# parse the options
my ( $buffsize, $dumpfile );
GetOptions(
    'buffsize=i' => \$buffsize,
    'dumpfile=s' => \$dumpfile,
);
$buffsize ||= $dbuffsize;

# set up the signal handler and initialize a counter
die "USAGE: $0 [--buffsize=<lines>] --dumpfile=<filename>"
  unless ( length($dumpfile) );

$SIG{'USR1'} = \&dumpnow;     # set a signal handler for dump

# and away we go! (with just a simple
# read line-store line loop)
while ( defined( $_ = <> ) ) {

    # Insert line into data structure.
    # Note: we do this first, even if we've caught a signal.
    # Better to dump an extra line than lose a line of data if
    # something goes wrong in the dumping process.

    $buffer[$whatline] = $_;

    # where should the next line go?
    $whatline = ++$whatline % $buffsize;

    # if we receive a signal, dump the current buffer
    if ($dumpnow) {
        dodump();
    }
}

# simple signal handler that just sets an exception flag,
# see perlipc(1)
sub dumpnow {
    $dumpnow = 1;
}
```

```
# dump the circular buffer out to a file, appending to file if
# it exists
sub dodump {
    my $line;        # counter for line dump
    my $exists;      # flag, does the output file exist already?
    my $DUMP_FH;     # filehandle for dump file
    my ( @firststat, @secondstat );    # to hold output of lstats

    $dumpnow = 0;                      # reset the flag and signal handler
    $SIG{'USR1'} = \&dumpnow;

    if ( -e $dumpfile and ( ! -f $dumpfile or -l $dumpfile ) ) {
        warn 'ALERT: dumpfile exists and is not a plain file, '.
            "skipping dump.\n";
        return undef;
    }

    # We have to take special precautions when we're doing an
    # append. The next set of "if" statements performs a set of
    # security checks while opening the file for appending.
    if ( -e $dumpfile ) {
        $exists = 1;
        unless ( @firststat = lstat $dumpfile ) {
            warn "Unable to lstat $dumpfile, skipping dump.\n";
            return undef;
        }
        if ( $firststat[3] != 1 ) {
            warn "$dumpfile is a hard link, skipping dump.\n";
            return undef;
        }
    }
    unless ( open $DUMP_FH, '>>', $dumpfile ) {
        warn "Unable to open $dumpfile for append, skipping dump:$!.\n";
        return undef;
    }
    if ($exists) {
        unless ( @secondstat = lstat $DUMP_FH ) {
            warn "Unable to lstat opened $dumpfile, skipping dump.\n";
            return undef;
        }

        if (
            $firststat[0] != $secondstat[0] or    # check dev num
            $firststat[1] != $secondstat[1] or    # check inode
            $firststat[7] != $secondstat[7]       # check sizes
          )
        {
            warn "SECURITY PROBLEM: lstats don't match, skipping dump.\n";
            return undef;
        }
    }

    $line = $whatline;
    print {$DUMP_FH} '-' . scalar(localtime) . ( '-' x 50 ) . "\n";
```

```
    do {
        # print only valid lines in case buffer was not full
        print {$DUMP_FH} $buffer[$line] if defined $buffer[$line];
        $line = ++$line % $buffsize;
    } until $line == $whatline;

    close $DUMP_FH;

    # zorch the active buffer to avoid leftovers
    # in future dumps
    $whatline = 1;
    @buffer   = ();

    return 1;
}
```

A program like this can stir up interesting implementation issues. We'll look at a few of them here.

Input blocking in log-processing programs. I mentioned earlier that this is a simplified version of *bigbuffy*. For ease of implementation, especially across platforms, this version has an unsavory characteristic: while dumping data to disk, it can't continue reading input. During a buffer dump, the OS may tell the program sending output to *bigbuffy* to pause operation pending the drain of its output buffer. Luckily, the dump is fast, so the window where this could happen is very small, but this is still less passive than you might like.

Possible solutions to this problem include:

- Rewriting *bigbuffy* to use a double-buffered, multitasking approach. Instead of using a single storage buffer, it would use two. Upon receiving the signal, the program would begin to log to a second buffer while a child process or another thread handled dumping the first buffer. At the next signal, the buffers would be swapped again.

- Rewriting *bigbuffy* to interleave reading and writing while it is dumping. The simplest version of this approach would involve writing some number of lines to the output file each time a new line is read. This gets a bit tricky if the log output being read is "bursty" instead of arriving as constant flow, though, as you wouldn't want to have to wait for a new line of output before you could receive the requested log buffer dump. You'd have to use some sort of timeout or internal clock mechanism to get around this problem.

Both approaches are hard to pull off portably in a cross-platform environment, hence the simplified version shown in this book.

Security in log-processing programs. You may have noticed that *bigbuffy* takes considerable care with the opening and writing of its output file. This is an example of the defensive coding style mentioned earlier, in the section "Log rotation" on page 388. If this program is to be used to debug server daemons, it is likely to be run by privileged users on

---

a system. It is therefore important to think about unpleasant situations that might allow the program to be abused.

One possible scenario would be swapping the link to the output file with a link to another file. If we opened and wrote to the file without checking its identity, we might find ourselves inadvertently stomping on an important file like */etc/passwd*. Even if we check the output file before opening it, it might be possible for a malicious party to switch it on us before we begin writing to it. To avoid this scenario:

- We check if the output file exists already. If it does, we `lstat()` it to get the file-system information.
- We open the file in append mode.
- Before we actually write to the file, we `lstat()` the open filehandle and check that it is still the same file we expect it to be and that it hasn't been switched since we initially checked it. If it is not the same file (e.g., if someone swapped the file with a link right before the **open**), we do *not* write to the file and we complain loudly. This last step avoids the potential race condition mentioned in Chapter 1.

If we didn't have to append, we could instead open a temporary file with a randomized name (so it couldn't be guessed ahead of time) and then rename the temporary file into place. Perl ships with Tim Jenness's `File::Temp` module to help you do things like this.

These sorts of gyrations are necessary on most Unix systems because Unix was not originally designed with security as a high priority. Windows also has "junctions,"[*] the rough equivalent of symbolic links, but I have yet to see any indication that they pose the same sort of security threat due to their implementation.

Log Parsing and Analysis

Some system administrators never get past the rotation phase in their relationships with their log files. As long as the necessary information exists on disk when it is needed for debugging, they never put any thought into using their log file information for any other purpose. I'd like to suggest that this is a shortsighted view, and that a little log file analysis can go a long way. We're going to look at a few approaches you can use for performing log file analysis in Perl, starting with the most simple and getting more complex as we go along.

Most of the examples in this section use Unix log files for demonstration purposes, since the average Unix system has ample logs just waiting to be analyzed, but the approaches offered here are not OS-specific.

---

[*] You'll also hear the term "reparse point" in this context, because Microsoft has been refining its terminology about these sorts of things over the course of several OS releases. At the time of this writing, junctions are considered to be created from reparse points.

Stream read-count

The easiest approach is the simple "read and count," where we read through a stream of log data looking for interesting data, and increment a counter when we find it. Here's a simple example that counts the number of times a machine has rebooted based on the contents of a Solaris 10 *wtmpx* file:

```
# template for Solaris 10 wtmpx
my $template = 'A32 A4 A32 l s s s x2 l l l x20 s Z257 x';

# determine the size of a record
my $recordsize = length( pack( $template, () ) );

# open the file
open my $WTMP, '<', '/var/adm/wtmpx' or die "Unable to open wtmpx:$!\n";

my ($ut_user, $ut_id,               $ut_line,  $ut_pid,
    $ut_type, $ut_e_termination, $ut_e_exit, $tv_sec,
    $tv_usec, $ut_session_pad,     $ut_syslen, $ut_host
   )
   = ();

my $reboots = 0;

# read through it one record at a time
while ( read( $WTMP, $record, $recordsize ) ) {
    (   $ut_user, $ut_id,               $ut_line,  $ut_pid,
        $ut_type, $ut_e_termination, $ut_e_exit, $tv_sec,
        $tv_usec, $ut_session,        $ut_syslen, $ut_host
    )
    = unpack( $template, $record );

    if ( $ut_line eq 'system boot' ) {
        print "rebooted " . scalar localtime($tv_sec) . "\n";
        $reboots++;
    }
}

close $WTMP;
print "Total reboots: $reboots\n";
```

Let's extend this methodology and explore an example of statistics gathering using the Windows Event Log facility. As mentioned before, Windows has a well-developed and fairly sophisticated system-logging mechanism. This sophistication makes it a bit trickier for the beginning Perl programmer. We'll have to use some Windows-specific Perl module routines to get at the basic log information.

Windows programs and operating system components log their activities by posting "events" to one of several different event logs. The OS records in the log basic information such as when the event was posted, which program or OS function posted it, what kind of event it is (informational or something more serious), etc.

Unlike in Unix, the actual description of the event, or log message, is not actually stored with the event entry. Instead, an `EventID` is posted to the log. This `EventID` contains a reference to a specific message compiled into a program library (*.dll*). Retrieving a log message given an `EventID` is tricky. The process involves looking up the proper library in the registry and loading the library by hand. Luckily, the current version of Win32::EventLog performs this process for us automatically (see `$Win32::EventLog::GetMessageText` in our first `Win32::EventlLog` example, in the section "Using the OS's Logging API" on page 384).

For our next example, we're going to generate some simple statistics on the number of entries currently in the *System* log, where they have come from, and their level of severity. We'll write this program in a slightly different manner from how we wrote the first Windows logging example in this chapter.

Our first step is to load the `Win32::EventLog` module, which contains the glue between Perl and the Windows event log routines. We then initialize a hash table that will be used to contain the results of our calls to the log-reading routines. Perl would normally take care of this for us, but sometimes it is good to add code like this for the benefit of others who will be reading the program. Finally, we set up a small list of event types that we will use later for printing statistics:

```
use Win32::EventLog;

# this is the equivalent of $event{Length => NULL, RecordNumber =>NULL, ...}
my %event;
my @fields = qw(Length RecordNumber TimeGenerated TimeWritten EventID
    EventType Category ClosingRecordNumber Source Computer Strings Data);
@event{@fields} = (NULL) x @fields;

# partial list of event types: Type 1 is "Error",
# 2 is "Warning", etc.
my @types = ('','Error','Warning','','Information');
```

Our next step is to open up the *System* event log. The `Open()` call places an *EventLog* handle into `$EventLog` that we can use as our connection to this particular log:

```
my $EventLog    = '';     # the handle to the event Log
my $event       = '';     # the event we'll be returning
my $numevents   = 0;      # total number of events in log
my $oldestevent = 0;      # oldest event in the log
Win32::EventLog::Open($EventLog,'System','')
   or die "Could not open System log:$^E\n";
```

Once we have this handle, we can use it to retrieve the number of events in the log and the ID of the oldest record:

```
$EventLog->GetNumber($numevents);
$EventLog->GetOldest($oldestevent);
```

We use this information as part of our first `Read()` statement, which positions us at the place in the log right before the first record. This is the equivalent of `seek()`ing to the beginning of a file:

```
$EventLog->Read( ( EVENTLOG_SEEK_READ | EVENTLOG_FORWARDS_READ ),
    $numevents + $oldestevent, $event );
```

From here on in, we use a simple loop to read each log entry in turn. The EVENTLOG_SEQUENTIAL_READ flag says "continue reading from the position of the last record read." The EVENTLOG_FORWARDS_READ flag moves us forward in chronological order.[†] The third argument to Read() is the record offset: in this case it's 0, because we want to pick up right where we left off. As we read each record, we record its Source and EventType in a hash table of counters:

```
my %source;
my %types;
for ( my $i = 0; $i < $numevents; $i++ ) {
$EventLog->Read( ( EVENTLOG_SEQUENTIAL_READ | EVENTLOG_FORWARDS_READ ),
        0, $event );
    $source{ $event->{Source} }++;
    $types{ $event->{EventType} }++;
}

# now print out the totals
print "--> Event Log Source Totals:\n";
for ( sort keys %source ) {
    print "$_: $source{$_}\n";
}
print '-' x 30, "\n";
print "--> Event Log Type Totals:\n";
for ( sort keys %types ) {
    print "$types[$_]: $types{$_}\n";
}
print '-' x 30, "\n";
print "Total number of events: $numevents\n";
```

My results look like this:

```
--> Event Log Source Totals:
Application Popup: 4
BROWSER: 228
DCOM: 12
Dhcp: 12
EventLog: 351
Mouclass: 6
NWCWorkstation: 2
Print: 27
Rdr: 12
RemoteAccess: 108
SNMP: 350
Serial: 175
Service Control Manager: 248
Sparrow: 5
Srv: 201
msbusmou: 162
```

[†] Here's another place where the Win32 event log routines are more flexible than usual. Our code could have moved to the end of the log and read backward in time if we wanted to do that for some reason.

```
msi8042: 3
msinport: 162
mssermou: 151
qic117: 2
----------------------------
--> Event Log Type Totals:
Error: 493
Warning: 714
Information: 1014
----------------------------
Total number of events: 2220
```

As promised, here's some sample code that relies on a *last*-like program to dump the contents of the event log. It uses a program called *ElDump* by Jesper Lauritsen, which you can download from *http://www.ibt.ku.dk/Jesper/NTtools/*. *ElDump* is similar to *DumpEl*, which can be found in several of the resource kits (and online at *http://www .microsoft.com/windows2000/techinfo/reskit/tools/existing/dumpel-o.asp*):

```perl
my $eldump = 'c:\bin\eldump';    # path to ElDump

# output data field separated by ~ and without full message
# text (faster)
my $dumpflags = '-l system -c ~ -M';

open my $ELDUMP, '-|', "$eldump $dumpflags" or die "Unable to run $eldump:$!\n";

print 'Reading system log.';

my ( $date, $time, $source, $type, $category, $event, $user, $computer );
while ( defined ($_ = <$ELDUMP>) ) {
    ( $date, $time, $source, $type, $category, $event, $user, $computer ) =
        split('~');
    $$type{$source}++;
    print '.';
}
print "done.\n";

close $ELDUMP;

# for each type of event, print out the sources and number of
# events per source
foreach $type (qw(Error Warning Information AuditSuccess AuditFailure))
{
    print '-' x 65, "\n";
    print uc($type) . "s by source:\n";
    for ( sort keys %$type ) {
        print "$_ ($$type{$_})\n";
    }
}
print '-' x 65, "\n";
```

Here's a snippet from the output:

```
ERRORs by source:
BROWSER (8)
```

```
Cdrom (2)
DCOM (15)
Dhcp (2524)
Disk (1)
EventLog (5)
RemoteAccess (30)
Serial (24)
Service Control Manager (100)
Sparrow (2)
atapi (2)
i8042prt (4)
-------------------------------------------------------------
WARNINGs by source:
BROWSER (80)
Cdrom (22)
Dhcp (76)
Print (8)
Srv (82)
```

A simple stream read-count variation

A simple variation of the stream read-count approach involves making multiple passes through the data. This is sometimes necessary for large data sets and cases where it takes an initial scan to determine the difference between interesting and uninteresting data. Programmatically, this means that after the first pass through the input, you do one of the following:

- Move back to the beginning of the data stream (which could just be a file) using seek() or an API-specific call.
- Close and reopen the filehandle. This is often the only choice when you are reading the output of a program like *last*.

Here's an example where a multiple-pass read-count approach might be useful. Imagine you have to deal with a security breach where an account on your system has been compromised. One of the first questions you might want to ask is, "Has any other account been compromised from the same source machine?" Finding a comprehensive answer to this seemingly simple question turns out to be trickier than you might expect. Let's take a first shot at the problem. This code takes the name of a user as its first argument and an optional regular expression as a second argument for filtering out hosts we wish to ignore:

```
use Perl6::Form;
use User::Utmp qw(:constants);

my ( $user, $ignore ) = @ARGV;
my $format
    = '{<<<<<<<} {<<<<<<<<<<<<<<<<<<<<<<<<<<<<<<<<<} {<<<<<<<<<<<<<<<<<<<<<<<}';

User::Utmp::utmpxname('/var/adm/wtmpx');

print "-- scanning for first host contacts from $user --\n";
```

```
my %contacts = ();# hostnames that have contacted us for specified user
while ( my $entry = User::Utmp::getutxent() ) {
    if ( $entry->{ut_user} eq $user ) {
        next if ( defined $ignore and $entry->{ut_host} =~ /$ignore/o );
        if ( $entry->{ut_type} == USER_PROCESS
            and !exists $contacts{ $entry->{ut_host} } )
        {
            $contacts{ $entry->{ut_host} } = $entry->{ut_time};
            print form $format, $entry->{ut_user}, $entry->{ut_host},
                scalar localtime( $entry->{ut_time} );
        }
    }
}

print "-- scanning for other contacts from those hosts --\n";
User::Utmp::setutxent();     # reset to start of database

while ( my $entry = User::Utmp::getutxent() ) {

    # if it is a user's process, and we're looking for this host,
    # and this is a connection from a user *other* than the
    # compromised account, then output this record
    if (    $entry->{ut_type} == USER_PROCESS
        and exists $contacts{ $entry->{ut_host} }
        and $entry->{ut_user} ne $user )
    {
        print form $format, $entry->{ut_user}, $entry->{ut_host},
            scalar localtime( $entry->{ut_time} );
    }
}
User::Utmp::endutxent();     # close database (not strictly necessary)
```

First the program scans through the *wtmpx* data looking for all logins from the compromised user. As it finds them, it compiles a hash of all the hosts from which these logins took place. It then resets the database so the next scan will start at the beginning of the file. The second scan looks for connections from that host list, printing matches as it finds them. We could easily modify this program to scan all of the files in a directory of rotated *wtmp* log files. To do that, we'd just have to loop over the list, calling `User::Utmp::utmpxname()` with each filename in turn.

One problem with this program is that it is too specific. That is, it will only match exact hostnames. If the intruder is coming in from an ISP's pool of DSL or cable modem addresses (which they often are), chances are the hostnames could change with each connection. Still, partial solutions like this often help a great deal.

Besides its simplicity, the stream read-count approach we've been discussing has the advantage of being faster and less memory-intensive than the method we'll consider next. It works well with the stateless type of log files we discussed early on in the chapter. But sometimes, especially when dealing with stateful data, we need to use a different plan of attack.

Read-remember-process

The opposite extreme of our previous approach, where we passed by the data as fast as possible, is to read it into memory and deal with it after reading. Let's look at a few versions of this strategy.

First, an easy example: let's say you have an FTP transfer log and you want to know which files have been transferred the most often. Here are some sample lines from a *wu-ftpd* FTP server transfer log. Blank lines have been added to make it easier to see where these long lines begin and end:

```
Sun Dec 27 05:18:57 2008 1 nic.funet.fi 11868
/net/ftp.funet.fi/CPAN/MIRRORING.FROM a _ o a cpan@perl.org ftp 0 *

Sun Dec 27 05:52:28 2008 25 kju.hc.congress.ccc.de 269273
/CPAN/doc/FAQs/FAQ/PerlFAQ.html a _ o a mozilla@ ftp 0 *

Sun Dec 27 06:15:04 2008 1 rising-sun.media.mit.edu 11868
/CPAN/MIRRORING.FROM b _ o a root@rising-sun.media.mit.edu ftp 0 *

Sun Dec 27 06:15:05 2008 1 rising-sun.media.mit.edu 35993
 /CPAN/RECENT.html b _ o a root@rising-sun.media.mit.edu ftp 0 *
```

Table 10-4 lists the fields in each line of the output (please see the `wu-ftpd` server man-page *xferlog(5)* for details on each field).

Table 10-4. Fields in a wu-ftpd server transfer log

Field #	Field name
0	current-time
1	transfer-time (in seconds)
2	remote-host
3	filesize
4	filename
5	transfer-type
6	special-action-flag
7	direction
8	access-mode
9	username
10	service-name
11	authentication-method
12	authenticated-user-id

Here's some code to show which files have been transferred most often:

```perl
my $xferlog = '/var/adm/log/xferlog';
my %files   = ();

open my $XFERLOG, '<', $xferlog or die "Unable to open $xferlog:$!\n";

while (defined ($line = <$XFERLOG>)){
    $files{(split(' ',$line))[8]}++;
}

close $XFERLOG;

for (sort {$files{$b} <=> $files{$a}||$a cmp $b} keys %files){
    print "$_:$files{$_}\n";
}
```

We read each line of the file, using the name of the file as a hash key and incrementing the value for that key. The name of the file is extracted from each log line using an array index that references a specific element of the list returned by the split() function:‡

```perl
$files{(split)[8]}++;
```

You may notice that the specific element we reference (8) is different from the eighth field listed in Table 10-4. This is an unfortunate result of the lack of field delimiters in the original file. We are splitting on whitespace (the default for split()), so the date field becomes five separate list items.

One subtle trick in this code sample is in the anonymous **sort** function we use to sort the values:

```perl
for (sort {$files{$b} <=> $files{$a}||$a cmp $b} keys %files){
```

Note that the places of $a and $b have been switched from their alphabetical order in the first portion. This causes **sort** to return the items in descending order, thus showing us the more frequently transferred files first. The second portion of the anonymous **sort** function (||$a cmp $b) assures that we list files with the same number of transfers in a sorted order.

If we wanted to limit this script to counting only certain files or directories, we could let the user specify a regular expression as the first argument to this script. For example, adding this:

```perl
next unless /$ARGV[0]/o;
```

to the **while** loop allows you to specify a regular expression to limit which log lines will be counted.

---

‡ Just FYI, a split() is likely to break if you have filenames with whitespace in them. In that case you'd probably need to use a regexp to take apart the line instead.

Let's take a look at another example of the read-remember-process approach, using our "breach-finder" program from the previous section. Our earlier code only showed us *successful* logins from the intruder sites. What if we want to find out about unsuccessful attempts? For that information, we're going to have to bring in another log file.

 This scenario exposes one of Unix's flaws: Unix systems tend to store log information in a number of different places and formats. Few tools are provided for dealing with these disparities (luckily, we have Perl). It is not uncommon to need more than one data source to solve problems like this one.

The log file that will be the most help to us in this endeavor is the one generated through *syslog* by Wietse Venema's Unix security tool *tcpwrappers*. *tcpwrappers* provides gatekeeper programs and libraries that can be used to control access to network services. An individual network service like *telnet* can be configured so that a *tcpwrappers* program handles all network connections. When a connection attempt is made, the *tcpwrappers* program will *syslog* it and then either pass the connection off to the real service or take some action (like dropping the connection). The choice of whether to let the connection through is based on some simple user-provided rules (e.g., allow connections from only certain hosts). *tcpwrappers* can also take preliminary precautions to make sure the connection is coming from the place it purports to come from using a DNS reverse-lookup. It can even be configured to log the name of the user who made the connection (via the RFC 931 *ident* protocol) if possible. For a more detailed description of *tcpwrappers*, see Simson Garfinkel, Gene Spafford, and Alan Schwartz's book *Practical Unix & Internet Security (http://oreilly.com/catalog/9780596003234/)* (O'Reilly).

For our purposes, we can just add some code to our previous breach-finder program that scans the *tcpwrappers* log (*tcpdlog* in this case) for connections from the suspect hosts we found in our scan of *wtmp*. If we add the following code to the end of our previous code sample:

```
# tcpd log file location
my $tcpdlog = '/var/log/tcpd/tcpdlog';

print "-- connections found in tcpdlog --\n";
open my $TCPDLOG, '<', $tcpdlog or die "Unable to read $tcpdlog:$!\n";
my ( $connecto, $connectfrom );
while ( defined( $_ = <$TCPDLOG> ) ) {
    next if !/connect from /;    # we only care about connections
    ( $connecto, $connectfrom ) = /(.+):\s+connect from\s+(.+)/;
    $connectfrom =~ s/^.+@//;

    print
        if ( exists $contacts{$connectfrom}
        and $connectfrom !~ /$ignore/o );
}
close $TCPDLOG;
```

we get output that looks like this:

```
-- first host contacts from baduser --
user        hostxx.ccs.example.edu  Thu Apr  3 13:41:47 2008
-- other connects from suspect machines --
user2       hostxx.ccs.example.edu  Thu Oct  9 17:06:49 2008
user2       hostxx.ccs.example.edu  Thu Oct  9 17:44:31 2008
user2       hostxx.ccs.example.edu  Fri Oct 10 22:00:41 2008
user2       hostxx.ccs.example.edu  Wed Oct 15 07:32:50 2008
user2       hostxx.ccs.example.edu  Wed Oct 22 16:24:12 2008
-- connections found in tcpdlog --
Jan 12 13:16:29 host2 in.rshd[866]: connect from user4@hostxx.ccs.example.edu
Jan 13 14:38:54 host3 in.rlogind[4761]: connect from user5@hostxx.ccs.example.edu
Jan 15 14:30:17 host4 in.ftpd[18799]: connect from user6@hostxx.ccs.example.edu
Jan 16 19:48:19 host5 in.ftpd[5131]: connect from user7@hostxx.ccs.example.edu
```

You may have noticed that this output contains connections from two different time ranges: we found connections in *wtmpx* from April 3 to October 22, while the *tcpwrappers* data appeared to show only January connections. The difference in these dates is an indication that our *wtmpx* files and our *tcpwrappers* files are rotated at different speeds. You need to be aware of these details when writing code that tacitly assumes the two log files being correlated refer to the same time period.

For a final and more sophisticated example of the read-remember-process approach, let's look at a task that requires combining stateful and stateless data. If you wanted a more comprehensive picture of the activity on a *wu-ftpd* server, you might want to use code to correlate the login and logout activity logged in a machine's *wtmp* file with the file transfer information recorded by *wu-ftpd* in its *xferlog* file. It might be nice if you could see output that showed when an FTP session started and finished, and what transfers took place during that session.

Here's a snippet of sample output from the code we're about to assemble. It shows four FTP sessions in March. The first session shows one file being transferred to the machine, the next two show files being transferred from that machine, and the last shows a connection without any transfers:

```
Thu Mar 12 18:14:30 2008-Wed Mar 12 18:14:38 2008 pitpc.host.ed
        -> /home/dnb/makemod

Sat Mar 14 23:28:08 2008-Fri Mar 14 23:28:56 2008 traal-22.host.edu
        <- /home/dnb/.emacs19

Sat Mar 14 23:14:05 2008-Fri Mar 14 23:34:28 2008 traal-22.host.edu
        <- /home/dnb/lib/emacs19/cperl-mode.el
        <- /home/dnb/lib/emacs19/filladapt.el

Wed Mar 25 21:21:15 2008-Tue Mar 25 21:36:15 2008 traal-22.host.edu
        (no transfers in xferlog)
```

Producing this output turns out to be nontrivial, since we need to pigeonhole stateless data into a stateful log. The *xferlog* transfer log shows only the time and the host that initiated the transfer. The *wtmpx* log shows the connections and disconnections from other hosts to the server. Let's walk through how to combine the two types of data using a read-remember-process approach. First, we'll define some variables for the program and load some supporting modules:

```perl
use Time::Local; # for date->Unix time (secs from Epoch) conversion
use User::Utmp qw(:constants);
use Readonly;    # to create read-only constants for legibility

# location of transfer log
my $xferlog = '/var/log/xferlog';

# location of wtmpx
my $wtmpx = '/var/adm/wtmpx';

# month name to number mapping
my %month = qw{Jan 0 Feb 1 Mar 2 Apr 3 May 4 Jun 5 Jul 6
    Aug 7 Sep 8 Oct 9 Nov 10 Dec 11};
```

Now let's look at the procedure that reads the *wu-ftpd xferlog* log file:

```perl
# scans a wu-ftpd transfer log and populates the %transfers
# data structure
print 'Scanning $xferlog...';
open my $XFERLOG, '<', $xferlog or die "Unable to open $xferlog:$!\n";

# fields we will parse from the log
my ( $time, $rhost, $fname, $direction );
my ( $sec, $min, $hours, $mday, $mon, $year );
my $unixdate;  # the converted date
my %transfers; # our data structure for holding transfer info

while (<$XFERLOG>) {

    # using an array slice to select the fields we want
    ( $mon, $mday, $time, $year, $rhost, $fname, $direction )
        = (split)[ 1, 2, 3, 4, 6, 8, 11 ];

    $fname =~ tr/ -~//cd;   # remove "bad" chars
    $rhost =~ tr/ -~//cd;   # remove "bad" chars
```

```
    # 'i' is "transferred in"
    $fname = ( $direction eq 'i' ? '-> ' : '<- ') . $fname;

    # convert the transfer time to Unix epoch format
    ( $hours, $min, $sec ) = split( ':', $time );
    $unixdate = timelocal( $sec, $min, $hours, $mday, $month{$mon}, $year );

    # put the data into a hash of lists of lists, i.e.:
    # $transfers{hostname} = ( [time1, $filename1],
    #                          [time2, $filename2],
    #                          ...)
    push( @{ $transfers{$rhost} }, [ $unixdate, $fname ] );
}
close $XFERLOG;
print "done.\n";
```

Three lines of Perl in the previous code deserve a little explanation. The first two are:

```
$fname =~ tr/ -~//cd;    # remove "bad" chars
$rhost =~ tr/ -~//cd;    # remove "bad" chars
```

This is just a primitive attempt to prevent nasty things from showing up in our output later in the program. This line strips control characters from the filename, so if a user has transferred a file with a funky name (either unintentionally or maliciously) we don't have to suffer later when we go to print the name and our terminal program freaks out. You'll see a similar cleanup take place to the hostnames we read in later in the code. If we wanted to be really thorough (and we should want this), we could write a regular expression to accept only "legitimate" filenames and use what it captured. But for now, this will do.

A more complicated piece of Perl is the push() statement:

```
push( @{ $transfers{$rhost} }, [ $unixdate, $fname ] );
```

This line creates a hash of lists of lists that looks something like this:

```
$transfers{hostname} =
  ([time1, filename1], [time2, filename2],[time3, filename3]...)
```

The %transfers hash is keyed on the name of the host that initiated the transfer.

For each host, we store a list of transfer pairs, each pair recording when a file was transferred and the name of that file. We're choosing to store the time in "seconds since the epoch"[*] for ease of comparison later. The subroutine timelocal() from the module Time::Local helps us convert to that standard. Because we're scanning a file transfer log written in chronological order, these lists of pairs are built in chronological order as well (a property that will come in handy later).

---

[*] This is seconds since some arbitrary starting point. For example, the epoch on Unix machines is 00:00:00 GMT on January 1, 1970.

Let's move on to scanning *wtmpx*:

```
# scans the wtmpx file and populates the @sessions structure with ftp sessions
my ( %connections, @sessions );

print "Scanning $wtmpx...\n";
User::Utmp::utmpxname($wtmpx);
while ( my $entry = User::Utmp::getutxent() ) {
    next if ( $entry->{ut_id} ne 'ftp' ); # ignore non-ftp sessions

    # "open" connection record using a hash of lists of lists (where the LoL
    # is used like a a stack stored in a hash, keyed on the device name)
    if ( $entry->{ut_user} and $entry->{ut_type} == USER_PROCESS ) {
        $entry->{ut_host} =~ tr/ -~//cd;     # remove "bad" chars

    push(
            @{ $connections{ $entry->{ut_line} } },
            [ $entry->{ut_host}, $entry->{ut_time} ]
        );
    }

    # found close connection entry, try to pair with open
    if ( $entry->{ut_type} == DEAD_PROCESS ) {
        if ( !exists $connections{ $entry->{ut_line} } ) {
            warn "found lone logout on $entry->{ut_line}:"
                . scalar localtime( $entry->{ut_time} ) . "\n";
            next;
        }

        # create a list of sessions, where each session is represented by
        # a list of this form: (hostname, login, logout)
        push(
            @sessions,
            [   @{ shift @{ $connections{ $entry->{ut_line} } } },
                $entry->{ut_time}
            ]
        );

        # if there are no more connections under that tty, remove it from hash
        delete $connections{ $entry->{ut_line} }
            unless ( @{ $connections{ $entry->{ut_line} } });
    }
}
User::Utmp::endutxent();
print "done.\n";
```

Let's look at what's going on in this code. We read through *wtmpx* one record at a time. If the current record takes place on the special device name ftp, we know that this is an FTP session. Given an entry in the *wtmpx* database for ftp, we see if it describes the opening (ut_type is USER_PROCESS) or closing (ut_type is DEAD_PROCESS) of an FTP session.

If it describes the opening of a connection, we record that info in a data structure that keeps tabs on all the open sessions, called %connections. Like %transfers in our previous subroutine, it is a hash of lists of lists, this time keyed on the device (i.e., tty/pty) of each connection. Each of the values in this hash is a set of pairs detailing the name of the host from which the connection originated and the time.

Why use such a complicated data structure to keep track of the open connections? Unfortunately, there isn't a simple "open-close open-close open-close" pairing of lines in *wtmpx*. For instance, take a look at these lines from *wtmpx* (as printed by our first *wtmpx* program earlier in this chapter):

```
ftpd1833:dnb:ganges.example.edu:Thu Mar 27 14:04:47 2008
ttyp7:dnb:(exit):Thu Mar 27 14:05:11 2008
ftpd1833:dnb:hotdiggitydog.example.edu:Thu Mar 27 14:05:20 2008
ftpd1833:dnb:(exit):Thu Mar 27 14:06:20 2008
ftpd1833:dnb:(exit):Thu Mar 27 14:06:43 2008
```

Notice the two open FTP connection records on the same device (lines 1 and 3). If we just stored a single connection per device in a plain hash, we'd lose the first connection record when we found the second one.

Instead, we use the list of lists keyed off every device in %connections as a stack. When we see a connection opening, we add a (*host, login-time*) pair for the connection to the stack kept for that device. Each time we see a close connection line for this device, we "pop" one of the open connection records off the stack and store our complete information about the session as a whole in another data structure called @sessions. That's the purpose of this statement:

```
push(
     @sessions,
     [   @{ shift @{ $connections{ $entry->{ut_line} } } },
         $entry->{ut_time}
     ]
);
```

Let's untangle this statement from the inside out to make sure everything is clear. The part in bold type returns a reference to the stack/list of open connection pairs for a specific device (ut_line):

```
push(
     @sessions,
     [   @{ shift @{ $connections{ $entry->{ut_line} } } },
         $entry->{ut_time}
     ]
);
```

This pops the reference to the first connection pair off that stack:

```
push(
     @sessions,
     [   @{ shift @{ $connections{ $entry->{ut_line} } } },
         $entry->{ut_time}
     ]
);
```

We dereference it to get at the actual (*host, login-time*) connection pair list. If we place this pair at the beginning of another list that ends with the connection time, Perl will interpolate the connection pair and we'll have a single, three-element list. This gives us a triad of (*host, login-time, logout-time*):

```
push(
    @sessions,
    [   @{ shift @{ $connections{ $entry->{ut_line} } } },
        $entry->{ut_time}
    ]
);
```

Now that we have all of the parts of an FTP session (initiating host, connection start time, and end time) in a single list, we can push a reference to a new anonymous array containing that list on to the @sessions list of lists for future use:

```
push(
    @sessions,
    [   @{ shift @{ $connections{ $entry->{ut_line} } } },
        $entry->{ut_time}
    ]
);
```

We have a list of sessions thanks to this one very busy statement.

To finish the job, we check if the stack is empty for a device (i.e., if there are no more open connection requests pending). If this is the case, we can delete that device's entry from the hash, as we know the connection has ended:

```
delete $connections{ $entry->{ut_line} }
    unless ( @{ $connections{ $entry->{ut_line} } });
```

Now it's time to do the actual correlation between our two data sets. For each session, we want to print out the connection triad, and then the files transferred during that session:

```
# constants to make the connection triad data structure more readable;
# the list consists of ($HOSTNAME,$LOGIN,$LOGOUT) in those positions
Readonly my $HOSTNAME => 0;
Readonly my $LOGIN    => 1;
Readonly my $LOGOUT   => 2;

# iterate over the session log, pairing sessions with transfers

foreach my $session (@sessions) {

    # print session times
    print scalar localtime( $session->[$LOGIN] ) . '-'
        . scalar localtime( $session->[$LOGOUT] ) . ' '
        . $session->[$HOSTNAME] . "\n ";

    # returns all of the files transferred for a given connect session

    # easy case, no transfers in this login
    if ( !exists $transfers{ $session->[$HOSTNAME] } ) {
```

```
            print " \t( no transfers in xferlog ) \n ";
            next;
        }

        # easy case, first transfer we have on record is after this login
        if ( $transfers{ $session->[$HOSTNAME] }->[0]->[0] > $session->[$LOGOUT] )
        {
            print " \t( no transfers in xferlog ) \n ";
            next;
        }

        my (@found) = ();     # to hold the transfers we find per each session

        # find any files transferred in this session
        foreach my $transfer ( @{ $transfers{ $session->[$HOSTNAME] } } ) {

            # if transfer happened before login
            next if ( $transfer->[0] < $session->[$LOGIN] );

            # if transfer happened after logout
            next if ( $transfer->[0] > $session->[$LOGOUT] );

            # if we've already reported on this entry
            next if ( !defined $transfer->[1] );

            # record that transfer and mark as used by undef'ing the filename
            push( @found, " \t " . $transfer->[1] . " \n " );
            undef $transfer->[1];
        }
        print( scalar @found ? @found : " \t( no transfers in xferlog ) \n" )
            . " \n ";
    }
```

The code starts by eliminating the easy cases: if we haven't seen any transfers initiated by this host, or if the first transfer associated with this host occurs after the session triad we are checking has ended, we know no files have been transferred during this session.

If we can't eliminate the easy cases, we need to look through our lists of transfers. We check each transfer made from the host in question to see if it occurred after the session started but before the session ended. If either of these conditions isn't true, we skip to the next transfer. Also, as soon as we've found a transfer that takes place after the session has ended, we avoid testing the other transfers for the host. Remember I mentioned that all of the transfers are added to the data structure in chronological order? Here's where that pays off.

The last test we make before considering a transfer entry to be valid may look a little peculiar:

```
# if we've already used this entry
next if ( !defined $transfer->[1] );
```

If two anonymous FTP sessions from the same host overlap in time, we have no way of knowing which session is responsible for initiating the transfer of any files uploaded or downloaded during that window. There is no information in either of our logs that can help us make that determination. The best we can do in this case is make up a standard and keep to it. The standard used here is "attribute the transfer to the first session possible." The preceding test line and the subsequent undefing of the filename value as a flag enforce that standard.

If this final test passes, we declare victory and add the filename to the list of files transferred in the current session (@found). The session and its accompanying file transfers are then printed.

Read-remember-process programs that have to do this sort of correlation can get fairly sophisticated, especially when they are bringing together data sources where the correlation is a bit fuzzy. So, in good Perl spirit, let's see if we can take an easier approach.

Black boxes

In the Perl world, if you are trying to write something generally useful, it's always possible that another person has beaten you to it and published his code for the task. In that case, you can simply feed your data into that person's module in a prescribed way and receive results without having to know how the task was actually performed. This is often known as a "black box approach." This approach can have its perils, though, so be sure to heed the warning in the following sidebar.

Congratulations! You Are the New Module Maintainer!

Though I tend to go for the black box approach more often than not, it is not without its perils. Let me tell you a cautionary tale.

In the first edition of this book I gushed about a module called SyslogScan. This was a swell module for the parsing of *syslog* with especially good support for the mail logs the *sendmail* mail transfer agent produced. It handled the drudgework of parsing a raw *sendmail* log and pairing up the two log lines associated with the handling of a single mail message. It provided a lovely, simple interface for iterating through the log file one message at a time. These iterators could then be handed to other parts of the package, and it would produce summary reports and summary objects. Those objects could in turn be handed to yet another part of the package, and even more impressive reports would be generated. It was beautiful.

But at some point, the developers of *sendmail* made a few small changes to the format of their log file. SyslogScan ceased being able to parse the log file as well as it did before. In time, it stopped working entirely.

In most cases this sort of change wouldn't be too much of a hassle, because the module author would notice the problem and issue a new release to address the log format change. Unfortunately, the author of SyslogScan seems to have disappeared from the Perl world some time in 1997. And that's where the module sits as of this writing on CPAN: frozen in time and broken.

If you depended on the module after the log format change, you had three choices:

---

1. Start using another module (perhaps not viable if this was the only module for that purpose).

2. Write your own replacement module (could be lots of work).

3. Try to patch SyslogScan yourself to deal with the format change.

Of the three choices, #3 probably involves the least work. Chances are the changes necessary to get it working again are small. But from this point on, congratulations, you are now the maintainer of the module (at least for your small world)! If it breaks again for some reason, the onus will be on you to fix it again. This may not be a big deal for you, but it is a potential drawback worth knowing about before you commit to relying on somebody else's code.

One of the strengths of the Perl community is its generosity in sharing code. There are many log-parsing modules available on CPAN. Most of them are designed to perform very specific tasks. For example, the Log::Procmail module by Philippe "BooK" Bruhat makes iterating through the log produced by the *procmail* mail filter and parsing it as we go easy. To print a list of addresses we received mail from and where each of those messages were filed, we can just write code like this:

```
use Log::Procmail;

my $procl = new Log::Procmail '/var/log/procmail';

while (my $entry = $procl->next){
    print $entry->from . ' => ' . $entry->folder . "\n";
}
```

There are a number of Apache log file parsers (for example, Apache::ParseLog, Parse::AccessLogEntry, and Apache::LogRegex) that perform similar heavy lifting for that log format.

Several modules are also available for building your own special-purpose parsers. Some of these are themselves more "black box" than others. On the Unix side of the house, Parse::Syslog continues to be a good black-box choice for taking apart *syslog*-style lines. As an added spiffy feature, Parse::Syslog's new() method will also take a File::Tail object instead of just your average, boring filehandle. Given this object, Parse::Syslog will operate on a log file that is still being written to, like so:

```
use File::Tail;
use Parse::Syslog;

my $file = File::Tail->new( name => '/var/log/mail/mail.log' );

my $syslg = Parse::Syslog->new( $file );

while ( my $parsed = $syslg->next ) {
    print $parsed->{host} . ':'
        . $parsed->{program} . ':'
        . $parsed->{text} . "\n";
}
```

If you'd like to build a parser using more basic building blocks, you may want to look at the set of modules that help in the construction of regular expressions. For example, Dmitry Karasik's `Regexp::Log::DateRange` module helps you construct the gnarly regular expression necessary for selecting a date range in *syslog* files:

```
use Regexp::Log::DateRange;

# construct a regexp for May 31 8:00a to May 31 11:00a
my $regexp = Regexp::Log::DateRange->new('syslog', [ qw(5 31 8 00) ],
                                                    [ qw(5 31 11 00) ]);
# $regexp now contains: 'may\s+31\s+(?:(?:0?[8-9]|10)\:|11\:0?0\:)'
# compile that regular expression for better performance
$regexp = qr/$regexp/i;

# now use that regexp
if ($input =~ /$regexp/) { print "$input matched\n" };
```

If you want to go up one level of meta, Philippe "BooK" Bruhat's `Regexp::Log` module allows you to build other modules that build regular expressions for you. The easiest way to see how these derived modules function is to look at one of the modules built using it. `Regexp::Log::Common`, a parser module for the Common Log Format (used by packages like Apache) by Barbie, is a good example of a derived module.

Here's how a derived module like `Regexp::Log::Common` is used:

```
use Regexp::Log::Common;

my $rlc = Regexp::Log::Common->new( format => ':extended' );
$rlc->capture( qw(:none referer) );
my $regexp = $rlc->regexp;

# now we have a regexp that will capture the referer field
# from each line in the Extended Common Log Format
# as in
#      ($referer) = $logline =~ /$regexp/
```

After loading the module, we tell it that we will be dealing with a file that has lines following the Extended Common Log Format. (`:extended` is just a shortcut for specifying all of field names found in that format; we could have listed them by hand if we really wanted.)

We then tell the module which of these fields we want to capture using `capture()`. `capture()` may look like a simple method call to set the list of fields to capture, but it actually adds those fields to the current capture list. This list starts off defaulting to the entire set of fields, so we need to use the special `:none` keyword to zero out the list before telling it the one field we are looking to capture ("referer").

To end this section on using the black box method of programming, we're going to look at one of the black box analysis modules that can help make the writing of log analysis modules considerably easier. Alex White has written a module called `Log::Statistics` that can perform simple (i.e., count-based) analyses of log files. Let's take a look at how it works.

The first step after the usual loading of the module and creation of a new object is to teach the module how to parse your log file into fields. For this example, we'll use the *stats* log file format generated by the PureFtpd server (*http://www.pureftpd.com*). It has the following fields:

```
<date> <session id> <user> <ip> <U or D> <size> <duration> <file>
```

Here are three example lines (with extra separator lines) so you can get a sense of what they look like:

```
1151826125 44a778cc.1a41 ftp bb.67.1333.static.
theplanet.com D 29 0 /home/ftp/net/mirrors/ftp.funet.fi/pub/
languages/perl/CPAN/authors/02STAMP

1151826483 44a77a32.1cf4 ftp ajax-1.apache.org D 11 0
 /home/ftp/net/mirrors/dev.apache.org/dist/DATE

1151829011 44a78408.1eca ftp 69.51.111.252 D 1809 0 /home/ftp/net
/mirrors/squid.nlanr.net/pub/squid-2/md5s.txt
```

To parse this sort of line, we tell `Log::Statistics` to use a custom regular expression that will capture each field:

```
use Log::Statistics;

my $ls = Log::Statistics->new();
$ls->add_line_regexp(
    '^(\d+)\s+(.*)\s+(\w+)\s(.*)\s+(U|D)\s+(\d+)\s+(\d+)\s+(.*)');
```

At this point, we tell the module which fields it should summarize and at which positions they are found in the regular expression:

```
$ls->add_field( 3, 'ip' );
$ls->add_field( 4, 'direction' );
```

All that remains is the actual reading of the log file and its parsing:

```
open my $LOG, '<', 'pureftpd.log';

my $line = '';
while ( defined ($line = <$LOG>) ) {
    $ls->parse_line($line);
}

close($LOG);
print $ls->get_xml();
```

The end result is an XML-based report that looks something like this:

```
<?xml version="1.0" standalone="yes"?>

<log-statistics>
  <fields name="direction">
    <direction name="D" count="4674" />
  </fields>
  <fields name="ip">
    <ip name="0x530f53.hrnxx2.adsl-dhcp.tele.dk" count="2" />
```

```
        <ip name="12.135.144.8" count="6" />
        <ip name="12.24.221.254" count="1" />
        <ip name="124.14.4.223" count="1" />
        <ip name="125.13.133.183" count="2" />
        ...
    </fields>
</log-statistics>
```

In it, we can see that 4674 downloads have been recorded; we also get a list of the IP addresses or hostnames that did the downloading and how many downloads each performed. If we wanted to get fancier and show the files each host downloaded, we could change the `add_field()` section to:

```
$ls->register_field( 'ip', 3 );
$ls->register_field( 'file', 7 );
$ls->add_group(['ip','file']);
```

The first two lines associate names to those positions in the regexp (without generating statistics for them, like `add_field()` does); the last line specifies the two fields to group on when calculating the statistics. Now the XML output looks like this:

```
<?xml version="1.0" standalone="yes"?>

<log-statistics>
    <groups name="ip-file">
        <ip name="12.135.144.8">
            <file name="/home/ftp/net/mirrors/ftp.funet.fi/pub/languages/perl/CPAN/
authors/01mailrc.txt.gz" count="1" />
            <file name="/home/ftp/net/mirrors/ftp.funet.fi/pub/languages/perl/CPAN/
authors/id/H/HA/HAKANARDO/CHECKSUMS" count="1" />
            <file name="/home/ftp/net/mirrors/ftp.funet.fi/pub/languages/perl/CPAN/
authors/id/Y/YV/YVES/CHECKSUMS" count="1" />
            <file name="/home/ftp/net/mirrors/ftp.funet.fi/pub/languages/perl/CPAN/
authors/id/Y/YV/YVES/MIME-Lite-3.01.tar.gz" count="1" />
            <file name="/home/ftp/net/mirrors/ftp.funet.fi/pub/languages/perl/CPAN/
modules/02packages.details.txt.gz" count="1" />
            <file name="/home/ftp/net/mirrors/ftp.funet.fi/pub/languages/perl/CPAN/
modules/03modlist.data.gz" count="1" />
        </ip>
        ...
    </groups>
</log-statistics>
```

Prefer to see who downloaded which files? Simply reverse the last line of the preceding code so it reads:

```
$ls->add_group(['file','ip']);
```

The output will now have a section like this:

```
    ...
    <groups name="file-ip">
        <file name="/home/ftp/ls-lR.gz">
            <ip name="dau.cgr.ru" count="1" />
        </file>
        <file name="/home/ftp/net/mirrors/dev.apache.org/dist/DATE">
```

```
    <ip name="ajax-1.apache.org" count="14" />
    <ip name="month.cs.uu.nl" count="20" />
    <ip name="minotaur.apache.org" count="26" />
  </file>
  ...
</groups>
```

This XML output can be transformed for display in a pretty table (perhaps using an XSLT stylesheet) or parsed and graphed to make pretty pictures.

If you like modules that do this sort of statistical work for you, there are a few worth looking at (including `Algorithm::Accounting` and `Logfile`). Be sure to check them all out before embarking on your next project in this vein.

As a way of ending this section, let me remind you that the black box approach should be used carefully. The plus side of this approach is that you can often get a great deal done with very little code of your own, thanks to the hard work of the module or script author. The minus side to using the black box approach is that you have to place your trust in another author's code. It may have subtle bugs or use an approach that does not scale for your needs. It is best to look over the code carefully before you drop it into production in your site.

Using databases

The last approach we'll discuss requires the most knowledge outside of the Perl domain to implement. As a result, we'll only take a very simple look at a technique that over time will probably become more prevalent.

The previous examples we've seen work fine on reasonably sized data sets when run on machines with a reasonable amount of memory, but they don't scale. For situations where you have lots of data, especially if the data comes from different sources, databases are the natural tool.

There are at least two ways to make use of databases from Perl. The first is one I'll call a "Perl-only" method. With this method, all of the database activity takes place in Perl, or libraries tightly coupled to Perl. The second way uses Perl modules like the DBI family to make Perl a client of another database, such as MySQL, Oracle, or Microsoft SQL Server. Let's look at an example of using both of these approaches for log processing and analysis.

Using Perl-only databases. As long as the data set is not too large, we can probably stick to a Perl-only solution. We'll extend our ubiquitous breach-finder program for an example. So far our code just dealt with connections on a single machine. If we wanted to find out about logins from intruders on any of our machines, how would we do it?

Our first step is to drop all of the *wtmpx* data for our machines into a database of some sort. For the purpose of this example, assume that all the machines in question have direct access to some shared directory via some network filesystem, like NFS. Before we proceed, we need to choose a database format.

My "Perl database format" of choice is the Berkeley DB format. I use quotes around "Perl database format" because, while the support for DB is shipped with the Perl sources, the actually DB libraries must be procured from another source (*http://www .oracle.com/database/berkeley-db/index.html*) and installed before the Perl support can be built. Table 10-5 provides a comparison between the different supported database formats.

Table 10-5. Comparison of the supported Perl database formats

Name	Unix support	Windows support	Mac OS X support	Key or value size limits	Byte-order independent
"old" dbm	Yes	No	No	1K	No
"new" dbm	Yes	No	Yes	4K	No
Sdbm	Yes	Yes	Yes	1K (default)	No
Gdbm	Yes[a]	Yes[b]	Yes[a]	None	No
DB	Yes[a]	Yes[b]	Yes[a]	None	Yes

[a] Actual database libraries may have to be downloaded separately.

[b] Database library and Perl module must be downloaded from the Web (*http://www.roth.net* has an old version, or you'll need to use the Cygwin distribution of Perl). At some point, you may be able to use Strawberry Perl as well (see Chapter 1).

I like the Berkeley DB format because it can handle larger data sets and is byte-order-independent. Byte-order independence is particularly important for the Perl code we're about to see, since we'll want to read and write to the same file from different machines, which may have different architectures. If byte-order independence is important to you but you don't want to build and link in external libraries, the module DBM::Deep is another good option.

We'll start by populating the database. For the sake of simplicity and portability, we're calling the *last* program to avoid having to unpack() several different *wtmpx* files ourselves. Here's the code, with an explanation to follow:

```
use DB_File;
use FreezeThaw qw(freeze thaw);
use Sys::Hostname;
use Fcntl;
use strict;

# note for Solaris, if you don't want the hostnames truncated you can use
# last -a, but that requires a change to the field parsing code below
my $lastex = '/bin/last' if ( -x '/bin/last' );
$lastex = '/usr/ucb/last' if ( -x '/usr/ucb/last' );

my $userdb    = 'userdata';
my $connectdb = 'connectdata';
my $thishost  = &hostname;

open my $LAST, '-|', "$lastex" or die "Can't run the program $lastex:$!\n";
```

```perl
my ( $user, $tty, $host, $day, $mon, $date, $time, $when );
my ( %users, %connects );
while ( defined( $_ = <$LAST> ) ) {
    next if /^reboot/ or /^shutdown/ or /^ftp/ or /^account/ or /^wtmp/;
    ( $user, $tty, $host, $day, $mon, $date, $time ) = split;
    next if $tty =~ /^:0/ or $tty =~ /^console$/;
    next if ( length($host) < 4 );
    $when = $mon . ' ' . $date . ' ' . $time;

    push( @{ $users{$user} },    [ $thishost, $host, $when ] );
    push( @{ $connects{$host} }, [ $thishost, $user, $when ] );
}

close $LAST;

tie my %userdb, 'DB_File', $userdb, O_CREAT | O_RDWR, 0600, $DB_BTREE
    or die "Unable to open $userdb database for r/w:$!\n";

my $userinfo;
for my $user ( keys %users ) {
    if ( exists $userdb{$user} ) {
        ($userinfo) = thaw( $userdb{$user} );
        push( @{$userinfo}, @{ $users{$user} } );
        $userdb{$user} = freeze $userinfo;
    }
    else {
        $userdb{$user} = freeze $users{$user};
    }
}

untie %userdb;

tie my %connectdb, 'DB_File', $connectdb, O_CREAT | O_RDWR, 0600, $DB_BTREE
    or die "Unable to open $connectdb database for r/w:$!\n";

my $connectinfo;
for my $connect ( keys %connects ) {
    if ( exists $connectdb{$connect} ) {
        ($connectinfo) = thaw( $connectdb{$connect} );
        push( @{$connectinfo}, @{ $connects{$connect} } );
        $connectdb{$connect} = freeze($connectinfo);
    }
    else {
        $connectdb{$connect} = freeze( $connects{$connect} );
    }
}
untie %connectdb;
```

Our code takes the output from the *last* program and does the following:

1. Filters out the lines that are not useful.

2. Squirrels away the output in two hashes of lists of lists data structures that look like this:

```
$users{username} =
    [[current host, connecting host, connect time],
     [current host, connecting host, connect time]
     ...
    ];
$connects{host} =
    [[current host, username1, connect time],
     [current host, username2, connect time],
     ...
    ];
```

3. Takes this data structure in memory and attempts to merge it into a database.

This last step is the most interesting, so let's explore it more carefully. We tie the hashes %userdb and %connectdb to database files.[†] This magic allows us to access those hashes transparently, while Perl handles storing data in and retrieving it from the database files behind the scenes. But hashes only store simple strings, so how do we get our "hashes of list of lists" into a single hash value for storage?

Ilya Zakharevich's FreezeThaw module is used to store our complex data structure in a single scalar that can be used as a hash value. FreezeThaw can take an arbitrary Perl data structure and encode it as a string. There are other modules like this, including Data::Dumper by Gurusamy Sarathy (shipped with Perl) and Storable by Raphael Manfredi, but FreezeThaw offers the most compact representation of a complex data structure (hence its use here). Each of these modules has its strong points, so be sure to investigate all three if you have a task like this one to perform.

In our program, we check whether an entry for this user or host exists. If it doesn't, we simply "freeze" the data structure into a string and store that string in the database using our tied hash. If it does exist, we "thaw" the existing data structure found in the database back into memory, add our data, then re-freeze and re-store it.

If we run this code on several machines, we'll have a database with some potentially useful information to feed to the next version of our breach-finder program.

 An excellent time to populate a database like this is just after a log rotation of a *wtmp* file has taken place.

The database population code presented here is too bare-bones for production use. One glaring deficiency is the lack of a mechanism to prevent multiple instances of the program from updating the database at the same time. Given that file locking over NFS is known to be dicey at best, it might be easier to call code like this from a larger program that serializes the process of collecting information from each machine in turn.

[†] You don't usually have to use the BTree form of storage when using DB_File, but this program can store some very long values. Those values caused the version 1.85 DB_HASH storage method to croak in testing (causing corrupted data), while the BTree storage method seemed to handle the pounding. Later versions of the DB libraries may not have this bug.

Now that we have a database full of data, let's walk through our new improved breach-finder program that uses this information:

```
use DB_File;
use FreezeThaw qw(freeze thaw);
use Perl6::Form;
use Fcntl;

my ( $user, $ignore ) = @ARGV;

my $userdb      = 'userdata';
my $connectdb   = 'connectdata';
my $hostformat = '{<<<<<<<<<<<<<<<} -> {<<<<<<<<<<<<<<<} on {<<<<<<<<<<<}';
my $userformat
    = '{<<<<<<<<}: {<<<<<<<<<<<<<<<} -> {<<<<<<<<<<<<<<<} on {<<<<<<<<<<<}';

tie my %userdb, 'DB_File', $userdb, O_RDONLY, 666, $DB_BTREE
    or die "Unable to open $userdb database for reading:$!\n";
tie my %connectdb, 'DB_File', $connectdb, O_RDONLY, 666, $DB_BTREE
    or die "Unable to open $connectdb database for reading:$!\n";
```

We've loaded the modules we need, taken our input, set a few variables, and tied them to our database files. Now it's time to do some work:

```
# we can exit if we've never seen a connect from this user
if ( !exists $userdb{$user} ) {
    print "No logins from that user\n";
    untie %userdb;
    untie %connectdb;
    exit;
}

my ($userinfo) = thaw( $userdb{$user} );

print "-- first host contacts from $user --\n";
my %otherhosts;
foreach my $contact ( @{$userinfo} ) {
    next if ( $ignore and $contact->[1] =~ /$ignore/o );
    print form $hostformat, $contact->[1], $contact->[0], $contact->[2];
    $otherhosts{ $contact->[1] } = 1;
}
```

This code says: if we've seen this user at all, we reconstitute the user's contact records in memory using thaw(). For each contact, we test to see if we've been asked to ignore the host from which it came. If not, we print a line for that contact and record the originating host in the %otherhosts hash.

We use a hash here as a simple way of collecting the unique list of hosts from all of the contact records. Now that we have the list of hosts from which the intruder may have connected, we need to identify all the other users who have connected from these potentially compromising hosts.

Finding this information will be easy, because when we recorded which users logged into which machines, we also recorded the inverse (i.e., which machines were logged into by which users) in another database file. We can now look at all of the records from the hosts we identified in the previous step. If we are not told to ignore a host, and we have connection records for it, we capture a unique list of users who have logged into that host using the %userseen hash:

```perl
print "-- other connects from suspect machines  --\n";
my %userseen;
foreach my $host ( keys %otherhosts ) {
    next if ( $ignore and $host =~ /$ignore/o );
    next if ( !exists $connectdb{$host} );

    my ($connectinfo) = thaw( $connectdb{$host} );

    foreach my $connect ( @{$connectinfo} ) {
        next if ( $ignore and $connect->[0] =~ /$ignore/o );
        $userseen{ $connect->[1] } = 1;
    }
}
```

The final act of this three-step drama has a nice circular flair. We return to our original user database to find all of the connections made by suspect users from suspect machines:

```perl
foreach my $user ( sort keys %userseen ) {
    next if ( !exists $userdb{$user} );

    ($userinfo) = thaw( $userdb{$user} );

    foreach my $contact ( @{$userinfo} ) {
        next if ( $ignore and $contact->[1] =~ /$ignore/o );
        print form $userformat, $user, $contact->[1], $contact->[0],
            $contact->[2]
            if ( exists $otherhosts{ $contact->[1] } );
    }
}
```

All that's left to do then is sweep up the theater and go home:

```perl
untie %userdb;
untie %connectdb;
```

Here's some example output from the program (again, with the user- and hostnames changed to protect the innocent):

```
-- first host contacts from baduser --
badhost1.example -> machine1.hogwarts.ed on Jan 18 09:55
badhost2.example -> machine2.hogwarts.ed    on Jan 19 11:53
-- other connects from suspect machines  --
baduser2:  badhost1.example -> machine2.hogwarts.e on Dec 15 13:26
baduser2:  badhost2.example -> machine2.hogwarts.e on Dec 11 12:45
baduser3:  badhost1.example -> machine1.hogwarts.e on Jul 13 16:20
baduser4:  badhost1.example -> machine1.hogwarts.e on Jun 9 11:53
baduser:   badhost1.example -> machine1.hogwarts.e on Jan 18 09:55
baduser:   badhost2.example -> machine2.hogwarts.e on Jan 19 11:53
```

This is a lovely example program, but it doesn't really scale past a small cluster of machines. For every subsequent run of the program, it may have to read a record from the database, thaw() it back into memory, add some new data to the record, freeze() it again, and store it back in the database. This can be CPU time- and memory-intensive. The whole process potentially happens once per user and machine connection, so things slow down very quickly.

Using Perl-cliented SQL databases. If you have a very large data set, you may need to load your data into a more sophisticated SQL database (commercial or otherwise) and query the information you need from it using SQL. If you're not familiar with SQL, I recommend you take a quick peek at Appendix D before looking at this section.

Populating the database could be done with code that looks like the following. This example uses SQLite as the backend, but swapping in most other database backends (e.g., MySQL, Microsoft SQL Server, Oracle, DB2, etc.) would be easy; the only things you'd need to change are the DBI connect string and the code for making sure a table with that name exists/is created. That said, let's dive in:

```
use DBI;
use Sys::Hostname;
use strict;

my $db    = 'lastdata';
my $table = 'lastinfo';

# field names we'll use in that table
my @fields = qw( username localhost otherhost whenl );

my $lastex = '/bin/last' if ( -x '/bin/last' );
$lastex = '/usr/ucb/last' if ( -x '/usr/ucb/last' );

# database-specific code (note: no username/pwd used, unusual)
# RaiseError is used so we don't have to check that each operation succeeds
my $dbh = DBI->connect(
    'dbi:SQLite:dbname=$db.sql3',
    '', '',
    {   PrintError         => 0,
        RaiseError         => 1,
        ShowErrorStatement => 1,
    }
);

# Determine the names of the tables currently in the database.
# This code is mildly database engine-specific because of the
# need to map() to strip off the quotes DBD::SQLite returns around
# table names. Most database engines don't require that handholding,
# so $dbh->tables()'s results can be used directly.
my %dbtables;
@dbtables{ map { /\"(.*)\"/, $1 } $dbh->tables() } = ();

if ( !exists $dbtables{$table} ) {

# More database engine-specific code.
```

```
# This creates the table with all fields of type text. With other database
# engines, you might want to use char and varchar as appropriate.
    $dbh->do(
        "CREATE TABLE $table (" . join( ' text, ', @fields ) . ' text)' );
}

my $thishost = &hostname;

# this constructs and prepares a SQL statement with placeholders, as in:
# "INSERT INTO lastinfo(username,localhost,otherhost,whenl)
#     VALUES (?, ?, ?, ?)"
my $sth = $dbh->prepare( "INSERT INTO $table ("
        . join( ', ', @fields )
        . ') VALUES ('
        . join( ', ', ('?') x @fields )
        . ')' );

open my $LAST, '-|', "$lastex" or die "Can't run the program $lastex:$!\n";

my ( $user, $tty, $host, $day, $mon, $date, $time, $whenl );
my ( %users, %connects );
while ( defined( $_ = <$LAST> ) ) {
    next if /^reboot/ or /^shutdown/ or /^ftp/ or /^account/ or /^wtmp/;
    ( $user, $tty, $host, $day, $mon, $date, $time ) = split;
    next if $tty =~ /^:0/ or $tty =~ /^console$/;
    next if ( length($host) < 4 );
    $whenl = $mon . ' ' . $date . ' ' . $time;

# actually insert the data into the database
    $sth->execute( $user, $thishost, $host, $whenl );
}

close $LAST;
$dbh->disconnect;
```

This code creates a table called lastinfo with username, localhost, otherhost, and whenl columns. We iterate over the output of *last*, inserting non-bogus entries into this table.

Now we can use our databases to do what they do so well. Here is a set of sample SQL queries that could easily be wrapped in Perl using the DBI or ODBC interfaces we explored in Chapter 7:

```
-- how many entries in the database?
select count (*) from lastinfo;


-----------
      10068


-- how many users have logged in?
select count (distinct username) from lastinfo;


-----------
       237
```

```
-- how many separate hosts have connected to our machines?
select count (distinct otherhost) from lastinfo;

-----------
      1000

-- which local hosts has the user "dnb" logged into?
select distinct localhost from lastinfo where username = "dnb";
 localhost
----------------------------------------
 host1
 host2
```

These examples should give you a taste of the sort of "data mining" you can do once all of the data is in a real database. Each of those queries took only a second or so to run. Databases can be fast, powerful tools for system administration.

Writing Your Own Log Files

I've intentionally held back any discussion of how to create your own log files until the very end of this chapter for one simple reason: if you have a good understanding of how to read, parse, and analyze random log files, you are much more likely to write code that will produce log files that are easy to read, parse, and analyze. The actual mechanics of writing log files is pretty easy, as you'll see in a moment, but knowing how to write good/useful log files is a learned art.

There are a relatively large number of Perl modules available to help you with log file production. In the interest of saving space, we'll look at three options that do a good job of representing the varying levels of functionality and complexity the cornucopia of modules has to offer.

 One simple admission before we look at some modules: you don't actually need any modules at all to write to a log file. This process can be as simple as:

```
open my $LOGFILE, '>>', 'logfile' or
  die "can't open logfile for append: $!\n";
print $LOGFILE 'began logfile example: ' .
           scalar localtime . "\n";
close $LOGFILE;
```

But as you've probably guessed, we're going to get much spiffier than that....

Logging Shortcuts and Formatting Help

The first option is to use log modules that try to make writing the actual lines of a log easier, more structured, or both. For example, `Tie::LogFile` by Chris Reinhardt makes it easy to write lines to a log file with a preset format. Here's a piece of sample code:

```
use Tie::LogFile;

tie( *LOG, 'Tie::LogFile', 'filename', format => '(%p) [%d] %m' );

print LOG 'message';    # (pid) [dt] message

close(LOG);
```

The `tie()` line creates a `tie()`d filehandle with special properties. Each time we print to that filehandle, it will format the output using the format string specified and then add it to the file. In this case, we're specifying that each line contain:

(%p)
> The PID of the running process

[%d]
> A date/time stamp

%m
> The actual message

If we run the preceding program three times, we get a file that looks like this:

```
(19064) [Wed Jun 21 12:01:46 2008] message
(19719) [Wed Jun 21 12:09:02 2008] message
(19725) [Wed Jun 21 12:10:12 2008] message
```

Basic/Intermediate Logging Frameworks

Eventually, your desires for more sophisticated logging functionality may outgrow the types of modules we've seen so far. At that point you'll find yourself looking for a module with at least a basic framework for handling logging tasks. Two such frameworks that have found favor in the Perl community are `Log::Dispatch`, by Dave Rolsky, and `Log::Agent`, originally by Raphael Manfredi and now maintained by Mark Rogaski. We'll take a look at the first one, but you should feel free to compare the two and see which one appeals to you.

Here's how `Log::Dispatch` works. First, you create a log dispatch object through which all logging is done:

```
use Log::Dispatch;
my $ld = Log::Dispatch->new;
```

That object isn't particularly useful to start, but (and here comes the fun part) it acts as the hub for a set of modules that handle the disposition of every log message. For example, if you wanted log messages to go to a file, you would use a line like this to add it to the dispatch object:

```
$ld->add(
    Log::Dispatch::File->new(
        name     => 'to_file',
        filename => 'filename',
        min_level => 'info',
```

```
            max_level => 'alert',
            mode      => 'append'
        )
    );
```

This line says that output should go to an object called `to_file` whose job it will be to log data to the file `filename`. That object will log any message it receives that has a log level anywhere from `info` to `alert`.

But why stop with logging to a file? How about configuring it to send out messages via an email message? You can do that as follows:

```
$ld->add(
    Log::Dispatch::Email::MailSend->new(
        name      => 'to_email',
        min_level => 'alert',
        to        => [qw ( operators@example.com )],
        subject   => 'log alert'
    )
);
```

Similarly, you might want to send messages to a *syslog* server for further aggregation and processing:

```
$ld->add(
    Log::Dispatch::Syslog->new(
        name      => 'to_syslog',
        min_level => 'warning',
        facility  => 'local2'
    )
);
```

One of the great things about `Log::Dispatch` is that it has so many of these dispatch objects available. The module ships with other modules that can write to a file, send email, or log to the screen. Others have created modules for logging to a database via DBI, writing to files that are automatically rotated for you, sending messages via a Jabber IM server, and so on.

Observant readers are probably getting a bit impatient at this point, because they've noticed we haven't actually *logged* anything yet. No problem, that's easy:

```
$ld->log( level => 'notice', message => 'here is a log message' );
```

Or, we could use a shortcut to send a message at the notice level:

```
$ld->notice( 'here is a log message' );
```

This code will send that message to each of the dispatch objects we've `add()`ed that are set to listen to messages at this log level. If at this point we did the equivalent of screaming bloody murder:

```
$ld->emergency( 'printer on fire!' );
```

a message would get recorded to the file and sent to *syslog*, and an email message would be dispatched. To send a message to a specific dispatch object, the `log_to` method is used:

```
$ld->log_to( name    => 'to_syslog',
             level   => 'debug',
             message => 'sneeble component is failing' );
```

A basic/intermediate logging framework like this gives us significantly more control over when messages are logged, and where. This is often all of the flexibility and control one needs for a project. But there are cases where a really large project demands even more control. For those cases, there is an advanced logging framework available.

Advanced Logging Framework

The next step up in complexity and power is the `log4perl` logging framework, by Mike Schilli and Kevin Goess. This is a direct port of the `log4j` framework that is so popular in the Java community. The `log4perl` package is so compatible with its progenitor that it will even parse and use many `log4j` configuration files without modification.

Code examples and a deeper exploration of `log4perl`'s functionality would take considerably more space in this chapter than makes sense, especially considering that one of its authors has created an excellent tutorial (see the references section at the end of this chapter for a pointer). Instead, let me give you a quick rundown of the features of the framework and how they can benefit you.

Let's start with the features we've already seen:

- `log4perl` offers the same ability to multiplex logging messages out to different output destinations as `Log::Dispatch`. In fact, it actually uses the same `Log::Dispatch::*` output modules as `Log::Dispatch`, so all of that flexibility comes along for the ride.

- `log4perl` supports logging levels (and has the ability to tell parts of the framework to pay attention to only messages of a certain level).

- `log4perl` has similar convenience methods (`$object->error()`, `$object->warn()`, `$object->debug()`, etc.) for logging at all of the standard levels.

Now let's add the exciting parts:

- `log4perl` has something called "categories" that let you name a particular section of your code for logging purposes. For example, for an online banking application, you might have `GetBalance`, `MakeWithdrawal`, and `MakeDeposit` categories for each section of your code. The logging for each of these categories can be turned off/on and have its level set independently. Only want logging information about withdrawals at debug level? No problem with `log4perl`.

- If you are building big systems with lots of code, chances are they are written in an OOP-ish style with classes and subclasses, objects and sub-objects, and all that other good stuff. `log4perl` handles all of this complexity, because its categories are actually hierarchical in nature. Each category can correspond to a class in your system; you can have a `Withdrawal`, `Withdrawal::CheckBalance`, `Withdrawal::Check Balance::Overdraft`, and so on. Log levels can be set at a place high in the tree of categories, and all subcategories under that level will inherit the setting. Want logging enabled for only a piece of your complex code hierarchy? Easily done.

- As I alluded to earlier, `log4perl` can read configuration files that describe precisely how logging should be enabled for your complex code jungle. As an added bonus, `log4perl` can be set to periodically check this file for modifications and load a new configuration if it changes. This means you can change the kind of logging your massive system is doing *while it's running*. Pretty slick.

If this description has piqued your interest, visit *http://log4perl.sourceforge.net* for more details.

The subject of log creation, manipulation, and analysis is a vast one. Hopefully this chapter has given you a grasp of a few tools and a little inspiration.

Module Information for This Chapter

Modules	CPAN ID	Version
Win32::EventLog (ships with ActivePerl)		0.074
File::Copy (ships with ActivePerl)		2.09
Logfile::Rotate	PAULG	1.04
File::Temp (ships with Perl)		0.17
Getopt::Long (ships with Perl)		2.35
Time::Local (ships with Perl)		1.13
Perl6::Form	DCONWAY	0.04
User::Utmp	MPIOTR	1.8
Readonly	ROODE	1.03
Log::Procmail	BOOK	0.11
SyslogScan	RHNELSON	0.32
File::Tail	MGRABNAR	0.99.3
Parse::Syslog	DSCHWEI	1.09
Regexp::Log::DateRange	KARASIK	0.01
Regexp::Log	BOOK	0.04
Regexp::Log::Common	BARBIE	0.04
Log::Statistics	VVU	0.047
DB_File (ships with Perl)	PMQS	1.72

Modules	CPAN ID	Version
DBM::Deep	RKINYON	0.983
FreezeThaw	ILYAZ	0.3
Sys::Hostname (ships with Perl)		1.11
Fcntl (ships with Perl)		1.05
DBI	TIMB	1.52
DBD::Sqlite	MSERGEANT	1.13
Tie::LogFile	CREIN	0.1
Log::Dispatch	DROLSKY	2.13
Log4perl	MSCHILLI	1.07

References for More Information

Essential System Administration, Third Edition (*http://oreilly.com/catalog/9780596003432/*), by Æleen Frisch (O'Reilly) has a good, short intro to *syslog*.

http://www.heysoft.de/index.htm is the home of Frank Heyne software, a provider of Win32 Event Log-parsing software. It also has a good Event Log FAQ list.

http://www.le-berre.com is Philippe Le Berre's home page; it contains an excellent write-up on the use of Win32::EventLog and other Windows packages.

Practical Unix & Internet Security, Third Edition (*http://oreilly.com/catalog/9780596003234/*), by Simson Garfinkel, Gene Spafford, and Alan Schwartz (O'Reilly), is another good (and slightly more detailed) intro to *syslog*; also includes *tcpwrappers* information.

http://www.geekfarm.org/wu/muse/LogStatistics.html is the home of the Log::Statistics package and contains some good documentation on the project.

http://log4perl.sourceforge.net is the home of the log4perl project. Be sure to see the tutorial linked off that site at *http://www.perl.com/pub/a/2002/09/11/log4perl.html*.

http://www.loganalysis.org is the site set up by Tina Bird and Marcus Ranum, two security researchers who are working to bring more attention to log analysis issues as they relate to security. They also host a mailing list on the subject at *http://www.loganalysis.org/mailman/listinfo/loganalysis/*.

USENIX held a workshop on analysis of system logs in 2008 (WASL '08). More information can be found at *http://www.usenix.org/events/wasl08/*.

For interactive log analysis, the products provided by Splunk (*http://www.splunk.com*) are pretty phenomenal. They also allow for free usage when analyzing data under a certain size.

Microsoft makes a (poorly publicized but very cool) package called *Log Parser*. I last found it on the download site at *http://www.microsoft.com/downloads/details.aspx?Fam ilyID=890cd06b-abf8-4c25-91b2-f8d975cf8c07*, but given how often Microsoft shuffles URLs, you may have to search for it at *http://www.microsoft.com/downloads/*. Microsoft describes it like this:

> Log parser is a powerful, versatile tool that provides universal query access to text-based data such as log files, XML files and CSV files, as well as key data sources on the Windows® operating system such as the Event Log, the Registry, the file system, and Active Directory®. You tell Log Parser what information you need and how you want it processed. The results of your query can be custom-formatted in text based output, or they can be persisted to more specialty targets like SQL, SYSLOG, or a chart.

## CHAPTER 11

Security

Any discussion of security is fraught with peril, for at least three reasons:

- Security means different things to different people. If you walked into a conference of Greco-Roman scholars and asked about Rome, the first scholar might rise dramatically to her feet and begin to lecture about aqueducts (infrastructure and delivery), while the second focused on *Pax Romana* (ideology and policies), a third expounded on the Roman legions (enforcement), a fourth on the Roman Senate (administration), and so on. The need to deal with every facet of security at once is security's first trap.

- Security is a continuum, not a binary. People often mistakenly think that a program, a computer, a network, etc. can be "secure." This chapter will never claim to show you how to make anything secure, though it will try to help you to make something *more* secure, or at least to recognize when something is *less* secure.

- Finally, one of the most deadly traps in this business is specificity. It is true that you can often address security issues by paying attention to the details, but the set of details is ever-shifting. Patching security holes A, B, and C only ensures that those particular holes will not be a problem—*if* the patches work as promised. It does nothing to help when hole D is found. That's why this chapter will focus on general principles and tools for improving security, rather than telling you how to fix any particular buffer overflow, vulnerable registry key, or world-writable system file.

One good way to lead into a discussion of these principles is to examine how security manifests itself in the physical world. In both the real and virtual worlds, it all comes down to *fear*. Will something I care about be damaged, lost, or revealed? Is there something I can do to prevent this from happening? What is the likelihood of something happening, and what are the consequences if it does? Is it happening *right now*?

If we look at how we face fear in the physical world, we can learn ways to deal with it in the system administration domain as well. When we want to protect real-world objects, we invent stronger ways of partitioning physical space (e.g., bank vaults) so that only certain people can get to their contents. When we want to protect real-world intellectual property and secrets, we create methods of restricting access, like top-secret clearance policies or, in spy-vs.-spy situations, data encryption. The computer equivalents of these things are remarkably similar; they too include permission systems, access lists, encryption, etc. But both on and off the computer, security is a never-ending pursuit. For every hour spent designing a security system, there is at least an hour spent looking for a way to evade it. In our case, threats may come from hordes of bored teenagers with computers looking for something to do with their excess energy, or disgruntled former employees with vengeance on their minds.

One approach to improving security that has persisted over the ages is appointing a designated person to allay the public's fears. Once upon a time, there was nothing so comforting as the sound of the night watchman's footsteps as he walked through the town, jiggling door handles. We'll use this quaint image as the jumping-off point for our exploration of security and network monitoring with Perl.

Noticing Unexpected or Unauthorized Changes

A good watchman notices change. She knows when things are in the wrong place or go missing. If your precious Maltese Falcon gets replaced with a forgery, the watchman is the first person who should notice. Similarly, if someone modifies or replaces key files on your system, you want sirens to blare and klaxons to sound. More often than not, the change will be harmless. But the first time someone breaches your security and mucks with */bin/login*, *system32/*.dll*, or *Finder*, you'll be so glad you noticed that you will excuse any prior false alarms.[*]

Local Filesystem Changes

Filesystems are an excellent place to begin our exploration of change-checking programs. We're going to investigate ways to check whether important files, like operating system binaries and security-related files (e.g., */etc/passwd* or *system32/*.dll*), have changed. Changes to these files made without the administrator's knowledge are often signs of an intruder. Some relatively sophisticated cracker toolkits available on the Web install Trojan versions of important files, then cover their tracks. That's a malevolent kind of change that we have the ability to detect.[†] On the other end of the spectrum, sometimes it is just nice to know when important files have been changed (especially in environments where multiple people administer the same systems). The techniques we're about to explore will work equally well in both cases.

---

[*] This is not to say that you shouldn't work hard to reduce false positives. If you get too many alerts, you'll start ignoring them or (worse) automatically sending them to the bitbucket.

[†] Though if you are dealing with a particularly nasty rootkit that changes the OS-level functions that Perl calls, all bets are off. Sorry.

The easiest way to tell if a file has changed is to use the Perl functions `stat()` and `lstat()`. These functions take a filename or a filehandle and return an array containing information about that file. The only difference between the two functions manifests itself on operating systems such as Unix that support symbolic links. In these cases, `lstat()` returns information about the symbolic link itself, while `stat()` returns info about the target of the link. On all other operating systems, the information `lstat()` returns should be the same as that returned by `stat()`.

Using `stat()` or `lstat()` is easy:

```
my @information = stat('filename');
```

As demonstrated in Chapter 2, we can also use Tom Christiansen's `File::Stat` module to provide this information using an object-oriented syntax.

The information `stat()` or `lstat()` returns is operating system-dependent. `stat()` and `lstat()` began as Unix system calls, so the Perl documentation for these calls is skewed toward the return values for Unix systems. Table 11-1 shows how these values compare to those returned by `stat()` on Windows-based operating systems. The first two columns show the Unix field number and description.

Table 11-1. stat() return value comparison[a]

Field #	Unix field description	Valid for Windows-based operating systems?
0	Device number of filesystem	Yes (drive #)
1	Inode number	No (always 0)
2	File mode (type and permissions)	Yes
3	Number of (hard) links to the file	Yes (for NTFS)
4	Numeric user ID of file's owner	No (always 0)
5	Numeric group ID of file's owner	No (always 0)
6	Device identifier (special files only)	Yes (drive #)
7	Total size of file, in bytes	Yes (but does not include the size of any alternate data streams)
8	Last access time since the epoch	Yes
9	Last modify time since the epoch	Yes
10	Inode change time since the epoch	Yes (but is file *creation* time)
11	Preferred block size for filesystem I/O	No (always null)
12	Actual number of blocks allocated	No (always null)

[a] Fans of the first edition of this book might notice that this chart has lost a column. The transition from Mac OS to Mac OS X brought along a massive amount of compatibility changes (unusually, making it *more* compatible), rendering the Mac OS column unnecessary.

If dealing with time values on Windows systems in a way that is consistent with Unix systems is important to you, you will want to install the module Win32::UTCFileTime, by Steve Hay, and read its documentation carefully. Windows systems have some issues reporting file times as they relate to daylight savings time. This module can override the standard Perl stat() and other calls to fix the problems.

In addition to stat() and lstat(), some versions of Perl have special mechanisms for returning attributes of a file that are particular to a specific OS. See Chapter 2 for discussions of functions like Win32::FileSecurity::Get().

Once you have queried the stat() values for a file, the next step is to compare the "interesting" values against a known set of values for that file that you've pre-generated and kept secure. If the values have changed, something about the file must have changed. Here's a program that both generates a string of lstat() values and checks files against a known set of those values. We intentionally exclude field #8 from Table 11-1 (last access time) because it changes every time a file is read.

This program takes either a -p *filename* argument to print lstat() values for a given file or a -c *filename* argument to check the lstat() values for all of the files recorded in *filename*:

```
use Getopt::Std;

# we use this for prettier output later in PrintChanged()
my @statnames = qw(dev ino mode nlink uid gid rdev
    size mtime ctime blksize blocks);

getopt( 'p:c:', \my %opt );

die "Usage: $0 [-p <filename>|-c <filename>]\n"
    unless ( $opt{p} or $opt{c} );

if ( $opt{p} ) {
    die "Unable to stat file $opt{p}:$!\n"
        unless ( -e $opt{p} );
    print $opt{p}, '|', join( '|', ( lstat( $opt{p} ) )[ 0 .. 7, 9 .. 12 ] ),
        "\n";
    exit;
}

if ( $opt{c} ) {
    open my $CFILE, '<', $opt{c}
        or die "Unable to open check file $opt{c}:$!\n";
    while (<$CFILE>) {
        chomp;
        my @savedstats = split('\|');
        die "Wrong number of fields in line beginning with "$savedstats[0]\n"
            unless ( scalar @savedstats == 13 );
        my @currentstats = ( lstat( $savedstats[0] ) )[ 0 .. 7, 9 .. 12 ];
```

```
            # print the changed fields only if something has changed
            PrintChanged( \@savedstats, \@currentstats )
                    if ( "@savedstats[1..12]" ne "@currentstats" );
        }
        close $CFILE;
    }

    # iterates through attribute lists and prints any changes between
    # the two
    sub PrintChanged {
        my ( $saved, $current ) = @_;

        # prints the name of the file after popping it off of the array read
        # from the check file
        print shift @{$saved}, ":\n";

        for ( my $i = 0; $i <= $#{$saved}; $i++ ) {
            if ( $saved->[$i] ne $current->[$i] ) {
                print "\t" . $statnames[$i] . ' is now ' . $current->[$i];
                print ' (should be ' . $saved->[$i] . ")\n";
            }
        }
    }
```

To use this program, we might type `checkfile -p /etc/passwd >> checksumfile`. `check sumfile` should then contain a line that looks like this:

```
/etc/passwd|1792|11427|33060|1|0|0|24959|607|921016509|921016509|8192|2
```

We would then repeat this step for each other file we want to monitor. Then, running the script with `checkfile -c checksumfile` will show any changes. For instance, if we remove a character from *etc/passwd*, the script will complain like this:

```
/etc/passwd:
        size is now 606 (should be 607)
        mtime is now 921020731 (should be 921016509)
        ctime is now 921020731 (should be 921016509)
```

Before we move on, there's one quick Perl trick in this code that I want to mention. The following line demonstrates a quick-and-dirty way of comparing two lists for equality (or lack thereof):

```
if ("@savedstats[1..12]" ne "@currentstats");
```

Perl automatically "stringifies" the contents of the two lists by concatenating the list elements with a space between them, doing essentially this:

```
join(' ',@savedstats[1..12]))
```

Then, the resulting strings are compared. For short lists where the order and number of the list elements is important, and the elements themselves do not contain the list separator ($", normally a space character), this technique works well. In most other cases, modules like `Array::Compare` can be of service.

Now that you have file attributes under your belt, I've got bad news for you. Checking to see that a file's attributes have not changed is a good first step, but it doesn't go far enough. It is not difficult to alter a file while keeping attributes like the last access and modification times the same. Perl even has a function, `utime()`, for changing the access or modification times of a file. Time to pull out the power tools.

Detecting changes in data is one of the fortés of a particular set of algorithms known as "message-digest algorithms." Here's how Ron Rivest describes a particular message-digest algorithm called the "RSA Data Security, Inc. MD5 Message-Digest Algorithm" in RFC 1321:

> The algorithm takes as input a message of arbitrary length and produces as output a 128-bit "fingerprint" or "message digest" of the input. It is conjectured that it is computationally infeasible to produce two messages having the same message digest, or to produce any message having a given prespecified target message digest.

For our purposes, this means that if we run a message digest algorithm such as MD5 (or, better, SHA) on a file we'll get a unique fingerprint. If the data in this file were to change in any way, no matter how small, the fingerprint for that file would change.

MD5 Considered Harmful?

With apologies to Dan Kaminsky (one of my favorite security researchers), who wrote the paper called "MD5 To Be Considered Harmful Someday" cited in the references section at the end of this chapter, here's a brief note about why none of the MD5 code from the first edition is still found in this chapter.

Since the first edition of this book was published, Ron Rivest's conjecture from 1992 "that it is computationally infeasible to produce two messages having the same message digest" turned out to be a bit, umm, optimistic, especially in the face of some interesting mathematical attacks and the aggregate computing power (clusters and spare cycle scavenging contests) now available. It's now somewhat easier to construct two files that have the same MD5 message digest.

Note that I said "easier" and not "easy." This sidebar may seem equally optimistic some day, but it is *my* conjecture that if someone is going to go to the (currently) considerable trouble to create a substitute file with the same MD5 hash as one of your important files, you've got bigger problems than the message digest algorithm in use.

That being said, it took me maybe 5 seconds per program to swap in SHA-256 for MD5, because the `Digest::SHA` module by Mark Shelor has an almost identical interface to Gisle Aas's `Digest::MD5`. It supports other members of the SHA-2 family as well, so feel free to ratchet up the digest length should you want even more warm fuzziness. I've swapped out the MD5 code in this chapter to make sure you don't get taunted about weak message digest algorithms at work.

The easiest way to harness this magic from Perl is through the `Digest` module family and its `Digest::SHA` module.

The `Digest::SHA` module is easy to use. You create a `Digest::SHA` object, add the data to it using the `add()` or `addfile()` method, and then ask the module to create a digest (fingerprint) for you.

To compute the SHA-256 fingerprint for a password file on Unix, we could use something like this:

```
use Digest::SHA;

my $sha = Digest::SHA->new(256);

# 'p' means 'portable mode'; it converts line endings in
# data to Unix format so the same code yields the same
# digest on different operating systems. Feel free to
# leave that out if that is not a concern for you.
$sha->addfile( '/etc/passwd', 'p' );

print $sha->hexdigest . "\n";
```

We can also string methods together to make the program more compact:

```
use Digest::SHA;

print Digest::SHA->new(256)->addfile( '/etc/passwd', 'p' )->hexdigest, "\n";
```

Both of these code snippets print out:

```
c0e541600943622fe8ddf4142072107f076a8da35d1e39bc1c8c91a3892a46da
```

If we make even the slightest change to that file, the output changes. Here's the output after I transpose just *two characters* in the password file:

```
ef88f8ce4c24eaa2d5937e929955d0eb63caf4813026ca8c877e3cc4b123c3ac
```

Any change in the data now becomes obvious. If we were to change it back, the fingerprint would return to the previous one, but the `stat()` information would reflect that the file had been updated.

Let's extend our previous attribute-checking program to include SHA-256:

```
use Getopt::Std;
use Digest::SHA;

# we use this for prettier output later in PrintChanged()
my @statnames = qw(dev ino mode nlink uid gid rdev
    size mtime ctime blksize blocks SHA-256);

getopt( 'p:c:', \my %opt );

die "Usage: $0 [-p <filename>|-c <filename>]\n"
    unless ( $opt{p} or $opt{c} );

if ( $opt{p} ) {
    die "Unable to stat file $opt{p}:$!\n"
        unless ( -e $opt{p} );

    my $digest = Digest::SHA->new(256)->addfile( $opt{p}, 'p' )->hexdigest;
```

```perl
            print $opt{p}, '|', join( '|', ( lstat( $opt{p} ) )[ 0 .. 7, 9 .. 12 ] ),
                "|$digest", "\n";
            exit;
}

if ( $opt{c} ) {
    open my $CFILE, '<', $opt{c}
        or die "Unable to open check file $opt{c}:$!\n";
    while (<$CFILE>) {
        chomp;
        my @savedstats = split('\|');
        die "Wrong number of fields in line beginning with $savedstats[0]\n"
            unless ( scalar @savedstats == 14 );
        my @currentstats = ( lstat( $savedstats[0] ) )[ 0 .. 7, 9 .. 12 ];
        push( @currentstats,
            Digest::SHA->new(256)->addfile( $savedstats[0] )->hexdigest );

        # print the changed fields only if something has changed
        PrintChanged( \@savedstats, \@currentstats )
            if ( "@savedstats[1..13]" ne "@currentstats" );
    }
    close $CFILE;
}

# iterates through attributes lists and prints any changes between
# the two
sub PrintChanged {
    my ( $saved, $current ) = @_;

    # prints the name of the file after popping it off of the array read
    # from the check file
    print shift @{$saved}, ":\n";

    for ( my $i = 0; $i <= $#{$saved}; $i++ ) {
        if ( $saved->[$i] ne $current->[$i] ) {
            print "\t" . $statnames[$i] . ' is now ' . $current->[$i];
            print " (should be " . $saved->[$i] . ")\n";
        }
    }
}
```

One last tip on monitoring filesystem changes before we switch topics: many operating systems have a built-in way to look for changes to a filesystem—Linux has *inotify* (previously *dnotify* was available), Mac OS X 10.5+ has a filesystem events API (available for use from Perl using Andy Grundman's Mac::FSEvents module), and Windows has the built-in auditing mechanism we looked at in Chapter 4. One of these facilities may come in handy for you.

Changes in Data Served Over the Network

We've looked at ways to detect changes on our local filesystem. How about noticing changes on other machines or in the services they provide? In Chapter 5, we saw ways to query NIS and DNS. It would be easy to check repeated queries to these services for changes. For instance, if our DNS servers are configured to allow this, we can pretend to be a secondary server and request a dump (i.e., a "zone transfer") of that server's data for a particular domain:

```
use Net::DNS;

# takes two command-line arguments: the first is the name server
# to query, the second is the domain to query from that name server
my $server = new Net::DNS::Resolver;
$server->nameservers( $ARGV[0] );

print STDERR 'Transfer in progress...';
my @zone = $server->axfr( $ARGV[1] );
die $server->errorstring unless @zone;
print STDERR "done.\n";

foreach my $record (@zone) {
    $record->print;
}
```

 All correctly configured DNS servers should be set to strictly control which hosts can perform a zone transfer. Code like this must run on one of those permitted hosts.

Let's combine this idea with SHA-256. Instead of printing the zone information, let's take a digest of it:

```
use Net::DNS;
use FreezeThaw qw(freeze);
use Digest::SHA;

my $server = new Net::DNS::Resolver;
$server->nameservers( $ARGV[0] );

print STDERR 'Transfer in progress...';
my @zone = $server->axfr( $ARGV[1] );
die $server->errorstring unless @zone;
print STDERR "done.\n";

my $zone = join( '', sort map { freeze($_) } @zone );

print "SHA-2 fingerprint for this zone transfer is: \n";
print Digest::SHA->new(256)->add($zone)->hexdigest, "\n";
```

SHA-256 (or any message digest algorithm) works on a scalar chunk of data (a message), not a Perl list-of-hashes data structure like @zone. That's where this line of code comes into play:

```
my $zone = join( '', sort map { freeze($_) } @zone );
```

We're using the FreezeThaw module introduced in Chapter 10 to flatten each @zone record data structure into a plain text string. Any other module like this (e.g., Data::Dumper) could also be used. Once flattened, the records are sorted before being concatenated into one large scalar value. The sort step allows us to ignore the order in which the records are returned in the zone transfer.

Dumping the contents of an entire zone file is a bit extreme, especially for large zones, so it may make more sense to monitor only an important subset of addresses. It is also a good idea to restrict the ability to do zone transfers to as few machines as possible, for security reasons.

The material we've seen so far doesn't get you completely out of the woods. Here are a few questions you might want to ponder:

- What if someone tampers with your database of SHA-256 digests and substitutes valid fingerprints for their Trojan file replacements or service changes?
- What if someone tampers with your script so it only *appears* to check the digests against your database?
- What if someone tampers with the SHA module on your system?
- For the ultimate in paranoia, what if someone manages to tamper with the Perl executable, one of its shared libraries, or the operating system core itself?[‡]

The usual ways of dealing with these threats (poor as they may be) involve keeping known good copies of everything related to the tamper-checking process (digest databases, modules, statically linked Perl, etc.) on read-only media.

This conundrum is another illustration of the continuum of security. It is always possible to find more to fear. The trick is to find a balance between paranoia and laziness.

Noticing Suspicious Activities

A good night watchman needs more than just the ability to monitor for change. He also needs to be able to spot suspicious activities and circumstances. Someone needs to notice holes in the perimeter fence and unexplained bumps in the night. We can write programs to play this role.

Local Signs of Peril

It's unfortunate, but a talent for spotting signs of suspicious activity often comes as a result of experiencing pain and the desire to avoid it in the future. After the first few security breaches, you'll start to notice that intruders often follow certain patterns and

---

[‡] If you haven't read Ken Thompson's seminal paper "Reflections on Trusting Trust" (*http://cm.bell-labs.com/who/ken/trust.html*), you really must.

leave behind telltale clues. Spotting these signs, once you know what they are, is often easy in Perl.

> After each security breach, it is vitally important that you take a few moments to perform a postmortem of the incident. Document (to the best of your knowledge) where the intruders came in, what tools or holes they used, what they did, who else they attacked, what you did in response, and so on.
>
> It is tempting to return to normal daily life and forget the break-in. If you can resist this temptation, you'll find later that you've gained something from the incident, rather than just wasting time and effort. The Nietzschean principle of "that which does not kill you makes you stronger" is often applicable in the system administration realm.

For instance, intruders—especially the less sophisticated kind—often try to hide their activities by creating "hidden" directories to store their data. On Unix systems they will put exploit code and sniffer output in directories with names like "..." (dot dot dot), ". " (dot space), or " Mail" (space Mail). These names are likely to be passed over in a cursory inspection of *ls* output.

We can easily write a program to search for these names using the tools introduced in Chapter 2. Here's a program based on the `File::Find` module that looks for anomalous directory names:

```
use File::Find;

find( \&wanted, '.' );

sub wanted {

    ( -d $_ ) and       # is a directory
        $_ ne '.' and $_ ne '..' and      # is not . or ..
        (
        /[^-.a-zA-Z0-9+,:;_~\$#()]/ or    # contains a "bad" character
        /^\.{3,}/               or    # or starts with at least 3 dots
        /^-/                          # or begins with a dash
        ) and print "'" . nice($File::Find::name) . "'\n";
}

# Print a "nice" version of the directory name, i.e., with control chars
# displayed. This subroutine is barely modified from &unctrl() in Perl's
# stock dumpvar.pl. If we wanted to be less of a copycat we could
# use something like Devel::Dumpvar instead.
sub nice {
    my $name = shift;
    $name =~ s/([\001-\037\177])/'^'.pack('c',ord($1)^64)/eg;

    return $name;
}
```

A prettier option is the `File::Find::Rule` equivalent of the same code:

```
use File::Find::Rule;

my @problems
    = File::Find::Rule->name( qr/[^-.a-zA-ZO-9+,:;_~\$#()]/,
                              qr/^\.{3,}/,
                              qr/^-/ )
                ->in('.');

foreach my $name (@problems) {
    print "'" . nice($name) . "'\n";
}

# Print a "nice" version of the directory name, i.e., with control chars
# explicated. This subroutine is barely modified from &unctrl() in Perl's
# stock dumpvar.pl. If we wanted to be less of a copycat we could
# use something like Devel::Dumpvar instead.
sub nice {
    my $name = shift;
    $name =~ s/([\001-\037\177])/'^'.pack('c',ord($1)^64)/eg;

    return $name;
}
```

The effectiveness of filesystem-sifting programs often hinges on the quality and quantity of their regular expressions. If you use too few regexps, you miss things you might want to catch. If you use too many regexps or regexps that are inefficient, your program runs for too long and uses too many resources. If you use regexps that are too loose, the program will generate many false positives. It's a delicate balance.

Finding Problematic Patterns

We've just talked about looking for suspicious objects; now let's move on to looking for *patterns* that may indicate suspicious activity. We can demonstrate this with a program that does some primitive log file analysis to identify potential break-ins.

This example is based on the following premise: most users logging in remotely do so consistently from the same place or a small list of places. That is, they usually log in remotely from a single machine, or from the same ISP each time. If you find an account that has logged in from more than a handful of domains, it's a good indicator that this account has been compromised and the password has been widely distributed. Obviously this premise does not hold for populations of highly mobile users (especially if they are using a VPN or company proxy server), but if you find an account that has been logged into from Brazil and Finland in the same two-hour period, that's a pretty good indicator that something is fishy.

Let's walk through some code that looks for this indicator. This code is Unix-centric, but the techniques demonstrated in it are platform-independent. First, here's our built-in documentation. It's not a bad idea to put something like this near the top of your program for the sake of other people who will read your code.[*] Before we move on, be sure to take a quick look at the arguments the rest of the program will support:

```
sub usage {
    print <<"EOU";
lastcheck - check the output of the last command on a machine
            to determine if any user has logged in from > N domains
            (inspired by an idea from Daniel Rinehart)

    USAGE: lastcheck [args], where args can be any of:
     -i <class>    for IP #'s, treat class <B|C> subnets as the same "domain"
     -f <domain>   count only foreign domains, specify home domain
     -l <command>  use <command> instead of default /usr/bin/last -a
                   note: no output format checking is done!
     -m <#>        max number of unique domains allowed, default 3
     -u <user>     perform check for only this username

     -h            this help message

EOU
    exit;
}
```

First we parse the user's command-line arguments. The getopts line in the following code will look at the arguments to the program and set $opt{<*flag letter*>:} appropriately. The colon after the letter means that option takes an argument:

```
use Getopt::Std;
use Regexp::Common qw(net);

getopts( 'i:hf:l:m:u:', \my %opt );     # parse user input

usage() if ( defined $opt{h} );

# number of unique domains before we complain (default 3)
my $maxdomains = $opt{m} ||= 3;

# keep network block upcased, provide default of 'C'-sized
if ( exists $opt{i} ) {
    $opt{i} = uc $opt{i};
    $opt{i} ||= 'C';
}
```

The following lines reflect the portability versus efficiency decision we discussed in Chapter 4. If you wanted to make the program a little more efficient (but less portable), you could use unpack(), as discussed in that chapter. Here, we're opting to call an external program:

```
my $lastex = $opt{l} ||= '/usr/bin/last -a';

open my $LAST, '-|', $lastex || die "Can't run the program $lastex:$!\n";
```

---

[*] If you want to be really cool and impress all your friends, use something like Pod::Usage's pod2usage() to allow your program to display its own manual page based on embedded documentation in POD format.

Before we get any further into the program, let's take a quick look at the hash-of-hashes data structure this program uses as it processes the data from last. This hash will have a username as its key and a reference to a sub-hash with the unique domains that user has logged in from as its keys. The values of the sub-hash don't really matter. We're just using a sub-hash instead of a sub-list because it makes it very easy to keep the list of domains associated with a user unique.

For instance, a sample entry might be:

```
$userinfo { 'laf' } = { 'ccs.example.edu' => undef,
                        'xerox.com'       => undef,
                        'tpu.edu'         => undef }
```

This entry shows that the user *laf* has logged in from the *ccs.example.edu*, *xerox.com*, and *tpu.edu* domains.

We begin by iterating over the input we get from last. On my system, the output looks like this:

```
cindy    pts/145  Thu Jan  1 20:57    still logged in nwbdfsd42.hsd1.ma.comcast.net
michael  pts/145  Thu Jan  1 20:27 - 20:27  (00:00)  pool-68-25-87.bos.verizon.net
david    pts/113  Thu Jan  1 18:51    still logged in 65.64.24.204
deborah  pts/110  Thu Jan  1 14:48 - 15:42  (00:54)  nat-service4.example.net
barbara  pts/158  Thu Jan  1 10:25 - 11:22  (00:57)  65.96.246.34
jerry    pts/81   Thu Jan  1 10:04 - 12:13  (02:09)  athedsl-4392.home.otenet.gr
```

Early on in the while loop, we try to skip lines that contain cases we don't care about. In general, it is a good idea to check for special cases like these at the beginning of your loops before any actual processing of data (e.g., data extraction with //) takes place. This lets the program quickly identify when it can skip a particular line and continue reading input:

```perl
my %userinfo;
while (<$LAST>) {

    # ignore special users
    next if /^reboot\s|^shutdown\s|^ftp\s/;

    # if we've used -u to specify a specific user, skip all entries
    # that don't pertain to this user (whose name is stored in $opt{u}
    # by getopts for us)
    next if ( defined $opt{u} && !/^$opt{u}\s/ );

    # ignore X console logins
    next if /:0\s+(:0)?/;

    chomp;    # chomp if we think we still might be interested in the line

    # find the user's name, tty, and remote hostname
    my ( $user, $host ) = /^([a-z0-9-.]+)\s.*\s([a-zA-Z0-9-.]+)$/;

    # ignore if the log had a bad username after parsing
    next if ( length($user) < 2 );
```

```
    # ignore if no domain name or IP info in name
    next if $host !~ /\./;

    # find the domain name of this host (see explanation following code)
    my $dn = domain($host);

    # ignore if you get a bogus domain name
    next if ( length($dn) < 2 );

    # ignore this input line if it is in the home domain as specified
    # by the -f switch
    next if ( defined $opt{f} && ( $dn =~ /^$opt{f}/ ) );

    # store the info for this user
    $userinfo{$user}{$dn} = undef;
}
close $LAST;
```

There's one utility subroutine, domain(), that takes a fully qualified domain name
(FQDN)—i.e., a hostname with the full domain name attached—and returns its best
guess at the domain name of that host. It has to make a few choices because not all
hostnames in the logs will be actual names; they may be simple IP addresses. In this
case, if the person running the script has set the -i switch, we assume any IP address
we get is a class B or C network subnetted on the standard byte boundary. In practical
terms, this means that we treat the first two or three octets as the "domain name" of
the host. This allows us to treat logins from 192.168.1.10, for example, as coming from
the same logical source as logins from 192.168.1.12. This may not be the best of
assumptions, but it is the best we can do without consulting another source of information (and it works most of the time). If the user does not use the -i switch, we treat
the entire IP address as the domain of record.

Here's the code for this subroutine, followed by one quick comment:

```
# take an FQDN and attempt to return the FQD
sub domain {
    my $fdqn_or_ip = shift;

    if ( $fdqn_or_ip =~ /^$RE{net}{IPv4}{-keep}$/ ) {
        if ( exists $opt{i} ) {
            return ( $opt{i} eq 'B' ) ? "$2.$3" : "$2.$3.$4";
        }
        else { return $fdqn_or_ip; }
    }
    else {

        # Ideally we'd check against $RE{net}{domain}{-nospace}, but this
        # (as of this writing) enforces the RFC 1035 spec, which
        # has been updated by RFC 1101. This is a problem
        # for domains that begin with numbers (e.g., 3com.com).

        # downcase the info for consistency's sake
        $fdqn_or_ip = lc $fdqn_or_ip;
```

```
            # then return everything after first dot
            $fdqn_or_ip =~ /^[^.]+\.(.*)/;
            return $1;
        }
    }
```

The most interesting thing about this code is the use of `Regexp::Common` to do some of its dirty work. The match that determines whether the input to the subroutine was an IP address has someone else's smarts embedded in it. Using `Regexp::Common` means we don't have to think hard about constructing the right regexp to both identify the correct format and dice it properly. With the `{-keep}` subkey, it not only matches valid IP addresses but also sets (as per the documentation):

- `$1` to the entire match
- `$2` to the first component of the address
- `$3` to the second component of the address
- `$4` to the third component of the address
- `$5` to the final component of the address

We first saw `Regexp::Common` in Chapter 8, but I thought it deserved a second cameo because of its usefulness.

That's it for iterating over the output of `last` and building our data structure. To wrap up this program, let's run through all the users we found and check how many unique domains each has logged in from (i.e., the number of keys we've stored for each user). For those entries that have more domains than our comfort level, we print the contents:

```
foreach my $user ( sort keys %userinfo ) {
    if ( scalar keys %{ $userinfo{$user} } > $maxdomains ) {
        print "\n\n$user has logged in from:\n";
        print join( "\n", sort keys %{ $userinfo{$user} } );
    }
}
print "\n";
```

Now that you've seen the code, you might wonder if this approach really works. Here's some real sample output from our program (with some of the hostnames truncated to protect the innocent) for a user who had her password sniffed at another site:

```
username has logged in from:
38.254.131
bu.edu
ccs.neu.ed
dac.neu.ed
hials.no
ipt.a
tnt1.bos1
tnt1.bost
tnt1.dia
tnt2.bos
tnt3.bos
```

```
tnt4.bos
toronto4.di
```

Some of these entries look normal for a user in the Boston area. However, the *toronto4.di* entry is a bit suspect, and the *hials.no* site is in Norway. Busted!

This program could be further refined to include the element of time or correlations with another log file, like that from *tcpwrappers*. But as you can see, pattern detection is often very useful by itself.

Danger on the Wire, or "Perl Saves the Day"

Here's a true story that shows how Perl can help in crisis times. One Saturday evening I casually logged into a machine on my network to read my email. Much to my surprise, I found our mail and web servers near death and fading fast. Attempts to read and send mail or look at web content yielded slow responses, hung connections, and outright connection failures. Our mail queue was starting to reach critical mass.

I looked first at the state of the servers. The interactive response was fine, and the CPU load was high, but not deadly. One sign of trouble was the number of mail processes running. According to the mail logs, there were more processes running than expected because many transactions were not completing. Processes that had started up to handle incoming connections from the outside were hanging, driving up the load. This load was then capping any new outgoing connections from initiating. This strange network behavior led me to examine the current connection table of the server using netstat.

The last column of the netstat output told me that there were indeed many connections in progress on that machine from many different hosts. The big shocker was the state of those connections. Instead of looking like this:

```
tcp    0    0  mailhub.3322    mail.mel.aone.ne.smtp   ESTABLISHED
tcp    0    0  mailhub.3320    edunet.edunet.dk.smtp   CLOSE_WAIT
tcp    0    0  mailhub.1723    kraken.mvnet.wne.smtp   ESTABLISHED
tcp    0    0  mailhub.1709    plover.net.bridg.smtp   CLOSE_WAIT
```

they looked more like this:

```
tcp    0    0  mailhub.3322    mail.mel.aone.ne.smtp   SYN_RCVD
tcp    0    0  mailhub.3320    edunet.edunet.dk.smtp   SYN_RCVD
tcp    0    0  mailhub.1723    kraken.mvnet.wne.smtp   SYN_RCVD
tcp    0    0  mailhub.1709    plover.net.bridg.smtp   CLOSE_WAIT
```

At first, this looked like a classic denial of service attack called a SYN flood or a SYN-ACK attack. To understand these attacks, we have to digress for a moment and talk a little bit about how the TCP/IP protocol works.

Every TCP/IP connection begins with a handshake between the participants. This little dance lets both the initiator and the recipient signal their readiness to enter into a conversation. The first step is taken by the initiating network entity. It sends a SYN (for

SYNchronize) packet to the recipient. If the recipient wishes to talk, it will send back a SYN-ACK, an ACKnowledgment of the request, and record that a conversation is about to begin in its pending connection table. The initiator then replies to the SYN-ACK with an ACK packet, confirming that the SYN-ACK was heard. The recipient hears the ACK, removes the entry from its pending table, and away they go.

At least, that's what should happen. In a SYN flood situation, a nogoodnik will send a flood of SYN packets to a machine, often with spoofed source addresses. The unsuspecting machine will send SYN-ACKs to all the spoofed source addresses and open an entry in its pending communication table for each SYN packet it has received. These bogus connection entries will stay in the pending table until the OS ages them out using some default timeout value. If enough packets are sent, the pending communication table will fill up and no legitimate connection attempts will succeed. This leads to symptoms like those I was experiencing at the time, and similar netstat output.

The one anomaly in the netstat output that made me question this diagnosis was the variety of hosts represented in the table. It was possible that the attacker had a program with superb spoofing capabilities, but you usually expect to see many connections from a smaller set of bogus hosts (unless they are using a botnet to launch a distributed denial of service attack). Many of these hosts also seemed perfectly legitimate and unlikely to be zombies. Further clouding the situation were the results of a few connectivity tests I ran. Sometimes I could ping or traceroute to a randomly selected host listed in my netstat output, and sometimes I couldn't. I needed more data. I needed to get a better grasp on the connectivity to these remote hosts. That's where Perl came in.

Because I was writing code under the gun, I wrote a very simple script that relied on the output of two other external network programs to handle the hard parts of the task. Let me show you that version, and then we'll use this task as a springboard for some more advanced programming.

The task in this case boiled down to one question: could I reach the hosts that appeared to be trying to connect to me? To find out which hosts were trying to contact my machine, I turned to a program called *clog* written by Brian Mitchell, found at *http://coast.cs.purdue.edu/pub/tools/unix/logutils/clog/*. *clog* uses the Unix libpcap library from Lawrence Berkeley National Laboratory's Network Research Group to sniff the network for TCP connection requests (i.e., SYN packets). This is the same library used by the seminal network monitoring program *tcpdump*. Found at *http://www.tcpdump.org*, libpcap works for most Unix variants. A libpcap port for Windows can be found at *http://www.winpcap.org*.

clog reports SYN packets like this:

```
Mar 02 11:21|192.168.1.51|1074|192.168.1.104|113
Mar 02 11:21|192.168.1.51|1094|192.168.1.104|23
```

The preceding output shows two connection requests from 192.168.1.51 to 192.168.1.104. The first was an attempt to connect to port 113 (*ident*), and the second to port 23 (*telnet*).

With *clog*, I was able to learn which hosts were attempting to connect to me, and now I needed to know whether I could also reach them. That task was left to a program called *fping*, written by Roland J. Schemers III and now maintained by Thomas Dzubin. *fping*, which can be found at *http://www.fping.com*, is a fast and fancy *ping* program for testing network connectivity on Unix and variants. Putting these external commands together, we get this little Perl program:

```perl
use Readonly;

# location/switches of clog
Readonly my $clogex => '/tmp/clog';

# location/switches of fping
Readonly my $fpingex => '/arch/unix/bin/fping -r1';

Readonly my $localnet => '192.168.1';    # local network
my %cache;

open my $CLOG, '-|', "$clogex" or die "Unable to run clog:$!\n";
while (<$CLOG>) {
    my ( $date, $orighost, $origport, $desthost, $destport ) = split(/\|/);
    next if ( $orighost =~ /^$localnet\b/ );
    next if ( exists $cache{$orighost} );
    print `$fpingex $orighost`;
    $cache{$orighost} = 1;
}

# we'd never really get here because we were in an infinite loop,
# but this is just good practice should we change the code above
close $CLOG;
```

This program runs the `clog` command and reads its output *ad infinitum*. Since our internal network connectivity wasn't suspect, it checked each originating host against the local network's addressing prefix and ignored traffic from the local network.

We perform some rudimentary caching in this code. To be a good net citizen we want to avoid hammering outside machines with multiple *ping* packets, so we keep track of every host we've already queried. The `-r1` flag to *fping* is used to restrict the number of times *fping* will retry a host (the default is three retries).

This program has to be run with elevated privileges, since both *clog* and *fping* need privileged access to the computer's network interface. On my system, the program printed output like this:

```
199.174.175.99 is unreachable
128.148.157.143 is unreachable
204.241.60.5 is alive
199.2.26.116 is unreachable
199.172.62.5 is unreachable
130.111.39.100 is alive
207.70.7.25 is unreachable
198.214.63.11 is alive
129.186.1.10 is alive
```

Clearly something fishy was going on here. Why would half of the sites be reachable, and the other half unreachable? Before we answer that question, let's look at what we could do to improve this program. A first step would be to remove the external program dependencies. Learning how to sniff the network and send *ping* packets from Perl opens a whole range of possibilities. Let's take care of removing the easy dependency first.

The `Net::Ping` module (written by Russell Mosemann and now maintained by Steve Peters), found in the Perl distribution, can help us with testing connectivity to network hosts. `Net::Ping` allows us to send three different flavors of *ping* packets—ICMP, TCP, and UDP—and check for a return response. Internet Control Message Protocol (ICMP) echo packets are "*ping* classic," the kind of packet sent by the vast majority of the command-line *ping* programs. This particular packet flavor has one major disadvantage, though: like our previous *clog/fping* code, any `Net::Ping` scripts using ICMP need to be run with elevated privileges.

If you don't like the "run with elevated privileges" restriction, I'd recommend using `Net::Ping::External` by Alexandr Ciornii and Colin McMillen.

`Net::Ping::External` is a wrapper that knows how to call the `ping` command in your path on many different operating systems and parse the results. Since the operating system's `ping` command is already set up in some fashion (e.g., the executable might be marked *setuid root*) to work when called by mere mortal users, calling it from Perl means your code will also have this ability. If you want to cut out the middleman on Windows systems, Toby Ovod-Everett's `Win32::PingICMP` uses `Win32::API` to call *ICMP.DLL* just like the standard `ping` command does.

I'll stick to `Net::Ping` in this particular example (since we'll need to run with elevated privileges to sniff the network) but switching to either of these two alternatives is quite easy.

The other two choices for `Net::Ping` packets are TCP (Transmission Control Protocol) and UDP (User Datagram Protocol). Both of these choices send packets to a remote machine's *echo* service port. Using these options gains you portability, but you may find them less reliable than ICMP. ICMP is built into all standard TCP/IP stacks, but all machines may not be running the *echo* service. As a result, unless ICMP is deliberately filtered, you are more likely to receive a response to an ICMP packet than to the other types.

`Net::Ping` uses the standard object-oriented programming model, so the first step is the creation of a new `ping` object instance:

```
use Net::Ping;
my $p = Net::Ping->new('icmp');
```

Using this object is simple:

```
if ( $p->ping($host) ) {
    print "ping succeeded.\n";
}
else {
    print "ping failed\n";
}
```

Now let's dig into the hard part of our initial script, the network sniffing. Earlier, we used the *clog* program to handle that work, but it was written for Unix systems so using it on another operating system may be dicey (or downright impossible). We're going to need a different solution if we expect to perform this function on anything but a Unix variant.

The first step toward using Perl in this case is to build and/or install `libpcap` (or, if you're on Windows, `winpcap`) on your machine. I recommend you also build and/or install *tcpdump*. *tcpdump* can be used to explore `libpcap` functionality before coding Perl or to double-check that code.

With `libpcap` built, it's easy to build the `Net::Pcap` module (originally written by Peter Lister, completely rewritten by Tim Potter, and now maintained by Sébastien Aperghis-Tramoni). This module gives you full access to the power of `libpcap`. Let's first take a look at a very simple `Net::Pcap` example, and then develop it into something that we can use to find `SYN` packets, similar to *clog*.

Our example code begins by requesting a packet capture descriptor for the specified device (in this case, the wireless adaptor on my laptop):

```
use Net::Pcap qw(:functions);

# could also use lookupdev and findalldevs to find the right device
my $dev = 'en1';

# prepare to capture 1500 bytes from each packet,
# promiscuously (i.e., all traffic, not just sent to us),
# with no packet timeout, placing any error messages
# for this call in $err
my $err;
my $pcap = open_live( $dev, 1500, 1, 1, \$err )
    or die "Unable to open_live device $dev: $err\n";
```

 If you'd like your code to be smarter about which device to open, check out the `Net::Pcap::FindDevice` module in Max Maischein's `Sniffer::HTTP` package. It has the best set of heuristics I've seen for that purpose.

Now we ask `Net::Pcap` to begin the actual capture:

```
# capture packets until interrupted
my $ret = loop( $pcap, -1, \&printpacketlength, '' );
warn 'Unable to perform capture:' . geterr($pcap) . "\n"
    if ( $ret == -1 );

Net::Pcap::close($pcap);
```

This says to start capturing packets (`-1` says do so until interrupted; we could give a set number of packets here instead). Each time we capture a packet, we hand it to the callback code in `printpacketlength()` for processing. Should we not capture any packets, we print an error and attempt to nicely close the device associated with our packet capture descriptor.

Callback subroutines like `printpacketlength()` receive a few pieces of data from `loop()`:

- A user ID string, optionally set when starting a capture, that allows a callback procedure to distinguish between several open packet capture sessions
- A reference to a hash describing the packet header (timestamps, etc.)
- A copy of the entire packet

It's the third item in that list that lets us trivially compute the packet length for every packet:

```
sub printpacketlength {
    my ( $user_data, $header, $packet ) = @_;
    print length($packet), "\n";
}
```

If we run the code at this point, it will start spewing the packet length for every packet. That's the basics of using `Net::Pcap`.

OK, so let's get to the SYN capture question. `libpcap` gives you the ability to capture all network traffic or a select subset based on filter criteria of your choosing. Its filtering mechanism is very efficient, so it is often best to invoke it up front, rather than sifting through all the packets via Perl code. In our case, we need to look at only SYN packets.

So what's a SYN packet? To understand that, you need to know a little bit about how TCP packets are put together. Figure 11-1 shows a picture (from RFC 793) of a TCP packet and its header.

A SYN packet, for our purposes, is simply one that has only the SYN flag (highlighted in Figure 11-1) in the packet header set. In order to tell `libpcap` to capture packets like this, we need to specify which byte it should look at in the packet. Each tick mark above is a bit, so let's count bytes. Figure 11-2 shows the same packet with byte numbers.

We'll need to check if byte 13 is set to binary 00000010, or 2. The filter string we'll need is `tcp[13] = 2`. If we wanted to check for packets that had *at least* the SYN flag set, we could use `tcp[13] & 2 != 0`.

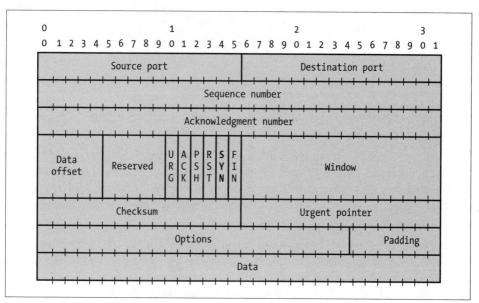

Figure 11-1. Diagram of a TCP packet

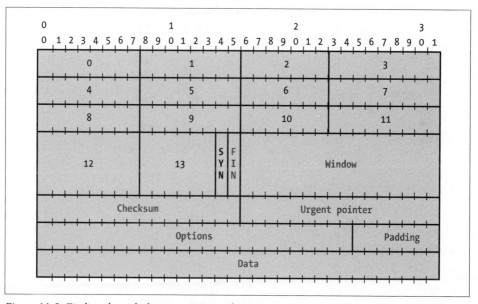

Figure 11-2. Finding the right byte in a TCP packet

To use this information in a `Net::Pcap` program, we need just a few additional lines of code before we begin the capture with `loop()`. The filter string we just constructed first gets compiled into a *filter program* and then set on the packet capture descriptor:

```
    my $filter_string = 'tcp[13] = 2';

    # compile and set our "filter program"
    Net::Pcap::compile( $pcap, \my $filter, $filter_string, 1, 0 )
        and die "unable to compile $filter_string\n";

    Net::Pcap::setfilter( $pcap, $filter ) and die "unable to set filter\n";
```

If we run the modified version of the code, we now see packet lengths only for those TCP packets with just the SYN flag set.

This code captures SYN packets and prints their lengths, but that's not quite where we wanted be when we started this section. We need a program that watches for SYN packets from another network and attempts to *ping* the originating hosts. We have almost all of the pieces; the only thing we are missing is a way to determine the sources of the SYN packets we've received.

As with our nitty-gritty DNS example in Chapter 5, we'll need to take a raw packet and dissect it. Usually this entails reading the specifications (RFCs) and constructing the necessary unpack() templates. Fortunately, Tim Potter has done this hard work for us, producing a set of NetPacket modules now maintained by Yanick Champoux: NetPacket::Ethernet, NetPacket::IP, NetPacket::TCP, NetPacket::ICMP, and so on. Each of these modules provides two methods: strip() and decode().

strip() simply returns the packet data with the network layer stripped from it. Remember, a TCP/IP packet on an Ethernet network is really just a TCP packet embedded in an IP packet embedded in an Ethernet packet. So, if $pkt holds a TCP/IP packet, NetPacket::Ethernet::strip($pkt) will return an IP packet (having stripped off the Ethernet layer). If you needed to get at the TCP portion of $pkt, you could use NetPacket::IP::strip(NetPacket::Ethernet::strip($packet)) to strip off both the IP and Ethernet layers.

decode() takes this one step further, breaking a packet into its component parts and returning an instance of an object that contains all of those parts. The following line returns an object instance with the fields detailed in Table 11-2:

```
    my $pobj = NetPacket::TCP->decode(
               NetPacket::IP::strip(NetPacket::Ethernet::strip($packet)))
```

Table 11-2. Fields accessible from the object returned by NetPacket::TCP's decode() method

Field name	Description
src_port	Source TCP port
dest_port	Destination TCP port
seqnum	TCP sequence number
acknum	TCP acknowledgment number
hlen	Header length
reserved	6-bit "reserved" space in the TCP header

Field name	Description
flags	URG, ACK, PSH, RST, SYN, and FIN flags
winsize	TCP window size
cksum	TCP checksum
urg	TCP urgent pointer
options	Any TCP options in binary form
data	Encapsulated data (payload) for this packet

These should look familiar to you from Figure 11-2. To get the destination TCP port for a packet, we can use:

```
my $dport = NetPacket::TCP->decode(
            NetPacket::IP::strip(
                NetPacket::Ethernet::strip($packet)))->{dest_port};
```

Let's tie this all together and then throw in two quick ways to make this task easier. Tim Potter created a small wrapper for the Net::Pcap initialization and loop code and released it in his Net::PcapUtils module. It handles several of the packet capture descriptor initialization steps we just performed, making our code shorter. Here it is in action, along with everything else we've learned along the way in the last section:

```
use Net::PcapUtils;
use NetPacket::Ethernet;
use NetPacket::IP;
use Net::Ping;
use Readonly;

Readonly my $dev      => 'en0';
Readonly my $localnet => '192.168.1';

# filter string that looks for SYN-only packets
# not originating from local network
Readonly my $filter_string => "tcp[13] = 2 and src net not $localnet";

my %cache;

$| = 1;    # unbuffer STDIO

# construct the ping object we'll use later
my $p = Net::Ping->new('icmp');

# and away we go
my $ret = Net::PcapUtils::loop(
    \&grab_ip_and_ping,
    FILTER => $filter_string,
    DEV    => $dev
);
die "Unable to perform capture: $ret\n" if $ret;
```

```
# find the source IP address of a packet, and ping it (once per run)
sub grab_ip_and_ping {
    my ( $arg, $hdr, $pkt ) = @_;

    # get the source IP adress
    my $src_ip
        = NetPacket::IP->decode( NetPacket::Ethernet::strip($pkt) )->{src_ip};

    print "$src_ip is "
        . ( ( $p->ping($src_ip) ) ? 'alive' : 'unreachable' ) . "\n"
        unless $cache{$src_ip}++;
}
```

If you like the idea of using wrapper modules to eliminate code, a relatively recent addition to the module scene can take things still further. Paul Miller's `Net::Pcap::Easy` attempts to provide built-in routines for the sorts of operations you find yourself rewriting over and over again when using `Net::Pcap`. Here's a rewrite of the previous code, with a brief explanation to follow:

```
use Net::Pcap::Easy;
use Net::Ping;
use Readonly;

Readonly my $dev       => 'en1';
Readonly my $localnet  => "192.168.1";

# filter string that looks for SYN-only packets
# not originating from local network
Readonly my $filter_string => "tcp[13] = 2 and src net not $localnet";

my %cache;

$| = 1;     # unbuffer STDIO

# construct the ping object we'll use later
my $p = Net::Ping->new('icmp');

# set up all of the Net::Pcap stuff and
# include a callback
my $npe = Net::Pcap::Easy->new(
    dev               => $dev,
    filter            => $filter_string,
    packets_per_loop  => 10,
    bytes_to_capture  => 1500,
    timeout_in_ms     => 1,
    promiscuous       => 1,

    tcp_callback => sub {
        my ( $npe, $ether, $ip, $tcp ) = @_;

        my $src_ip = $ip->{src_ip};
```

```
        print "$src_ip is "
            . ( ( $p->ping($src_ip) ) ? 'alive' : 'unreachable' ) . "\n"
            unless $cache{$src_ip}++;
    }
);

while (1) { $npe->loop(); }
```

Only the last half of the code has changed, so we'll focus on that in this explanation. Most of the magic is in the new() call, where we can very simply set the parameters for the capture, including the filter string and any callbacks we need. Net::Pcap::Easy lets us define callbacks for the different packet types (TCP, UDP, ICMP, etc.). Since our filter string specifies only TCP packets, we've only defined the TCP callback. One really cool thing about Net::Pcap::Easy's callbacks is that they are handed NetPacket::* objects instead of raw packets. We no longer have to write the code to strip() or decode(); we can just access the right object attributes, like src_ip. When we call the loop() method, Net::Pcap::Easy captures the number of packets specified by packets_per_loop in the new() call. Once it has captured this number of packets, it parcels them out one packet at a time to the appropriate callbacks and returns. To be consistent with the other versions of our program, we call loop() again and again until interrupted.

Now that we've achieved our goal of writing a program completely in Perl that would have helped diagnose my server problem (albeit using some modules that are Perl wrappers around C code), let me tell you the end of the story.

On Sunday morning, the central support group outside of my department discovered an error in its router configuration. A student in one of the dorms had installed Linux on his machine and misconfigured the network routing daemon. This machine was broadcasting to the rest of the university that it was a default route to the Internet. The misconfigured router that fed our department was happy to listen to this broadcast and promptly changed its routing table to add a second route to the rest of the universe. Packets came to us from the outside world, and this router dutifully doled out our response packets evenly between both destinations. This "a packet for the real router to the Internet, a packet for the student's machine, a packet for the real router, a packet for the student's machine..." distribution created an asymmetric routing situation. Once the bogus route was cleared and filters were put in place to prevent it from returning, our lives returned to normal. I won't tell you what happened to the student who caused the problem (or the employee who configured the router that way!).

In this section, you have now seen one diagnostic application of the Net::Pcap, Net::PcapUtils/Net::Pcap::Easy, and NetPacket::* family of modules. Don't stop there! These modules give you the flexibility to construct a whole variety of programs that can help you debug network problems or actively watch your wire for danger.

Preventing Suspicious Activities

The very last night watchman's attribute that we will consider is an eye toward prevention. This is the voice that says "You know, you shouldn't leave those fresh-baked pies on the windowsill to cool."

We're going to conclude this chapter with an example that, when properly deployed, could positively impact a single machine, or even an entire computing infrastructure. As a symbolic gesture, instead of making use of somebody else's work, we'll build our own module.

The goal I have in mind is the prevention, or at least reduction, of bad passwords. Good security mechanisms have been thwarted by the selection of bad passwords since the dawn of time. Oog's password to get back into the clan's cave was probably "oog".[†] Nowadays, the situation is exacerbated by the widespread availability of sophisticated password-cracking programs like *John the Ripper* by Solar Designer and Alec Muffett's *Crack*.

The only way to prevent the vulnerability in your systems that these programs expose is to avoid bad passwords in the first place. You need to help your users choose and retain hard-to-crack passwords. There are two complementary ways to do this: suggest good passwords and prevent bad passwords from being used.

Suggest Better Passwords

Picking a good password is actually pretty hard if you have no idea what makes a password "good." There are a number of psychological, sociological, and contextual factors contributing to why people pick and keep bad passwords. One important factor is the "blank-page" problem. If someone says to you "quick, pick something you'll need to be able to remember, but don't make it something anyone else can guess," that's a lot of pressure.

To help people get over this pressure, it can often be helpful to pre-generate suggested passwords for them to use. There are several Perl modules designed to generate more secure passwords. Some of them create passwords that are truly random. Others produce passwords that are close to random, but have the nice property of being pronounceable in someone's native language (and hence perhaps more memorizable). Random passwords are in theory more secure, but there have been some good debates over the years in the security community about whether providing users with something so complex that they have to write it down on a sticky note is any better than giving them something less random that they are more likely to be able to keep in their heads.

All the Perl modules in this space are very easy to use. You ask for a password, and the module hands you one. You may have to (or want to) provide some parameters

---

† It was only later that he changed it to 00g.

describing the kind of password you want, or perhaps provide some hints on what "pronounceable" entails in your language, but that's all the thinking you need to do to use them. Let's look at a couple of examples. The first, `Data::SimplePassword`, prints a random password of 10 characters long:

```
use Data::SimplePassword;

my $dsp = Data::SimplePassword->new();

# 10-char-long random password; we could specify which
# characters to use if we cared via the chars() method
print $dsp->make_password(10),"\n";
```

When I have to generate random passwords, I tend to use `Crypt::GeneratePassword` by Jörg Walter, because it generates pronounceable passwords that are slightly more secure than those that rely strictly on the NIST standard (FIPS-181) for creating them. It also provides the functionality for screening the generated password for naughty words of your choice (one of the hazards of creating pronounceable passwords is that it's possible to generate passwords containing character sequences that might offend those with delicate sensibilities). To use it, we call either the `word()` function for pronounceable passwords or the `chars()` function for purely random passwords. Both functions take two required arguments: the minimum and maximum lengths of the password to return. For example, the following code:

```
use Crypt::GeneratePassword;

for (1..5) {
    print Crypt::GeneratePassword::word( 8, 8 ),"\n";
}
```

might print something like:

```
ecloorfi
neleappw
xchanedo
noutoone
nopenule
```

Reject Bad Passwords

Suggesting good passwords to your users is an excellent start, but it's also important to have a mechanism in place to reject bad passwords should they ignore your suggestions. One way to do this on Unix machines is to use *CrackLib*, also by Alec Muffett. In the process of writing *Crack*, Muffett did the system administration community a great service by taking some of the methods used in *Crack* and distilling them to a single password-checking library written in C.

This library has exactly one function for its user interface: `FascistCheck()`. This function takes two arguments: a string to check and the full pathname prefix of the dictionary file created when installing *CrackLib*. It returns either `NULL` if the string is a "safe" password, or an explanatory piece of text (e.g., "is a dictionary word") if it is vulnerable to cracking. It would be extremely handy to be able to use this functionality as part of any Perl program that sets or changes a password, so let's look at how we would build a module that would incorporate it. This foray will require a very brief peek at some C code, but I promise it will be quick and painless.

> In the interest of full disclosure, I should mention that there is a module to do exactly this available on CPAN: `Crypt::Cracklib` by Dan Sully. I wasn't aware of this module at the time I wrote this section for the first edition; I've updated this discussion and left it in the book in this new edition because I think it's useful to know how to roll your own modules. Sully's module works well, though, and I recommend it if you don't want to use the one we'll build together here.
>
> One tip: as of this writing, the tests for that module haven't been updated to match the newer *CrackLib* responses, so you may have to force the install.

Our first step is to build the *CrackLib* package, available from *http://sourceforge.net/projects/cracklib*. The process detailed in the distribution is straightforward. Let me offer three hints:

- The larger the dictionary you can build, the better. Two good sources of wordlists to be included in that dictionary are *ftp://ftp.ox.ac.uk/pub/wordlists* and the wordlist CD for sale via the Openwall project at *http://www.openwall.com/wordlists*. The dictionary build process requires a significant amount of temporary disk space (for the *sort* process in *utils/mkdict*), so plan accordingly.

- Be sure to build *CrackLib* with the same development tools used to build Perl. For instance, if you used *gcc* to compile Perl, be sure to use *gcc* for the *CrackLib* build process as well. This is true of all modules that need to link in additional C libraries.

- The example code in this section uses *CrackLib* version 2.8.12. Make sure the version you are building against is sufficiently up-to-date (even if it means downloading the new version from the site referenced earlier and building it instead of relying on the version that shipped with your OS distribution).

Once we've built the C library *libcrack.a* (or the shared library equivalent), we need to set up the method for calling the `FascistCheck()` function in that library from within Perl. This method is called `XS`.[‡]

The easiest way to begin with `XS` is to use the *h2xs* program to create a proto-module for us:

[‡] In the first edition of this book I also mentioned using SWIG as an interface method, but as far as I can tell that has fallen out of favor in the Perl community (at least for modules published to CPAN).

```
$ h2xs -b 5.6.0 -A -n Cracklib
Writing Cracklib/ppport.h
Writing Cracklib/lib/Cracklib.pm
Writing Cracklib/Cracklib.xs
Writing Cracklib/Makefile.PL
Writing Cracklib/README
Writing Cracklib/t/Cracklib.t
Writing Cracklib/Changes
Writing Cracklib/MANIFEST
```

Table 11-3 describes the files created by this command.

Table 11-3. Files created by h2xs -b 5.6.0 -A -n Cracklib

Filename	Description
Cracklib/ppport.h	Cross-version portability header file
Cracklib/lib/Cracklib.pm	Perl stub and documentation
Cracklib/Cracklib.xs	C code glue
Cracklib/Makefile.PL	*Makefile*-generating Perl code
Cracklib/t/Cracklib.t	Stub test code
Cracklib/Changes	Version documentation
Cracklib/MANIFEST	List of files shipped with module

We only need to change a few of these files to get the functionality we seek. Let's take on the hardest part first: the C code glue. Here's how the function is defined in the *CrackLib* include file (*crack.h*):

```
const char *FascistCheck(const char *pw, const char *dictpath);
```

 To save you some hassle, here's a quick warning: the XS tools are finicky about whitespace, so if you're following along at home and copying the following code to make your own *Cracklib/Cracklib.xs*, be sure you preserve the whitespace as written.

In our *Cracklib/Cracklib.xs* glue file, we repeat this definition:

```
#include <crack.h>

PROTOTYPES: ENABLE

const char *
FascistCheck(pw,dictpath)
    char *pw
    char *dictpath
```

The PROTOTYPES directive will create Perl prototypes for the functions in our glue file. This isn't an issue for the code we're writing, but we include the directive to stifle a warning message in the build process.

Right after the function definition, we describe how it's called and what it returns:

```
CODE:

    RETVAL = FascistCheck((const char*)pw, (const char*)dictpath);

    OUTPUT:
    RETVAL
```

RETVAL is the actual glue here. It represents the transfer point between the C code and the Perl interpreter. Here, we tell Perl that it should receive a string of characters returned from the `FascistCheck()` C library function and make that available as the return value (i.e., OUTPUT) of the Perl `Cracklib::FascistCheck()` function.

We can also remove the `#include "ppport.h"` line that was added to this file by `h2xs` because we're not doing anything that it (and the `Devel::PPPort` module) was designed to help. If you run the Perl interpreter on that include file, it will tell you whether it is needed:

```
$ perl ppport.h
Scanning ./Cracklib.xs ...
=== Analyzing ./Cracklib.xs ===
No need to include 'ppport.h'
Suggested changes:
--- ./Cracklib.xs        2009-01-03 22:08:28.000000000 -0500
+++ ./Cracklib.xs.patched    2009-01-03 22:08:30.000000000 -0500
@@ -2,7 +2,6 @@
 #include "perl.h"
 #include "XSUB.h"

-#include "ppport.h"

 #include <crack.h>
```

When we remove it from *Cracklib/Cracklib.xs*, we should also remove the actual file, and its mention in *Cracklib/MANIFEST*.

That's all the C code we'll need to touch.

The other file we need to modify needs only a couple of lines changed. To be sure Perl can find the `libcrack` library and its *crack.h* include file, we need to modify the arguments to the `WriteMakefile()` call in *Cracklib/Makefile.PL*. Here are the additional and changed lines, in context:

```
    LIBS            => [''], # e.g., '-lm'
        DEFINE      => '', # e.g., '-DHAVE_SOMETHING'
        MYEXTLIB    => '/opt/local/lib/libcrack$(LIB_EXT)',
        INC         => '-I. -I/opt/local/include',
```

That's the bare minimum we need to do to make this module work.[*] If we type:

---

[*] I had to add `-lintl` to LIBS to get the module to link properly in my Mac OS X-based *macports* setup, but that's not a generic requirement so I did not include it in the example text.

```
$ perl Makefile.PL
$ make
$ make install
```

we can begin to use our new module like this:

```
use Cracklib;
use Term::Prompt;
use Readonly;

Readonly my $dictpath => '/opt/local/share/cracklib/pw_dict';

my $pw = prompt( 'p', 'Please enter password:', '', '' );
print "\n";

my $result = Cracklib::FascistCheck( $pw, $dictpath );
if ( defined $result ) {
    print "That is not a valid password because $result.\n";
}
else {
    print "That password is peachy, thanks!\n";
}
```

Don't skip right to using the module yet, though. Let's make this a professional-grade module before we install it.

First, let's modify the skeleton test script h2xs created to test that the module is working correctly. First we'll change it to use the more fully featured test module Test::More. Test::More helps us to provide output in a specific format for the test harness to use. The Test::More module makes this easy, we just need to do two things:

- Specify how many tests we plan to run by changing the tests => 1 line.
- Use the is() function to call our function with some known values (and specify the known results we expect to get back).

Here are the contents of *Cracklib/t/Cracklib.t* with the changes made to run our tests. I've removed the boilerplate comments from h2xs to make for easier reading:

```
use Test::More tests => 6;
BEGIN { use_ok 'Cracklib' };

# location of our cracklib dictionary files
#
# to make this test file portable we'd write out this test
# file with the pointer to the dictionary files supplied
# by the user at Makefile.PL runtime
my $dictpath = '/opt/local/share/cracklib/pw_dict';

# test strings and their known cracklib responses
my %tests =
  ('happy'         => 'it is too short',
   'a'             => 'it is WAY too short',
   'asdfasdf'      => 'it does not contain enough DIFFERENT characters',
   'minicomputer'  => 'it is based on a dictionary word',
   '1ftm2tgr3fts'  => undef);
```

```
foreach my $pw (sort keys %tests){
    is(Cracklib::FascistCheck($pw,$dictpath), $tests{$pw}, "Passwd = $pw");
}
```

Now, we can type `make test` and *Makefile* will run the test code to check that our module is working properly:

```
PERL_DL_NONLAZY=1 /opt/local/bin/perl "-MExtUtils::
Command::MM" "-e" "test_harness(0, 'blib/lib', 'blib/arch')" t/*.t
t/Cracklib....ok
All tests successful.
Files=1, Tests=6,  0 wallclock secs ( 0.02 cusr +  0.01 csys =  0.03 CPU)
```

A test script is certainly important, but our script won't be nearly respectable if we omit one crucial component: documentation. Take some time to flesh out the stub information in the *Cracklib/Cracklib.pm* and *Cracklib/Changes* files. It is also a good idea to edit the *Cracklib/README* file† and perhaps add a *Cracklib/INSTALL* file describing how to build the module, where to get the component parts like *CrackLib*, example code, etc. New files and the earlier deleting of the *pport.h* file should be noted in the *Cracklib/MANIFEST* file to keep the generic module-building code happy.

Finally, install your module everywhere in your infrastructure. Sprinkle calls to `Cracklib::FascistCheck()` everywhere you need to set or change passwords. As the number of bad passwords diminishes in your environment, so shall the night watchman smile kindly upon you.

Module Information for This Chapter

Module	CPAN ID	Version
Getopt::Std (ships with Perl)		1.06
Digest::SHA	MSHELOR	5.47
Net::DNS	OLAF	0.64
FreezeThaw	ILYAZ	0.43
File::Find (ships with Perl)		1.13
File::Find::Rule	RCLAMP	0.30
Regexp::Common	ABIGAIL	2.122
Net::Ping (ships with Perl)	SMPETERS	2.35
Net::Pcap	SAPER	0.16
Net::PcapUtils	TIMPOTTER	0.01

† One of my pet peeves are the *README* files in modules published to CPAN that haven't been modified one whit from the stock one created by h2xs and other module-building tools. I think it is very bad form to leave the generic file untouched, reflecting badly on the module and its author. It doesn't take much effort to add a modicum of real documentation to that file, so what does that say about the actual code?

Module	CPAN ID	Version
NetPacket	YANICK	0.41
Net::Pcap::Easy	JETTERO	1.32
Data::SimplePassword	RYOCHIN	0.04
Crypt::GeneratePassword	JWALT	0.03
Readonly	ROODE	1.03
Term::Prompt	PERSICOM	1.04

References for More Information

http://www.tcpdump.org is the home of `libpcap` and *tcpdump*. `winpcap` can be found at *http://www.winpcap.org*.

RFC 793: Transmission Control Protocol, by J. Postel (1981), documents TCP.

"MD5 To Be Considered Harmful Someday," by Dan Kaminsky (2004), can be found at *http://www.doxpara.com/md5_someday.pdf*.

http://www.perlmonks.org/?displaytype=print;node_id=431702 is a lovely (only slightly out of date) guide to writing your own modules.

The section "Suggest Better Passwords" on page 460 was adapted from text originally published in the column I wrote for `;login` magazine (*http://www.usenix.org/publications/login/*) called "This Column is Password Protected."

RFC 1321: The MD5 Message-Digest Algorithm, by R. Rivest (1992), documents MD5.

FIPS 180-2: Secure Hash Standard (SHS) documents the SHA-1 and SHA-2 standards (as of this writing) and can be downloaded from *http://csrc.nist.gov/publications/fips/fips180-2/fips180-2withchangenotice.pdf*.

tripwire used to be the canonical free tool for filesystem change detection. After it was commercialized, the company stopped selling a filesystem change-detection program as a product *per se*. A number of other open source tools, such as *yafic (http://www.saddi.com/software/yafic/)* and *AIDE (http://www.cs.tut.fi/~rammer/aide.html)*, stepped in to fill the void.

## CHAPTER 12

SNMP

The Simple Network Management Protocol (SNMP) offers a general way to remotely monitor and configure network devices and networked computers. Once you master the basics of SNMP, you can use it to keep tabs on (and often configure) practically every device on your network.

Truth be told, the "Simple" Network Management Protocol isn't particularly simple. There's a respectable learning curve associated with this subject. If you aren't already familiar with SNMP, see Appendix G for a tutorial.

Using SNMP from Perl

One way you can use SNMP from Perl is to call command-line programs. In Appendix G I show how to use the programs in the Net-SNMP distribution as one example of this. It's a straightforward process, no different from any of the examples of calling external programs earlier in this book. Since there's nothing new to learn there, we won't spend any time on this technique.

One caveat: if you are using SNMPv1 or SNMPv2c, chances are you'll be tempted to put the community name on the command line. But if the program runs on a multiuser box, anyone who can list the process table may be able to see this community name and steal the keys to the kingdom. This threat is present in our command-line examples in Appendix G, but it becomes more acute with automated programs that repeatedly make external program calls. For demonstration purposes only, the examples in this chapter are invoked with the target hostname and community name string on the command line. You should change that for production code.[*]

If we don't call an external program to perform SNMP operations from Perl, our other choice is to use a Perl SNMP module. There are at least three separate but similar modules available: Net::SNMP, by David M. Town; SNMP_Session.pm, by Simon Leinen;

---

[*] Another way around this problem is to use a well-protected *snmp.conf* file, as documented in the Net-SNMP package.

and a module that has had several names, including NetSNMP, Perl/SNMP, and "The Perl5 'SNMP' Extension Module v5.0 for the Net-SNMP Library," originally written by G. S. Marzot and now maintained by the Net-SNMP Project. We'll refer to that last module as `SNMP` because of the way it is loaded. All of these modules implement SNMPv1. `Net::SNMP` and `SNMP` additionally offer some SNMPv2c and SNMPv3 support. Table 12-1 gives a comparison of these modules versus calling the Net-SNMP command-line tools from Perl.

Table 12-1. Comparison of SNMP methods from Perl

Feature	SNMP_Session	Net::SNMP	SNMP	Net-SNMP command line
SNMPv1 support	Y	Y	Y	Y
SNMPv2c support	Y	Y	Y	Y
SNMPv3 support	N	Y	Y	Y
OID resolution	N	N	Y	Y
Send version 1 traps	Y	Y	Y	Y
Receive version 1 traps	Y	N	N	Y
Send v2 notifications	Y	Y	Y	Y
Receive v2 notifications	Y	N	N	Y
Send v3 notifications	N	N	Y	Y
Receive v3 notifications	N	N	N	Y
Send informs	N	Y	Y	Y
Receive informs	Y	N	N	Y
All Perl	Y	Y for v1 and v2c, N for v3	N	Y

The most significant difference between these three modules (other than their level of SNMP support) is their reliance on libraries external to the core Perl distribution. The first two (`Net::SNMP` and `SNMP_Session.pm`) are largely implemented in Perl alone,[†] while `SNMP` needs to be linked against a separate prebuilt Net-SNMP library. The main drawback to using `SNMP` is this added dependency and build step (presuming you can build the Net-SNMP library on your platform).

The plus side of depending on the Net-SNMP library is the extra power it provides to the module. For instance, `SNMP` can parse Management Information Base (MIB) description files and print raw SNMP packet dumps for debugging, two functions the other modules do not provide. There are other modules that can help reduce this disparity in functionality, but if you are looking for one module to do the whole job, `SNMP` is your best bet.

[†] `Net::SNMP` relies on a few C-based modules (such as `Crypt::DES`, `Digest::MD5`, and `Digest::SHA1`) if you use it for SNMPv3, so it is not strictly pure Perl.

Be sure to install the version of the SNMP module found in the *perl* directory of the Net-SNMP source distribution. The version found on CPAN is likely to be less up-to-date than this version and may be out of sync with the current Net-SNMP libraries.

Let's start with a small Perl example. If we need to know the number of interfaces a particular device has, we can query the interfaces.ifNumber variable. Using Net::SNMP, it's this easy:

```
use Net::SNMP;

# requires a hostname and a community string as its arguments
my ($session,$error) = Net::SNMP->session(Hostname => $ARGV[0],
                                           Community => $ARGV[1]);

die "session error: $error" unless ($session);

# iso.org.dod.internet.mgmt.mib-2.interfaces.ifNumber.0 =
#    1.3.6.1.2.1.2.1.0
my $result = $session->get_request('1.3.6.1.2.1.2.1.0');

die 'request error: '.$session->error unless (defined $result);

$session->close;

print 'Number of interfaces: '.$result->{'1.3.6.1.2.1.2.1.0'}."\n";
```

When pointed at a workstation with Ethernet and loopback interfaces, this program will print Number of interfaces: 2; a laptop with Ethernet, loopback, and PPP interfaces returns Number of interfaces: 3; and a small router might return Number of interfaces: 7.

One key thing to notice is the use of object identifiers (OIDs) instead of variable names. Both Net::SNMP and SNMP_Session.pm handle SNMP protocol interactions only; they don't convert numerical OIDs to human-readable names by handling peripheral SNMP-related tasks like parsing SNMP MIB descriptions. For this functionality you will have to look to other modules, such as SNMP::MIB::Compiler or SNMP_util.pm by Mike Mitchell for use with SNMP_Session.pm.‡

If you want to use textual identifiers instead of numeric OIDs without coding in the mapping yourself or using an additional module, your only choice is to use the SNMP module, which has a built-in MIB parser. Let's do a table walk of a machine's Address Resolution Protocol (ARP) table using this module:

---

‡ SNMP_util.pm should not be confused with the similarly named module SNMP::Util, by Wayne Marquette. Marquette's module serves a very different purpose as a helper to the SNMP module.

```
use SNMP;

# requires a hostname and a community string as its arguments
my $session = new SNMP::Session(DestHost      => $ARGV[0],
                               Community     => $ARGV[1],
                               Version       => '1',
                               UseSprintValue => 1);

die "session creation error: $SNMP::Session::ErrorStr" unless
   (defined $session);

# set up the data structure for the getnext() command
my $vars = new SNMP::VarList(['ipNetToMediaNetAddress'],
                            ['ipNetToMediaPhysAddress']);

# get first row
my ($ip,$mac) = $session->getnext($vars);
die $session->{ErrorStr} if ($session->{ErrorStr});

# and all subsequent rows
while (!$session->{ErrorStr} and
       $vars->[0]->tag eq 'ipNetToMediaNetAddress'){
   print "$ip -> $mac\n";
   ( $ip, $mac ) = $session->getnext($vars);
};
```

Here's an example of the output this produces:

```
192.168.1.70 -> 8:0:20:21:40:51
192.168.1.74 -> 8:0:20:76:7c:85
192.168.1.98 -> 0:c0:95:e0:5c:1c
```

This code looks similar to the previous Net::SNMP example. We'll walk through it to highlight the differences:

```
use SNMP;

my $session = new SNMP::Session(DestHost      => $ARGV[0],
                               Community     => $ARGV[1],
                               Version       => '1',
                               UseSprintValue => 1);
```

After loading the SNMP module, we create a session object just like we did in the Net::SNMP example. The additional Version => 1 sets the protocol version (the default is version 3), and the UseSprintValue => 1 argument just tells the SNMP module to pretty-print the return values. If we didn't set the latter, the Ethernet (MAC) addresses in the output would be printed in an encoded form.

The next line creates the object that getnext() will use:

```
my $vars = new SNMP::VarList (['ipNetToMediaNetAddress'],
                             ['ipNetToMediaPhysAddress']);
```

SNMP uses simple strings like `interfaces.ifNumber.0` with its commands, but `getnext()` requests need to use special objects called `VarBind`s. In RFC 1157 it says, "A variable binding, or `VarBind`, refers to the pairing of the name of a variable to the variable's value. A `VarBindList` is a simple list of variable names and corresponding values." If you're thinking that a `VarBind` sounds like a Perl hash key/value pair and a `VarBindList` sounds like a list of hashes, you're on the right track. They aren't implemented that way in the SNMP module, but you've got the right idea. The preceding line of code uses `VarList()`, which creates an object containing a list of two `VarBind`s, each of which is a reference to an anonymous array with just the `obj` element filled in.

`VarBind`s are actually implemented as anonymous Perl arrays with four elements—`obj`, `iid`, `val`, and `type`—because that is closer to the way they are specified in the encoding system used for SNMP. For our purposes, we only need to worry about `obj` and `iid`. The first element, `obj`, is the object you are querying. `obj` can be specified in one of several formats. In this case, we are using a *leaf identifier* format (i.e., specifying the leaf of the tree we are concerned with). `ipNetToMediaNetAddress` is the leaf of the tree (this is all one long string, broken into two lines):

```
.iso.org.dod.internet.mgmt.mib-2.ip.ipNetToMediaTable.
ipNetToMediaEntry.ipNetToMediaNetAddress
```

The second element in a `VarBind` is the `iid`, or instance identifier. In our previous discussions, we've always used a `0` here (e.g., `system.sysDescr.0`), because we've been dealing with objects that only have a single instance. Shortly, however, we'll see examples where the `iid` can be something other than `0`. For instance, later we'll want to refer to a particular network interface on a multiinterface Ethernet switch.

`obj` and `iid` are usually the only two parts of a `VarBind` you need to specify for a `get()` operation; SNMP will fill in suitable values for the rest. If you are only using `getnext()` calls, you don't even need to specify `iid`, since that method returns the next instance by default. That's why the preceding code can specify just the first element of the `VarBind` (the `obj`) when creating the two `VarBind`s that make up the `VarList`.

For our purposes you can think of `VarBind`s as buckets of information for passing data to and from SNMP queries. For example, the preceding code calls the `getnext()` method to send a `GetNextRequest`, just like in the IP route table example in Appendix G. We get back some data, the indices of which we'll use in our next call to `getnext()`. SNMP stores the returned `iid`s in a `VarBind` for us so we don't have to keep track of them by hand. The next call to `getnext()` passes in the `VarList` object with the two `VarBind`s that are holding the last values we received, and does the right thing.

We feed the `VarList` object we created to the `getnext()` method:

```perl
# get first row
my ($ip,$mac) = $session->getnext($vars);
die $session->{ErrorStr} if ($session->{ErrorStr});
```

getnext() returns the values it received from our request and updates the VarList data structure accordingly. Now it's just a matter of calling getnext() until we fall off the end of the table:

```
while (!$session->{ErrorStr} and
       ($vars->[0]->tag eq 'ipNetToMediaNetAddress')){
    print "$ip -> $mac\n";
    ($ip,$mac) = $session->getnext($vars);
};
```

For our final SNMP module example, let's use a scenario from the world of security. We'll pick a task that would be tricky, or at least annoying, to do well with the command-line SNMP utilities.

Here's the scenario: you're asked to track down a misbehaving user on your switched Ethernet network. The only info you have is the Ethernet address of the machine that user is on. It's not an Ethernet address you have on file (such addresses could be kept in our host database from Chapter 5 if we extended it), and you can't easily sniff your switched net, so you're going to have to be a little bit clever about tracking down this machine. Your best bet in this case may be to ask one or all of your Ethernet switches if they've seen that address on one of their ports (i.e., is it in the switch's dynamic CAM table?). Doing this by hand can be a big pain, involving connecting to multiple network boxes and running multiple commands on each.

Just to make this example more concrete so we can point at specific MIB variables, we'll say that your network consists of several Cisco Catalyst 6500 and 4500 switches. The basic methodology we're going to use to solve this problem will apply to other products and other vendors as well. Any switch- or vendor-specific information will be noted as we go along. Let's walk through this problem step by step.

As before, first we have to search through the correct MIB module files. With a little jumpstart from Cisco's tech support, we realize we'll need to access five separate objects:

- The vmMembershipTable, found here (it's one long string, listed on two lines):

      enterprises.cisco.ciscoMgmt.ciscoVlanMembershipMIB.
      ciscoVlanMembershipMIBObjects.vmMembership

  in the CISCO-VLAN-MEMBERSHIP-MIB description.[*]

- The dot1dTpFdbTable (transparent port forwarding table), found at dot1dBridge.dot1dTp in the RFC 1493 *BRIDGE-MIB* description.

---

[*] In the first edition of this book, we used the vlanTable from CISCO-STACK-MIB. That still works for older Cisco equipment, but the vmMembershipTable is the only available way to get this information for the more current gear.

- The `dot1dBasePortTable`, found at `dot1dBridge.dot1dBase` in the same RFC.
- The `ifXTable`, found in the RFC 1573 *IF-MIB* (interfaces) description.
- The `vlanTrunkPortTable`, found at:

    `enterprises.cisco.ciscoMgmt.ciscoVtpMIB.vtpMIBObjects.vlanTrunkPorts`

  in the `CISCO-VTP-MIB` description.

Why five different tables? Each table has a piece to contribute to the answer, but no one table has all the information we seek. The first table provides us with a list of the virtual local area networks (VLANs), or virtual "network segments,"[†] on the switch. Cisco has chosen to keep separate tables for each VLAN on a switch, so we will need to query one VLAN at a time (more on this in a moment).

The second table provides us with a list of Ethernet addresses and the number of the switch's *bridge port* on which each address was last seen. Unfortunately, a bridge port number is an internal reckoning for the switch; it does not correspond to the name of a physical port on that switch. We need to know the physical port name (i.e., from which card and port the machine with that Ethernet address last spoke), so we have to dig further.

There is no table that maps bridge ports to physical port names (that would be too easy), but the `dot1dBasePortTable` can provide a mapping from bridge ports to interface numbers. Once we have the interface number, we can look it up in `ifXTable` and retrieve the port name.

And finally, we use the `vlanTrunkPortTable` to help us determine if a particular interface number is trunked (i.e., configured so it will pass traffic to another network box). We can ignore all matches for the Ethernet address in question found on trunked ports. A trunked port will report back the addresses it has learned from its peer. Information about another switch that saw the address isn't helpful when we're trying to track down the physical port on the current device.

Figure 12-1 shows a picture of a four-layer dereference necessary to perform our desired task.

[†] Technically VLANs are actually "broadcast domains," but most people think of them as ways to partition their networks so that the hosts on a given VLAN see only the traffic from the other hosts on the same VLAN.

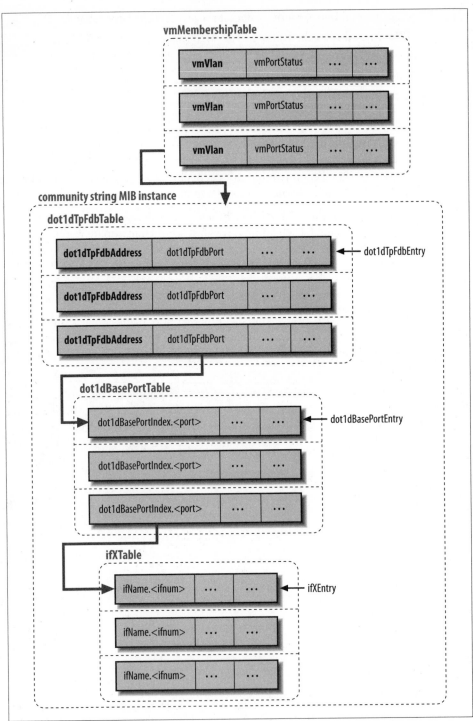

Figure 12-1. The set of SNMP queries needed to find the port name on a Cisco 6500 or 4500

Here's the code to put these five tables together and dump the information we need:

```perl
use SNMP;

my ($switchname, $community, $macaddr) = @ARGV;

# here are the MIBs we need and why
$ENV{'MIBS'}=join(':', ('CISCO-VLAN-MEMBERSHIP-MIB', # VLAN listing and status
                        'BRIDGE-MIB',                # MAC address to port table
                        'CISCO-VTP-MIB',             # port trunking status
                       ));

# connect and get the list of VLANs on this switch
$session = new SNMP::Session(DestHost  => $switchname,
                             Community => $community,
                             Version   => 1);
die "session creation error: $SNMP::Session::ErrorStr" unless
    (defined $session);

# enterprises.cisco.ciscoMgmt.
#   ciscoVlanMembershipMIB.ciscoVlanMembershipMIBObjects.vmMembership.
#     vmMembershipTable.vmMembershipEntry
# in CISCO-VLAN-MEMBERSHIP-MIB
my $vars = new SNMP::VarList (['vmVlan'],['vmPortStatus']);

my ( $vlan, $vlanstatus ) = $session->getnext($vars);
die $session->{ErrorStr} if ($session->{ErrorStr});

my %vlans;
while (!$session->{ErrorStr} and $vars->[0]->tag eq 'vmVlan'){
    $vlans{$vlan}++ if $vlanstatus == 2; # make sure the vlan is active (2)
    ( $vlan, $vlanstatus ) = $session->getnext($vars);
};

undef $session,$vars;

# make sure the MAC address is in the right form
my $findaddr = massage_mac($macaddr);

# for each VLAN, see if there is a bridge port that has seen a particular
# macaddr; if so, find the interface number associated with that port, and
# then the interface name for that interface number
foreach my $vlan (sort keys %vlans) {

    # for caching query results
    #  (we keep the cache around only for a single VLAN)
    my (%ifnum, %portname);

    # note our use of "community string indexing" as part
    # of the session setup
    my $session = new SNMP::Session(DestHost => $switchname,
                                    Community => $community.'@'.$vlan,
                                    UseSprintValue => 1,
                                    Version       => 1);
```

```perl
    die "session creation error: $SNMP::Session::ErrorStr"
        unless (defined $session);

    # see if the MAC address is in our bridge forwarding table
    # note: the $macaddr has to be in XX.XX.XX.XX.XX.XX form
    #
    # from transparent forwarding port table at
    # dot1dBridge.dot1dTp.dot1dTpFdbTable.dot1dTpFdbEntry
    # in RFC 1493 BRIDGE-MIB
    my $portnum  = $session->get(['dot1dTpFdbPort',$findaddr]);

    # nope, it's not there (at least in this VLAN), try the next VLAN
    next if $session->{ErrorStr} =~ /noSuchName/;

    # convert the forwarding table port number to interface number
    #
    # from dot1dBridge.dot1dBase.dot1dBasePortTable.dot1dBasePortEntry
    # in RFC 1493 BRIDGE-MIB

    my $ifnum =
        (exists $ifnum{$portnum}) ? $ifnum{$portnum} :
            ($ifnum{$portnum} =
                $session->get(['dot1dBasePortIfIndex',$portnum]));

    # skip it if this interface is a trunk port
    #
    # from ciscoVtpMIB.vtpMIBObjects.vlanTrunkPorts.vlanTrunkPortTable.
    # vlanTrunkPortEntry in CISCO-VTP-MIB
    next if
        $session->get(['vlanTrunkPortDynamicStatus',$ifnum]) eq 'trunking';

    # convert the interface number to port name (i.e., module/port)
    #
    # from ifMIB.ifMIBObjects.ifXTable.ifXEntry in RFC 1573 IF-MIB
    my $portname =
        (exists $portname{$ifnum}) ? $portname{$ifnum} :
            ($portname{$ifnum}=$session->get(['ifName',$ifnum]));

    print "$macaddr on VLAN $vlan at $portname\n";

}

# take in a MAC address in the form of XX:XX:XX:XX:XX:XX,
# XX-XX-XX-XX-XX-XX, or XXXXXXXXXXXX (X is hex) and return it in the
# decimal, period-delimited format we need for queries
sub massage_mac {
    my $macaddr = shift;

    # no punctuation at all (becomes colon-separated)
    $macaddr =~ s/(..)(?=.)/$1:/g if (length($macaddr) == 12);

    # colon- or dash-separated
    return join('.', map (hex,split(/[:-]/,uc $macaddr)));
}
```

If you've read Appendix G, most of this code will look familiar. Let's take a look at the new stuff:

```
$ENV{'MIBS'}=join(':', ('CISCO-VLAN-MEMBERSHIP-MIB', # VLAN listing and status
                        'BRIDGE-MIB',               # MAC address to port table
                        'CISCO-VTP-MIB',            # port trunking status
                       ));
```

This code sets the `MIBS` environment variable for the Net-SNMP package library. When set, this variable instructs the library to parse the listed set of additional MIB modules for object definitions. These files should be in the default search path for the Net-SNMP distribution. If you don't want to place them in the standard spot, you can set the `MIBFILES` environment variable to make their location more explicit.

There's a common misunderstanding about the Net-SNMP `MIBS` environment variable. My own understanding of it used to be weak, so let me clear it up for you before it gets in your way. `MIBS` contains a list of SNMP MIB *module* names, not SNMP MIB module *file* names. You do not place the name of the file that holds the module definition in this list; instead, you use the module's name. That name is usually found as the first non-commented piece of text in a MIB module file. For example, Cisco distributes a file called *CISCO-VLAN-MEMBERSHIP-MIB-V1SMI.my*. That file's first non-comment line says:

```
CISCO-VLAN-MEMBERSHIP-MIB DEFINITIONS ::= BEGIN
```

So in this case, we would use `CISCO-VLAN-MEMBERSHIP-MIB` when populating the MIB environment variable.

You might also have noticed that we don't include `IF-MIB` and `BRIDGE-MIB`, even though the program references objects from both of them. This is because they are both in the Net-SNMP library's default list of MIB modules to load. That list is created at Net-SNMP compile time, during the configure stage (both `IF-MIB` and `BRIDGE-MIB` are among the recommended choices). It would be perfectly reasonable to include these in the setting of `MIBS` here just to explicitly declare their use in your program; it's a matter of personal taste.

Moving on in our code, here's another strange statement:

```
foreach my $vlan (sort keys %vlans) {

    my $session = new SNMP::Session(DestHost => $switchname,
                                    Community => $community.'@'.$vlan,
                                    UseSprintValue => 1,
                                    Version        => 1);
```

Instead of just passing on the community name as provided by the user, we're appending something in the form @*VLAN-NUMBER*. In Cisco parlance, this is known as "community string indexing." When dealing with VLANs and bridging, Cisco devices keep track of several "instances" (duplicate internal copies) of the MIB, one for each

VLAN. Our code makes the same queries once per each VLAN found on the switch. Here are two such queries:

```
my $portnum = $session->get(['dot1dTpFdbPort',$findaddr]);

# nope, it's not there (at least in this VLAN), try the next VLAN
next if $session->{ErrorStr} =~ /noSuchName/;
```

and:

```
my $ifnum =
    (exists $ifnum{$portnum}) ? $ifnum{$portnum} :
        ($ifnum{$portnum} =
            $session->get(['dot1dBasePortIfIndex',$portnum]));
```

For the first piece of code, the key thing to note is that we're performing a lookup in the dot1dTpFdbTable of the *massaged* version (i.e., $macaddr) of the Ethernet address we're looking up. This table is indexed by dot1dTpFdbAddress (MAC address). To actually perform this lookup, we need to query using a period-delimited decimal format: NNN.NNN.NNN.NNN.NNN.NNN. The massage_mac() subroutine handles the work of taking a MAC address in one of several common formats and returning the canonical format we need to use for queries.

In the second piece of code, we're doing some very simple caching. Before we actually perform a get(), we look in a simple hash table (%ifnum) to see if we've already made this query. If we haven't, we make the query and populate the hash table with the result. This is a good technique to remember when programming SNMP code. It is important to query for as little data and as seldom as possible if you want to be kind to your network and network devices. A device may have to take horsepower away from its usual tasks to respond to your slew of queries if you are not prudent.

Here's the output of our code:

```
00:60:b0:b7:1e:ed on VLAN 116 at "Gi4/2"
```

It's not hard to see how this program could be enhanced. Besides prettier or more orderly output, it could save state between runs. Each time it ran, the program could let you know how things have changed: new addresses appearing, ports being changed, etc. One quick caveat: most switches are of the "learning" variety, so they will age out entries for addresses that they haven't heard from in a while. This means that your program will need to run at least as often as the standard port aging time (by default this is three minutes in most Cisco gear).

Sending and Receiving SNMP Traps, Notifications, and Informs

Working with SNMP traps, notifications, and informs from Perl is pretty straightforward, so this section will be brief. Just to quickly review the background from Appendix G, traps, notifications, and informs are ways for an SNMP agent (in v1 and v2c terms) or SNMP entity (in v3 terminology) to send important messages to designated management stations without being polled first. The asynchronous messages could be something serious, like "Hey, I'm on fire!," or something less dramatic, like "A route has gone down." The protocol specifies a special way to transmit this information because the messages are considered either a) important enough not to wait for another SNMP entity to poll the device, or b) a poor fit for the polling model (you wouldn't want to constantly send out messages like, "Are you on fire yet? Are you on fire yet? How about now? Still not on fire?"). These asynchronous messages are called *traps* in v1; in v2 and v3 the name became *notification*.‡

Informs are just a fancier form of notification. With most SNMP notifications, the notifying device sends the message to the listening station, and that's the end of the interaction until the next notification is sent. The tricky part here is that these messages are most likely being sent over UDP.* UDP, by design, makes no guarantees that the intended recipient will actually receive the data after it has been sent. SNMPv2c provides a simple response to this concern through the use of informs, sometimes known as "acknowledged notifications." When an inform listener receives a "legitimate" message (see the RFCs for details), it responds with an acknowledgment of receipt. And yes, before you ask, the response is most likely coming back over UDP, so the response's receipt isn't guaranteed either. The RFCs specifically do not dictate how the initial sender should behave if does not receive an acknowledgment. Still, this is better than no mechanism at all.

Let's take a quick look at how you send and receive traps, notifications, and informs from Perl. We'll look at the mechanisms for sending first because that's the most common operation.

As I mentioned in Appendix G, the format of trap messages changes significantly from SNMPv1 to v2 (remember: the name also changes from "trap" to "notification" in v2). Luckily, the sending process is almost the same. Here's the code for sending a v1 trap using the SNMP module:

```
my $s = new SNMP::TrapSession(..., Version => 1);
$s->trap(enterprise => '.1.3.6.1.4.1.2021',    # Net-SNMP MIB extension
        agent       => '192.168.0.1',
        generic     => 2,                       # link down
        specific    => 0,
        uptime      => 1097679379,              # leave out to use current time
        [['ifIndex', 1, 1],                     # which interface
         ['sysLocation', 0, 'dieselcafe']]);    # in which location
```

SNMP::TrapSession() takes the same arguments as SNMP::Session() that we've seen all along (DestHost, Community, etc., represented by the ellipsis). Version is included here to indicate that this is an SNMPv1 trap. The SNMPv2c notification sending code is a little easier to read:

---

‡ I have also seen the term "trap notification" used to cover both cases.

* Unless they are using TCP for the transport, as defined in RFC 3430 (or one of the other transports listed in RFC 3417)—but in practice, that's very rare.

```
my $s = new SNMP::TrapSession(..., Version => '2c');
$s->trap(oid   => 'linkDown',
          uptime => 1097679379,              # leave out to use current time
          [['ifIndex', 1, 1],                # which interface
           ['ifAdminStatus', 1, 1],          # administratively up
           ['ifOperStatus', 1, 2]]);         # operationally down
```

Sending a v3 inform (v2 informs are not implemented as of this writing) looks almost exactly the same as sending an ordinary notification. Here's an example with the differences highlighted:

```
sub callback {...};
my $s = new SNMP::TrapSession(..., Version => '3');
$s->inform(oid   => 'linkDown',
            uptime => 1097679379,            # leave out to use current time
            [[ifIndex, 1, 1],                # which interface
             [ifAdminStatus, 1, 1],          # administratively up
             [ifOperStatus, 1, 2]],          # operationally down
            [\&callback, $s]);
```

Switching from trap to inform and 2c to 3 is pretty obvious, but that callback part looks a little weird. The code is there because we need a way to receive acknowledgments back from the receiver. When the acknowledgment returns or the process times out waiting for it, a subroutine called "callback" (we could have called it "message" or "got_it" or anything we liked) is invoked with arguments that contain the response message or an indication that the request has timed out. See the SNMP module documentation for more specifics on these arguments. Two comments on this idea before we move on:

- You don't need to include callback code if you don't want to—the last argument isn't mandatory. It really doesn't make sense to send an acknowledgment-requested notification and not listen for the response, but hey, it's your prerogative. The only reason I can see for sending an inform rather than a vanilla notification without caring about the response—and it is a stretch—is to comply with some internal enterprise standard that all SNMP notifications must be informs.

- Mentioning callbacks like this is actually a sneaky way to peek at a more sophisticated way of using the SNMP module. Though we won't be exploring this functionality, most of the SNMP module's methods (get(), getnext(), set(), etc.) can accept a callback reference as their last argument. When they receive this reference, they act in an asynchronous manner. That's a big word for "method calls run in the background without waiting and report back when they get an answer."

  Usually when you call get(), your program waits around (blocks) until whatever you've asked to get has been gotten (or the request times out). But in asynchronous mode, the program starts the request going and then immediately continues to process the next statement. Once the request completes, the code designated for callback is run with the answer to the original request passed in through its arguments. This way of working can be very useful when it is efficient to spin off a number of requests in the background without causing the entire program to grind to a halt for each one. One of the classical uses for this is in network management GUI programming, where you'd like the user to retain the ability to scroll a window even while an SNMP query is in progress.

Now that you've seen how to send traps, notifications, and informs, it's natural to want to know how to write programs that can receive them. It's less common to *need* to do this, because sites often deploy a larger network-monitoring package whose job it is to sit around receiving distress calls and alerting personnel as necessary. Those packages can be expensive, though, or sometimes too heavyweight for small tasks, so we'll take a quick look here at how to roll our own receivers.

The simplest and most boring method is to launch *snmptrapd*, which ships with the Net-SNMP distribution, and monitor its output. Though this method isn't exciting, as of this writing it is the only way to receive SNMPv3 notifications using Perl. We will shortly discuss a much more interesting way to use *snmptrapd*, so look for its triumphant return in a few moments.

If you need a pure Perl solution to handle v1 traps and v2c notifications, you can turn to a module we've largely neglected so far in this chapter: SNMP_Session.pm by Simon Leinen. This module is mostly known because of its association with the network-monitoring program the Multi Router Traffic Grapher (MRTG), but it can be useful by itself. SNMP_Session.pm is not available on CPAN as of this writing, so see the Module Information table at the end of this chapter for a pointer on where to get it if you want to use it.

Here's an example from the SNMP_Session.pm documentation that demonstrates how to listen for an SNMPv1 trap:

```
use SNMP_Session;
use BER;
my $trap_session = SNMPv1_Session->open_trap_session()
    or die 'cannot open trap session';
my ($trap, $sender_addr, $sender_port) = $trap_session->receive_trap()
    or die 'cannot receive trap';
my ($community, $enterprise, $agent,
    $generic, $specific, $sysUptime, $bindings) =
        $trap_session->decode_trap_request($trap)
    or die 'cannot decode trap received';
...
# this is how we would decode the bindings (e.g., if dealing
# with v2c notification)
my ($binding, $oid, $value);
while ($bindings ne '') {
    ($binding,$bindings) = decode_sequence($bindings);
    ($oid, $value) = decode_by_template($binding, "%O%@");
    print BER::pretty_oid($oid),' => ',pretty_print ($value),"\n";
}
```

First we open a session, then we sit and wait to receive the data from that session. Once the data is received, it gets decoded into its individual parts. The last of these parts in the request is the encoded sequence of data fields (OID/value pairs) called VarBinds that we saw in an earlier example. We iterate through this sequence, unpacking the individual OID/value pairs into a form we can use as we go. SNMPv2c notifications are received in a similar way (we replace `SNMPv1_Session` with `SNMPv2c_Session`), with the one important difference being the location where the important part of the message is encoded. In v1, most of the data is available to us after we've performed the `decode_trap_request()`. Extra information on that request can be found in the bindings, but we don't have to decode any further to know most of what we need to know about the message. This is largely reversed for v2 notifications: the key information is in the bindings, so we have to do a dual decode, as seen in the preceding code.

Before we move on, I should briefly mention the most interesting development to date in the world of trap and notification receipt. Versions 5.2 and greater of the Net-SNMP package let you build *snmptrapd* with an embedded Perl interpreter. If you add `perl ...` directives to the *snmptrapd* configuration file, the daemon will run your code at startup and then fire off code (e.g., a subroutine) as traps, notifications, and informs are received. This essentially gives you the best of both worlds, because it means you don't have to worry about the gnarly details of listening on the network, receiving messages, decoding them, running as a daemon, etc. Instead, your Perl coding time can be spent writing the programs that will react to these messages in some way.

Alternative SNMP Programming Interfaces

We've now seen all of the standard ways to do SNMP programming in Perl. Once you get the hang of them, and of SNMP in general, they are pretty straightforward to use. Still, as demonstrated in the multi-table lookup example earlier in this chapter, more involved tasks can sometimes be a bit more tedious to code than we'd like. In this section we'll explore a few of the additions and alternatives to the standard modules that aim to make the job easier. Be sure to do a search for "snmp" on *http://search.cpan .org* to see the breadth of modules available.

Some of the helper modules try to save you the labor of remembering specific SNMP variable names or OIDs. They have methods that return the most commonly requested information. For example, `Net::SNMP::Interfaces` by Jonathan Stowe and `Net::SNMP::HostInfo` by James Macfarlane augment `Net::SNMP` by providing method calls like:

```
$interface->ifInOctets()
$interface->ifOperStatus()
$interface->ifOutErrors()
```

and:

```
$hostinfo->ipForwarding()
$hostinfo->ipRouteTable()
$hostinfo->icmpInEchos()
```

SNMP::BridgeQuery by John D. Shearer also uses Net::SNMP to make retrieving certain tables from bridge devices (e.g., network switches) easy. With a single function you can retrieve a device's forwarding bridge table or address translation table.

A more sophisticated family of modules in the same vein is SNMP::Info, originally written for the netdisco project by Max Baker. SNMP::Info is a framework that includes a set of vendor- and device-specific submodules like:

```
SNMP::Info::Layer1::Allied
SNMP::Info::Layer2::Aironet
SNMP::Info::Layer2::Bay
SNMP::Info::Layer2::HP
SNMP::Info::Layer3::Foundry
SNMP::Info::Layer3::C6500
```

Using SNMP::Info, you can make queries for generic information (e.g., the duplex setting on an interface) without having to worry about which vendor-specific SNMP variable needs to be queried for that particular device. This means that the code can be this simple:

```perl
use SNMP::Info;

my $c = SNMP::Info->new(AutoSpecify => 1,
                        DestHost    => $ARGV[0],
                        Community   => $ARGV[1],
                        Version     => '2c');

my $duplextable = $c->i_duplex();

print "Duplex setting for interface $ARGV[2]: " .
    $duplextable->{$ARGV[2]} . "\n";
```

This code snippet takes the name of the host, the community string, and the interface number to query and returns the duplex setting of that interface. The code should be very easy to read, in part because:

- We didn't have to write vendor/model-specific code for all of the possible devices we might want to query, with each special case full of esoteric SNMP variable names or OIDs.

- We didn't even have to write code to determine the vendor or model of the device. Just setting AutoSpecify => 1 in the object constructor tells the module to do this on our behalf.

- To get the table of duplex settings, we didn't have to bother writing table-walking code that makes getnext() calls. We just called a single function.

SNMP::Info is worth exploring for a number of problems you may encounter. It is a good way to help make the Simple Network Management Protocol simpler.

Module Information for This Chapter

Module	CPAN ID/URL	Version
Net::SNMP	DTOWN	5.01
SNMP	http://www.net-snmp.org	5.2.1
SNMP_Session.pm	http://www.switch.ch/misc/leinen/snmp/perl/	1.07
SNMP::MIB::Compiler	FTASSIN	0.05
SNMP_util.pm	http://www.switch.ch/misc/leinen/snmp/perl/	1.04
SNMP::Util	WMARQ	1.8
Net::SNMP::Interfaces	JSTOWE	1.1
Net::SNMP::HostInfo	JMACFARLA	0.04
SNMP::BridgeQuery	JSHEARER	0.58
SNMP::Info	MAXB	0.90

References for More Information

There are over 70 RFCs with SNMP in their titles (and more than 100 that mention SNMP elsewhere). Here are just the RFCs referenced in this chapter or in Appendix G:

- *RFC 1157: A Simple Network Management Protocol (SNMP)*, by J. Case, M. Fedor, M. Schoffstall, and J. Davin (1990)
- *RFC 1213: Management Information Base for Network Management of TCP/IP-based Internets: MIB-II*, by K. McCloghrie and M. Rose (1991)
- *RFC 1493: Definitions of Managed Objects for Bridges*, by E. Decker, P. Langille, A. Rijsinghani, and K. McCloghrie (1993)
- *RFC 1573: Evolution of the Interfaces Group of MIB-II*, by K. McCloghrie and F. Kastenholz (1994)
- *RFC 1905: Protocol Operations for Version 2 of the Simple Network Management Protocol (SNMPv2)*, by J. Case, K. McCloghrie, M. Rose, and S. Waldbusser (1996)
- *RFC 1907: Management Information Base for Version 2 of the Simple Network Management Protocol (SNMPv2)*, by J. Case, K. McCloghrie, M. Rose, and S. Waldbusser (1996)
- *RFC 2011: SNMPv2 Management Information Base for the Internet Protocol using SMIv2*, by K. McCloghrie (1996)
- *RFC 2012: SNMPv2 Management Information Base for the Transmission Control Protocol using SMIv2*, by K. McCloghrie (1996)
- *RFC 2013: SNMPv2 Management Information Base for the User Datagram Protocol using SMIv2*, by K. McCloghrie (1996)

- *RFC 2274: User-based Security Model (USM) for Version 3 of the Simple Network Management Protocol (SNMPv3)*, by U. Blumenthal and B. Wijnen (1998)
- *RFC 2275: View-based Access Control Model (VACM) for the Simple Network Management Protocol (SNMP)*, by B. Wijnen, R. Presuhn, and K. McCloghrie (1998)
- *RFC 2578: Structure of Management Information Version 2 (SMIv2)*, by K. McCloghrie, D. Perkins, and J. Schoenwaelder (1999)

A variety of good general SNMP resources are also available.

http://www.simpleweb.org is a superb collection of all things related to network management, a big chunk of which is SNMP-related.

http://net-snmp.sourceforge.net is the home of the Net-SNMP project.

http://www.cisco.com/public/sw-center/netmgmt/cmtk/mibs.shtml is the location of Cisco's MIB files. Other vendors have similar sites.

http://www.snmpinfo.com is the home of the company SNMPinfo and David Perkins (an SNMP guru who actively posts to *comp.protocols.snmp*, and one of the authors of *Understanding SNMP MIBs*).

http://www.ibr.cs.tu-bs.de/ietf/snmpv3/ is an excellent resource on version 3 of SNMP.

http://www.mrtg.org and *http://cricket.sourceforge.net* are the homes of MRTG and its descendant Cricket (written in Perl!), two good examples of how SNMP can be used to do long-term monitoring of devices.

Understanding SNMP MIBs, by David Perkins and Evan McGinnis (Prentice Hall) is a good resource on MIBs.

http://www.snmp.org is the home of the company SNMP Research. The "protocol" section of the site has some good references, including the *comp.protocols.snmp* FAQ.

## CHAPTER 13

Network Mapping and Monitoring

People who administer networks of machines, even if they don't officially have the title "network administrator," care about the answers to at least two basic questions: "What's on my network?" (mapping) and "Are the nodes doing what I think they should be doing?" (monitoring). Even though you'd probably like to think the first question is an easy one (after all, it is your network, right?), the answer turns out to be less simple in these days of $20 mini-hubs and wireless access. Making sure that the web servers are constantly serving HTTP or HTTPS, the routers are moving packets, and the database servers can be queried has become really important. Perhaps even more important is knowing when the web servers suddenly start serving SMTP, the database servers unexpectedly begin offering web access, or the routers are dropping packets. This chapter is about answering both the mapping and monitoring questions. Its goal is to help you identify and understand the various components necessary to build the custom solutions you need in these areas.

Network Mapping

We'll start by looking at the mapping question, because it's generally a good idea to know exactly what you have before you start trying to monitor it. Back in the Mesozoic age of computing, it was much easier to map one's environment. The most sophisticated tools you needed were a pencil and paper and a few moments of quiet reflection. There were fewer computers, all ran services you'd installed, and the difficulty of adding a machine or a service to the network was beyond the ken of most users (packet drivers, anyone?). These days, anyone can roll in with a laptop ready to start spewing packets onto your network with a single click (or less)—and believe me, they will.

Now that we've had a lovely nostalgic moment, let's come back to the cold, harsh present reality and get specific about just what we plan to map. There are a number of choices, but here are some of the more common possibilities:

- Host existence
- Network gear configuration

- Network topology
- Network services
- Physical locations of network hosts

Of these, the last item turns out to be both one of the most common requests and one of the hardest. We'll save some tips on that until the very end of this section so we can concentrate on the more easily accomplished tasks.

Discovering Hosts

We can take one of two tacks when trying to determine which hosts are actually out on the network: active or passive. The active approach requires sending probe packets of some sort onto the network, while the passive approach simply requires listening. Let's look at how we perform each approach. Then we'll discuss their relative merits.

The simplest and most common active probe involves sending ICMP `ECHO_REQUEST` datagrams (i.e., "ping" packets) to a range of network addresses and listening for ICMP `ECHO_RESPONSE` datagrams. There are a few modules that make sending *ping* packets easy:

Net::Ping
: This may be the grandpappy of all the `Ping` modules, but it has aged quite well. Over the years, the options for checking host reachability via a *ping*-ish packet have expanded to include a number of protocols besides ICMP. Russell Mosemann, the original author, and other contributors, including Rob Brown, the current maintainer, have kept up admirably with these developments. `Net::Ping` supports sending packets to a host's TCP or UDP `echo` service, standard ICMP requests, and even partial TCP handshakes. It can also call the next module in our list when needed.

Net::Ping::External
: Classic *ping* packets often pose a conundrum for Perl scripters. On the one hand, a random host is more likely to respond to an ICMP packet than it is to respond to a request for either TCP or UDP `echo` service.* On the other hand, many operating systems require scripts that wish to undertake ICMP-related activities to be run with elevated privileges. `Net::Ping::External` seeks to help security-conscious programmers by allowing them to call the native OS's *ping* executable. That executable already has the privileges necessary for the job and (in theory) has been vetted for security issues surrounding that level of privilege. `Net::Ping::External` provides a simple layer around this process so your scripts don't have to bother with the nitty-gritty of calling executables with different input or output formats on different operating systems.

---

* Over time, largely in response to the wild and woolly nature of the current Internet (e.g., ICMP attacks, malevolent probes, etc.), ICMP has been blocked at more and more network gateways and hosts. By default, the Windows XP SP2+ firewall blocks ICMP. If you need to probe a host that is blocked like this, `Net::Ping`'s `syn` protocol mode may be your best bet.

Win32::PingICMP

If calling another executable just to get around the privilege issue bothers you, there is one more avenue available for Perl users on machines running Windows-based operating systems. Before raw sockets capabilities were introduced in Windows, it used a special *ICMP.dll* for ICMP packet sending and receipt. Largely undocumented by Microsoft, this DLL ties into the OS in a way that allows nonprivileged programs, like the standard *ping* program, to do their stuff. Toby Ovod-Everett's Win32::PingICMP calls this same DLL. This gives Perl access to even more precise packet timing data than the previous module, which can only report on what the *ping* program returned. One caveat if you are planning to use this module: Microsoft has been promising for some time to remove this DLL from the OS. When (if) this happens, the Win32::PingICMP will cease to function.

So, let's see one of these modules in action. The following code implements a simple *ping* sweep for an entire network block. It uses the Net::Netmask module to make the network block calculations easy:

```
use Net::Ping;
use Net::Netmask;

my $ping = Net::Ping->new('icmp');       # must run this script w/root privileges

# hand this script a network/netmask specification
die $Net::Netmask::error
    unless my $netblock = new2 Net::Netmask( $ARGV[0] );

my $blocksize = $netblock->size() - 1;

# this loop may take a while since nonreachable addresses have to time out
my (@addrs);
for ( my $i = 1; $i <= $blocksize; $i++ ) {
    my $addr = $netblock->nth($i);
    push( @addrs, $addr ) if $ping->ping( $addr, 1 );
}
print "Found\n", join( "\n", @addrs ), "\n" if scalar @addrs;
```

The Net::Ping code is pretty easy to suss—it's just a new() followed by a ping() of an address—so let's skip straight to the Net::Netmask methods in this example. We first construct a Net::Netmask object using new2. The difference between new, the constructor you are used to seeing, and new2 has to do with how the module responds to bad data: new2 will return undef if it receives a network specification it can't understand, while plain old new will hand back an empty object. I think this default is too subtle (I'd rather have the program blow up if it gets bad input); hence the use of new2 in the example. This object has a few handy method calls, such as size to return the size of the address block and nth to return the Nth address in that block. This makes it easy for us to iterate over the entire block, *ping*ing as we go. Net::Netmask also has an enumerate() method that you can call like so:

```
for my $address ($netblock->enumerate) {...}
```

but it can be dangerous to use if the network block size is large (it will generate a huge list of items).

A related, but slightly more dangerous active probe technique is the Address Resolution Protocol (ARP) scan. ARP is used to help a machine determine the unique hardware address that another machine on its local segment uses for communication so it can talk to that machine. The host broadcasts a question like, "Which host is 192.168.0.11?" and the host with that address is supposed to reply, "Here I am, I'm at 00:1e:c2:c2:a1:f1." To perform an ARP scan, you send out ARP requests for all the possible IP addresses on the segment and see which hosts reply. There are two reasons why I call this "slightly more dangerous":

- The ARP protocol is a fundamental building block of your network. If your program impedes its functioning, either intentionally (as in the case of an ARP spoof attack) or unintentionally (in the case of an ARP storm), that's a *very bad thing*. Be sure you know what you are doing before going down this path.

- Some operating systems like Windows get *very* unhappy if they see replies to handcrafted ARP requests (i.e., responses to requests the OS itself didn't make) involving the machine's current IP address. How unhappy? Well, if you manually send an ARP request for a given machine from that machine, the OS may decide to shut down the interface, in addition to the klaxons and sirens going off. You need to be careful not to probe for the address of the machine sending the probe.

Now that I've warned you about playing with fire, let's go find some matches. Constructing random ARP packets, sending them out, and then listening for the responses turns out to be really hard to do in a platform-independent fashion. Finding one approach that properly builds and functions under multiple operating systems can be very tricky. We'll look at three possibilities, at least one of which is likely to work for you.

This may seem like a cop-out, but the closest thing to a multiplatform method for ARP packet manipulation is the use of an external binary. There are a number of packet construction suites available on the Web, including spak, ipsend, rain, arp-sk, hping, and nemesis. We're going to look at the last one in that list, because creators Mark Grimes and Jeff Nathan have put considerable effort into making sure nemesis runs under a wide range of platforms, including the BSD flavors, Linux, Solaris, OS X, and Windows. The rest compile on only a subset of those platforms.

 nemesis was written to use (and only works with) libnet 1.0.2. It does not work with libnet 1.1, the version that is included in most modern Linux distributions. Tips on getting nemesis working using the old libnet version can be found at *http://codeidol.com/security/anti-hacker -tool-kit/TCP-IP-Stack-Tools/NEMESIS-PACKET-WEAVING-101*.

Producing the ARP packet you want via nemesis is easy:

```
nemesis arp -v -S 192.168.0.2 -D 192.168.0.1
```

That command line will return something like this:

```
ARP/RARP Packet Injection -=- The NEMESIS Project Version 1.4 (Build 26)

                [MAC] 00:0A:95:F5:92:56 > FF:FF:FF:FF:FF:FF
      [Ethernet type] ARP (0x0806)

  [Protocol addr:IP] 192.168.0.4 > 192.168.0.1
 [Hardware addr:MAC] 00:0a:95:f5:92:56 > 00:00:00:00:00:00
        [ARP opcode] Request
   [ARP hardware fmt] Ethernet (1)
   [ARP proto format] IP (0x0800)
    [ARP protocol len] 6
    [ARP hardware len] 4
```

It's easy to wrap a Perl script around this, similar to the one we saw a moment ago, and cause Net::Ping to send a flurry of queries. However, unlike the situation with our Net::Ping code, it then becomes incumbent on us to catch the responses that come back. We already saw how to capture packets in Chapter 11. When sniffing the traffic, we can trap just ARP replies by using this filter:

```
arp[7]=2
```

Let's look at how that filter is constructed. The =2 part is easy: the ARP reply opcode (ares_op$REPLY) is defined in RFC 826 as 2. The harder part is determining where in the packet to look using the *proto*[*N*] notation. However, this isn't a big deal either if you have a diagram of an ARP packet like the one in Figure 13-1 handy.

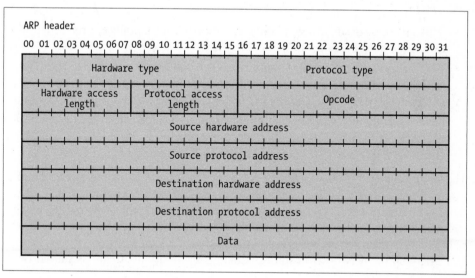

Figure 13-1. ARP packet diagram

Besides calling an external binary, there are two remaining approaches available for ARP probing. First, there's the do-it-yourself approach involving the modules we explored in detail in Chapter 5. It is possible to create your own ARP requests and place them on the wire. The Net::Packet module has explicit support for the construction of ARP packets. Net::Pcap can read the responses off the wire. We've already seen how these modules work, so we'll skip right to the final approach.

Oleg Prokopyev's Net::Arping module provides this last approach for ARP probing. It is similar to the two previous approaches in that it is built on the same fundamental libraries, libnet[†] (by Mike Schiffman) and libpcap (originally by Van Jacobson, Craig Leres, and Steven McCanne of the Lawrence Berkeley National Laboratory and now maintained by a group of volunteers at tcpdump.org (*http://tcpdump.org*)). Windows users build against an enhanced port of libpcap called WinPcap.

Net::Arping has syntax similar to what we saw earlier for Net::Ping. Namely:

```
use Net::Arping;

my $arping = Net::Arping->new();
# arping() returns the MAC address from the ARP response if received
my $return = $arping->arping($ARGV[0]);
print "$ARGV[0] " .
   ($return) ? "($return) is up\n" : "is down\n";
```

By now you're probably starting to get sick of modules with the word "ping" in them, so let's switch tracks and look at passive approaches to mapping host existence. These are the approaches that don't involve asking each host to respond in some fashion to a probe. They typically take more time to complete but are useful in the following circumstances:

- When there's a desire to avoid calling attention to the mapping efforts. Penetration tests often have a stealth component to them.

- When there's a concern about adding to the amount of network traffic. This is especially important when dealing with slow or saturated links.

- When there's a concern about damaging the network's operation. As mentioned previously, there's a certain amount of risk associated with playing with ARP packets and the like. Passive approaches are much less likely to have an adverse effect.

The first passive approach we'll look at can be described as "just sit and listen." Though it sounds more like a technique for meditation than for network mapping, this is often the easiest and most effective way to start. It involves using the same packet-sniffing techniques mentioned earlier (and described in detail in Chapter 11) to listen for the right things on the network. What are "the right things"? That depends on your network and where on the network you sniff, but here is a laundry list to get us started (with some code to follow):

---

† The same warning about libnet versions (only works with 1.0.2) that I gave for nemesis applies to Net::Arping as well.

- ARP traffic
- DHCP lease requests/renewals and server responses
- Traffic to a central gateway
- SNMP or other network-monitoring requests

Everything but the last item should make immediate sense, so here's a quick explanation of that item before we see some actual code. If there is another network monitor of some sort running on your network that probes individual hosts or network gear for status, you can piggyback on its efforts by listening for its probes/responses. You may be wondering, "If there's another monitoring system on the network, why are we bothering to write code?" There are a bunch of reasons to do this. Here's one good one: the monitoring system may be set to monitor a select set of hosts, while you are trying to map the entire network and/or find the ones it's missing. Gathering data from the probes sent from the existing system will give you a good start toward this goal. When you are mapping a network, it is good to make use of as many hints as are available to get the most complete picture.

Let's look at some code that actually sniffs the network and shows us the request and reply ARP traffic. This code (like the rest of our network-sniffing code) must be run with elevated privileges to work:

```
use Net::PcapUtils;
use NetPacket::Ethernet;
use NetPacket::ARP;

my $filter = 'arp';
my $dev    = 'en1'; # device for my wireless card
my %addresses = ();

die 'Unable to perform capture: ' . Net::Pcap::geterr($dev) . "\n"
  if ( Net::PcapUtils::loop(\&CollectPackets,
                          FILTER    => $filter,
                          DEV       => $dev,
                          NUMPACKETS => 100,
      )
  );

print join( "\n", keys %addresses ),"\n";

sub CollectPackets {
    my ( $arg, $hdr, $pkt ) = @_;

    # convert the source protocol address (i.e., IP address)
    # in hex form to dotted quad format (i.e., X.X.X.X)
    my $ip_addr = join(
        '.',
        unpack(
            'C*',
            pack( 'H*',
                NetPacket::ARP->decode( NetPacket::Ethernet::strip($pkt) )
                ->{'spa'} )
```

```
          )
     );

          $addresses{$ip_addr}++;
     }
```

This code will run until it has seen 100 packets, collecting IP addresses from ARP requests and replies as it goes. It will then print all of the unique hosts found so far. Changing this code to look for any of the other signs of life mentioned earlier is just a matter of changing the libpcap filter string and the line that decodes the packet. For instance, this code will find DHCP response traffic and show you the DHCP servers found:

```
use Net::PcapUtils;
use NetPacket::Ethernet;
use NetPacket::IP;

my $filter = 'dst port 68';     # DHCP response port
my $dev    = 'en1';             # device for my wireless card

my %addresses = ();

die 'Unable to perform capture: ' . Net::Pcap::geterr($dev) . "\n"
  if (
    Net::PcapUtils::loop(
        \&CollectPackets,
        FILTER     => $filter,
        DEV        => $dev,     # device for my wireless card
        NUMPACKETS => 100,
    )
  );

print join( "\n", keys %addresses ), "\n";

sub CollectPackets {
    my ( $arg, $hdr, $pkt ) = @_;

    # convert the IP address in hex form to dotted quad
    my $ip_addr =
        NetPacket::IP->decode( NetPacket::Ethernet::strip($pkt) )->{'src_ip'};

    $addresses{$ip_addr}++;
}
```

This code is pretty simplistic. It doesn't try to interpret the contents of an ARP or DHCP packet, because it doesn't need to. All we care about is the fact there's a host talking (that protocol). We really don't care what it's saying, just that it's out there. If we did want to get more sophisticated, we could look at the contents of the DHCP packets, see which IP addresses the server handed out or renewed, and add that to our knowledge of the network.

As simple as these programs are, the listening approach itself has its limitations. In order for it to be effective, the program has to be run from a place on the network that hears the traffic of interest. On wireless networks, that's easy: anywhere within broadcast range of the talking nodes will do.‡ On a wired network that is switch-based, however, it's considerably more difficult. The easiest way is to use a "mirrored" or "spanned" port specially configured to see all the traffic on that network. If you are not the network administrator, you'll need that person or group to set this up for you. If that's not an option, there are ways to redirect traffic through your node (e.g., involving ARP spoofing and packet forwarding), but that sort of skullduggery is beyond the scope of this book.*

Since we've brought network administrators into the picture, let's look at another passive approach for discovering host existence. This approach barely squeaks in under the definition of passive discovery, since it involves talking on the network (it's more of an active but indirect approach): we'll send packets, just not to the actual hosts we're trying to find. In this case we're interested in querying the network gear to which those hosts are connected. There are three possible questions we might ask a network device:

- What hosts have you seen using IP (i.e., as part of populating your ARP table)?
- What hosts have you seen on your ports at the Ethernet level (i.e., in the dynamic CAM table)?
- Do you know about any other network devices?†

In the section "Using SNMP from Perl" on page 469 in Chapter 12, we talked about using SNMP to retrieve both a device's ARP table and its dynamic CAM table (i.e., the table containing all of the Ethernet addresses heard on its ports). That discussion covers the first two questions. Modifying the scripts we saw in that chapter to collect the information over time is easy, so we won't rehash the actual query code here.

Here's a repeat of the caveat I mentioned at the end of that section in Chapter 12, because it especially bears repeating in this context: most switches are of the "learning" variety, so they will age out entries for addresses in the dynamic CAM table that they haven't heard from in a while. This means that your program will need to run at least as often as the standard port aging time (by default this is three minutes in most Cisco gear).

---

‡ Assuming you can associate with the access point, have the right WEP/WPA keys, etc.

* If you'd like to get deeper into this topic, one place to start is Dug Song's *dsniff* package, available at *http://monkey.org/~dugsong/dsniff/*.

† This question comes into play mostly when dealing with larger, dynamic, or unfamiliar infrastructures. If you are working on your own small and static network, writing code to discover other network devices probably isn't worth your time.

The third question is either very easy or more work to answer, depending on how your network gear is configured. Many vendors provide some sort of discovery protocol to facilitate broadcasting information to and receiving it from other network devices from the same manufacturer. For example, the Cisco Discovery Protocol (CDP) is fairly common, with others, like the Foundry Discover Protocol and the SynOptics Network Management Protocol (for SynOptics, Bay, and Nortel gear), serving a similar role. This makes it simple to answer the third question of our questions. If one of these protocols is turned on, we can query one of two ways: with a dedicated module (e.g., `Net::CDP` by Michael Chapman) or a more general framework (like that provided by Max Baker's `SNMP::Info`). I'm partial to the latter approach, because it means I don't have to find, install, learn, or write a new module every time I perform a similar discovery task. Here's an excerpt from the sample code in the `SNMP::Info::CDP` documentation to show you just how easy it is to query a network device's neighbors:

```
use SNMP::Info::CDP;

my $cdp = new SNMP::Info (
                            AutoSpecify => 1,
                            Debug       => 1,
                            DestHost    => 'router',
                            Community   => 'public',
                            Version     => 2
                         );

my $interfaces = $cdp->interfaces();
my $c_if       = $cdp->c_if();
my $c_ip       = $cdp->c_ip();
my $c_port     = $cdp->c_port();

foreach my $cdp_key (keys %$c_ip){
    my $iid           = $c_if->{$cdp_key};
    my $port          = $interfaces->{$iid};
    my $neighbor      = $c_ip->{$cdp_key};
    my $neighbor_port = $c_port->{$cdp_key};
    print "Port : $port connected to $neighbor / $neighbor_port\n";
}
```

Now, what if the network gear in question isn't running a discovery protocol like this? That's actually a very likely scenario, because turning off this sort of protocol is high up on most security lists for ways to "harden" a network infrastructure. If something like CDP is blabbing router topology information in clear text onto the wire, it makes it much easier for nogoodniks to locate and target the central networking gear in an unfamiliar infrastructure. This is one of those places where we're going to have to work a little harder to get the answer.

To discover other networking gear when we're not being handed those devices' information on a silver platter, we need to hunt around to locate higher-level routing information.‡ We're looking for the routers we've located through some sort of routing protocol, like BGP, OSPF, or RIPvN, or manually inserted via static routes. Looking at the routing table for other machines to query requires a simple `snmpwalk` followed by some filtering:

```
use SNMP;

my $c = new SNMP::Session(DestHost => 'router',
                          Version   => '2c',
                          Community => 'secret');

my $routetable = $c->gettable('ipRouteTable');

for my $dest (keys %$routetable){
  # 3 = "direct" route (see RFC 1213 for the other values)
  next unless $routetable->{$dest}->{ipRouteType} == 3;
  print "$routetable->{$dest}->{ipRouteNextHop}\n";
}
```

This information gives us a starting place to go look for additional information.*

Discovering Network Services

Ordinarily we'd work our way up to the most sophisticated approach to a problem, but this time let's go right for the atomic destructo-ray option. When looking for what services are running on a network, we could try simple approaches using modules like `IO::Socket` or Spider Boardman's `Net::UDP` to attempt to make TCP and UDP contact with select ports. But that would be slow, tedious, and hardly whiz-bang.

For scanning a network segment to find open ports, *nmap* by Fyodor (*http://nmap .org*) is most often the tool of choice. It is optimized for speed and efficiency; we can probably do no better than an *nmap* scan driven and processed by Perl. The most complete module for initiating *nmap* scans from Perl is `Nmap::Scanner` by Max Schubert. If you need to parse and analyze the output of *nmap* (in XML mode), `Nmap::Parser` by Anthony G. Persaud is also an excellent tool. Be sure to look at both before you begin a project like this.

`Nmap::Scanner` has two programming styles available: batch and event-driven. In batch mode, we tell it, "Here's what I want you to scan and how. Go off and do it and then come back and give me the results when you're done." In event mode, we register

---

‡ We could also look for trunked ports, but the problem is there isn't a good way to determine the IP address of the network device on the *other* side of the trunk. If CDP were on, we could look at the `cdpCacheTable` for this info, but without it, we're stuck.

* And this is just the tip of the iceberg. Michal Zaleweski's book, cited in the references at the end of the chapter, is a good place to start, but there are other good places to look as well (e.g., the DHCP leases file, the log files of services such as IMAP, NetBIOS requests, etc.).

callbacks (snippets of code) we want run after certain events take place before, during, and after the scan. For example, we might tell it, "Let me know every time you find an open port so my code can do something (write to a database, ring a bell, deploy a SWAT team to rappel down the cubicle wall, etc.)." Let's look at a sample of each style. Here's an example of batch mode:

```
use Nmap::Scanner;

my $nscan = new Nmap::Scanner;

# Location of nmap binary. We're being explicit
# here as a matter of precaution, but if you leave
# this out it will be found in your $PATH.
$nscan->nmap_location('/usr/local/bin/nmap');

# scan the 192.168.0.x subnet for port 80 (http) open
my $nres = $nscan->scan('-p 80 192.168.0.0/24');

# retrieve the list of host objects found by the scan
my $nhosts = $nres->get_host_list();

# iterate over that list, printing out hostnames for
# the hosts with open ports
while( my $host = $nhosts->get_next() ){
    print $host->hostname()."\n" if
        $host->get_port("tcp",80)->state() eq 'open';
}
```

Here's that code modified to use event mode:

```
use Nmap::Scanner;

my $nscan = new Nmap::Scanner;

$nscan->nmap_location('/sw/bin/nmap');

# every time we find a port, run &PrintIfOpen
$nscan->register_port_found_event( \&PrintIfOpen );

my $nres = $nscan->scan('-p 80 129.10.116.0/24');

sub PrintIfOpen {

    # we receive a scanner object, a host object
    # and a port object each time this event
    # handler is called
    my ( $self, $host, $port ) = @_;

    print $host->hostname() . "\n"
      if $port->state() eq 'open';
}
```

We get two additional bonuses by using *nmap* for network discovery: version and OS identification. By default *nmap* will find open ports, but that's not precisely the same as finding network services. An open port 80 is probably but not necessarily a web server, 22 is likely but not always an SSH server, and so on. If we change this line from our examples from:

```
my $nres = $nscan->scan('-p 80 192.168.0.0/24');
```

to:

```
my $nres = $nscan->scan('-p 80 -sV 192.168.0.0/24');
```

nmap will take the extra step of attempting to connect to the open ports it finds and doing its best to determine what actual services are being provided on those ports. Furthermore, if it finds an open port that appears to be serving SSL or TLS, it will engage OpenSSL's client routines and attempt to determine what service is being offered over that encrypted channel. Pretty cool.

 Our code doesn't display or do anything with the extra info returned when using the -sV flag. To get at that info, you can call methods like these:

```
$host->get_port('tcp',80)->service->extrainfo()
$host->get_port('tcp',80)->service->product()
$host->get_port('tcp',80)->service->version()
```

Adding OS detection to the script is equally as easy: just add -O, remove the port specification (or add to it—*nmap* needs to talk to at least one open port to perform the detection), and run the script with elevated privileges.

Physical Location

This is the holy grail of network discovery. Everyone would really like to be able to figure out where network hosts are physically located, but it is often the hardest task. When a machine gets infected with a worm that forces it to saturate a network segment, you can shut down its network port (and probably should), but what you really want is to be able to visit the machine itself to disinfect it. Merely shutting down the port often just encourages the unwitting user to switch to a working network wall jack, and the game starts again.

There are a few impediments that make this task impossible in the abstract. Wireless networking is the easiest one to point at, but even wired networks make this difficult. The vast majority of networks use patch panels to connect the network gear to the room ports. Network switch ports can be queried for their configuration, but unless you have very expensive patch panels, there's no infallible way to determine which switch port was plugged into which physical port in the panel besides a visit to the wiring closet.[†] Even if you visit the closet, if you don't know the local network well (e.g., in a large organization) tracking down the errant machine can be a big pain.

Unfortunately, there are no sure-fire technical solutions for this problem that will work for everyone. At best, there are a few technology-aided approaches that can help. Here are two general observations that may spark your own ideas.

Observation 1: Proximity can help

If you can identify a specific part of your network that the host is close to, it's easier to track it down. Follow these steps:

1. Narrow down the search to the last piece of network gear that saw that host. In Chapter 12, we saw how to query a network switch for its dynamic CAM table using SNMP. If your wireless access points are SNMP-manageable (recommended for just this reason), you should be able to query their lists of associated nodes to find the MAC address in question. In both cases, your search scope narrows significantly.

2. Once you've narrowed the search, consider the various things you know about proximity in your network. Wireless access points are the most obvious epicenters, since users need to be within a certain distance of such an access point[‡] (depending on the flavor of wireless network and antennae in use) to associate with it.

   For wired networks, sometimes you can make use of known hosts, like servers, as an initial starting place. For example, if you know where some of the servers are found on the patch panel in your network, that may offer you an idea of where the machine you seek is located.[*] And finally, you may be able to discern something about the machine's location based on the logs of a print server. Most people print to the nearest printer. If you know which printer that machine has accessed, it might be a good clue as to the location of the host in question.

Observation 2: Conventions can help

Thinking about the conventions used in your network (naming, wiring, etc.) can also help you identify the location of the errant machine:

1. Narrow the search scope (as in the preceding section).

[†] And sometimes that doesn't even help. Having a good record of all of your patches and a process for maintaining it is important, but I have yet to meet a network administrator who hasn't had to trace cables at least once.

[‡] Although that could be anywhere from 150 to >300 feet in three dimensions, depending on the antennae in use. "Different floor" and even "next building over" are becoming pretty common search locations.

[*] The scenario being something like this: the infected machine is found on switch port 5/11, and you know that the mail server living in the machine room is plugged into the same switch on port 5/5. If your patch panel isn't too spaghetti-like, you might be able to make a reasonable guess that the infected machine is in a room relatively near your machine room.

---

2. If you have a local wiring/networking convention (and most people do, even if they didn't intentionally create it), bring it to bear on this problem. Are your patch panels laid out in a particular way? Do you name your network ports for the rooms they serve? Can you use reverse DNS information to narrow down the list of possible network segments on which the host could be located?

I realize that neither of these approaches is perfect when attempting to track down a rogue node, but hopefully they are a start.

Presenting the Information

When rolling your own network-monitoring code, there are four components to the task: data acquisition (i.e., probing), data presentation, controlling framework, and finally analysis and notification. We've just spent a bunch of time on the first item in that list, so let's move on to the second.

Textual Presentation Tools

In Hollywood movies network monitors all have shiny graphics, big maps, blinky lights, and the occasional sonar "ping" noise thrown in for good effect. In reality, this isn't the normal (or arguably even the most useful) way for data about network status to be presented. A great deal of information is presented in pure text form. Plain text works best for email reports, status checks from smartphones, and a whole host of other data and contexts.

In this section we're going to look at a number of Perl tools that can help make this presentation easier and more professional. Though we'll be using network-monitoring data in our examples, these tools are great for any time you need to present output in textual form. Use them often, and with great gusto.

 There's a whole class of related tools we *won't* be looking at that are worth mentioning. These are the multipart suites and modules available for general template work. They define little mini-languages or markup that can be inserted into textual template documents to generate reports, web pages, and any other cookie-cutter output. Example packages include the Template Toolkit, `Text::Template`, and `HTML::Template`.

These tools can be used to perform all of the tasks I'll be mentioning (most can embed Perl code to be executed, so they can do anything Perl can), but they are more complex and intricate than necessary for everyday simple tasks. We're going to be looking at the best simple, single-purpose tools for the job. For larger tasks, definitely look at the larger suites/modules, because they work very well.

Let's start off with some generic tools to make the text you present look better, and then get progressively fancier with our output. There are a number of good modules for reformatting text into something more legible.[†] This reformatting usually consists of wrapping lines where appropriate, stripping extra whitespace and punctuation characters, making capitalization changes, and so on. Modules in this category include `Text::Wrap` by David Muir Sharnoff and `Text::Beautify` by José Alves de Castro. More and more, though, I find myself using `Text::Autoformat` by Damian Conway in preference to these other modules. By default it tries very hard to reformat text the way you'd probably do it if you were working on it by hand. It preserves indentation, respects list formats and quoting conventions, and so on. All of this is configurable, but the module rarely requires tweaking.

Using `Text::Autoformat` is commendably simple:

```
use Text::Autoformat;
my $a= 'This is an example of really long text that blathers on and on.
        Strangely formatted, too.
Should it be presented to
        a user in this form? Probably not.
Here are three good reasons:
 1) we really don't want our lists to look bad. Ideally we'd
 like the numbered lists to wrap properly too.
 2) it looks unprofessional
 3) we need an example
';
print autoformat ($a, {all=>1});
```

This yields:

```
This is an example of really long text that blathers on and on.
Strangely formatted, too. Should it be presented to a user in this form?
Probably not. Here are three good reasons:
 1) we really don't want our lists to look bad. Ideally we'd like the
    numbered lists to wrap properly too.
 2) it looks unprofessional
 3) we need an example
```

This lovely reformatting was achieved with a single call to `autoformat()`. The only nonobvious part of the code is the optional parameter: by default, `autoformat()` will reformat only the first paragraph of the text; `all` tells it to reformat all of the paragraphs.

 Be sure you are using the latest version of `Text::Autoformat` (1.14.0 as of this writing), since it fixes an issue when interpreting lines that end with a colon, as in our example.

---

† The modules we'll be discussing are mostly geared toward making English or English-like text prettier. I don't know how well they will play with non-Anglo-centric text.

Now that we've seen an easy way to format text into good-looking paragraphs, let's talk about presenting it in other shapes. Column and table are the next two most common forms. We often have lists of things we'd like to show to a user or send in an email. Putting a list into sorted columns can make it easier to read. Alan K. Stebbens's `Array::PrintCols` performs this task well. For instance, this:

```
use Array::PrintCols;

my @a = ('Martin Balsam','John Fiedler','Lee J. Cobb','E.G. Marshall',
         'Jack Klugman','Ed Binns','Jack Warden','Henry Fonda',
         'Joseph Sweeney','Ed Begley','George Voskovec','Robert Webber');

$Array::PrintCols::PreSorted = 0; # the data is not presorted, so sort

print_cols \@a;
```

prints the following:

```
E.G. Marshall   George Voskovec Jack Warden    Lee J. Cobb
Ed Begley       Henry Fonda     John Fiedler   Martin Balsam
Ed Binns        Jack Klugman    Joseph Sweeney Robert Webber
```

`Array::PrintCols` can be configured to print out a set number of columns or change the column widths. See the documentation for details.

The very next step toward spiffing up your output, once you have column creation under your belt, is table creation. Here's an example of the sort of output you'll be able to easily generate:

```
+----------+--------+--------+
| Host     | Status | Owner  |
+----------+--------+--------+
| brady    | passed | fmarch |
| drummond | passed | stracy |
| hornbeck | passed | gkelly |
+----------+--------+--------+
```

For some reason it seems like text-formatting tasks inspire authors to write new modules even if similar modules already exist. When it comes to creating textual tables, choices include (at least) `Text::TabularDisplay` by Darren Chamberlain, `Text::Format Table` by David Schweikert, `Text::ASCIITable` by Håkon Nessjøenand, and `Data::ShowTable` by Alan K. Stebbens. From this pack, I tend to employ `Text::Format Table` most often because of its simplicity and ease of use.

Here's the code that generated the table just shown:

```
use Text::FormatTable;

# imagine we generated this data structure through some
# complicated network probe process
my %results = (
    'drummond' => {
        status => 'passed',
        owner  => 'stracy'
```

```
        },
        'brady' => {
            status => 'passed',
            owner  => 'fmarch'
        },
        'hornbeck' => {
            status => 'passed',
            owner  => 'gkelly'
        }
);

my $table = Text::FormatTable->new('| l | l | l |');
$table->rule('-');
$table->head(qw(Host Status Owner));
$table->rule('-');

for ( sort keys %results ) {
    $table->row( $_, $results{$_}{status}, $results{$_}{owner} );
}

$table->rule('-');
print $table->render();
```

Creating a table with this module is essentially a three-step process:

1. Create a new table object. The number of columns and how they should be justified (i.e., whether the text should be centered or aligned to the left or right of the column) are specified at object-creation time.

2. Fill in the table content, starting with a table header. Creating a table header is as simple as drawing a separator line with $table->rule('-'), specifying the column names, and then drawing another line. To populate the rows of the table, call row() once for every row to be added. row() takes the data for each column as its parameters, in the order specified when the table was created. After populating all of the rows, add another separator line at the bottom to close the table and make it look pretty.

3. Generate the table with render() and print the results.

One last useful module to wrap up this section is Text::BarGraph, by Kirk Baucom. With a simple program like this:

```
use Text::BarGraph;

# imagine these are important statistics collected for each machine
my %hoststats = ( 'click'  => 100,
                  'clack'  => 37,
                  'moo'    => 75,
                  'giggle' => 10,
                  'duck'   => 150);

my $g = Text::BarGraph->new();

$g->{columns} = 70; # set column size
```

```
$g->{num}     = 1; # show values next to bars

print $g->graph(\%hoststats);
```

We can draw a textual bar graph like this:

```
  clack ( 37) #############
  click (100) ####################################
   duck (150) ######################################################
 giggle ( 10) ###
    moo ( 75) ###########################
```

Graphs like this one can easily be sent in mail messages for reporting purposes.

Graphical Presentation Tools

The textual graph we talked about in the last section offers an excellent segue into a discussion on a few toolsets for presenting information using pictures instead of text.

Using the GD::Graph module family

When people think of displaying information in this context, they often think of producing pretty graphs. There are a plethora of ways to create graphs using Perl, ranging from remote controlling other dedicated graphing programs (e.g., *gnuplot* or *ploticus*) or generalized number-crunchers (e.g., Excel or Matlab) to using sophisticated ray-tracers and OpenGL scene generators. The easiest (and perhaps most direct, in this context) way to create graphs is through the GD::Graph family of modules, by Martien Verbruggen and other contributors.

 The one thing that may not be easy about the modules we're about to explore is the process of building them. GD::Graph modules rely upon the GD module by Lincoln Stein. The GD module relies upon the GD (C) library by Thomas Boutell. The GD library tries to rely on at least five other C libraries (zlib, libpng, FreeType, JPEG, and XPM). Several of those rely on other libraries. Getting the picture? Building the whole kit and kaboodle can be a good example of the term "shaving a yak." Ultimately it's probably worth it, but if you can get someone else's build (e.g., if your Unix distribution offers a prebuilt package), all the better.

The first step when using these modules is to choose the kind of graph desired. Given the number of choices, this isn't always easy. At the time of this writing the chart type alternatives included area, bar (both horizontal and vertical), histogram, lines, lines with points, pie, sparklines, and timeline.

Once you've chosen the graph type, the process for graphing is straightforward:

1. Load the appropriate submodule. For example, to make a vertical bar graph similar to our earlier textual example, we would pick GD::Graph::hbars:

```
use GD::Graph::hbars;
```

2. Make sure the data is in the correct form. It should consist of at least two array references. The first array reference should point to an array with the label values. This essentially lists the labels for the x/horizontal axis or, if creating a pie chart, the slice names. Subsequent array references describe the values to plot on the y/vertical axis or the sizes of the slices in the pie chart:

```
my @data=([qw(click clack moo giggle duck)],[100,37,75,10,150]);
```

3. Create a new object of the desired type:

```
my $g = new GD::Graph::hbars;
```

4. Plot the data:

```
$g->plot(\@data);
```

5. Write it out to disk:

```
open my $T, '>', 't.png' or die "Can't open t.png:$!\n";
binmode $T;
print $T $g->gd->png;
close $T;
```

Everything in that snippet is pretty basic except for the mention of `binmode`. This is one of the more obscure Perl commands that you don't typically find out about until your code requires it to operate properly. In short, it makes sure that data gets written with no end-of-line remapping or funny business that can take place on operating systems that distinguish between types of I/O handling. The most common place this shows up is in Windows Perl programming, since the Windows family of operating systems has text and binary modes.

Figure 13-2 shows the resulting graph from our code.

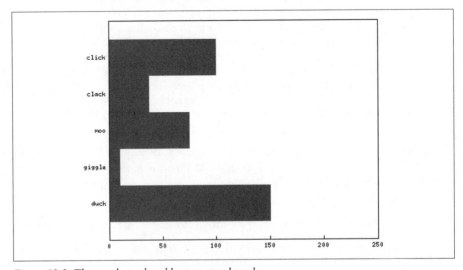

Figure 13-2. The graph produced by our sample code

Pretty boring, eh? Boring in a chart isn't always bad (see Edward Tufte's lucid arguments against "chartjunk," referenced at the end of this chapter, for more details), but a little prettier surely would be better. To improve the appearance, we can set some options right after creating the object and before plotting the data:

```
$g->set(
        x_label           => 'Machine Name',
        y_label           => 'Bogomips',
        title             => 'Machine Computation Comparison',
        x_label_position => 0.5,
        bar_spacing       => 10,
        values_space      => 15,
        shadow_depth      => 4,
        shadowclr         => 'dred',
        transparent       => 0,
        show_values       => $g
);
```

Now we get the result shown in Figure 13-3.

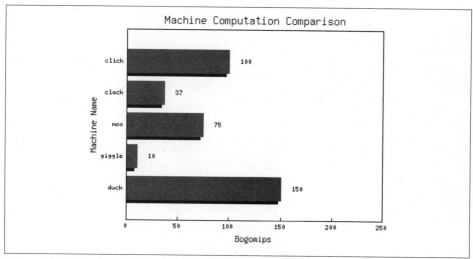

Figure 13-3. Improved graph with formatting

Much nicer. There are many options for changing the look of the graph. If making things as shiny as possible is your aim, there is a GD::Graph3d module by Jeremy Wadsack that is a drop-in replacement for parts of GD::Graph. If we change hbars to bars3d in our code, we get the chart shown in Figure 13-4.

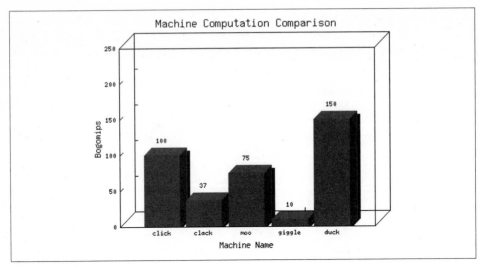

Figure 13-4. 3D version of our graph

Using GraphViz

Charts and graphs aren't the only graphical presentation available to us. I have yet to meet someone who deals with networks who isn't delighted by a tool that makes drawing diagrams easy. The GraphViz visualization software by AT&T (*http://www.graphviz .org*), driven by Leon Brocard's `GraphViz` module, is just such a tool.

Figure 13-5 shows a very simple diagram created with GraphViz.

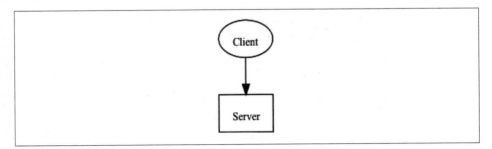

Figure 13-5. GraphViz diagram

The code to generate it is equally simple:

```
use GraphViz;

my $g = GraphViz->new();

$g->add_node('Client');
$g->add_node('Server', shape=>'box');
$g->add_edge('Client' => 'Server');
```

```
$g->as_jpeg('simple.jpg');
```

Create the object, add two nodes, add the connector, write the file out as a JPEG file—can't get much simpler than that. Though it isn't apparent in this example, the GraphViz module really starts to shine when it comes to creating more complex diagrams. The GraphViz software itself goes to considerable lengths to try to compute how to lay out diagrams in an aesthetically pleasing way, so you don't have to bother. If you were going to create your diagrams using a drawing package, you'd probably spend considerable time writing code to place the nodes so they didn't overlap and lines didn't cross. GraphViz handles all of that for you.

Let's look at a slightly more complex example so you can see the power of this tool. The following code sniffs the network for 50 SYN packets destined for the HTTP port and keeps a hash of all of their unique HTTP source/destination pairs. It then graphs this information so we can get a picture of which machines are browsing content from which servers. The sniffing code is the same as that in Chapter 11 with just the addition of a few GraphViz commands, so the whole program should be pretty straightforward:

```
use NetPacket::Ethernet qw(:strip);
use NetPacket::IP qw(:strip);
use NetPacket::TCP;
use Net::PcapUtils;
use GraphViz;

my $filt = 'port 80 and tcp[13] = 2';
my $dev  = 'en1';
my %traffic;    # for recording the src/dst pairs

die 'Unable to perform capture: '
    . Net::Pcap::geterr($dev) . "\n"
    if ( Net::PcapUtils::loop(
        \&grabipandlog,
        DEV        => $dev,
        FILTER     => $filt,
        NUMPACKETS => 50 )
    );

my $g = new GraphViz;

for ( keys %traffic ) {
    my ( $src, $dest ) = split(/:/);
    $g->add_node($src);
    $g->add_node($dest);
    $g->add_edge( $src => $dest );
}

$g->as_jpeg('syn80.jpg');

sub grabipandlog {
    my ( $arg, $hdr, $pkt ) = @_;
```

```
    my $src = NetPacket::IP->decode( NetPacket::Ethernet::strip($pkt) )
        ->{'src_ip'};

    my $dst = NetPacket::IP->decode( NetPacket::Ethernet::strip($pkt) )
        ->{'dest_ip'};

    $traffic{"$src:$dst"}++;
}
```

Some example output appears in Figure 13-6.

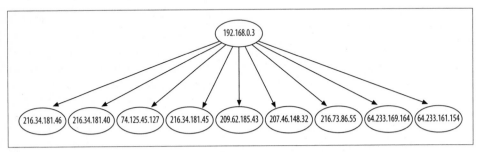

Figure 13-6. Default output

That's with the default output format. If we change this line:

```
    my $g = new GraphViz;
```

to:

```
    my $g = new GraphViz(layout => 'circo');
```

the diagram changes to what you see in Figure 13-7.

Changing the line to the following:

```
    my $g = new GraphViz(layout => 'fdp');
```

results in different formatting again, as illustrated in Figure 13-8.

`GraphViz` has many formatting options; see the documentation for more information.

 As an aside, I'd also recommend that you check out the `Graph::Easy` family of modules by Tels. It has a really comfortable user interface that you may prefer over plain `GraphViz`. It also has some spiffy features (e.g., ASCII diagram output).

Before finishing our discussion of `GraphViz`, it's important to mention that there are a number of modules that have been built on the `GraphViz` module from which you can draw inspiration. The module itself ships with submodules that can produce diagrams from Perl data structures, regular expressions, parsing grammars, and XML files. Other people have written modules to visualize database structures via DBI, arbitrary graphs,

---

Makefile dependencies, mail threads, and DNS zones, just to name a few. There's no telling what uses you can find for `GraphViz`.

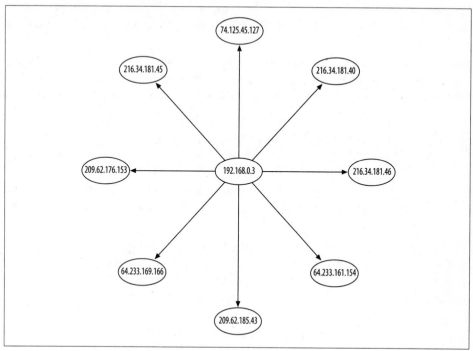

Figure 13-7. Output with "circo" layout

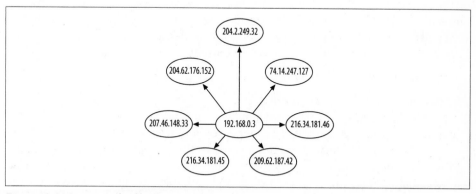

Figure 13-8. Output with "fdp" layout

Using RRDtool

I've saved one more type of graphical presentation tool for last because it is potentially the most complex: RRDtool. We're only going to skim the surface of this package to get you going, but once you've got the basics down you can explore the rest of the functionality at will.

People often find RRDtool a bit daunting at the start because they come to it with some misunderstandings about what it is good for and how it should work based on experiences with other programs. Let's try to banish two misconceptions right away so you don't fall into the same trap:

- RRDtool is not a general-purpose plotting package. In most cases, you don't just hand it a data set and expect it to plot the data in an X, Y coordinate graph. If this is your primary need, see the `GD::Graph` family of modules we just discussed.
- RRDtool is not a general database tool for storing a data set, like the Berkeley DB or {s,n,g}bm databases. Use modules like `BerkeleyDB` or `DBM::Deep` for applications that require this storage model.

The key to easy entry into the RRDtool world is to have the right mental model for the tool when you start. If you think about it as either a plotting package or a relational database, it will be more confusing than is necessary. We'll hit the core concepts of RRDtool first and then take a look at the actual command lines and such for implementing them.

One way to get the right mental model is to start with an RRDtool-appropriate goal in mind and figure out what is necessary to achieve it. A classic use for RRDtool is monitoring a router. There are many possible bits of information we might want to monitor on the average router, but we'll pick just three for this example: incoming bandwidth, outgoing bandwidth, and router temperature. To keep track of these three statistics, we'll poll the router for the information and store the data every 2 minutes. That should be often enough to get a good picture of the current operation of the router.

To go about this, we need to understand five fundamental RRDtool concepts:

RRDtool fundamental #1: Periodic update

An RRDtool database consists of a number of time buckets that hold data. RRDtool stores data at fixed intervals (the step size), and it expects you to hand it data accordingly. Unfortunately, in the real world you are not always able to acquire and provide data at exactly the defined interval. So, to make it easier for you, RRDtool will take the data you provide and resample it to match the time buckets set up in the database. RRDtool assumes your data to be continuous and calculates accordingly.

I use my own made-up term, "time bucket," rather than "timeslot" because RRDtool has the ability to handle a certain amount of wiggle room in the time between your updates. For example, an RRDtool database set to be updated every 5 minutes can be configured so that data stored at the 6-minute mark is handled properly (by calculating an average for the interval). A good mental image for this is an old milk bucket with a funnel built into the top. These buckets are able catch the milk poured directly into the narrow opening and the milk poured very close to the opening. Keep that picture in your head, and you'll have the right idea.

RRDtool fundamental #2: Unknown values

You are expected to update the database with the latest values once per period to fill each bucket. If you don't update once per period, you will get unknown values. If more than 50% of the values across the duration of a bucket are unknown, the whole bucket will be marked *UNKNOWN*.

UNKNOWN values come into play when subsequent calculations (e.g., daily averages) are made. RRDtool can be told the percentage of known to unknown values to allow for that calculation before marking the whole calculation *UNKNOWN*. This is similar to the way an error in a spreadsheet cell will cause any formulas based on that cell to show an error as well.

RRDtool fundamental #3: Finite number of buckets

When an RRDtool database is created, it is predefined with a set number of buckets (enough to hold the specified number of samples over the specified time period). RRDtool uses the same circular buffer approach we saw in Chapter 10 with bigbuffy. Data values are added from the beginning of the database one at a time until the end of database has been reached. At that point RRDtool wraps back to the beginning and starts writing from the top again. This is where the term "round robin database" comes from in the tool's name. The circular buffer approach allows RRDtool to store values for a specified window of time without taking up more storage space than is necessary.

RRDtool fundamental #4: Primary data points (PDPs) and consolidated data points (CDPs)

Each time new values are presented to RRDtool for an update, two things come into play: the primary data point (the actual value after it is stored for processing) and the consolidated data points calculated from it and other PDPs collected in the same bucket. For example, if RRDtool is told to keep a one-hour average for a statistic, it will store the new value (PDP) and the average (CDP) in that time bucket in the database. CDPs are important because more often than not they are the values that actually appear in the graphs we'll be producing. RRDtool handles incoming data in such a way that the averages you can get out of it are quite accurate.

This point illustrates how RRDtool is not like a normal database. With most data stores, you expect to retrieve the same values you put into them. With RRDtool, that's not the case. In our router example, we'll be graphing a measure of the router's average incoming bandwidth as it changes over time. With bandwidth measurements one is often looking for trends, so it is the average, not the actual stored byte count that matters.

RRDtool fundamental #5: Data source types (DSTs)

When creating an RRDtool database, you have to choose the type of data each data source will represent. This describes the structure of the data you are planning to feed to RRDtool. You are given a choice between `counter`, `derive`, `absolute`, `gauge`, and `compute`.

In a second, the most important phrase of this section will be mentioned again. That phrase is "rate of change."

RRDtool is largely concerned with presenting pieces of data *as they change over time*. Though you can record data values by themselves, RRDtool is designed to help you display the *rate of change*. It's useful when first starting out with this stuff to keep repeating to yourself "rate of change, change over time, rate of change..." to make sure you are clear on just what data RRDtool will store and graph.

`counter` is the most frequently used DST. It is used to store the rate of change in ever-increasing counters, as its name suggests. Most counters (e.g., in routers) have an upper limit after which they wrap around to zero. RRDtool handles this case: if the value presented to RRDtool for a `counter` PDP is smaller than the previous value, it assumes the counter has wrapped and is actually the sum of the distance of the last value from the wrap point plus the current value. This wrapping feature of the `counter` type can be an issue in cases where the device has reset or rebooted, throwing the start value back to zero again. RRDtool has no way to tell the difference between a wrap and a reset if you have not specified an upper and lower bound for the data source, so it assumes the former. If this is a concern for you, there are two ways to deal with it: you can explicitly update with a value of "U" (unknown) to prevent RRDtool from making any wrong wrapping assumptions, or you can use the `derive` type instead and set the lower bound to 0.

`derive` is like `counter` but without the wrap logic. More precisely (according to the documentation), it is "the derivative of the line going from the last to the current value of the data source." Before you whip out your calculus text, this means that the `derive` type can deal with both positive and negative rates of change. For example, available disk space is a statistic whose rate of change can be either positive (more space has been freed up) or negative (more disk space has been used).

`absolute` is usually described as being useful for counters that automatically reset back to zero each time you read them. Those are fairly rare, so I find it easier to think of this type as saying to RRDtool, "the rate of change should be whatever value I'm handing you divided by the amount of time between updates." For example, let's say the goal is to measure trends in virus handling on a mail server. If you check the number of virus messages rejected by the mail server every 5 minutes, and 30 more have been rejected since you last checked 5 minutes ago, an `absolute` data source would treat the rate of change as `30/(5 * 60 seconds)`.

gauge is probably the second most common type used. Unlike the other types we've seen so far, gauge values aren't computed over time. They are not rates; they are the simple values as supplied to RRDtool. If you wanted to see the sheer numbers of rejected mail messages from the last example (as opposed to the rate at which that number has changed from one time bucket to the next), you would use gauge.

compute is a type that does not get mentioned much in RRDtool tutorials, because it leads to one of the parts of the tool known to scare beginners. RRDtool uses Reverse Polish Notation (RPN) for specifying certain calculations. In this case, RPN is used to specify a data source computed from other data sources. This is similar to storing a formula in a spreadsheet cell (only that formula gets expressed in RPN). There's a good RPN tutorial distributed with RRDtool if you find your RPN skills are rusty from the days of your first calculator.

OK, enough theory. Let's actually use what we've just learned in practice to set up an RRDtool database, update it, and then graph the results. First comes the creation of the database:

```
$ rrdtool create router.rrd --start `perl -e 'print time-1'` \
                    --step 120                              \
            DS:bandin:COUNTER:240:0:10000000    \
            DS:bandout:COUNTER:240:0:10000000   \
            DS:temp_in:GAUGE:240:0:100          \
            RRA:AVERAGE:0.5:30:24
```

Let's look at this piece by piece. First we create the database, starting at the current time, and set it to be updated every 2 minutes (120 seconds):

```
$ rrdtool create router.rrd --start `perl -e 'print time-1'` \
                    --step 120                          \
```

We're going to be feeding it three sets of information every 2 minutes (bandwidth in, bandwidth out, and the temperature of the air flowing into the router). If we haven't updated each value within 240 seconds of the last update, that time bucket gets marked as *UNKNOWN*. The bandwidth data sources have their minimum and maximum set to 0 and 10 MB, respectively (let's assume we're monitoring a 10 MB router interface). This is important because it allows RRDtool to detect counter resets. We similarly declare reasonable maximum and minimum bounds for the temperature data source by stating that the temperature of the air flowing into the router will remain between the freezing and the boiling point of water (0–100° Celsius):‡

```
DS:bandin:COUNTER:240:0:10000000  \
            DS:bandout:COUNTER:240:0:10000000 \
            DS:temp_in:GAUGE:240:0:100        \
```

And finally, we want to store a day's worth of consolidated data points (CDPs), each representing an hourly average (there are 30 2-minute intervals in an hour and 24 total hours in a day). An hourly average is kept for each of the three data sources we defined.

---

‡ Though I don't want to be anywhere near your data center if it ever approaches those temperatures!

The 0.5 parameter here is the setting I mentioned in RRDtool fundamentals #2 a few pages back. It indicates that half of the buckets used to calculate this average can be *UNKNOWN* before we give up on the whole CDP and call it *UNKNOWN* too:

```
RRA:AVERAGE:0.5:30:24
```

We can store as many round robin archives (RRAs) as we want (e.g., for calculating a monthly or yearly average), but we'll only use this one to keep the example simple.

The Perl version of this `create` command line is a direct translation:

```
use RRDs;
my $database = "router.rrd";
RRDs::create ($database, '-start', time-1, '-step', '120',
              'DS:bandin:COUNTER:240:0:10000000',
              'DS:bandout:COUNTER:240:0:10000000',
              'DS:temp_in:GAUGE:240:0:100',
              'RRA:AVERAGE:0.5:30:24');

my $ERR=RRDs::error;
die "Can't create $database: $ERR\n" if $ERR;
```

Database in hand, we can start to feed in data values every two minutes:

```
rrdtool update router.rrd N:25336600490171:159512031730187:26
 (2 minutes go by)
rrdtool update router.rrd N:25336612743804:159512154231472:26
...
rrdtool update router.rrd N:25336810864361:159513632487313:26
...
rrdtool update router.rrd N:25336950227556:159515045447411:26
...
rrdtool update router.rrd N:25337088963449:159516528948027:26
...
rrdtool update router.rrd N:25337088963449:159516528948027:26
...
```

The first parameter is the name of the RRDtool database being updated. This is followed by the actual data for the update. The first field of that data is the time or the shortcut N for Now, representing the current time. If for some reason we didn't want the update to be associated with the current time via N (e.g., if we were loading in a data set already collected), we would use the time in the format shown previously in the `rrdtool cre ate` command (as with `time()`). The fields after the timestamp are the values for each data source in the order they were specified in our `rrdtool create` or `RRDs::create()`.

As you probably guessed, the Perl version of each line is also a direct translation, as in:[*]

```
RRDs::update('router.rrd', 'N:25336600490171:159512031730187:26');
RRDs::update('router.rrd', 'N:25336612743804:159512154231472:26'); ...
```

---

[*] In case you're wondering where these large data numbers come from, they are the respective values returned from my Cisco router by an snmpget (using SNMPv2c) for the OIDs `1.3.6.1.2.1.31.1.1.1.6.74` (ifHCInOctets), `1.3.6.1.2.1.31.1.1.1.10.74` (ifHCOutOctets), and `1.3.6.1.4.1.9.9.13.1.3.1.3.1` (ciscoEnvMonTemperatureStatusValue). I've omitted the snmpget command lines to keep the focus on RRDtool.

Although in a program, you'd probably write something like this:

```
while (1) {
    ($in,$out,$temp)= snmpquery(); # query the router with SNMP
    RRDs::update($database, "N:$in:$out:$temp");
    my $ERR=RRDs::error;
    die "Can't update $database: $ERR\n" if $ERR;
    sleep (120 - time % 120);       # sleep until next step time
}
```

We started to talk about RRDtool because it is a graphing tool, but we haven't seen a single picture yet. Your patience is about to be rewarded: we're now going to look at how to use everything we've done so far to generate pretty graphs. We'll be drawing two separate graphs (for reasons that will become clear in a moment).

The graphing features of RRDtool are the second speed bump beginners encounter, because they can get complex fast. As with the other parts of this survey, we're only going to skim the top so you can get started. Be sure to consult the RRDtool documentation when you're ready to dive deeper.

To graph the information we've collected so far, we need to specify at a minimum three things:

- The name of the output file where the graph will be stored. A dash (-) can be used if you'd like the data sent to *stdout* instead.

- One or more data definitions, so RRDtool knows which value or values to extract from the database for graphing or calculation.

- A graph specification (i.e., what to actually draw).

Let's graph the router bandwidth information first. A command line to do this might be:

```
rrdtool graph bandw.png \
            DEF:bandwin=router.rrd:bandin:AVERAGE \
            DEF:bandwout=router.rrd:bandout:AVERAGE \
            LINE2:bandwin\#FF0000 \
            LINE2:bandwout\#000000
```

This yields a picture like the one shown in Figure 13-9.

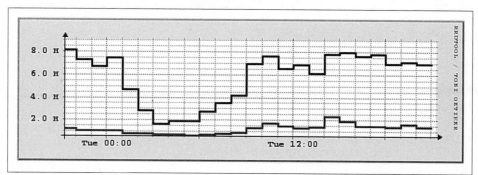

Figure 13-9. Router bandwidth graph

Let's break this down some more. We'll start with the data definition:

```
DEF:banwdin=router.rrd:bandin:AVERAGE \
DEF:banwdout=router.rrd:bandout:AVERAGE \
```

This says to pull the averaged values from the data sources `bandin` and `bandout` in the `router.rrd` database and refer to them by the names `bandwin` and `bandwout`:

```
LINE2:bandwin\#FF0000 \
LINE2:bandwout\#000000
```

We then graph both `bandwin` and `bandwout` using a medium line (`LINE2`) with the colors specified in hex form. That wasn't so bad, right? By default the graph shows about a day's worth of data. We can narrow down the display to specific hours by specifying a start and end time. For fun, let's generate a graph that displays data from 1 p.m. to 5 p.m. using Perl code:

```
use RRDs;
RRDs::graph('dayband.png',
            '-start', '1234893600','-end', '1234908000',
            '--lower-limit 0',
            'DEF:bandwin=router.rrd:bandin:AVERAGE',
            'DEF:bandwout=router.rrd:bandout:AVERAGE',
            'LINE2:bandwin#FF0000',
            'LINE2:bandwout#000000');
```

The resulting graph appears in Figure 13-10.

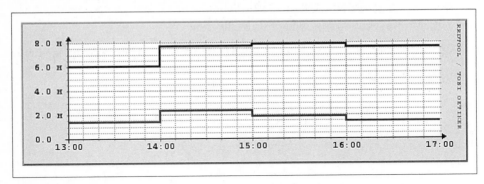

Figure 13-10. 4-hour bandwidth graph

Now let's get to the temperature graph. If we again create a graph using the minimum amount of code, like this:

```
use RRDs;
RRDs::graph('temp.png',
            'DEF:temp=router.rrd:temp_in:AVERAGE',
            'LINE2:temp#000000');
```

we get the result shown in Figure 13-11.

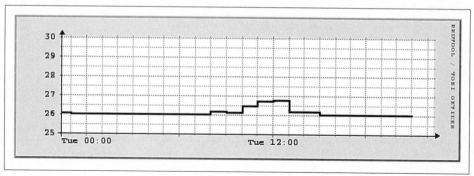

Figure 13-11. Temperature graph

There are a few things to say about this graph. First, it's boring. But boring is good! The graph is meant to display the temperature of the air as it enters the router.[†] If it were any less boring, it would mean there were serious issues with the cooling systems in our data center. The second thing to note about the graph is that the values are all in the 26–27° Celsius range. The scale and units of this graph are sufficiently different from that of the bandwidth graphs we just completed that it was necessary to create a separate graph to display the temperatures.

If we wanted to make the picture a little (but only a little) less boring, there are a number of things we could do. Most Americans aren't used to reading temperatures in Celsius, so we'll use RRDtool's built-in RPN calculation engine to convert the temperature values to Fahrenheit. We'll also gussy up the graph with both a legend and a warning line at 85° Fahrenheit:

```
use RRDs;
RRDs::graph('tempf.png',
            'DEF:temp=router.rrd:temp_in:AVERAGE',
            'CDEF:tempf=temp,9,*,5,/,32,+',
            'LINE2:tempf#000000:Inflow Temp',
            "LINE:85#FF0000:Danger Line\r");
```

Now we get the result shown in Figure 13-12.

[†] There's a separate SNMP OID for the outtake temperature that you may also want to track (e.g., to see if your router's electronics have caught fire, or more likely, if there is fan/internal ventilation problem). That OID is 1.3.6.1.4.1.9.9.13.1.3.1.3.3.

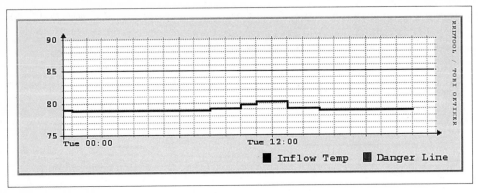

Figure 13-12. Temperature graph in Fahrenheit

Let's look at the lines from the preceding code that are different from the previous examples. First, there is this pair:

```
'CDEF:tempf=temp,9,*,5,/,32,+',
'LINE2:tempf#000000:Inflow Temp',
```

The first line is one of those RPN calculations I warned you about earlier. It takes the value we pulled from the RRDtool database, multiplies it by 1.8 (9/5), and then adds 32 to convert the value from Celsius to Fahrenheit. The Fahrenheit value is then graphed and an entry for it is added to the graph's legend.

The other line we haven't seen before is:

```
"LINE:85#FF0000:Danger Line\r"
```

This is meant to simply draw a line at the 85° F mark and place an entry for it in the graph's legend.

With this, we've come to the end of our exploration of RRDtool. RRDtool is a tremendously powerful tool. It has a large set of documentation, a very responsive developer, and an active user community. Hopefully this overview has given you a start with it; I encourage you to explore the more sophisticated aspects on your own.

Monitoring Frameworks

It's time to pull together everything we've covered so far to create a framework for network monitoring. We've seen how to gather the information and how to present it. Now we just need something to drive the whole process. We'll look at one option for building a home-brewed system here, and then we'll end with a peek at how to integrate our work into other, larger pre-existing packages.

One of the simplest frameworks we can use to construct a monitoring system actually ships with Perl. In 2003 Randal Schwartz wrote a column for *Linux Magazine* about using the `Test::More` module to test a website's health. `Test::More` is a module that provides a framework for writing a set of test scripts. You tell it which tests to run and what the expected output of those tests should be, and the module takes it from there.

Schwartz's article described how to construct a `Test::More` script that connected to a website and checked that the site returned reasonable data. With very little effort, we can extend this basic idea to monitoring an entire network. As long as we can write a set of tests to determine that your network and its hosts are functioning, `Test::More` will do the rest. It runs these tests in the desired order, skips tests that don't make sense (e.g., if you can't *ping* the mail server, there's no use trying to connect to its SMTP port), and provides coherent output.

Getting started with `Test::More` is really simple. The first step is to load the module and tell it how many tests will be run:

```
use Test::More tests => 5;
```

If you don't know how many tests will be run in your script (e.g., while you are still developing it), you can say this instead:

```
use Test::More 'no_plan';
```

Now we write the actual tests:

```
is(check_dns('my_server'),$known_ip,
    'DNS query returns right address for server');
is(sha2_page('http://www.example.com'),
    '6df23dc03f9b54cc38a0fc1483df6e21',
    'Home page has correct data');
```

`Test::More` just defines `is()` and a few other simple testing routines. It's up to code defined or loaded earlier in the script to define subroutines like `check_dns()`, `sha2_page()`, `router_interface_up()`, `correct_ports_open()`, or anything else we need checked. The script will generate output like this when everything is working OK:

```
ok 1 - DNS query returns right address for server
ok 2 - Home page has correct data
```

However, if something breaks, we might see output like this:

```
not ok 1 - DNS query returns right address for server
#     Failed test (test.pl at line 5)
#          got: '192.168.0.4'
#     expected: '192.168.0.6'
ok 2 - Home page has correct data
```

Once the results have been returned, we can feed them into a script that displays the information (perhaps using some of the tools we looked at earlier in this chapter in the sections "Textual Presentation Tools" on page 503 and "Graphical Presentation Tools" on page 507).

Since writing tests is generally pretty easy, you may quickly amass a large collection of `Test::More` scripts to test different parts of your infrastructure. At a certain point, it becomes unwieldy to keep track of all of the different possible tests and their results. `Test::Harness`, shipped with Perl, can handle this task for you. You pass it a list of files to run, and it runs the tests and returns a summary of which failed and which succeeded. There are other, more sophisticated testing modules and options available if you want to go further down this path. For more info, *Perl Testing: A Developer's Notebook (http: //oreilly.com/catalog/9780596100926/)*, by Ian Langworth and chromatic (O'Reilly), is a good reference.

Once you've written your framework (whether it's a `Test::Harness` script or a collection of `Test::More` subroutine calls), you can run it from *cron*, *launchd*, or the *scheduler* service. If you'd prefer to keep even the scheduling part entirely in Perl, Roland Huß's `Schedule::Cron` module provides a *cron*-like scheduler for Perl subroutines.

If you need something more sophisticated in a monitoring system framework, there are at least two directions you can pursue:

- For more complex, but still Perl-centric tasks, the best bet is to begin to use the Perl Object Environment (POE). For example, if you needed to gather data from multiple network devices at once (for a large infrastructure) while summarizing yet another set of data at the same time, POE would be a natural choice. POE is essentially a mini-operating system with process-like thingies that are run by a central kernel/scheduler in a multitasking-like fashion. POE has a considerable learning curve because it requires a solid grasp of OOP programming, the learning of new POE-specific terminology (sessions, wheels, handlers, drivers, etc.), and a little aptitude for multitasking programming. Rather than trying to cram a substantial POE tutorial into this already full chapter, let me direct you to the chapter devoted entirely to POE in Simon Cozen's *Advanced Perl Programming*, Second Edition *(http://oreilly.com/catalog/9780596004569/)* (O'Reilly). The POE home page also provides several tutorials that can be helpful.

- If a roll-your-own-in-Perl solution starts to be untenable, extending an existing monitoring package can be an attractive option. All good packages offer some way to plug in custom probe modules. In the next section we'll explore the general ideas necessary to write these plug-ins and then look at some concrete examples using a few of the popular packages.

Extending Existing Monitoring Packages

The vast majority of the extendable packages available at the time of this writing operate on a simple principle for their extensions: they periodically call some code you've written, with the expectation that your code will return status information (in a prescribed manner). For example, once every 5 minutes, the monitoring system will call your code (perhaps kept in a Perl script), and your code will return the string "OK" or "NOT OK". What your code does to determine which answer to return is totally up to you. Maybe it queries the outgoing packet count of a router via SNMP and makes sure that number has increased by the correct percentage since the last time it ran. Maybe it attempts to connect to your LDAP server to look up a test entry. Or perhaps it connects to your company's web application via a proprietary API and requests a status check.

All of this is totally up to you. The key thing here is that your code encapsulates a test in which a predetermined input will yield a specific predetermined output.

To make things more concrete, let's look at a specific example. The Big Brother monitoring package (*http://www.bb4.org* and *http://www.quest.com/bigbrother/*) lets you write plug-ins (called "external scripts") that are responsible for reporting back status to the main server each time they run. Though you could contact the server directly using Perl's socket support, it is usually easier to do this (even from Perl) by calling the bb command with the right arguments:

```
# bb machine_name color_code_for_display status_message
system("bb mymachine green everything_groovy")
```

If you don't want to do this by hand, there is a third-party module called BigBrother.pm, available at *http://www.deadcat.net*, that can make writing Big Brother plug-ins from within Perl easier.

Virtually all of the extension mechanisms we'll see in this section are variations on this theme. Let's take a quick tour of three open source monitoring packages to see how this plays out.

Two notes about the selection of monitoring packages:

1. There are several good open source monitoring packages out there. The ones discussed here were selected because, as of this writing, they are under active development and have vibrant user communities. Others, such as Spong (*http://spong.sourceforge.net*) and Big Sister (*http://www.bigsister.ch/bigsister.html*), are also worth looking at, but their development seems to have stalled. Be sure to factor this into your investigation when evaluating potential systems to use.

2. This tour includes only open source packages (not any of the fine commercial products available) because they offer the lowest initial monetary impediment to implementation. The same principles shown here for extending an open source package apply to the commercial packages as well.

Xymon

Xymon (*https://sf.net/projects/xymon/*), formerly known as "Hobbit" (*https://sf.net/projects/hobbitmon/*) is a descendant of Big Brother that attempts to offer good legacy compatibility. As a result, it too has a bb command that can be used just like in our earlier example.

Mon

Mon (*http://www.kernel.org/software/mon/*) describes itself as "fundamentally a scheduler which executes the monitors (each test a specific condition), and calls the appropriate alerts if the monitor fails." Each monitor is essentially a separate program or script, so extending the basic system is easy. The main configuration file, *mon.cf*, lists the programs to be run and the arguments to be passed to them. The program then signals success to Mon by exiting with a status of 0, the standard shell return code for success—or, if things didn't go so well, it exits with a different status to indicate that something has gone wrong. It can also print out more detail, the first line of which Mon treats as a summary of the problem.

This is all very simple to code, which is one of the reasons that Mon has built up a following of people who have written monitors for all sorts of services and devices. There's also room for greater complexity within this simple framework. Each time a monitor is run, Mon hands it data about previous runs through environment variables (e.g., MON_LAST_SUCCESS for the time of the last successful run, MON_LAST_OUTPUT for the text last output by the monitor, and so on). Perl scripts can access this data with code similar to this:

```
my $lastfailure = $ENV{MON_LAST_FAILURE};
```

With this sort of data, the monitor script can make much more sophisticated decisions about what tests to run and how to react to the current condition.

Nagios

Nagios (*http://www.nagios.org*) is the most sophisticated of the monitoring packages discussed here. Luckily, the basic plug-in interface mirrors that of Mon in that Nagios expects a return code based on the success of the test and a line of output to provide more information. The possible return codes are documented in Nagios's plug-in documentation (this is the one package amongst all the ones mentioned here that actually has plug-in documentation).

Nagios does have stricter rules about how Perl plug-ins have to be coded (largely due to its embedded Perl interpreter environment) than the other packages, but these rules are excellent guidelines for coding plug-ins for any package. For example, plug-in authors are responsible for making sure their plug-ins properly time out. This keeps a plug-in from gumming up the works should the service it is testing hang the test connection forever. It is well worthwhile reading the plug-in documentation even if you don't plan to use Nagios.

What's Left?

With the probing, display, and framework components all set, you have most of a simple network-monitoring system built. The other piece, which can be as simple or as complex as you want, is the analysis/notification mechanism. This is the code that looks at the results of the framework and decides when and how to let you know about problems. We talked in depth about these elements earlier in Chapters 8 and 10, so be sure to refer to those chapters when you are ready to tackle the final piece of this puzzle.

Module Information for This Chapter

Module	CPAN ID/URL	Version
Net::Ping	Bundled with Perl	
Net::Ping::External	COLINM	0.11
Win32::PingICMP	TEVERETT	0.02
Net::Netmask	MUIR	1.9012
NetPacket	ATRAK	0.04
Net::Packet	GOMOR	2.04
Net::Arping	RIIKI	0.02
SNMP::Info	MAXB	0.9.0
Nmap::Scanner	MAXSHUBE	0.8.0
Text::Autoformat	DCONWAY	1.14.0
Array::PrintCols	AKSTE	2.1
Text::FormatTable	DSCHWEI	1.01
Text::BarGraph	KBAUCOM	1.0
GD::Graph	MVERB	1.43
GD::Graph3d	WADG	0.63
GraphViz	LBROCARD	2.02
RRDs	Bundled with RRDtool	
Test::More	Bundled with Perl	
Test::Harness	Bundled with Perl	

References for More Information

http://www.packetfactory.net/projects/nemesis/ is the nemesis home page.

Silence on the Wire: A Field Guide to Passive Reconnaissance and Indirect Attacks, by Michal Zalewski (No Starch Press), is an entire book on finding information about a network and its hosts without directly probing for it.

http://www.tcpdump.org is the home page for *tcpdump* and the libpcap library.

http://www.winpcap.org is the home page for the Windows port of libpcap.

http://www.insecure.org/nmap/index.html is the Nmap Security Scanner home page.

http://rrdtool.org is a pointer to the RRDtool home page.

http://poe.perl.org is the POE home page.

Randal Schwartz's November and December 2003 columns on checking a website's health using `Test::More` can be found in the *Linux Magazine*'s archive at *http://www.linux-mag.com/magazine/backissues*.

Perl Testing: A Developer's Notebook (http://oreilly.com/catalog/9780596100926/), by Ian Langworth and chromatic (O'Reilly), is a useful guide to Perl testing modules and options.

Edward Tufte has written and self-published (as of this writing) four superb books on the presentation of information: *The Visual Display of Quantitative Information, Envisioning Information, Visual Explanations: Images and Quantities, Evidence and Narrative*, and *Beautiful Evidence*. They are well worth the read for anyone who has to take data, understand it, and present it to others.

## CHAPTER 14

Experiential Learning

My apologies for foisting such a buzzword-compliant chapter title on you. I didn't want your boss to see you reading something called "SysAdmins Just Want to Have Fun," which probably would have been a better title for this chapter. If you *are* the boss (and you didn't come up through the sysadmin ranks), I have a secret to share—just don't tell upper management (and if you are upper management, feel free to tell anyone you'd like, because no one will believe you).

This secret revolves around something I wrote in the foreword of Thomas Limoncelli's book *Time Management for System Administrators (http://oreilly.com/catalog/9780596007836/)* (O'Reilly):

> By and large, sysadmins find what they do to be fun. All of this tinkering, integrating, installing, building, reinstalling, puttering, etc., is fun. So fun, in fact, that they work all day and then go home and do it some more.
>
> I once shared a bus ride with a professional chef who told me she hated to cook on her days off. "Postmen don't like to take long walks when they come home from work" is how she put it. Most of the sysadmins I know have never heard of this idea. You'll find them (and me, as my spouse would be quick to point out) curled up at home in front of a laptop "mucking about" virtually all the time. The notion of "play" and "work" are best described as a quantum superposition blur for a sysadmin....

The vast majority of the people I respect who are doing system administration in some guise or another (and enjoy it) seem to get tremendous value out of their play time. Things they learn from their experimentation outside of work invariably get funneled back into their work lives. They are more efficient at work because they already have both the right and the wrong answers to many problems at hand.

This chapter provides a small sampling of examples where playing with something fun (for a sysadmin) can yield real rewards in the work world. While I won't be making an argument for more play time at work,* perhaps this chapter will help you form your own opinions on the subject.

---

* Google's 20% time, anyone?

Playing with Timelines

In January 2008, the following message was posted to the *SAGE* mailing list (lightly excerpted and anonymized, but reprinted with permission):

> From: ...
>
> Date: January 9, 2008 2:10:14 PM EST
>
> Subject: Re: [SAGE] crontabs vs /etc/cron.[daily,hourly,*] vs.
>
> /etc/cron.d/
>
> On a more specific aspect of this (without regard to best practice), does anyone know of a tool that converts crontabs[†] into Gantt charts?
>
> I've always wanted to visualize how the crontab jobs (on a set of machines) line up in time. Each entry would need to be supplemented with an estimate of the duration of the job (3 minutes vs. 3 hours).
>
> JM

This seemed like a fun sysadmin-related visualization project, so I decided to see how hard it would be to undertake. Let me share what I learned along the way. We'll tackle this challenge in three parts: parsing *crontab* files, displaying a timeline, and writing some XML output that will be used to generate that timeline. At the end we'll put the pieces together and show the results.

Task One: Parsing crontab Files

The first subtask that comes up with this project is the parsing and interpretation of a standard *crontab* file. Reading in the file and having our program make sense of the individual fields is easy enough, but having a *crontab* file sliced and diced into some data structure or object doesn't actually help us all that much, because our end goal is to be able to plot what happens when *cron* interprets those pieces. We'll need some way to determine all of the times *cron* would have run a particular line during some set time period.

For example, let's say we take a very basic *crontab* file like this:[‡]

```
45 * * * * /priv/adm/cron/hourly
15 3 * * * /priv/adm/cron/daily
15 5 * * 0 /priv/adm/cron/weekly
15 6 1 * * /priv/adm/cron/monthly
```

[†] *crontab* files are a Unix-specific mechanism for specifying that certain tasks on the system should be run at certain set times or intervals. Run `man 5 crontab` or `man crontab` for more information.

[‡] This is the basic *crontab* format. The modules we are using expect that format, rather than some of the newer extensions. For example, if you include a username before the command (as some formats allow), that will be interpreted as the command line.

The first line tells us that at 45 minutes past the hour the */priv/adm/cron/hourly* program is run, so we'll be plotting that event at 1:45 a.m., 2:45 a.m., 3:45 a.m., and so on. The second line indicates that at 3:15 a.m. each day we run */priv/adm/cron/daily*, and so on.

Figuring all of this out is doable, but truth be told, kind of a pain. Luckily, we've been spared that effort because Piers Kent has written and published a module called `Schedule::Cron::Events` that makes this really easy. It calls upon another module (`Set::Crontab` by Abhijit Menon-Sen) to parse a *crontab* file line and then provides a simple interface for generating the discrete events we'll need.

To use `Schedule::Cron::Events`, we'll need to pass it two pieces of information: the line from the *crontab* file we care about and some indication of when we'd like `Schedule::Cron::Events` to begin calculating the events the file line creates:

```
my $event = Schedule::Cron::Events( $cronline, Seconds => {some time} );
```

(where *{some time}* is provided using the standard convention of describing time as the number of seconds that have elapsed since the epoch).

Once we've created that object, each call to `$event->nextEvent()` returns back all of the fields we'd need to describe a date (year, month, day, hour, minutes, second).

Task Two: Displaying the Timeline

Creating a pretty timeline is a nontrivial undertaking, so let's let look for another pre-built solution. There are some decent Perl timeline representation (`Data::Timeline`) and display (`Graph::Timeline`) modules available, but there's one way to create timelines that is so spiffy that I'm actually going to forsake using Perl for it. The SIMILE project at MIT created a tool called *Timeline* that it describes as a "DHTML-based AJAXy widget for visualizing time-based events." You can find more info on it at *http://simile .mit.edu/timeline/*.

To make use of this widget we need to create two files: an HTML file that references/initializes/displays the widget from MIT and an XML file containing the events we want displayed. That last requirement will be the task for the next section. In the meantime, let me show you the HTML file in question. I should mention that my JavaScript skills are larval at best, so most of the following is cribbed from the tutorial found at the SIMILE. If this is all gobbledygook to you, feel free to just read the comments (marked as `<!-- -->` and `//`):

```
<!DOCTYPE html PUBLIC "-//W3C//DTD HTML 4.01//EN">
<html>
  <head>
    <!-- Reference the widget -->
    <script src="http://simile.mit.edu/timeline/api/timeline-api.js"
            type="text/JavaScript">
    </script>

    <script type="text/JavaScript">
```

```
function onLoad() {
  // tl will hold the timeline we're going to create
  var tl;
  // get ready to specify where we'll get the data
  var eventSource = new Timeline.DefaultEventSource();

  // Create a timeline with two horizontal bars, one displaying
  // the hours and the other the days that contain the hours.
  // Note: both bands are set to display things relative
  // to my time zone (-5 GMT).
  var bandInfos = [
    Timeline.createBandInfo({
      eventSource:    eventSource,
      timeZone:       -5, // my timezone in Boston
      width:          "70%",
      intervalUnit:   Timeline.DateTime.HOUR,
      intervalPixels: 100 }),
    Timeline.createBandInfo({
      timeZone:       -5,
      width:          "30%",
      intervalUnit:   Timeline.DateTime.DAY,
      intervalPixels: 100 }),
  ];

  // keep the two bands in sync, highlight the connection
  bandInfos[1].syncWith = 0;
  bandInfos[1].highlight = true;

  // create a timeline and load its data from output.xml
  tl = Timeline.create(document.getElementById("cron-timeline"), bandInfos);
  Timeline.loadXML("output.xml", function(xml, url) {
    eventSource.loadXML(xml, url); });
  }

  // boilerplate code as specified in the tutorial
  var resizeTimerID = null;
  function onResize() {
    if (resizeTimerID == null) {
      resizeTimerID = window.setTimeout(function() {
        resizeTimerID = null;
        tl.layout();
      }, 500);
    }
  }
}
</script>
<title>My Test Cron Timeline</title>
</head>

<!-- run our custom code upon page load/resize -->
<body onload="onLoad();" onresize="onResize();">

<!-- actually display the timeline here in the document -->
<div id="cron-timeline"
     style="height: 150px;
     border: 1px solid #aaa">
```

```
        </div>

      </body>
    </html>
```

Rather than repeating the explanations for each part of this file here, I'll just refer you to the Timeline tutorial (*http://simile.mit.edu/timeline/docs/create-timelines.html*) instead.

The one last non-Perl thing I need to show you to complete this subtask is an example of the event data we'll need (in a file called *output.xml*). This will give you an idea of what data the widget is expecting us to provide. Here's an example that assumes we're showing the *cron* events for January 2008:

```
<data>
  <event start="Jan 01 2008 00:45:00 EST" title="/priv/adm/cron/hourly"></event>
  <event start="Jan 01 2008 01:45:00 EST" title="/priv/adm/cron/hourly"></event>
  <event start="Jan 01 2008 02:45:00 EST" title="/priv/adm/cron/hourly"></event>
  <event start="Jan 01 2008 03:45:00 EST" title="/priv/adm/cron/hourly"></event>
  ...
  <event start="Jan 01 2008 03:15:00 EST" title="/priv/adm/cron/daily"></event>
  <event start="Jan 02 2008 03:15:00 EST" title="/priv/adm/cron/daily"></event>
  <event start="Jan 03 2008 03:15:00 EST" title="/priv/adm/cron/daily"></event>
  <event start="Jan 04 2008 03:15:00 EST" title="/priv/adm/cron/daily"></event>
  ...
  <event start="Jan 06 2008 05:15:00 EST" title="/priv/adm/cron/weekly"></event>
  <event start="Jan 13 2008 05:15:00 EST" title="/priv/adm/cron/weekly"></event>
  <event start="Jan 20 2008 05:15:00 EST" title="/priv/adm/cron/weekly"></event>
  <event start="Jan 27 2008 05:15:00 EST" title="/priv/adm/cron/weekly"></event>
  <event start="Jan 01 2008 06:15:00 EST" title="/priv/adm/cron/monthly"></event>
</data>
```

Task Three: Writing Out the Correct XML File

So far we've vanquished the tricky parts of the project having to do with determining what data we need and what will consume this data. The last task is to make sure we format the data in a workable form. In this case we're looking to create an XML file with specific tags and contents. As you saw in Chapter 6, there are a whole bunch of ways to generate XML files with Perl. We'll repeat a technique we saw in that chapter and press `XML::Writer` (now maintained by Joseph Walton) into service. This requires code something like the following:

```
use IO::File;
use XML::Writer;

# set up a place to put the output
my $output = new IO::File('>output.xml');

# create a new XML::Writer object with some pretty-printing turned on
my $writer
    = new XML::Writer( OUTPUT => $output, DATA_MODE => 1, DATA_INDENT => 2 );
```

```
# create a <sometag> start tag with the given attributes
$writer->startTag('sometag', Attribute1 => 'value', Attribute2 => 'value' );

# just FYI: we could leave out the tag name here and it will try to
# figure out which one to close for us
$writer->endTag('sometag');

$writer->end();
$output->close();
```

Putting It All Together

Now that we have all of the pieces in place, let's see the final script. I'll only explicate the parts of the code that are new to the discussion.

First, we load the modules we need:

```
use Schedule::Cron::Events;
use File::Slurp qw( slurp );   # we'll read the crontab file with this
use Time::Local;               # needed for date format conversion
use POSIX qw(strftime);        # needed for date formatting
use XML::Writer;
use IO::File;
```

Next, we get the info we'll need for Schedule::Cron::Events ready. We're going to have to tell Schedule::Cron::Events where to begin its event iteration—basically, we have to pick a start date. It seems like it might be useful to display a timeline showing the events for the current month, so let's calculate the seconds from the epoch at the beginning of the first day of the current month:

```
my ( $currentmonth, $currentyear ) = ( localtime( time() ) )[4,5];
my $monthstart = timelocal( 0, 0, 0, 1, $currentmonth, $currentyear );
```

We then read the *crontab* file into memory and start writing our XML output file:

```
my @cronlines = slurp('crontab');
chomp(@cronlines);

my $output = new IO::File('>output.xml');
my $writer
    = new XML::Writer( OUTPUT => $output, DATA_MODE   => 1,
                                          DATA_INDENT => 2 );

$writer->startTag('data');
```

Now let's do the actual work and iterate over the contents of the *crontab* file. As we iterate, we need to enumerate all of the events produced by each line we find. Schedule::Cron::Events is happy to provide nextEvent()s *ad infinitum*, so we'll have to pick an arbitrary place in time to stop. As we're planning on our timeline showing events for the month, our code stops asking for a nextEvent() as soon as that call returns something not in the current month. We hand each line in the *crontab* file that is not a comment or a variable definition to Schedule::Cron::Events, with a start time of the beginning of the current month. Then we iterate for as long as we're still in the current month:

```perl
foreach my $cronline (@cronlines) {
  next if $cronline =~ /^#/;          # skip comments
  next if $cronline =~ /^\s*\w+\s*=/; # skip variable definitions
  my $event
      = new Schedule::Cron::Events( $cronline, Seconds => $monthstart );

  my @nextevent;
  while (1) {
    @nextevent = $event->nextEvent;

    # stop if we're no longer in the current month
    last if $nextevent[4] != $currentmonth;
```

For each event, we're going to want to generate an `<event></event>` element with the start attribute showing the time of that event and the title attribute listing the command *cron* would run at that time. We'll be calling the `strftime()` function from the POSIX module to get the date formatted the way the Timeline widget likes it. After this iteration we close the outer tag in the XML file, stop `XML::Writer`'s processing, and close the file itself:

```perl
$writer->startTag('event',
    'start' => strftime('%b %d %Y %T %Z',@nextevent),
    'title' => $event->commandLine(),
    );
    $writer->endTag('event');
  }
}

$writer->endTag('data');
$writer->end();
$output->close();
```

We could add an `<end></end>` attribute to this element if we knew how long each event would last, but unfortunately there is no easy way to know or estimate the length of time a particular *cron* job takes (as suggested in the email that started this section). However, you could imagine writing more code to analyze past *crontab* file logs to try to guess that information.

So, how does this look? Figure 14-1 shows a screenshot from the widget when loaded into a browser using our newly created data file.

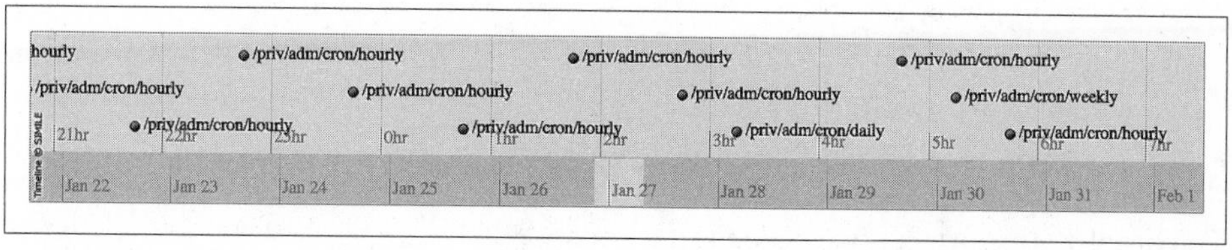

Figure 14-1. Timeline from a simple crontab

This is even cooler in person because you can scroll back and forth in the month.

I realize that this code doesn't fulfill the original correspondent's wishes, for two reasons:

1. It's not a Gantt chart (that requires analyzing the different *cron* jobs and seeing how they connect).

2. It doesn't show multiple machines overlaid.

Defect #1 turns out to be pretty hard to remedy. As another person pointed out in a followup to this message, dependency tracking in this context takes you into the fairly complex world of batch processing, and that's not something we can address in this chapter. Defect #2, on the other hand, is pretty easy to fix; it just requires opening more than one *crontab* file and doing the same work on each file.

Even with these defects, the diagram seemed pretty spiffy to me. I wanted to see what would happen if I fed the script real-world data from another site, so I contacted the original message writer, and he was kind enough to send me a set of *crontab* files from his workplace. Running my code against one of the *crontab* files (and changing the HTML file that displayed it so it had a larger display area) yielded the results in Figure 14-2, which the correspondent described as "Sweet!"

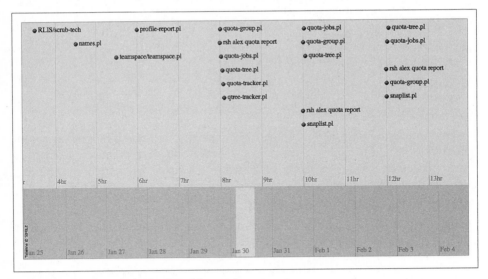

Figure 14-2. Timeline from a real-world crontab

Summary: What Can We Learn from This?

To complete this project, we needed to learn:

- How to deal with *crontab* files

- How to work with SIMILE's Timeline widget (this will come in handy at work the next time you need to visualize a timeline of events—perhaps when documenting an equipment failure, or while you're planning for some project)
- Some JavaScript

(Not to mention continuing to hone skills centered around problem decomposition.)

Playing with Geocoding

Wikipedia (as of this writing) defines geocoding as "the process of finding associated geographic coordinates (often expressed as latitude and longitude) from other geographic data, such as street addresses, or zip codes (postal codes)." It also can refer to the process of attempting to geographically locate an IP address. Geocoding is one of those activities that is entertaining because it knits together the virtual and the physical world.

Geocoding from Postal Addresses

Let's start with one of the standard geocoding tasks: given a postal address of some sort, is it possible to locate that address on the planet such that we could plot it on a map, etc.? Doing geocoding well (where "well" means "could use it for commercial applications") is actually fairly difficult for a number of reasons, the most difficult being that all the data is suspect. Postal addresses can be ambiguous, the geographical data is sometimes incomplete/incorrect, and both man and nature are always changing the surface features of the planet.

 Disclaimer 1: I have no relationship, commercial or otherwise, to the various service providers mentioned in this chapter beyond occasionally paying for the cheaper web services so I can play with them.

Disclaimer 2: Often when people in the U.S. talk about geocoding, they really mean "North America geocoding" and are minimally concerned with finding points outside of the U.S. Setting aside the standard U.S.-ethnocentrism, this phenomenon is partly a function of the availability of data. The U.S. government makes a passable data set available for free; most other countries don't have an equivalent. If you are interested in non-U.S. geocoding, the people at NAC Geographic Products, Inc. (*http://www.nacgeo.com*) have a relatively inexpensive commercial offering that may suit your needs.

If we leave out the expensive for-pay geocoding services, there are still a few methods available to us. The first one Perl people tend to turn to is *geocoder.us*, which provides not only a free set of web services but also the `Geo::Coder::US` module on CPAN (should you desire to set up your own server). *geocoder.us* offers several different flavors of web service, including XML-RPC, SOAP, REST, and "plain-text" REST. We're going to pick XML-RPC to start with because the code to use it is very simple:

```perl
use XMLRPC::Lite;

my $reply = XMLRPC::Lite
        -> proxy ( 'http://rpc.geocoder.us/service/xmlrpc' )
        -> geocode('1005 Gravenstein Highway North, Sebastopol, CA')
        -> result;

foreach my $answer (@{$reply}){
    print 'lat: '   . $answer->{'lat'}
          . ' long: ' . $answer->{'long'} . "\n";
}
```

First we load the `XMLRPC::Lite` module that is bundled in the `SOAP::Lite` distribution. The `proxy()` method (which, despite its name, doesn't have anything to do with a web proxy or any other kind of proxy) is used to specify where the query will be directed. We make our remote call out to that server using the `geocode()` method and ask `XMLRPC::Lite` to return the result.

The code for printing the result may look a little more complex than necessary. `geocode()` returns a list of hashes, one hash per result of the query. Some queries can yield multiple answers (e.g., if we asked for "300 Park, New York, NY" there might be a 300 Park Street, a 300 Park Drive, and a 300 Park Lane). There's only one Gravenstein Highway North in Sebastopol, so it would have been easier (but less robust) to write:

```perl
print 'lat: '   . $reply->[0]->{'lat'} .
        'long: ' . $reply->[0]->{'long'} . "\n";
```

If you decide for some reason that you don't like the results you receive from *geocoder.us*, there are a number of other cheap geocoding services available, including Yahoo!'s REST-based geocoding API (for less than 5000 queries a day). Let's look at that now. To use Yahoo!'s service, we need to apply for a free application ID at *http://developer.yahoo.com/wsregapp/*. With that ID, we can then use the API described at *http://developer.yahoo.com/maps/rest/V1/geocode.html*. Here's some sample code to do that:

```perl
use LWP::Simple;
use URI::Escape;
use XML::Simple;

# usage: scriptname <location to geocode>

my $appid  = '{your API key here}';
my $requrl = 'http://api.local.yahoo.com/MapsService/V1/geocode';

my $request
    = $requrl . "?appid=$appid&output=xml&location=" . uri_escape( $ARGV[0] );

my $response = XMLin( get($request), forcearray => ['Result'] );
```

```
foreach my $answer ( @{ $response->{'Result'} } ) {
    print "Lat: $answer->{Latitude} Long: $answer->{Longitude} \n";
}
```

One of the pleasant properties of REST interfaces is that they are really easy to query. If you know how to retrieve a web page in Perl using a GET or PUT, you can use a REST interface. In the preceding example, we constructed the URL by taking the base Yahoo! REST request URL and adding a few parameters: the required `appid`, our preferred output format, and a URL-encoded version of the location to query. This gets handed to `LWP::Simple`'s `get()` routine, the output of which we immediately parse using `XML::Simple`.

If the geocode server returned a single response, `XML::Simple` would ordinarily hand us back a hash that contained a single hash. If the server returned several answers—remember the ambiguous address case mentioned earlier—it would provide a hash that contained a list of hashes (one for each answer). When it came time to display the results, we could have written code to distinguish between the single-answer data structure and the multianswer data structure using `ref()` and act accordingly, but that's too much work. Instead, we take the easy way out and ask `XML::Simple` (via `forcearray=>['Result']`, as we saw in Chapter 6) to always hand us back a hash with a list of hashes. The code for results output then gets to do an easy `foreach` walk over that list.

 If this code seemed a little too complex for you, there's an even a simpler way to do it courtesy of the `Geo::Coder::Yahoo` module, by Ask Bjørn Hansen. This module has exactly two calls in it, one to create the search object and another to call the Geocoding API. The latter call returns a list of hashes, with no XML parsing required. Use whichever one suits your fancy.

Now that we've seen a couple of ways to turn an address into its corresponding latitude and longitude, what can we do with that information? The obvious answer to this question is to plot the information on a map. There are a number of good web services for doing this, including Google Maps (*http://www.google.com/apis/maps/*), Yahoo! Maps (*http://developer.yahoo.com/maps/*), and TerraServer (*http://terraservice.net/web services.aspx*). For fun, you can generate KML or KMZ (compressed KML) files for Google Earth (*http://earth.google.com/kml/*) and fly between your data points.

The process of plotting geocoded data onto one of these maps usually involves fiddling with HTML and that icky JavaScript stuff. In Perl, we luck out for Google Map creation because Nate Mueller has written an `HTML::GoogleMaps` module that makes the process really easy. Here's a sample CGI script that displays a map with a labeled marker pointing at the O'Reilly mothership:

```perl
use HTML::GoogleMaps;

# '1005 Gravenstein Highway North, Sebastopol, CA'
# though we could also specify the address and let the module call
# Geo::Coder::Google for us
my $coords = [ -122.841571, 38.411239 ];

my $map
    = HTML::GoogleMaps->new( key => '{your API KEY HERE}' );
$map->center($coords);      # center it on the address
$map->v2_zoom(15);          # zoom closer than the default

# add a marker at the address using the given html as a label
# (and don't change the size of that label)
$map->add_marker(
    point   => $coords,
    noformat => 1,
    html    => "<a href='http://www.oreilly.com'>O'Reilly</a> HQ"
);

# add some map controls (zoom, etc.)
$map->controls( 'large_map_control', 'map_type_control' );

# create the parts of the map
my ( $head, $map_div ) = $map->onload_render;

# output the HTML (plus CGI-required Content-Type header) for that map
print "Content-Type: text/html\n\n";
print <<"EOH";
<html>
  <head>
    <title>Otter Demo</title>
    $head
  </head>
EOH

print
    "<body onload=\"html_googlemaps_initialize()\" onunload=\"GUnload()\">
     $map_div </body> </html>\n";
```

It produces output that looks like Figure 14-3.

As with the Yahoo! service, to use Google Maps you'll have to apply for an API key from Google at *http://code.google.com/apis/maps/signup.html*.

There's much more that can be done with Google Maps and the other services, so be sure to check out the respective documentation for these services and products.

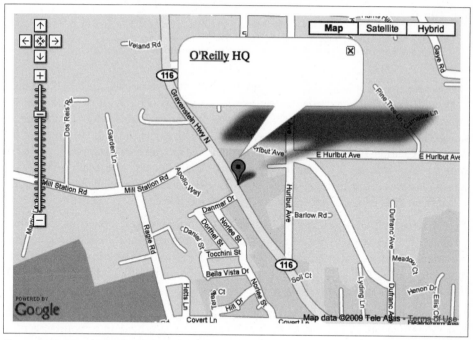

Figure 14-3. Sample map generated with HTML::GoogleMaps

Geocoding from IP Addresses

It seems eminently doable that one could take a postal address and look it up on some list some place to find its coordinates. That seems like something you can picture rows and rows of clerks in little green visors doing in a big, nondescript office somewhere in the Midwest. It sounds a lot more magical if I tell you, "Give me the name of your computer on the Internet and I can make a guess as to where that computer is located." There's something about crossing over the virtual/physical divide I mentioned earlier that makes this task seem all the more impressive.

The first step of the process is to turn the DNS fully qualified domain name into an IP address. That's straightforward with the `Net::DNS` module we've used throughout the book:

```
use Net::DNS;

my $resolv = Net::DNS::Resolver->new;

my $query = $resolv->search( $ARGV[0] );

die 'No response for that query' if !defined $query;
```

```
# only print addresses found in A resource records
foreach my $resrec ( $query->answer ){
    print $resrec->address . "\n" if ($resrec->type eq 'A');
}
```

Chances are you won't be geocoding any names that have more than one IP address associated with them, but this code still tries to give you back all of the addresses returned in response to your query. Note that if you plan to do this sort of lookup many times (e.g., when parsing a log file), you'll want to maintain a cache of your results like we did in Chapter 11. If you plan to process massive amounts of data, you'll probably want to look into some of the asynchronous DNS libraries, like adns (*http://www.chiark.greenend.org.uk/~ian/adns*), that handle parallel queries well. adns can be called from Perl using the Net::ADNS or EV::ADNS modules.

Now that we have an IP address in hand, let's use a different web service to get the data we need. There are a few fairly cheap (for the amount of data I push through them) providers. The following examples use the service provided by MaxMind, because that's the one I've played with the most.[*] You can find more info on this service at *http://www.maxmind.com/app/ip-location*.

MaxMind and several other providers offer both a web services interface to their data and a database subscription that allows you to download the data to your server for faster lookups. We'll look at examples of both methods here because the code required for each is really small.

For MaxMind's web service, we just need to construct a simple HTTP GET (or PUT, if that's your fancy), similar to what we did for the Yahoo! API earlier in this chapter. The main difference between that example and this one is the format returned. Here we get Comma/Character-Separated Values (CSV) results instead of something in XML format:

```
use LWP::Simple;
use Text::CSV_XS;    # this is the faster version of Text::CSV

# usage: scriptname <IP address to geocode>

my $maxmkey = '{your API key here}';

my $requrl = "http://maxmind.com:8010/f?l=$maxmkey&i=$ARGV[0]";

my $csvp = Text::CSV_XS->new();    # (or Text::CSV->new())

$csvp->parse( get($requrl) );

my ($country, $region, $city,        $postal,
     $lat,     $lon,    $metro_code, $area_code,
```

---

[*] A small piece of trivia: MaxMind was founded by noted Perl hacker T. J. Mather (*http://search.cpan.org/~tjmather*).

```
    $isp,    $org,    $err
 ) = $csvp->fields();
```

The non-web services version of this service requires downloading a database and then pointing MaxMind's module at it. The data is available in an optimized binary format or CSV format for importing into a SQL database. Here's how to use the binary version:

```
use Geo::IP;

my $gi = Geo::IP->open( 'GeoIPCity.dat', GEOIP_STANDARD );

my $record = $gi->record_by_name( $ARGV[0] );

print join( "\n",
    $record->country_code, $record->country_code3, $record->country_name,
    $record->region,       $record->region_name,   $record->city,
    $record->postal_code,  $record->latitude,      $record->longitude,
    $record->time_zone,    $record->area_code,     $record->continent_code,
    $record->metro_code );
```

OK, one last geocoding-related fun project for this section—if we geocode an IP address associated with a U.S. address and get back a zip code, it is easy to provide the current weather forecast for that zip code. I know of at least four U.S. weather services that are free for noncommercial use:

- NOAA's National Weather Service has a SOAP-based service (details at *http://www .weather.gov/xml/*).

- Weather.com provides an XML-based service (details at *http://www.weather.com/ services/xmloap.html*). However, this service comes with a whole boatload of requirements you have to satisfy if you want to use it on your website.

- Yahoo! provides weather information via RSS (see *http://developer.yahoo.com/ weather/*). You'll need to parse the RSS format using something like `XML::RSS` (or even `XML::Simple`).

- *http://www.rssweather.com* also provides weather info via RSS.

This project lets us bring together what we learned in the other sections. The following is a CGI script that attempts to determine the zip code for the connecting IP address's location and then queries Yahoo! for the current weather conditions and forecast:

```
use LWP::Simple;
use Text::CSV_XS;
use XML::RSS;

my $maxmkey = '{your API key here}';
my $requrl  = "http://maxmind.com:8010/f?l=$maxmkey&i=$ENV{'REMOTE_ADDR'}";

my $csvp = Text::CSV_XS->new();

$csvp->parse( get($requrl) );
my ($country, $region, $city,      $postal,
    $lat,     $lon,    $metro_code, $area_code,
    $isp,     $org,    $err
```

```
    ) = $csvp->fields();

print "Content-Type: text/html\n\n";
print << "EOH";
    <html><head><title>Otterbook test</title></head>
    <body>
EOH
print "<p>Hi there " . $ENV{'REMOTE_ADDR'} . "!</p>\n";

if ($postal) {
    my $rss = new XML::RSS;
    $rss->parse( get("http://xml.weather.yahoo.com/forecastrss?p=$postal") );
    print '<h1>' . $rss->{items}[0]->{'title'} . "</h1>\n";
    print $rss->{items}[0]->{'description'}, "\n";
}
print "</body></html>\n";
```

Summary: What Can We Learn from This?

In order to complete this project, we needed to learn:

- A bit more about XML-RPC (useful for all sorts of web services)

- How to work with several geocoding services (likely to come in handy the next time your boss asks, "So... what regions of the country and world do we get web hits from?" or the next time you want to set up a service that redirects people to their closest local mirrors).

- How to work with APIs from both Yahoo! and Google to retrieve maps, address info, weather reports, and more on demand.

Playing with an MP3 Collection

I've had the pleasure of getting to know many people who do system administration over the years. As I sit and talk with people at conferences like LISA (the Large Installation System Administration Conference, see *http://www.usenix.org* for details), one thing I've found in common amongst this crowd is their (sometimes voracious) love of music. Many have huge (legal) music collections that they have ripped to MP3 or Ogg/FLAC/Shorten format.[†]

Many of us baby our digital collections, making sure each file has the appropriate tags (if just to keep our portable MP3 players' displays tidy). Some of us treat this pile of sound as another interesting data source to play with. Here are a few resources I've used in that process:

For operating on individual files, there are two modules in heavy use: `MP3::Info`, originally written by Chris Nandor and now maintained by Dan Sully, and Ilya

---

[†] I'm fond of saying that the disposable income of a sysadmin coupled with a lack of a drug habit can yield a pretty sizable collection.

Zakharevich's `MP3::Tag` (which actually uses `MP3::Info` for certain functions). The latter is more complete when it comes to writing information back to MP3 files, but it is an interesting use of `MP3::Info` that I want to explore here.

A key function from that module is the `get_mp3info()` call. It takes a filename and returns a reference to a hash containing information about that file. For example, this:

```
use MP3::Info;

my $mp3 = get_mp3info($file);
```

will let you access some basic info about the file, like:

```
$mp3->{SECS};    # total number of seconds of audio
$mp3->{BITRATE}; # bitrate in kbps
```

There's a similar call, `get_mp3tag()`, which is a little more fun. With that, we can write:

```
my $mp3 = getmp3tag($file);
```

and see something like this:

```
DB<1> x $mp3

0  HASH(0x439c00)
   'ALBUM' => 'Feel Good Ghosts'
   'ARTIST' => 'Cloud Cult'
   'COMMENT' => 'ISRC US 786 08 00002'
   'GENRE' => 'Other'
   'TAGVERSION' => 'ID3v1.1 / ID3v2.3.0'
   'TITLE' => 'Everybody here is a Cloud'
   'TRACKNUM' => 2
   'YEAR' => 2008
```

or:

```
DB<1> x $mp3

0  HASH(0x95a6dc)
   'ALBUM' => 'Little Creatures'
   'ARTIST' => 'Talking Heads'
   'COMMENT' => '6F091209'
   'GENRE' => 'rock/pop'
   'TAGVERSION' => 'ID3v2.3.0'
   'TITLE' => 'Road To Nowhere'
   'TRACKNUM' => '9/9'
   'YEAR' => 1985
```

`MP3::Info` lets you set tags on individual files too, but that's not the interesting part.

For me, it becomes more interesting when we throw a little `File::Find::Rule` into the mix. There's a `File::Find::Rule::MP3Info` module that lets you write code like this (to use the examples from the documentation):

```
use File::Find::Rule::MP3Info;

# Which mp3s haven't I set the artist tag on yet?
```

```
my @mp3s = find( mp3info => { ARTIST => '' }, in => '/mp3' );

# What have I got that's 3 minutes or longer?
@mp3s = File::Find::Rule::MP3Info->file()
                              ->mp3info( MM => '>=3' )
                              ->in( '/mp3' );

# What have I got by either Kristin Hersh or Throwing Muses?
# I'm sometimes lazy about case in my tags.
@mp3s = find( mp3info =>
                  { ARTIST => qr/(kristin hersh|throwing muses)/i },
              in => '/mp3' );
```

I won't show you a full project for this section, but I'm hoping I've already started your imagination running about the sorts of scripts that can be written to do things like create playlists, find badly tagged files, etc.

Summary: What Can We Learn from This?

This project should have taught you:

- How to work with MP3 files (not particularly utilitarian, but hey).
- How to get even more familiar with `File::Find::Rule`. This subject, plus `File::Find::Rule::Permissions`, which lets you write code like this:

```
# Which files can the 'nobody' user read in the current directory?
@readable = File::Find::Rule::Permissions->file()
    ->permissions(isReadable => 1, user => 'nobody')
    ->in('.');
```

inspired me to explore the `File::Find::Rule` module, leading to its inclusion in Chapter 2 (and use in my work).

One Final Exploration

Let's look at one final bit of play that combines some handy knowledge of web scraping with some more of the geocoding/mapping material we saw earlier in this chapter.

To set the scene, the book you have in front of you wouldn't be nearly as good as it is without the help of an entire cadre of technical reviewers (see the acknowledgments section of this book for further gushing about their efforts). While setting up the reviewing infrastructure, I noticed that the people who had graciously offered their time to review the text seem to be geographically diverse. This observation was just based on casual glances at their email addresses and the timestamps on the messages I received from them. Just for a lark, I asked the reviewers if they would enter their home locations into a wiki page for me. I was amazed to see just how geographically diverse they really were, and hence this example project was born. For this section, let's grab the live information from that page and map the results.

Part One: Retrieving the Wiki Page with WWW::Mechanize

Downloading the contents of a single web page is pretty easy, as evidenced by the LWP::Simple examples earlier in this chapter. It gets a bit trickier, however, if that web page is protected in some fashion. In this particular case, the web page is on a password-protected wiki page that is part of the *trac (http://trac.edgewall.org)* instance I was using to coordinate work on this book. To get to the page, we're going to first have to log on by submitting the right information to a web form.

The tool I reach for almost exclusively when it comes to web scraping/crawling/etc. is the module WWW::Mechanize, by Andy Lester (and the other related modules in its orbit). I know of no better tool for tasks like these. Let's take a brief look at how to use the module first, and then we'll attack the password-protected page problem.

Almost all WWW::Mechanize scripts start out like this:

```
use WWW::Mechanize;

my $mech = WWW::Mechanize->new();

# get() can also take a ":content_file" parameter
# to save the returned information to a file
$mech->get($url);
```

We initialize a new object and ask it to go fetch some web page. If we have the necessary SSL support installed (Crypt::SSLeay or IO::Socket::SSL), we can get() pages served by both http and https.

If want the contents of the page we just fetched, we call:

```
my $pagecontents = $mech->content();
```

It's not uncommon to hand the results of the content() method off to some other module to do more sophisticated parsing. We'll do exactly that in the next subsection.

So far, the code has been really simple. So simple, in fact, that LWP::Simple could have handled it. Let's take things to the next level:

```
use WWW::Mechanize;

my $mech = WWW::Mechanize->new();

$mech->get( 'http://www.amazon.com' );
$mech->follow_link( text => 'Help' );
print $mech->uri . "\n";

# prints out something like:
# http://www.amazon.com/gp/help/customer/display.html?ie=UTF8&nodeId=508510
```

What happened here? WWW::Mechanize retrieved the home page for Amazon.com and then found the link on the page with the text "Help." It followed the link in the same way you would in a browser and retrieved the contents of the URL specified in the link.

At this point, if we called $mech->content(), we'd get back the contents of the new page found by browsing to the selected link.

If we wanted to, we could use an even cooler feature and write something like:

```
$mech->follow_link ( text_regex => qr/rates.*policies/ );
# or
$mech->follow_link ( url_regex => qr/gourmet.*food/ );
```

The first line of code will find and then follow the first link whose text matches the given regular expression. This means we can follow links in a page without knowing the precise text used (e.g., if each page was generated dynamically and had unique links). The second line of code performs a similar find and follow, this time based on the URL in the link.

follow_link() has a number of other options as well. For instance, there's a related url => 'http://...' option, equivalent to the text => 'text' option, that will take a fully specified URL to follow. Alternatively, though this is more fragile, follow_link() can take an n => option to allow you to choose the Nth link on the page. All of the options mentioned so far can be compounded. If we wanted the third "help"-related link on a page with a URL that includes "forum" in its path, for example, we could write:

```
$mech->follow_link( text => 'help', url_regex => 'forum', n => 3 );
```

If for some reason we wanted to just find the links on a page without navigating to their targets, WWW::Mechanize provides find_link() and find_all_links() methods that take the same selector arguments as follow_link(). WWW::Mechanize can also find images on a page via find_images() and find_all_images(), using similar arguments.

Let's get back to the situation where we need to log into the website before we can access the content we need. WWW::Mechanize has equally good support for dealing with forms like login pages, as long as you understand what information the form requires. WWW::Mechanize ships with a utility called mech-dump that can help you gain this understanding. You have the option to install mech-dump when you install WWW::Mechanize.

mech-dump uses the WWW::Mechanize module for its heavy lifting, thus giving you a little bit of insight into how WWW::Mechanize is parsing a particular page. It offers four choices:

- Display all forms found on a page
- Display all links found on a page
- Display all images found on a page
- Display all of the above

Let's see it in action:

```
$ mech-dump --links http://www.amazon.com
http://www.amazon.com/access
/
/gp/yourstore/ref=pd_irl_gw?ie=UTF8&signIn=1
/gp/yourstore/home/ref=topnav_ys_gw
...
```

I cut that list off quickly, because:

```
# count the number of links on that page
$ mech-dump --links http://www.amazon.com|wc -l
  247
```

Finding links can be helpful, but this command really shines when it comes time to interact with forms (something we're going to do in just a moment):

```
$ mech-dump --forms http://www.boingboing.net
```

```
GET http://www.google.com/search
   ie=UTF-8                      (hidden readonly)
   oe=UTF-8                      (hidden readonly)
   domains=boingboing.net        (hidden readonly)
   sitesearch=boingboing.net     (hidden readonly)
   q=                            (text)
   btnG=Search                   (submit)

POST http://www.feedburner.com/fb/a/emailverify
   email=                        (text)
   url=http://feeds.feedburner.com/~e?ffid=18399 (hidden readonly)
   title=Boing Boing             (hidden readonly)
   loc=en_US                     (hidden readonly)
   <NONAME>=Subscribe            (submit)
```

The output shows us that each form has a number of fields. Some are hidden fields set in the form by the form's author, but the useful information in the output is the fields that someone sitting at a browser would need to fill in and select. For example, the blog Boing Boing has an option to allow people to subscribe via email using a Feedburner service. The output of mech-dump lets us know that we'd need to fill in a field called email (rather than address or user_email or any number of similar possibilities).

If we point mech-dump at the *trac* site that is hosting the wiki we need to scrape, it shows:

```
$ mech-dump --forms http://otterbook.example.org/otterbook/wiki
```

```
GET http://otterbook.example.org/otterbook/search

POST http://otterbook.example.org/otterbook/login
   __FORM_TOKEN=d157f83e443347c3a36efe1f (hidden readonly)
   referer=                      (hidden readonly)
   user=                         (text)
   password=                     (password)
   <NONAME>=Login                (submit)
```

So we know we're going to need to fill in the fields user and password.

In WWW::Mechanize we can use the submit_form() method to fill in a form like so:

```
use WWW::Mechanize;
use Readonly;

Readonly my $loginurl => 'http://otterbook.example.org/otterbook/login';
Readonly my $revurl =>
    'http://otterbook.example.org/otterbook/wiki/ReviewerLocation';
```

```
Readonly my $user     => 'username';
Readonly my $pass     => 'password';

my $mech = WWW::Mechanize->new();
$mech->get($loginurl);
$mech->submit_form(
    form_number => 2,
    fields      => { user => $user, password => $pass },
);
```

submit_form() chooses the form to use, fills in the given fields, and performs the "submit" action (the equivalent of selecting the "Login" element on the page). Now the script is "logged in" to the wiki and can proceed to fetch the protected page:

```
$mech->get($revurl);
```

Now that we've fetched the page, what can we do with it?

Part Two: Extracting the Data

The location information for each reviewer on that page is in an HTML table with each row containing City, State/etc, and Country columns. There are a number of ways to extract this data from the HTML page (see Kevin Hemenway and Tara Calishain's *Spidering Hacks (http://oreilly.com/catalog/9780596005771/)*, also from O'Reilly, for several of them), but we're going to use another one of my favorite modules—HTML::TableExtract, by Matt Sisk—to make short work of the process. This module lets us specify the table we are looking for and the data we want from that table in a number of ways. The easiest way is to request it by providing the column headers:

```
use HTML::TableExtract;

my $te = HTML::TableExtract->new( headers => [qw(City State/etc Country )] );
```

Now we can feed HTML::TableExtract the contents of the fetched page to parse, as suggested in Part One:

```
$te->parse( $mech->content() );
```

Once the content is parsed, we can get to the data by asking for the info row by row:

```
# rows() with no arguments works with the first table found by default.
# Since there's only one table on the page, this is a safe thing to do.
#
# $row is a reference to an anonymous array, and each element is a column
# from that row

my @reviewlocations;
foreach my $row ( $te->rows ) {
    # the trac wiki adds spurious newlines into its HTML table code
    chomp (@$row);
    push @reviewlocations, $row;
}
```

Part Three: Geocoding and Mapping the Data

For the final fun we are going to have with this project, let's use a cousin of the `HTML::GoogleMaps` module we saw earlier in the chapter. Google also offers a service that serves static images of maps (rather than interactive maps that use JavaScript). The `Geo::Google::StaticMaps` module by Martin Atkins let us use this service. The documentation for the module assumes you understand the Google API docs, so be sure to read the material at *http://code.google.com/apis/maps/documentation/staticmaps* before beginning (or if you're like me, throughout) your development process. The other piece of this puzzle comes in the form of `Geo::Coder::Google` by Tatsuhiko Miyagawa. The two Google Maps APIs require us to send them already-geocoded data. The `HTML::GoogleMaps` module we used earlier in the chapter was kind enough to call `Geo::Coder::Google` for us on the fly to satisfy that restriction, but in this example we're going to have to do our own geocoding. We'll do that using this routine:

```
use Geo::Coder::Google;
use Geo::Google::StaticMaps;

...

sub locate {
    my $place = shift;

    # we could initialize this outside of this routine and pass the object
    # in to the routine with the query
    my $geocoder
        = Geo::Coder::Google->new( apikey => '{your API key here}' );

    my $response;
    until ( defined $response ) {
        $response = $geocoder->geocode( location => $place );
    }

    my ( $long, $lat ) = @{ $response->{Point}{coordinates} };
    return $lat, $long;
}
```

`locate()` takes a place and returns a list with the latitude and longitude.

When I was working on this example I found that for some reason either the service or the module sometimes just (seemingly at random) didn't return good data for perfectly valid queries. If I repeated the query again, even during the same session, it would return valid data.

Consequently, in the preceding code I do something very dangerous for most applications: if it doesn't get a reasonable response, it tries again until it does. If you are going to geocode with addresses where there is any chance at all that the query could legitimately fail, don't write code that is this persistent.

So, let's briefly see how we use the module. The first step will be to construct a data structure that includes all of the locations we're going to want to mark on the map. Once we have that, the rest is basically encapsulated in a single method call. Here's what the code looks like:

```
my @markers;
# create a list of hashes, each hash containing the info for
# that marker (lat/long, size, etc.)
foreach my $location (@reviewlocations) {
    push @markers, {
        point => [ locate( join( ',', @$location ) ) ],
        size  => 'mid' };
}

my $url = Geo::Google::StaticMaps->url(
    key     => '{your API key here}',
    size    => [ 640, 640 ],
    markers => [@markers],
);
```

Calling url() hands back a huge URL that looks something like this:

```
http://maps.google.com/staticmap?format=png&
markers=42.389121,-71.097145,midred%7C34.052187,-118.243425,midred%7C39.951639,
-75.163808,midred%7C35.231402,-80.845841,midred%7C42.503450,-71.
207985,midred%7C40.567095,-105.077036,midred%7C42.375392,-71.118487,
midred%7C33.754487,-84.389663,midred%7C32.718834,-117.163841,midred%7C49.203705,
-122.914588,midred%7C50.940664,6.959911,midred%7C-33.867139,151.207114,
midred%7C37.775196,-122.419204,midred%7C37.369195,-122.036849,midred%7C42
.886875,-78.877875,midred%7C61.216583,-149.899597,midred%7C47.350102,
7.902589,midred%7C33.179521,-96.492980,midred%7C49.263588,-123.138565,
midred%7C44.250871,-79.604822,midred%7C42.125291,-71.102576,
midred%7C45.423494,-75.697933,midred%7C37.279132,-121.956295,midred%7C51
.500152,-0.126236,midred%7C32.055400,34.759500,midred%7C39.762445,
-84.205247,midred%7C50.087811,14.420460,midred%7C52.663857,-8.626773,
midred%7C43.670233,-79.386755,midred%7C42.540904,-76.658372,midred%7C32.
832207,-85.763611,midred&key=YOURKEY&size=640x640
```

And a URL like that one, believe it or not, returns a picture of a map that displays where most of the reviewers for this book live (see Figure 14-4).

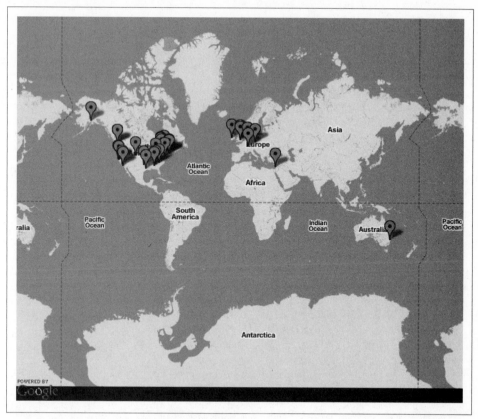

Figure 14-4. Map displaying all reviewers' locations

If we wanted to be more explicit about what is drawn (e.g., if we just wanted to see the North American/U.S. reviewers' locations), we could add a few more fields to that last call to center the map and zoom it:

```
my $url = Geo::Google::StaticMaps->url(
    key    => '{your API key here}',
    size   => [ 640, 640 ],
    markers => [@markers],
    center => [ locate('Kansas, US') ],
    zoom => 3,
);
```

Figure 14-5 shows the centered and zoomed version.

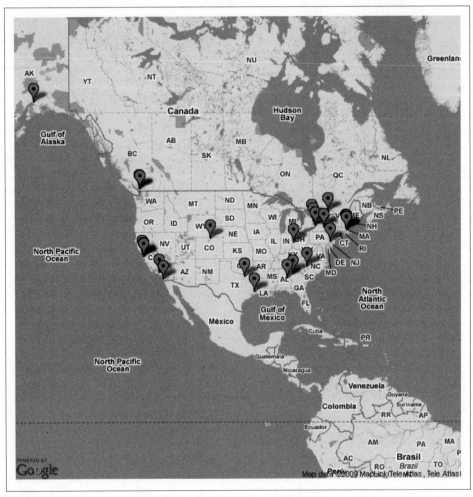

Figure 14-5. Centered and zoomed map displaying locations of U.S. reviewers

And with that, let's end this example and get ready to part company in this book.

Summary: What Can We Learn from This?

This project illustrates:

- How to use `WWW::Mechanize` (tremendously useful in this age of proliferating web interfaces for various system administration tools and applications)
- How to use `HTML::TableExtract` (an easy way to extract and reuse tabular data on a web page)
- How to use another geocoding and mapping API

- That the Perl community, especially those kind enough to help with this book, are a far-flung and generous lot

Remember to Play

There are many more projects like these that we could have looked at in this chapter. Just off the top of my head, here are some tasks you might consider:

- Parsing EXIF metadata from photographs
- Polling a cheap temperature sensor on the net in your house via SNMP and graphing the results via RRDtool
- Work with info from a barcode scanner
- Using CDDB for identifying CDs
- Controlling everything in your house from Perl (like with the MisterHouse project, at *http://misterhouse.sourceforge.net*)
- Computer speech production (e.g., via Win32 SAPI) or recognition
- Package tracking
- Parallel processing
- Cloud computing

All of these would lead to the acquisition of some great knowledge and skills immediately transferable to your workplace. If you can learn to play—to play with Perl, to play with anything sysadmin-related—the joy and learning you gain can improve all facets of your life.

Remember to play.

Module Information for This Chapter

Name	CPAN ID	Version
Schedule::Cron::Events	PKENT	1.8
IO::File (part of IO dist)	GBARR	1.2301
XML::Writer	JOSEPHW	0.606
File::Slurp	DROLSKY	9999.13
Time::Local	DROLSKY	1.1901
POSIX (ships with Perl)		1.15
XMLRPC::Lite (part of the SOAP-Lite dist)	MKUTTER	0.710.6
URI::Escape (part of the URI dist)	GAAS	3.29
XML::Simple	GRANTM	2.18
LWP::Simple (part of the libwww/LWP dist)	GAAS	5.810

Name	CPAN ID	Version
HTML::GoogleMaps	NMUELLER	10
Net::DNS	OLAF	0.64
Text::CSV_XS	HMBRAND	0.58
Geo::IP	BORISZ	1.36
XML::RSS	SHLOMIF	1.42
MP3::Info	DANIEL	1.24
File::Find::Rule::MP3Info	KAKE	0.01
File::Find::Rule::Permissions	DCANTRELL	1.3
WWW::Mechanize	PETDANCE	1.52
Readonly	ROODE	1.03
HTML::TableExtract	MSISK	2.10
Geo::Google::StaticMaps	MART	0.1
Geo::Coder::Google	MIYAGAWA	0.03

Source Material for This Chapter

Much of the material in this chapter was adapted and expanded from columns I've published in USENIX's ;login magazine (*http://www.usenix.org/publications/login/*).

The Eight-Minute XML Tutorial

One of the most impressive features of XML (eXtensible Markup Language) is how little you need to know to get started. This appendix gives you some of the key pieces of information you'll need. The references at the end of Chapter 6 point you to many excellent resources that you can turn to for more information.

XML Is a Markup Language

Thanks to the ubiquity of XML's older and stodgier cousin, HTML, almost everyone is familiar with the notion of a markup language. Like HTML, XML consists of plain text interspersed with little bits of special descriptive or instructive text. HTML has a rigid definition for which bits of markup text, called *tags*, are allowed, while XML allows you to make up your own.

Consequently, XML provides a range of expression far beyond that of HTML. One example of this range of expression is found in Chapter 6, but here's another simple example that you should find easy to read even if you don't have any prior XML experience:

```
<hosts>
  <machine>
    <name> quiddish </name>
    <department> Software Sorcery </department>
    <room> 314WVH </room>
    <owner> Horry Patter </owner>
    <ipaddress> 192.168.1.13 </ipaddress>
  </machine>
  <machine>
    <name> dibby </name>
    <department> Hardware Hackery </department>
    <room> 310WVH </room>
    <owner> Harminone Grenger </owner>
    <ipaddress> 192.168.1.15 </ipaddress>
  </machine>
</hosts>
```

XML Is Picky

Despite XML's flexibility, it is pickier in places than HTML. There are syntax and grammar rules that your data must follow. These rules are set down rather tersely in the XML specification found at *http://www.w3.org/TR/REC-xml/*. Rather than poring through the official spec, I recommend you seek out one of the annotated versions, such as Tim Bray's version (available at *http://www.xml.com*) or Robert Ducharme's book *XML: The Annotated Specification* (Prentice Hall). The former is online and free; the latter has many good examples of actual XML code.

Here are two of the XML rules that tend to trip up people who know HTML:

- If you begin something, you must end it. In the preceding example, we started a machine listing with `<machine>` and finished it with `</machine>`. Leaving off the ending tag would not have been acceptable XML.

- In HTML, tags like `<img src="picture.jpg">` are legally allowed to stand by themselves. Not so in XML. This would have to be written as either:

  ```
  <img src="picture.jpg"> </img>
  ```

  or:

  ```
  <img src="picture.jpg" />
  ```

  The extra slash at the end of this last tag lets the XML parser know that this single tag serves as both a start and an end tag. A pair of start and end tags and the data they contain are together called an *element*.

- Start tags and end tags must mirror one another exactly. Changing the case is not allowed, because XML is case-sensitive. If your start tag is `<MaChINe>`, your end tag must be `</MaChINe>` and cannot be `</MACHine>` or any other case combination. HTML is much more forgiving in this regard.

These are three of the general rules in the XML specification. But sometimes you want to define your own additional rules for an XML parser to enforce (where by "enforce" I mean "complain vociferously" or "stop parsing" while reading the XML data if a violation is encountered). If we use our previous machine database XML snippet as an example, one additional rule we might to enforce is "all `<machine>` entries must contain a `<name>` and an `<ipaddress>` element." You may also wish to restrict the contents of an element to a set of specific values, like YES or NO.

How these rules get defined is less straightforward than the other material we'll cover, because there are several complementary and competitive definition "languages" afloat at the moment.

The current XML specification uses a Document Type Definition (DTD), the SGML standby. Here's an example piece of XML code from the XML specification that has its definition code at the beginning of the document itself:

```
<?xml version="1.0" encoding="UTF-8" ?>
<!DOCTYPE greeting [
  <!ELEMENT greeting (#PCDATA)>
]>
<greeting>Hello, world!</greeting>
```

The first line of this example specifies the version of XML in use and the character encoding (Unicode) for the document. The next three lines define the types of data in this document. This is followed by the actual document content (the `<greeting>` element) in the final line of the example.

If we wanted to define how the `<hosts>` XML code at the beginning of this appendix should be validated, we could place something like this at the beginning of the file:

```
<?xml version="1.0" encoding="UTF-8" ?>
<!DOCTYPE hosts [
  <!ELEMENT hosts       (machine)*>
  <!ELEMENT machine     (name,department,room,owner,ipaddress)>
  <!ELEMENT name        (#PCDATA)>
  <!ELEMENT department  (#PCDATA)>
  <!ELEMENT room        (#PCDATA)>
  <!ELEMENT owner       (#PCDATA)>
  <!ELEMENT ipaddress   (#PCDATA)>
]>
```

This definition requires that a `hosts` element contains `machine` elements and that each `machine` element consists of `name`, `department`, `room`, `owner`, and `ipaddress` elements (in this specific order). Each of those elements is described as being #PCDATA (see the section "Leftovers" on page 560 for details).

The World Wide Web Consortium (W3C) has also created a specification for data descriptions called *schemas* for DTD-like purposes. Schemas are themselves written in XML code. Here's an example of schema code that uses the 1.0 XML Schema recommendation syntax found at *http://www.w3.org/XML/Schema* (version 1.1 of this recommendation was still in process while this book was being written):

```
<?xml version='1.0' ?>
<xsd:schema xmlns:xsd="http://www.w3.org/2001/XMLSchema">

  <xsd:complexType name="MachineType">
    <xsd:sequence>
      <xsd:element name="name" type="xsd:string"/>
      <xsd:element name="department" type="xsd:string"/>
      <xsd:element name="room" type="xsd:string"/>
      <xsd:element name="owner" type="xsd:string"/>
      <xsd:element name="ipaddress" type="xsd:string"/>
    </xsd:sequence>
  </xsd:complexType>
  <xsd:complexType name="ListOfMachines">
    <xsd:sequence>
      <xsd:element name="machine" type="MachineType"
                   minOccurs="1" maxOccurs="unbounded" />
    </xsd:sequence>
  </xsd:complexType>
```

```
      <xsd:element name="hosts" type="ListOfMachines" />
   </xsd:schema>
```

Both the DTD and schema mechanisms can get complicated quickly, so we're going to leave further discussion of them to the books that are dedicated to XML/SGML.

Two Key XML Terms

You can't go very far in XML without learning two important terms. First, XML data is said to be *well-formed* if it follows all of the XML syntax and grammar rules (matching tags, etc.). Often a simple check for well-formed data can help you spot typos in XML files. That's an advantage when the data you are dealing with holds configuration information, as in the machine database excerpted in the last section.

Second, XML data is said to be *valid* if it conforms to the rules we've set down in one of the data definition mechanisms mentioned earlier. For instance, if your data file conforms to its DTD, it is valid XML data.

Valid data by definition is well-formed, but the converse does not have to be true. It is possible to have perfectly wonderful XML data that does not have an associated DTD or schema. If it parses properly, it is well-formed, but not valid.

Leftovers

Here are three terms that appear throughout the XML literature and may stymie the XML beginner:

Attribute
> The descriptions of an element that are part of the initial start tag. To reuse a previous example, in the element `<img src="picture.jpg" />`, `src="picture.jpg"` is an attribute. There is some controversy in the XML world about when to use the contents of an element and when to use attributes. The best set of guidelines on this particular issue is found at *http://www.oasis-open.org/cover/elementsAndAttrs .html*.

CDATA
> The term CDATA (Character Data) is used in two contexts. Most of the time it refers to everything in an XML document that is not markup (tags, etc.). The second context involves *CDATA sections*. A CDATA section is declared to indicate that an XML parser should leave that section of data alone even if it contains text that could be construed as markup. CDATA sections look a little strange. Here's the example from the XML spec:
>
> ```
> <![CDATA[<greeting>Hello,world!</greeting>]]>
> ```

In this case the `<greeting></greeting>` tags get treated like just plain characters and not as markup that needs to be parsed.

PCDATA

Tim Bray's annotation of the XML specification (mentioned earlier) gives the following definition:

> The string PCDATA itself stands for "Parsed Character Data." It is another inheritance from SGML; in this usage, "parsed" means that the XML processor will read this text looking for markup signaled by < and & characters.

You can think of this as data composed of CDATA and potentially some markup. Most XML data falls into this classification.

Here are two final tips about things that experienced XML users say may trip up people new to XML:

- Pay attention to the characters that, as in HTML, cannot be included in your XML data without being represented as entity references. These include <, >, &, ' (single quote), and " (double quote). These are represented using the same convention as in HTML: <, >, &, ', and ". Lots of new users get stymied because they leave an ampersand somewhere in their data and it doesn't parse.

- If you are going to place non-UTF-8 data into your documents, be sure to specify an encoding. Encodings are specified in the XML declaration:

  ```
  <?xml version="1.0" encoding="iso-8859-1" ?>
  ```

  A common mistake is to either omit this declaration or declare the document as UTF-8 when it has other kinds of characters in it.

XML has a bit of a learning curve, but this small tutorial should help you get started. Once you have the basics down, you can begin to look at some of the more complex specifications that surround XML, including XSLT (for transforming XML to something else, such as HTML), XPath (a way of referring to a specific part of an XML document; see the next appendix), and SOAP/XML-RPC (used to communicate with remote services using messages written in XML).

References for More Information

See the end of Chapter 6 for more references on XML-related topics.

The 10-Minute XPath Tutorial

Before we launch into XPath, we need to get three caveats out of the way.

First, in order to understand this appendix, you'll need to have at least a moderate grip on the subject of XML. Be sure to read Appendix A if you haven't already.

Second, XPath is a language unto itself. The XPath 1.0 spec consists of 34 relatively dense pages; the XPath 2.0 spec is 118 pages long. This appendix is not going to attempt to do any justice to the richness, expressiveness, and complexity of XPath (especially v2.0). Instead, it is going to focus on the subset of XPath that will be immediately useful to a Perl programmer.

Finally, this appendix will be sticking to XPath 1.0. As of this writing there are no solid Perl modules that I know of that support XPath 2.0.

With all of that aside, let's get to questions like "What is XPath?" and, perhaps more importantly, "Why should I care?" XPath is a W3C spec for "a language for addressing parts of an XML document." If you ever have to write code that attempts to select or extract certain parts of an XML document, XPath may make your life a great deal easier. It is a fairly terse but quite powerful language for this task and has a lovely "make it so" quality to it. If you can describe what data you are looking for using the XPath language (and you usually can), the XPath parser can fetch it for you, or allow you to point your program at the right part of the XML document. You can often achieve this with a single line of Perl.

XPath Basic Concepts

There are several basic concepts that you need to understand to be able to start using XPath. Let's look at them one at a time in order of increasing complexity.

Basic Location Paths

To understand XPath, you have to start with the notion that an XML document can be parsed into a tree structure. The elements of the document (and the other stuff, but we'll leave that out for now) serve as the nodes of the tree. To make this clearer, let's pull in the sample XML file from Chapter 6. I'll reprint it here so you don't have to keep flipping back and forth to refer to it:

```
<?xml version="1.0" encoding="UTF-8"?>

<network>
    <description name="Boston">
        This is the configuration of our network in the Boston office.
    </description>
    <host name="agatha" type="server" os="linux">
        <interface name="eth0" type="Ethernet">
            <arec>agatha.example.edu</arec>
            <cname>mail.example.edu</cname>
            <addr>192.168.0.4</addr>
        </interface>
        <service>SMTP</service>
        <service>POP3</service>
        <service>IMAP4</service>
    </host>
    <host name="gil" type="server" os="linux">
        <interface name="eth0" type="Ethernet">
            <arec>gil.example.edu</arec>
            <cname>www.example.edu</cname>
            <addr>192.168.0.5</addr>
        </interface>
        <service>HTTP</service>
        <service>HTTPS</service>
    </host>
    <host name="baron" type="server" os="linux">
        <interface name="eth0" type="Ethernet">
            <arec>baron.example.edu</arec>
            <cname>dns.example.edu</cname>
            <cname>ntp.example.edu</cname>
            <cname>ldap.example.edu</cname>
            <addr>192.168.0.6</addr>
        </interface>
        <service>DNS</service>
        <service>NTP</service>
        <service>LDAP</service>
        <service>LDAPS</service>
    </host>
    <host name="mr-tock" type="server" os="openbsd">
        <interface name="fxp0" type="Ethernet">
            <arec>mr-tock.example.edu</arec>
            <cname>fw.example.edu</cname>
            <addr>192.168.0.1</addr>
        </interface>
        <service>firewall</service>
    </host>
    <host name="krosp" type="client" os="osx">
        <interface name="en0" type="Ethernet">
            <arec>krosp.example.edu</arec>
            <addr>192.168.0.100</addr>
        </interface>
```

```
        <interface name="en1" type="AirPort">
            <arec>krosp.wireless.example.edu</arec>
            <addr>192.168.100.100</addr>
        </interface>
    </host>
    <host name="zeetha" type="client" os="osx">
        <interface name="en0" type="Ethernet">
            <arec>zeetha.example.edu</arec>
            <addr>192.168.0.101</addr>
        </interface>
        <interface name="en1" type="AirPort">
            <arec>zeetha.wireless.example.edu</arec>
            <addr>192.168.100.101</addr>
        </interface>
    </host>
</network>
```

If we parse this into a node tree, it will look something like Figure B-1.

The root of the tree points to the document's root element (`<network></network>`). The other elements of the document hang off of the root. Each element node has associated attribute nodes (if it has any attributes) and a child text node that represents the contents of that element (if it has any character data in it). For example, if the XML said `<element attrib="value">something</element>`, the XPath parse would have one `<element></element>` node with an attribute node of `attrib` and a text node holding the string `something`. Be sure to stare at Figure B-1 until the XML document-to-node tree idea is firmly lodged in your head, because it is crucial to the rest of this material.

If this diagram reminds you of the tree-like diagrams in Chapter 2, that's good. The resemblance is intentional. XPath uses the concept of a *location path* to navigate to a node or set of nodes in a document. Location paths start either at the top of the tree (an absolute path) or at some other place in the tree (a relative path). Just like in a filesystem, "/" at the beginning means "start at the root of the tree," "." (dot) refers to the current node (also known as the "context node"), and ".." (dot-dot) refers to the parent of the context node.

If you want, you can think of location paths as a way to point at a specific node or set of nodes in a diagram. For example, if we wanted to point at the `<description></description>` node, the location path would be `/network/description`. If we used a location path of `/network/host`, we would be referring to all of the `<host></host>` nodes at that level of the tree. Pointing at a node any further down the tree would require a way to distinguish between the different `<host></host>` nodes. How to do that leads to a whole other XPath topic; we'll hold off on that question for just a moment so we can look at a few more of the navigational aspects of walking a node tree.

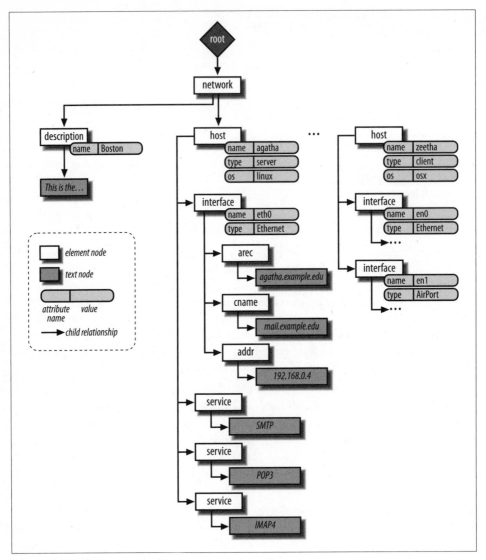

Figure B-1. XML document node tree

The information in our sample file consists of more than just markup tags; the file has real data in it. The elements themselves often have attributes (e.g., `<interface name="en1" type="AirPort">`) or act as labels for data (e.g., `<addr>192.168.0.4 </addr>`). How do we get to those parts of the document? To get to an element's attributes, we use an @ in front of the attribute name. For example, `/network/description/ @name` gets us `name="Boston"`. To access the contents of an element's text node, we end the location path with `text()`, as in `/network/description/text()`. This returns the data `This is the configuration....`

Wildcards in XPath can function similarly to their filesystem analogs. `/network/host/*/arec/text()` finds all element nodes[*] under a `<host></host>` node that have `<arec></arec>` sub-nodes and then returns the contents of those `<arec></arec>` elements. In this case, we get back the DNS A resource record name associated with each interface:

```
agatha.example.edu
gil.example.edu
baron.example.edu
mr-tock.example.edu
krosp.example.edu
krosp.wireless.example.edu
zeetha.example.edu
zeetha.wireless.example.edu
```

Attributes can be wildcarded in a similar fashion by using `@*`. `/network/host/@*` would return all of the attributes of the `<host></host>` elements.

There's one last piece of syntax worth mentioning before we get to the next section. XPath has what I call a "magic" location path operator. If you use two slashes (`//`) anywhere in the location path, it will search from that point down in the tree to try to locate the subsequent path elements. For example, if we say `//arec/text()`, we will get back the same set of interface A resource record names as in our previous example, because the operator will search from the root of the tree down to find all of the `<arec></arec>` elements that have text nodes. You can also place double slashes in the middle of a location path, as in `/network//service/text()`. Our sample file has a very shallow node tree, but you can imagine how the ability to describe a path without specifying all of the intervening parts of the tree might come in handy.

Predicates

In the last section we daintily stepped over the question of how one specifies which branch or branches of a tree to follow if the elements at that level in the tree have the same name. In our example document, we have five `<host></host>` elements at the third level of the tree. They have different attributes and the data in each is different, but that doesn't help if the location path is constructed with just element names. If we say `/network/host`, the word `host` is (in the parlance of the spec) acting as a "node test." It selects which network branch or branches to take when moving down the tree in our location path. But the node test in this example isn't giving us the granularity we need to select a single branch.

That's one place where XPath *predicates* come into play. Predicates allow you to filter the set of possible nodes provided by a node test to get just the ones you care about. `/network/host` returned all of the host nodes; we'd like a way to narrow down

---

[*] At the beginning of the chapter I mentioned that XPath parses the document into a set of nodes that include both the elements and "other stuff." The wildcard `*` matches just element nodes, whereas `node()` matches all kinds of nodes (element nodes and the "other stuff").

that set. Predicates are specified in square brackets ([ ]) in the location path itself. You insert a predicate right at the point where a filtering decision has to be made.

The simplest predicate example looks like an index number, as in `/network/host[2]/interface/arec/text()`. This location path returns the interface name(s) for the second host node (second in document order). If you were standing and looking at all of the host nodes, the predicate would tell you which branch of the tree to take: in this case, the one in the second position.

 Perl programmers should be familiar with this index-like syntax, but don't get too comfortable. Unlike in Perl, the index numbers in XPath start with 1, not 0.

If index numbers were the only possible predicate, that would be a bit ho-hum. But here's where XPath starts to get really cool. XPath has a relatively rich set of predicates available for use. The next level of predicate complexity looks something like this: `/network/host[@name="agatha"]`. This selects the correct `<host></host>` by testing for the presence of a specific attribute with a specific value.[†]

Predicates aren't always found at the very end of a location path, either. You can work them into a larger location string. Let's say we wanted to find the names of all of the Linux servers in our network. To get this information we could write a location path like `/network/host[@os="linux"]/service/../@name`. This location path uses a predicate to select all the `<host></host>` elements that have an os attribute of linux. It walks down the branch for each of the nodes in that set that have a `<service></service>` subelement (i.e., selecting only the hosts that are servers). At this point we've walked the tree all the way down to a `<service></service>` node, so we use `../@name` to get to the name attribute of its parent (the `<host></host>` that contains the `<service></service>` we just found).

We can test the contents of a node like this: `//host/service[text()='DNS']`. This location path says to start at the root of the tree looking for branches that have a `<service></service>` node embedded in a `<host></host>` node. Once XPath finds a branch that fits this description, it compares the contents of each of those service nodes to find the one whose contents are "DNS".

The location path is being nicer to the parser than it needs to be by calling `text()`. If we just use a "." (dot) instead of `text()` (meaning the current node), XPath will perform the comparison against its contents.

[†] Before we go any further, it is probably worthwhile making something implicit in this discussion explicit: if a node test fails (e.g., if we tried to find the node or nodes at /network/admin/homephonenumber in this document), it doesn't return anything. There's no error, the program doesn't stop, etc.

Testing for equality is only one of the comparison operators. Our sample data doesn't offer a good way to demonstrate this, but predicates like [`price > 31337`] can be used to select nodes as well.

It's starting to look like a real computer language, no? It gets even closer when we bring functions into the picture. XPath defines a whole bunch of functions for working with node sets, strings, Boolean operations, and numbers. In fact, we've seen some of them in action already, because `/network/host[2]/interface/arec/text()` really means `/network/host[position()=2]/interface/arec/text()`.

Just to give you a taste of this, here's a location path that selects the HTTP and HTTPS service nodes (allowing for any whitespace that might creep in around the service name): `//host/service[starts-with(normalize-space(.),'HTTP')]`. The string function `starts-with()` does just what you would expect it to: it returns true if the thing being compared (the contents of the current node) begins with the string provided in the second argument. The XPath spec has a list of the available functions, though it is a little less beginner-friendly than one might like. Searching for "XPath predicate" on the Web can lead to other resources that help explain the spec.

Abbreviations and Axes

This appendix started with the simplest core ideas of XPath, and each section along the way has incorporated more complexity and nuance. Let's add one last level of subtlety by circling back to the original discussion of location paths. It turns out that all of the location paths we've seen so far have been written in what the spec calls an "abbreviated syntax." The *un*abbreviated syntax is one of those things that you almost never need, but when you do, you *really* need it. We're going to look at it quickly here just so you know it is available if you get into one of those situations.

So what exactly got abbreviated in the location paths we've seen so far? When we said `/network/host[2]/service[1]/text()`, it actually meant:

1. Start at the root of the tree.
2. Walk toward the children of the root node (i.e., down the tree), looking for the child node or nodes with the element name `network`.
3. Arrive at the `<network></network>` node. This becomes the context node.
4. Walk toward the children of the context node, looking for the child node or nodes with the element name `host`.
5. Arrive at the level in the tree that has several `<host></host>` nodes. Filter to choose the node in the second position. This becomes the context node.
6. Walk toward the children of the context node, looking for the child node or nodes with the element name `service`.
7. Arrive at the level in the tree that has several `<service></service>` nodes. Filter to choose the node in the first position. This becomes the context node.

8. Walk toward the text node associated with the context node. Done.

If we were to write that out in the unabbreviated syntax, it would look like the following (this is all one long location path split onto two lines):

```
/child::network/child::host[position()=2]/child::service[position()=1]/
child::text()
```

The key things we've added in this path are the axes (plural of axis, we're not talking weaponry here). For each step in the location path, we can include an axis to tell the parser which direction to go in the tree relative to the context node. In this case we're telling it at each step to follow the child:: axis; that is, to move to the children of the context node. We're so used to filesystem paths that describe a walk from directory to subdirectory to target file that we don't think too hard when faced with the */dir/ sub-dir/file* syntax. This is why the abbreviated XPath syntax works so nicely. But XPath doesn't restrict us to moving from child node to child node down the tree. We've seen one example of this freedom already with the // syntax. When we say /network//cname, we are really indicating /child::network/descendant-or-self::cname. That is:

1. Start from the root.
2. Move to its child nodes to find a <network></network> node or nodes. When we find one, it becomes the context node.
3. Look at the context node or descend farther in the tree until we find a <cname></cname> node or nodes.

The other three axes you already know how to reference in abbreviated form are self:: (.), parent:: (..), and attribute:: (@). The unabbreviated syntax lets us use all of the other axes—eight more, believe it or not: ancestor::, following-sibling::, preceding-sibling::, following::, preceding::, namespace::, descendant::, and ancestor-or-self::.

Of these, following-sibling:: is probably the most useful, so I'm only going to describe and demonstrate that one. The references section of this appendix points you at other texts that have good descriptions of the other axes. The following-sibling:: axis tells the parser to move over to the next element(s) in the tree at that level. This references the context node's siblings. If we wanted to write a location path that tried to find all of the hosts with multiple interfaces, we could write (again, as one long line):

```
/child::network/child::host/child::interface/following-sibling::interface/
parent::host/attribute::name
```

This essentially says, "Walk down from the network node until you find a host with an interface node as its child, then see if it has a sibling interface at the same level in the tree. If it does, walk back up to the host node and return its name attribute."

Further Exploration

If you find XPath really interesting and you want to get even deeper into it, there are definitely some places you can explore outside the scope of this chapter. Be sure to read the specification and other references listed in the next section. Learn about the other predicates and axes available to you. Become acquainted with XPath 2.0, so when a Perl module that can use it becomes available, you'll be ready. And in general, just play around with the language until you feel comfortable with it and it can become another handy tool in your toolchest.

References for More Information

http://www.w3.org/TR/xpath and *http://www.w3.org/TR/xpath20* are the locations of the official XPath 1.0 and 2.0 specifications. I'd recommend reading them after you've had a chance to read a good tutorial or two (like those listed here).

XML in a Nutshell, Third Edition (*http://oreilly.com/catalog/9780596007645/*), by Elliotte Rusty Harold and W. Scott Means (O'Reilly), and *Learning XML*, Second Edition (*http://oreilly.com/catalog/9780596004200/*), by Erik T. Ray (O'Reilly), both have superb sections on XPath. Of the tutorials I've seen so far, they are best.

http://www.zvon.org/xxl/XPathTutorial/General/examples.html is a tutorial that consists mostly of example location paths and how they map onto a sample document. If you like to learn by example, this can be a helpful resource.

There are various tools that allow you to type an XPath expression and see what it returns based on a sample document. Some parsers (e.g., the *libxml2* parser) even ship with tools that provide this functionality. Get one, as they are really helpful for creating and debugging location paths. The one I use most of the time is built into the Oxygen XML editor (*http://www.oxygenxml.com*).

Another cool tool for working with XML documents via XPath is XSH2 (*http://xsh.sf .net*) by Petr Pajas, the current maintainer of `XML:LibXML`. It lets you manipulate them using XPath 1.0 as easily as you can manipulate files using filesystem paths.

The 10-Minute LDAP Tutorial

The Lightweight Directory Access Protocol (LDAP) is the protocol[*] for accessing the preeminent directory services deployed in the world today. Over time, system administrators are likely to find themselves dealing with LDAP servers and clients in a number of contexts. For example, Active Directory and Mac OS X Open Directory are both LDAP-based. This tutorial will give you an introduction to the LDAP nomenclature and concepts you'll need when using the material in Chapter 9.

The action in LDAP takes place around a data structure known as an *entry*. Figure C-1 is a picture to keep in mind as we look at an entry's component parts.

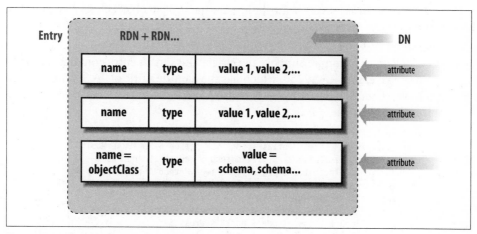

Figure C-1. *The LDAP entry data structure*

An entry has a set of named component parts called *attributes* that hold the data for that entry. To use database terms, they are like the fields in a database record. In

---

[*] Just to stress this point: LDAP is a protocol. It is not a relational database; it is the protocol through which you can communicate with a database-like directory service. More on the difference between databases and directory services can be found in Chapter 9.

Chapter 9 we use Perl to keep a list of machines in an LDAP directory. Each machine entry will have attributes like `name`, `model`, `location`, `owner`, etc.

Besides its name, an attribute consists of a type and the value for the attribute. The value has to be of the type defined for the attribute. For example, if you are storing employee information, your entry might have a `phone` attribute that has a type of `telephoneNumber`. The value of this attribute might be that employee's phone number. A type also has a syntax that dictates what kind of data can be used (strings, numbers, etc.), how it is sorted, and how it is used in a search (is it case-sensitive, etc.?). To accommodate multiple values, you can store multiple attributes of the same name in a single entry. An example of this would be a group entry where you would have multiple member attributes in the entry, each holding a group member.

An entry's contents and structure are defined by its object class. The object class (along with server and user settings) specifies which attributes must and may exist in that particular entry. Each entry can be in multiple object classes, in which case the specifications are essentially merged. The object class (or classes) of an entry is recorded in that entry in a special attribute named `objectClass`.

Let's look a little closer at the `objectClass` attribute, because it illustrates some of the important qualities of LDAP and allows us to pick off the rest of the jargon we haven't encountered yet. If we consider the `objectClass` attribute, we notice the following:

LDAP is object-oriented.

Each value in an `objectClass` attribute is the name of an object class. As mentioned earlier, these classes either define the set of attributes that can or must be in an entry, or expand on the definitions inherited from another class.

Let's look at an example. Suppose the `objectClass` in an entry contains the string `residentialPerson`. RFC 2256, which has the daunting title of "A Summary of the X.500(96) User Schema for Use with LDAPv3," defines the `residentialPerson` object class like this:

```
residentialPerson
   ( 2.5.6.10 NAME 'residentialPerson' SUP person STRUCTURAL MUST l
     MAY ( businessCategory $ x121Address $ registeredAddress $
     destinationIndicator $ preferredDeliveryMethod $ telexNumber $
     teletexTerminalIdentifier $ telephoneNumber $
     internationaliSDNNumber $
     facsimileTelephoneNumber $ preferredDeliveryMethod $ street $
     postOfficeBox $ postalCode $ postalAddress $
     physicalDeliveryOfficeName $ st $ l ) )
```

This definition says that an entry of object class `residentialPerson` must have a l attribute (short for locality) and may have a whole other set of attributes (`registeredAddress`, `postOfficeBox`, etc.). The key part of the specification is the `SUP person` string. It says that the superior class (the one from which `residentialPerson` inherits its attributes) is the `person` object class. That class's definition looks like this:

```
person
    ( 2.5.6.6 NAME 'person' SUP top STRUCTURAL MUST ( sn $ cn )
      MAY ( userPassword $ telephoneNumber $ seeAlso $ description ) )
```

So, an entry with object class of residentialPerson must have sn (surname), cn
(common name), and l (locality) attributes and may have the other attributes listed
in the MAY sections of these two RFC excerpts. We also know that person is the top
of the object hierarchy for residentialPerson, since its superior class is the special
abstract class top.

In most cases, you can get away with using the predefined standard object classes.
If you need to construct entries with attributes not found in an existing object class,
it is usually good form to locate the closest existing object class and build upon it,
like residentialPerson builds upon person.

LDAP has its origins in the database world.

A second quality we see in objectClass is LDAP's database roots. A collection of
object classes that specify attributes for the entries in an LDAP server is called a
schema. The RFC I just quoted is one example of an LDAP schema specification.
We won't be addressing the considerable issues surrounding schema in this book.
Like database design, schema design can be a book topic in itself, but you should
at least be familiar with the term "schema" because it will pop up later.

LDAP is not limited to storing information in strict tree structures.

There's one last thing I should mention about objectClass to help us move from
our examination of a single entry to the larger picture. Our previous object class
example specified top at the top of the object hierarchy, but there's another quasi-
superclass worth mentioning: alias. If alias is specified, this entry is actually an
alias for another entry (specified by the aliasedObjectName attribute in that entry).
LDAP strongly encourages hierarchical tree structures, but it doesn't demand
them. It's important to keep this flexibility in mind when you code to avoid making
incorrect assumptions about the data hierarchy on a server.

LDAP Data Organization

So far we've been focused on a single entry, but there's very little call for a directory
that contains only one entry. When we expand our focus and consider a directory
populated with many entries, we are immediately faced with one important question:
how do we find anything?

The stuff we've discussed so far all falls under what the LDAP specification calls its
"information model." This is the part that sets the rules for how information is represented. But for the answer to our question, we need to look to LDAP's "naming model,"
which dictates how information is organized.

If you refer back to Figure C-1, you'll see that we've discussed all of the parts of an
entry except for its name. Each entry has a name, known as its distinguished name

(DN). The DN consists of a string of relative distinguished names (RDNs). We'll return to DNs in a moment, but first let's concentrate on the RDN building blocks.

An RDN is composed of one or several attribute name/value pairs. For example, cn=Jay Sekora (where cn stands for "common name") could be an RDN. The attribute name is cn and the value is Jay Sekora.

Neither the LDAP nor the X.500 specification dictates which attributes should be used to form an RDN. They do require RDNs to be unique at each level in a directory hierarchy, however. This restriction exists because LDAP has no inherent notion of "the third entry in the fourth branch of a directory tree," so it must rely on unique names at each level to distinguish between individual entries at that level. Let's see how this restriction plays out in practice.

Take, for instance, another example RDN: cn=Robert Smith. This is probably not a good RDN choice, since there may be more than one Robert Smith in an organization of even moderate size. If you have a large number of people in your organization and your LDAP hierarchy is relatively flat, name collisions like this are to be expected. A marginally better entry would combine two attributes: perhaps cn=Robert Smith + l=Boston. (Attributes in RDNs are combined with a plus sign.)

Our revised RDN, which appends a locality attribute, still has problems, though. We may have postponed a name clash, but we haven't eliminated the possibility. Furthermore, if Smith moves to some other facility, we'll have to change both the RDN for the entry and the location attribute in the entry. Perhaps the best RDN we could use would be one with a unique and immutable user ID for this person. For example, we could use the username component of the person's email address, so the RDN would be uid=rsmith. This example should give you a taste of the decisions involved in the world of schemas.

Astute readers will notice that we're not really expanding our focus; we're still puttering around with a single entry. The RDN discussion was a prelude to this. Here's the real jump: entries live in a tree-like[†] structure known as a directory information tree (DIT), or just a directory tree. The latter is probably the preferred term to use, because in X.500 nomenclature DIT usually refers to a single universal tree, similar to the global DNS hierarchy or the management information base (MIB) we'll be seeing in Appendix G when we discuss SNMP.

Let's bring DNs back into the picture. Each entry in a directory tree can be located by its distinguished name. A DN is composed of an entry's RDN followed by all of the RDNs (separated by commas or semicolons) found as you walk your way back up the tree toward the root entry. If we follow the arrows in Figure C-2 and accumulate RDNs as we go, we'll construct DNs for each highlighted entry.

[†] I say "tree-like" rather than just "tree" because the alias object class I mentioned earlier allows you to create a directory structure that is not strictly a tree (at least from a computer-science, directed-acyclic-graph perspective).

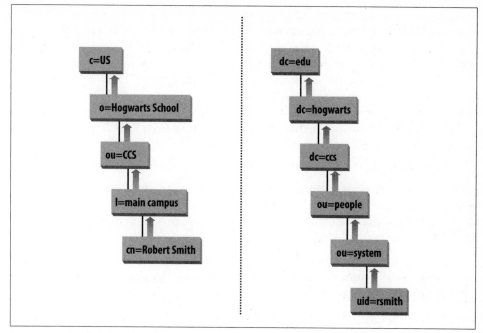

Figure C-2. Walking back up the tree to produce a DN

In the first picture, our DN would be:

```
cn=Robert Smith, l=main campus, ou=CCS, o=Hogwarts School, c=US
```

In the second, it is:

```
uid=rsmith, ou=system, ou=people, dc=ccs, dc=hogwarts, dc=edu
```

ou is short for organizational unit, o is short for organization, dc stands for "domain component" à la DNS, and c is for country (Sesame Street notwithstanding).

An analogy is often made between DNs and absolute pathnames in a filesystem, but DNs are more like postal addresses because they have a "most specific component first" ordering. In a postal address like this:

Doreen Hodgkins
288 St. Bucky Avenue
Anywhere, MA 02104
USA

you start off with the most specific object (the person) and get more vague from there, eventually winding up at the least specific component (the country). So too it goes with DNs.

You can see this ordering in our DN examples. The very top of the directory tree is known as the directory's *suffix*, since it is the end portion of every DN in that directory tree. Suffixes are important when constructing a hierarchical infrastructure using multiple delegated LDAP servers. Using an LDAPv3 concept known as a *referral*, it is possible to place an entry in the directory tree that essentially says, "for all entries with this suffix, go ask that server instead." Referrals are specified using an LDAP URL, which looks similar to your run-of-the-mill web URL except that it references a particular DN or other LDAP-specific information. Here's an example from RFC 2255, the RFC that specifies the LDAP URL format:

```
ldap://ldap.itd.umich.edu/o=University%20of%20Michigan,c=US?postalAddress
```

The other place directory suffixes come into play is in the client/server authentication process, since a client usually is connecting to access a single directory tree on the server: it "binds" to the server using this suffix. We'll see this process and details on querying an LDAP server in Chapter 9.

By now you have some idea of how data is organized and specified in LDAP terms. With that grounding, the discussion of the manipulation of this data in Chapter 9 should be much clearer.

The 15-Minute SQL Tutorial

Relational databases can be excellent tools for system administration. A relational database is accessed and administered using Structured Query Language (SQL) statements. As a result, it is a good idea for system administrators to learn at least the basics of SQL. The goal of this appendix is not to make you a full-time database programmer or even a real database administrator; that takes years of work and considerable expertise. However, we can look at enough SQL that you can begin to fake it. You may not be able to speak the language, but you'll at least get the gist if someone speaks it at you, and you'll know enough to go deeper into the subject if necessary. These basic building blocks are used extensively in Chapter 7, where we integrate SQL and Perl.

SQL is a command language for performing operations on relational databases and their component parts. Tables are the component parts you'll deal with most often. Their column and row structure makes them look a great deal like spreadsheets, but the resemblance is only surface-level. Table elements are not used to represent relationships to other elements—that is, table elements don't hold formulas, just data. Most SQL statements are devoted to working with the data in these rows and columns, allowing the user to add, delete, select, sort, and relate it between tables.

Let's go over some of the operators offered by SQL. If you want to experiment with the operators we'll be discussing, you'll need access to a SQL database. You may already have access to a server purchased from Oracle, Sybase, IBM, Microsoft, or elsewhere. If not, you can download an excellent open source database called MySQL from *http://www.mysql.org*. Another, simpler (no server required) open source database engine can be found at *http://www.sqlite.org*.

For this appendix, we'll be using a mostly generic SQL dialect, though each database server has its own SQL quirks. SQL statements particular to a specific database implementation will be noted.

The SQL code that follows will be shown using the capitalization standard found in most SQL books. This standard capitalizes all reserved words in a statement.

Most of the example SQL code in this appendix will use a table that mirrors the flat-file machine database we saw in Chapter 5. As a quick refresher, Table D-1 shows how that data looks in table form.

Table D-1. Our machine table

name	ipaddr	aliases	owner	dept	bldg	room	manuf	model
shimmer	192.168.1.11	shim shimmy shimmydoodles	David Davis	Software	Main	909	Sun	M4000
bendir	192.168.1.3	ben bendoodles	Cindy Coltrane	IT	West	143	Apple	Mac Pro
sander	192.168.1.55	sandy micky mickydoo	Alex Rollins	IT	Main	1101	Dell	Optiplex 740
sulawesi	192.168.1.12	sula su-lee	Ellen Monk	Design	Main	1116	Apple	Mac Pro

Creating/Deleting Databases and Tables

In the beginning, the server will be empty and void of objects useful to us. Let's create our database:

```
CREATE DATABASE sysadm ON userdev=10 LOG ON userlog=5
GO
```

This SQL statement creates a 10 MB database on the device **userdev** with a 5 MB log file on the **userlog** device. This statement is Sybase/Microsoft SQL Server-specific: database creation (when performed at all) takes place in different ways on different servers.* In this case, it is placing the database in a predefined storage device (an area defined as part of the storage allocation for the database server) and keeping the logging information (all of the info about the operations on the database and other housekeeping info) in a separate device.

 The GO command is used with some interactive database clients to indicate that the preceding SQL statement should be executed. (These clients also often provide additional commands beyond just plain SQL for working with the databases; e.g., MySQL has a **DESCRIBE** command for displaying information about tables.) It is not a SQL statement itself. Other databases require you to type a semicolon at the end of each statement. In the following examples, we'll assume that GO or a semicolon will follow each individual SQL statement if you are using one of these clients. We'll also be using the SQL commenting convention of `--` for comments in the SQL code.

---

* In fact, different servers even have different ideas about what the meaning of "database" is. The term is broader for an Oracle DBA than it is for a MySQL DBA.

To remove this database, we can use the DROP command:

```
DROP DATABASE sysadm
```

Now let's actually create an empty table to hold the information shown in Table D-1:

```
USE sysadm
-- Last reminder: you need to type GO or ; here (if you are using
-- an interactive client that requires this) before entering the
-- next statement
CREATE TABLE hosts (
    name      varchar(30)    NOT NULL,
    ipaddr    varchar(15)    NOT NULL,
    aliases   varchar(50)    NULL,
    owner     varchar(40)    NULL,
    dept      varchar(15)    NULL,
    bldg      varchar(10)    NULL,
    room      varchar(4)     NULL,
    manuf     varchar(10)    NULL,
    model     varchar(10)    NULL
)
```

First we indicate which database we wish to use (sysadm). The USE statement takes effect only if it is run separately before any other commands are executed; hence, it gets its own statement.

Next, we create a table by specifying the name, data type/length, and NULL/NOT NULL settings for each column. Let's talk a little bit about data types.

It is possible to hold several different types of data in a database table, including numbers, dates, text, and even images and other binary data. When each column is created, the kind of data it will hold is specified. Our needs are modest, so this table is composed of a set of columns that hold simple strings of varchars (non-space-padded characters). Some SQL servers allow you to create user-defined aliases for data types, like ip_address or employee_id. User-defined data types are used in table creation to keep table structures readable and data formats consistent between columns across multiple tables.

The last parameter in our previous command declares a column to be either mandatory or optional. If this parameter is set to NOT NULL, a row cannot be added to the table if it lacks data in this column. In our example, we need a machine name and IP address for a machine record to be useful to us, so we declare those fields NOT NULL. All the rest (though highly desirable) are optional, so we declare them NULL. There are other constraints besides NULL/NOT NULL that can be applied to a column for the purposes of data consistency. For instance, in some SQL dialects, we could ensure that two machines cannot have the same name by changing this:

```
    name      varchar(30)    NOT NULL,
```

to:

```
    name      varchar(30)    NOT NULL CONSTRAINT unique_name UNIQUE,
```

where `unique_name` is the name of this particular constraint. Naming your constraints makes the error messages generated by constraint violations more useful. See your server documentation for other constraints that can be applied to a table.

Deleting entire tables from a database is considerably simpler than creating them:

```
USE sysadm
DROP TABLE hosts
```

Inserting Data into a Table

Now that we have an empty table, let's look at two ways to add new data. Here's the first form:

```
USE sysadm
INSERT hosts
   VALUES (
      'shimmer',
      '192.168.1.11',
      'shim shimmy shimmydoodles',
      'David Davis',
      'Software',
      'Main',
      '309',
      'Sun',
      'Ultra60'
   )
```

The first line tells the server we are going to work with objects in the `sysadm` database. The second line selects the `hosts` table and adds a row, one column at a time. This version of the `INSERT` command is used to add a complete row to the table (i.e., one with all columns filled in).[†]

To create a new row with a partial record we can specify the columns to fill, like so:

```
USE sysadm
INSERT hosts (name,ipaddr,owner)
   VALUES (
      'bendir',
      '192.168.1.3',
      'Cindy Coltrane'
   )
```

The `INSERT` command will fail if we try to insert a row that does not have all of the required (`NOT NULL`) columns.

`INSERT` can also be used to add data from one table to another; we'll see this usage later. For the rest of our examples, assume that we've fully populated the `hosts` table using the first form of `INSERT`.

---

† Experienced SQL users would probably suggest you always specify the column destinations for each piece of data (even when inserting a complete row), as per the next example. This makes the `INSERT` statement more robust, because it isn't prone to errors in order (e.g., if you should add another field to the database).

Querying Information

As an administrator, the SQL command you'll probably use the most often is SELECT. SELECT is used to query information from a server. Before we talk about this command, a quick disclaimer: SELECT is a gateway into a whole wing of the SQL language. We're only going to explore some of its simpler forms. There is an art to constructing good queries (and designing databases so they can be queried well), but more in-depth coverage of this topic is best found in books entirely devoted to SQL and databases.

The simplest SELECT form is used mostly for retrieving server- and connection-specific information. With this form, you do not specify a data source. Here are three examples:

```
-- Sybase/MS-SQL - retrieve server name
SELECT @@SERVERNAME

-- MySQL - retrieve current version
SELECT VERSION();

-- Oracle - retrieve STARTUP_TIME
SELECT STARTUP_TIME from v$instance;
```

These examples show significant differences in the retrieval of database-specific information.

Retrieving All of the Rows in a Table

To get at all of the data in our hosts table, we can use this SQL code:

```
USE sysadm
SELECT * FROM hosts
```

This returns all of the rows and columns, in the column order in which our table was created:

```
name      ipaddr       aliases                    owner           dept
bldg  room  manuf  model
--------- ------------- -------------------------- --------------- ---------
----- ----- ------ -------------
shimmer   192.168.1.11  shim shimmy shimmydoodles David Davis     Software
Main  309   Sun    M4000
bendir    192.168.1.3   ben bendoodles             Cindy Coltrane  IT
West  143   Apple  Mac Pro
sander    192.168.1.55  sandy micky mickydoo       Alex Rollins    IT
Main  1101  Dell   Optiplex 740
sulawesi  192.168.1.12  sula su-lee                Ellen Monk      Design
Main  1116  Apple  Mac Pro
```

If we want to see specific columns, we just need to specify them by name:

```
USE sysadm
SELECT name,ipaddr FROM hosts
```

When we specify the columns by name they are returned in the order we specify them, independent of the order used when the table was created. For instance, to see IP addresses per building, we could use this query:

```
USE sysadm
SELECT bldg,ipaddr FROM hosts
```

This returns:

```
bldg       ipaddr
---------- ----------------
Main       192.168.1.11
West       192.168.1.3
Main       192.168.1.55
Main       192.168.1.12
```

Retrieving a Subset of the Rows in a Table

Databases wouldn't be very interesting if you couldn't retrieve a subset of your data. In SQL, we use the SELECT command and add a WHERE clause containing a conditional:

```
USE sysadm
SELECT * FROM hosts WHERE bldg='Main'
```

This shows:

```
name      ipaddr        aliases                    owner          dept      bldg
room  manuf  model
--------- ------------- -------------------------- -------------- --------- -----
----- ------ -------------
shimmer   192.168.1.11  shim shimmy shimmydoodles  David Davis    Software  Main
309   Sun    M4000
sander    192.168.1.55  sandy micky mickydoo       Alex Rollins   IT        Main
1101  Dell   Optiplex 740
sulawesi  192.168.1.12  sula su-lee                Ellen Monk     Design    Main
1116  Apple  Mac Pro
```

The set of available conditional operators for WHERE clauses contains the standard programming fare:

```
=     >     >=     <     <=     <>
```

Unlike Perl, SQL does not have separate string and numeric comparison operators.

Conditional operators can be combined with AND/OR and negated with NOT. We can test for an empty column using IS NULL, or for a non-empty column with IS NOT NULL. For instance, this SQL code will show all of the machines without owners listed in our table:

```
USE sysadm
SELECT name FROM hosts WHERE owner IS NULL
```

If you want to find all of the rows that have a column whose content is one of several specified values, you can use the IN operator to specify a list of values:

```
USE sysadm
SELECT name FROM hosts WHERE dept IN ('IT', 'Software')
```

This shows all of the machines in use in either the IT or software departments. SQL will also allow you to return rows that match a certain range of values (most useful with numeric or date values) with the BETWEEN operator. Here's an example that shows all of the machines in the main building between the 10th and 19th floors (presuming you use a simple convention for room numbers):

```
USE sysadm
SELECT name FROM hosts
  WHERE (bldg = 'Main') AND
        (room BETWEEN '1000' AND '1999')
```

Finally, the WHERE clause can be used with LIKE to choose rows using weak pattern matching (weak, that is, in comparison to Perl's regular expressions). For instance, this will select all of the machines that have the string "doodles" somewhere in their aliases:

```
USE sysadm
SELECT name FROM hosts WHERE aliases LIKE '%doodles%'
```

Table D-2 lists the supported LIKE wildcards.

Table D-2. LIKE wildcards

Wildcard	Meaning	Closest Perl regexp equivalent
%	Zero or more characters	.*
_	A single character	.
[]	A single character that is one of a specified set or range	[]

Some database servers have added extensions to SQL to allow for regular expression use in SELECTs. For instance, MySQL offers the REGEXP operator for use with SELECT. REGEXP doesn't have all the power of Perl's regular expression engine, but it offers a substantial increase in flexibility over the standard SQL wildcards.

Simple Manipulation of Data Returned by Queries

Three useful clauses for a SELECT statement are COUNT, DISTINCT, and ORDER BY. The first returns the number of rows retrieved:

```
USE sysadm
SELECT COUNT(*) FROM hosts
```

The second allows us to eliminate duplicate records returned by a query. If we want a list of all of the distinct manufacturers represented in our hosts table, we can use DISTINCT:

```
USE sysadm
SELECT DISTINCT manuf FROM hosts
```

The third clause allows us to specify the order of the returned results. If we want to see our data returned in a sorted order, we can use ORDER BY:

```
USE sysadm
SELECT name,ipaddr,dept,owner FROM hosts ORDER BY dept
```

Experienced database users often habitually add `ORDER BY` clauses to queries that return multiple rows because it makes dealing with the returned information easier.

SQL has several operators that can be used to modify the output returned by a query. They allow you to change column names, do summary and intra/intercolumn calculations, reformat how fields are displayed, perform subqueries, and a whole host of other things. Please see a dedicated SQL book for more detail on `SELECT`'s many clause operators.

Adding the Query Results to Another Table

A new table containing the results of a query can be created on the fly by using an `INTO` clause on some SQL servers:

```
USE sysadm
SELECT name,ipaddr INTO itmachines FROM hosts WHERE dept = 'IT'
```

This statement works just like those we've seen previously, except that the results of the query are added to another table called `itmachines`. With some servers, this table is created on the fly if it does not exist. You can think of this operator clause as the equivalent of the > operator in most Unix- and Windows-based operating system command-line shells.

 Some database servers (like MySQL[‡]) do not support `SELECT INTO`; they require the use of different syntax. For example, Oracle uses something like this:

```
CREATE TABLE COPY AS SELECT name,ipaddr FROM hosts WHERE dept = 'IT'
```

Some other servers instead use an `INSERT` command to perform this action. Still others, such as Microsoft SQL Server and Sybase, require that a special flag be set on a database before `SELECT INTO` can be used within that database, or the command will fail.

Changing Table Information

Our working knowledge of the `SELECT` command comes into play with other commands as well. For instance, the `INSERT` command we saw earlier can also take a `SELECT` clause. This allows us to insert query information into an existing table. If our software department were to merge with IT, we could add their machines to the `itmachines` table:

[‡] Just to be clear: MySQL 5.x does have a `SELECT .. INTO`, but it dumps data to a regular file, not to a database, as we've been discussing. For MySQL, you'll want to use `INSERT .. INTO` instead.

```
USE sysadm
INSERT itmachines
  SELECT name,ipaddr FROM hosts
  WHERE dept = 'Software'
```

If we want to change any of the rows in our table, we can use the UPDATE command. For example, if all of the departments in the company moved into a single facility called Central, we could change the name of the building in all rows like so:

```
USE sysadm
UPDATE hosts
  SET bldg = 'Central'
```

It's more likely that we'll need to change only certain rows in a table. For that task, we use the handy WHERE clause we saw when discussing the SELECT operator:

```
USE sysadm
UPDATE hosts
  SET dept = 'Development'
  WHERE dept = 'Software'
```

That changed the name of the Software department to Development. This moves the machine called *bendir* to our Main building:

```
USE sysadm
UPDATE hosts
  SET bldg = 'Main'
  WHERE name = 'bendir'
```

If we want to remove a row or set of rows from a table instead of updating them, we can use the DELETE command:

```
USE sysadm
DELETE FROM hosts
  WHERE bldg = 'East'
```

While there's no standardized way to undo a straight DELETE operation,[*] you can gain some safety using transactions (outside the scope of this appendix). In many cases you can run the DELETE command as a SELECT first to gain an understanding of just what effect the DELETE will have. Still, be careful with these operations.

Relating Tables to Each Other

Relational databases offer many ways to forge connections between the data in two or more tables. This process is known as "joining" the tables. Joins can get complex quickly, given the number of query possibilities involved and the fine control the programmer has over the data that is returned. There are different flavors of joints (inner,

---

[*] Oracle 10g and beyond offer a flashback facility that can undo DELETE and DROP operations, depending on the amount of data in play and how much the database has changed since the destructive operations were performed.

outer, etc.) but we're not going to get into those here. If you are interested in this level of detail, your best bet is to seek out a book devoted to SQL.

Here is one example of a join in action. For this example we'll use another table called `contracts`, which contains information on the maintenance contracts for each of our machines. That table is shown in Table D-3.

Table D-3. Our contracts table

name	servicevendor	startdate	enddate
bendir	IBM	09-09-2005	06-01-2008
sander	Dell	03-14-2008	03-14-2009
shimmer	Sun	12-12-2008	12-12-2009
sulawesi	Apple	11-01-2005	11-01-2008

Here's one way to relate our `hosts` table to the `contracts` table using a join:

```
USE sysadm
SELECT contracts.name,servicevendor,enddate,bldg,room
  FROM contracts, hosts
  WHERE contracts.name = hosts.name
```

The easiest way to understand this code is to read it from the middle out. `FROM contracts, hosts` tells the server that we wish to relate the `contracts` and `hosts` tables. `WHERE contracts.name = hosts.name` says we will match a row in `contracts` to a row in `hosts` based on the contents of the `name` field in each table. Note that we say `contracts.name` because we need to distinguish which `name` field we are using (the one on the `contracts` table). Finally, the `SELECT` line specifies the columns we wish to appear in our output.

SQL Stragglers

Before we close this tutorial section, there are a few more advanced SQL topics you may encounter in your travels.

Views

Most SQL servers allow you to create different *views* of a table. Views are like magic permanent `SELECT` queries. Once you create a view using a special `SELECT` query, the specification of your query sticks around. Each time you access anything from the view, the original query is run to provide that information. Views can be queried like any other table. Modifications to a view, with a few restrictions, are propagated back to the original table or tables.

Note I said *tables*. Here's where the magic of views comes in: a view on a table can be created that consists of a join between that table and another. This view behaves as one large virtual table. Changes to this view are propagated back to the original tables that are part of the join that created the view.

A view can also be created with a new column consisting of calculations performed between other columns in that table, almost like in a spreadsheet. Views are also useful for more mundane purposes, such as query simplification (e.g., you may be able to SELECT fewer columns) and data restructuring (e.g., table users see a view of the data that doesn't change, even if other columns in the underlying table structure are modified).

Here's a view-creation example that demonstrates query simplification:

```
USE sysadm
CREATE VIEW ipaddr_view AS SELECT name, ipaddr FROM hosts
```

Now we can use a very simple query to get back just the information we need:

```
USE sysadm
SELECT * FROM ipaddr_view
```

The result of this query is:

```
name                             ipaddr
-----------------------------    ---------------
shimmer                          192.168.1.11
bendir                           192.168.1.3
sander                           192.168.1.55
sulawesi                         192.168.1.12
```

Like tables, views are dropped using a form of the DROP command:

```
USE sysadm
DROP VIEW ipaddr_view
```

Dropping the view has no effect on the underlying data tables.

Cursors

In all the queries we've seen thus far, we've asked the server to hand us back all of the results once the query has completed. But sometimes it is preferable to receive the answer to a query one line at a time. This is most often the case when embedding SQL queries in other programs. If your query returns tens of thousands of lines, chances are pretty good that you'll want to process the results one line at a time, rather than storing them all in memory for later use. SQL programming in Perl often uses this line-at-a-time method. Here's a small native-SQL program that demonstrates cursor use on a Sybase or Microsoft SQL Server:

```
USE sysadm
-- declare our variables
DECLARE @hostname varchar(30)
DECLARE @ip varchar(15)

-- declare our cursor
DECLARE hosts_curs CURSOR FOR SELECT name,ipaddr FROM hosts

-- open this cursor
OPEN hosts_curs

-- iterate over the table, fetching rows one at a time,
-- until we receive an error
FETCH hosts_curs INTO @hostname,@ip
WHILE (@@fetch_status = 0)
  BEGIN
    PRINT "----"
    PRINT @hostname
    PRINT @ip
    FETCH hosts_curs INTO @hostname,@ip
  END

-- close the cursor (not strictly necessary when followed
-- by a DEALLOCATE)
CLOSE hosts_curs

-- undefine cursor def
DEALLOCATE hosts_curs
```

This produces the following output:

```
----
shimmer
192.168.1.11
----
bendir
192.168.1.3
----
sander
192.168.1.55
----
sulawesi
192.168.1.12
```

Stored Procedures

Most database systems allow you to upload SQL code to the server, where it is stored in an optimized, post-parsed form for faster execution. Such uploads are known as *stored procedures*. Stored procedures are often a critical component of SQL for administrators, because large parts of server administration for some servers rely on them. For example, to change the owner of the **sysadm** database in Sybase, you might do this:

```
USE sysadm
sp_changedbowner "jay"
```

Some databases also support something called "triggers." Triggers are stored procedures that automatically fire when some event takes place in the database (e.g., when a row gets INSERTed). Each database vendor implements triggers slightly differently, so check the documentation of the database you are using for the details on how to use CREATE TRIGGER and DROP TRIGGER.

Now that you've seen the basics of SQL, you're ready to tackle Chapter 7.

The Five-Minute RCS Tutorial

This quick tutorial will teach you everything you need to know to use the Revision Control System (RCS) for system administration. RCS is useful for applying version control to all of your system files. It has considerably more functionality than we'll discuss here, so be sure to take a look at the manual pages and the references at the end of this appendix if you plan to use it heavily. You may also be wondering why we're bothering with RCS when more modern systems, such as Git and Subversion, exist. That's a good question, and I'll address it at the end of the tutorial. In the meantime, though, let's get the RCS basics down; they'll help with the explanation later.

RCS functions like a car rental agency. Only one person at a time can actually rent a particular car and drive it off the lot. The agency can only rent out a new car after adding it to its pool. Customers can browse the list of cars (and their features) at any time, but if two people want to rent the same car, the second person must wait for the car to be returned to the lot. Finally, car rental agencies inspect cars very carefully after they have been returned and record any changes that took place during the rental. All of these properties hold true for RCS as well.

In RCS, a file is like a car. If you wish to keep track of a file using RCS (i.e., add it to the rental lot), you must "check it in" for the first time:

```
$ ci -u inetd.conf
```

ci stands for "check in," and the -u tells RCS to leave *inetd.conf* in place during the check-in. When a file is checked in (i.e., made available for rental), RCS does one of two things to remind the user that the file is under RCS's control:

1. Deletes the original file, leaving only the RCS archive file behind. It sometimes distresses new users of RCS when the file seems to disappear after being checked in, but in fact the data has just been squirreled away in its archive file. This archive file is usually called *filename,v* and is kept either in the same directory as the original file or in a subdirectory called *RCS* (if the user creates it). You must protect the *RCS* directory and archive file (using filesystem permissions) at least as strongly as the original file.

2. If -u is used (as in our earlier command), it checks the file out again, leaving the permissions on the file set to "read-only."

To modify a file under RCS's control (i.e., rent a car), you first need to "check out" (co) that file:

```
$ co -l services
```

The -l switch tells RCS to "strictly lock" *services* (i.e., do not allow any other user to check out *services* at the same time). This lock is respected only by RCS; the file is not actually locked using filesystem capabilities (ACLs, attributes, etc.). Other switches that are commonly used with co include:

- -r <revision number> to check out an older revision of a file
- -p to print a past revision to the screen without actually checking it out

Once you are done modifying a file, you need to check it back in using the same command you used to put the file under RCS's control (ci -u *filename*). The check-in process stores any changes made to this file in a space-efficient manner.

Each time a file that has been modified is checked in, it is given a new revision number. At check-in time, RCS will prompt you for a comment to be placed in the change log it automatically keeps for each file. This log and the listing of the current person who has checked out a file can be viewed using rlog *filename*.

If someone neglects to check her changes to a particular file back into RCS (perhaps having gone home for the day) and you have a real need to change the file yourself, you can break that person's lock using rcs -u *filename*. This command will prompt for a break-lock message that is mailed to the person who owns the lock.

After breaking the lock, you should check to see how the current copy differs from the RCS archive revision. rcsdiff *filename* will show you this information. If you wish to preserve these changes, check the file in (with an appropriate change-log comment), and then check it back out again before working on it. rcsdiff, like co example, can also take a -r <revision number> flag to allow you to compare two past revisions.

Table E-1 lists some common RCS operations and their command lines.

Table E-1. Common RCS operations

RCS operation	Command line
Initial check-in of file (leaving file active in filesystem)	ci -u *filename*
Check out with lock	co -l *filename*
Check in and unlock (leaving file active in filesystem)	ci -u *filename*
Display version *x.y* of a file	co -p*x.y filename*
Undo to version *x.y* (overwrites file active in filesystem with the specified revision)	co -r*x.y filename*
Diff file active in filesystem and last revision	rcsdiff *filename*
Diff versions *x.y* and *x.z*	rcsdiff -r*x.y* -r*x.z filename*

RCS operation	Command line
View log of check-ins	`rlog filename`
Break an RCS lock held by another person on a file	`rcs -u filename`

Believe it or not, this is really all you need to get started using RCS. Once you start using it for system administration, you'll find it pays off handsomely.

Choosing RCS over CVS, Git, SVN, etc.

Given that there are modern version control systems available that are much cooler than RCS, why do I still suggest people learn and use RCS? The fact is that the newer systems (which I use for my own version control in other contexts) have a model that is not nearly as conducive for this specific sysadmin need as RCS.

With systems like CVS and SVN, the user checks out the file or files in question into a "working directory" from the central repository. Changes are made and then re-synced to the repository. Multiple people can check out the same files, and (if possible) all of their changes are automatically merged/reconciled when the file is returned to the repository. The Subversion documentation refers to this process as "copy-modify-merge."

There are a few reasons why this model doesn't mesh well with our usual sysadmin workflow around things like configuration files:

- The presence of config files in a specific place in the filesystem is dreadfully important. */etc/passwd* doesn't do you any good if it isn't in */etc* or is stored in a special repository format. It is possible to force people to use */etc* as the working directory, but that can be fraught with peril. RCS lets you simply keep your files in the live filesystem after they've been checked back in.

- The copy-modify-merge approach often doesn't jive with how sysadmins work. The notion that multiple people might be making concurrent edits to a configuration file that later will automatically be reconciled (without regard for how parts of that file might interact with other parts) is a very scary thought. Both CVS and SVN have at least some support for locking a file so others won't edit it at the same time, but this runs contrary to the spirit of those systems. RCS only thinks in terms of locking, likely making it a better fit. If you need data to be concurrently edited, I'd suggest that using a database from which config files are generated is probably a better approach.

- CVS and SVN are "directory-based": they deal with directory trees that contain files. Git is content-based (it manages the data under source control). RCS is file-based.

- Though the newer distributed version control systems allow for a certain amount of disconnected operation, using a centralized networked file repository for crucial files can sometimes get you into trouble. If your machine is off the net for some reason and you are trying to fix it, as long as you have your RCS repository and the RCS binaries you are in okay shape. But if you use a version control system

---

that requires network access to get to the file you need to fix the lack of network access, you've got a problem. Git's fully distributed model is better in this sense, but it has its own issues in this context.

In short, while CVS, SVN, Git and the rest of the pack of version control systems are probably much better at version control for most software development environments, RCS is better suited to managing system files.

References for More Information

ftp://ftp.gnu.org/pub/gnu/rcs has the latest source code for the RCS package (though it is available through most standard packaging mechanisms if it doesn't ship with your OS).

http://cygwin.com is a source for an RCS package (and many, many other Unix-born programs). If you'd like to install RCS without requiring the entire Cygwin environment, there is a version available at *http://www.cs.purdue.edu/homes/trinkle/RCS*.

Applying RCS and SCCS: From Source Control to Project Control (http://oreilly.com/catalog/9781565921177/), by Don Bolinger and Tan Bronson (O'Reilly), is an excellent RCS reference.

http://www.nongnu.org/cvs and *http://subversion.tigris.org* are the places to go if you find you need features not provided in RCS. The next step up is either the Concurrent Versions System (CVS) or Subversion (SVN).

The next step up from CVS and SVN is the crop of relatively new distributed version control systems, such as *git*, *mercurial*, *bazaar*, and *darcs*. For more info, check out the article at *http://en.wikipedia.org/wiki/Distributed_Version_Control_System*.

The Two-Minute VBScript-to-Perl Tutorial

Heresy to talk about VBScript in a book largely focused on Perl tools? Perhaps, but if you put down the pitchfork for a second, I'll explain why it is useful to spend two minutes learning a little VBScript. The following rationale assumes you have some familiarity with machines running Windows-based operating systems. If you've never had any contact with Windows machines, and never expect to, please skip to the next appendix. The rest of you, follow me.

It may border on the tautological to say this, but Microsoft expects administrators to automate their tasks using Microsoft technologies. Perl has been shoehorned into this realm largely thanks to the efforts of Jan Dubois and the other contributors to the `Win32::OLE` module. This module gives us a way to communicate with other parts of the Microsoft software universe on an almost equal footing with Microsoft scripting languages like VBScript.

`Win32::OLE` makes communication possible, but it doesn't always make it easy. Perl doesn't share the same DWMM (Do What Microsoft Means) language idioms as VBScript, so it's not always clear how an apparently simple piece of VBScript code that performs some behind-the-scenes magic for the programmer can be translated. This difficulty is compounded by the lack of reference and teaching material written in our native language. Barring a few notable exceptions, like David Roth's books, the vast majority of the material on Windows scripting is written using VBScript as its implementation language. For example, Microsoft's excellent Script Center website (*http://www.microsoft.com/technet/scriptcenter/default.mspx*) (based on the equally good Windows 2000 Scripting Guide) would be a perfect reference for us, except that it's all in icky VBScript.

I'm not a VBScript programmer, nor do I expect you to be one. You won't even be able to fake it by the end of this appendix. Luckily, you don't have to know very much about VBScript or even Win32 programming to be able to convert simple VBScripts to Perl using `Win32::OLE`. This appendix will give you some basic translation hints and demonstrate how they are put into practice on a few of the real scripts posted at Microsoft's Script Center.

Translation Tactics

The first four tactics that I want to show you can be illustrated by a step-by-step translation of the following simple VBScript:

```
' Lists all the members of the Managers group in fabrikam.com

Set objGroup = GetObject _
("LDAP://cn=managers,ou=management,dc=fabrikam,dc=com")
For each objMember in objGroup.Members
Wscript.Echo objMember.Name
Next
```

We'll look at a few more sample scripts later, but for now let's see about translating this one into a more palatable language.[*]

Tactic 1: Loading Your Modules

All translated programs begin by loading the Win32::OLE module:

```
use Win32::OLE;
```

If you think you are going to be using container and contained objects,[†] you'll want to either import the in primitive or load Win32::OLE::Enum:

```
# 'in' is another way to say Win32::OLE::Enum->All()
use Win32::OLE qw(in);
        # or
use Win32::OLE;
use Win32::OLE::Enum;
```

It can also be helpful to load Win32::OLE::Const and use it to import constants from an application or OS library for use in your programs. We'll see an example of this later in this appendix.

There are other primitives, such as with and valof, that you might also want to consider importing if you are translating more sophisticated scripts. However, using them typically requires more in-depth knowledge of Windows programming principles. See the Win32::OLE doc for more info on these primitives and their usage.

---

[*] One reason I call VBScript less palatable is that it requires a line continuation character when a single statement spans two lines in a file (and uses the underscore, _, for this purpose). It also uses a single quote (') as its comment character. But hey, who are we to pick on another language's syntax?

[†] For more on container objects, see the section "Dealing with Container/Collection Objects" on page 359.

Tactic 2: Referencing an Object

The translation is straightforward:

```
my $objGroup =
    Win32::OLE->
        GetObject('LDAP://cn=managers,ou=management,dc=fabrikam,dc=com');
```

To make the mapping between the VBScript and the Perl as easy as possible, we'll retain the VBScript variable names, mixed case and all.

Tactic 3: Accessing Object Properties Using the Hash Dereference Syntax

VBScript uses the dot (.) character to access an object's properties (or attributes, in LDAP or OOP parlance). The Perl equivalent[‡] is the hash dereference syntax (i.e., `$object->{property}`).

So, this VBScript code:

```
objGroup.Members
```

becomes this Perl code:

```
$objGroup->{Members}
```

Tactic 4: Dealing with Container Objects

Both the original VBScript and the Perl code in the preceding section return a container object. That object contains a set of user objects (the users who are members of the *managers* group). VBScript accesses the individual objects in the container object using in, and strangely enough, thanks to our import in "Tactic 1: Loading Your Modules," so will we:

```
for my $objMember (in $objGroup->{Members}){
    # using the access syntax we saw in tactic #3
    print $objMember->{Name},"\n";
}
```

And there you have it—your first VBScript-to-Perl program:

```
# Lists all the members of the managers group in fabrikam.com

use Win32::OLE qw(in);

my $objGroup =
    Win32::OLE->
        GetObject('LDAP://cn=managers,ou=management,dc=fabrikam,dc=com');
```

[‡] Just to be clear, this is the Perl 5 equivalent. Perl 6, still in its implementation stages as of this writing, is due to use the dot character as well.

```
for my $objMember (in $objGroup->{Members}){
    print $objMember->{Name},"\n";
}
```

If that looked simple, that's a good sign. The goal here is to let you take simple sysadmin VBScript code and convert it to Perl without having to think too hard. If it seemed complicated, don't worry, you'll find that this sort of translation will become easier the more you grapple with specific examples. Let's take a look at another VBScript example from the Microsoft Script Center so we can bring in another translation tactic.

Tactic 5: Converting Method Invocations

```
' Creates a new global security group -- atl-users02 -- within Active
' Directory.

Set objOU = GetObject("LDAP://OU=management,dc=fabrikam,dc=com")
Set objGroup = objOU.Create("Group", "cn=atl-users02")
objGroup.Put "sAMAccountName", "atl-users02"
objGroup.SetInfo
```

The first line of code should be an easy rewrite, so let's look at the remaining lines. In these lines, the dot character (.) is used for a different purpose than we saw in tactic #3: this time the dot is used invoke an object's methods (i.e., the verbs for the object) rather than to access the object's properties (i.e., what pieces of data it holds). In a serendipitous twist of fate, like VBScript, Perl uses a similar syntax for method invocations and for hash dereferences. Perl uses the arrow operator (->) for both, so the remaining lines of code in our example get translated to:

```
my $objGroup = $objOU->Create('Group', 'cn=atl-users02');
$objGroup->Put('sAMAccountName', 'atl-users02')
$objGroup->SetInfo;
```

Here's the finished translation:[*]

```
# Creates a new global security group -- atl-users02 -- within Active
# Directory.

use Win32::OLE;

my $objOU = Win32::OLE->
    GetObject('LDAP://OU=management,dc=fabrikam,dc=com');

my $objGroup = $objOU->Create('Group', 'cn=atl-users02');

$objGroup->Put('sAMAccountName', 'atl-users02')

$objGroup->SetInfo;
```

---

[*] I've left it out because this is meant to be a strict translation, but it would be good to add error checking at various places in the script (e.g., checking the value returned from `Win32::OLE::LastError()`).

Pretty easy, no? The one marginally tricky conversion is the last `SetInfo` line. How did we know this was supposed to be a method invocation rather than a property access? In this case we got a strong hint because no assignment operator is present. When we access a property we usually expect something to be returned—a value, another object, etc. The VBScript doesn't indicate that it is going to use any data returned, so we can safely assume this is a method invocation. The other tip here (probably more helpful to native English speakers who would pick up on this naturally) is that "SetInfo" sounds like an action and not a piece of data. If it sounds like it should be doing something rather than holding something, that's probably what it does. While these tips aren't foolproof, they can help you hazard a good guess. If worst comes to worst, try the translation as a property access and then, if that doesn't work, attempt it as a method invocation.

Tactic 6: Dealing with Constants

Let's look at one last VBScript example to illustrate our final translation tactic:

```
' Removes user MyerKen from the group Sea-Users.

Const ADS_PROPERTY_DELETE = 4

Set objGroup = GetObject _
  ("LDAP://cn=Sea-Users,cn=Users,dc=NA,dc=fabrikam,dc=com")

objGroup.PutEx ADS_PROPERTY_DELETE, _
  "member", _
    Array("cn=MyerKen,ou=Management,dc=NA,dc=fabrikam,dc=com")

objGroup.SetInfo
```

The very first line of this code probably jumps out at you. In VBScript, `Const` is used to define a constant. The constants you need for scripting are defined by OS and application developers and stored in a component's or application's type library. One of VBScript's limitations (as of this writing) is that it can't read these constants from the library. Instead, VBScript authors have to hardcode operational constants like `ADS_PROPERTY_DELETE` into their scripts. Perl, thanks to the `Win32::OLE::Const` module, doesn't have this limitation. Instead of hardcoding in the constant in our translation (a move always fraught with peril), we can do the following:

```
use Win32::OLE::Const 'Active DS Type Library';
```

and the ADSI constants become available to us. The next obvious question is, where did the magic string "Active DS Type Library" come from? How did we know to use it instead of something like "ADSI TypeLib" or even "ADS Constants Found Here"? The string comes from the registration in the Windows registry for the *actiuveds.tlb* file found in either *HKCR\TypeLib* or *HKLM\Software\classes\TypeLib*. If that doesn't mean much to you, a more useful answer might be: poke around in your registry, look at the

SDK and other documentation Microsoft publishes, and/or search on the Web for someone else's example code until you find a string that works for you.

The second and fourth lines of the code are things we've seen before, so let's look at the third line. We've already seen how to translate a method invocation, and we know how to import constants, so the only remaining concern is how to deal with the `Array("cn=MyerKen...")` part. The good news is that VBScript's `Array()` creation keyword maps nicely to Perl's anonymous array reference creation syntax:

```
$objGroup->PutEx(ADS_PROPERTY_DELETE,
                 'member',
                 ['cn=MyerKen,ou=Management,dc=NA,dc=fabrikam,dc=com']);
```

Here's the final result of our work:

```
# Removes user MyerKen from the group Sea-Users.

use Win32::OLE::Const 'Active DS Type Library';

my $objGroup = Win32::OLE->
    GetObject('LDAP://cn=Sea-Users,cn=Users,dc=NA,dc=fabrikam,dc=com');

$objGroup->PutEx(ADS_PROPERTY_DELETE,
                 'member',
                 ['cn=MyerKen,ou=Management,dc=NA,dc=fabrikam,dc=com']);

$objGroup->SetInfo;
```

These six tactics should get you surprisingly far on the road to your own conversions.

References for More Information

If you haven't yet, you must download the Microsoft Scriptomatic tool (version 2 as of this writing) from *http://www.microsoft.com/technet/scriptcenter/tools/scripto2.mspx*. This Windows tool from "the Microsoft Scripting Guys" lets you poke around the WMI namespaces on your machine. When you find something you might be interested in using, it can write a script to use it for you. Really. But even better than that, it can write the script for you in VBScript, JScript, Perl, or Python. I can't think of a better tool for comparing how one language is translated into another. I'm raving about this tool both here and in the other chapters that mention WMI because I like it so much. If you want to use it under Vista, though, be sure to read the section on Vista in Chapter 1.

Finally, I should mention that if you don't want to do your own translation from VBScript to Perl, there is a commercial product available that can do a much more sophisticated job than you're likely to be able to manage after only a simple introduction like this. The VBScript Converter is part of ActiveState's Perl Dev Kit (PDK). More information on the product can be found at *http://activestate.com/perl_dev_kit/*.

The 20-Minute SNMP Tutorial

The Simple Network Management Protocol (SNMP) is the ubiquitous protocol used to manage devices on a network. Unfortunately, as mentioned at the beginning of Chapter 12, SNMP is not a particularly simple protocol (despite its name). This longish tutorial will give you the information you need to get started with version 1 of SNMP.

SNMP is predicated on the notion of a management station polling SNMP agents running on remote devices for information. An agent can also signal the management station if an important condition arises, such as a counter exceeding a threshold. When we programmed SNMP in Perl in Chapter 12, we essentially acted as a management station, polling the SNMP agents on other network devices.

We're going to concentrate on version 1 of SNMP in this tutorial. Seven versions of the protocol (SNMPv1, SNMPsec, SNMPv2p, SNMPv2c, SNMPv2u, SNMPv2*, and SNMPv3) have been proposed; v1 is the one that has been most widely implemented and deployed, though v3 is expected to eventually ascend thanks to its superior security architecture.

Perl and SNMP both have simple data types. Perl uses a scalar as its base type. Lists and hashes are just collections of scalars in Perl. In SNMP, you also work with scalar *variables*. SNMP variables can hold any of four primitive types: integers, strings, object identifiers (more on this in a moment), or null values. And just like in Perl, in SNMP a set of related variables can be grouped together to form larger structures (most often *tables*). This is where their similarity ends.

Perl and SNMP diverge radically on the subject of variable names. In Perl, you can, given a few restrictions, name your variables anything you'd like. SNMP variable names are considerably more restrictive. All SNMP variables exist within a virtual hierarchical storage structure known as the management information base (MIB). All valid variable names are defined within this framework. The MIB, now at version MIB-II, defines a tree structure for all of the objects (and their names) that can be managed via SNMP.

In some ways the MIB is similar to a filesystem: instead of organizing files, the MIB logically organizes management information in a hierarchical tree-like structure. Each node in this tree has a short text string, called a *label*, and an accompanying number that represents its position at that level in the tree. To give you a sense of how this works, let's go find the SNMP variable in the MIB that holds a system's description of itself. Bear with me; we have a bit of a tree walking (eight levels' worth) to do to get there.

Figure G-1 shows a picture of the top of the MIB tree.

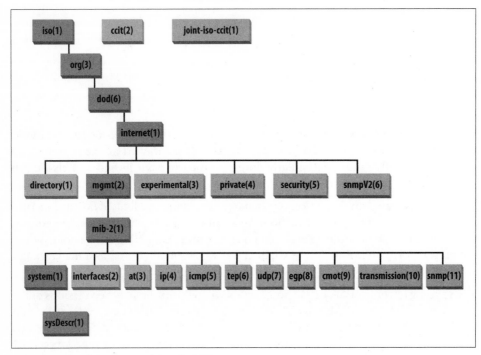

Figure G-1. Finding sysDescr(1) in the MIB

The top of the tree consists of standards organizations: `iso(1)`, `ccitt(2)`, `joint-iso-ccitt(3)`. Under the `iso(1)` node, there is a node called `org(3)` for other organizations. Under this node is `dod(6)`, for the Department of Defense. Under that node is `internet(1)`, a subtree for the Internet community.

Here's where things start to get interesting. The Internet Architecture Board has assigned the subtrees listed in Table G-1 under `internet(1)`.

Table G-1. Subtrees of the internet(1) node

Subtree	Description
directory(1)	OSI directory
mgmt(2)	RFC standard objects
experimental(3)	Internet experiments
private(4)	Vendor-specific

Subtree	Description
security(5)	Security
snmpV2(6)	SNMP internals

Because we're interested in using SNMP for device management, we will want to take the mgmt(2) branch. The first node under mgmt(2) is the MIB itself (this is almost recursive). Since there is only one MIB, the only node under mgmt(2) is mib-2(1).

The real meat (or tofu) of the MIB begins at this level in the tree. We find the first set of branches, called object groups, which hold the variables we'll want to query:

```
system(1)
interfaces(2)
at(3)
ip(4)
icmp(5)
tcp(6)
udp(7)
egp(8)
cmot(9)
transmission(10)
snmp(11)
```

Remember, we're hunting for the "system description" SNMP variable, so the system(1) group is the logical place to look. The first node in that tree is sysDescr(1). Bingo—we've located the object we need.

Why bother with all this tree-walking stuff? This trip provides us with sysDescr(1)'s object identifier (OID), which is the dotted set of the numbers from each label of the tree we encountered on our way to this object. Figure G-2 shows this graphically.

So, the OID for the Internet tree is 1.3.6.1, the OID for the system object group is 1.3.6.1.2.1.1, and the OID for the sysDescr object is 1.3.6.1.2.1.1.1.

When we want to actually use this OID in practice, we'll need to tack on another number to get the value of this variable. That is, we will need to append a .0, representing the first (and only, since a device cannot have more than one description) *instance* of this object.

Let's do that now, to get a sneak preview of SNMP in action. In this appendix we'll be using the command-line tools from the Net-SNMP package for demonstration purposes. This package (*http://www.net-snmp.org*) is an excellent free SNMPv1 and v3 implementation. We're using this particular implementation because one of the Perl modules links to its library, but any other client that can send an SNMP request will do just as nicely. Once you're familiar with command-line SNMP utilities, making the jump to the Perl equivalents is easy.

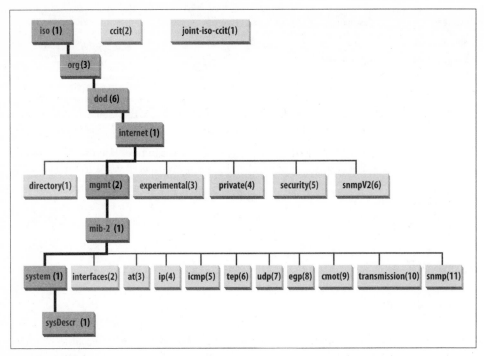

Figure G-2. Finding the OID for our desired object

The Net-SNMP command-line tools allow us to prepend a dot (.) if we wish to specify an OID/variable name starting at the root of the tree. Here are two ways we might query the machine *solarisbox* for its systems description (note that the second command should appear on one line; it's broken here with a line continuation marker for readability):

```
$ snmpget -v 1 -c public solarisbox .1.3.6.1.2.1.1.1.0
$ snmpget -v 1 -c public solarisbox \
.iso.org.dod.internet.mgmt.mib-2.system.sysDescr.0
```

These lines both yield:

```
system.sysDescr.0 = Sun SNMP Agent, Ultra-1
```

Back to the theory. It is important to remember that the P in SNMP stands for *Protocol*. SNMP itself is just the protocol for the communication between entities in a management infrastructure. The operations, or "protocol data units" (PDUs), are meant to be *simple*. Here are the PDUs you'll see most often, especially when programming in Perl:[*]

---

[*] The canonical list of PDUs for SNMPv2 and v3 is found in RFC 3416; it builds upon the list of PDUs in SNMPv1's RFC 1157. The list in the RFC doesn't contain many more PDUs than are cited here, so you're not missing much.

get-request

> get-request is the workhorse of the PDU family: it is used to poll an SNMP entity for the value of some SNMP variable. Many people live their whole SNMP lives using nothing but this operation.

get-next-request

> get-next-request is just like get-request, except it returns the item in the MIB just *after* the specified item (the "first lexicographic successor" in RFC terms). This operation comes into play most often when you are attempting to find all of the items in a logical table object. For instance, you might send a set of repeated get-next-requests to query for each line of a workstation's ARP table. We'll see an example of this in practice in a moment.

get-bulk-request

> get-bulk-request is an SNMPv2/v3 addition that allows for the bulk transfer of information. With other PDUs, you typically ask for and receive one piece of information. get-bulk lets you make one query and receive a whole set of values. This can be a much more efficient way to transfer chunks of information (like whole tables).

set-request

> set-request does just what you would anticipate: it attempts to change the value of an SNMP variable. This is the operation used to change the configuration of an SNMP-capable device.

trap/snmpV2-trap

> trap is the SNMPv1 name, and snmpV2-trap is the SNMPv2/3 name. Traps allow you to ask an SNMP-capable box to signal its management entity about an event (e.g., a reboot, or a counter threshold being reached) without being explicitly polled. Traps report events right when they happen, rather than when the agent is polled.

inform-request

> inform-request is an SNMPv2/3 addition to the PDU list. It provides trap-like functionality with the addition of confirmation. (With normal trap requests, the agent sends a notification but has no way of knowing if that notification was received. Informs provide this mechanism.)

response

> response is the PDU used to carry back the response from any of the other PDUs. It can be used to reply to a get-request, signal if a set-request succeeded, and so on. You rarely reference this PDU explicitly when programming, since most SNMP libraries, programs, and Perl modules handle SNMP response receipt automatically. Still, it is important to understand not just how requests are made, but also how they are answered.

If you've never dealt with SNMP before, a natural reaction to this list might be, "That's it? Get, set, tell me when something happens, that's all it can do?" But *simple*, as SNMP's creators realized early on, is not the opposite of *powerful*. If the manufacturer of an SNMP device chooses his variables well, there's little that cannot be done with the protocol. The classic example from the RFCs is the rebooting of an SNMP-capable device. There may be no "reboot-request" PDU, but a manufacturer could easily implement this operation by using an SNMP trigger variable to hold the number of seconds before a reboot. When this variable is changed via `set-request`, a reboot of the device can be initiated in the specified amount of time.

Given this power, what sort of security is in place to keep anyone with an SNMP client from rebooting your machine? In earlier versions of the protocol, the protection mechanism was pretty puny. In fact, some people have taken to expanding the acronym as "Security Not My Problem" because of SNMPv1's poor authentication mechanism. To explain the *who*, *what*, and *how* of this protection mechanism, we have to drag out some nomenclature, so bear with me.

SNMPv1 and SNMPv2c allow you to define administrative relationships between SNMP entities called *communities*. Communities are a way of grouping SNMP agents that have similar access restrictions with the management entities that meet those restrictions. All entities that are in a community share the same *community name*. To prove you are part of a community, you just have to know the name of that community. That is the *who can access?* part of the scheme.

Now for the *what can they access?* part. RFC 1157 calls the parts of a MIB applicable to a particular network entity an *SNMP MIB view*. For instance, an SNMP-capable toaster[†] would not provide all of the same SNMP configuration variables as an SNMP-capable router.

Each object in an MIB is defined by its accessibility: `read-only`, `read-write`, or `none`. This is known as that object's *SNMP access mode*. If we put an SNMP MIB view and an SNMP access mode together, we get an *SNMP community profile* that describes the type of access available to the applicable variables in the MIB by a particular community.

When we bring together the *who* and *what* parts, we have an *SNMP access policy* that describes what kind of access members of a particular community offer each other.

How does this all work in real life? You configure your router or your workstation to be in at least two communities, one controlling read and the other controlling read/write access. People often refer to these communities as the `public` and `private` communities, named after popular default names for these communities. For instance, on a Cisco router you might include this as part of the configuration:

```
! set the read-only community name to MyPublicCommunityName
snmp-server community MyPublicCommunityName RO
```

[†] There used to be several SNMP-capable soda machines on the Web, so it isn't all that far-fetched. Scoff if you will, but the Internet Toaster (controlled via SNMP over a SLIP connection) first made its debut in 1990!

```
! set the read-write community name to MyPrivateCommunityName
snmp-server community MyPrivateCommunityName RW
```

On a Solaris machine, you might include this in the */etc/snmp/conf/snmpd.conf* file:

```
read-community  MyPublicCommunityName
write-community MyPrivateCommunityName
```

SNMP queries to either of these devices would have to use the `MyPublicCommunity Name` community name to gain access to read-only variables or the `MyPrivateCommunity Name` community name to change read/write variables on those devices. In other words, the community name functions as a pseudo-password used to gain SNMP access to a device. This is a poor security scheme. Not only is the community name passed in clear text in every SNMPv1 packet, but the overall strategy is "security by obscurity."

Later versions of SNMP—in particular, v3—added significantly better security to the protocol. RFCs 3414 and 3415 define a User Security Model (USM) and a View-Based Access Control Model (VACM): USM provides crypto-based protection for authentication and encryption of messages, while VACM offers a comprehensive access-control mechanism for MIB objects. We won't be discussing these mechanisms here, but it is probably worth your while to peruse the RFCs since v3 is increasing in popularity. I'd also recommend reading the SNMPv3 tutorials provided with the Net-SNMP distribution. If you are interested in USM and VACM and how they can be configured, the SNMP vendor NuDesign Technologies has also published a good tutorial on the subject (*http://www.ndt-inc.com/SNMP/HelpFiles/v3ConfigTutorial/v3ConfigTutorial.html*).

SNMP in Practice

Now that you've received a healthy dose of SNMP theory, let's do something practical with this knowledge. You've already seen how to query a machine's system description (remember the sneak preview earlier), so now let's look at two more examples: querying the system uptime and the IP routing table.

Until now, you just had to take my word for the location and name of an SNMP variable in the MIB. Querying information via SNMP is a two-step process:

1. Find the right MIB document. If you are looking for a device-independent setting that could be found on any generic SNMP device, you will probably find it in RFC 1213.‡ If you need a vendor-specific variable name (e.g., the variable that holds the color of the blinky-light on the front panel of a specific VoIP switch) you will need to contact the switch's vendor and request a copy of the vendor's *MIB module*. I'm being pedantic about the terms here because it is not uncommon to hear people incorrectly say, "I need the MIB for that device." There is only one MIB in the

---

‡ RFC 1213 is marginally updated by RFCs 4293, 4022, and 4113. RFC 3418 adds additional SNMPv2 items to the MIB.

world; everything else fits somewhere in that structure (usually off of the private(4) branch).

2. Search through MIB descriptions until you find the SNMP variable(s) you need.

To make this second step easier for you,* let me help decode the format.

MIB descriptions aren't all that scary once you get used to them. They look like one long set of variable declarations similar to those you would find in source code. This is no coincidence, because they *are* variable declarations. If a vendor has been responsible in the construction of its module, that module will be heavily commented like any good source code file.

MIB information is written in a subset of Abstract Syntax Notation One (ASN.1), an Open Systems Interconnection (OSI) standard notation. A description of this subset and other details of the data descriptions for SNMP are found in the Structure for Management Information (SMI) RFCs that accompany the RFCs that define the SNMP protocol and the current MIB. For instance, the latest (as of this writing) SNMP protocol definition can be found in RFC 3416, the latest base MIB manipulated by this protocol is in RFC 3418, and the SMI for this MIB is in RFC 2578. I bring this to your attention because it is not uncommon to have to flip between several documents when looking for specifics on an SNMP subject.

Let's use this knowledge to address the first task at hand: finding the system uptime of a machine via SNMP. This information is fairly generic, so there's a good chance we can find the SNMP variable we need in RFC 1213. A quick search for "uptime" in RFC 1213 yields this snippet of ASN.1:

```
sysUpTime OBJECT-TYPE
                SYNTAX   TimeTicks
                ACCESS   read-only
                STATUS   mandatory
                DESCRIPTION
                        "The time (in hundredths of a second) since the
                        network management portion of the system was last
                        re-initialized."
                ::= { system 3 }
```

Let's take this definition apart line by line:

sysUpTime OBJECT-TYPE
    This defines the object called sysUpTime.

SYNTAX TimeTicks
    This object is of the type TimeTicks. Object types are specified in the SMI I mentioned a moment ago.

---

* This task can become even easier if you use a good GUI MIB browser like *mbrowse (http://kill-9.org/ mbrowse)* or *jmibbrowser (http://jmibbrowser.sf.net)*. You can often get a hunch about the MIB contents by performing an snmpwalk on the device.

ACCESS read-only

This object can only be read via SNMP (i.e., with `get-request`); it cannot be changed (i.e., with `set-request`).

STATUS mandatory

This object must be implemented in any SNMP agent.

DESCRIPTION...

This is a textual description of the object. Always read this field carefully. In this definition, there's a surprise in store for us: `sysUpTime` only shows the amount of time that has elapsed since "the network management portion of the system was last re-initialized." This means we're only going to be able to tell a system's uptime since its SNMP agent was last started. This is almost always the same as when the system itself last started, but if you spot an anomaly, this could be the reason.

::= { system 3 }

Here's where this object fits in the MIB tree. The `sysUpTime` object is the third branch off of the system object group tree. This information also gives you part of the OID, should you need it later.

If we wanted to query this variable on the machine *solarisbox* in the read-only community, we could use the following Net-SNMP tool command line:

```
$ snmpget -v 1 -c MyPublicCommunityName solarisbox system.sysUpTime.0
```

This returns:

```
system.sysUpTime.0 = Timeticks: (5126167) 14:14:21.67
```

indicating that the agent was last initialized 14 hours ago.

> The examples in this appendix assume our SNMP agents have been configured to allow requests from the querying host. In general, if you can restrict SNMP access to a certain subset of "trusted" hosts, you should.
>
> "Need to know" is an excellent security principle to follow. It is good practice to restrict the network services provided by each machine and device. If you do not need to provide a network service, turn it off. If you do need to provide it, restrict the access to only the devices that "need to know."

Time for our second and more advanced SNMP example: dumping the contents of a device's IP routing table. The complexity in this example comes from the need to treat a collection of scalar data as a single logical table. We will have to invoke the `get-next-request` PDU to pull this off. Our first step toward this goal is to look for an MIB definition of the IP routing table. Searching for "route" in RFC 1213, we eventually find this definition:

```
-- The IP routing table contains an entry for each route
-- presently known to this entity.
ipRouteTable OBJECT-TYPE
    SYNTAX  SEQUENCE OF IpRouteEntry
    ACCESS  not-accessible
    STATUS  mandatory

    DESCRIPTION
            "This entity's IP Routing table."
    ::= { ip 21 }
```

This doesn't look much different from the definition we took apart just a moment ago. The differences are in the ACCESS and SYNTAX lines. The ACCESS line is a tip-off that this object is just a structural placeholder representing the whole table, not a real variable that can be queried. The SYNTAX line tells us this is a table consisting of a set of IpRouteEntry objects. Let's look at the beginning of the IpRouteEntry definition:

```
ipRouteEntry OBJECT-TYPE
    SYNTAX  IpRouteEntry
    ACCESS  not-accessible
    STATUS  mandatory
    DESCRIPTION
            "A route to a particular destination."
    INDEX   { ipRouteDest }
    ::= { ipRouteTable 1 }
```

The ACCESS line says we've found another placeholder—the placeholder for each of the rows in our table. But this placeholder also has something to tell us. It indicates that we'll be able to access each row by using an index object, the ipRouteDest object of each row.

If these multiple definition levels throw you, it may help to relate this to Perl. Pretend we're dealing with a Perl hash of lists structure. The hash key for the row would be the ipRouteDest variable. The value for this hash would then be a reference to a list containing the other elements in that row (i.e., the rest of the route entry).

The ipRouteEntry definition continues as follows:

```
ipRouteEntry ::=
    SEQUENCE {
        ipRouteDest
            IpAddress,
        ipRouteIfIndex
            INTEGER,
        ipRouteMetric1
            INTEGER,
        ipRouteMetric2
            INTEGER,
        ipRouteMetric3
            INTEGER,
        ipRouteMetric4
            INTEGER,
        ipRouteNextHop
            IpAddress,
```

```
        ipRouteType
            INTEGER,
        ipRouteProto
            INTEGER,
        ipRouteAge
            INTEGER,
        ipRouteMask
            IpAddress,
        ipRouteMetric5
            INTEGER,
        ipRouteInfo
            OBJECT IDENTIFIER
    }
```

Now you can see the elements that make up each row of the table. The MIB continues by describing those elements. Here are the first two definitions for these elements:

```
ipRouteDest OBJECT-TYPE
    SYNTAX  IpAddress
    ACCESS  read-write
    STATUS  mandatory
    DESCRIPTION
            "The destination IP address of this route. An
            entry with a value of 0.0.0.0 is considered a
            default route. Multiple routes to a single
            destination can appear in the table, but access to
            such multiple entries is dependent on the table-
            access mechanisms defined by the network
            management protocol in use."
    ::= { ipRouteEntry 1 }

ipRouteIfIndex OBJECT-TYPE
    SYNTAX  INTEGER
    ACCESS  read-write
    STATUS  mandatory
    DESCRIPTION
            "The index value which uniquely identifies the
            local interface through which the next hop of this
            route should be reached. The interface identified
            by a particular value of this index is the same
            interface as identified by the same value of
            ifIndex."
    ::= { ipRouteEntry 2 }
```

Figure G-3 shows a picture of the ipRouteTable part of the MIB to help summarize all of this information.

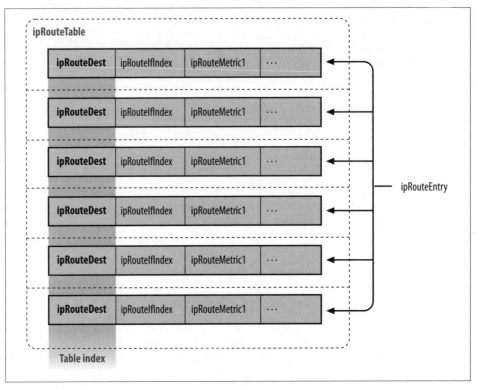

Figure G-3. The ipRouteTable structure and its index

Once you understand this part of the MIB, the next step is querying the information. This is a process known as "table traversal." Most SNMP packages have a command-line utility called something like *snmptable* or *snmp-tbl* that will perform this process for you, but they might not offer the granularity of control you need. For instance, you may not want a dump of the whole routing table; you may just want a list of all of the ipRouteNextHops. On top of this, some of the Perl SNMP packages do not have tree-walking routines. For all of these reasons, it is worth knowing how to perform this process by hand.

To make this process easier to understand, I'll show you up front the information we're eventually going to be receiving from the device. This will let you see how each step of the process adds another row to the table data we'll collect. If I log into a sample machine (as opposed to using SNMP to query it remotely) and type netstat -nr to dump the IP routing table, the output might look like this:

```
default          192.168.1.1      UGS       0    215345  tu0
127.0.0.1        127.0.0.1        UH        8    5404381 lo0
192.168.1/24     192.168.1.189    U        15    9222638 tu0
```

This shows the default internal loopback and local network routes, respectively.

Now let's see how we go about obtaining a subset of this information via the Net-SNMP command-line utilities. For this example, we're only going to concern ourselves with the first two columns of the output (route destination and next hop address). We make an initial request for the first instance of those two variables in the table. Everything in bold type is one long command line and is only printed here on separate lines for legibility:

```
$ snmpgetnext -v 1 -c public computer \
ip.ipRouteTable.ipRouteEntry.ipRouteDest \
ip.ipRouteTable.ipRouteEntry.ipRouteNextHop
ip.ipRouteTable.ipRouteEntry.ipRouteDest.0.0.0.0 = IpAddress: 0.0.0.0
ip.ipRouteTable.ipRouteEntry.ipRouteNextHop.0.0.0.0 = IpAddress: 192.168.1.1
```

We need to pay attention to two parts of this response. The first is the actual data: the information returned after the equals sign. `0.0.0.0` means "default route," so the information returned corresponded to the first line of the routing table output. The second important part of the response is the `.0.0.0.0` tacked onto the variable names. This is the index for the `ipRouteEntry` entry representing the table row.

Now that we have the first row, we can make another `get-next-request` call, this time using the index. A `get-next-request` always returns the *next* item in an MIB, so we feed it the index of the row we just received to get back the next row after it:

```
$ snmpgetnext -v 1 -c public computer \
ip.ipRouteTable.ipRouteEntry.ipRouteDest.0.0.0.0\
ip.ipRouteTable.ipRouteEntry.ipRouteNextHop.0.0.0.0
ip.ipRouteTable.ipRouteEntry.ipRouteDest.127.0.0.1 = IpAddress: 127.0.0.1
ip.ipRouteTable.ipRouteEntry.ipRouteNextHop.127.0.0.1 = IpAddress: 127.0.0.1
```

You can probably guess the next step. We issue another `get-next-request` using the `127.0.0.1` part (the index) of the `ip.ipRouteTable.ipRouteEntry.ipRouteDest. 127.0.0.1` response:

```
$ snmpgetnext -v 1 -c public computer \
ip.ipRouteTable.ipRouteEntry.ipRouteDest.127.0.0.1 \
ip.ipRouteTable.ipRouteEntry.ipRouteNextHop.127.0.0.1
ip.ipRouteTable.ipRouteEntry.ipRouteDest.192.168.1 = IpAddress: 192.168.1.0
ip.ipRouteTable.ipRouteEntry.ipRouteNextHop.192.168.11.0 = IpAddress: 192.168.1.189
```

Looking at the sample `netstat` output shown earlier, you can see we've achieved our goal and dumped all of the rows of the IP routing table. How would we know this if we had dispensed with the dramatic irony and hadn't seen the `netstat` output ahead of time? Under normal circumstances, we would have to proceed as usual and continue querying:

```
$ snmpgetnext -v 1 -c public computer \
ip.ipRouteTable.ipRouteEntry.ipRouteDest.192.168.1.0 \
ip.ipRouteTable.ipRouteEntry.ipRouteNextHop.192.168.1.0
ip.ipRouteTable.ipRouteEntry.ipRouteIfIndex.0.0.0.0 = 1
ip.ipRouteTable.ipRouteEntry.ipRouteType.0.0.0.0 = indirect(4)
```

Whoops, the response did not match the request! We asked for `ipRouteDest` and `ipRouteNextHop` but got back `ipRouteIfIndex` and `ipRouteType`. We've fallen off the edge of the `ipRouteTable` table. The SNMP `get-next-request` PDU has done its sworn duty and returned the "first lexicographic successor" in the MIB for each of the objects in our request. Looking back at the definition of `ipRouteEntry` in the previous excerpt from RFC 1213, we can see that `ipRouteIfIndex(2)` follows `ipRouteDest(1)`, and `ipRouteType(8)` does indeed follow `ipRouteNextHop(7)`.

The answer to the question of how you know when you're done querying for the contents of a table is "When you notice you've fallen off the edge of that table." Programmatically, this translates into checking that the same string or OID prefix you requested is returned in the answer to your query. For instance, you might make sure that all responses to a query about `ipRouteDest` contained either `ip.ipRouteTable.ipRouteEntry.ipRouteDest` or `1.3.6.1.2.1.4.21.1.1`.

Now that you have the basics of SNMP under your belt, you may want to turn to Chapter 12 to see how you can use it from Perl. You should also check out the references at the end of Chapter 12 for more information on SNMP.

Index

We'd like to hear your suggestions for improving our indexes. Send email to *index@oreilly.com*.

read-remember process, 402–412
  stream read-count, 396–399
ancestor-or-self:: axis, 570
ancestor:: axis, 570
anonymous binding, 323
Apache Directory Studio, 373
Apache SpamAssassin (see SpamAssassin)
Apache web server, 385
Apache::LogRegex module, 413
Apache::ParseLog module, 413
Aperghis-Tramoni, Sébastien, 453
APNIC registry, 318
App::REPL module, 114
Apple System Log facility, 378
AppleScript, 266
Application object, 267
ARF (Abuse Reporting Format), 303
ARP (Address Resolution Protocol), 471, 492–
  499
arp-sk tool, 492
Array::Compare module, 437
Array::PrintCols module, 505
Atkins, Martin, 551
Atkins, Steve, 303
attribute:: axis, 570
attributes
  DBI metadata, 248
  defined (LDAP), 573
  defined (XML), 560
  FAT filesystems, 17
  modifying for LDAP, 337–339
  quoting values for LDAP, 326
  RDN support (LDAP), 576
  viewing possible names (ADSI), 361
  XML elements and, 209
Authen::SASL module, 325
Authen::SASL::Cyrus module, 325
authentication
  anonymous binding, 323
  Kerberos, 51, 323, 325
  LDAP support, 323–324
  SASL support, 323, 325
  simple binding, 323
axes, XPath, 570

B

backward slash (\), 17, 326
Baecker, Renee, 127
Baker, Max, 485, 498

Barclay, Alan R., 47
Barr, Graham, 177, 269, 322, 325
base DN, 325, 341
Baucom, Kirk, 506
Berkeley Fast File System (FFS), 16
Berkeley Software Distribution (BSD), 57
BerkeleyDB module, 514
BETWEEN operator, 585
Big Brother monitoring package, 525
Big Sister monitoring package, 525
bigbuffy program, 391–395, 515
binary format, configuration files, 188
binary log files
  calling, 383–384
  logging API, 384
  overview, 378
  unpack function, 378–382
BIND DNS server, 156–165, 191
binding
  ADSI support, 358
  anonymous (LDAP), 323
  LDAP support, 340, 341
  print queues to queries (ADSI), 370
  simple (LDAP), 323
  variable (VarBind in SNMP), 473, 483
binding to the server (LDAP), 323
binmode command, 508
black box approach, 412–417
Blazer, Mike, 47
Boardman, Spider, 499
Boing Boing blog, 549
bots, IRC
  defined, 123
  eggdrop, 123
Boumans, Jos, 235
Boutell, Thomas, 507
Bray, Tim, 561
British Telecom, 151
Brocard, Leon, 510
Brown, Hugh, 187
Brown, Rob, 490
Bruhat, Philippe, 413, 414
BSD (Berkeley Software Distribution), 57
bulk emailers, 303–305
Bunce, Tim, 240, 253
byte-order independence, 418

C

cache, property (ADSI), 358

kernel process structures, 120
overview, 99
proc filesystem, 120
Proc::ProcessTable module, 121–125
Unix-based, 119–125
Windows-based, 100–118
WMI support, 111–118
procmail mail filter, 413
progIDs (programmatic identifiers), 356
Prokopyev, Oleg, 494
properties
defined, 355
in different ADSI namespaces, 367
interface-defined, 355, 358, 362
schema-defined, 355, 361, 362
property cache (ADSI), 358
protocol data units (PDUs), 606
PROTOTYPES directive, 463
ps command, 79, 119
PsTools utilities suite, 100
Pugh, Kake, 38
pulist.exe program, 100
PureFtpd daemon, 415

Q

queries
adding results to tables, 586
ADSI searches, 363–365
binding print queues, 370
creating views, 588
cursor use, 589
data manipulation, 585
filesystem usage, 46
LDAP searches, 325–329, 340
Microsoft SQL Server via ODBC, 255–257
MySQL server via DBI, 252
Oracle server via DBI, 254–255
property cache and, 358
retrieving all table rows, 583
retrieving subset of rows, 584
SELECT statement support, 583–586
SNMP process, 609–616
WHOIS information, 320
quota command, 39
Quota module, 44
quotation marks, 326
quotatool package, 40

R

race conditions, avoiding, 12
rain tool, 492
Ramdane, Amine Moulay, 127
RCS (Revision Control System)
ci command, 593
co command, 594
comparisons to other systems, 595
features, 149
rcs command, 594
rcsdiff command, 150, 594
reference information, 596
rlog command, 594
tutorial, 593–596
rcs command (RCS), 594
Rcs module, 149
rcsdiff command (RCS), 150, 594
RDN (relative distinguished name)
defined, 576
modifying, 335–337
quoting attribute values, 326
read function, 120
Read-Eval-Print Loop (REPL), 114
Readonly module, 187
recursive code
defined, 22
examples, 22, 342
references
continuation, 340, 342–343
LDAP, 339–343
object, 599
referrals (LDAP), 339–343
REGEXP operator (MySQL), 585
Regexp::Assemble module, 295
Regexp::Common module, 294, 296, 448
Regexp::Log module, 414
Regexp::Log::Common module, 414
Regexp::Log::DataRange module, 414
regular expressions
reference information, 404
SQL support, 585
Reinhardt, Chris, 425
relative distinguished name (see RDN)
relative ID (RID), 61
rename function, 388
REPL (Read-Eval-Print Loop), 114
repositories for prebuilt packages, 8
resource kits (Microsoft), 69
response PDU, 607

REST web service, example, 538
reverse mapping, 159, 164
Revision Control System (see RCS)
RFC 1035, 168, 169, 184
RFC 1101, 169, 184
RFC 1157, 473, 486
RFC 1213, 486, 610, 611
RFC 1288, 315, 317, 373
RFC 1321, 438, 467
RFC 1493, 486
RFC 1573, 475, 486
RFC 1833, 374
RFC 1905, 486
RFC 1907, 486
RFC 1939, 285, 286, 312
RFC 2011, 486
RFC 2012, 486
RFC 2013, 486
RFC 2045, 270, 287, 312
RFC 2046, 270, 312
RFC 2047, 270, 312
RFC 2077, 270, 312
RFC 2131, 175, 184
RFC 2222, 323, 374
RFC 2251, 329, 340, 341, 345, 374
RFC 2252, 374
RFC 2254, 326, 374
RFC 2255, 339, 356, 374, 578
RFC 2274, 487
RFC 2275, 487
RFC 2578, 487, 610
RFC 2821, 265, 268, 312
RFC 2822, 265, 287, 291, 293, 298, 312
RFC 2830, 324, 344
RFC 2849, 331, 374
RFC 2891, 344
RFC 3062, 344
RFC 3416, 606, 610
RFC 3418, 610
RFC 3501, 287, 312
RFC 3834, 312
RFC 4288, 270, 312
RFC 4289, 270, 312
RFC 793, 454, 467
RFC 849, 184
RFC 881, 184
RFC 882, 184
RFC 931, 404
RFC 954, 373

RID (relative ID), 61
RIPE registry, 318
Rivest, Ron, 438
rlog command (RCS), 594
Rogaski, Mark, 426
Rogers, Jay, 82, 316
Rolsky, Dave, 272, 426
root distinguished name (LDAP), 323, 332
root DSE (LDAP), 345
Rose::DB::Object module, 76
Rosler, Larry, 147
Roth, David, 60, 63, 597
RRDtool, 514–522
RSS feeds, 543
runas.exe utility, 7
Russinovich, Mark, 100, 125, 129

S

SAGE mailing list, 530
SAM (Security Accounts Manager)
    ADSI support, 355
    background, 59
    binary data support, 59
    storing user identities, 64
    WinNT namespace support, 356
Samba software suite, 151
Santiago, Ed, 152
Sarathy, Gurusamy, 420
SASL (Simple Authentication and Security
        Layer), 323, 325
SAX2, 216–228
Schedule::Cron module, 524
Schedule::Cron::Events module, 531, 534
schema (LDAP)
    defined, 575
    DSML support, 346
    LDAP support, 361
    namespace comparisons, 367
    updating, 348
schema properties
    accessing, 361, 362
    defined, 355
    name considerations, 362
Schemers, Roland J., III, 451
Schiffman, Mike, 494
Schilli, Mike, 428
Schubert, Max, 499
Schutz, Austin, 82, 316
Schwartz, Alan, 404

Schwartz, Randal, 522, 528
Schweikert, David, 192, 505
Search tool (Windows), 21
searches
    ADSI support, 363–365
    LDAP support, 325–329, 340, 342
secondary NIS/DNS servers (see slave servers)
Secure Sockets Layer (see SSL)
security
    LDAP server setup, 332
    log processing programs, 394
    Logfile::Rotate module, 390
    noticing changes, 434–442
    noticing suspicious activities, 442–449
    preventing suspicious activities, 460–466
    real-life example, 449–459
    reference information, 467
Security Accounts Manager (see SAM)
security identifier (SID), 61
SELECT statement (SQL)
    BETWEEN operator, 585
    creating views, 588
    data manipulation, 585
    IN operator, 584
    INSERT statement and, 586
    INTO clause, 586
    LIKE clause, 585
    querying information, 583–586
    regular expression support, 585
    retrieving all table rows, 583
    retrieving subset of rows, 584
    WHERE clause, 245, 584
self:: axis, 570
Sergeant, Matt, 217
service element, 200, 217, 220, 230
set-request PDU, 607
Set::Crontab module, 531
SetACL binary, 62
setpgrp function, 119
setpriority function, 119
setquota command (Linux), 40
SetSystemtimePrivilege, 69
SHA message digest algorithm family, 438, 441
shadow password files, 58
Sharnoff, David Muir, 133, 504
Shearer, John D., 485
shell globbing, 327
Shell::Perl module, 114

Shelor, Mark, 438
SHOW COLUMNS statement (MySQL), 253
SHOW command (MySQL), 252
SHOW TABLES statement (MySQL), 253
SID (security identifier), 61
Signes, Ricardo, 269, 271, 294, 296
SIMILE project, 531
Simple Authentication and Security Layer
    (SASL), 323, 325
simple binding (LDAP), 323
Simple Mail Transfer Protocol (SMTP), 268–
    272
Simple Network Management Protocol (see
    SNMP)
Sisk, Matt, 550
slave servers, 152, 156
SMTP (Simple Mail Transfer Protocol), 268–
    272
SNMP (Simple Network Management
    Protocol)
    alternative interface modules, 484–485
    data type support, 603
    functionality, 469–480
    mapping physical locations, 502
    query process, 609–616
    reference information, 486
    sending/receiving data, 480–484
    tutorial, 603–616
    variable names, 603
    walking tables, 485
    WBEM support, 112
SNMP module
    functionality, 470–480
    TrapSession method, 481
snmp.conf file for Net-SNMP, 469
SNMP::BridgeQuery module, 485
SNMP::Info module, 485, 498
SNMP::Info::CDP module, 498
SNMP::MIB::Compiler module, 471
SNMP::Util module, 471
snmptrapd daemon, 483, 484
snmpV2-trap PDU, 607
SNMP_Session.pm module, 469, 471, 483
SNMP_util.pm module, 471
SOA (Start of Authority) resource record, 156
SOAP::Lite module, 538
Solaris operating system
    classic Unix password file, 50
    DNS support, 156

documentation, 120
parsing data, 120
UPDATE statement (SQL)
    changing table information, 587
    WHERE clause, 587
URI::LDAP module, 341
Urist, Daniel J., 121
URLs
    ADsPath comparison, 356
    LDAP support, 339–342
use constants pragma, 186
USE statement (SQL), 581
use strict pragma, 204
use vars pragma, 28
USENIX Association, 237, 556
User Account Control (UAC), 7
user accounts
    account system to manage, 71–96
    creating, 368
    reference information, 97
    retrieving user rights, 70
    Unix creation/deletion routines, 78–83
    Unix user identities, 50–59
    Windows creation/deletion routines, 83–89
    Windows-based user identities, 59–71
user activity
    file operations, 99, 125–135
    network operations, 99, 125–135
    OS-specific, 99
    process management, 99, 100–125
    reference information, 136
User Datagram Protocol (UDP), 452, 481, 490
user ID (see UID)
user rights, Windows
    retrieving, 70
    Windows-based, 68–71
user shell, 55
User:: module, 55
User::Utmp module, 401
useradd command (Solaris), 81
users, Windows, 63
    Unix support, 50–59
    user rights, Windows, 68–71
    Windows numbers, 61–63
    Windows storage and access, 59–61, 64
utime function, 438

V

valid XML data, 560
variable binding, 473, 483
variables
    Perl support, 603
    SNMP support, 603
    tied, 358
VBScript
    ADSI support, 357
    conversion to Perl, 597–602
    reference information, 602
VBScript Converter, 602
VBScript-to-Perl
    tutorial, 597–602
Venema, Wietse, 404
Verbruggen, Martien, 507
VFAT filesystem, 17
VIEW ANY DEFINITION permission, 255
views, SQL, 588
Vincent, Jesse, 6
virtual local area networks (VLANs), 475
Vista (Microsoft), 7
Vixie, Paul, 174
vlandTrunkPortTable, 475
VLANs (virtual local area networks), 475
vmMembershipTable, 474
von Löwis, Martin, 15

W

Wadsack, Jeremy, 509
walking the filesystem
    by hand, 21–26
    using File::Find module, 26–35
    using File::Find::Rule module, 36–38
Wall, Larry, 217
Walter, Jörg, 461
Walton, Jose, 533
Wayback Machine, 127
WBEM (Web-Based Enterprise Management), 112
Web-Based Enterprise Management (WBEM), 112
well-formed XML data, 560
WHERE clause (SQL)
    SELECT statement, 245, 584
    UPDATE statement, 587
White, Alex, 414
whitespaces in filenames, 403